# LIGHT TO THE NATIONS

Part One

*The History of Christian Civilization*

SECOND EDITION

*"I will give you as a light to the nations,
that my salvation may reach to the end of the earth."*

—*Isaiah: 49:6*

# LIGHT TO THE NATIONS

Part One

## The History of Christian Civilization

SECOND EDITION

*General Editor*
Rollin A. Lasseter

*Editor and Chief Storyteller*
Christopher Zehnder

*President and Founder, CTP*
Michael J. Van Hecke

Produced and developed by:

Editing: Bridget Neumayr and Christianne Thillen

Design and Production: Hespenheide Design, Gary Hespenheide, Laurie Miller, Randy Miyake, and Naomi Valdivia

Acknowledgments:
Research Contributed to *Light to the Nations: The History of Christian Civilization: Part One*

Rollin A. Lasseter, Ph.D.: the ancient world, medieval England, Chaucer, Malory

John R. Sommerfeldt, Ph.D.: medieval Germany and France, the medieval reform movement

Alexandra Wilhelmsen, Ph.D.: medieval Spain

Archduchess Alexandra von Habsburg: Queen Isabella

Philipp W. Rosemann, Ph.D.: the birth of the universities, Abelard of Paris

Theresa M. Kenney, Ph.D.: the troubadours

Raymond D. DiLorenzo, Ph.D.: Dante

William A. Frank, Ph.D.: William of Ockham

Ruth D. Lasseter: copy editing and "Highways and Byways"

Patricia B. Bozell: copy editing and advice.

Helen T. Lasseter, Ph.D.: copy editing and research

Benjamin F. Lasseter, Ph.D.: research and proofreading

Janet Matulka: copy editing and proofreading

2022 VERSION
UPDATED AND RE-PRINTED
FROM ORIGINAL ©2017

©2017 Catholic Textbook Project
www.catholictextbookproject.com
All rights reserved
ISBN 978-1-935644-24-8
Printed in United States

**Cover Image**
Statue of Charlemagne © Michael Van Hecke; Stained glass window © Dean Conger/Corbis; Teresa of Avila © Kunsthistorisches Museum, Wien oder KHM, Wien; Hagia Sophia © Gavin Hellier/JAI/Corbis

**Photo Credits**
**p. 2** (tl) © Awe Inspiring Images/Shutterstock; **p. 2** © Steve Estvanik/Shutterstock (tr); **p. 2** © Zvonimir Atletic/Shutterstock (b); **p. 3** © Renata Sedmakova/Shutterstock (tl); **p. 3** © Jurand/Shutterstock (tr); **p. 3** © Kamira/Shutterstock (bl); **p. 3** © Paolo Gallo/Shutterstock (br); **p. 4** © Carsten Medom Madsen/Shutterstock; **p. 7** © Awe Inspiring Images/Shutterstock; **p. 8** (tl) © Steve Estvanik/Shutterstock; **p. 8** © Phillip Minnis/Shutterstock; **p. 12** © Brannend/Shutterstock; **p. 13** © Zvonimir Atletic/Shutterstock; **p. 17** © Renata Sedmakova/Shutterstock; **p. 19** © Lucy/Shutterstock; **p. 20** © Gregory James Van Raalte/Shutterstock; **p. 21** © Renata Sedmakova/Shutterstock; p 23 © Zvonimir Atletic/Shutterstock; **p. 24** © Zvonimir Atletic/Shutterstock; **p. 25** © Oleg Golovnev/Shutterstock; **p. 28** © Vladimir Wrangel/Shutterstock; **p. 29** © kiyanochka1/Shutterstock; **p. 31** © Faraways/Shutterstock; **p. 32** © Tupungato/Shutterstock; **p. 33** © arly/Shutterstock; **p. 35** © neko92vl/Shutterstock; **p. 36** © Zvonimir Atletic/Shutterstock; **p. 37** © Renata Sedmakova/Shutterstock; **p. 41** © iofoto/Shutterstock; **p. 49** © wjarek/Shutterstock; **p. 52** © mountainpix/Shutterstock; **p. 53** © Lagui/Shutterstock; **p. 54** © Sergey Kohl/Shutterstock; **p. 56** © Sailorr/Shutterstock; **p. 57** © Passion Images/Shutterstock; **p. 59** © Matteo Volpone/Shutterstock; **p. 60** © Renata Sedmakova/Shutterstock; **p. 61** © Kamira/Shutterstock; **p. 63** © Paul Prescott/Shutterstock; **p. 64** © mountainpix/Shutterstock; **p. 70** © mountainpix/Shutterstock; **p. 74** © mountainpix/Shutterstock; **p. 77** © Valery Shanin/Shutterstock; **p. 78** © I. Pilon/Shutterstock; **p. 80** © anshar/Shutterstock; **p. 81** © Wikipedia; **p. 82** © zebra0209/Shutterstock; **p. 83** © m.bonotto/Shutterstock; **p. 90** © Wikipedia; **p. 91** © Boris Stroujko/Shutterstock; **p. 94** © kavring/Shutterstock; **p. 95** © mountainpix/Shutterstock; **p. 96** © IgorGolovniov/Shutterstock; **p. 97** © PavleMarjanovic/Shutterstock; **p. 98** © Tupungato/Shutterstock; **p. 100** © Renata Sedmakova/Shutterstock; **p. 101** © Renata Sedmakova/Shutterstock; **p. 102** © Paolo Gallo/Shutterstock; **p. 104** © Wikipedia (t); **p. 104** © Wikipedia (b); **p. 105** © Wikipedia; **p. 105** © Wikipedia; **p. 106** © Wikipedia; **p. 107** © Viacheslav Lopatin/Shutterstock; **p. 109** ©Wikipedia; **p. 116** © Hermann Vogel/Getty Images;

*Credits continue on page 674*

# Contributors

**Rollin A. Lasseter**, General Editor, retired in 2003 from the English faculty of the University of Dallas. He graduated *summa cum laude* from Vanderbilt University, and took the M.A. and Ph.D. from Yale University. He was Director of the Honors Program at the University of Kentucky, where he received the Great Teacher Award twice. He was given tenure in the English Department at North Carolina State University. He did postgraduate work at the University of Notre Dame, and taught at St. Mary's College, South Bend, and Indiana University at South Bend before joining the English faculty in 1992 at the University of Dallas. For several years he taught Latin, ancient history and literature, and English composition at an exemplary secondary school, Trinity School at Greenlawn, where his six children attended. He was Director of Curriculum at an independent Catholic school and continued as a consultant for curriculum. Dr. Lasseter passed away on May 12, 2008.

**Christopher Zehnder** is a graduate of Thomas Aquinas College. He has taught history, theology, Latin, English grammar, composition, English literature, and universal literature at Catholic secondary schools in Connecticut and California. He has edited two news monthlies and written for various publications on historical, political, and theological subjects. He lives with his wife, Katherine, and seven children in Tehachapi, California, raising goats, chickens, and vegetables.

**John R. Sommerfeldt**, Professor of history and past president of the University of Dallas, holds a Ph.D. in history from the University of Michigan. He did additional graduate study at Albert-Ludwigs-Universität, Freiburg im Breisgau, the University of Notre Dame, and Western Michigan University. At WMU, he was the founding Director of the Medieval Institute and founder of the International Medieval Congress. Also at WMU, he served as Executive Director of the Institute of Cistercian Studies and Director of the Center for Contemplative Studies. An authority on Cistercian history, he has taught medieval history and German history at the University of Dallas, and is author or editor of twenty-six books, especially *The Spiritual Teachings of Bernard of Clairvaux* (1991). His newest book is titled *Bernard of Clairvaux on the Life of the Mind* (May 2004).

**Alexandra Wilhelmsen**, Professor of Spanish and Adjunct Professor of History at the University of Dallas, holds degrees from the University of Dallas (politics and Spanish), Rice University (history) and a Doctorate of History from the University of Navarra. Her study of nineteenth-century Spanish Catholic political thought, *La formación del pensamiento politico del Carlismo 1810–1875*, published in Madrid in 1995, won the Luis Hernando de Larramendi Award. She has published over sixty articles, mainly on Spanish topics, in various countries and languages and currently is the director of the interdisciplinary Spanish Program at the University of Dallas.

**Philipp W. Rosemann**, associate professor of philosophy, University of Dallas, holds degrees from the University of Hamburg, Queen's University of Belfast, and the licentiate and *Doctor Philosophiae* from Université Catholique de Louvain. His forthcoming study, *Peter Lombard*, will appear in the Great Medieval Thinkers series, published by Oxford University Press.

**Theresa M. Kenney**, associate professor of English at the University of Dallas, holds degrees from Pennsylvania State University, the University of Notre Dame, and the Ph.D. from Stanford University. She teaches medieval and renaissance poetry and narrative, and has published a study of the renaissance Italian nun and essayist, Arcangela Tarraboti. Her recent books include *Women Are Not Human: an Anonymous Treatise and Responses*, and articles such as "John Donne's Conversion from Mysogyny," and "From Francesca to Francesco: Transcribing the Tale of Passion from the *Inferno* to the *Paradiso*."

**Raymond D. DiLorenzo**, associate professor of English at the University of Dallas, is a graduate of John Carroll University, and holds the Ph.D. from the University of Toronto, and the (MSL) Licentiate in Mediaeval Studies from the Pontifical Institute of Mediaeval Studies. He publishes in medieval studies journals, and his stimulating courses on St. Augustine, Chaucer, and Dante at the University of Dallas are famous with students.

**William A. Frank**, professor of philosophy at the University of Dallas, holds the Ph.D. from the Catholic University of America. Former Dean of Braniff Graduate School of Liberal Arts, he teaches medieval philosophy and the philosophy of education. He is past Academic Director of the University of Dallas Rome Program. His recent book, *Duns Scotus, Metaphysician*, coauthored with Allan B. Wolter, is published by Purdue University Press, 1995.

**Ruth D. Lasseter** is the wife of Rollin Lasseter and mother of their six children, now adults and teachers. She was Director of Admissions at a private Catholic school. She was Assistant Editor of *Canticle*, a magazine for Catholic women, where she wrote a regular column. She has published and lectured in several Catholic forums.

# Dedication to Professor Rollin A. Lasseter

By 1969, when Yale University conferred a Ph.D. in English on him, Rollin Lasseter had already achieved an array of honors. Before graduating Summa Cum Laude and being awarded a Woodrow Wilson Fellowship to graduate school at Yale, he led his Vanderbilt team for three contests on national television's popular "College Bowl." In addition, he was editor of The Vagabond, Vanderbilt's literary magazine, published a volume of poetry, *Flags and Other Poems*, and received several academic and literary awards. At the University of Kentucky, his first academic position, he was named "Teacher of the Year" three times and was invited to direct the Honors Program. A few years later, he joined the English faculty at North Carolina State University, where he was given tenure. During that time at Raleigh, Dr. Lasseter and his wife, Ruth, became parents to their six children, all of whom have followed their father's example and entered the teaching profession.

In the 1970s and 80s, academic institutions everywhere in America abandoned the good of Christianity and its heritage of Western Civilization, but Dr. Lasseter embraced the Faith and defended the tradition more firmly. Following the example of his teachers and mentors, Donald Davidson and Cleanth Brooks, who were champions of the Western literary tradition, Dr. Lasseter looked to the future, even while defending the past. It was with hope that in the following decades he dedicated himself to learning, teaching, and writing. His articles on Catholic education have been published in *Catholic Faith* magazine and *This Rock*, and his poetry has been printed in several journals. He has, in addition, designed a K–12 curriculum for private Catholic schools, served on the faculty of the University of Dallas for several years prior to his retirement, and shaped the Catholic Textbook Project as director, editor and main writer. A new volume of his poetry, *The Cast of Valor*, published in April 2008, is available from St. Augustine Press. Dr. Lasseter passed away on May 12, 2008 after a long battle with cancer.

Dr. Helen Lasseter, his youngest daughter, recently praised her father in these words: "He has always been influential and encouraging to his colleagues, as well as being a great teacher. If he had looked only to his personal advancement when he was a young professor, instead of balancing his career and his care of our family, he might be really famous today; but, had he done so, he would not have been our daddy."

For my part, Dr. Lasseter has been the mind behind our Catholic Textbook Project. I could never have made it to page one had it not been for his tireless dedication and expansive knowledge and experience. All of us who have worked so hard and long to offer these textbooks to Catholic schoolchildren would like to honor the memory of Dr. Lasseter, a true teacher, by dedicating this volume to him. Thank you, Dr. Lasseter, for bringing Catholic culture to the classroom and into our minds and hearts.

—Michael J. Van Hecke, M. Ed.
President

[Thank you to Mrs. Ruth Lasseter and family for providing the above information, and for your own hand in countless hours of support, reading and contributing to your husband and father's work.]

# Table of Contents

| | | |
|---|---|---|
| From the Founding General Editor | | x |
| Introduction: History's Beginnings | | 1 |
| **Chapter 1** | A Light to the Nations | 17 |
| **Chapter 2** | Emperors and Madmen | 47 |
| **Chapter 3** | The Blood of Martyrs | 69 |
| **Chapter 4** | The Christian Empire | 89 |
| **Chapter 5** | Germanic Kingdoms in the West | 115 |
| **Chapter 6** | Founders of Christendom—A.D. 500–700 | 139 |
| **Chapter 7** | The Rise of Islam—A.D. 624–800 | 167 |
| **Chapter 8** | The Defense and the Building of Christendom | 193 |
| **Chapter 9** | The Achievements of Feudalism: A.D. 800–1000 | 219 |
| **Chapter 10** | The Medieval Reformation | 243 |
| **Chapter 11** | The New Nations: Spain, England, and France | 267 |
| **Chapter 12** | The Crusades | 295 |
| **Chapter 13** | The Great Century | 327 |
| **Chapter 14** | Decline and Decay of the Middle Ages | 359 |
| **Chapter 15** | Two Centuries of Conflict | 381 |
| **Chapter 16** | The Birth of a New World | 413 |
| **Chapter 17** | The Protestant Reformation | 443 |
| **Chapter 18** | Catholic Renewal and Religious War | 483 |
| **Chapter 19** | Europe Before the Flood | 521 |
| **Supplemental Chapters** | | |
| | China: The Middle Kingdom | 558 |
| | Japan: The Land of the Rising Sun | 576 |
| | Africa: The Enduring Continent | 588 |
| | Latin America: Lands of Many Cultures | 604 |
| | The Scientific Revolution | 624 |
| | Two Revolutions: Industrial and Agricultural | 644 |
| | The Age of Enlightenment | 653 |
| **Index** | | 677 |

# From the Founding General Editor, CTP

History is a treasure chest of riches. In its stories are the most exciting, the saddest and the happiest moments of human life. All the great souls and heroes of the world are to be met in the pages of a good history book.

A Christian interpretation of History is the story of God's love for mankind. As a long and complex story, it can tell of tragedies as well as comedies, of famines as well as feasts, of exiles and homecomings, defeats and victories. There is among the many stories of history some story to entertain or to edify everyone. But over all, the story of history is the tale of God's acts in time and space, the story of rebellious mankind, and the Mercy of God for human folly. History is a story, a story of hope.

However, events in our own time tend to leave most people in fear of the future, despite the watchword of our culture, which remains: "Progress! Be always Optimistic!" Current secular ideologies have given "history" a god-like power, that makes sometimes wild proclamations: "Someday, History will look back and say . . . "; or "History will show the wisdom of . . . "; or "History will prove he was right . . . "; or "History will leave this 'whatever' behind in the dust of the ages." This ideological sense of the name "History" is more than a little idolatrous in its foolish optimism. Our Holy Father, Pope Benedict XVI has written in several places about "optimism" as but a shallow mockery of Hope.

The evidence of the stories that come down to us from the ancient world and the medieval era do not promise all good endings. Humanity makes costly mistakes. Great men and women pay for those mistakes with their lives. Great empires collapse. Utopias are not realistic, nor realized.

The Hope that the Christian Faith offers is more than an optimistically happy ending. The end of history will be the return of Our Lord in Glory and the end of time. Providence does not mean every time a happy ending—only a blessed one. It is God's abiding care and love, in History and in individual lives. It is the vision of the perfection in Christ to which all people are called, not just what society and cultures—however great—have been.

May you, the readers of this book, young and old, find in its tales the traces of that Providence that keeps all of us safe in his Everlasting Arms.

—Rollin A. Lasseter, Ph.D.
Founding General Editor, CTP

# Introduction: History's Beginnings

History is the story of God's dealings with mankind. Through the long roll of centuries, God's **grace**, his gift of himself, has never abandoned mankind. Through all the moments of change in the world, God has given his grace to mankind. History witnesses to moments of grace-filled change in the lives of people and of nations.

In the story of Adam and Eve, we have one grace-filled moment: Adam and Eve knew they were created in God's own image and had an eternal destiny, which they lost by rejecting the grace that God gave them. Yet, despite Adam and Eve's rejection of grace, God promised them and their descendents that he would not abandon them.

God has continued to speak his truth to mankind. He speaks through the order, beauty, and grandeur of creation. He speaks through the inspiration he gives human beings to perfect the order in creation—to build a more useful and more beautiful world. But God also speaks in extraordinary ways. Through Moses, he sent a law as a guide for life. Through spokesmen called the prophets, God explained creation and his Law for human beings.

God's final and most wonderful word, however, was heard through the *fiat* of a humble maiden from the humble people of Israel. With Mary's cooperation, God revealed himself through Jesus, his Son. That event, the coming of God as a man to live among people, is called the **Incarnation.**

Jesus Christ is the light of the world, a light no darkness can extinguish. Because this volume and the next tell the story of the Christian Church and the civilization it has formed, they are titled *A Light to the Nations*.

**grace:** God's love and protection given to mankind; a strength or power beyond human nature given by God to human beings

***fiat*:** the Latin word for "let it be so," drawn from Mary's response to the Angel of the Annunciation, as translated into Latin in the Vulgate Bible: *fiat mihi secundum verbum tuum.* ("Let it be so with me according to thy word.") The Latin word *fiat* has become an English word, meaning a decision to accept what is to be.

**the Incarnation:** God's taking on the nature of man in the person of Jesus of Nazareth. (From the Latin *in carne,* "in the flesh.")

# 2  LIGHT TO THE NATIONS: The History of Christian Civilization

Humanity has received no greater light than Christ Jesus, who came down from heaven, lived among us, taught us how to live justly and to love rightly, died as a sacrifice for our sins, and gave us a Church that continues in his name to tell the Truth about God and man and to nourish us with the sacraments.

## A.D. and B.C.—Telling Time

God's becoming man in Jesus of Nazareth was humanity's greatest moment of grace-filled change. The Incarnation changed history, and it changed humanity. All events that came after and all that went before are measured by the Incarnation. For that reason, we number years based on whether they precede or follow Jesus' birth.

The years *after* the birth of Jesus are called "in the Year of the Lord"—or, in Latin, *Anno Domini* ("A.D.," as in A.D. 2000). We count backward when speaking of the years *before* the birth of Jesus: The larger the number, the farther that year is from his birth. These years are called Before

Timeline 50,000 B.C. to 200 A.D.

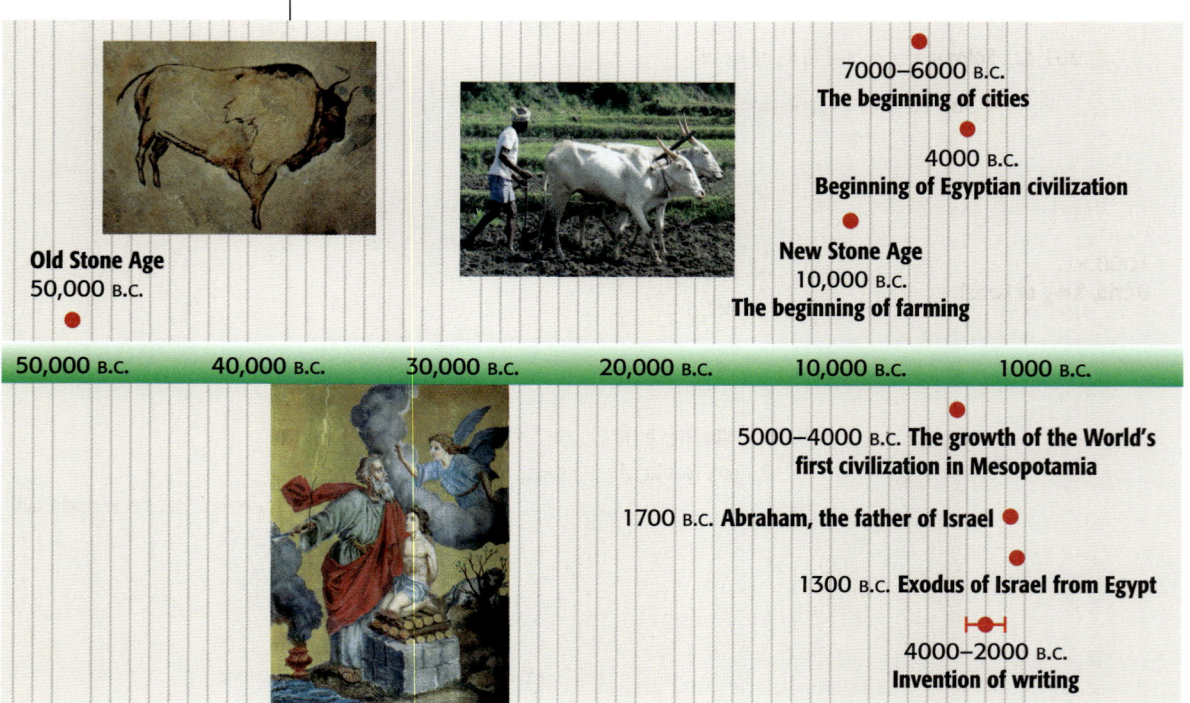

*Christ* ("B.C.," as in 2000 B.C.). The year A.D. 2000 is as far from the birth of Jesus in one direction as 2000 B.C. is in the other.

## The Long March of Years

We know very little of what happened between the creation of the first man and woman and the rise of what are called the first "civilizations." Though certain scientists called **archaeologists** and **paleontologists** have made many discoveries—uncovering ancient tools made by humans and even ancient cities—these years are dark to us. Our lack of knowledge stems from the fact that we possess no *written* accounts of what happened in the long period between God's creation of mankind and the rise of the civilization called Mesopotamia.

It is important to understand that **history** is concerned with what men and women in different times and places have written about themselves. Without the written word, there really is no history. To understand this better, imagine that you have dug up an American Indian encampment.

**archaeologist:** a scientist who studies the evidence of the human past

**paleontologist:** a scientist who studies the evidence of all past life, human and nonhuman

**history:** the study of what people did and what happened to them based on written records of past ages

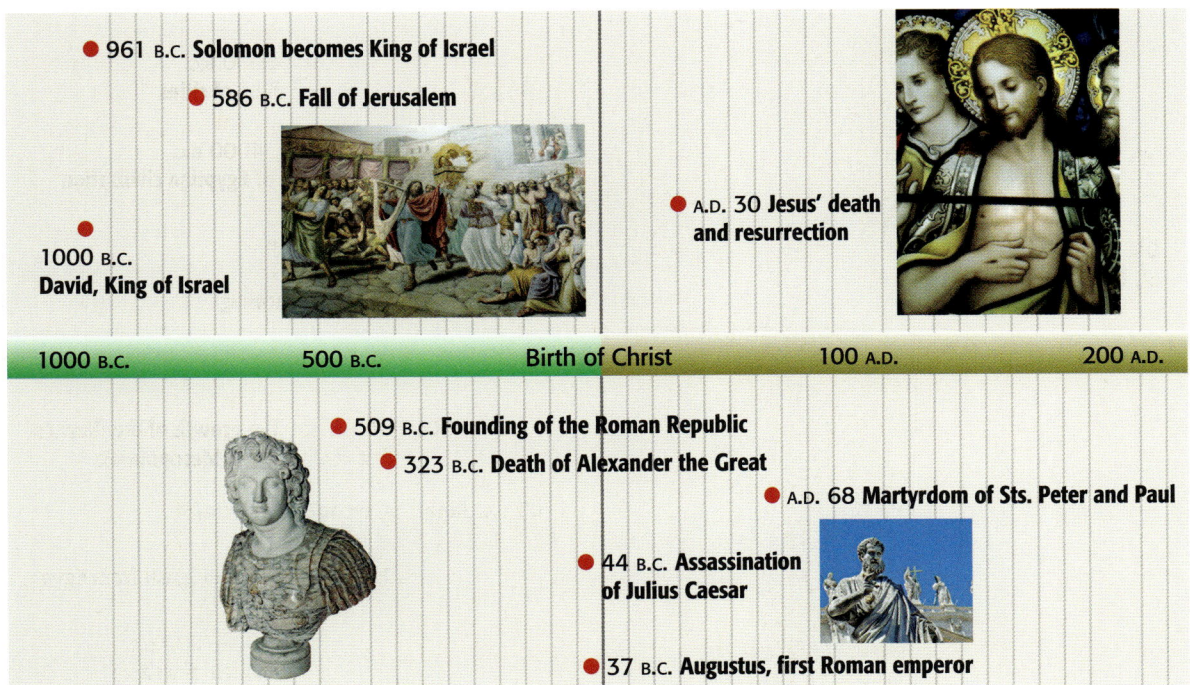

- 961 B.C. **Solomon becomes King of Israel**
- 586 B.C. **Fall of Jerusalem**
- 1000 B.C. **David, King of Israel**
- A.D. 30 **Jesus' death and resurrection**

1000 B.C. — 500 B.C. — Birth of Christ — 100 A.D. — 200 A.D.

- 509 B.C. **Founding of the Roman Republic**
- 323 B.C. **Death of Alexander the Great**
- A.D. 68 **Martyrdom of Sts. Peter and Paul**
- 44 B.C. **Assassination of Julius Caesar**
- 37 B.C. **Augustus, first Roman emperor**

A Neolithic stone ax

You find arrowheads, tools made from stone or bone, campfire rings. Maybe you even find rock paintings nearby. Based on what you have found, you can understand certain things about how the Indians in question lived. But you cannot know what deeds they did, what wars they fought, when they first came to that place, or what finally happened to them. You cannot know these things because you have no one to tell you the story. Likewise, we have no written records to tell us what happened in those ancient times before people wrote about their deeds. So it is that we call those long ago times, not history, but **prehistory.**

Writing allows people to tell other people about themselves and what has happened to them. Through the written word, people of one age can communicate with those of future ages. Writing allows us to learn stories even from thousands of years ago and pass those stories on to others.

The first book of the Bible, Genesis, gives us some account of the years between Adam and Eve and those human societies we call the first civilizations. But Genesis actually tells us very little of those times. Genesis is concerned with telling a particular story—the true story of God's dealings in love with mankind. Of course, this story is the most important of all. It is the story behind all the stories that make up the history of mankind. For history is finally the tale of God's gift-giving to fallen mankind and of mankind's response.

**prehistory:** the period of human life on Earth before the invention of writing

# What Is Civilization?

The first and most important gift God has given human beings is the capacity to think and create. We can discover new ways of doing old tasks and solving old problems. Some things we discover by thinking hard about them, but most discoveries come to us in flashes of insight, what we often call gifts of God. Are these discoveries merely the operation of human brains? Or are they God's gift to individuals entrusted with his insight and direction? In the long years before recorded history, humans made many important discoveries, some of which we rely on even in our own day. We can call these discoveries natural and the result of human thinking, or we can recognize in them the power of God working through natural human creativity.

## The Stone Age—Paleolithic and Neolithic

Ancient humans did not have what we call *civilization*, but there would have been no civilization today without their discoveries. Modern historians divide prehistory into two periods, both called the Stone Age. The first period (dated from approximately 50,000 B.C. to approximately 10,000 B.C.) is longer by far than the second period (from 10,000 to 2,000 B.C.) During the first period, called **Paleolithic** or the Old Stone Age, human beings lived nomadically, hunting and gathering wild foods. They formed family groups and had a sense of religious wonder about the natural order around them. But during this period they also discovered the use of tools and began to make art. The second period, lasting only from around 10,000 B.C. to around 2,000 B.C., is called **Neolithic** or the New Stone Age. During this period, human beings discovered agriculture and thus formed settled human habitations, villages, and cities

> **paleolithic:** (from Greek *palai–*, "old," and *lithos*, "stone") the Old Stone Age
> **neolithic:** (from Greek *neo–*, "new," and *lithos*, "stone") the New Stone Age

Because humans lived nomadically during the Old Stone Age, they spread across all the continents except Antarctica by about 40,000 B.C. They walked and even sailed in crude boats from the Asian mainland to the South Pacific islands and then to Australia. They sailed or walked down the west coasts of the Americas and into the eastern seacoasts of North America. Traces of settlements as old as 30,000 B.C. have been found on South America's southernmost coasts. Human beings were great travelers from the beginning.

### Paleolithic Discoveries

The discoveries of the Old Stone Age were both spiritual and technical. Among the technical discoveries, perhaps the most important was the discovery of how to make and control fire. Fire for cooking made some foods edible by human beings. Fire for heating enabled people to survive through the cold of winter. Other technical discoveries included the use of stone and wood weapons and tools, which increased people's ability to shelter, feed, and protect themselves and those they loved.

**6** LIGHT TO THE NATIONS: The History of Christian Civilization

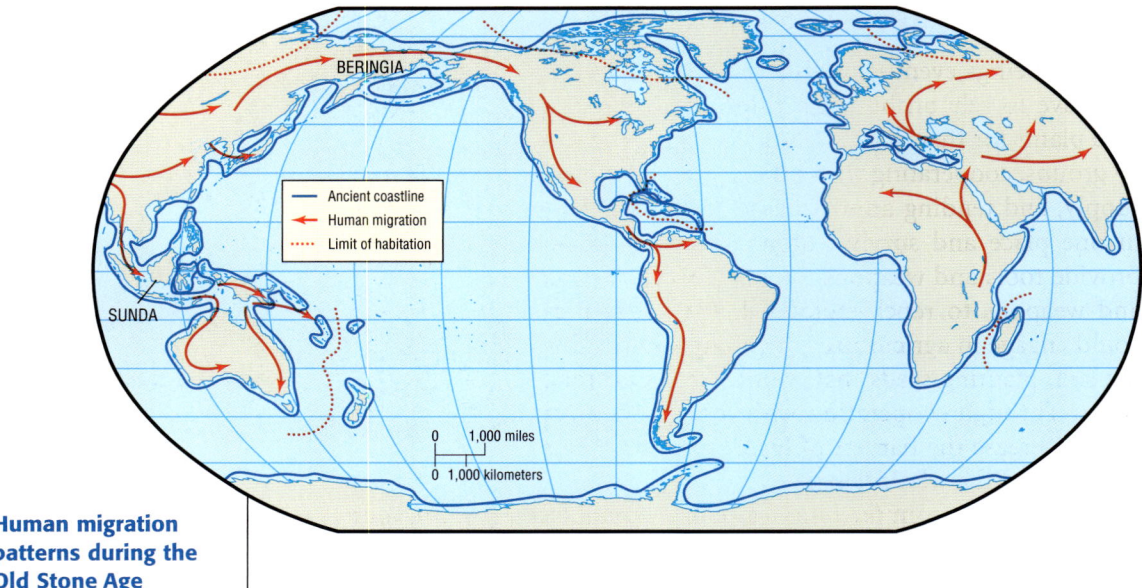

**Human migration patterns during the Old Stone Age**

Human beings, however, were not content with usefulness alone. As if in response to the beauty of God's creation, they loved beauty, too. From archaeological excavations, we know that ancient peoples covered their tools, clothing, weapons, and homes with elaborate carving and painting. They decorated things they used for even the most ordinary tasks with pictures and designs to give them a special and sacred beauty. Often these designs expressed religious ideas; for even though it seems most ancient peoples did not worship the one true God, they believed that the world was filled with spiritual beings who demanded worship and service and from whom people could gain favors. Ancient people feared these spirits and made stories about them and heroes of the far distant past.

Worship of nature gods was the religion of the Stone Age. The forces of nature seemed to have human personalities and human desires as well as the characteristics of animals. Because these forces had human-like qualities, ancient people thought they could persuade them to grant favors, just as each one of us can persuade other people to do things for us. Their sense of the beauty in nature and their awe of natural forces led early humans to decorate the walls of deep caves with paintings of their gods depicted as animals. These painted caves were temples and places of worship, not living quarters for the tribe.

But nature worship was terrible. Human beings saw only the terrors of nature and the fragility of human life. Most died young, and few saw old age. Their gods were dark and frightening, not loving or forgiving.

## The Neolithic Revolution

Human beings eventually discovered that they did not have to rely on hunting, fishing, or gathering wild plants for their food. Instead, by living in family groups, cooperating with others, growing a food supply, and tending animal herds, they could stay in one place and survive. Stone and bone could provide tools and weapons—tools to work the soil and weapons to repel enemies. Using tools, they could engage in agriculture—breaking and turning the soil, planting seeds that would grow into food crops. Through cooperation with others, one man could increase the harvest of his labor and make a crop to feed the whole tribe.

**Paleolithic cave art in Altamira, Spain**

The harvests from farming fed and enlarged human communities far beyond what hunting or gathering wild foods could have allowed. The first farming seems to have begun sometime around 10,000 B.C. Farming, which allows people to develop a stable food supply, is called **agriculture.** This practice began with the preservation and planting of once wild grains and the taming and domestication of certain friendly animals—the sheep, cow, dog, and horse. Historians call the discovery of agriculture the Neolithic Revolution.

The human beings of the New Stone Age also discovered building, the beginnings of **architecture.** Again, by cooperating with others, people could make a building to house several families. Farming and building changed human life forever. No longer would human families wander the Earth searching for food or shelter. Whole peoples began to settle in one place for generations, and the human family began to increase while continuing to make new discoveries.

The natural human love of beauty and worship of the nature gods led people to build monuments and temples of stone, earth, and wood. They raised the great stone-circle monuments of Europe and Asia and the earthworks of America.

Because farming gave populations a better and more trustworthy supply of food, people had more time for leisure. Families, bands, and tribes could join their efforts in pursuit of a common good. Shared customs, technologies, and a common religion—elements of what we call "culture"—bound tribes together. With a more stable life, people dwelt together in villages, some of which eventually became cities. The first cities seem to have been forts, built for defense. Walls and close-built houses

**agriculture:** the art of cultivating crops and domesticating herd animals for human food and use

**architecture:** the science of designing and raising houses and other buildings

**8** LIGHT TO THE NATIONS: The History of Christian Civilization

A man guides a wooden plow in India today, as was done in early times.

made for easy cooperation. They allowed easier defense and mutual support in wartime and protected the farmers and their harvests. The first cities appeared around 7,000–6,000 B.C. From these cities grew what we call **civilization.**

What is a civilization? A civilization is a culture that builds and supports cities. God gave this discovery to men and women to further their lives and development. Rule of law, the common good, justice, and improvement of life are the marks of civilization. These gifts to mankind were all the results of the cooperation required by life in cities and evidence of divine intervention in human life.

**civilization:** a culture that builds and supports cities

**Mesopotamia:** Greek for "the land in the middle of the rivers." The region between the Tigris and Euphrates rivers in what is now modern-day Iraq.

# The First Civilizations

The first civilizations grew up along four great rivers: the *Tigris and Euphrates Rivers,* in the land called **Mesopotamia** (Greek for "the land in the middle of the rivers"); the *Nile River,* in the land later called Egypt;

Megaliths were moved long distances to build the prehistoric monument of Stonehenge, in England, shown here.

the *Indus River*, in what is now northern India; and the *Yellow River* in northern China. These rich river valleys fed growing populations, and their waterways allowed for an easy interchange of ideas and ways of doing things.

**Map of early civilizations**

These ancient civilizations grew and ruled over the known world for two thousand years. Their religions remained close to the nature religions of the Stone Age, though they were more refined. People recognized moral truths and drew up laws and organized governments.

## In The Fullness of Time

Egypt was the first great center of civilization on the Mediterranean Sea. The center of civilization around the Mediterranean then shifted to the Syrian and Mesopotamian empires of Assyria and Babylon. Then came a wave of invaders called the Aryans or Indo-Europeans. These people swept over the lands of modern Turkey, Iran, and into India. Their invasion disrupted the older empires and kingdoms for centuries. But amid the rise and fall of old empires, the little people of Israel, the Hebrew kingdoms, held to the revelation God had given them. Israel and its **covenant** with God held the hope of light amid the darkness of the hardships, conquering armies, and exile.

> **covenant:** a binding agreement between two or more individuals to cooperate in a mutual task

The empire of Alexander the Great

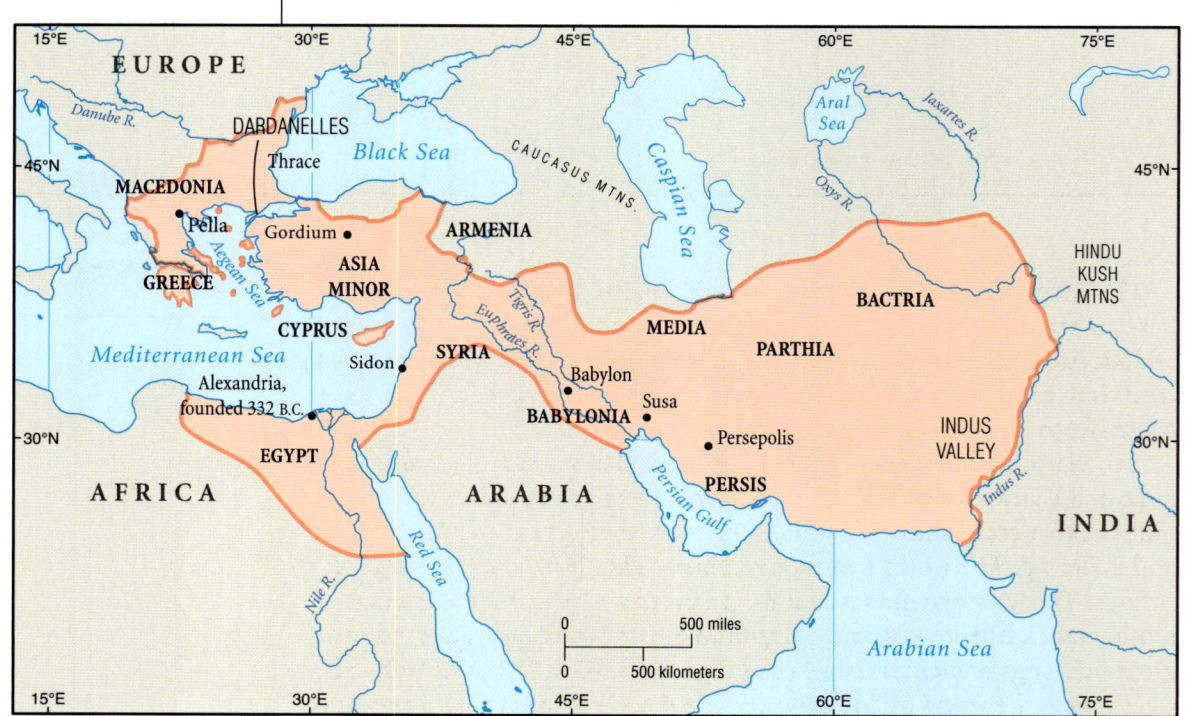

**Introduction** History's Beginnings **11**

Map of the Roman Empire at its greatest extent

The Mediterranean world was first organized under one rule by the Persian empire, then by the Greek empires under Alexander the Great and his successors, and then by Rome. Rome organized the Mediterranean lands into one empire, and all the shores of the Mediterranean Sea became *Mare Nostrum,* "Our Sea," as the Romans called it.

Yet, despite the growth of empires and the spread of civilization, human life lacked what it always had wanted—the satisfaction or sense of purpose that could make life something more than a prison house of pain and suffering. The world had received many gifts from the ancient civilizations. The Mesopotamians and Egyptians gave the world such things as mathematics, astronomy, and the technology by which people could raise great buildings and cities. Israel gave the world God's law and truth. The Greeks gave the world philosophy, a rational understanding of human and natural order. The Romans gave the world universal law and justice. Civilization gave material security and practical laws, but it did not satisfy the human spirit and its longing for the one true God.

The ancient world understood that when humans obeyed the natural law or the rules of right conduct, they had a happier and more successful life. In some ways, religion became more developed over time. The gods were more human than the Stone Age spirits had been. But the gods of the great civilizations had human flaws and desires, and they were often cruel and petty.

The philosophers of Greece and Rome had given people a reasonable way of understanding the natural order of the world. But people did not change. They were as greedy and violent as ever. The Creator God had revealed his law for mankind in nature, if people had been willing to see it and live by it. But they were not willing.

To the little people of Israel, God sent prophets. First there was Moses, who gave Israel the divine Commandments. Moses was followed by others who instructed the people in the will of God for us and for our happiness. The Old Testament records stories of good men and women trying to live by the will of God but falling back into the trap of slavery to the laws of nature.

**A statue of the Greek god Hermes**

## God Enters History

Then God took a great step. He himself entered human history to show humanity how it ought to live and to draw human souls to his friendship through personal contact. When teaching failed to change the world, God undertook a next step; he submitted to death for our sake. Mankind received a second chance at finding the eternal life our first parents forsook. "For as in Adam all die, so in Christ shall all be made alive" (1 Corinthians 15:20). The story of Jesus the Christ and the new life found by the Church was a new direction in history. The mystery revealed in Jesus' life, sacrifice, and resurrection transformed the story of human life and death.

It was into a civilized world that Jesus and his Church came. The peace and order of the Roman Empire provided the opportunity for the rapid spread of a new faith. Travelers, merchants, and missionaries, finding it safe to travel and welcomed in foreign towns and cities, carried the news to every corner of the empire.

The apostles took the news to all the civilized world. St. Paul, sometimes called "the Thirteenth Apostle," founded churches and wrote letters that gave a theology to the whole Church. The fast-growing Christian Church became a force for good and righteousness in all classes of society. The Church would survive persecution and scorn, separate itself from the customs of the Jewish religion, and carry the Good News from the Apostolic Age into the future.

What was the appeal of this little group of Jesus' followers in the very civilized world of the great Roman Empire? It was the message of the forgiveness of sins and eternal life. Forgiveness of sins meant, and means, a renewed life and a chance to live as human beings are supposed to live—at peace with God and each other. Eternal life meant just that—life that does not end with physical death. How the event of Jesus' Incarnation brought these gifts to humanity is a mystery worthy of lifelong study. But that mystery is a fact in the lives of generations of believers. These were the gifts Jesus gave to all ages through his sacrifice of himself on the cross.

**A fresco of the Nativity of Christ**

# Introduction Review

## Summary

- History is the story of God's dealings with humanity. It tells the tale of God's gift-giving to fallen mankind and of mankind's response.
- God speaks truth to mankind through the order, beauty, and grandeur of creation, but he also speaks to mankind in extraordinary ways. God gave his word and law through Moses and the prophets, but he spoke in a final and most wonderful way through the coming of Jesus Christ.
- The Incarnation of Jesus Christ was humanity's greatest moment of grace-filled change. It changed history and it changed humanity.
- The Incarnation measures all events that came after it and before it. The years before the birth of Jesus are called *Before Christ,* B.C. The years after the birth of Jesus are called *Anno Domini,* or "in the Year of the Lord."
- History is concerned with what men and women in different times and places have written about themselves and their societies. Without the written word, there is no history.
- Whatever happened in the years before people wrote about their deeds or what happened to them is called prehistory.
- During the Paleolithic (Old Stone Age) period of prehistory, human beings were nomadic hunters and gatherers, but they also began making tools and discovered art. Old Stone Age humans discovered the use of fire, among other things. They worshipped the forces of nature, which they called gods.
- During the Neolithic (New Stone Age) period of prehistory, human beings began to engage in agriculture and domesticated animals. Farming allowed people to settle in villages, some of which eventually became walled cities. Civilization arose from city life.
- The first civilizations grew up along four great rivers: the Tigris and Euphrates (Mesopotamia); the Nile River (Egypt); the Indus River (India); and the Yellow River (northern China).
- The center of civilization along the Mediterranean Sea passed from Egypt, to Assyria and Babylon, then to the Persians, then to the Greeks, and then to Rome.
- The great civilizations gave mankind many benefits, but none of these benefits could finally satisfy the human heart. God did not reveal himself to the great civilizations but to the humble nation of Israel. God made a covenant with the people of Israel, gave them divine laws, and

spoke to them through prophets. Finally, God himself became man in Jesus Christ. Jesus' life, sacrifice, and resurrection transformed the story of human life and death.

## Key Concepts
**the Incarnation:** God's taking on the nature of man in the person of Jesus of Nazareth. From the Latin *in carne,* "in the flesh."
**history:** the study of what people did and what happened to them based on written records of past ages
**agriculture:** the cultivation of crops and domestication of herd animals for human food and use
**civilization:** a culture that builds and supports cities

## Dates to Remember
**ca. 10,000 B.C.:** the beginning of farming
**ca. 7000–6000 B.C.:** the first cities appear

## Questions for Review
1. What does A.D. mean? What does B.C. mean? Do we call the years following the birth of Christ A.D. or B.C.? Of the two dates 200 B.C. or 25 B.C., which one indicates a year closer to our time? Which date is farther from our time?
2. What is prehistory? Why might a historian give us a clearer understanding of the past than either an archaeologist or paleontologist?
3. What were the important discoveries of the Paleolithic period? Of the Neolithic period?
4. How did agriculture make civilization possible? What are the benefits of civilization?
5. The first civilizations arose along four great rivers. Please name these rivers and the lands through which they run.
6. What human problems did God answer through the gift of Jesus' life and death?

## Ideas in Action
1. Imagine yourself as a prehistoric man or woman. You experience various natural forces—pleasant things, such as rain, snow, spring breezes, sunlight and moonlight. You also experience unpleasant and disastrous things, such as hurricanes, earthquakes, tornadoes, bitter cold, sweltering heat, and raging fire. Write an essay or story describing how you, living in prehistoric times, would imagine the gods or

spirits, based on your experience of the natural world. What would these gods or spirits look like? How would they act? (Maybe describe certain deeds you imagine them to perform.) Would they be lovable or terrible?

2. Imagine you are an archaeologist in the distant future, uncovering the remains of a school or household trash heap. You possess no written records of the time period. You find remnants of furniture, such as school desks or chairs, couches, and so on. Perhaps you find some religious pictures or a crucifix, and maybe there are disintegrating books. You find cups and saucers and plates; you find televisions and computers, which, of course, no longer work. What could be learned about our society from such an archaeological dig? Would future archaeologists be able to understand the uses of everything they discover? How would they know to what uses the room was given? Would they think us a very religious people? Would they think that we are great lovers of beauty?

# Chapter 1  A Light to the Nations

The birth of a baby is not the sort of event that historians or chroniclers would have thought worth recording. But they might have thought the birth of the baby, Jesus of Nazareth, worthy of recording, if they had known who he is.

There is little record of Jesus' life apart from the accounts now called the Gospels: Matthew, Mark, Luke, and John. From these same Gospels, we learn of Jesus' teachings, what he did, and his final sacrifice for mankind. Jesus did not write his teachings down, but his disciples, inspired by the Holy Spirit, wrote their memories of his words and deeds.

**Christ and four evangelists, from a windowpane from the church of Saint Denis, Paris, France**

# Herod, the King of Judea, 73–04 B.C.

**Testament:** a contract. The covenant of God with Israel, recorded in the books of the Hebrew Scriptures, is called the Old Testament. The covenant with all mankind made through the sacrifice of Christ on the cross and recorded in the books of the Christian Scriptures is called the New Testament.

When Jesus was born, his homeland, the land of the Jewish people, was under Roman control. Rome had stepped into Palestine to quiet civil strife there in 47 B.C. Eventually the Romans made a Jewish ally, named Herod, king of Judea, and placed him under Roman "protection," or control. Herod was not a Judean; he was an Idumean, or Edomite, from a desert tribe in the south that had only recently converted to Judaism.

King Herod is known to history as "Herod the Great." But Herod was great only in outliving all his rivals; he ruled for about 33 years, from 37 to 4 B.C. He executed his wife, fearing her disloyalty. He also killed his two eldest sons for plotting against him, killed or blinded other relatives he suspected of plotting his overthrow, and taxed and terrorized his subjects—who called him not the Great, but the Terrible.

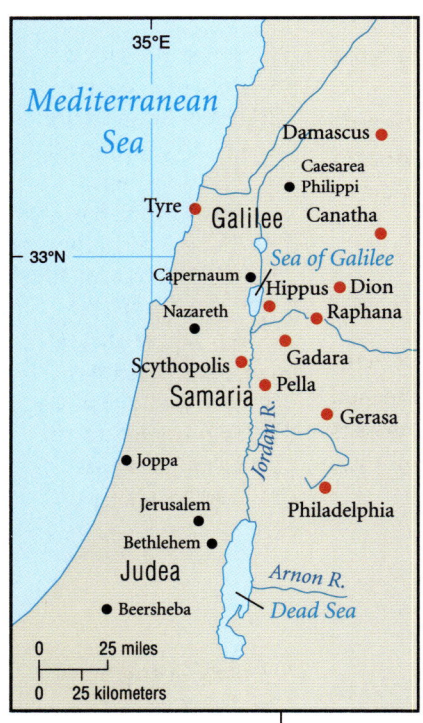

**Roman-era Palestine**

## A Divided People

Herod ruled over a deeply divided nation. Though all Israelites worshiped the one true God, they disagreed about how to live that faith.

One small group of Israelites were the Samaritans, who were descended from the kingdom of Israel, made up of the ten northern Israelite tribes and destroyed by the Assyrians five hundred years before. The Samaritans worshiped God at their holy place on Mount Gerizim, near the ruins of ancient Samaria. The Samaritans claimed that only the Torah, or five books of the Law—Genesis, Exodus, Leviticus, Numbers, and Deuteronomy—were inspired. All other writings of our Old **Testament**, they thought, were merely human. Since the days of the Babylonian exile, the Samaritans had resisted being united with the majority group—the Judeans, or Jews. By Herod's time, the Samaritans were a despised and oppressed group, living in the hills of Palestine.

The Jews were united, in that all of them worshiped at the Temple in Jerusalem. Yet, they were divided into two major religious groups with political as well as religious differences. These were the Sadducees and Pharisees.

**Model of the Jerusalem temple at the time of Christ**

The *Sadducees* (the "Righteous") came chiefly from old aristocratic families. They were not strict in observing the Law and did not believe in an afterlife of heaven and hell. Like the Samaritans, they accepted only the Torah as inspired **scripture**. The high priest was always chosen from the Sadducees.

The *Pharisees* (the "Separated") were closer to the ordinary people and concerned with matters of practical justice and easing the misery of the poor. They accepted belief in the afterlife. They made study of the Law, the Torah, the center of their religious lives. They accepted the rest of the scripture, the prophets and the other writings, as inspired by God. The greatest Jewish thinkers of the time, Hillel and Shammai, were both Pharisees.

The Pharisees came from merchant and professional families, with connections and ties to the Jewish communities in Judea and dispersed throughout the cities of the Roman Empire. From among the Pharisees came the scribes, judges, and teachers of the Law, who decided how Jews were to practice the commands of the Law.

**scripture:** the sacred writings of a religion. The Hebrew Scripture is what Christians call the Old Testament. It consisted of the first five books, called the Torah, that recounted the origins and Law of the Hebrew people, as well as books of Israel's history, books of the prophets' teachings, and literature such as the poetry of the Psalms.

# The Birth of Jesus

Our Lord Jesus the Christ was born sometime before Herod's death in 4 B.C., in the year of Augustus' great **census** of the empire, "when Quirinius was governor of Syria," as St. Luke's Gospel puts it. No official

**census:** an enumeration or count of the population

**20** LIGHT TO THE NATIONS: The History of Christian Civilization

**The nativity of Christ from a medieval stained glass**

Roman records document this birth. No notice was taken of it by the world at large. The most important birth in the history of the world occurred not in a palace but in a cave—used as a stable for horses and cattle—on the edge of a small town in Judea called Bethlehem. Jesus' mother, Mary, and Joseph, her husband, had traveled from Nazareth up into the hills to Bethlehem to comply with the Roman order for a general census of the empire's population. They went to Bethlehem because Joseph was "of the house and lineage of David." Bethlehem was David's birthplace and, thus, the center for David's descendants in a census. When the child was born, the parents named him Jesus (Hebrew *Yehoshua*, or *Yeshua*, meaning "God's Salvation").

## Jesus' Infancy and Hidden Life

In his last years, King Herod was full of dread. Enemies, he feared, were plotting against him to seize his throne. So it was that when he heard of the birth of an infant "king of the Jews," his only desire was to destroy the child.

The king had received some exotic visitors—*magi*, wise men from the East—who had come to find the promised child-king of the Jews (Matthew 2:1–12). They had stopped at Herod's court to find out what he knew about the child. They told him the prophecies had named Bethlehem as the site of the birth. Herod asked them, if they found the child, to return and tell him; Herod said he himself wanted to worship the infant king.

The magi did find the child, but they returned to their homes without going back to tell Herod. When the magi did not return, Herod was enraged. He ordered all male babies in Bethlehem killed (Matthew 2:16–18), to be sure that the prophesied babe should be destroyed.

### The Four Periods of Jesus' Life

Christians divide the life of Jesus into four periods. These are: the Infancy and Hidden Life, the Public Ministry, the Passion, and the Resurrection.

**The Adoration of the Magi**

But the child, Jesus, was not destroyed. His foster father, Joseph, warned by an angel in a dream, took his wife and the child down to Egypt to escape Herod's wrath. When news of Herod's death reached Joseph, he returned to Galilee and the town of Nazareth, where the family lived a normal, unremarkable life.

When the boy Jesus was about 12 years old, Joseph and Mary again journeyed to Jerusalem, to make the pilgrimage all Jews were to undertake at least once in their lives to worship at the Temple of Jerusalem. When they were returning home after having traveled some miles from the city, Joseph and Mary discovered their son was missing. Hurrying back to Jerusalem, they found Jesus, still in the temple, talking with a group of learned men about the things of God.

To his mother and Joseph, who wondered why he had worried them so, Jesus said, "Did you not know that I must be in my Father's house?"

When Jesus was still a boy, the Romans divided Herod's kingdom into two territories, Judea and Galilee. The larger territory, old Judea and Samaria, went to Herod's eldest surviving son, Herod Archelaus. But when he proved too incompetent to keep the peace, the Romans, in A.D. 6, made his kingdom a Roman province and placed it under the control of a Roman official, known as a procurator, or governor. Under the procurator's supervision, the Romans allowed the Jews a form of self-government under a council (the Sanhedrin) directed by the Jewish high priest.

To the north and east, Herod's possessions in Galilee and across the Jordan were given to his younger son, Herod Antipas, who ruled four districts as Rome's agent or *tetrarch* (meaning "ruler of four regions"). Joseph and his family lived in Nazareth of Galilee, the territory ruled by Herod Antipas.

In Galilee, the boy Jesus grew up without incident or notice, though he must have studied the sacred Scriptures intently and prepared himself for the years ahead. These are the years of the Hidden Life, about which we know nothing. Joseph, it appears, died in Jesus' youth, and the son may have taken up the trade of carpentry.

# Jesus' Public Life and Ministry

When Jesus was about 30 years old, a Jewish prophet and preacher appeared on the desert fringes of Herod Antipas' territory, calling on all Jews to repent of their sins and be baptized in the Jordan River. This preacher was Jesus' cousin John—the son of Mary's cousin Elizabeth.

Many crowds followed this prophet called John the Baptist, or Baptizer. He taught that the kingdom of God was at hand and that all who repented of their sins and received his baptism would be part of that kingdom when it came.

One of those who came to ask John for baptism was Jesus.

When John saw who stood before him, he balked at baptizing him and said, "I have need of being baptized by you. And yet you are coming to me?"

Jesus answered him, "Allow this now, for it is proper for us to fulfill all righteousness." Both knew that the entire history of the Jews was a history of salvation—the history of the Lord's mighty deeds among his chosen people, who strived through righteousness to be worthy. In submitting to baptism, Jesus was both fulfilling the ancient prophecies and purifying the waters of baptism through his own sinlessness. When Jesus came up out of the water, a voice from heaven declared, "This is my beloved Son, with whom I am well pleased."

**The Baptism of Christ**

After his baptism, Jesus withdrew into the desert of Judea, where he fasted for forty days and was tempted by Satan, the Enemy. After this he returned to the region of the Baptist's ministry, Galilee, and was acknowledged by John again. Jesus then began to collect around him a group of friends with whom he lived and taught.

At Cana in Galilee, at a wedding feast, Jesus performed his first miracle: the changing of water into wine. His mother asked him to do something to save the young groom from embarrassment, for the wine had run out. Jesus at first refused; but his mother said to the servants, "Do whatever he tells you." Obeying Jesus' command, the servants filled large jugs with water, which was then poured out as fine wine.

Jesus and his followers journeyed through the countryside and villages of Galilee. He spent his days in teaching anyone who would listen, forgiving sins, healing the sick, driving out demons, and bringing the dead back to life. His miracles drew large crowds to him, and they listened to his teaching.

## The Death of John the Baptist

Meanwhile, John the Baptist was scolding both Pharisees and Sadducees for neglecting their duties. But then, John did a dangerous thing; he denounced the tetrarch, Herod Antipas, for his immoral life and oppression of the poor. Herod had taken his brother Philip's wife, Herodias, and kept her as his wife. John publicly condemned this adultery, and Herod arrested him.

Though Herod feared John as a prophet of God, Herodias hated him. She laid plans for his death. One night at a feast, her daughter danced before Herod and the assembled guests. So pleased was Herod with his stepdaughter's dancing that he promised to give her anything she desired. The young girl, coached by her mother, asked for the head of John the Baptist on a platter. Even though he was afraid of John, Herod was obliged by his hasty promise to give her what she wanted. After John's death, many of those John had baptized became followers of Jesus.

Fresco of the beheading of St. John the Baptist

Chapter 1  A Light to the Nations  25

"Christ and the Woman with an Issue of Blood," by Paolo Veronese

## Jesus Calls the Twelve

Many, both men and women, followed Jesus. From these followers, Jesus selected 12 men as his closest companions to accompany him on his journeys through the towns of Galilee.

Jesus preached to large crowds and explained that the Law of God was a law of love—love of neighbor and of God. Jesus spoke of God as his father and explained the righteous life as the love of God, our father in heaven. He taught that true righteousness is mercy and kindness, not just obedience to the rules. He worked wonders and miracles that cured the sick and troubled and commanded the forces of nature. He raised from sickness the daughter of a synagogue official and the servant of a Roman centurion and revived from death the son of a poor widow in the village of Nain. His followers saw him calm the waves on the Sea of Galilee and even walk over the waters. He began to be known

**Messiah:** (Hebrew *Mashiach*; Greek *Christos*) the "Anointed One," a king or royal person

throughout the country as a miracle worker as well as a teacher with authority. Was this Jesus another prophet, the people asked, or could he be the long-awaited **Messiah** (the Christ)?

## The Teachings of Jesus

Jesus' insistence that the love of God and neighbor is the primary message behind the Law and the prophets was a familiar teaching in the Jewish tradition. In the books of Deuteronomy and Leviticus, the people could read: "Thou shalt love the lord thy God with all thy heart, and with all thy soul, and with all thy strength, and with all thy mind" (Deuteronomy 6:5) and "Love thy neighbor as thyself" (Leviticus 19:18). To the question, "Who is my neighbor?" Jesus answered with the parable of the Good Samaritan. Jesus taught that the one who shows mercy on the afflicted is the true neighbor of him. He said:

> *You have heard that it was said, "You shall love your neighbor and hate your enemy." But I say to you, Love your enemies and pray for those who persecute you, so that you may be the sons of your Father who is in heaven. (Matthew 5:43–44)*

Jesus preached a radical courage emboldened by faith in God. "Be not afraid," Jesus said, "not a sparrow falls but that the Father sees it. You are more valuable than sparrows and will not be forgotten before God" (Luke 12:7).

St. Luke (5:20–24) tells us that Jesus once said to a paralyzed man who was brought to him by friends and let down through the roof into the room where Jesus was teaching, "Man, your sins are forgiven you." When Jesus did this, the scribes and Pharisees whispered among themselves that this was blasphemy (claiming to be the equal of God): "Who can forgive sins but God only?" Jesus knew their thoughts, and replied, "'but that you may know that the Son of Man has authority on earth to forgive sins' (he turned to the paralyzed man and said), 'I say to you, rise, take up your bed and go home.'" Immediately the man rose and went home, praising God.

The forgiveness of sins was a focal point of Jesus' ministry, arising from his insistence on love as the first element of the kingdom of heaven. He forgave sins, and he told his followers to forgive the sins others commit against them.

Peter said to him, "Lord, how often shall my brother sin against me, and I forgive him? As many as seven times?"

Jesus replied to Peter, "I do not say to you seven times, but seventy times seven" (Matthew 18:21).

Greater even than Jesus' powerful teaching was his personality, drawing many to him in friendship. His example moved others to find the meaning behind the Law rather than to despair of keeping it. He said, "Think not that I have come to abolish the law and the prophets; I have come not to abolish them but to fulfill them" (Matthew 5:17).

Jesus dared to forgive sins and accept the repentant sinner back into the company of the righteous. He dared to reinterpret the Law to bring people to God, as when he said, "Man was not made for the Sabbath; the Sabbath was made for man" (Mark 2:27). The final authority would not be the letter of the Law, but Jesus' actions and his teachings about the true meaning of the Law.

## Jesus the Messiah, Son of the Father

Jesus spoke and acted not as a mere representative of God, as the Jewish tradition had expected of the Messiah, but as the Son of the Father. The Jews who opposed him accused him of blasphemy when he called himself the "Son of Man," a title of the Messiah. He left no doubt of who he claimed to be when he said that as the Son he was one with the Father in heaven: "The Father and I are one."

His last and greatest example would be the acceptance of the pain and death his enemies would force on him in the Crucifixion.

## Jesus' Passion

Jesus had known for some time that he would have to go down to Jerusalem for one last attempt to speak to the leaders of the people. He had prophesied that he would die and be raised again on the third day: "Destroy this temple and I will build it up in three days" (John 2:19). He knew also that the officials of the Jewish government would try to silence him, even kill him. On the first day of the week before **Passover**, Jesus entered the city.

Like the Hebrew kings of old, Jesus rode through the gates on a colt. The acclaim of the people, throwing down their cloaks and palm branches, crying out to Jesus, "Hosanna to the Son of David," disturbed the temple officials. They paid one of his disciples, Judas Iscariot, to lead the guards to arrest Jesus privately so that his arrest would not provoke a riot.

On the Thursday before the Passover, Jesus arranged for a room where he and his closest disciples could celebrate the Passover together. Jesus'

**passion:** painful suffering (from Latin *passio*, endurance). Christian tradition has long referred to Christ's suffering and death on the Cross as his Passion.
**Passover:** (Hebrew *pesach*) the Jewish ceremonial meal and feast commemorating the escape and deliverance of the Hebrew people from the bondage of Egypt

**28** LIGHT TO THE NATIONS: The History of Christian Civilization

**Eucharist:** so named from the Greek word for "thanksgiving." The central sacrament of the Christian Faith. In the Mass, the Church gives thanks for Christ's sacrifice and redemption of sinners by repeating the words of Our Lord and consecrating the sacred bread and wine.

action at this Last Supper was the institution (or start) of the greatest sacrament of Christian life—the Holy **Eucharist**. Since that night, Christians have joined themselves to Jesus the Christ by taking, as he commanded, the bread of his Body and the cup of his Blood and repeating his words, "Take, this is my body" and "This is my blood of the new covenant which is shed for many" (Luke 22:19–20). The Catholic Church has defined that in this sacrament the bread and wine are changed to become the body and blood of Jesus. This change the Church calls "transubstantiation."

After the supper, Jesus went out from the city with his 12 disciples to a public garden on the Mount of Olives, east of the city. He went off from the others to pray and to ask God to spare him from what he knew was ahead: "Father, if thou art willing, remove this cup from me;

**The Kiss of Judas Iscariot. a detail of the Magdeburg (Sigtuna) Gate of Sophia Cathedral in Novgorod, Russia**

nevertheless not my will, but thine, be done" (Luke 22:42). Knowing where Jesus would likely be, Judas brought the temple soldiers to arrest him.

After his arrest, Jesus was taken first to the palace of Caiaphas, the high priest, for trial. The temple officials found Jesus guilty of blasphemy. But they were afraid to act without Roman permission; so they sent him to the Roman governor, Pilate, who sent him to Herod Antipas, the tetrarch, who was in the city for the Passover. Herod was afraid to make a judgment, for his treatment of John the Baptist had made him many enemies among the people, so he sent Jesus back to Pontius Pilate.

Pilate saw Jesus in the early hours of the morning, but Jesus would not respond to the governor's questions. Being reluctant to put Jesus to death, Pilate looked for a way to put the burden on others. It was the custom to offer two condemned men to the mob, letting the people choose one to be executed and one to be pardoned. Pilate brought Jesus and a well-known rioter and murderer, Barabbas, to the porch of the governor's palace and let the people in the square decide which man to release. The temple officials incited the people to choose Barabbas for release. And when asked what then to do with Jesus, the mob cried, "Crucify him! Crucify him!"

The governor had sent Jesus to his guards for flogging. They scourged Jesus with whips, as Roman law required. Then, because Jesus had claimed to be the Messiah, or King of the Jews, the soldiers mocked him by forcing on him a crown of thorns and an old cloak to be his royal costume.

Rejected and alone, Jesus was forced to walk to the place of execution. On his bleeding back he had to drag his own crossbeam—possibly

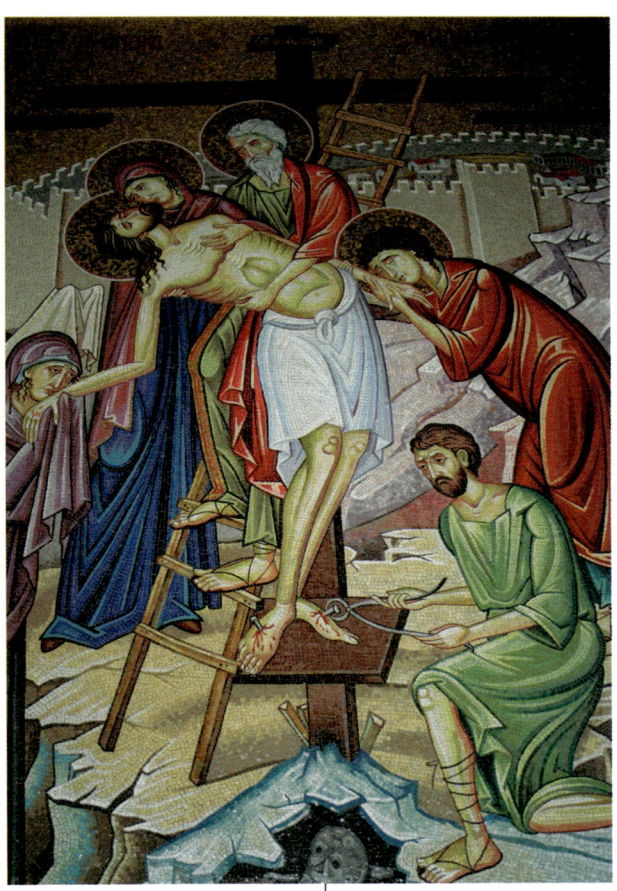

**The deposition from the cross, a fresco in the Church of the Holy Sepulchre, Jerusalem**

### Roman Scourging

Roman law prescribed a serious and torturous whipping with both rods and a lead-weighted leather whip of several strands, a Roman version of the later "cat-o-nine-tails." This scourging was so severe that many of the condemned died in the beating.

as much as 125 pounds of heavy wood—from the Roman headquarters, across the streets of Jerusalem, outside the walls, to the hill of Golgotha.

Jesus was nailed to the cross on Friday morning and lifted upright to hang there until dead. Jesus hung between two other crucified men, both criminals. On Jesus' cross Pilate had ordered the placing of an inscription to proclaim Jesus' crime: "Jesus of Nazareth, King of the Jews."

Toward evening, the Jewish officials asked that Jesus and the other two criminals hanging with him be killed and taken down so that no bodies would be there for the Holy Days of the Passover. Soldiers went to break the legs of the condemned; unable to push themselves up to take a breath, the condemned would die of suffocation. When, however, the soldiers went to break Jesus' legs, they found he was already dead—after only three hours, an unexpectedly short time. To be certain, a soldier plunged his spear into Jesus' side. Both blood and water, a sign of death, came forth. The soldiers did not break Jesus' legs; as the Hebrew Scriptures had prophesied of him, "not a bone of his shall be broken" (Psalm 34:20).

## Jesus' Resurrection and Ascension

Because the Jewish Sabbath was approaching and Jewish tradition forbade anyone to prepare a body for burial on the Sabbath, Jesus was hastily buried in a borrowed, unused tomb set in a garden. The tomb had been prepared for Joseph of Arimathea, one of Jesus' followers and also one of the Sanhedrin. Remembering that Jesus had said he would rise up on the third day and fearing a plot by the apostles, the chief priests and Pharisees set a guard by the tomb.

Sometime in the early morning of Easter Sunday, a tremendous physical disturbance—something like an earthquake—stunned the guards. By the time they recovered their senses, the stone had been rolled back and the tomb was empty. The guards went to the Pharisees, afraid they would be punished for neglecting their duty. Instead, they were given money and told to spread a story that the apostles had stolen the body while the soldiers were asleep. This they did.

Later that same morning, several of the women who had followed Jesus came to the tomb. Mary Magdalene, Mary the mother of James, and Salome brought spices to complete the embalming of the body. Arriving first, the two Marys saw that the tomb was empty; and an angel appeared, telling them, "He is not here, for he has risen as he said" (Matthew 28:6). Mary Magdalene immediately went to tell the disciples.

The other women then arrived and were greeted by an angel, who gave them the message that Jesus had risen and instructed them to report this

**Jesus delivering Adam and Eve from Hades, from Chora Church, Constantinople**

news to the disciples. When the women brought this incredible story to the apostles, John and Peter ran immediately to the tomb to see for themselves. John, arriving first, saw the shroud in which Christ had been buried; it was neatly folded, something no thief would have done. Peter ran into the empty tomb to confirm that no dead body was there.

However, the other apostles were stubborn men who refused to believe the women or the other men. But that night, when they were behind locked doors, Jesus suddenly appeared in their midst. To prove that he had truly returned to life and was not a disembodied ghost, he sat down and ate with them.

One disciple, however, was absent from that meeting—Thomas. On hearing of it, he refused to be convinced until he personally saw Jesus' wounds. But the following Sunday, Christ appeared again and spoke to Thomas directly and by name. Thomas fell on his knees, saying, "My Lord and my God" (John 20:28).

A mosaic depicting the Ascension of Jesus Christ, in Saint Mark's Basilica, Venice, Italy

Forty days after his resurrection, Jesus led his disciples to the Mount of Olives and mysteriously left the world. Before his wondering followers Jesus rose up, ascended, into heaven (Acts 1:9–10). But though he had departed from them, Jesus left in their hearts a strength and courage they had not held before, empowering them to "go and teach all nations" the good news of their salvation. "I am with you always, to the close of the age" (Matthew 28:20), he said before leaving them.

Jesus' promise to be with his followers would have a new significance in the years to come, when they—like he—had to meet opposition and persecution, torture and death for their faith.

# Pentecost and the Jerusalem Church

After Jesus' death, the disciples were in hiding for fear the temple authorities would arrest them. On a Jewish holy day called **Pentecost**, only 10 days after Jesus' ascension into heaven, the disciples assembled in the same upper room where they had shared the Last Supper. Suddenly, a strong, driving wind filled the house. Those present were crowned with tongues

## The Holy Eucharist

Following Jesus' death and resurrection, in the very beginnings of the Church, the disciples held weekly gatherings, sharing the bread and the cup and repeating Jesus' words. The weekly sacred meal became a moment of union with Jesus as brought to them through his words and command, "Do this in remembrance of me."

St. Paul, in an account that was written earlier than the Gospels (1 Corinthians 10:16), says of this meal, "The cup of blessing which we bless, is it not a participation in the blood of Christ? The bread which we break, is it not a participation in the body of Christ?" Then later in the same epistle (1 Corinthians 11:23–26), Paul gives the words of Jesus as "This is my body which is for you" and "This cup is the new covenant in my blood. Do this as often as you drink it in remembrance of me." From the earliest records of the Church, it is clear that the apostles and their flock took the words of the Lord seriously and made of the weekly meal a sacred moment of participation in the Lord's body and blood.

The early Church's weekly gatherings gave thanks for what had been done for them and what had been revealed to them about the nature of their lives through the life of Jesus. The meal was called a Thanksgiving, a Eucharist (Greek *eucharistos*). In other places it was called an *agapeia*, a "love feast," because of the expression of love that the sharing commanded.

*The Last Supper*, from the Beram Church of Saint Mary, Croatia

of flame, and they each began to speak in different languages previously unknown to them (Acts 2:1–2). Those present were given a new courage. They immediately ran out into the city to begin preaching to the crowds of pilgrims, who had come to Jerusalem for the feast, that Jesus of Nazareth had risen from the dead and held the promise of salvation and spiritual light for all nations.

**Pentecost:** a Jewish holy day of thanksgiving for the wheat harvest. It was held 50 days after Passover (from the Greek word *pentekoste*, meaning "fiftieth").

**apostle:** (from Greek *apostolos*) one sent forth, a messenger

## The Twelve Apostles

Just as the people of Israel had been made up of 12 tribes descended from the 12 sons of Jacob, so the Church was established on the witness of 12 men—Jesus' disciples. Since these men were to go forth as Jesus' messengers to all the world, they were called **apostles**.

There was a problem, however. The traitor, Judas Iscariot, was no longer with them. He had killed himself soon after the death of Jesus on the cross, and Judas' place as one of the Twelve had to be filled. The apostles voted to restore their significant number by naming Matthias to the twelfth place. Matthias had been a disciple from the beginning and could bear witness to Jesus' Resurrection.

As in so many other critical moments of history, the hope of the future rested with unlikely heroes. The Twelve were ordinary workmen. The chief of the apostles, Simon Peter, once had been just Simon, a humble fisherman on Lake Galilee; then Jesus had called him, along with his brother Andrew, to follow him and become "fishers of men." As an apostle, Simon was also called Cephas (*Petros* in Greek, *Cephas* in Aramaic, both meaning "rock"). Simon had received his new name, Peter, from Jesus, who said, "And I tell you, you are Peter, and on this rock I will build my church" (Matthew 16:18).

Jesus' apostles had been far from perfect men. James and John, the sons of Zebedee, had also been simple fishermen, given to displays of such hot temper that they were called the "sons of thunder." Matthew had been a tax collector, despised by the Jews for working under the Roman oppressor. Simon the Zealot had been a member of one of the rebel bands that annoyed the Romans and terrorized the villagers with demands for supplies. Thomas had refused to believe in the Resurrection until he had touched the wounds in Jesus' hands and side.

Jesus had said, "I came not to call the righteous, but sinners to repentance." The Twelve were all sinful men and unimportant peasants, but in their new faith they found the strength to be great heroes and saints.

The disciples included many women. Among them was Jesus' mother, Mary, known to all his friends as the first disciple. Because of Mary's love, obedience, and holiness, and because of her special relationship with Jesus, she has been honored above all other disciples and women through the ages. "All generations shall call me blessed," she had proclaimed in the "Magnificat" (Luke 1: 46–55), her hymn of joy at the great things that God had done in his love for human beings.

There were also other Marys, the mother of James and John, who had followed her sons up to Jerusalem with Jesus; and Jesus' friends, Mary and

## The Twelve

The Twelve, as named in the Gospels, were

1. Simon Peter (Cephas bar-Jona)
2. Andrew (Peter's brother)
3, 4. James and John (the sons of Zebedee)
5. Philip
6. Bartholemew
7. Thomas (Didymus)
8. Matthew (Levi, the tax collector)
9. James the Less (the son of Alpheus)
10. Jude (Lebbaeus, Thaddaeus)
11. Simon the Zealot
12. Judas Iscariot (who betrayed the Lord)

Martha of Bethany, sisters of Lazarus, whom Jesus had raised from the dead. Then there were also unhappy and disreputable women—like Mary of Magdala (a town in Galilee), who had been cured of demonic possession. To these women, as to his male friends, Jesus entrusted the deepest mysteries of the religious life: incarnation, forgiveness of sins, and resurrection.

At first, after Jesus' ascension, the disciples stayed in the city of Jerusalem. They pooled all their resources to support every member of the community and appointed James (Jesus' cousin, not one of the Twelve) the leader of the community. They held all their possessions in common while they waited for the return of Jesus. However, this arrangement did not work well. Some held back their property, and some ate at the common table but did not contribute to it. The disciples finally abandoned communal living after the Roman siege and capture of Jerusalem in A.D. 71.

*The Last Judgment, from the portal of Notre Dame de Paris*

St. Stephen, the first martyr

## The First Martyr

The first Christians were eager to share their new faith with others, especially with their fellow Jews. At first, most converts to the Church were Jews; but after he baptized a Roman named Cornelius, Peter convinced his fellow Christians to admit non-Jews, or gentiles, into the community.

The young Church attracted more and more followers and appointed deacons (from Greek *diakonos*, meaning "servant") to teach and serve the new converts. The common life of the community in Jerusalem centered on the common meal (the Eucharist) and prayer on the first day of the Jewish week, Sunday, when the stronger members cared for the weaker by providing the food and drink.

But the growing number of converts threatened the Jewish authorities. Angered at the public preaching of a deacon named Stephen, they ordered him to be stoned to death as a blasphemer (Acts 7:60). Stephen became the first Christian **martyr**. He died in around A.D. 34 or 36, not long after the death of Jesus.

Stephen's death had a great effect on at least one young man present at the stoning. He was Saul, a wealthy and learned Pharisee from the city of Tarsus in Asia Minor.

**martyr:** (from Greek *martyros*, "witness") a witness, later coming to mean someone who dies rather than deny his faith

## The Life and Journeys of St. Paul

Saul was a Pharisee, a learned and respected teacher of the Law. He was from the city of Tarsus in Asia Minor, and he had studied at Jerusalem with the great teachers of the Pharisees, Hillel and Gamaliel. By family connections he was a Roman citizen, with the right to travel throughout the empire.

Saul did not himself take part in the stoning of Stephen, but he watched it without protest and sympathized with the Jewish authorities. It is recorded that he "held the cloaks" of those who did the stoning. After Stephen's death, Saul volunteered to take the orders from the Jerusalem authorities to the Jewish leaders of Damascus in Syria to punish the followers of Jesus living in Syria.

**St. Paul, from the Basilica of St. Paul, Rome**

## Saul Becomes Paul

On the road to Damascus, Saul was struck down by a blinding light. He heard a voice saying, "Saul, Saul, why do you persecute me? I am Jesus, whom you are persecuting" (Acts 9:4–5). For three days Saul could see nothing, and he ate and drank nothing.

Following Jesus' instructions given to him in his vision, Saul went on to Damascus. Instead of going to the authorities, he went to the Christians, who baptized him and tended him until his sight was miraculously restored. After Saul could see again, he began speaking in the synagogues of Damascus about Jesus as the promised Messiah. Over time, he began to use his Roman name, Paul, rather than his Hebrew name, Saul. Paul called himself an apostle, just like the Twelve, or the "least of the apostles."

Taking Jesus' command to heart, to "go and teach all nations" of the salvation brought by Jesus, over the next 30 years, A.D. 36–68, Paul traversed thousands of miles, winning converts among both Jews and Gentiles, establishing churches in dozens of cities throughout Syria, Asia Minor, Greece, and as far away as Spain.

**38** LIGHT TO THE NATIONS: The History of Christian Civilization

**The journeys of St. Paul**

## The Epistles

Of the 21 epistles contained in the New Testament, the first 14 are by St. Paul. They are Romans, 1 Corinthians, 2 Corinthians, Galatians, Ephesians, Philippians, Colossians, 1 Thessalonians, 2 Thessalonians, 1 Timothy, 2 Timothy, Titus, Philemon, and Hebrews. They were arranged in this order in the early Church, and are positioned according to the importance of the church community addressed, not the order of their composition or their subject. The remaining epistles collected in the New Testament are called the "Catholic," or Universal epistles, and are addressed to all the churches at once about more general topics rather than local concerns. They are James; 1 and 2 Peter; 1, 2, and 3 John; and Jude.

He met opposition at every step along the way. Once, his enemies stoned Paul and, supposing he was dead, dragged his unconscious body out of their city. The next day, Paul rose up and returned to the city. Paul and Barnabas then established a community of believers, appointing elders to guide them.

After Paul departed from a city, leaving behind a new Christian church, he wrote letters back to the community he had begun there, continuing to teach his distant friends and converts through the written word. These letters were treasured heirlooms of the churches that he founded and have continued down through the ages to teach us in the new millennium. The surviving letters are collected in Christian Bibles as the Letters or **Epistles** of Paul. The Epistles are the oldest books in the New Testament.

**epistle:** letter (from Greek *epistole*)

## The Teachings of St. Paul

Paul witnessed to the love of Christ. He taught that Jesus' sacrifice on the cross brought salvation to all mankind, not just the Jewish people. Salvation, he said, does not come through observing Jewish rituals. Non-Jews, he insisted, do not have to become Jews before baptism. Salvation, Paul taught, is a free gift of God's grace through faith in Christ. Grace transforms the human heart by hope and charity and promises believers a share in Christ's resurrection. "For as in Adam all men die, so in Christ will all be made alive" (1 Corinthians 15:20).

Paul's teachings made him enemies, both Jewish and gentile. They engineered disturbances, beat him up, drove him out of towns, and complained about him to the Jewish elders or to the city police officials. Everywhere he went, Paul's missionary work brought him into conflict with the Jewish authorities—and sometimes with the Romans, who were trying to keep the peace and prevent local disturbances. His three journeys, each lasting many years, were full of troubles—both from natural causes and human attacks. St. Paul became known to the Church as the model of faithful endurance of suffering for Christ's sake.

Paul returned to Jerusalem about A.D. 58. There, the Jewish elders accused him of blasphemy, and the Roman procurator arrested him to save his life from the elders. He was sent to the Roman provincial capital at Caesarea on the coast and there kept under house arrest while two successive Roman governors tried to think of some way to let him go. Finally, Paul claimed his rights as a Roman citizen and asked to be sent directly to the emperor in Rome to be tried. He was sent under guard by ship but was shipwrecked off the coast of Malta, where he spent some time at liberty.

Paul then traveled to Syracuse in Sicily and to Rhegium on the toe of Italy. Paul finally arrived at Rome, where he spent two years in comparative liberty while waiting for the imperial courts to hear his case. During this time he lived in a private house where he prayed, wrote, and daily received visitors from the Christian community in Rome.

## Peter and Paul Martyred

Paul of Tarsus and Simon Peter were the two most prominent and important figures in the early years of the Church. Peter was the head and

**The miraculous catch of fish, from Notre Dame Cathedral, Paris**

spokesman for the Twelve Apostles, while Paul was the greatest missionary and founder of churches.

Both Peter and Paul were in Rome during the first imperial persecution of Christians. In A.D. 68, a great fire laid waste to much of Rome. The Emperor Nero, knowing that many Romans blamed the fire on him, was looking for a scapegoat. He found it in the strange, new sect called Christians. Nero blamed the fire on the Christians and began brutally persecuting them. Paul was condemned to death and executed by beheading, the punishment for a condemned citizen of Rome. His death occurred about A.D. 68. His body, at first buried outside the city, is now contained in the basilica of St. Paul's Outside the Walls in Rome.

Tradition says that Peter's death took place in the same year as Paul's. According to the later Christian writer, Origen, Nero's judges condemned Peter to be crucified. However, deeming himself unworthy to suffer the same death, in the same way, as his Lord and Savior, Peter asked to be nailed to the cross head down. The bones of Peter are buried in St. Peter's Basilica in Rome. A statue of St. Peter in the front of the basilica is near the actual site where Peter was crucified.

**Saint Peter Enthroned, Saint Peter's Basilica, Rome**

All but one of the Twelve suffered martyrdom. Tradition relates that only St. John died a natural death, after his exile to the tiny island of Patmos off the coast of Asia Minor. He returned to Ephesus in Asia Minor, where he died in old age. The churches the Twelve left behind grew and survived the persecutions that followed. They carried faith and courage to the highest and the lowliest alike, across the empire and beyond into Europe, Africa, and India—and finally, many centuries later, to the Americas.

# Jesus' Gifts to Civilization

Jesus' death on the Cross for our salvation was his greatest gift to humanity. But his death also gave gifts to civilization that cannot be ignored—hope, and an image of God in human form, a story of sacrifice and promise. The followers of Jesus and missionaries like St. Paul brought a new hope to the empire's great and small, rich and poor. Life without fear was promised to all who believed in Jesus and accepted him as Lord. As Jesus had taught, "He that loveth his life shall lose it, and that hateth his life in this world shall keep it unto life eternal. If any man serve me, let him follow me; and where I am, there shall also my servant be" (John 12:25–26). "This is my commandment, that you love one another as I have loved you" (John 16:12). God was in Christ Jesus, and the human heart could love him as he had loved us.

In the light of this hope, civilization could follow paths of thought and invention not possible before. Individuals could develop ideas and practices that had not occurred to anyone caught in the old worship of nature. A civilization of love and forgiveness of sins was now possible. Jesus gave civilization a new purpose and goal, union in love with God.

# Chapter Review

## Summary

- Christian history begins with the birth of Jesus. His parents, Mary and Joseph, raised him in Nazareth of Galilee. This period of Jesus' life is known as the Infancy and Hidden Life.
- The second period of Jesus' life is known as the Public Life. After being baptized by John, Jesus journeyed through Galilee and Judea teaching, healing the sick, casting out demons, and bringing the message of hope and forgiveness. Jesus taught that love of God and neighbor is our proper response to God's forgiveness and love for us.
- At last, in the Passion and Death, the Jewish leaders plotted against Jesus, paying Judas Iscariot, one of the disciples, to betray him. On the Thursday before the Passover, Jesus instituted the sacrament of the Eucharist in a last supper with his disciples. That night, Jesus was arrested and brought before the Roman authority, Pontius Pilate; the Jewish leaders accused him of blasphemy of God and treason to Rome. Pilate condemned Jesus to death by crucifixion. Jesus endured this terrible torture and died on the cross.

- When the third day had dawned after his death, Jesus rose and was seen by several of his disciples and followers. His followers saw him ascend to Heaven on the fortieth day after his Resurrection.
- Jesus' followers experienced a renewal of their fervor 50 days after his death. On the feast of Pentecost, the Holy Spirit filled them with new life and zeal to carry Jesus' good news of forgiveness to all the world.
- The Twelve Apostles remained in Jerusalem after Pentecost, organizing the first community of believers in Jesus. Peter, the chief of the apostles, convinced his fellow Christians, who had all been Jewish, to admit Gentiles into the Church of the believers.
- Although he at first persecuted Jesus' followers, St. Paul was converted by a miraculous vision of the Lord and became the chief apostle and missionary to the people of the Roman world. His letters (epistles) to the churches he founded are now part of the Christian Scriptures. Paul and Peter together suffered martyrdom in Rome in the reign of the Emperor Nero.

## Key Concepts

**testament:** a contract, the covenant between God and Mankind. The covenant of God with Israel recorded in the books of the Hebrew Scriptures is called the Old Testament. The covenant with all mankind made through the sacrifice of Christ on the cross and recorded in the books of the Christian Scriptures is called the New Testament.

**Passover:** (Hebrew *pesach*) the Jewish ceremonial meal and feast commemorating the escape and deliverance of the Hebrew people from the bondage of Egypt

**Eucharist:** so named from the Greek word for "thanksgiving." The central sacrament of the Christian Faith. In the Catholic Mass, the Church gives thanks for Christ's sacrifice and redemption of sinners by repeating the words of Our Lord and the consecration of the sacred bread and wine.

**Messiah:** (Hebrew *Mashiach*; Greek *Christos*) the "Anointed One," a king or royal person

**scripture:** the sacred writings of a religion. The Hebrew Scripture is what Christians call the Old Testament. It consisted of the first five books, called the Torah, that recounted the origins and Law of the Hebrew people, as well as books of Israel's history, books of the prophets' teachings, and literature such as the poetry of the Psalms.

**apostle:** (from Greek *apostolos*) one sent forth, a messenger

**martyr:** (from Greek *martyros*, "witness") a witness, later coming to mean someone who dies rather than deny his faith

## Dates to Remember

**37–4 B.C.:** reign of Herod the Great
**6 or 4 B.C.:** birth of Jesus Christ
**A.D. 28 or 30:** death and resurrection of Jesus
**A.D. 68:** deaths of Sts. Peter and Paul by martyrdom in Rome

## Central Characters

**Jesus:** the Son of God and Jewish Messiah, who brought salvation to Jews and Gentiles alike and gave new light and hope to civilization
**John the Baptist:** cousin of Jesus; a Jewish prophet and preacher who preached a baptism for the forgiveness of sins. John announced the coming of Jesus.
**Herod the Great:** king of Judea when Jesus was born
**Mary:** mother of Jesus
**Joseph:** foster father of Jesus, husband of Mary
**the Twelve Apostles:** Jesus' closest companions and disciples
**Peter:** a fisherman who became the chief of the apostles of Jesus
**Pontius Pilate:** Roman procurator, or governor, of Judea, under whom Jesus was crucified
**Paul:** Saul the Pharisee, who persecuted Christians but was converted after receiving a vision of Christ. Paul spread the Gospel throughout the Mediterranean basin.

## Questions for Review

1. What written evidence do we have for Jesus' life?
2. What are the four periods of Jesus' life? Which period or periods do we know most about? Which period do we know least about? Why?
3. What does *Eucharist* mean? Why was, and is, weekly celebration of the Eucharist so important to Christians?
4. Why do you think the Christian faith spread so quickly?
5. What is a martyr? Who was the first martyr?
6. Where were Peter and Paul martyred?

## Ideas in Action

1. Attend Mass. Read the accounts of the Last Supper in the Gospels. Then discuss as a class: How is the Mass like the Last Supper? How is it different? What are the major divisions of the Mass? Why do we

read Scripture from the Old Testament and the New? What is going on in the consecration? What is said and what is done? How does the Communion of the congregation repeat the early Church's thanksgiving love-feast meal?
2. Read from one of St. Paul's epistles (for instance, Ephesians or Colossians), and discuss what he is saying. Why would he say these things to an audience of the ancient world? What is he saying to people who were pagans? What is he saying to Jewish Christians?
3. How does the Church in our day spread the Gospel? Do we have preachers like Sts. Peter and Paul? In what ways can Christians spread the Gospel among their friends and family?

# Highways and Byways

### From St. Peter's Sermon on Pentecost Day

"Peter stood up with the Eleven and addressed them in a loud voice: 'Men of Judaea, and all you who live in Jerusalem, make no mistake about this, but listen carefully to what I say. This is what the prophet spoke of:

> *In the days to come — It is the Lord who speaks —*
> *I will pour out my spirit on all mankind.*
> *Their sons and daughters shall prophesy,*
> *your young men shall see visions,*
> *your old men shall dream dreams.*
> *Even on my slaves, men and women,*
> *in those days, I will pour out my spirit,*
> *I will display portents in heaven above*
> *and signs on earth below.*
> *The sun will be turned into darkness*
> *and the moon into blood*
> *before the great Day of the Lord dawns.*
> *All who call on the name of the Lord will be saved.*

"Men of Israel, listen to what I am going to say; Jesus the Nazarene was a man commended to you by the miracles and portents and signs that God worked through him when he was among you, as you all know. This man, who was put into your power by the deliberate intention and foreknowledge of God, you took and had crucified by men outside the Law. You killed him, but God raised him to life, freeing him from the pangs of Hades; for it was impossible for him to be held in its power:"

—Acts 2:14–25 (trans. *Jerusalem Bible*, 1966)

# Chapter 2: Emperors and Madmen

On August 19, A.D. 14, only a few years after Jesus of Nazareth was born, the great Augustus, master of the civilized world, died.

At Augustus' death, the Roman Empire over which he had ruled included the entire Mediterranean world, from the Atlantic Ocean to the Caucasus Mountains, from the deserts of Morocco to the valleys of the Rhine and Danube rivers in Europe.

Augustus had inherited the empire from his uncle, Julius Caesar. For centuries, the Roman state had been a republic. It was ruled by a body of prominent men, called the Senate, and administered by various officials. As the republic spread east, west, and south across the Mediterranean world, its form of government grew incapable of keeping peace. Civil war between factions continually troubled Rome.

Finally, Julius Caesar, a brilliant general and the hero of the common people of Rome, seized power. The Senate named Caesar dictator—sole ruler—for life. He did not enjoy his power for long, however. His enemies, fearing Caesar would make himself king and so forever bury the republic, assassinated him.

## The First Caesar

Gaius Julius Caesar was the full name of Julius Caesar. As with other Roman names, the second name, Julius, was the name of the clan or greater family to which he belonged while Caesar was the name of his branch of the Julian family. Gaius was his personal name.

## The Principate

After Julius Caesar's death, Augustus, then called Octavian (Gaius Julius Caesar Octavianus), defeated his uncle's enemies. He divided the rule of the empire with two other men, Marcus Lepidus and Marc Antony,

**the principate:** the new organization of government begun by Augustus, giving real power to the emperor or princeps ("first citizen")

47

**48** LIGHT TO THE NATIONS: The History of Christian Civilization

**Map of the Roman Empire at the beginning of the second century A.D.**

**emperor:** "commander in chief," "supreme commander"; title of a commander of several legions, given by the Senate first to Augustus and then held by all his successors

in what was called the Second Triumvirate (rule of three men). Lepidus, accused of attempting rebellion and exiled, soon died. Octavian and Antony then struggled for power in a fight that Octavian won. As sole ruler of the empire, Octavian set up a government to preserve the Roman state from further civil war.

The Senate gave Octavian the title "Augustus" (meaning "majestic," "venerable") in token of his remaking of the Roman system of government into what was called the **principate**. The new government was an organization governing the Mediterranean world, directed by officials and defended by a paid army. Both the officials and the army answered to one man, Augustus himself, who was called the *princeps*, or "first citizen"—the **emperor**. Though the emperor needed the Senate's approval and support, the senators basically did his bidding. Before Augustus came to power, the

Senate largely ruled the empire. Under Augustus, however, the Senate lost most of its power.

The principate lasted almost unchanged for about 270 more years after Augustus' death. The Mediterranean world prospered under the **Pax Romana**, the Roman Peace, that Augustus' rule brought to it. Augustus and his successors steadily extended citizenship to all the leading families of the empire outside Italy. The empire's law courts and administrators combined local customs and Roman principles of law into a universally respected system of law. Trade and manufacturing united all the corners of the empire.

The poet Virgil's lines in the *Aeneid*, addressed to Aeneas, expressed well the Roman ideal of government:

> *Remember, Roman, by your strength to rule*
> *Earth's peoples—for your arts are to be these:*
> *To pacify, to impose the rule of law,*
> *to spare the conquered, battle down the proud.*

(Aeneid VI. 851–53)

A marble portrait of young Augustus

However, the power and wealth in the hands of Augustus' successors corrupted them. Army commanders learned that they could become emperors by using their **legions** as a threat. When good men held the principate, they resisted the pull of crime and thought about the good of the empire. But being emperor offered too many opportunities for self-indulgence—something weak, greedy, and sensual men found difficult to resist.

Many terrible and shocking stories are told about the emperors who followed Augustus, but the imperial system survived in spite of bad emperors. Lifelong **bureaucrats**, who made the real decisions of daily government, maintained the principate. And since these men did more real work of government than the emperors, the empire sought out only the best and most qualified men to serve as bureaucrats.

*Pax Romana:* the "Roman Peace," a long period of relative peace in the Mediterranean world, lasting from 27 B.C. to A.D. 180

**legion:** the name of a division of the Roman army, numbering about five thousand soldiers. Several legions would be combined into an army commanded by an *imperator* or "general."

**bureaucrat:** a government official, appointed by a ruler, who takes care of the day-to-day workings of government. A government run by bureaucrats is called a bureaucracy.

### Imperial Patron of the Arts

Augustus worked to reform the Roman government, but he was interested in renewing the arts as well. His friends supported Virgil, Horace, and Ovid—poets who made Latin poetry the equal of Greek poetry and wrote works that influenced European literature for all ages to come.

Virgil spent his last years creating an epic poem about the legendary founder of Rome, Aeneas. This epic, called *The Aeneid*, tells of Aeneas' travels from Troy after the Trojan War and his coming to Italy and fighting for a new home for his people. From that new home, called Latium, would come the city and republic of Rome.

Horace wrote lyrical poems, songs, and odes. In them he praised famous people and places and celebrated the simple but joyful country life of old Rome.

The third great Roman poet, Ovid, is remembered for his long poem called *The Metamorphoses*. A book of tales from the Greek myths about mortals and gods, *The Metamorphoses* became the textbook for schoolchildren to read when learning Latin in Europe during the Middle Ages and early modern times. But because of Ovid's scandalous life, Augustus sent him into exile in the last years of his life. Ovid died on the shores of the Black Sea, still writing letters to Augustus asking to be pardoned.

---

Nevertheless, in the years after Augustus, a shocking gulf widened between rich and poor. The ruling classes lost a sense of duty toward the government they served, while the hearts of the lower classes were turned to anger and despair. Widespread distrust, and even hatred, between classes and individuals threatened to destroy civilization. Where could people turn for help in a crumbling world? The old Roman gods offered no comfort or hope, and the human wisdom found in philosophy could do nothing against the temptations of greed and power A great emptiness seemed to settle on the heart of the world. Civilization lost its way.

Into this world of despair and sadness came a new message, the Good News of Jesus the Messiah. The Christian message spread across the Roman world in only a few decades. The new Christian faith and its message of forgiveness, love, and hope was the answer long awaited by a civilized yet empty world.

Within only 50 years after the death of Jesus in about A.D. 30, the Christian Church grew from a few loyal Jewish disciples to an international and non-Jewish church, with assemblies and houses of prayer all over the Mediterranean world. The new faith had its order of worship and its recognized ministry of leaders, who were successors of the first apostles. Moreover, the new faith reformed individual lives through acceptance of Jesus as Lord and Savior.

But the Roman world was not ready to accept this message of love so easily. Those who declared themselves Christian seemed to their neighbors to be traitors to the empire or blasphemers of the old gods. Local officials tried to discourage further growth of the Church by ordering the death or torture of professed Christians. Mobs took out their anger and discontent on these "different" people in their midst. But the imperial government took no overt action against the new faith. Officially, Roman law recognized the Christians as another **sect** among the Jews, who were already officially recognized as a religious group and tolerated in the empire. But that too would change, and the harshest attacks on the faith would come from the imperial offices.

**sect:** a division or small group of believers within a larger religious group.

# The Reign of the Julians

Because he outlived all his children, Augustus was plagued by the problem of who would succeed him as emperor. Like Julius Caesar, who had adopted him as his heir, Augustus adopted his grandsons; but they had died while still young men. In A.D. 4, Augustus adopted Tiberius Claudius Nero, his wife Livia's son by a previous marriage. Tiberius was already a grown man, acknowledged as a brilliant general of the northern legions in Germany, and an experienced administrator. He was an obvious successor to the principate.

Because Augustus was the adopted heir of Julius Caesar, all the heirs of Augustus are called the Julians. The Julians held the principate beginning with Tiberius in 14 A.D. and lasting until the death of Nero, Augustus' great grandson, in A.D. 68. The family would give Rome two great rulers, Tiberius and Claudius, and two moral criminals, Caligula and Nero.

### Augustus Poisoned?

The Roman historian Suetonius claimed that Augustus' wife Livia poisoned him to ensure that her son Tiberius should become emperor; she was afraid the old emperor would change his mind and appoint another successor. To escape the many attempts on his life by professional assassins, Augustus himself picked his favorite fruit and cooked it by his own hand. Rumor reported that Livia poisoned the pears of his garden while he slept.

Though the Julian line ended with Nero, the magic of the Julian name continued to enchant the Romans for centuries afterward. Each emperor added the name Julius Caesar Augustus to his name, like a sort of royal title.

## The Unwilling Emperor

**Bust of Emperor Tiberius**

Tiberius (reigned A.D. 14–37) never wanted the principate. His mother's ambition pushed him into it, and he accepted it only because all other candidates from the Julian family had already died or been eliminated. He had made a name for himself as a general in a campaign against the German tribes along the Rhine, and he had governed Gaul for some years with success and acclaim. Augustus left him the problems of ruling the empire without any advice or encouragement.

Though an unwilling emperor, Tiberius was an able one. As soon as possible, however, he retired to his villa atop the Isle of Capri. From there he governed through ministers and messengers, who carried his will to the Senate and the governors of provinces.

During Tiberius' principate, Jesus was crucified as a rebel against Rome, and St. Paul began his missionary travels to the far corners of the eastern Mediterranean. The emperor knew nothing of all this, because he had turned over the rule of the provinces to governors, such as Pontius Pilate in Judea. When Tiberius died, the churches Paul founded in the cities of Asia Minor and Greece were thriving. The new faith was already firmly implanted in the ailing imperial civilization.

## "Little Boots"

Since Tiberius had no living son, he passed his wealth and power to his nephew, Gaius. The son of Tiberius' brother, the general Germanicus, Gaius grew up in military camps. The soldiers gave the boy the nickname Caligula because of his habit of wearing soldier boots (called *caligae* in Latin.)

After becoming emperor in A.D. 37 at the age of 25, Caligula soon proved he was unfit for the task of ruling. He was self-indulgent, cruel, and possibly mad, which made him feared and hated. The Senate plotted to kill him; the army looked for someone to succeed him as emperor. It was

Caligula's palace guards, called the Praetorian Guard, who assassinated him after a brief four-year reign.

## The Able Fool

After assassinating Caligula, the palace guards took to robbing the imperial palace. Searching for loot, the soldiers found the elderly historian, Claudius, hiding fearfully under the stairs. Claudius was a member of the Julian family; but his uncle, Tiberius, had overlooked him as his successor because Claudius stammered and had a lame leg that made him limp ridiculously. His family thought him a fool, and Claudius encouraged this opinion because he did not want to be emperor.

The Praetorians, too, thought Claudius weak and foolish—just weak and foolish enough to be an emperor they could control. The Senate agreed because they, too, thought they could control Claudius.

Claudius surprised both the Praetorians and the Senate. He proved to be a very capable ruler, restoring the prestige and good name of his family and ruling the principate wisely. He added Britain to the empire and made peace with the Parthians in the East. He ruled for 13 years, from A.D. 41 to 54, and left the empire a better place than he had found it. But, like his predecessors, he had no son; and so the empire went to his stepson and grandnephew, Nero.

Nero

## The Last of the Julians

Under the guidance of his tutor, the philosopher Seneca, Nero at first earned the goodwill of the Roman people and the Senate. During the first five years of Nero's reign, the imperial government protected people in the provinces from oppression and lowered taxes.

Nero had a deep interest in the arts and learning and thought himself a great artist. He tried to revive the golden age of Augustus' poets and thinkers by encouraging the best writers and statesmen of his time to move to Rome and give their works to the empire. The **satirist** Petronius was Nero's friend and received from the emperor the official title *Arbiter Elegantiae*, "Judge of Fashion."

**satirist:** a writer of satire, a literary form that cleverly ridicules human vices and folly

**Nero and the Great Fire of Rome**

**Palatine hill:** one of the seven hills on which ancient Rome was built

Nero, however, soon began to show a dark side to his character. In A.D. 58, he had his mother, Agrippina, murdered. Under the influence of Poppaea Sabina, a woman he loved, Nero became more self-indulgent. He divorced his wife, Octavia, and then had her murdered. He married Poppaea and under her influence became more and more brutal.

In A.D. 60, a revolt of the Celtic tribes in Britain almost lost the island for Rome. Queen Boadicea led the British tribes to a brief independence but was ultimately defeated by the Romans. Boadicea took poison and died. This was a triumph for Nero, but it was quickly countered by a disaster that almost brought down his government.

### The Great Fire and Persecution

In A.D. 64, a terrible fire broke out in the crowded tenements of Rome, sweeping through the mansions of the wealthy as well as the hovels of the poor. The imperial palace itself was destroyed. Though some blamed Nero himself for the fire, he worked hard to help those whose possessions the fire had destroyed and to rebuild housing for the poor. At the same time, however, he built a large and glorious palace, called the "golden house," for himself. The house lay on the slopes of the **Palatine** and neighboring hills. The splendor of the palace angered the suffering and struggling citizens.

Soon, the public was looking for someone to blame the fire on. Nero found a scapegoat in the new sect of Christians and the Jewish residents of the city. With great cruelty, officials carried out this first imperial persecution of Christians amid lavish theatrical displays and public distributions of wine and bread. Christians were burned alive in the public gardens and torn apart by beasts in the arenas. Pity for these obviously innocent victims, however, eventually turned the people against Nero and gave fuel to his enemies' plots.

Nero's fear of the people and of his opponents in the Senate made him suspicious even of his former friends. The emperor's suspicions forced his old tutor, Seneca, to commit suicide. The poet Lucan went into exile. Petronius Arbiter killed himself before Nero could arrest him. The emperor was left without friends and advisors, and his own guards feared him. A revolt of the legions, beginning first in the province of Gaul, spread to the rest of the empire. Finally, in A.D. 68, Nero committed suicide while fleeing from his own Praetorian Guards.

## Year of the Four Emperors

After Nero's death, the empire was left to become the spoils of powerful generals. Within one year, four different men claimed the title of Caesar. Nero brought the Julian family to an unlamented end and left a legacy of violence and political intrigue that threatened the empire again with civil war.

The period from A.D. 68 to 69, called the "Year of the Four Emperors," showed that emperors could be made by the will and might of the legions. The legions in Hispania (Spain) proclaimed their general, Galba, emperor. But when he marched on Rome, the Praetorians proclaimed their commander, Otho, to be emperor. Otho was deposed by Vitellius, who was supported by the legions of Germany. Vitellius was quickly replaced by Flavius Vespasian, commander of the legions stationed along the Danube.

# The Flavians

Flavius Vespasian (reigned A.D. 69–79) was the most successful and highly regarded general of his time. He won not only Rome, but the support of the Senate. He was a strong and wise ruler who brought the empire a long period of stability. A man of the army who came of humble origins, Vespasian restored the finances of the government that had been squandered by Nero and the civil war. He reorganized the army to reward merit and created a new **aristocracy** of provincial leaders. These new aristocrats and the emperor himself tried to restore the old Roman virtues of frugality, self-control, and simplicity. Vespasian undertook great public works, of which the Colosseum at Rome is the most striking example.

Vespasian and his son Titus ruled an empire on the verge of breaking apart. One of the major rebellions they faced was a revolt of the Jews in Judea. The Romans subdued this revolt, known as the First Jewish

**aristocracy:** an upper class of persons thought to be the "best" or most able to govern

## Pompeii, the Buried City: A.D. 79

An eruption of Mount Vesuvius in A.D. 79 was a major tragedy of Titus' reign. The volcano buried the resort towns of Pompeii and Herculaneum near Naples under a layer of volcanic ash that perfectly preserved the cities' houses and made plaster-cast forms of many of the cities' fleeing inhabitants. The Roman scientist Pliny the Elder met his death on the slopes of the "quiet" volcano, where he had climbed to observe the beginnings of the eruption he thought would be a minor one.

In the 19th century, archeologists unearthed the ruins of Pompeii and remains of its inhabitants. They offered a sad but intriguing look at daily life in Roman times.

War, only after a three-year siege of Jerusalem. The siege ended with the destruction of Jerusalem and its temple in A.D. 71. The Arch of Titus that greets visitors to the now-ruined forum in Rome shows scenes of that siege and the Roman triumph.

Vespasian's son Titus succeeded his father but died soon after, leaving the empire to his brother, Domitian. Domitian at first worked for the good of the empire and encouraged the arts and sciences. He too wanted to revive the spirit of Augustus and the old Roman virtues.

Domitian restored the ancient Roman religious cults that had dropped out of favor and suppressed religious cults that had crept into Rome from the empire's eastern provinces. The cults of Isis, from Egypt; of Helios the Sun God, from Syria; and Mithras, from Persia had become the fashionable worship of the bored and spiritually starved upper classes. The cult of Mithras had taken hold in the army and had become the religion of most of the legions, east and west.

Domitian's character changed for the worse, however, when the legions in Germany revolted against him. The rebellion was crushed, but Domitian began to mistrust everyone around him and condemned many to death. In the end he suffered death by being stabbed while in his own bedroom.

# The "Good Emperors"

After the death of Domitian, the Senate saw to it that one of its own held the imperial office. Marcus Cocceius Nerva (reigned A.D. 96–98) was an old man of simple habits, wise and restrained. He spared Domitian's murderers and elevated Domitian's military supporters to high office. At his death, the Senate followed his advice and acclaimed as emperor his adopted son, Marcus Ulpius Trajanus (Trajan), a prominent army commander of the legions in Germany.

## The "Best" Emperor

Born in Hispania, Trajan was the first emperor to come from the provinces outside of Italy. Because he made a practice of consulting with the Senate and taking their advice, he reestablished mutual respect between Senate and emperor.

Trajan revived the morale of the legions stationed in Syria and Mesopotamia on the Parthian border by building new fortifications and granting lands to retiring legionaries. The Senate gave him the title *Optimus*, "the Best," recognizing what his troops already called him.

Trajan conquered the plains of Dacia (the southern end of the valley of the Danube River) and made it a military colony, strong enough to defend the empire from European barbarians. Veterans who retired from the legions received land in Dacia along the Danube River to set up farms and villages with their families and form military units able to defend themselves and hold the border. Modern Romania gets its name and its language from these Roman soldiers.

**Bust of Trajan**

In A.D. 116, while Trajan was engaged in campaigns in Mesopotamia against the Parthian kings, Jewish communities all over the empire broke out in revolt. Joining the revolt were the islands of Rhodes and Cyprus and the cities of Egypt and North Africa, all home to large Jewish communities. Much of the eastern Mediterranean was in arms. But before Trajan could leave his Parthian campaign and move against the rebels, he died suddenly in Babylon.

## Law Reformer, Patron of the Arts, Warrior

After Trajan's death, the Senate and the army recognized as his successor Publius Aelius Hadrianus, Trajan's nearest male relative and the governor of Syria. Hadrian was a wise ruler, a patron of architecture and the arts. He wanted to assure justice throughout the empire and so instituted humane laws, including one forbidding masters to put their slaves to death and another that punished a master who treated his slaves poorly. Though he angered some powerful men by doing so, Hadrian abandoned the territories conquered by Trajan east of the Euphrates River—Assyria, Mesopotamia, and Armenia.

Hadrian forbade Jews in the empire to practice their religion. The emperor forbade circumcision, reading the Law, and observance of the Sabbath. To prevent further civil wars, Hadrian brought the imperial armies of the East and West under his one command. Independent generals were dismissed. Hadrian decided against expansion of the empire's territory by war and sought instead to preserve peace within well-defended frontiers. His empire became a fortress against the uncivilized world. Where there were no natural border defenses, such as mountains and rivers, he set up strong fortifications. And to ensure that all his governors and generals were loyal, he frequently visited all the provinces of the empire. In Britain he built a wall across the island to keep out the wild Picts of Scotland. In Germany he erected a wall of forts and earthworks to join the Rhine River forts to the Danube's banks.

In about the year 130, Hadrian ordered the rebuilding of Jerusalem, which had been destroyed in A.D. 71. But the rebuilt Jerusalem was not to be a Jewish city; it would be a Roman colony, called Aelia Capitolina. Furious at this desecration of the sacred city, one Judah Bar Kochbar led the Jews in another revolt against the Romans. After three years (132–135), Hadrian crushed the revolt. The emperor ordered mass executions that reduced the population of Jerusalem to that of a small town. It was to be repopulated not with Jews, but with Gentile legionary veterans. From that time on, Jews were forbidden to enter Jerusalem.

Hadrian expected his death for many years before it came. On the banks of the Tiber he built for himself a massive round tomb, visible from all over the city. His tomb was so large and well-constructed that it became a fortress in the Middle Ages, the private castle of the popes. Today it is known as Castel Sant'Angelo.

Like Augustus, Hadrian had no son of his own and searched throughout his reign for a successor. Finally he chose Titus Aurelius Antoninus, a 51-year-old senator. Antoninus was not related to Hadrian in any way, but he was respected for his upright life. To further ensure the stability of the empire, Hadrian made Antoninus adopt two youths to succeed him in turn as emperor—Marcus Aurelius, 16 years old, and Lucius Verus, who was only 7.

Castel Sant'Angelo

## The Pious Emperor

One of Antoninus' first acts after becoming emperor was to persuade the Senate to proclaim Hadrian a god. The Senate had done so for previous emperors from the days of Augustus, but not for Hadrian. For this act, done out of respect for his predecessor, Antoninus received the title *Pius*, meaning "affectionately dutiful."

Antoninus Pius' reign was a time of prosperity and peace. Unlike Hadrian, he traveled little. Coins with the words *Tranquillitas* (peace) and *Concordia* (harmony) were the marks of his rule. His armies pushed the frontier further into Germany and Dacia, and he built a new wall in Britain to the north of Hadrian's, thus bringing the lowlands of Scotland into Roman territory.

## The Philosopher Emperor

Antoninus' successor as emperor, the young Marcus Aurelius was raised to be a soldier and spent his youth among the legions defending the Danube border.

Marcus Aurelius is remembered today more for his **Stoic philosophy** and his beautifully written *Meditations* than for being emperor, though his rule was impressive and colorful. Marcus began his reign by making Antoninus' other heir, Lucius Verus, co-emperor with him, though Verus was too young and of weak character. Marcus took command of the Danube legions himself and sent young Verus to Mesopotamia. Verus' generals gave him great victories, taking the army all the way to Ctesiphon, the capital of Parthia.

An event in about 167 was a sign of trouble to come. German peoples of the northern European plains and forests were threatening the empire's

**Statue of Marcus Aurelius**

**Stoic philosophy:** or stoicism, a philosophy that teaches that happiness can only be found by one who practices self-control and follows the natural law

northern borders. In 167, a German people called the Marcomanni invaded the Roman province of Pannonia and lay siege to the city of Aquileia on the northern coast of the Adriatic Sea. Marcus Aurelius moved north over the Danube River against the Marcomanni and drove them out of Roman territory. This was not the end of the Germanic threat, however. Until his death in 180, Marcus Aurelius was engaged in war with the Marcomanni and other German peoples. Though a victory for Rome, these wars revealed the weaknesses of the empire.

### Last of the Good Emperors

The exhausted Marcus Aurelius died at Vindobona (Vienna) in 180. Since Verus had died in 169 and Marcus had not named an heir, his lieutenants appointed his 19-year-old son, Commodus, to be emperor. Commodus was conceited, changeable, spoiled with luxury, and totally unprepared for the office he was to fill.

The young emperor devoted himself to sensual pleasure and to the production of gladiatorial games in the Roman arenas, the cost of which exhausted the Roman treasury. After an attempt had been made on his life, Commodus became a tyrant, putting to death many prominent Romans. Finally, on the last day of the year 192, he himself was assassinated. Commodus' bad rule and death brought the line of the good emperors to a disgraceful end.

### Claudius Ptolemy, the Astronomer

The reigns of the Good Emperors saw little literary achievement. But much important work was accomplished in the sciences and history by men who wrote in Greek and lived in the eastern Mediterranean world. In about A.D. 150, the astronomer Claudius Ptolemy produced his mathematical description of the heavens, the *Almagest,* and his *Geographical Outline.* The *Almagest* was to remain the authority on astronomy until the 16th century.

# The Fifty Years of the Fifty Emperors: 218–268

After the Good Emperors, the empire endured a century of military emperors. Some were better administrators than others, but all were more concerned with their own enrichment and the rewards they gave to their soldier supporters than with the good of the empire as a whole. Under the family of the Severii, Septimius Severus and his sons (who reigned from 193 to 235), the empire continued to prosper and the legions held the borders against invaders. After the Severii, the third century A.D. saw the steady decline of the prosperous empire left by Augustus to his heirs. Military commanders seized the imperial office by force and threats.

Between 218 and 268, fifty different men claimed the title of emperor, either at Rome or in other parts of the empire. Out of the 27 legitimate emperors, 17 were killed by their own troops and 2 were forced to commit suicide. The armies were more loyal to their own commanders than to the empire, and a change of emperors meant that their commanders were obliged to give the armies lavish gifts.

**Bust of Emperor Septimius Severus**

## The Sassanids of Persia Defeat a Roman Emperor

The rebellions and civil wars that rocked the empire came at a time when it could least afford them. The Germanic tribes of the north joined in a confederacy organized by the chieftains of the Goths. In the east, the Parthian kingdom, Rome's old enemy, came under the control of a new ruling family, called the Sassanids. These new rulers of Iran, or Persia, claimed the right to all the Roman Empire's eastern territories once ruled by their Persian ancestors. The new Persian army was the most up-to-date attacking force of the age, heavily armored and mounted on horseback. Re-arming and recruiting new legions for the East now became an urgent necessity for the emperors, but it was hugely expensive and not very effective.

In 260 the Persians captured the Emperor Valerian near Edessa in Mesopotamia. Valerian remained a prisoner of the Persians for the rest of his life. His son Gallienus did not succeed in rescuing him or did not try. Only the Persian kings' savage treatment of the Roman provinces they conquered saved the territories for Rome. The Persians made the empire's citizens more afraid of the Persians than of the Romans.

Valerian's defeated legions straggled back into Syria. With them, they may have carried the beginnings of the bubonic plague—an epidemic that raced across the empire, reducing the population of major cities by horrific numbers of deaths.

Before marching out to battle the Persians, Valerian had divided the empire. No one man, he realized, could command the troops of both the German and eastern frontiers at once. He took the east for himself and placed his son Gallienus in charge of the west. Gallienus was murdered by one of his officers, after winning the bloodiest battle of the empire's history, the defeat of the Goths at Niš on the Balkan Peninsula. Fifty thousand Gothic warriors died, and Roman deaths exceeded the numbers of a whole legion (about five thousand men).

But such military victories came at an enormous price. War and plague reduced the population in the cities of the empire to dangerously low levels. The imperial currency of gold and silver had so lost its value that silver coins hardly contained any recognizable silver at all, and gold merely covered a base metal core. People no longer accepted the official money but bought and sold with private currency. Prices in many parts of the empire rose by nearly 1,000 percent. Epidemics, war, high prices, and taxes became an unendurable burden for the common people to bear.

# The Reform of Diocletian

In 284, Roman troops in the eastern provinces of the empire proclaimed their general, Diocletian, emperor. Soon the entire empire recognized him. The new emperor began a reorganization of the empire that buried forever the principate of Augustus.

Diocletian divided the empire into eastern and western sections. Each section was ruled by an "Augustus" who had a "Caesar" to assist him. Diocletian, as Augustus of the East, remained the supreme ruler of the empire.

As Augustus of the East, Diocletian commanded the eastern Mediterranean—Asia Minor, Syria, Mesopotamia, and Egypt. His Caesar, Galerius, commanded Greece, the Danube frontier and Balkans, and the Black Sea. Diocletian made his friend and fellow commander, Maximian, Augustus of the West. Maximian commanded the Rhine valley border

Chapter 2  Emperors and Madmen  63

**Ruins of Diocletian's palace**

A statue in the wall of St. Mark's Basilica in Venice depicting the two augustuses and caesars of Diocletian's reform

and the coasts of Hispania and North Africa. His Caesar was Constantius, who commanded Gaul and Britain.

Diocletian built himself a new capital at Nicomedia on the Asian side of the Bosporus straits in order to protect the approaches to the Black Sea grain supply. Galerius imitated him by building a military fortress-palace at Thessalonica in Macedonia. In Italy, Maximian established his capital at Milan. In Gaul, Constantius headquartered at Trier to be near the Rhine and Britain.

Diocletian then split each of the 50 provinces of the empire in two, thus making 100 new provinces, each too small to support a rebel general or make serious trouble for the emperor. The total military strength of the empire was now more than half a million men in arms. Paying them, feeding them, and keeping them in armor and weapons as well as transporting them put a tremendous strain on the empire.

## The Failure of Economic Reform

In an effort to help the poor, Diocletian set a limit above which prices and the wages of workers could not rise. However, he and his co-rulers could not enforce this limit. Goods disappeared from the market, and prices soared again. To make collecting taxes easier, the government told workers they could not change jobs, nor could they move from one city or region to another unless the local tax collector allowed them to.

Diocletian's taxes angered ordinary people. Diocletian and the later emperors tried all sorts of propaganda to persuade the people that the government was in fact doing things for the general good and saving the empire from invaders and plagues.

## The New Face of the Empire

With Diocletian's removal of the Roman capital to the east, Rome, the "City of the West," would no longer rule over the Mediterranean world.

Instead, it would become a backwater town, known only for its Christian bishop and its faded glories. But the Christian religion, not the emperors, would become the chief force directing the movement of history, both of the east and west. The Church would unite the traditions of Mesopotamia and Egypt, of Israel and European Greece and Rome, and create a new civilization called Christendom. How that change came about is the subject of the history of the early Church, a history of martyrs and teachers.

# Chapter Review

## Summary

- When Caesar Augustus died in A.D. 14, he left the principate, which survived to rule the empire for five centuries.
- Augustus' successors were both good and bad as rulers of an empire. Four families commanded the empire in the first two centuries after Christ—Augustus' own Julian family, the Flavians, the family of the Good Emperors, and the Severii.
- Tiberius, the second of the Julians, reigned during the last years of Jesus' life. His heir, Caligula, was assassinated by his own guards. Claudius, his nephew, proved a wise and successful ruler. But Claudius' adoptive grandson Nero carried the empire to civil war and ordered the first official persecution of Christians in Rome.
- The Flavian emperors Vespasian and Titus worked to restore the glory of Augustus' empire. They besieged and destroyed Jerusalem in A.D. 70–71.
- The so-called Good Emperors were Nerva, Trajan, Hadrian, Antoninus Pius, and Marcus Aurelius.
- Pressure from the growing Germanic tribes on the north and the renewed threat of the Persian Empire on the east forced the Roman Empire to increase the size of its armies. Taxation, to pay for the huge armies that were needed, began to impoverish the common people who paid these taxes.
- Military commanders declared themselves emperors. Fifty emperors in 50 years brought chaos to the empire.
- In A.D. 260, the emperor Valerian led an army to defend the eastern empire against the kings of Persia. He was captured by the Persians and held for ransom.
- Diocletian, a general of the Danube legions, took command of the empire in 290 and reorganized it under four commanders.

- Diocletian moved his capital to Nicomedia in Asia Minor for the eastern empire, and Maximian moved his capital to Milan in Italy for the western empire. Old Rome became only the symbolic capital.
- Diocletian's attempts at reforming the tax system only made the financial life of the empire worse. Common workers were forbidden to leave their trade or place of birth.

## Key Concepts

**Senate:** the body of elected aristocrats or patricians that governed Rome. After Augustus, the Senate lost its powers to the emperors.

**principate:** the new organization of government begun by Augustus, giving real power to the emperor or *princeps* ("first citizen")

**emperor:** "commander in chief," "supreme commander"; title of a commander of several legions, given by the Senate first to Augustus and then held by all his successors

**Augustus:** title given by the Roman Senate to Octavian, nephew of Julius Caesar and founder of the principate

**legion:** the name of a division of the Roman army, numbering about five thousand soldiers. Several legions would be combined into an army commanded by an *imperator* or "general."

**Caesar:** family name of Gaius Julius Caesar. The name was taken as a title by all succeeding emperors.

## Dates to Remember

**A.D. 14:** the death of Augustus

**27 B.C.–A.D. 68:** the years of the Julian emperors

**A.D. 64:** burning of Rome under Nero and the first imperial persecution of Christians

**284–305:** Diocletian's rule

## Central Characters

**Augustus Caesar (63 B.C.–A.D. 14):** Gaius Julius Caesar Octavianus, nephew and adopted son of Julius Caesar, given the title emperor by the Senate in 29 B.C. He established the principate, the imperial system of government.

**Tiberius Caesar (42 B.C.–A.D. 37):** Tiberius Julius Caesar Augustus, born to Augustus' wife, Livia, and her previous husband. Tiberius was emperor when Jesus was crucified.

**Nero (A.D. 37–68):** Nero Claudius Caesar, adopted by the Emperor Claudius. Nero was the son of Domitius Ahenobarbus and Agrippina, later the wife of Claudius. Nero was the first Roman emperor to order a persecution of the Christians.

**Trajan (A.D. 53–117):** Marcus Ulpius Trajanus, emperor, A.D. 98–117. He was born in Hispania, was adopted by Nerva, and was a respected general.

**Hadrian (A.D. 76–138):** Publius Aelius Hadrianus, emperor A.D. 117–138. He was adopted by Trajan and became reformer and advocate of just treatment of the poor.

**Antoninus Pius (A.D. 86–161):** Titus Aurelius Fulvus Boionius Antoninus, emperor A.D. 137–161. He was counselor to Hadrian, adopted by Hadrian as his successor.

**Marcus Aurelius (A.D. 121–180):** Marcus Aelius Aurelius Verus Caesar, adopted by Antoninus Pius, emperor A.D. 161–180. Marcus Aurelius was a scholar and author of the *Meditations*, a collection of Stoic wisdom.

**Diocletian (A.D. 245–316):** Gaius Valerius Diocletianus, general of the Danube legions, was emperor from A.D. 284 to 305. He reorganized the imperial principate, dividing the empire into eastern and western territories in 293.

## Questions for Review

1. What is a "triumvirate"? Who made up the Second Triumvirate?
2. What was the principate? Who was the head of government in the principate?
3. What was the Senate of Rome? How did its role in governing the Roman state change after Augustus?
4. Who were the good emperors and who were the bad? Why are they now thought of as "good or bad"?
5. What were some of the signs that the Roman Empire was breaking apart?
6. How did Diocletian change the government of the empire?
7. Why was Diocletian unsuccessful in reforming the empire?

## Ideas in Action

1. Discuss what might have been some difficulties of ruling an empire like Rome. Why was the job too big for one man?
2. Research these questions: Why was assassination a fear for emperors after Augustus? Which emperors were in fact assassinated?
3. Compile a class time-line display of the emperors and their dates. Find any portraits of the emperors that may exist.

## Highways and Byways

### The Death of Augustus Caesar: A.D. 14

He gathered his closest friends, all old men by now; Livia, his wife of many years; and his stepson and heir, Tiberius, to be with him in his last moments. The old Emperor Augustus ordered his servants to dress his hair and tie up his sagging cheeks with a silken bandage. He jokingly asked his friends whether he had played his role in life's comedy well enough. Then he recited the last verse of a Roman play:

> *Since I have made you laugh, clap your paws;*
> *And cheer me from the stage with loud applause.*

He dismissed everyone except his wife from the room and passed away peacefully.

# Chapter 3: The Blood of Martyrs

In about the year A.D. 155, a most bitter persecution arose against the Christians in Asia Minor. Many believers became martyrs, showing such bravery in the face of the most terrible tortures that they amazed even their tormentors. One man, Germanicus, particularly astounded the crowd. He encouraged his fellow Christians and spurred the wild beasts, to which he had been thrown, to slay him.

The example of such courage only stirred the pagans to rage. They cried out, "Away with the atheists" (as they called the Christians). "Seek Polycarp!" The 86-year-old Polycarp was an important figure in the Christian community. He was bishop of the church of Smyrna, and he was one of the last living links with the age of the apostles. It was said he had spoken with the Apostle John himself. Eventually, Polycarp was seized and brought before the governor.

The governor, who wanted to save the beloved old man, urged him to curse Christ and save himself from death. Polycarp refused. He declared, "Eighty-six years I have served him, and he never did me any wrong. How can I blaspheme my King who saved me?"

Since the games were done, Polycarp could not be thrown to the beasts. He was condemned to be burned alive. As the flames roared up around Polycarp in a wall of fire so hot the executioners had to fall back, the old man did not cry out or beg for mercy or release. Finally the executioner, in tears, stabbed through the flames to end Polycarp's life quickly. His fellow believers rescued his bones from the ashes and kept them "as more precious than gold."

# The Courage of the Martyrs

St. Polycarp was one of countless Christian martyrs of the Roman Empire who underwent tortures and death out of love for Jesus Christ. They counted the loss of this world's goods and life itself as nothing if, to win them, they must lose Christ. The courage of the martyrs often sparked the wrath of the pagans. But just as often, the pagans were filled with awe at the Christians' courage.

**Christ with a martyr's crown, a mosaic from the church of St. Vitalis, Ravenna, Italy**

Though the authorities often considered Christians to be lawbreakers, the emperor had no more faithful subjects than they. While Christians believed their first duty was to their Lord and Savior, Jesus Christ, their leaders taught that as citizens of the empire they were bound to obey the emperor and his governors and magistrates. The first Epistle of Peter says:

*Be subject for the Lord's sake to every human institution, whether it be to the emperor as supreme, or to governors as sent by him to punish those who do wrong and to praise those who do right. . . . Honor all men. Love the brotherhood. Fear God. Honor the emperor. (1 Peter 2:13–17)*

To follow the will of their Savior, Christians tried to be both exemplary citizens and virtuous individuals. From the Church's earliest beginnings, Christian communities in every city collected money to support the poor and needy. The Christians tried to live at peace with, and to win the respect of, their non-Christian neighbors.

Nevertheless, before the end of the first century, Roman authorities began to worry about the growing number of Christians in the big cities. Christians steadfastly refused to acknowledge the emperor as a god and pay him worship. Roman officials began to see this refusal as a possible source of revolt and civil disorder. The empire's pagan majority was not disturbed by emperor worship—among so many gods, what was one more? Worshiping the emperor as a god meant doing business without trouble from the police, so it was acceptable. For Jews, however, worshipping the emperor meant denying the One True God. For Christians it also meant denying the Lordship of Jesus. But while imperial law had exempted the Jews from this emperor worship because of their ancient and respected tradition, Christians, who no longer claimed to be part of the Jewish communities, were seen to have no excuse for disobeying the law of the empire.

Beyond refusing to acknowledge the emperor—and the sun, moon, and heavenly stars—as divine, some Christians refused to serve in the army or to kill other men. The authorities thus feared Christianity could undermine legitimate authority and the social order.

## Blood of the Martyrs, Seed of the Church

Nero was the first, but not the last, emperor to persecute the Christians. The Emperor Domitian, the first emperor to call himself a god during his own lifetime, ordered the persecution of Christians as **atheists** because they refused to worship the Roman gods—and, more importantly, they

**atheist:** (from Greek *atheos*– ("no-god"); one who believes there are no gods

refused to worship him. Under Domitian's persecution, the Apostle John was exiled to the Island of Patmos in the Aegean Sea, where he received the vision that became the Apocalypse, or the Book of Revelation, in the Bible.

During the next two centuries, Christians around the empire would endure attacks from local authorities and mobs and then from the imperial authorities as well. In an effort to be fair, Emperor Trajan issued an edict that no one could be condemned merely for being a Christian. But if a person were accused, he or she could be sentenced to death for refusing to perform the token public worship of the emperor. Thus Christians were to be left alone—until someone or some event forced them to face the test of making sacrifice to the deified Caesars.

During the reign of the philosopher emperor, Marcus Aurelius, the empire saw another wave of persecution. Attacks against Christians came from the local authorities or the mob, and the empire was not able to control them. In the western part of the Roman Empire—during the year 177—at Lyons in the Rhône River valley of Gaul, the governor incited

## The Martyrdom of St. Perpetua and St. Felicity

The reign of Emperor Septimius Severus (A.D. 193–211) was marred by another wave of officially sponsored persecution. Among the most famous of the Christian martyrs of this persecution were the young Carthaginian noblewoman, St. Perpetua (Vibia Perpetua), and her maid and fellow Christian, St. Felicitas (or Felicity).

Perpetua was a catechumen and the mother of a small infant. When she came before the Roman procurator for examination, her aged father appeared. A pagan, he begged Perpetua to pity him and her child and offer sacrifice for the emperor. Though moved to pity for her father and tenderness for her child, Perpetua refused to sacrifice. When the procurator asked her, "Are you a Christian?" She answered resolutely, "Yes."

Felicity was expecting a child when she was imprisoned. While in prison, she delivered her child. Her jailers taunted her, saying that if she groaned so loudly now in childbirth, she would be screaming in the pains of the arena. She replied that she was the one who suffered now but, in the arena, her Savior would suffer for her.

Felicity was also a catechumen. She and her mistress, Perpetua, received baptism in jail. When brought into the arena, the women faced a mad cow that charged Perpetua, tossing her but not killing her. The crowds in the arena, who that day had seen so many martyrs killed by wild beasts, were tired of such spectacles and cried out that the women should be led away. After giving each other the kiss of peace, Perpetua and Felicity were killed by gladiators. Since the day of their martyrdom on March 7, 203, Perpetua and Felicity have been venerated by the Church as great martyrs.

the mobs to attack and loot Christian shops and homes. The assault on Christians spread throughout all of Gaul, with mobs torturing and killing many Christians. The victims' bones were thrown into the river to prevent surviving Christians from revering them as relics.

Despite the danger of accepting Jesus as Lord, more and more converts flocked to the Church. They were drawn by the example of these brave men and women, the martyrs. In trying to destroy the new religion and restore the old paganism, the persecutions succeeded instead in attracting most of the empire's people to the Faith. As Tertullian, an early church father, wrote in the third century, "The blood of the martyrs is the seed of Christians."

# The Threat of Heresy

The early Church suffered attacks from without—persecution—as well as assaults from within its own ranks. False teaching or heresy was a greater danger to the Church than persecution; for, while persecution was directed toward the body, heresy struck at the mind and soul.

A **heresy** is an idea that takes a part of God's revelation and exaggerates or distorts it to the point of denying the revelation given to the Church. Yet heresy was not simply a danger, for it gave the Church the opportunity to define and clarify her teachings. In answering heretical errors, the Church came to a better and deeper understanding of the revelation her Lord had given her.

## Early Heretics

One of the earliest and most powerful heresies was **Gnosticism**. The Gnostics (from the Greek *gnosis*, meaning "secret knowledge") tried to combine pagan thought with Christian revelation in new mythologies about the powers of the natural universe.

For the Gnostic, the material world, including our bodies, is evil. Only the spiritual world is good. Gnostics believed that this world and all material existence is an evil and painful prison in which the pure spirit is held until liberated or released by divine power. According to Gnosticism, the spirits or "powers" of nature try to prevent the soul's liberation and keep our spirits enslaved to do their will in the material world. Many Christians tried to interpret the life and message of Jesus in a Gnostic way.

A preacher named *Marcion* (died A.D. 160) formed a movement, called **Marcionism** after him. Marcion sought to divide the New Testament from the Old Testament. He taught that Christ had come to reveal a God of love who was opposed to the God of judgment presented in the Old

**heresy:** a teaching that emphasizes part of the received faith and ignores or denies the rest of the received tradition; a false teaching (from Greek *hairesis*, a "choice," a "faction")

**Gnosticism:** One of the most powerful heresies in the early Church. Gnostics claimed there is a secret knowledge (Greek *gnosis*) necessary for salvation. Most Gnostics held the material world to be evil and a prison for the soul.

**Marcionism:** Heretical sect founded by Marcion that rejected the Old Testament and most of the New. Marcion taught that the God of the Old Testament was not the God of Love revealed in the New Testament.

**An ancient (fourth century) Christian wall painting from the Catacombs of Saints Marcellinus and Peter in Rome, depicting Christ healing the woman with the issue of blood (Mark 5:25-34)**

Testament. Marcion called the Old Testament God a false God. Marcion rewrote and edited the Scriptures, removing most of the Hebrew books and all the harsher moral passages from the Christian texts. He said the only true Gospel was Luke and rejected all but 10 of the epistles of the New Testament.

Although Marcion damaged the Christian Faith among his followers, his attempt to remove all Jewish elements from the New Testament gave historians a record of what works the early Church did, in fact, recognize as part of Sacred Scripture. It is a proof of the New Testament's authority that so much of it was already known to the whole Church and revered by the middle of the second century A.D.

Among the developments of the second century was that Christian thinkers began to use Greek philosophy to help them better understand the Scriptures. Some Christians, however, were opposed to using Greek philosophy because it was pagan. A Christian teacher and evangelist, Montanus, was one of those who rejected the use of Greek philosophy to understand Christian revelation. For Montanus, only those who lived a severe and **ascetic** life could be worthy of the sacrifice of Jesus and the love of the Father.

Montanus began to teach that whatever he said had the same authority as Scripture. He claimed to be a prophet of the Paraclete, or the Holy Spirit, and had prophetesses among his followers. The **Montanists** removed themselves from ordinary life and shunned Christians who did not keep the strict moral and theological customs of the heretical sect.

## Christian Theologians Fight Heresy

Christian thinkers were forced by attacks from without and within to begin a thoughtful defense of the Faith and to develop a Christian theology to explain and defend true Christian positions.

Justin, known to history as St. Justin Martyr (ca. 100–165), had been a student of Greek philosophy before becoming a Christian when he was around 30 years old. Justin was a prolific writer, penning defenses of the Christian faith against the pagans and a Jewish scholar named Trypho.

Justin wrote a treatise against the heretic, Marcion, arguing that Jesus fulfilled the prophecies of the Old Testament. Justin tried to show that Christianity was not contrary to Greek philosophy. Jesus, he said, was the **Logos**, the Word of God, or divine Reason itself, in human form. All truth can be found in Jesus, he said; but the pagan philosophers recognized only traces of truth in nature and its laws.

---

**ascetic:** practicing self-denial—fasting and other penances—to achieve spiritual discipline; ascetic practice is called *asceticism*

**Montanists:** followers of a heretical sect, founded by Montanus, which held that only severe asceticism and strict adherence to the divine law would save a soul

**Logos:** (Greek for "word.") The Word of God is the Son of God by whom God made and continues to make all creation what it is. Recorded in the Scriptures, the Word is the record of God's saving acts in history, his commandments. In Jesus, God's Word takes a human face.

Justin was martyred in 165 in a local persecution.

One of the greatest defenders of the Christian faith against heresy was St. Irenaeus, bishop of Lyons in Gaul. While still very young, Irenaeus had heard St. Polycarp. The most important of Irenaeus' works was *Adversus Haereses* (meaning "Against Heresies"), which was written primarily against Gnosticism but dealt with the major heresies of his age. In this work, Irenaeus witnessed to the unique authority of the bishop of Rome, the successor of St. Peter, in the Church.

Athenagoras of Alexandria, who lived around the same time as Justin, argued in his writings that not only were Christian moral standards exceptionally high, but Christians had always tried to be loyal citizens. Athenagoras used Greek philosophy to show that the Christian concepts of One God and of the divinity of Christ were similar to the Greek concept of the unity of God. He may have been the first to defend the Trinity, demonstrating that the Father, the Son, and the Holy Spirit are one Substance.

Tertullian of Carthage (ca. 160–230), himself well educated in philosophy and **rhetoric**, at first taught that philosophy could be used in defense of the Christian belief. He had been a stalwart defender of the Church, especially against the pagans, but he eventually refused to think about Christianity in a philosophic light. He concluded that thinking philosophically would lead to the sin of pride. He wrote, "What has Athens to do with Jerusalem?"—thus setting the seat of Greek philosophy (Athens) against Jerusalem, the birthplace of the Church.

Tertullian later joined the Montanists, separating himself from the Church. He eventually split from the Montanists and founded his own sect.

> **rhetoric:** the art of speaking and writing well and eloquently

# Founding Christian Schools

Many Christian converts naturally thought about their experience of faith according to the ideas of their education, the philosophical language of Greece. Early Christians knew that the pagan philosophy of the Greeks, if understood properly, could lead to a deeper understanding of Christian revelation.

To encourage a thoughtful response to heresies, bishops founded Christian schools in the empire's major cities, and Christian writers joined the intellectual life of the empire. In about 190, a catechetical school (offering preparation for Christian preaching) was begun in Alexandria. The school was later headed by St. Clement, bishop of Alexandria, himself a poet and theologian. For hundreds of years, that school was the most important center for Christian thought. Christian schools grew up and flourished in other Christian centers, such as Carthage and Rome.

# Origen, Theologian and Philosopher

During the persecution decreed by the Emperor Septimius Severus in 202, a young man in Alexandria named Origen (185–254) looked on helplessly as his own father was seized and martyred. When it was possible to go about again in safety, Origen found that he was now the sole supporter of his family, which included his mother and six younger brothers. He found work as a teacher and sold all his possessions. The 18-year-old scholar already had mastered the learning of his day and was recognized by his teachers and by Bishop Clement as an authority on Platonic philosophy.

**Roman stadium in ancient Carthage**

Platonic philosophy, the thought of the Athenian philosopher Plato (ca. 428–348 B.C.), had been revived in the first two centuries of the Christian era. Origen's study of Platonism had strengthened his faith in the Christian message. To develop better the connection of Christian revelation and pagan thought, Bishop Clement left the direction of his school to this young genius, Origen.

Origen became one of the most famous writers of his time, read by Christians and pagans alike. He wrote so much and so fast that he employed a dozen stenographers and copyists to work in shifts, trying to keep up with him in writing down his words and thoughts. Origen held that Christ's love is so strong that all men and angels (including Satan) would be redeemed before the end of time. Because of this teaching, later ages called Origen a heretic. But some of the greatest Church Fathers have acknowledged and revered Origen's ideas and his work on Scripture.

# The Last Persecutions: 250–313

In the first half of the third century after Christ, the Christian faith achieved intellectual maturity and penetrated to the highest circles of society, converting many of those who shaped imperial policy and culture. Indeed, the Christian faith was now a respectable alternative to the official pagan religion of Rome. The imperial state would either have to recognize the Faith or exterminate it. The Roman officials opted for extermination.

In 248, Rome celebrated its thousand-year anniversary with festivities and the reopening of the Secular Games. The Secular Games were great shows held at the end of every hundred-year cycle (in Latin, the *saeculum*, from which the word "secular" comes). All the pagan world relished the games, which, involving fights to the death along with other competitions, were often quite bloody; but Christians were forbidden by their Faith to attend these shows, which honored the pagan gods. It appeared to the pagans that the Christians scorned the city's great heritage or even that they wished Rome ill, and public prejudice ran high against them.

The empire was faltering because of economic troubles and bad management. The Emperor Decius, commander of the Danube legions, tried to rebuild the morale of the empire by restoring the old pagan religion and demanding worship of the emperors as the mark of citizen loyalty. In 250, he began a new and bloody persecution of Christians throughout the empire—the first official and empire-wide persecution of the Church. The government's purpose was not to kill Christians but to convince them to accept the state religion. Everyone was required to obtain a certificate stating that he had sacrificed to the pagan Roman gods. For Christians, obtaining a certificate would require denying Christ; for that reason, many of them refused to accept the pagan religion.

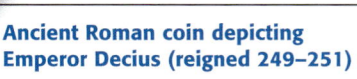

**Ancient Roman coin depicting Emperor Decius (reigned 249–251)**

But the systematic persecution of so large a minority in the empire as the Christians only weakened the Roman state further. Especially in the army, where there were many Christians, there was increasing opposition to the persecution. After only two years, Decius had to call off the persecution. While harassment of Christians would continue over the next 50 years, it was without public support and often faced the opposition of prominent pagan citizens.

## "The Long Peace"

Persian assaults in the eastern part of the Roman Empire and German invasion from the north left the empire in need of friends, not more enemies. Emperor Gallienus began to court the loyalty of Christians, particularly those who now filled the ranks of his armies. He restored Christian property and halted persecution with an **edict** of **toleration** in 260. Christians called the period of some 40 years that followed the edict "the Long Peace."

There had been universal suffering throughout the empire, not just among the persecuted Christians. The government levied crushing taxes and confiscated private property to support its huge armed campaigns in Mesopotamia and on the Danube-Rhine frontiers. The middle classes were ruined, small farmers destroyed, and the urban poor left in misery and near starvation. As the empire began to crumble under the succession of military emperors, the strong organization of the Christian Church stepped in to establish the order that the government could not provide. Bishops became organizers and administrators of large estates left by wealthy converts for the relief of the poor.

It was the Christian spirit of mutual love and brotherly charity that most impressed the pagans. Christians left their fortunes to the relief of the poor; ordinary people donated their tithes to Church associations that fed the poor; took care of orphans; provided aid to old slaves, retired sailors, and soldiers; rescued prisoners in the mines and prison islands; and cared for girls left orphaned or without dowries to secure husbands. The well-organized Christian Church had set up a miniature welfare state in an empire lacking any social services.

> **edict:** proclamation of a law
> **toleration:** official recognition of the rights of individuals or groups to hold dissenting opinions, especially in religion
> **currency:** coins or government notes used in the buying and selling of goods

## The Great Persecution

The Edict of Toleration remained in effect from 260 to 303 through the reigns of three reforming emperors. Then, in 284, the legions in the east-

**80** LIGHT TO THE NATIONS: The History of Christian Civilization

**The Four Tetrarchs: the two Augusti (Diocletian and Maximian) and their Caesars**

ern parts of the Roman Empire acclaimed their commander, Diocletian, emperor.

The large numbers of Christians serving in the government and the military had been able to keep the emperors from abandoning the Edict of Toleration. However, an unfortunate event gave Diocletian an excuse to change this policy.

At a sacrifice, Diocletian and his fiercely anti-Christian Caesar, Galerius, surrounded by their staff and courtiers, were observing the pagan priests. The priests were slaughtering animals and then examining the livers of the beasts for omens that would, they believed, predict the empire's future. But the priests failed to find any signs at all. To hide their failure to get a clear "omen," they blamed nonbelievers present at the sacrifice. The Christian historian Lactantius, who was present, recorded that Caesar Galerius had noticed certain members of the staff and court crossing themselves before the sacrifice. Galerius concluded that they must have been making a "magic spell" to spoil the emperor's ceremony.

Diocletian was furious. He had been publicly embarrassed. He ordered all those present to sacrifice to the gods then and there or be flogged. Everyone in the court, both Christian and non-Christian, obeyed. Diocletian soon forgot the incident; but Galerius did not. He began to insist that Christians be forced to comply with the state religion.

On February 23, 303, the Emperor Diocletian, through Galerius, proclaimed an edict, ordering that all Christian churches everywhere were to be torn down, all Christian books were to be turned over to the state authorities and burned, and all Christians were to be dismissed from public office of any kind. Those who protested the sweeping violence of the edict were swiftly and cruelly silenced.

Churches were broken into; and copies of the Scriptures, both Jewish and Christian, were seized and burned. Christians tried to hide these, their most precious documents—the Gospels and the treasured copies of letters of the founding apostles. Some clergy, however, thought they could save themselves and their flocks by handing over their irreplaceable Scriptures to the magistrates. Their compromise, however, did not save them.

Instead, Diocletian issued a second edict condemning to prison all Christian clergy throughout the empire. Even the compromisers were arrested. So many bishops, priests, and deacons were imprisoned that the overcrowded jails and prisons could not be maintained. So many prisoners filled the jails of Egypt that the government sent thousands to the copper mines of southern Palestine, where they met their deaths by exposure to the poison in these mines.

In the autumn of 303, Diocletian fell ill. He left the powers of government in the hands of his anti-Christian assistant, Caesar Galerius, who in 304 issued a further edict. The edict commanded all men, women, and children of the empire to sacrifice to the old gods on pain of death. In the eastern part of the Roman Empire, thousands of Christians who refused to sacrifice were killed. In Asia Minor, all the Christians in a town were burned to death, and their houses were pulled down. In the western part of the Roman Empire, reprisals against Christians were less severe; the western Augustus, Maximian, and his Caesar, Constantius, discreetly ignored the enforcement of Galerius' edicts.

The next year, in 305, Diocletian abdicated rule to Galerius and persuaded the western Augustus, Maximian, to retire with him. Galerius was to rule the eastern empire and Constantius, the western empire.

Galerius, however, quickly seized complete power over the empire. He refused to allow Constantine and Maxentius, the sons of Constantius and Maximian, to become Caesars. Instead, Galerius appointed his nephew, Maximinus Daia, as Caesar in the Eastern Roman Empire and a friend, Severus, as Caesar in the Western Roman Empire. To impress his uncle, Maximinus Daia intended to force Christians back to the old pagan religion. He ordered everyone, regardless of sex or age, to sacrifice to the divine emperors or die. However, the Christian resistance was so firm that he had to change the death sentence to mutilation or slavery in the quarries and mines.

**Maximian**

# The Triumph of Constantine

For seven more years the unwise edicts of Diocletian continued to cause misery and disruption throughout the eastern provinces of the empire. Galerius, mistrusting Constantius, held his son Constantine hostage

# 82   LIGHT TO THE NATIONS: The History of Christian Civilization

**Bas-relief of Constantine**

in the east. But in 305 Constantine escaped; riding over hundreds of miles to the west and eluding his pursuers, he joined his father in Gaul. There, the armies hailed both father and son as supreme commanders. Constantius and his son then crossed to Britain, where Constantius died at York in 306. The army then conferred the title of Augustus on Constantine. Knowing that accepting the title would mean war with Galerius, Constantine took the lesser title of Caesar.

When Severus died in 307, Maximinus Daia moved into Italy—he assumed his uncle Galerius would promote him to Augustus of the west. But fearing his nephew's ambition, Galerius instead made his brother-in-law, Licinius, Augustus. Both Constantine and Maximinus Daia then proclaimed themselves Augusti of the west, ignoring Licinius.

In the spring of 311, Galerius became mortally sick with a painful illness, probably a cancer. His wife convinced him that he was suffering because he had offended the god of the Christians. In April 311, he issued an Edict of Toleration, freeing Christian prisoners, allowing Christian assemblies, and removing penalties for refusing to sacrifice to the gods. He wrote that he hoped the Christians "will be bound to entreat their god for our well-being."

The last official persecution was over. Clergy came out of hiding. The sacred texts, hidden from the book burners, were returned to their places of honor. The stripped and ravaged churches were reopened amid psalms and hymns of praise. Galerius died within a week after issuing his Edict of Toleration.

## Chi Rho

Chi and rho (English *ch* and *r*) are the first two letters in the Greek word *Christos*. The PX symbol served in place of the Cross, forbidden by the Roman authorities, as a mark of Christian allegiance. Constantine carried the Chi Rho into battle.

### In hoc signo vinces

While Constantine was at war on the Rhine trying to hold back the German Franks, Maxentius, son of Maximian, seized Italy. Maximinus Daia fled Italy to Asia Minor, where he claimed for himself Diocletian's capital of Nicomedia and declared himself the Augustus of the Eastern Roman Empire. Licinius, who was left to hold the Danube, made an alliance with Constantine on the Rhine to take away power from Maxentius in Rome and from Maximinus in the east.

In 312, outnumbered but determined, Constantine moved against Maxentius, marching his army down across the Alps at lightning speed. Maxentius drew up his forces along the Tiber River, some nine miles north of Rome. He was confident of victory, for he had a received a prophecy: "On this day the enemy of Rome shall perish." He took it as a good omen, for certainly the gods meant Constantine when they spoke of the "enemy of Rome." So confident was Maxentius that he made no plan for retreat. His only avenue of escape was over the narrow Milvian Bridge, which spanned the Tiber.

Before the battle, Constantine had a dream or vision. He saw a strange sign in the heavens and heard the words *en toutoi nika*—Greek for "in this, conquer." (The Latin is sometimes rendered as *In hoc signo vinces*, "In this sign you will conquer.") Constantine ordered that a new imperial standard bearing the sign be made immediately, and that the mysterious sign be painted on the shields of all his troops. The sign was formed from two Greek letters, *chi* (X) and *rho* (P), the first two letters of the title "Christ" (XPISTOS = CHRISTOS) in Greek.

**Ancient inscription with Chi Rho Monogram**

Though it was smaller, Constantine's army routed Maxentius' dispirited troops. They ran from the field, trying to retreat over the Milvian Bridge. So many people were fleeing across the bridge that thousands were thrown into the river from the narrow span and died in the flooded waters of the Tiber. Maxentius himself, the "enemy of Rome," perished that day in the river. Constantine was victorious—and was now the new Augustus of the western Roman Empire.

## The Edict of Milan

In the east, Licinius claimed the title Augustus after Maximinus Daia died by assassination; the new eastern Augustus then cemented his alliance with Constantine by marrying his sister. The two Augusti joined in issuing a new edict of toleration, the **Edict of Milan**, in A.D. 313. The edict granted

**Edict of Milan:** edict of toleration of all religions in the Roman Empire promulgated by Constantine and Licinius in 313. The Edict of Milan granted legal status to Christians.

**84** LIGHT TO THE NATIONS: The History of Christian Civilization

**The Roman Empire**

freedom of worship to all religious groups within the empire, making special mention of the Christians.

Licinius, however, grew jealous of Constantine and in 314 encouraged treasonous designs against him. Twice defeated in battle by Constantine, Licinius made peace with him. War again broke out between the two Augusti in 323, and Constantine defeated his rival in battle in February 324.

In a mere nine years, Constantine had become master of all the empire. To govern the huge territory and be available to oversee the difficult frontiers of Mesopotamia and the Danube, Constantine moved his capital from the west to the east.

### Nova Roma

For his new capital, Constantine chose the old Greek city of Byzantium. Set on a triangular ridge of high cliffs overlooking the Bosporus on one side and a deep bay—the Golden Horn—on the other side, Byzantium was a natural fortress that commanded the European side of the Bosporus, the route to the Black Sea. Constantine called his new city *Nova Roma*—New Rome. Later generations would name it Constantinople ("Constantine's City").

Constantine forced the Roman Senate and the army commanders to relocate to Nova Roma. With Constantine's support and encouragement, his city received a new Christian bishop and attracted the best preachers and teachers of the Christian Church. Gradually the entire administrative life of the empire moved from Rome and Milan in the west to the glittering new halls of Constantinople.

For the first time ever, there was a Christian emperor and a new, Christian capital city, free of the old dark memories of pagan and persecuting Rome. A new "Golden Age," a "Christian Empire," seemed to be dawning for the entire civilized world.

# Chapter Review

### Summary
- Roman officials saw the Christians' refusal to acknowledge the emperor as a god and pay him worship as a possible source of revolt and civil disorder.
- Domitian, the first emperor to call himself a god during his own lifetime, ordered the persecution of Christians as atheists because they refused to worship the Roman gods and the emperor.
- Local persecutions of Christians occurred under the "Good Emperors," though the Emperor Trajan issued an edict that no one could be condemned merely for being a Christian.
- The early Church was threatened not just by persecutions, but by heresy. Early heresies were Gnosticism, Marcionism, and Montanism.
- Christian theologians rose up to defend the Faith against heretics. These theologians included St. Justin Martyr, St. Irenaeus of Lyons, St. Athenagoras of Alexandria, and Tertullian of Carthage.
- Origen of Alexandria was an early Christian who tried to explain divine revelation in light of Greek philosophy. He became one of the most famous writers of his time, read by Christians and pagans alike.

- After a period of some 40 years of peace, the Emperor Diocletian initiated the most brutal persecution of Christians to that time.
- After seeing in a dream a strange sign and hearing the words, "In this, conquer," Constantine defeated his rival in battle and became Augustus of the Western Roman Empire. He and Licinius, the Augustus of the East, issued the Edict of Milan in 313, granting religious freedom to everyone in the empire, including the Christians.
- After becoming sole ruler of the empire, Constantine established his capital at Byzantium, calling it *Nova Roma*, "New Rome."

## Key Concepts

**martyrs:** those who gave their lives rather than deny Christ and the Faith
**heresy:** a teaching that emphasizes part of the received faith and ignores or denies the rest of the received tradition; a false teaching (from Greek *hairesis*, a "choice," a "faction")
**Marcionism:** heretical sect founded by Marcion that rejected the Old Testament and most of the New. Marcion taught that the God of the Old Testament was not the God of Love revealed in the New Testament.
**Gnosticism:** one of the most powerful heresies in the early Church. Gnostics claimed there is a secret knowledge (Greek *gnosis*) necessary for salvation. Most Gnostics held the material world to be evil and a prison for the soul.
**Montanists:** followers of a heretical sect, founded by Montanus, which held that only severe asceticism and strict adherence to the divine law would save a soul
**Edict of Milan:** edict of toleration of all religions in the Roman Empire promulgated by Constantine and Licinius in 313. The Edict of Milan granted legal status to Christians.

## Dates to Remember

**260–303:** Edict of Toleration under Emperor Gallienus
**303–313:** Great Persecution of Diocletian and Galerius
**313:** Constantine and Licinius' issuing of the Edict of Milan
**324:** capital of empire moved to Constantinople

## Central Characters

**St. Polycarp (A.D. 69–155):** Christian martyr and bishop of Smyrna who in his youth heard the Apostle John
**St. Irenaeus (b. ca. 130):** early Christian Church father and one of the greatest theologians and defenders of the faith in the early Church

**St. Justin Martyr (ca. 100–165):** theologian, martyr, and the first Christian philosopher
**Tertullian (ca. 160–230):** theologian and defender of the Faith who rejected philosophy as a means of understanding the Christian Faith
**Origen (185–254):** theologian and one of the most famous authors of his time. His works explained the connection between the Christian Faith and pagan thought.
**Diocletian (245–313):** Roman emperor who ordered the last persecution of Christians
**Galerius (d. 311):** Diocletian's Caesar and later Augustus of the East (reigned 305–311). Galerius instigated Diocletian's persecution of Christians and continued it after Diocletian's retirement.
**Constantine I (280–337):** first Christian Roman emperor (306–337). Constantine issued the Edict of Milan with the eastern emperor, Licinius.

## Questions for Review
1. The emperors persecuted Christians to make sure there would be fewer of them, but Tertullian said, "The blood of the martyrs is the seed of the church." Why did persecution increase the number of Christians?
2. When and under what emperor did the first imperial persecution occur?
3. What did Gnostics teach?
4. What did Montanists teach?
5. Why did Diocletian persecute the Christians? Why is his persecution called the Great Persecution?
6. What sign did Constantine see before going into battle? What did it stand for?

## Ideas in Action
1. The 20th century, it has been said, had more Christian martyrs than any other century since the birth of Christ. Do some research to discover in what countries and when in the 20th century persecution of Christians occurred. Why were Christians persecuted in these lands? Does persecution of Christians still occur in our time? If so, where, when, and why does it happen?
2. Prepare presentations or reports on individual martyrs.
3. Discuss whether Christians suffer persecution in our own country. If so, describe the persecution Christians suffer in our country; how does it differ from the Roman persecutions? If not, why are Christians in our country not persecuted?

## Highways and Byways

### The Martyrdom of St. Ignatius

When the bishop of Antioch, St. Ignatius (died early second century), refused to offer incense before the imperial image, he was brought before the Emperor Trajan himself. When cross-examined by Trajan, old Ignatius steadfastly refused to return to the pagan ways of his youth. Before his death as a martyr at the arena in Rome, he wrote that, if he was to be martyred for Christ at the jaws of the lions, he hoped that he would be "a tender little morsel."

Ignatius was one of the first in an unending line of martyrs who have welcomed their sacrifice. Fearful that his friends in Rome might intervene and prevent his execution, Ignatius wrote to them, "I must implore you to do me no such untimely kindness, pray leave me to be a meal for the beasts, for it is they who can provide my way to God. I am His wheat, ground fine by the lions' teeth to be made purest bread for Christ.... No power, visible or invisible, must grudge me my coming to Jesus Christ."

# Chapter 4: The Christian Empire

Under Constantine, the Roman Empire seemed to recover some of its former greatness. His issuing of the Edict of Milan in 313 offered a new hope for unity among the many peoples and provinces of the empire. His leadership, preserving the empire from civil war and strife and bringing new prosperity, made it seem stronger than, perhaps, it really was.

Though unbaptized himself (the emperor remained a **catechumen** nearly to the end of his life), Constantine believed the Christian Faith and gave the empire a new Christian direction. It was becoming a Christian empire. Though the emperor had not made the Christian Faith the official state religion, he bestowed benefits on the Church. At Rome, Constantine built large **basilicas** on the sites of St. Paul's tomb and St. Peter's martyrdom. At Jerusalem, he built a complex of buildings connected to a huge basilica over the site of Jesus' tomb; the basilica is called the Church of the Holy Sepulcher. In honor of the Cross of Christ, Constantine abolished crucifixion as a form of punishment. In 321, the emperor made Sunday a public holiday.

> **catechumen:** one being trained or educated in the faith but not yet baptized
>
> **basilica:** an early Christian church building based on the form of a Roman court of justice

## Contentious Christians

Although Constantine had little trouble ruling the empire, he found ruling the Church less easy. The Church was torn by divisions.

One of these divisions was a direct result of the hard feelings left behind by the persecutions. Christians who had remained firm during the

**Icon of Constantine I and Saint Helena**

**schismatic:** from Greek *schisma*, meaning "a division." A schismatic sets up a rival church, causing a division of a part of the Church from the whole.

persecution were suspicious of those clergy and laity who had tried to avoid disaster by obeying Diocletian's edict to turn over their churches' Scriptures. But these *traditores* ("those who give over," or "traitors") now wanted to be received back into the Church as if nothing had happened. Remembering what their faith had cost them, those who had not been traitors to Christ would not accept back into the Church those who had betrayed the Faith.

Faithful believers were themselves divided on how to treat the *traditores*. In Hispania (Spain), a council of bishops had met at Elvira, some years before Constantine came to the throne, and decided against receiving the *traditores* back into the Church unless they performed heavy penances and made public confessions, asking forgiveness from God and man for their betrayal. But some in North Africa, called Donatists, refused altogether to receive the *traditores* again into the Church. The Donatists eventually considered themselves the only true Church and insisted that Catholics who joined them be rebaptized.

Constantine attempted to assert his imperial authority to settle the question. The emperor sided with the North African bishops, who condemned the Donatists. But though condemned by Church and state, the Donatists formed **schismatic** churches—with their own bishops—that became an important fixture of the North African church for 100 years.

A far more serious controversy began in the eastern Mediterranean when Arius, a deacon and brilliant teacher in Alexandria, openly claimed that Jesus was not God equal to the Father. Arius asked how the Son could be "begotten by the Father" if he had not come later in time than the Father. Arius' answer was that the Son was greater than a man or an angel but of a lesser nature than the Father.

Chapter 4  The Christian Empire  **91**

**Detail of an ancient Byzantine fresco of the Council of Nicaea, from the church of St. Nicholas in Demre Turkey**

Controversy over Arius' teaching spread throughout the empire. Seeing the seriousness of the division in the Church and how it threatened the unity of the empire, Constantine decided to intervene. He called a general council of all the bishops of the Church to meet with him at Nicaea, a resort town in the hills of Asia Minor just south of Constantinople.

## The Son Is God

Late in the spring of 325, the bishops assembled in the great hall of the imperial residence in Nicaea. Their gathering was the first of what are called the **ecumenical councils**—gatherings of bishops that speak for the entire Church. More than 200 bishops had answered the summons; only a handful came from the western part of the empire. Pope St. Sylvester of Rome was ill and sent two priests to represent him. In the East, Alexander, the bishop of Alexandria, came with his young secretary, Athanasius, who would become the chief defender of the council's decision in the years to come.

The bishops' debate over the Arian doctrine was angry and emotional. The emperor had planned to attend only the opening session, but hav-

**ecumenical:** including the whole civilized world, universal (from *ekumene*, the Greek word for "household"). An **ecumenical council** is a gathering of bishops that represents the entire Church.

ing become so interested in the discussions, he stayed for the entire two months of the meetings. The question of the council touched the heart of the Gospel. The Christian Faith insisted on the divinity of Jesus the Christ. But how divine is he? Arius did not say that the Son is not divine at all, but that he is not God as the Father is God. The Son is not fully divine and is less than the Father, said Arius. His opponents said that the Son *is* God, equal to the Father.

Furthermore, Arians (the followers of Arius) preached that Jesus was a teacher of virtue and good morals, but that he could not redeem our fallen nature by baptism and his Body and Blood. Arians thus taught the importance of a good and virtuous life, but not the forgiveness of sins or a "born-again" new life. The council fathers fully understood the danger of the new heresy.

To settle the controversy between the pro-Arian and anti-Arian bishops, one bishop offered as a compromise an old baptismal creed recited in his country. The **creed** expressed traditional teaching and pleased Constantine. He recommended it to the council. Then the unexpected happened. Whether he was coached to do it or the idea simply came to him, the emperor himself suggested that perhaps the old creed could be amended to include the Greek word *homoousios*—meaning "**consubstantial**," "of one substance," "the same kind of thing"—to describe the relationship of the Son to the Father. If the Son and the Father are the same kind of thing, the Son cannot be less than the Father.

Perhaps Constantine, whose Greek was still a little shaky, was unaware that Arius and his followers had already rejected the word *homoousios*. But the fact that the emperor had suggested it made it necessary for the council to accept it. The anti-Arians were delighted. They amended the old creed to include the emperor's word.

Only Arius and two of the council fathers refused to go along with Constantine's suggestion. The council thus proclaimed the creed with the word *homoousios* as a formula of faith to be proclaimed throughout the empire.

The majority had won. Constantine sent the bishops home, thinking that he had solved the most difficult question of the age once and for all. Sadly, he had not solved it. The emperor exiled Arius and his closest followers to Illyria (modern Bosnia), but the Church was still divided between Arians and those called the **orthodox**, who held to the "straight truth" of the Church. Arianism appealed to the educated and the sophisticated because they thought it was more reasonable than the orthodox, Catholic belief in the Trinity. At the same time, Arianism had made great inroads among the German **mercenaries** who guarded the empire and its rulers.

---

**creed:** from the first word of the Creed in Latin, *credo*, "I believe . . ." A creed is a formal statement of religious belief that lays out what Christians must believe.

**consubstantial:** sharing "one substance," one essence; of the same nature; the word used in the creed of the Council of Nicaea to express the relation of God the Father and God the Son

**orthodox:** adhering to teaching, established, especially by a religious group; in the Christian Faith, adhering to the teachings revealed to the Church by Christ

**mercenary:** one who acts for pay, particularly soldiers who serve in the army for pay and not for loyalties or patriotism

## The Creed Proclaimed at Nicaea

The Church today repeats the creed of Nicaea, the "Nicene Creed," at every Sunday Mass. Today's creed is not exactly the same as the one agreed upon at the council, but it states the belief of the council's creed accurately. The original Nicene Creed reads:

*We believe in one God, the Father almighty, maker of all things visible and invisible;*

*And in one Lord Jesus Christ, the Son of God, only-begotten from the Father, that is, from the substance of the Father, God from God, Light from Light, true God from true God, begotten not made, of one substance* [homoousios] *with the Father, through whom all things came into being, things in heaven and things on earth, who for us men and for our salvation came down and became flesh, becoming man, suffered and rose again on the third day, ascended into heaven, and will come to judge the living and the dead;*

*And in the Holy Spirit. But as for those who say, "there was when he was not," and "before being born he was not," and that he came into existence out of nothing, or who assert that the Son of God is of a different reality or substance, or is subject to alteration or change, these the catholic and apostolic church anathematizes [condemns].*

And even though Constantine supported the Nicene Creed, the members of the imperial family were Arians who supported Arian bishops throughout the empire. Bishop Eusebius of Nicomedia (the old imperial capital), the foremost defender of Arius before and after the Council of Nicaea, personally guided and advised several members of the emperor's family. With such powerful and influential bishops objecting to the new creed, the council could not stamp out this new heresy. Arian bishops just ignored the creed. The ordinary citizens in the empire were orthodox Catholics; the ruling classes became Arian.

Constantine died in 337, leaving a religiously divided empire to his three sons: Constantine II, Constantius II, and Constans.

## The Trials of Athanasius

Though he had been a champion of the creed of Nicaea, Constantine, it seems, had never fully understood the controversy between the orthodox and the Arians. Under the influence of Bishop Eusebius of Nicomedia, an Arian, the emperor became less harsh toward the Arians; he even decided to allow Arius to return from exile. Since Arius belonged to the Church of Alexandria, Constantine ordered Athanasius, who had become archbishop of Alexandria in 328, to receive the **heresiarch** back into communion. Athanasius refused, and the emperor exiled him to Trier in Gaul.

Athanasius suffered several times over for his devotion to orthodox teaching. After Constantine's death, his son, Constantine II, restored Athanasius to Alexandria. But after Constantine II's death, a council of eastern bishops **deposed** Athanasius, who took refuge in Rome, where he enjoyed the support of the pope. With the backing of Constans, who ruled the western empire, Athanasius received permission from Constantius, the eastern emperor, to return to Alexandria in 346.

The bishops in the eastern empire had become almost entirely Arian—or, at least, many pretended to be Arian to please Constantius. So, when Constans died in 350, leaving Constantius sole ruler of the empire, the Arians again tried to destroy Athanasius. Even the orthodox bishops in the western empire abandoned the archbishop of Alexandria and condemned him. Athanasius left Alexandria and went into the Egyptian desert to live among ascetics who had gone there to seek God in solitude.

Constantius died in 361. His successor, Julian (known as the "Apostate" because he wanted to restore paganism as the religion of the empire), allowed all who had been exiled because of religion to return to their homes.

When Athanasius died in 373, orthodoxy had nearly triumphed in the empire, despite the support Arianism had received from emperors. There were other orthodox champions—Saint Basil, bishop of Caesarea; St. Gregory Nazianzus, archbishop of Constantinople; and St. Gregory of Nyssa—who by their preaching and writings demolished the teachings of Arius. Finally, in 381, the Ecumenical Council of Constantinople reaffirmed the creed of Nicaea, adding to it a section declaring the Holy Spirit to be God, equal to the Father and the Son.

**Bulgarian icon of Saint Athanasius**

**heresiarch:** the founder or the chief proponent of a heresy

**depose:** to remove from a high position in church or state, such as the kingship or the office of bishop

After the Council of Constantinople, Arianism died out utterly in the empire. It would continue, however, among the barbarian German tribes who were threatening the borders of the empire.

# The Gothic Threat

The chief threat to the empire in the years after Constantine's death was the Goths. The Gothic people were divided into two nations: the Visigoths or "West-Goths," who had moved into formerly Roman lands along the Danube, and the Ostrogoths, or "East-Goths," who were later to cross the Danube and take up those same lands from their migrating cousins.

Most of the Goths had already become Christians, but they were Arians. In the fourth century, a man named Wulfilas had been their great evangelist. Wulfilas had given the Goths translations into the Gothic language of all the major prayers and liturgies of the church as well as a Gothic translation of the Gospels.

The Goths were gathering along the Danube to face the Roman legions on the plains of Dacia. The Goths had been Roman allies; imperial officials had given them lands in Dacia in pay for their service on the border against other Germanic peoples. But later emperors decided to take back those lands and force the Goths to pay imperial taxes or leave. The Goths resisted.

Emperor Valentinian I drove the Gothic Germans back over the Danube but allowed other Germans—Franks and Vandals—to settle in the unpopulated lands of Gaul in exchange for military service. Emperor Valentinian I died of a heart attack while arguing with Gothic ambassadors, leaving his throne to his 16-year-old son, Gratian. In 378, the boy Gratian faced a catastrophe beyond his abilities. His uncle Valens, Valentinian's brother, who ruled the eastern empire, marched his legions from Asia to Europe to stop a major uprising of the Germanic Visigoths across the Danube. At Adrianople in Thrace, Valens and his legions fell, almost to a man, before the rebel Visigoth cavalry and spearmen. The East was left leaderless.

**Gold coins from the reign of Emperor Valens**

## Theodosius Makes Christianity Official

After the death of Valens, the Emperor Gratian realized he needed an able assistant. His choice was the young Spaniard, Theodosius. Theodosius was born in 346 near Toledo in the Roman province of Hispania. He was the son of Valentinian I's leading general. Theodosius' reputation for organization and bravery came to the attention of Gratian, who called him back from Hispania and in 379 made him co-Augustus of the East. Soon thereafter Gratian died in battle, and Theodosius inherited the real power in both East and West. With the aid of co-emperors and Caesars, Theodosius ruled a united empire and earned respect both as a formidable opponent in war and as an efficient administrator.

Theodosius took up residence at Milan in northern Italy, where he could be close to the dangerous frontiers of Gaul and the Balkans. The imperial government moved with Theodosius, and thus Milan became the unofficial capital of the empire.

**A relief carving of Emperor Theodosius and his court**

Theodosius decided that Christianity would be the official religion of the empire. On November 8, 391, Theodosius removed government support from the pagan religions while continuing to support Christian churches and clergy. This made Christianity the only religion supported by the empire and its official religion.

Revolts in Antioch and Gaul occupied Theodosius in the last year of his life, and the great emperor died in January 395. His two young sons, Arcadius and Honorius, inherited the empire, again splitting it into eastern and western halves.

# The Search for God in the Desert

Even before Constantine legalized the Christian Church, Christian ascetics in the East had been withdrawing from the cities to be alone with God in desert **hermitages**. The movement first began in Egypt, where ascetics like St. Anthony went out into the western desert to seek quiet and prayer. These **hermits** lived lives of utter poverty and prayer.

Almost a hundred years after the time of Anthony, St. Athanasius wrote a Life of St. Anthony, which persuaded many readers to leave their homes and follow the Egyptian hermits into the waste and desert places of the world. Others undertook life as **celibates** in small communities, pooling their money for common support.

These "single" Christians (**monks**, from Greek *monachos*, meaning "single") found that enduring the rigorous life of an ascetic, giving up the comforts and pleasures of ordinary life, brought them the inner freedom to speak directly with God and the time for prayer and contemplation. These monks gathered in small communities or "tables," and they built for themselves houses and churches called monasteries. The monks who shared a common table were called "cenobites," or table-monks, as distinct from "hermits," who lived alone.

The bishop of Caesarea in Asia Minor, St. Basil (ca. 329–379), enlisted the help of local monks to distribute food to the starving poor during a famine. Basil believed that monasteries should be less isolated, more closely involved in the needs of the greater Christian community. He wrote two sets of monastic instructions, or "rules," that are used today in Greek and Russian monasteries.

Monasticism spread from Egypt to all the Church in the eastern empire. In the west, Egyptian monasticism spread more slowly but became central to the religious life of the Irish after their conversion. Irish monks took their version of monastic life to Britain and northern Europe in the sixth and seventh centuries.

**hermit:** one who withdraws from society and lives alone, usually for religious reasons
**hermitage:** the dwelling place of a hermit
**celibate:** one who takes a vow not to be married (or a vow of *celibacy*)
**monk:** one who lives alone; a hermit; also, someone who lives in a community, called a monastery

The monastery of St. Katherine on Mt. Sinai in the Sinai Peninsula. The monastery is one of the oldest in the world and houses a rare book and icon collection.

# Three Saints Move the Church

During the reign of Emperor Theodosius, three great minds led the Church into the new Christian age, building on the wisdom of the early Church fathers. They were the bishop of Milan, *St. Ambrose*, Theodosius' friend and adviser; *St. Jerome*, the translator of the scriptures into Latin; and *St. Augustine*, the bishop of Hippo in North Africa. These three gave to the Western, Latin-speaking Church the unique character and theology that would characterize it for centuries to come.

## The Bishop Who Tamed an Emperor

While in Italy in 390, the Emperor Theodosius, his officials, and the bishops of the realm heard news of revolt in Thessalonica. Imperial officials had imprisoned a popular charioteer, and the mob rioted and stoned to death an imperial commander. The bishops of northern Italy—including Ambrose, the archbishop of Milan—asked Theodosius to show clemency to the rioters. Instead, he listened to his courtiers. The emperor ordered the slaughter of the citizens of Thessalonica; seven thousand men, women, and children died in a cruel bloodbath.

After the slaughter, Archbishop Ambrose learned that Theodosius would be in Milan. He wrote the emperor a letter in which he exhorted him to do penance for this sin of slaughter. And the Emperor Theodosius, master of the civilized world, heeded the bishop's voice. "Stripping himself of every emblem of royalty," Ambrose wrote later, "he publicly in church bewailed his sin. That public penance, which private individuals shrink from, an emperor was not ashamed to perform; nor was there afterwards a day on which he did not grieve for his mistake."

*Christ enthroned, from the Basilica of St. Ambrose, Milan*

This archbishop, St. Ambrose, was born the son of the Prefect of Gaul, one of the Emperor Valentinian's most trusted advisers. Trained as a lawyer, Ambrose became governor of north Italy. In 374, Ambrose used his authority to help settle a dispute between the Arians and Catholics over the election of the bishop of Milan. The choice lay between two men—one, an Arian; the other, orthodox.

At the cathedral in Milan, Ambrose begged those gathered for the election to be peaceful. So deeply did he impress the crowd that, as he left to allow the clergy to vote, a child shouted, "Ambrose for bishop!" The crowd took up the cry, and the electors saw they had little choice but to accept Ambrose in place of the two contesting candidates. Ambrose, however, was not a priest; in fact, he was only an unbaptized catechumen. But this fact did not discourage the clergy of Milan. Over the next eight days, they baptized him; ordained him deacon, then priest; and finally consecrated him as bishop of Milan.

Ambrose's personal talents and interests made him more suitable for the office of bishop than anyone else. All factions respected his personal holiness. In his spare time he wrote hymns and collected the musical heritage of Christian Italy. He was a spellbinding preacher.

Ambrose defended the Church against the Arians in Milan. He served as the advisor to the Emperor Gratian, and after the emperor's death he protected the Empress Justina and the young Valentinian II from assassins. However, Justina, an Arian, later demanded that Ambrose give over a basilica in Milan to the Arians. He refused, and crowds of Catholics gathered around the church to prevent the imperial court from seizing it. When the imperial guards came to seize the church, Ambrose told them to take this message to the empress: "The palaces belong to the emperor, but the church to the bishop." The basilica remained in Catholic hands.

### The Christian Scriptures

In 367, the aged Athanasius had assembled and published a list, or **canon**, of the divinely inspired Christian books. In 397, the Synod of Carthage made a final decision and recognized Athanasius' canon as the definitive Scripture of the Christian world. His canon is the list of books of the Bible that the Church recognizes today. Twenty years later, in 419, a second council at Carthage ratified the previous list and referred to it as "The New Testament," or "New Covenant."

**canon:** a list of, especially, sacred books

## Monk and Translator

In 382, Pope St. Damasus recalled a brilliant young scholar from his studies in Constantinople to Rome to be his secretary. Pope Damasus gave this scholar, named Hieronymus or Jerome, a towering mission that would consume 23 years of his life—to produce an authoritative Latin translation of the Scriptures for the use of the Church in the West.

The Christian Scriptures had been written in Greek while the Hebrew Scriptures were available in a Greek version, called the Septuagint. But in the West, the common speech was Latin. Translations of the Septuagint and the Christian Scriptures into Latin existed, but they were of very poor quality. Jerome's task was to remedy this problem.

**Saint Jerome, by Ludovico Carracci (1555–1619)**

Jerome moved to Bethlehem, the birthplace of Jesus, where he might be near the beginnings of the Faith. Two noblewomen, Paula and her daughter Eustochium, both accomplished scholars and translators, accompanied him and assisted him with the mammoth task of translation. For 23 years, Jerome and the two women worked on the translation, studying the Scriptures for their meaning. As Jerome translated, he wrote commentaries on every verse. When St. Jerome died at age 75, his Latin commentaries on Scripture filled 63 volumes.

Of all his work, however, St. Jerome's masterpiece is his Latin translation of the Bible, completed in 405. This translation is called the Vulgate, that is, the "Popular Version" (from Latin *vulgaris*, meaning "of the people"). It is a literary work of art as well as a very accurate translation, making use of Latin rhetoric (Jerome's inheritance from his classical studies), musical rhythms, and simplicity of phrasing. Jerome's Latin Bible served the Church in the West for more than a thousand years.

## St. Augustine of Hippo, Theologian of the West

In 395, the year of Emperor Theodosius' death, St. Augustine was consecrated as bishop of Hippo in North Africa. He had been born near

Carthage in North Africa in 354, the son of a pagan father and a Christian mother. Though she did not have him baptized as an infant, his mother, St. Monica, taught him about Christ; but Augustine rejected her Christian Faith and remained a pagan.

Though a pagan, Augustine was a high-minded youth and so was attracted to **Manicheanism**, a Persian philosophy that taught the material world is evil; only the spiritual world is good. Manicheans called for a severe self-control and piety. Manicheanism appealed to the educated and high-minded because it gave its adherents a sense of being above the ordinary run of mortals.

Augustine's parents gave him a very good education for a government post and sent him to Carthage at age 17 to complete his education. He would become a professor of rhetoric and a public orator.

In his early life Augustine lived like all other wealthy young pagans of the empire. He indulged in immorality and self-indulgence while congratulating himself on his superior understanding and disdain of ordinary concerns. While in Carthage, he lived with a young woman who was not his wife and fathered a son, Adeodatus. Augustine could not marry his son's mother legally, because she was beneath his social class. Meanwhile, Monica, although unable to prevent his pagan self-indulgences, never ceased to pray for her son and to remind him that he must live honorably as he taught his students to do.

Augustine eventually moved from Carthage to Rome and from Rome to Milan. Monica followed her son to be near him. In Milan, Augustine heard the preaching of Bishop Ambrose and gradually became convinced of the truth of the Christian Faith. Yet, he could not give up his sinful life, as he described it. But grace overcame his resistance. One day, after a great interior struggle, Augustine surrendered himself to God.

After he was baptized in 386, Augustine was determined to live the Christian life to its fullest: he would become a monk. After giving her a large sum of money for her support, he sent his son's mother home to Carthage. He kept his son, now a youth of 13 years, with him to educate.

Accompanied by Adeodatus and several friends, Augustine left Italy for his hometown of Tagaste, near Carthage, to found a monastic community. In 391, he was ordained a priest. Shortly after that he was elected bishop of Hippo, an important seaport town near Carthage.

**Manicheanism:** a Persian philosophy that taught the material world is evil; only the spiritual world is good. Manicheans called for a severe self-control and piety.

**Saint Augustine**

**A Shepherd Against the Wolves** As bishop, Augustine had to deal with the growing power of the Donatist faction in the North African Church. Augustine said the Donatist view of the Church was too restrictive. The true Church, said Augustine, is "a net that captures many kinds of fish." Both the holy and sinners belong to it; the Catholic Church welcomes both the "clean" and the "unclean," whom God will sort out at the Last Judgment.

Augustine, however, had to deal with a foe more dangerous than the Donatists. A British monk, Pelagius, was preaching a return to ascetic living and extreme self-denial. Pelagius had seen that the materialism and sensuality of many Christians in Rome were sapping the energy of the Church.

But Pelagius' solution to this problem was heretical. He said Christians could follow virtue and avoid sin by their own power, without God's Grace. All mankind, he taught, was born free of sin and chose either to sin or to live righteously. Pelagius said that by imitating Christ's behavior, we can assure our own salvation ourselves. Augustine replied that if Pelagius were right, people had no need of God's Grace—that Christ's sacrifice was for nothing.

Augustine knew that merely imitating Christ's behavior was not enough. He knew from Scripture and by experience that being a Christian meant being changed from within, becoming a new person, by the forgiveness of sin. Augustine insisted that only God's Grace allows our sinful nature to achieve anything worthwhile. In the controversy with Pelagius and his followers, Augustine clarified his definition of Original Sin and the nature of evil. Sin, he said, is present with us from the moment of our conception, because of Adam's first rebellion. Original Sin is the taint on human nature by reason of the first—the original—sin of our first parents. We are born with a deformed nature. Salvation, he said, comes only by the Grace of God given to us through Christ. Even our own cooperation with this grace, Augustine said, is by a gift of grace.

Augustine's influence on the theology of the Catholic Church was immense. Through his efforts the Church came to reject Pelagianism. Church councils embraced his teachings on grace and how it works on the human heart.

**Adam and Eve and the forbidden fruit, from the facade of Notre Dame Cathedral, Paris**

The Church eventually gave him the title "Doctor of Grace," in honor of his important contribution. His theology formed the theology of the Catholic Church in Western Europe for centuries to come and continues to influence it today.

Augustine clarified the nature of evil. Evil, he said, is not a thing in itself but a lack of good. It is a turning away from the good. He saw that the human will, though free to choose between good and evil, is weakened by Original Sin and evil desires; and so people tend to choose evil. Since the stain of Original Sin keeps human efforts from succeeding, Augustine said, God's Grace must intervene and bring good out of failed human effort.

St. Augustine saved the Christian Faith from becoming just a system of morality like the Greeks and Romans had had for centuries. The Faith does not just offer a list of do's and don'ts but is an encounter with a person, Jesus Christ, who brings us into friendship with God the Father through the Holy Spirit.

# The German Threat

The Emperor Theodosius, an able ruler, was the last emperor to rule over a united empire. His successors, however, proved not to be as able as he.

The dying emperor had charged his greatest general and brother-in-law, Stilicho, son of a Vandal chieftain and an aristocratic Roman mother, to watch over his two sons, the heirs to the imperial throne. But the boys' mother took the elder, Arcadius, to Constantinople, where her family and connections raised him. The younger, Honorius, was left in the West at Milan under Stilicho's care.

Though Theodosius was able to stem the Germanic advance into the empire, the Germans remained a threat. Stilicho watched with alarm the growing power of the Visigoths under their young king, Alaric. Alaric had the personality to draw others to him and quickly united the Gothic tribes behind him in a strong confederation. Stilicho tried to lessen Alaric's power by sending him large bribes of gold and by inviting two of the Gothic tribes to become Roman settlers and citizens if they would supply men for two Roman legions to patrol the Danube frontier. Stilicho settled the Gothic tribes in empty lands in the Balkans, the region between the Adriatic Sea and the Black Sea.

The Goths had been converted to Arian Christianity. They now had an alphabet, based on the Greek alphabet, and a written language of

**Obverse of *solidus* (gold coin) of Honorius (top) and Arcadius (bottom)**

their own, developed and taught them by the Arian missionary Wulfilas. Many of the Goths had served in the imperial armies and traveled over the European provinces of the empire. They knew the strengths, but also the weakness, of the Roman military.

To better protect the young Emperor Honorius, Stilicho moved him and the imperial court out of Milan to the newly fortified seaport of Ravenna on the east coast of Italy. Ravenna, an island city, offered a large harbor for the imperial navy and was protected from siege by the swampy ground surrounding it on all sides and by strong Roman walls and towers. No enemy could get close to the walls with siege engines, and the emperor could take ship and flee if the city seemed in serious danger. Stilicho himself and the imperial army command remained in Milan to defend Italy from any invasion from Gaul or the Balkans.

Alaric and his Visigoths, however, were not the only threat the empire faced. Another German tribe had quietly moved into Gaul over the Rhine River, where they had been employed as army auxiliaries and cavalrymen for the empire for many years. The pagan Franks found Gaul almost undefended and seized whatever towns or lands they wished from the few imperial troops left to guard them.

Then, one night in deep winter, the Arian Christian Vandals, a Germanic tribe, crossed the Rhine and advanced into southern Gaul unopposed. Potential invaders threatened Italy on both east and west. Stilicho appealed to the Emperor Arcadius in the East for help, but the East was itself pressed by the Goths that Stilicho had let into the Danube lands as his auxiliaries. Now, these Goths challenged the imperial troops to stop them. Arcadius had withdrawn to the impregnable walls of Constantinople.

At this critical time, the young Honorius had Stilicho assassinated and, to protect himself, withdrew the army from Milan to Ravenna. Learning of Stilicho's assassination, Alaric's Visigoths swept away the eastern legions and crossed the Danube, driving the Romans back to Constantinople.

Chapter 4   The Christian Empire   105

**Emperor Honorius in his court feeding birds**

## The Sack of Rome

With the Roman army holed up in Ravenna with Honorius, no sufficient force was left in Italy to oppose Alaric and the Goths. In 410, Alaric's Visigoths swept into Italy and, using Roman techniques, laid siege to Rome itself. A traitor within the walls of Rome opened the city gates, and the Visigoths poured in, looting and burning the helpless city for three days. Then, for reasons no one now knows, Alaric called off his men and took his army south into southern Italy, moving toward Naples. In southern Italy, Alaric caught a fever that killed him before the year was out.

The Visigoths, Alaric's people, left Italy and moved on into southern Gaul, pushing the Vandals before them over the Pyrenees into Hispania. The Visigoths seized all of southern Gaul, the old Roman provinces of Provincia and Aquitania, and made the Roman city of Tolosa (Toulouse) their royal capital. Finally they invaded Hispania, where they made themselves into a new

**Alaric, king of the Visigoths, who in 410 sacked Rome**

**Saint Augustine, by Sandro Botticelli**

military aristocracy. For the next 300 years, the Arian Visigoths ruled the Romanized Spanish populace, who were Catholic.

## The City of God

Augustine had learned about the sack of Rome from refugees fleeing Italy. After overrunning Hispania, the Vandals were moving across North Africa, toward Carthage. The Roman Empire, that vast edifice of civilization built by men, was crumbling to ruin.

Some pagans were saying that Rome fell because the empire had abandoned the ancient gods for the Christian Faith. To counter these claims, St. Augustine began to write a study of history, titled *De Civitate Dei* ("Concerning the City of God"). Completing this book occupied the last 15 years of his life. In the *City of God*, St. Augustine argues that the religion of Christ did not bring on the sack of Rome. In the second half of the work, he presents a parallel history of the "two cities," the City of God and the earthly city which arose when Satan and the angels rebelled against God. Both cities exist side by side in our world; but ultimately, Augustine shows, the City of God will triumph over the earthly city.

# The Popes Defend the West

The imperial court at Ravenna kept alive the name of the Western Roman Empire but actually ruled no more than the streets of the city itself. All of Italy fell into chaos and anarchy. In Rome, only local authority could rebuild the city. The wisdom and authority of the popes alone enabled the survival of Rome. The Church—the only organized institution left in the region—undertook the administration of the city and of central Italy. A generation later, in 440, a new pope—Leo I, known to us as St. Leo the Great—took office.

## Attila the Hun

In 452, Pope Leo climbed to the walls of Rome to direct the defense of the city against a ruthless and deadly invader—the Huns.

The Huns were not German, but a people from the Mongolian plains. They were not Christian, but they had long been in contact with Rome and had served in Roman armies. Like the Goths, the Huns wanted a share of the riches of the old empire. They had followed the Goths over the Danube into the plains of Dacia and Hungary, and from there they had invaded the Rhine Valley and crossed over into northern Italy. The Huns made no permanent settlements, but raided and looted where the whim struck them. Attila the Hun ruled from a tent city on the Hungarian plain, moving his "capital" wherever his army advanced.

The Huns were masters of horsemanship. They rode on light saddles and without stirrups. It was said that they ate and slept on horseback—that they were the fabled centaurs of Greek mythology, half horse and half

*The Meeting of Attila the Hun and Pope Leo I* **by Raphael**

man. The ferocity of their attacks, the destruction they left behind them everywhere, inspired terror in the lands they threatened. They swept over the Rhine Valley and into Gaul. Their king, Attila (the name means "Little Father"), had earned the nickname, "Scourge of God."

After invading Gaul, Attila turned his army around and moved south over the Alpine passes against Italy. Terrified, all defenders were swept away, and the Huns were at the walls of Rome in 452. Bravely, Pope Leo left the safety of the walls and went out to meet with the terrible Attila himself, near Mantua, a town north of the city. The pope convinced Attila not to enter the helpless city, but rather to receive gold to buy off his tribesmen and withdraw from Italy.

## St. Leo and the Vandals

But the danger to Rome did not end with the retreat of the Huns. After only two years of peace, Leo had to save his city again from a second enemy—the Vandals.

The Arian Vandals had taken Roman North Africa as their domain. St. Augustine lived to see their conquest of his home; he died, at the age of 76, during the Vandals' siege of Hippo in 430. Hippo held out through a prolonged siege before surrendering; but Augustine's beloved Carthage fell in 439. With it, the invaders took the whole of North Africa out of imperial control. Roman Africa became a Vandal kingdom.

The destructive path the Vandals tore through the lands they conquered has given the name "vandalism" to all senseless destruction of property. The Vandal king, Genseric, after defeating the Roman army sent to hold Carthage against him, took ship with his men for Italy and Rome itself. In 455, Pope Leo again disregarded his own safety and went out unarmed to meet the invaders.

Genseric had shown no mercy to Catholic Christians in North Africa, and he was not predisposed to honor even the pope. Neither with bribes nor persuasion could Leo turn the Vandals away from the city. Nevertheless, although he could not stop the pillaging and terrorizing of Rome, Leo persuaded this robber chieftain to spare the lives of its citizens.

Unopposed, Genseric's Vandals looted Rome for two weeks. The eastern and western emperors cooperated one last time by sending their combined fleets to punish Genseric. But in a sea battle off the coast of Carthage, the Vandals defeated the Roman ships and destroyed half their fleet. Genseric's Arian kingdom would survive for more than 50 more years.

Amid the destruction caused by the invading Huns and Germans, the Roman Empire in the West was tottering. Imperial authority in the

**Vandals sacking Rome**

western empire soon utterly collapsed, never to rise again. Only the Church remained, a sturdy bulwark protecting civilization against the rising tide of barbarism.

# Chapter Review

### Summary
- The Emperor Constantine not only legalized the Christian Faith, but took a deep interest in it. Besides building great basilicas and establishing Christian laws, the emperor took a hand in governing the Church.

- With the end of persecutions, the Church suffered from dangerous heresies. These heresies were Donatism, Arianism, and Pelagianism.
- The Arian heresy denied that the Son of God is equal to the Father. The Ecumenical Council of Nicaea condemned the heresy in 325. Though Constantine approved of the decisions of Nicaea, the imperial family continued to favor the Arians. In the empire, while most ordinary citizens held the orthodox Faith proclaimed at Nicaea, the ruling classes embraced Arianism. So did some of the Germanic peoples who had been converted by an Arian missionary.
- Germanic peoples, many of whom had been allowed to settle within the borders of the empire and were recruited into the Roman legions, began to threaten the empire from both within and without in the years following Constantine's death.
- Constantine's successors divided the empire into East and West, as Diocletian had done. In 379, the Emperor Gratian appointed Theodosius as co-emperor. After Gratian's death, Theodosius united the entire empire under his rule.
- Theodosius was a strong emperor who was able to hold back the Germans for a time. In 392, he removed government support from the old Roman pagan religion, establishing the Christian Faith as the sole religion of the empire.
- Even before Constantine, men and women had fled to the Egyptian desert to live the ascetic life. Many lived as hermits, but others formed communities in which they lived a life of prayer and mutual support. Monasticism spread from Egypt to the entire Church, East and West.
- Three great saints distinguished themselves under Theodosius' reign: St. Ambrose, the archbishop of Milan and advisor to the emperor; St. Jerome, who translated the Greek and Hebrew Scriptures into Latin (called the Vulgate); and St. Augustine, whose work became the foundation of theology in the Western, Latin Church for centuries to come.
- St. Augustine battled the Pelagian heresy, which taught that all men were born free of Original Sin and so had no need of God's Grace to live a virtuous life and attain salvation. Augustine taught that without God's Grace, men cannot live virtuously and attain salvation. He clarified the definition of Original Sin.
- After Theodosius' death, the empire was divided between his two sons: Honorius, in the West, and Arcadius, in the East. Under the general, Stilicho, the West was able to hold back the Visigoths under their king, Alaric. But, despite Germanic threats to the empire from the north, east, and west, Honorius had Stilicho assassinated.

- Hearing of Stilicho's death, Alaric led the Visigoths into Italy and sacked Rome in 410. After Alaric's death, the Visigoths left Italy and invaded southern Gaul and Hispania, where they established their military rule.
- Other threats to the empire came from the Huns, who invaded Gaul and pushed into Italy. Pope St. Leo the Great convinced their leader, Attila, to spare Rome and to withdraw from Italy.
- A Germanic tribe, the Vandals, being pushed out of Hispania by the Visigoths, invaded North Africa, where they established a kingdom. The Vandal king, Genseric, led an invasion of Italy and looted Rome.

## Dates to Remember
**325:** Council of Nicaea
**392:** Christianity declared the official religion of the Empire
**397:** canon of Scripture defined at the Synod of Carthage
**405:** Jerome completes the Latin translation of the Bible
**410:** fall of Rome to the Visigoths
**452:** the Huns' invasion of Italy
**455:** the sack of Rome by the Vandals

## Central Characters
**Arius (256–336):** heretical theologian who taught that the Son of God is not equal to the Father
**St. Athanasius (293–373):** archbishop of Alexandria; champion of the Trinitarian doctrine of the Council of Nicaea
**Theodosius I (347–395):** Roman emperor (379–395). He established Christianity as the official religion of the Roman Empire.
**St. Jerome: (340–420):** translator of the Vulgate Latin Bible
**St. Ambrose: (340–397):** archbishop of Milan; great preacher and collector of hymns
**St. Augustine (354–430):** theologian; bishop of Hippo
**Stilicho (359–408):** Roman general and counselor to the young Emperor Honorius
**Alaric the Visigoth (370–410):** king of the Visigoths; sacked Rome in 410
**St. Leo the Great (440–461):** pope; saved Rome from the Huns
**Attila the Hun (406–453):** king of the Huns
**Genseric the Vandal (d. 477):** king of the Vandals; conquered Roman North Africa and sacked Rome, 455
**Visigoths:** Germanic nation; the "Western Goths;" sacked Rome in 410; conquered southern Gaul and Hispania in the years following

**Vandals:** Germanic nation that conquered southern Gaul and Hispania and then moved to North Africa, where they established a kingdom around Carthage

**Huns:** Asiatic nomads who ravaged Western Europe in the fourth and fifth centuries

## Key Concepts

**Nicene Creed:** the creed recited in Catholic churches today at Mass; not the statement of faith of the Council of Nicaea, but a later version embodying that statement and accepted by the Church for liturgical use

**consubstantial:** sharing "one substance," one essence; of the same nature; the word used in the creed of the Council of Nicaea to express the relation of God the Father and God the Son

**ecumenical council:** a gathering of bishops that represents the entire Church

**Arianism:** the heretical teaching of Arius of Alexandria that God the Son was a later creation of God the Father and not coeternal with the Father

**Vulgate Bible:** the Latin translation of the Scriptures made by St. Jerome

**Pelagianism:** the heretical teaching of Pelagius, a British monk, who said that human beings could bring on their salvation by their own merits and works, without grace

**Donatists:** a schismatic sect that said that lay Christians and clerics who had cooperated with the Roman persecutors could not be legitimate Christians or priests

**schismatic:** from Greek *schisma*, meaning a division. A schismatic sets up a rival church, causing a division of a part of the Church from the whole.

**orthodox:** adhering to teaching, established, especially by a religious group; in the Christian Faith, adhering to the teachings revealed to the Church by Christ

**Manicheanism:** a Persian philosophy that taught the material world is evil; only the spiritual world is good. Manicheans called for a severe self-control and piety.

## Questions for Review

1. What were the errors of the Arian, Pelagian, and Manichean heresies? Why would educated people tend to favor these heresies over the orthodox Catholic Faith?
2. What key term did the Council of Nicaea define? What does it mean? Why would Arians object to this term?
3. How did German tribes become Arian?

4. Why did the pope ask Jerome to translate the Scriptures into Latin? In what languages were they originally written?
5. What event inspired Augustine to write the *City of God*? On what did some Romans blame the sack of the city?
6. How did Leo the Great save Rome?

## Ideas in Action
1. Discuss as a class the meaning of Augustine's concept of the two cities. What in this world belongs to the City of God and what to the earthly city?
2. Memorize the Nicene Creed as said in Mass. Discuss it in class. What does each part of the Creed mean in the daily life of a Christian?
3. Find several translations of the Bible. Compare them as to their easy-to-read language, their beauty of expression, their overall effect on the reader. Why is it important to have several translations of the Bible? Discuss why the Church needed a Latin translation of the Scriptures.

# Highways and Byways

## The Imperial Costume
Like Diocletian and Galerius, Constantine tried to inspire people with a sense of respect and awe for the imperial office, encouraging a court ceremony that was unlike the older, simpler Roman court ceremony. It was, in fact, based on the elaborate ceremonies surrounding the Persian kings. Though a believer in Christ, Constantine insisted on the observance of these rituals, which treated the emperor as if he were divine. He always appeared at state occasions looking like a being from the heavenly world.

The Council of Nicaea itself opened with the entrance of the august Emperor Constantine, who dressed in a way to impress and awe the quarreling bishops. He appeared like a god among men and commanded their silence. At the sound of the entrance gong, the bishops rose. Constantine entered and walked down the center aisle to his throne, a small gilded chair in the middle of the far wall. The rustling of his silks and the clicking pearls of his crown could be heard throughout the hushed room.

The emperor was then about 45 years old, weathered in appearance but still strong and hearty, broad-shouldered, muscular, large jawed. He was robed in heavy imperial robes and capes of gold-embroidered silk. The amount of silk on his person could have paid the ransom of hundreds of captives. His silken robes were colored with the imperial purple, green, and gold and swirled around him like clouds of color, giving off the scent of perfumes that struck the bishops as incense.

Constantine's hair was curled and stiffened into tight Persian ringlets. On his tightly coiffed head he wore the great imperial crown of gold and jewels, adorned with strings of pearls dangling down over his shoulders. The gold rings and bracelets were carefully displayed beneath the robes, and precious gems studded the whole costume like stars of light.

This did not seem to be the man who had led armies and won battles, who wore armor and rough wools, but a god-like being from a mythical realm. But this man was no immortal; and to prove his trust in these bishops as brother Christians, he refused armed security. Without guards, he walked down the aisle of bishops to his seat and asked them to be seated. When they declined to take their seats before the emperor took his, Constantine laughed and ordered them to sit at the same time as he did. They took their seats together, and the council began.

# Chapter 5: Germanic Kingdoms in the West

Writers in the 17th century called the five centuries between the years 400 and 900 the "Dark Ages" because they knew so little about them. These years were "dark" or hidden to their understanding. These writers of the 1600s knew only that "barbarians" had overrun the Roman Empire and that much of the ancient learning of Greece and Rome had been lost.

Much of classical civilization was indeed lost between 400 and 900. Travel was dangerous, commerce came almost to a standstill, and agricultural methods did not improve. Central political control and social order disappeared amid wars and their destructive effects. The standard of living in Gaul, Italy, and Germany fell disastrously from what it was in the days of the Roman Empire.

But the Dark Ages present more than just a tale of destruction. During those centuries, the Greco-Roman world and the "barbarians" were brought into the heart of the Christian Faith and its Church. The virtues of the northern people—heroism, perseverance, and personal loyalty—were being transformed by the Christian-Roman traditions of faith, intellectual investigation, compassion, moral responsibility, and legal wisdom. Greco-Roman civilization was not lost in the Dark Ages; it was remade into Christendom.

Christendom is the name given to the civilization that arose from the ancient civilizations of Greece, Rome, and Israel. Beginning in the Dark Ages, Christendom developed in western and eastern Europe and later spread to North and South America.

# The North Invades the South

**Germanic warriors pillage Rome**

The greatest migration of peoples in human history took place in the fourth through sixth centuries. During that time, Germanic tribes and nations descended on the provinces of the Roman Empire and claimed the lands of Gaul and Iberia.

The Germanic peoples were formerly spread across the forests south of the Baltic Sea and the plains and river valleys of Eastern Europe. During the later years of the Roman Empire, they moved with their families and herds into the Danube and Rhine valleys, and from there into Western Europe—Gaul, Italy, and the Iberian Peninsula. Beginning in the fourth century, a new wave of Germanic tribes moved down from the southern coasts and forests of the Baltic Sea region, through Dacia and Hungary, and into Roman lands.

For a hundred years, the imperial armies made use of some Germanic tribes as allies against other Germanic peoples. Then, in the later years of the empire, the Romans allowed several Germanic tribes to move their families as settlers and colonists into empty or underpopulated lands in Gaul or along the Danube River. Because of mistakes made by Roman commanders, the tribes finally moved into the empire of the West as conquerors, ruling over a much larger Romanized population. They set up kingdoms of their own, independent of the Roman emperors in Constantinople.

The Germanic tribes that had given warriors to the armies of Rome for a century or more regarded themselves as part of the Roman world. They did not think of themselves as Germans, but Romans. To these immigrants, to be Roman was to be Christian, to belong to the religion of the empire. Many of the Germanic tribes had been converted generations before by Arian missionaries and were proud of their faith.

Chapter 5   Germanic Kingdoms in the West   117

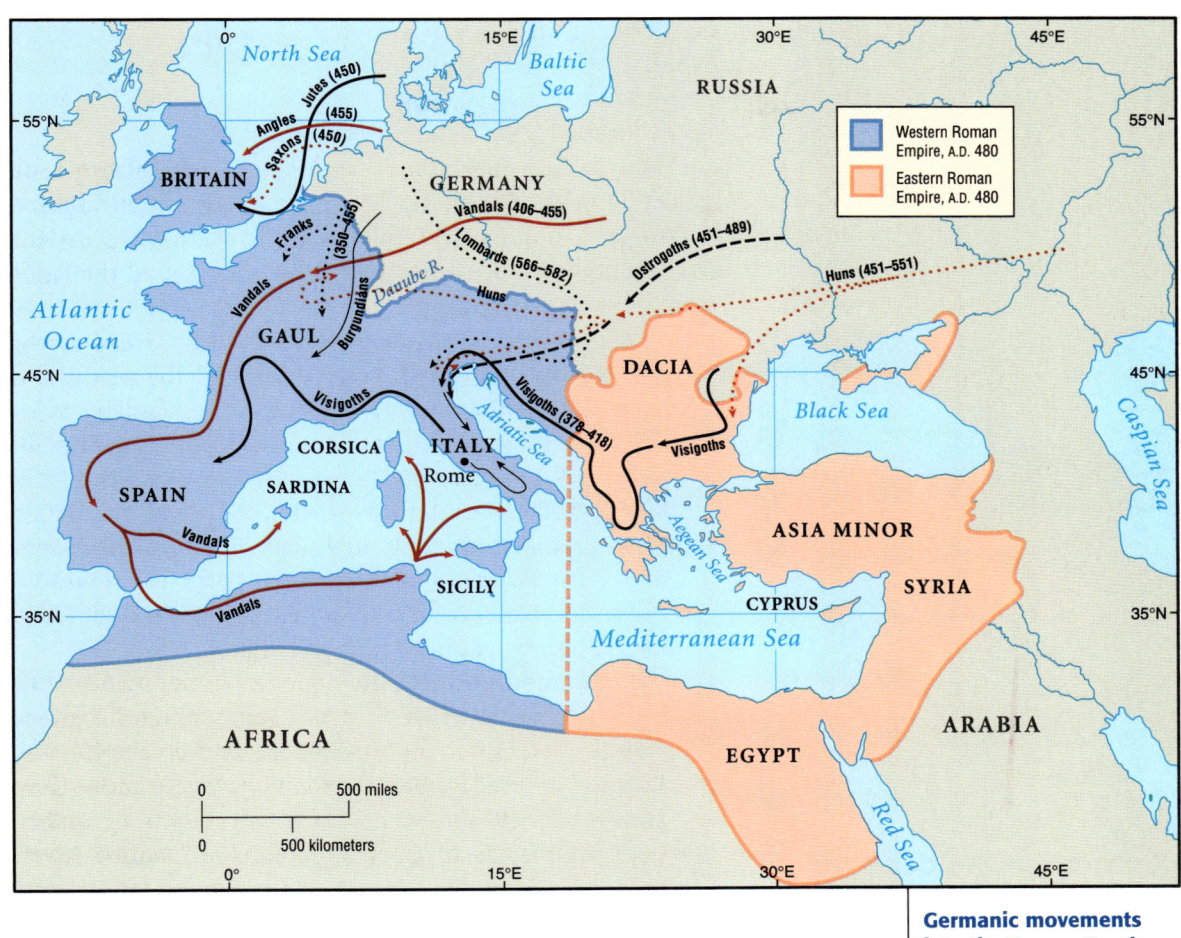

**Germanic movements into the Roman Empire**

# The Germanic World

Though they did not consider themselves one people, the Germanic nations had similar cultures that distinguished them from the peoples of the Mediterranean civilization. So it is that we can speak of Germanic languages, social organization, or law.

## Language and Social Classes

Though Germans of one tribe did not understand the language spoken by Germans of another tribe, their languages were related. Germanic language is a branch of the great Indo-European language family, which includes Persian, Greek, and Latin. There are three distinct Germanic language branches: Eastern, or Gothic (now wholly lost); Western (from which come modern German, Dutch, and English); and Northern (from which come Swedish, Norwegian, and Danish).

The Germans' long history of migration and their constant fights with the other peoples of the eastern plains had made them into a warrior-hunter society. War was necessary to defend the tribe, and the people devoted all their resources to it. All free men were expected to learn the use of arms—spear, sword, axe, and shield. Women, too, sometimes took up spear and shield and joined their men on the battle line. Those in the tribe who fought and hunted best were the elite, and from them came the kings and their circle of comrades in arms.

The Germanic "kings" traced their family lines back to mythological gods or **demigods** of an ancient heroic age. Germanic leaders were expected to rely on the counsel of the tribal elders, men who had earned their peers' respect or represented some powerful family. These elders also chose the next leader or deposed the present leader if they found him cowardly or unfit. The old songs tell tales of bad kings, like Hermanreich, who ruled the Goths so badly that they finally drove him out in disgust.

Germanic leaders were protected by a band of comrades—their cousins and friends, or the best warriors of the tribe who were supported by the king and fought beside him in battle. These companions were expected to protect their lord with their lives, and they swore oaths of loyalty that they dared not break. These warriors could expect a similar loyalty from their lord, who became famous through their deeds as well as by his generosity to them in dividing the spoils of battle and giving his own wealth to them and their families. One of the king's titles was "Ring-giver," for the gold rings he gave as gifts to his warriors.

**demigod:** a being who has more power than a human being but less than a god

## Germanic Law

The Germans were not ruled by written codes or by the edicts of kings or magistrates; for the Germans, the word "law" meant "age-old custom." Even the lowest free man could appeal to the customary law of the tribe for justice. But each tribe had a different law, and at first those laws were not written down. Instead, they were memorized and passed along by the bards or the council elders.

When people were accused of a crime under Germanic law, they were considered guilty until they proved their innocence. To prove their innocence, those who were accused could appeal to eyewitness testimony and to three kinds of "evidence": the oath, the ordeal, and the combat.

In taking an oath, the accused called on a god to support him for telling the truth or punish him for lying. Christian Germans swore by God's power or on the altar of a church. In an ordeal, the oath taker underwent severe pain or torture to prove he was telling the truth. The clean healing of the wound resulting from the injury was also a sign of a true oath.

Trial by combat involved a fight, perhaps to the death, with a court-appointed opponent or with one's accuser. It was believed that the god invoked in the oath would award the victory to the man who had sworn truthfully. Christian Germans said God would save the innocent. Some Christians, however, said God did not decide justice through violent combats or ordeals.

## The Gods of the North

Before accepting Christianity, the Germanic peoples worshiped fierce and frightening gods. In Germanic myth, the gods were forever at war with the giants and demons of the ice and cold. These divine beings were not thought to be very concerned with human life; indeed, they demanded human sacrifice. The human sacrifice of captives and slaves to the gods continued in the far northern part of Europe until the Christian Faith brought an end to the terrible practice.

**A Viking stone with runes**

What knowledge we have of Germanic gods we get through the stories of the Norse gods, who must have been similar to the gods of the other Germanic peoples. The major gods of the Norsemen were all war gods—the brothers Wodin, Thor, and Tiw ruled the Germanic **pantheon**. They required men's lives in battle. Recklessness on the battlefield was considered

### The Days of the Week

The names for the days of the week in English come from the names of ancient German gods: the Sun, the Moon, Tiw, Wodin, Thor, and Freia. The Roman god, Saturn, gave his name to the last day, Saturday. Can you spot the gods' names in our modern version of the days' names?

**pantheon:** the gods of a people or nation; also, a temple dedicated to all the gods

A scene from the tales of Thor, the Norse god of thunder. From an 18th century Icelandic manuscript.

a religious act, sacred to Thor. Men who were brave and fought well would be taken to Valhalla (the "gods' hall") after death to feast with the gods.

According to German myths, the world would end one day in a colossal battle of the gods with the giants. Mankind would perish in the conflict. The world would end in a final defeat. Because of this belief in universal destruction, the Germans believed that, in this life, only courage in the face of certain defeat proved human worth. Germanic songs and poems celebrated courageous defeat as much as victories and successes. Even when they became Christian, the Germans saw courage as the greatest virtue. No one was to give up the Christian Faith, not even under threat of torture and death. The Germanic soul rejoiced in the stories of the martyrs.

## The Visigoths in the Iberian Peninsula

As you learned in the previous chapter, the Visigoths moved into southern Gaul after the death of their leader, Alaric (who had sacked Rome in 410). Under a later king, Euric, who reigned from 466 to 481, the Visigoths invaded the Iberian Peninsula, conquering much of the Roman province of Hispania.

In southern Gaul and Hispania, the Visigoths made a huge kingdom centered on the city of Toulouse in Gaul. The kingdom stretched from the

Loire River to the Mediterranean coast, and it went from the Alps, over the Pyrenees, into the Iberian Peninsula. The family of Alaric, called the Baltings (because they claimed descent from the legendary hero, Balto), ruled the Visigothic kingdom for two centuries until the last Balting died in battle with the Franks.

Southern Gaul was, at first, the most important part of the Visigothic kingdom, since it contained both the capital and the richest lands. But in 507, in fierce battles, the Franks drove the Visigoths from most of Gaul. The Visigoths established their kingdom in Hispania, making Toledo their new royal capital.

These aggressive immigrants were only a tiny percentage of the population in Hispania, the Roman province that eventually became Spain. Arian Visigothic monarchs ruled the Catholic descendants of the Roman provincials in the peninsula from 466 until 713. With the Visigoths came Arian bishops and clergy; an Arian form of the liturgy (in Gothic and Latin), and a Gothic-language Bible that had been translated by Wulfilas in the fourth century. Most of the Visigoths, however, heard their own language only in the liturgy or the Gothic Bible, since they had come to speak Latin. To their Catholic subjects in Hispania and Gaul, whose liturgy and Scriptures were entirely in Latin, these Visigothic rulers were heretics and foreigners.

**San Pedro de la Nave—Visigothic church, Campillo, Spain**

The Visigoths were an unruly lot. They fought among themselves constantly, and they assassinated many of their kings. They elected their kings; but once elected, a king had to beware rivals in his own country as well as enemies from outside the kingdom.

The Visigoths preserved a significant part of the Greco-Roman heritage. For two-and-a-half centuries, largely through the efforts of great Catholic churchmen and monks, the Visigothic kingdom preserved much of the heritage of Greece and Rome.

Catholic monasticism flourished in Visigothic Hispania, especially in the sixth and seventh centuries. During this period, many saints were associated with these centers of Catholic spirituality. Monasteries were

**Crown of Recceswinth. The treasure of Guarrazar (Toledo, Spain) was discovered amongst the remains of a hidden Visigothic city in 1855. The most priceless items of the treasure are two votive crowns engraved with the names of the kings Suintila and Recceswinth.**

also centers of learning. Monks were often writers, editors, copyists, librarians, and school teachers.

## The Illustrious Family of Severianus

For two generations, one family of mixed Latin and Gothic blood greatly influenced the Visigothic kingdom. The family had no particular last name, but all its members in question were descendants and relatives of Severianus, a Catholic Latin. Severianus and his family lived in Cartagena (Murcia) on the Mediterranean coast of Spain. Later, they moved west to Seville.

Severianus' children, grandchildren, and in-laws included three bishops, a king, a martyr, a princess, an abbess, and a very successful mother. The Church venerates five members of the family as saints: Sts. Leander and Isidore, both bishops of Seville; St. Fulgentius, bishop of Ecija and Cartagena; St. Florentina, an abbess; and Queen Theodosia, who married Leovigild, a Visigothic king. (Though many historians think Theodosia was not related to Severianus.) The next generation of Theodosia's children was just as important: it included St. Hermenegild and his brother, King Reccared, as well as Hermenegild's wife, a Frankish princess named Ingunthis.

**Tragedy in a King's Family** Leovigild was one of the most formidable of the Visigothic monarchs. He subdued rebellions and conquered parts of the Iberian Peninsula not previously controlled by the Visigoths. He also sought to unify his kingdom. To do this, he tried to force Arianism on his Catholic subjects, who made up approximately 90 percent of the population. The attempt backfired, bringing personal tragedy to the king's own family.

Leovigild's first wife, Theodosia, was Catholic; but she died before he was elected to the throne. The newly elected monarch quickly married Goswintha, widow of the previous ruler and an enthusiastic Arian. She insisted that her stepsons be raised in the Arian faith. In 576, Leovigild married his eldest son, Hermenegild, to Goswintha's 13-year-old granddaughter, Ingunthis, a Frankish princess. The old queen tried to force Ingunthis to convert to Arianism, but Ingunthis was as fiercely Catholic as her grandmother the queen was passionately Arian. King Leovigild grew so tired of the quarreling in his palace that he sent Prince Hermenegild and his young wife south, to Seville, and gave him the grand title, Duke of Baëtica.

Leander, a member of the family of Severianus and Hermenegild's uncle, was bishop of Seville at the time. When Ingunthis arrived in Seville, she joined with Bishop Leander in converting Hermenegild. The Arian king and queen were furious. Because Leander had brought Hermenegild into the Catholic Church, Leovigild for a time banished the bishop from Seville.

Hearing of his son's conversion, Leovigild summoned him to return to Toledo. Hermenegild refused. Instead, seeing the harsh way Leovigild treated Catholics, Hermenegild led a rebellion against his father. Southwestern Spain declared its independence from Toledo, and Hermenegild was crowned king in Seville.

But Leovigild—a great warrior and strong leader—recaptured the rebel cities one by one. When Hermenegild was seized in Cordova, Leovigild banished him to distant Valencia. On Easter day, 585, Hermenegild was martyred because he refused to receive Easter communion from an Arian bishop. His young wife, Ingunthis, only 18 years old, died shortly after. Leovigild did not long survive them; he died a year later, leaving the kingdom to his second son, Reccared.

## The Arians Become Catholic

Ten months after ascending the throne, King Reccared privately accepted the Catholic Faith. He and his uncle, Bishop Leander, spent the next two years paving the way for the conversion of the Visigothic people. The arrangements included the celebration of an assembly of Catholic and Arian religious leaders.

On May 8, 589, in the city of Toledo, the Arian bishops—along with the Visigothic civil and military leaders and King Reccared himself—solemnly made a public announcement of their conversion to Catholicism. Reccared officially forbade Arianism in the realm. After more than a century of religious conflict, the small minority of ruling Arian Visigoths accepted the faith of the people they had conquered.

This momentous event, which would color so much of Spain's history from then on, took place at the Third Council of Toledo. The renowned assembly became the model for many future national assemblies. The councils of Toledo were to become one of the most important institutions of the Visigothic monarchy. They were a unique sign of the close cooperation that developed between Church and state.

After Reccared's long and productive reign, the Visigoths enjoyed little political stability. Reccared's grandson was assassinated, and the old cycle of quarrelsome rivalries began again. In this troubled state, the Church remained a source of stability. The bishops held the Visigothic kingdom

A 10th century miniature of Saint Isidore of Seville

together by their wisdom as well as by their spiritual authority. They counseled the kings and lords, saw to the administration of government, and handled foreign affairs. The Church took up some of the responsibilities the kings were unable to fulfill.

Adding to the civilizing work of the bishops, monasteries brought their orderly life and free schooling to all social classes. The Visigothic church made Spain a beacon of learning and civilization in the early Middle Ages. St. Isidore of Seville, one of the children of Severianus, wrote an encyclopedic work, the *Etymologies*, in which he collected all the learning known in his time. The *Etymologies* deals with grammar, logic, medicine, God, the angels, man, birds and beasts, geography, law, food, clothing, ships, and houses, among other topics. The *Etymologies* helped preserve much of Greek and Roman wisdom and knowledge. It was an important text for the centuries to come.

# The Vandals in North Africa

Over the frozen Rhine and into the province of Gaul in the winter of 406 poured the whole Vandal nation, bringing their wagon trains of children and household goods. The Emperor Gratian had not paid them for their services in guarding the imperial border, and so they descended on the southern half of Gaul. They were angry at Roman treachery and scornful of the civilized weaklings who had betrayed them.

Checked on the north by the Franks and harried by the Visigoths leaving Italy, the Vandals crossed into the Iberian Peninsula in 409 with their allies, the Suevi. There they looted the old Roman towns of Hispania and the cities on the coast. The arrival of Visigoth bands in the 420s forced the Vandals to move on to regions not yet plundered—the rich provinces of North Africa, the undefended grain lands of the empire.

Left without a male heir to their ancient royal family, the Vandals elected Genseric as king. Genseric was both a cripple (from a childhood accident) and the son of a slave, but he had overcome both these handicaps by his ferocity in battle and persuasive oratory. He achieved election as king through clever political maneuvering and the murder of rivals.

In 429, Genseric led his people across the Straits of Gibraltar on ships whose crews were forced to carry them or die. One by one the towns of the grain lands fell to the fierce warriors, until Genseric's horde was at the gates of Carthage. A Vandal army besieged Hippo, where St. Augustine rallied his townspeople to resist. The aged bishop died during the siege, falling ill from the general starvation and sickness that finally forced his people to open the gates to the barbarians. Carthage itself fell to Genseric's trickery when a traitor within the city opened a gate.

Knowing that the road to further loot was the sea, Genseric built a fleet of warships and trained his men to sail them. Piracy filled his coffers quickly. He conquered Sardinia and Corsica and left them suffering under a Vandal **garrison**. He landed in Sicily and overran the huge island in a year. Then he landed on Italian shores and marched on Rome. Despite the bribe paid by Pope St. Leo the Great, Genseric's warriors entered the city in 455 and looted and burned for two weeks. He took away the last treasures of pagan Rome, including the sacred vessels, the Great **Menorah** and the serving basins, brought to Rome by Titus in A.D. 71 from the sack of the Temple of Jerusalem.

The Vandals, lords as well as fighting men, carved out huge estates for themselves from the imperial grain fields of North Africa. The Roman population, helpless before them, was enslaved or reduced to serfdom. The Vandals were Arians, though they were less given to Christian forgiveness and virtue than their Germanic neighbors, the Visigoths, were. Genseric's Arianism gave him the excuse to loot Catholic churches and to confiscate Church lands. Catholics were made to pay a harsh tax for not converting to Arianism, and Catholic bishops were thrown into prison.

Vandal cruelty to Catholics only increased after Genseric's death. His successors used the excuse of religion to try to bleed more money out of their subjects. Medieval writers found many stories to tell of martyrdom at the hands of the Vandal lords.

> **garrison:** troops stationed in a territory or at a base camp
> **menorah:** a seven-branched candelabrum used in Jewish worship; in ancient times, the Jerusalem temple had a large menorah

**Menorah**

126   LIGHT TO THE NATIONS: The History of Christian Civilization

**A medieval depiction of the legend of King Clovis receiving the *fleur-de-lis*, the symbol of France**

But in becoming used to the luxuries and easy life of wealth, the warriors grew corrupt, fat, and lazy. Their sons were not made to learn the rigors of a warrior's life, and the Vandal ruling class lost its ferocity.

At his death, Genseric left his kingdom to his son, Hunneric, who kept the kingdom alive through the profits from piracy and the treacherous treaties his father had made with his neighbors. But after Hunneric, no king could stop the decline of the Vandal nation. Divided from their subjects who hated them, the Vandals could not stand against the armies of the Eastern Roman emperor Justinian in 533. They disappeared as a distinct people, mixing in with the highly diverse local population of North Africa.

# The First Catholic Germanic Kingdom

In the late 4th century, a confederation of tribes moved into Gaul to take service with the Roman armies. These *Franks* (meaning "free men"), as the tribes began to call themselves, had lived for centuries in what is now Belgium and along the Rhine and Main rivers in Germany. They had been allies of the Roman legions. The Frankish kings all claimed descent from a mythic hero, Merovech (after whom they called themselves Merovings).

When Roman power collapsed in Gaul, the Frankish kings moved their people onto the farms and into towns there which belonged to Romans. And there was no Roman opposition. Only the Catholic bishops and priests maintained what shreds of Roman government and order that remained.

The Franks were not Christian and had accepted little of the Roman way of life. They still fought without armor and on foot and went to war largely unclothed, armed with a spear, a sword, and a battle-axe called the *francisca* (or "little freedom"). They obeyed their chiefs only when those chiefs were successful in battle.

## The Merovings

In 481, Clodevech, the 16-year-old chief of one of the Frankish tribes, secured his father's claim to kingship by exterminating all his cousins and rivals. At age 21, this chief, known to history as Clovis, led his tribe into the Seine valley. He killed the Roman governor there, taking the towns of Soissons, Rouen, Reims, and Paris. Then he marched through the Loire River valley to the borders of Brittany and secured his western border. Safe on one front, he moved against his cousins along the Rhine and killed them one by one. By 491, Clovis held all the Frankish princedoms except Cologne. He slew every prince of Meroving blood who fell into his hands, and he did his best to exterminate all other members of rival families who could lay claim to his throne.

**An ancient Merovingian graveyard and chapel, dating to the 5th–8th centuries**

Clovis' conquests brought him into contact with the Burgundians, another Germanic invader nation, to the south. He sent ambassadors and married their princess, Clotilde, the Burgundian king's niece. Clotilde, a devout Catholic, was determined to convert her new husband to the Christian Faith. According to legend, when Clovis was awaiting a battle with the Germanic Alamanni, his wife said he would conquer only if he agreed to serve the one true God, the Lord of Hosts and Judge of all battles. Clovis cried out, "O Christ Jesus, as a suppliant I crave your glorious aid; and if you grant me victory over these enemies, I will believe in you and be baptized in your name!" The Franks then drove the Alamanni from the field in defeat.

**Tomb of Clovis from the church of St. Denis, Paris**

In fulfilling his contract with the Christian God, Clovis had himself baptized at Reims by Bishop Remigius (St. Remi) on Christmas Day, 496. Referring to Clovis' ancestor, Sigambris, a legendary Frankish villain, Remigius declared, "Bow your neck, Sigambrian, and adore that which you have burned and burn that which you have adored."

Clovis was the first Germanic king who adopted the faith of his Roman subjects; they and their clergy from then on served him with a loyalty no Arian Visigoth, Ostrogoth, or Vandal could ever win from his Roman subjects. The Catholic bishops, who had kept all local government from disappearing, gave Clovis a working governmental organization along with their faith. Their loyalty reinforced his sword. Bishop Avitus of Vienne declared, "Your faith is our triumph. Every battle you fight is a victory for us."

Clovis' conversion moved the rest of his people to follow him. In a single generation, the old Frankish paganism disappeared, and the Franks became Catholic. However, even after his baptism (if the old legendary histories can entirely be believed), Clovis remained as cruel, unscrupulous, and treacherous as he had ever been. In his later years, Clovis persuaded his cousin, the prince of Cologne, to kill his own father and claim the throne. For this crime (to which Clovis had pushed him), Clovis marched on the son and put him to death as a father-slayer. Thus he disposed of his last Meroving rival.

In 511 Clovis died, dividing his kingdom among his four quarrelsome sons. They followed their father's treacherous example more than that of their Catholic Faith. One of Clovis' sons ordered his own son burned alive for offending him. Another of Clovis' sons was killed by his conspiring sons, who then fought among themselves until only one was left. Clovis' last surviving son, Clothar, divided the Frankish realm between *his* two sons. For more than a century two Frankish kingdoms—Austrasia, the east kingdom along the Rhine Valley, and Neustria, the west kingdom comprised of northern Gaul—warred and plotted against each other and with their neighbors, the powerful dukes of Burgundy and Aquitaine.

## The Rise of the Mayor of the Palace

The Meroving kings were served by **chancellors**, called "mayors of the palace," who increasingly took on themselves the task of ruling the kingdom.

**chancellor:** the secretary or chief magistrate of a king

The last Merovings ruled no more than the lands of their small farms; the mayors of the palace commanded the armies and passed laws in the king's name. Because they believed the Meroving kings were sacred, the Franks refused to abandon the royal line. At last, in 688, a new mayor took office; he would rescue the Frankish kingdom from the corruption of the Merovings and advance both Frankish power and the Christian Faith at home and abroad. He was Pepin the Younger.

Pepin restored the Frankish kingdom to the boundaries it had in Clovis' time, and he defended the kingdom from outside attack. He sent missionaries into the forests and valleys of Germany to convert the last pagan tribes on his borders. St. Willebrord and his 12 companions preached the Gospel to the Frisians, and St. Boniface converted the heathen Hessians. Pepin's son, Charles, as mayor of the palace was so successful in putting down a rebellion among the tribes east of the Rhine that he was given the nickname of *Martellus* or *Martel* (meaning "Hammer.") Charles Martel established his rule over all the Frankish lands.

Pepin's grandson, Pepin the Short, finally removed the Merovingian kings from power and ruled in his own name as king. He was crowned by St. Boniface at Reims in 751. Pepin the Short began a new line of Frankish kings, called the Carolingians. They were named for his father, Charles Martel (Charles is *Karl* in Frankish and *Carolus* in Latin, from which comes the name "Carolingian"). Charles Martel's grandson was Charles (known to history as Charlemagne), who revived the Roman Empire in the West.

**Charles Martel halting the Moorish conquest of Europe at the Battle of Tours, 732**

# The Kingdom of The Ostrogoths

After the death of the Western Roman Emperor Valentinian III in 455, the imperial court withdrew into the walls of Ravenna. Since the imperial armies were composed entirely of German mercenaries, their commander —called the *magister militum* ("master of soldiers")—was the real ruler of the Western Roman Empire, not the emperor himself.

Romulus Augustulus surrenders to Odoacer the Insignia of Empire.

## The Last Emperor

In 475, one Orestes—a Roman who had served as Attila the Hun's Latin secretary and had married into the Roman aristocracy—bribed the Senate at Ravenna into naming his young son emperor. The new boy emperor was called Romulus Augustulus—*Romulus*, from the legendary founder of Rome, and *Augustulus*, "little Augustus," after the founder of the Roman Empire.

The German troops had been promised one-third of Italy for themselves if they went along with the election of the new emperor. But Romulus Augustulus and his father Orestes made the fatal mistake of refusing to honor the promise. So the troops elected as king their own commander—a Goth named Odoacer. In 476 Odoacer removed the boy emperor, giving him a villa at Naples and a fortune in gold; Orestes was beheaded. Odoacer styled himself king of the Germans in Italy, claiming the lands of the Western Roman Empire for himself. But only Italy and

Chapter 5   Germanic Kingdoms in the West   **131**

The Germanic kingdoms and the Eastern Roman Empire

the coasts of the Adriatic Sea were under his control. The imperial **regalia** were sent to the eastern emperor, Zeno, in Constantinople.

With this revolt, the great empire founded by Augustus almost 500 years earlier simply vanished from the West.

## The Amaling King

In 488, the Eastern Emperor Zeno financed an invasion of Odoacer's Italian territories and chose Theodoric, the young king of the Ostrogoths, to carry it out. Theodoric was the heir of the Amalings, the hereditary royal line of the Ostrogoths. To save Theodoric from family rivals, his father had sent him to the imperial court in Constantinople to be raised and trained in military skills.

**regalia:** the emblems or symbols of royalty (from the Latin *regalis*, meaning "regal" or "royal")

Theodoric spent 10 years among the Greeks and Romans. He then spent 20 years with his own people, whom he led in successful campaigns against the Huns, Burgundians, and Avars. He had already distinguished himself among his people as a great warrior and orator, a man wise in council and brave in war. Emperor Zeno thought that he could trust Theodoric to restore Italy to imperial control.

After subduing Odoacer, however, Theodoric declared himself king of Italy and took over the imperial court at Ravenna. A new emperor in Constantinople sent him the crown, robes, and regalia of the last western emperor, Romulus Augustulus.

As king, Theodoric set about rebuilding Italy. He repaired aqueducts and city walls, cleared drainage ditches, and dredged canals. Each year, he set aside 200 pounds of gold from his revenues to repair and maintain the public buildings and palaces of Rome and Ravenna.

Under Theodoric, the Ostrogoths continued to govern themselves by their tribal customs; but the king wisely used Roman law to govern his Italian subjects and had them tried in Roman courts of law. Theodoric's kingdom lasted 33 years under his rule and some 25 more years after his death.

Theodoric was determined to accustom his Goths to Roman ways—and he encouraged his Roman subjects to learn Gothic honesty and open-handedness. But the Ostrogoths were Arians, and they had their own Arian bishops and church organization. That meant dual churches in the one kingdom and constant friction between the Roman Italians and the Ostrogoths. Still, no other Germanic nation seemed so capable of forming a new civilized state on the ruins of the old Roman Empire. And no other Germanic prince was so fitted to the task of mediating between two cultures as was Theodoric. Though an Arian, Theodoric tolerated Catholic Christians and Jews. He had declared that "religion is a thing which the king cannot command, because no man can be compelled to believe against his will."

Theodoric's daughter married Alaric II, king of the Visigoths. When Alaric died at the hands of the Franks, she called on her father to defend his grandson, Amalric. Theodoric's armies drove the Franks out of Provence and Aquitaine and crossed the Pyrenees to defeat a rival claimant to the Visigoth throne. Theodoric ruled the Visigoths in his grandson's name for the next 11 years. The two Gothic kingdoms were one. At its height, Theodoric's kingdom included all of Italy, most of Sicily, Illyricum east of the Adriatic Sea, and the Visigothic kingdom in the West. The Danube River marked its northern border. It was the largest kingdom in the West since the days of the empire.

Toward the end of his life, Theodoric became afraid that the Eastern Roman Emperor Justin in Constantinople was plotting to kill him. Theodoric accused his Roman subjects, particularly the Senate, of planning to assassinate him. Theodoric condemned several senators to death because of anonymous letters that claimed they were plotting to assassinate him. Among the senators the king put to death was the philosopher Boethius. During the remaining years of his life, Theodoric grew ever more fearful and mentally unstable.

After his death, the Ostrogoth's kingdom passed to Theodoric's grandson, Amalaric. Since the new king was still a boy, his mother, Amalasuntha (Theodoric's daughter), served as **regent**. Amalric died in his late teens, and the kingdom fell into the usual Germanic disunity and feuding. A 20-year war with the armies of the Eastern Roman Empire ended the Ostrogoths' kingdom in the general ruin of Italy.

Ceiling mosaic of the Arian bapistry, Ravenna, erected by King Theodoric the Great, late 5th century

**regent:** one who governs a kingdom for a king or queen who is too young to govern. The reign of a regent is called a *regency*.

# Chapter Review

## Summary
- Germanic peoples came from the region of the Baltic Sea and the plains and river valleys of Eastern Europe. During the late Roman period, they moved south and east into Western Europe and then began to cross the boundaries of the empire.
- The Roman emperors allowed some Germanic tribes to settle within the empire, using them as allies against other Germanic tribes. Eventually, Germanic tribes moved into the empire as conquerors and permanent rulers.
- Germanic nations had similar cultures, though they did not consider themselves one people. They spoke related languages; were divided by similar social classes; governed themselves by customary, not written,

laws; and were warrior societies. Germanic nations held that courage was the highest virtue.
- Pagan Germans worshipped fierce gods who were thought to fight wars against giants and demons of the ice and cold. Brave warriors who died in battle were thought to be taken to the hall of these gods, called Valhalla. Many Germanic tribes were converted to Arianism.
- After sacking Rome in 410, the Visigoths withdrew from Italy and established a kingdom in southern Gaul and the Iberian Peninsula. Driven from southern Gaul by the Franks in 507, the Visigoths continued to rule Hispania for over two centuries. The Visigoths, who were Arian, ruled a much larger population of Romans, who were Catholic.
- A Visigothic king in Hispania, Leovigild, married Goswintha, a zealous Arian. Through her influence and to unify his kingdom, Leovigild tried to force Arianism on his Catholic subjects. But it did not work. Even his son, Hermenegild, who became Catholic through the influence of his wife, Ingunthis, refused to obey his father. After an unsuccessful rebellion, Hermenegild was martyred for refusing to receive communion from an Arian bishop.
- Leovigild's second son, Reccared, himself became Catholic; and with Bishop Leander of Seville, Recarred brought the Visigoths into the Catholic Church. He officially forbade Arianism in his realm.
- The Visigoths had driven another Germanic nation, the Vandals, out of the Iberian Peninsula. Led by their king, Genseric, the Vandals went to North Africa, where they set up a kingdom after plundering the Roman settlements and capturing Carthage. Genseric led his people in an invasion of Sicily and Italy, conquering Corsica and Sardinia, and in 455 looted and sacked Rome itself. The Arian Vandals persecuted the Christians in the conquered lands.
- Clovis, the Merovingian king of the Franks, conquered large sections of Gaul, seizing also the lands held by other Frankish kings. Though a pagan (along with the rest of his people), Clovis became the first Germanic king to become Catholic through the influence of his Burgundian wife, Clotilde.
- After Clovis' death, his kingdom was divided between his four sons. Over the next two centuries, the Merovingian kings became merely figureheads, their mayors of the palace carrying on the actual work of ruling. Finally, Pepin the Short, the Carolingian mayor of the palace, removed the last Merovingian rulers from power and was crowned king in 751.

- Theodoric, king of the Ostrogoths, overthrew Odoacer, the German king who had deposed the last Roman emperor in the West. Theodoric made himself king of Italy. He governed Italy and other lands he subsequently ruled wisely and well for most of his reign. Though an Arian, he treated Catholics with tolerance. But, at the end of his life, fearing a plot against him by the Eastern Roman emperor and the Catholic senators in Italy, he assassinated several senators. After Theodoric's death, his Ostrogothic kingdom fell into disunity.

## Key Concepts

**Council of Toledo:** held in 589; unified the Catholic and Arian churches of Spain
**king:** a Germanic title for the ruling chief of the people, either an hereditary office or elected by the principal nobles. A Germanic king ruled through custom and tribal connections.
**Germanic law:** age-old custom, traditional justice
**Merovings:** the line of the Frankish kings claiming descent from the legendary hero, Merovech
**Carolingian:** the line of Frankish kings descended from Charles Martel (Carolus Martellus)

## Dates to Remember

**400–900:** the "Dark Ages"
**476:** end of the Roman Empire in the West. The last emperor of Rome, Romulus Augustulus, abdicates to his Germanic master of horse, Odoacer.
**488:** Theodoric defeats Odoacer and is proclaimed king of Italy by the Eastern Emperor Zeno.
**496:** Clovis, king of the Franks, baptized as a Catholic by St. Remigius
**589:** King Reccared officially bans Arianism in Hispania.
**751:** Pepin the Short, Mayor of the Palace, is crowned king of the Franks.

## Central Characters

**Alaric (370–410):** king of the Visigoths, sacked Rome in 410
**St. Isidore (560–636):** bishop of Seville; wrote the famous *Etymologies*, the medieval encyclopedia
**Reccared (d. 601):** son of Leovigild, converted to the Catholic Faith and brought the whole Visigothic people into the Catholic Church

**Clovis (466–511):** king of the Franks, and the first German ruler to convert to the Catholic Faith

**Pepin the Short (714–768):** son of Charles Martel, grandfather of Charlemagne, Mayor of the Palace, crowned king of the Franks in 751; founded the Carolingian line of kings

**Romulus Augustulus (dates unknown):** last emperor of the Western Roman Empire; abdicated to Odoacer in 476, marking the end of the Roman Empire in the West

**Theodoric (454–526):** king of the Ostrogoths, king of Italy; ruled the largest territory of any kingdom in the West until his death

### Questions for Review

1. Why were the Germanic tribes able to sweep across the Roman Empire?
2. In what way were the Germanic kings different from the Roman emperors?
3. What were the main differences in government between the Germanic nations and the Roman Empire?
4. Did the Germans have a written law? How did they decide questions of justice? What is trial by combat? Trial by oath? Trial by ordeal?
5. After whom are the days of the week named?
6. Which Germanic peoples actually sacked the city of Rome?
7. What do the names "Visigoth" and "Ostrogoth" signify?
8. Who married the Frankish king, Clovis? How did she manage to convert him to the Catholic Faith?
9. What was a "mayor of the palace"? Which mayor of the palace became the king of the Franks?
10. Who were the Merovings? The Carolingians?
11. How did Theodoric bring peace between the Arians and Catholics in his kingdom?

### Ideas in Action

1. Write a report on the Germanic gods (a good source is Roger Lancelyn Green's *The Saga of Asgard*). How are they similar to the Roman and Greek gods?
2. Discuss why Germanic peoples valued courage so much. Why should such an idea have sprung from a pagan people like the Germans?

How is the Germanic ideal of courage acceptable to the Christian Faith? What is the value of suffering or defeat? Can one "lose" and still "win"?

3. Make a map of the Germanic kingdoms that replaced the Western Roman Empire.
4. On a map of Europe, find the original homelands of the Germanic peoples. Where are the Scandinavian lands? Where are the steppes? Where is the Danube River?

# Highways and Byways

### The Theory of Courage

The Germanic ideal of courage (which the English writer J.R.R. Tolkien called the "Theory of Courage") is summed up in the great Anglo-Saxon poem, "The Battle of Maldon." Here are the last words of an old warrior challenging his men to fight on even after their lord has been struck down. Outnumbered and outfought—but with unflinching courage—the band of English warriors, old men and boys, stand against a Viking raiding party:

J.R.R. Tolkien

> *Old Byrhtwold spoke then, bent in long service,*
> *Shaking his ash spear, shield-ready, after age:*
> *"Mind must be clearer, heart still the harder,*
> *Courage the keener, as our strength is strained.*
> *Lies here our leader, leveled by axes,*

*Bravery beaten down. Lost and lamenting,
Forever in sorrow, he who will shrink now
From war-play and peril. Old though I am, here
I purpose to perish, lie by my lord,
The hand loved and long-honored."*

# Chapter 6  Founders of Christendom— A.D. 500–700

## Justinian's Imperial Dream

In 527, fifty years after the abdication of the last Roman emperor of the West, a new emperor ascended to the throne of the East in Constantinople. His name was Justinian. Justinian ruled a territory from Mesopotamia to the Black Sea and commanded the riches of Thrace, Greece, Asia Minor, Syria, and Egypt.

Justinian had dreamed since boyhood of being as great an emperor as Constantine and Theodosius. He wanted more than anything to reunite the eastern and western parts of the Mediterranean world in a Catholic Christian empire, so that all civilized men and women might contribute to the creation of a City of God on Earth. Music, architecture, drama, painting and the visual arts, learning, and politics were all to be harnessed in an effort to build a Christian Empire.

**Eastern Roman Empire under Justinian**

**140** LIGHT TO THE NATIONS: The History of Christian Civilization

**Justinian, from the Basilica of San Vitale, Ravenna**

Justinian brought with him to the throne an immense talent for organization, dedication to long hours of work, great physical stamina, considerable skill as a poet and musician, and an ability to inspire loyalty and vision in others. Above all, he brought his amazing wife and helpmate, a former actress named Theodora.

Justinian and Theodora were an extraordinary couple for any age, but their marriage was rare in a time when there were few loving couples among the rich and powerful. They were deeply in love their entire lives, and they worked together as a team in all decisions. When Justinian's courage failed, he could count on Theodora's common sense, courage, and love to strengthen him. Likewise, his sense of justice tempered her passions and wrath.

The two weathered their first political crisis in 532 when a riot struck Constantinople. Rivalry between two sports clubs—called the Greens and Blues—had erupted into violence. (The rivalry was not just over sports; the Blues and Greens differed over politics as well.) Armed gangs passed through the streets shouting *Nika!* ("Conquer!"), setting fires, and attacking officers of the government. The emperor and empress and their officials took shelter in the palace, and the mob besieged its gates. This uprising was named the "Nika Revolt," from the mob's rallying cry.

Encouraged by Theodora, Justinian resolved to act; he ordered his general, Belisarius, to attack the mob and clear the streets. Belisarius brought in the Gothic mercenaries, and in less than one week more than 30,000 people lay dead in the city and surrounding areas. Justinian and Theodora had saved their throne, but at a very high cost.

## The Great Art of Byzantium

One month after the Nika Revolt had ended, Justinian set the workmen of the city to rebuilding *Hagia Sophia* ("Holy Wisdom"), the great cathedral built by Constantine nearly 200 years before. Justinian ordered several blocks of burned buildings around the old cathedral leveled. He then

Chapter 6   Founders of Christendom—A.D. 500–700   **141**

Hagia Sophia, the Church of Holy Wisdom, was commissioned by Byzantine Emperor Justinian and later converted into a mosque. Today, it is a museum.

instructed the builders to use the materials to build a new, much larger church. Justinian himself stripped off his fine clothes and laid the first stone with his own hands. The great church, completed in just six years, was intended to represent both the might of the empire and the glory of God's heaven.

Hagia Sophia was one of the glories of Christendom. Its interior shone like the court of heaven in gold, blue, and red. Its services filled its domes and vaults with an unearthly music. The cathedral's throngs of worshipers were made to feel that they stood in the forecourt of heaven.

The greatest gift Constantinople gave our civilization may be its distinctive music, art, and architecture. The style of painting known as "iconic" gave to the Eastern Church (in Greece, Asia Minor, and later, Eastern Europe and Russia) its images of saints and heaven. Some images were

**Carving on a pillar at the ruins of the St. John's Basilica, built in the 5th century AD by Emperor Justinian in Ephesus, Asia Minor**

**code:** an orderly and logical arrangement of rules or laws (from *codex*, Latin for "bound manuscript")

painted on wood or plaster, and some were "painted" in the bright mosaics of the walls and ceilings of churches.

The mosaic is an old Roman art form, developed and perfected by Byzantine artists. It is a picture composed of thousands of tiny tiles of colored glass and stone, set into concrete. Byzantine mosaics were designed to catch light and sparkle with color. The light reflected in the tiny tiles seemed like the light of heaven to worshipers below. The mosaics of Hagia Sophia and the other churches of Constantinople seemed to float in the air and be part of the heaven they depicted.

The architectural engineers of Constantinople found a way to cover larger and larger expanses with domes of stone. The Byzantine improvement of the Roman arch and dome gave to the Middle East and Russia the fantastic onion-shaped domes and the towers seen in Christian churches and Muslim mosques throughout Europe and Asia.

## Law for a Christian Empire

Justinian called Roman law that "holy temple of Roman justice." But being over one thousand years old, the Roman law **code** was large and confusing. To preserve this law for future generations, Justinian commanded that the code be reworked into a shorter summary of laws.

Justinian ordered this new summary of Roman law because he wanted to correct the abuses of corruption that had infected imperial government. He also wanted to make action in the law courts easier for the ordinary citizen. Justinian commissioned 10

**Backbones of medieval volumes of the Justinian Code**

famous lawyers to draft the new code, cutting away the many layers of court decisions and opinions and organizing the laws into easily found categories and subjects.

This legal code—called *Codex Justinianus*, or the Justinian Code—was published between 529 and 534. It became the model for medieval law and practice in all Europe. It was also used as the foundation for reforms of legal systems in the 19th century.

## Reconquest of the West

Justinian dreamed of recovering all the territories that once belonged to the Roman Empire in Asia, Africa, and Europe. This project required the reconquest of the West from its new Germanic masters.

For this conquest, Justinian enlisted the service of Belisarius, a military genius, who has often been compared to Julius Caesar for his grasp of battlefield tactics. This general was the personal friend of Justinian; Belisarius' wife, Antonina, was the best friend of Theodora—and, like her, a former actress.

Belisarius took command of a major expedition to regain North Africa and to return the Vandal kingdom of Carthage to imperial rule. Supported by a large fleet and army, Belisarius landed near Carthage in 533. After taking city after city in North Africa, the Roman general finally entered Carthage. There he was greeted by cheering Romans, happy to be freed from their Vandal masters. The defeated Vandals were never a military force again.

Belisarius returned to Constantinople with ships loaded with treasure. Justinian showered his friend with gifts and honors. But he gave him little rest, because another campaign was waiting—the reconquest of Italy.

For many years, Amalasuntha, the talented daughter of Theodoric, had ruled Italy as regent for her teenage son, Athalaric. Amalasuntha was highly educated, speaking and reading Greek and Latin as well as Gothic. Her son Athalaric and his wild friends tried to force her to give up the regency to him, though he was still too young

**Ostrogoth Italy, A.D. 544**

to rule. Amalasuntha refused. After Athalaric died suddenly following a drinking bout, his mother asked a cousin to join her as co-ruler. Instead, he had her strangled and declared himself king.

The murder of Amalasuntha gave Justinian the excuse he needed for action. In 535, he gave Belisarius and the armies a more difficult task than regaining Africa—a war on the Ostrogoths. Two armies set out against the Ostrogoths—one landed in Dalmatia, while the other invaded Italy. Leading the second army, Belisarius conquered all of Italy in a short time. The Ostrogothic kingdom was shattered like the Vandals' kingdom had been. Italy and North Africa were Roman again. Belisarius was ready to move to the next objective—Spain.

## Italy Laid Waste

Justinian's plans of further conquest, however, were ruined by suspicion and jealousy. Told by false witnesses that Belisarius had planned to set himself up as emperor of the West and declare war on his master, Justinian began to mistrust his former friend. In 541, he sent Belisarius to the Mesopotamian front to make war on the Parthians in hopes he would be defeated. But by 542, Belisarius had defeated the Parthians, winning a greater fame than the emperor. Justinian's suspicions of the general grew.

Roman aqueduct

Despite his suspicions, however, Justinian sent Belisarius to Italy in 544 after news reached Constantinople that the Ostrogoths had reconquered it. With even fewer men and supplies than the previous time, Belisarius had to perform miracles on the battlefield. But the Second Gothic War, as the campaign came to be called, could not be won so quickly as the first had been. It lasted into the next year, and then the next, and the next, and the next—dragging on for 20 years.

The two Gothic Wars turned Italy into a wasteland. Both Romans and Ostrogoths burned and sacked cities, leveling Roman monuments, such as the baths of Rome and other public buildings. They cut or destroyed aqueducts to deny water to enemy forces, and they tore up roads to impede the movement of heavy troops. Farms were raided and burned, and all harvesting ceased. When the war finally ended, the glory of Italy was no more.

During the Second Gothic War, Italians began referring to the invading easterners as "Byzantines," not Romans. **Byzantine** rule seemed more unbearable than that of the Goths; Byzantine tactics and war atrocities were the more "barbaric." Belisarius began to despair of any useful victory.

In July of 548, as the army's situation became desperate, Belisarius' wife, Antonina, who had accompanied her husband throughout the war, returned to Constantinople. She went to beg her old friend Theodora for help. She arrived too late. Theodora had died of cancer on June 28, 548.

Belisarius, tired and dispirited, resigned his commission. He retired to house exile on his estates, leaving the army to a general chosen by Justinian. The Gothic War dragged on until 554, leaving Italy a ruined wasteland.

> **Byzantine:** the name given to the civilization that came from the city of Byzantium, renamed Constantinople or *Nova Roma*; a term referring to the Eastern Roman Empire and its people.

# The End of the Ancient World

In 559, Justinian faced threats closer to home. The Huns had broken through the Byzantine lines and camped only 30 miles from Constantinople. Justinian called on his old friend Belisarius to come out of retirement and save the city. This time Belisarius had only a militia of volunteers from the city, no legion of trained and heavily armed troops. He used his genius for stratagems and tricked the Huns into thinking he had more men than he did. The Huns sued for peace.

After this victory, Justinian's jealousy of Belisarius only increased. He could not allow Belisarius to take credit for the success. The emperor himself went onto the battlefield with his household guard—all uniformed in gold and jeweled armor. There, he publicly fired his old general

**Hagia Sophia as it stands today**

and took personal command of the militia. The Huns, who had come to surrender, found that the emperor would pay them a huge ransom for their prisoners and then send them unharmed back to the Danube plains.

Belisarius himself returned peaceably to self-imposed house exile. He died quietly in his bed in 565, some said of a broken heart. He was not visited by his old friend and master, Justinian, who himself was worn down with his own grief for the loss of Theodora and the failure of his imperial dream.

On his 80th birthday, Justinian proclaimed a week of festivities to celebrate the reopening of Hagia Sophia after damage it had suffered in a great earthquake. The dome had been raised again, higher than before and better designed to withstand earthquakes. It remains standing to this day.

Justinian celebrated the event alone. His beloved wife, his loyal friend, and his best advisers and officers had all preceded him in death. For more than 35 years he had worked to forge the Christian Empire of his dream, but jealousy and forces beyond his control had destroyed it. Justinian died on November 14, 565. His death marked the end of the ancient, imperial age and the beginning of a new one—the age of Christendom that would be centered not on the eastern empire, but in the German-dominated West.

# Founders of the Christian West

In the eastern lands of Greece, Asia Minor, Palestine, and Egypt, Constantinople kept alive the civilization of ancient Greece and Rome. In what was once the Western Roman Empire, however, that civilization was becoming a distant memory. Yet it did not entirely disappear. It was kept alive in small and, apparently, insignificant ways.

Despite wars and barbarian rule, the Christian Faith preserved a spark of civilization. **Lay** Christians directed their efforts to recovering and rebuilding civilization, but they had only limited success. Strange as it may seem, it was those who sought nothing more than a life of prayer and the salvation of their souls who became the true preservers of civilized life and thought. Missionaries, too, whose chief aim was to win souls for Christ, were able to transplant civilization far from its native soil in the lands

**lay:** referring to those members of the Church who are not members of the clergy (bishops, priests, deacons). Lay Christians are called *laymen* or *laity*.

surrounding the Mediterranean. Civilization was to grow and flourish in the barbaric lands of Germany, England, Scotland, and Ireland. A new, Western European and Christian civilization was coming into being.

## St. Patrick of Ireland

Far to the north, civilization took root in a land that had never known Roman rule. It came to this land, Ireland, with the Catholic Faith preached by a former slave named Patrick.

Patrick was born in the late 300s in Roman Britain, the son of a Christian deacon. When Patrick was not quite 16, pagan Irish raiders landed on the coast and sacked his village. They carried him off to slavery in Ireland. After several years, however, Patrick escaped and returned home to Britain. But there he had a vision in which he heard voices calling to him, "Holy youth, come and walk among us once more!" These were voices of the Irish. The vision, he knew, was calling him to return to Ireland and preach the Gospel to its people.

St. Patrick, apostle of Ireland

Patrick, however, could barely read. And he had not memorized the words of Scripture that he would need for his missionary work. So he devoted himself to 14 years of intense study. Finally, he was consecrated a bishop and charged with a mission to Ireland.

Christian missionaries had gone to Ireland before but had made little progress. They failed to convert the fierce and hostile clans throughout most of the island. The Gaelic people of

**clan:** an extended family or association of families with loyalty to one head, the clan chief. The clan usually took its name from a legendary founder, adding to the name *Mac* or *Mhic*, meaning "son." Thus were created clan names such as McDonald or MacDougald. In Ireland the Irish form of "Mac" was *Uich*, pronounced "OO," which became the modern Anglo-Irish "O," as in O'Reilly.

**Druid:** a Gaelic priest belonging to a guild or caste of hereditary priests who came from the aristocracy or ruling class. The Gaels believed Druids could work magic and cast spells and curses.

Ireland thought the Christian gospel of forgiveness denied the heroic tradition on which their society depended.

The Irish were one of the Gaelic peoples who inhabited not only Ireland, but what are today England, Scotland, and Wales. Throughout the British isles, Gaelic life was bound by a rigid social order. The people were divided into clans or extended family groups, and each **clan** acknowledged one hereditary chief or king and his associates, who were the leaders in battle. Only men of the ruling class were allowed to learn the art of warfare, and they formed the ruling military elite. Free farmers and craftsmen formed the next social rank in Gaelic society. Slaves, who were outside the Gaelic clan system, had no rights at all in Gaelic society.

The **Druids**, a guild or caste of hereditary priests drawn from the aristocracy, handled all of a clan's legal and religious affairs. They were trained from birth to memorize long lists and stories and to repeat from memory anything they heard, no matter how long. The Irish Gaels believed the Druids were able to work magic and could place spells and curses on their enemies. The Druidic religion also practiced human sacrifice.

**An 18th century depiction of a Druid offering human sacrifice**

Patrick preached first to clan leaders. He hoped that if they became Christian, their clansmen would follow their example. But meeting with little success among clan leaders, Patrick took his mission to the common people. His preaching drew crowds and made many converts.

Patrick directly challenged the Druids. One Easter, Patrick lit the flame of the Paschal candle in front of a large crowd on the Hill of Slane. This act angered the Druids, for by law only Druids might kindle fire, a process they told their people was magic. The High King Leoghaire (the modern "Leary") was fearful of Patrick's success and sent for him; but Patrick ended up converting and baptizing the king.

Stories were soon circulating of many miraculous feats Patrick performed to combat the Druids' magic. In Ulster, Ireland's northern kingdom, he established his church at the tribal center of Armagh. It would become the **primatial see** of the island. Within 25 years, all of Ireland was at least **nominally** Catholic. Patrick lived and worked in Ireland for almost 60 years until his death.

> **primatial:** belonging to the "primate," or chief bishop of a land
> **see:** the town or place where a bishop has his seat, or "see"; the bishop's capital city
> **nominal:** in name only, not in actual fact; adverb, *nominally*

After Patrick's death, monasteries grew up all over Ireland. These monasteries became the centers of Church life in Ireland, and they were cultural centers as well. The monks continued the Druids' emphasis on learning and memorization, but made these abilities available to common people. The monasteries applied those skills to preserving the Latin Christian culture brought from Europe. Irish monks memorized whole books and a great part of the Christian Scriptures, the better to argue their faith with the Druids or other souls in need of evangelization. Irish monks left their homeland and evangelized their cousins in Scotland.

**Saint Patrick**

# 150 LIGHT TO THE NATIONS: The History of Christian Civilization

A color page from the Book of Kells, depicting Christ enthroned. The Book of Kells was a manuscript of the Gospels in Latin, found in the monastery of Kells, Ireland.

Through the efforts of Irish monks, Scotland and northern England became Christian lands.

## Boethius, the "Translator" of Antiquity

Among the laymen who worked to preserve ancient civilization, perhaps the most important was the Roman senator, Boethius. Boethius was the descendent of a noble Roman family, the Anicii. Born in Italy and educated in Athens, he entered the Senate while still a young man. Theodoric the Ostrogoth appointed Boethius to high office in 510 and relied on his counsel for important decisions in foreign affairs.

Boethius saw that his Roman countrymen no longer spoke or read the elegant Greek of the ancient philosophers. He realized that the inheritance of the past would be lost if the works of Greek philosophers were not translated into Latin. So, as St. Jerome had done with the Bible, Boethius undertook to translate Plato and Aristotle into the Romans' tongue.

Boethius began his project of translating Plato and Aristotle in 500. But by the time of his death 24 years later, he had completed only a few works. He chose the works that he considered central to understanding the thought of both philosophers. He also composed summaries of the **seven liberal arts**.

Boethius' summaries of ancient learning became the school textbooks of future generations for hundreds of years. Everything that people during the next several centuries knew about Plato and Aristotle, or about the subjects of music, arithmetic, and astronomy, they learned from Boethius' summaries.

Boethius' most famous work was the fruit of great suffering. As you read in Chapter 5, King Theodoric began to suspect all sorts of Catholic plots against him. Once a courtier accused two senators, Albinus and Boethius' father-in-law, Symmachus, of plotting against the king. Though the charges were clearly false, Theodoric had the senators

**seven liberal arts:** the disciplines that are the foundation of all learning. They are grammar, logic (the art which teaches orderly thinking), rhetoric (the art of public speaking), arithmetic, geometry, astronomy, and music.

Chapter 6  Founders of Christendom—A.D. 500–700   **151**

imprisoned. Boethius pleaded with the king to release the two men.

Because Boethius not only defended Albinus and Symmachus but also was a native Italian, a Catholic, and a senator, Theodoric thought Boethius must be in league with those who were plotting against him. The king tortured Boethius to make him confess. When Boethius did not confess, Theodoric left him in prison to await execution.

In the months of his imprisonment, Boethius wrote a personal account of his struggle to try to make sense of what had happened to him. The result was the *Consolation of Philosophy*, a work that would be one of the most influential books of the Middle Ages and an inspiration to readers into our own time. In this work Boethius sets out to prove to himself—without resorting to the arguments from Christian revelation but using only those available to human reason—that God's **Providence** directs all things to the good.

Happiness, Boethius saw, lies in seeing God in all things. God sees all and rewards and punishes. Therefore, Boethius concluded that human beings always seek for Justice; and God's Justice will make all things right in the end. Thus everything, even suffering, comes about through God's Providence.

In 524, Boethius died. He was strangled in prison by the king's executioner.

A lithograph of a 15th-century painting of Philosophy appearing to Boethius

**Providence:** God's foreknowledge of what history will bring, and his direction of history to serve his will

A 15th-century miniature depicting Boethius and Philosophy

## St. Benedict of Nursia

In 529, three years after King Theodoric died, a monk named Benedict founded a monastic community at Monte Cassino, 80 miles southeast of Rome. This monastery was the first of many similar monasteries that, spreading across Europe, would do more than perhaps any other institution to build up Christendom in the early Middle Ages.

Benedict was born to a noble family of Nursia in Italy. He left home when he was 20 to study the classics in Rome. Disgusted with the immorality he saw in the city, he gave up his studies. He went to live as a hermit in a cave near Subiaco, a mountain valley 30 miles southeast of Rome. For three years he lived alone, following a life of prayer and fasting.

Benedict's heroic way of life attracted others to live near him as hermits, following the example of the monks of the Egyptian deserts. Benedict established several small monasteries in the Subiaco region. Among them was a community of women for his twin sister, Scholastica, who had followed him into the wilderness.

The number of monks who gathered around Benedict eventually grew too many for the Subiaco region to support. Benedict moved with his closest friends and disciples to Monte Cassino, a rocky mountaintop, and there they built a new house. At Monte Cassino, Benedict set his mind to the question of how the new community was going to live together.

**Map of southern Italy**

## A Sister's Prayer

After embracing the monastic life, Scholastica and her brother, Benedict, would meet only once a year for a brief hour. One year, meeting in a cave on the Subiaco mountainside, they conversed, as was their habit, about the things of God. But Scholastica had a surprising request for her brother.

That day, Scholastica begged her brother to remain with her until the following day. But Benedict, fearing to break his monastic rule of life, refused. Scholastica then prayed to God, and a furious thunderstorm broke out. It was so furious that Benedict and the brothers who had accompanied him could not leave the cave.

"May almighty God spare you, sister! What have you done?" cried Benedict. But Scholastica replied, "Behold, I asked you, and you would not hear me; I asked my God, and he heard me. Even so, if you are able, dismiss me and go to your monastery." Seeing he could not leave, Benedict remained in the cave with his sister until early dawn.

Three days later, Benedict had a vision; he saw the soul of his sister ascending into heaven. Scholastica had died. Benedict had her body brought to his monastery, where he laid it in a tomb that had been prepared for him.

A 14th-century fresco depicting Saint Benedict and Saint Scholastica at table

Unlike the Egyptian hermits he had first imitated at Subiaco, who relied on the charity of neighbors for food and clothing, Benedict organized this new community as a self-sustaining village. The monastery at Monte Cassino had its own garden, flour mill, bakery, and chapel for communal prayer. For his new community, Benedict wrote a constitution and law that would become the model for all monastic foundations in the West. Although it is now known as the *Rule of St. Benedict*, Benedict himself called it "a little rule for beginners."

The *Rule* covers all aspects of a monk's daily life, down to the smallest detail. The *Rule* divides the monk's day into periods of prayer, work, and sleep. It prescribes communal prayer seven times a day, based on recitation of the Psalms. The *Rule* commands physical labor as a balance to the monk's life of prayer and meditative reading. The *Rule* prescribes the hours that the monk sleeps, as well as the hours of complete silence, to encourage rest.

**A 14th century fresco depicting Saint Benedict driving out the devil, who prevented the monks from moving a large stone**

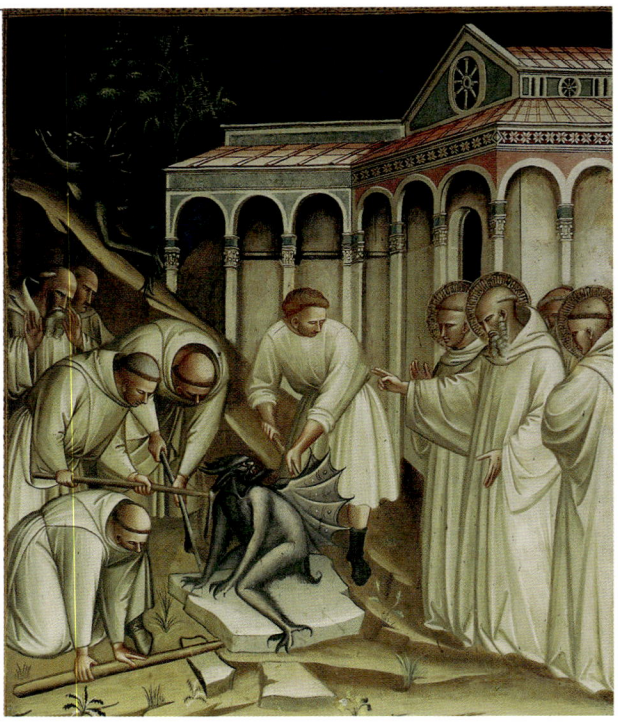

**cloistered:** separated from the world for the sake of prayer and contemplation

Benedict's rule opened the monastery to the outside world while preserving a life of **cloistered** prayer. It said hospitality was an obligation of every monastic house. Travelers and petitioners were never to be turned away empty from the gate. And the *Rule* required care for the poor from the surplus of the garden and the monks' labor.

Benedict's monks tried new agricultural techniques, opened new fields to planting, and made and sold cloth and other necessary products. They harvested their well-kept vineyards, made wine to be sold or given to the poor, and took in refugees and homeless travelers.

Life in the Eastern monasteries, based on the Egyptian model, was too ascetic for most people. Eastern monks practiced harsh penances and frequent fasting. Benedict's *Rule*, by contrast, emphasized old Roman virtues of cooperation and moderation. Physical health and moderate exercise, said the *Rule*, are necessary to prayer and contemplation. "Idleness is the enemy of the soul," Benedict wrote. *Ora et labora*—"Pray and work!"—is the motto of Benedictine monastic life.

Because the *Rule* was less harsh than those of Eastern monasteries, Benedict's monastic life could appeal to more men and women. The

**Abbey of Monte Cassino, rebuilt after World War II**

*Rule* opened up monasticism to more people. Other monasteries quickly saw the advantages of Benedict's *Rule* and adopted at least part of it as their own. Men from all classes of society joined these monastic families. Women, too, founded houses on the model of St. Scholastica's monastery for women. The orderly round of work, prayer, and sleep in these monasteries made them havens of safety and sanity in terrible times. They brought shelter to the poor, peace to the troubled and fearful, and increasing prosperity to the countryside around the monasteries.

# Pope St. Gregory the Great

After Emperor Justinian's 20-year war to reclaim Italy for the empire, Italy—and Rome itself—was a wasteland. Farming came to a halt for years. Only meager harvests were raised and gathered in secret or in remote valleys. Towns and cities had been burned and leveled. Abandoned by their citizens, many towns and villages sheltered only bandits, who preyed on the desperate survivors and pitiful refugees. The public works were ruined, torn apart for their building material or the precious bronze support rods within their concrete walls.

**A statue of Saint Augustine of Canterbury in front of the cathedral in Palermo, Italy**

**prefect:** the chief high official of the Roman government

Churchmen worked to ease this misery. Bishops and their clergy devoted themselves bravely to caring for the displaced and starving. The success of much of this effort was due to the work of one brilliant organizer and spiritual master: St. Gregory the Great.

Gregory belonged to the ancient Anicii family of Roman patricians (a family that had produced Boethius). In the early 570s, the young Gregory was **prefect** of Rome. He organized and commanded Rome's defenses against the advancing Lombards, another German tribe that was moving down into Italy. Gregory was heir to an old Roman fortune. But in 574, he gave away most of his inheritance and retired from his city office to enter a monastery near Rome.

Gregory would not long enjoy the peace of the cloister. The current pope had great need of the talented young man and sent Gregory to Constantinople as the pope's ambassador. Gregory went to plead for troops to drive the Lombards from Italy. The embassy failed, however—not because of Gregory's efforts, but because the emperor had no troops to send to Italy.

When Gregory returned to Rome with the bad news, he found things worse in the city than when he had left. Floods had destroyed the skimpy harvest of the previous year. A new outbreak of the plague was sweeping the countryside. The pope, Gregory's friend, was dying. And Italy and Rome were still threatened by roving war bands of Lombards and bandits. In 590, the Church in Rome elected Gregory as successor to the See of Peter. As pope, he immediately set about trying to save the ravaged country and cities.

Pope Gregory reorganized the administration of Rome. The pope governed estates left to the Church by wealthy landowners, as well as lands left ownerless by the warring armies and later taken over by the Church. On these lands, Gregory instructed farm overseers to rebuild lost herds, sell excess produce, and replant orchards and empty fields. They were also to clear ruined houses, rebuild or convert the area to growing space, and put an end to the waste of resources.

Within a few years, the reformed papal estates were able to feed much of Italy, as well as support the clergy and rebuild ruined churches. In all things, Gregory acted as the good steward of his papal office; he was, as he signed his letters, *servus servorum Dei*— "Servant of the servants of God." All popes since Gregory have used this title.

**Lombard warrior, medieval metalwork**

About 580, one of the roving Lombard war bands sacked the Abbey of Monte Cassino. The surviving monks and their abbot sought refuge in Rome. They brought with them Benedict's *Rule*, which they placed in the pope's keeping. Gregory had read it first as a monk and was deeply impressed by its common sense and practicality.

Gregory began a collection of the liturgical prayers of the Church of Rome. His goal was to establish a uniform liturgy for his missionaries to the Germanic nations. His collection, called the *Missale Romanum*, became the form of the liturgy for all lands in the Western Church. These books containing the Roman Rite of the liturgy of the Mass were sent to all the major missionary centers of the north. (Gregory is also said to have brought the chant melodies of the Church into a single style, called Gregorian chant. But this was probably done after his time and credited to the famous pope.) To the farthest reaches of the old Roman territories, Gregory sent missionary monks—among them St. Augustine of Canterbury, who converted the Germanic tribesmen of England.

Along with a copy of the Four Gospels in Latin, in the Vulgate version of St. Jerome, all the pope's missionaries were given a copy of Benedict's *Rule* and a *Missale Romanum* to take with them to the foreign lands. The Four Gospels, *The Rule*, and the Missal were the weapons of the spirit that drew men and women to rebuild and enlarge civilization.

*Saint Gregory the Great* by Carlo Saraceni

## St. Augustine of Canterbury

A famous legend tells that Pope Gregory, while still a young man, saw some fair-haired children captured in war and about to be sold in the slave market of Rome. Upon being told that these children were Angles, Gregory, mishearing the word as *angels,* said, "Indeed, well named, for they have the faces of angels. Such ought to be heirs with the angels in heaven!"

Years later, Gregory was able to act on that ambition. England had been conquered by the Saxons and another Germanic tribe, the Angles, beginning in the fifth century. Emissaries from Gaelic Iona and the Gaelic church in Wales arrived in Rome, asking the pope to send a mission to convert the Angles and Saxons. The Gaels knew that the pagan Saxons would never be converted by the Gaelic Church. The Saxons despised the Gaels, whom they had conquered and enslaved, and considered their Christian religion weak and worthless. Gregory sent a small band of Benedictine monks led by Augustine, a young monk of Gregory's own monastery, to Britain.

In 597, Augustine and the brothers landed in the southeast corner of England, the kingdom of Kent. They were taken to the king's seat at Canterbury and received with courtesy, for King Ethelbert was married to a devout Catholic princess of the Franks, and his contacts across the English Channel had convinced him of the advantages of Christian baptism.

King Ethelbert's council of tribal elders, the Witan, were not certain of the benefits of baptism and the Christian Faith. One of Ethelbert's elders, however, addressed the whole council. He compared man's life to a bird that flies into a lighted hall at night, sees the feasting, and then flies out again into the dark. "We do not know whence we came, or where we shall go," said the elder. "It is night outside the hall of this life. If this man and his religion can tell us of our fate after death, his words are worth our acceptance." Moved by these words, the Witan agreed to accept the Christian Faith.

**King Ethelbert as depicted in a stained glass window at All Souls College, Oxford, England**

## Conflict between Gaelic and Roman Christians

Pope Gregory had instructed Augustine, when he reached Britain, to consecrate Paulinus as archbishop of York. The new archbishop would have the authority to appoint 12 bishops for his territories. From the two sees of Canterbury and York, a network of missions and churches spread steadily across England. A hundred years later, the Angles and Saxons were Catholic Christians.

The constant feuding between the Saxons prevented unification of their many tiny kingdoms. At times the fighting delayed or even erased

**160**  LIGHT TO THE NATIONS: The History of Christian Civilization

**Paulinus, archbishop of York, baptizes Edwin, the king of Northumbria**

the gains made by the Church. The most serious problem, however, was a quarrel among Christians themselves, not over doctrine but jurisdiction. The Gaelic monks had been trying to convert the Saxons for 100 years before Augustine of Canterbury arrived. They had established Gaelic monastic houses throughout the ancient British country of Northumbria. The Gaelic populace, worn down and enslaved by the conquering Saxons, held to their Gaelic Catholicism despite oppression. The Gaelic Christians left under Saxon rule hated their barbarian masters, and they refused to acknowledge that these German Saxons could be legitimate Christians. The last Gaelic bishops felt betrayed by Augustine. He had appointed Saxon bishops over dioceses that formerly had Gaelic bishops.

The Saxon church and the Gaelic church had the same faith, but they had different practices. For instance, Gaelic monks shaved the whole front of their heads halfway back on the scalp. They allowed the remaining hair in the back to grow uncut, rolled into a knot on the back of the head or loose and uncombed over the shoulders. Augustine's monks, like other monks from the continent of Europe, wore the "tonsure," where the crown of the head is shaved, leaving only a fringe of hair to represent the crown of thorns.

Unlike Benedictine monks, Gaelic monks also acted independently of their abbots, though they looked to them for advice and spiritual direction. Gaelic monasteries encouraged a withdrawal from worldly activity and concerns and did harsh penances, unlike the more moderate

Benedictines. Even the worship of the two groups differed. The Gaelic liturgy was elaborate, like that of the Eastern Church, and lasted twice as long as the Roman liturgy.

The Gaelic and Saxon churches competed for converts and supremacy in England and all of Britain. The controversy between them confused the Saxons and slowed the missionary work of both churches.

**The Two Churches United** In 664, many years after the deaths of Augustine of Canterbury and Pope Gregory, Oswy, a Saxon king of Northumbria, called a **synod** (or grand council) of bishops. The rival churches met at Whitby, in northern England, to discuss whether the Church in Britain would follow Gaelic or Roman practices.

At the synod, Oswy heard both sides. But the real argument for him was the political support the Roman missionaries could offer him. The Franks on the continent, other Saxon kings, and the pope supported Roman practices. Only the hostile kings of Scotland, the cattle-raiding Gaelic chieftains of Wales and Cumbria, and the poor supported Gaelic practices. Finally, Oswy chose the Roman system.

After the Synod of Whitby, Gaelic monks were ordered to adopt the Roman tonsure in place of the Gaelic tonsure. Gaelic monasteries were ordered to accept the Benedictine *Rule*. Their churches had to accept the Roman liturgy and the authority of the new bishops. Because of the Synod of Whitby, the British Isles became part of Western European civilization and not a separate Gaelic culture.

Map showing Anglo-Saxon kingdoms in England

**synod:** a council or assembly of the clergy of one geographic region of the Church.

### The End of St. Gregory the Great's Papacy

The dream of a Christian Roman Empire was dead. Only the Church remained. Pope Gregory knew that no help for Italy or the West would come from the East; he alone had to defend and feed the city of Rome and central Italy.

Gregory sent papal emissaries to the courts of the Visigoths and Franks, and he sent missionaries to the heathens. He concluded treaties in his own name and appointed bishops and abbots to head churches that he would never visit. He appointed commanders, raised armies, paid the soldiers, fed thousands, and housed his new troops in Rome and throughout Italy.

No other pope before Gregory had wielded, or needed to wield, so much temporal power—making decisions that emperors or their governors usually made. After Gregory, the popes took on more and more **temporal power**. They became not just **spiritual** leaders, but temporal lords.

Even in his old age, Gregory's personal holiness and faith gave him energy to work 14 hours a day. He expected as much from others. He wrote the *Pastoral Rule*, a handbook to guide bishops. He wrote a collection of saints' lives and miracle stories, called *The Dialogues*, to encourage future monks to live a life of holiness. His many homilies and sermons became the models for preaching throughout the centuries to come.

Gregory died in 604. Italy was still not at peace, but the people were better fed and better ruled than they had been before Gregory became pope. The work of uniting the German and Roman cultures and saving the learning of antiquity continued due to the efforts and wisdom of this tireless servant of the servants of God.

**temporal power:** power over things having to do with life in this world, as opposed to **spiritual power**, which has to do with eternal or spiritual things. Making laws for a city or state, owning property, such as a farm or a house, or managing a business are things having to do with temporal power. Spiritual power has to do with things connected to administering the sacraments and teaching the Faith. The pope exercised temporal power when he made laws for the city of Rome or bought and sold farms and estates.

# Chapter Review

### Summary
- The Eastern Roman Emperor Justinian dreamed of making the Mediterranean world once again a Christian Empire. With his wife, Theodora, he established his power in Constantinople and then proceeded to conquer the western lands the Roman Empire had lost.
- Justinian's general Belisarius reconquered North Africa for the empire, ending the Vandal kingdom there. In the First and Second Gothic

Wars, Justinian's generals in a 20-year struggle took back Italy for the empire, laying it waste in the process.
- Justinian's reform of Roman law, called the *Codex Justinianus* (Justinian Code), simplified a thousand years of legal practice. It became the model for medieval law and practice in all Europe, as well as for reforms of legal systems in the 19th century.
- As a youth, St. Patrick was carried off into slavery in Ireland. Though he eventually escaped back to his homeland in Britain, he later returned to Ireland as a missionary. After Patrick's time, monasteries sprang up all over Ireland. Irish monks carried the Gospel to their fellow Gaels in Scotland and northern England.
- A descendant of a noble Roman family, Boethius tried to preserve Roman and Greek culture by translating the works of Plato and Aristotle from Greek into Latin. He composed books on the subjects included in the seven liberal arts, which became the schoolbooks of future generations for hundreds of years. He wrote the *Consolation of Philosophy* while in prison. Boethius was executed by order of Theodoric the Ostrogoth.
- St. Benedict fled the immorality of Rome to live as a hermit in the region of Subiaco. Eventually, men gathered around him, for whom he wrote a rule of monastic life, called today the *Rule of St. Benedict*. The *Rule* was more moderate than other monastic rules of the time, and monasteries following it sprang up over all Italy and Western Europe.
- Since the territories around Rome had been ravaged by disease and war, Pope St. Gregory I, the "Great," was the only authority who could bring order to those lands. Thus he established the temporal authority of the papacy.
- Pope Gregory collected the liturgical prayers of the city of Rome into the *Missale Romanum*. Missionaries throughout Europe carried the Missal and made the Roman Rite of the liturgy the rite followed by the peoples of Western Europe.
- St. Augustine, sent by Pope Gregory to Britain, converted the pagan Saxon peoples there. Augustine established Saxon bishops throughout England.
- The conflict over the different customs of the Gaelic Christians of England and the new Saxon Church was resolved by the Synod of Whitby. The synod determined that the Gaelic liturgical and monastic traditions had to give way to the Roman traditions.

## Key Concepts

**Byzantine:** the name given to the civilization that came from the city of Byzantium, renamed Constantinople or *Nova Roma*; a term referring to the Eastern Roman Empire and its people

**mosaic:** a picture made from thousands of little tiles of glass or stone

**Justinian Code:** *Codex Justinianus*, a compilation of Roman law made during Justinian's reign

**clan:** a family and tribal organization in Gaelic-speaking countries

*Servus Servorum Dei:* "Servant of the Servants of God." Title chosen by St. Gregory for himself and now given to all the popes

**Roman Rite:** the liturgy officially accepted by the pope as the liturgy for Rome and the Western Church

**Gregorian chant:** the form of sacred music sung in the churches of the Roman Rite

**seven liberal arts:** the disciplines that are the foundation of all learning. They are grammar, logic (the art which teaches orderly thinking), rhetoric (the art of public speaking), arithmetic, geometry, astronomy, and music.

*The Rule of St. Benedict:* the constitution of Western monastic life, first drawn up by St. Benedict for his monks at Monte Cassino

**temporal power:** power over things having to do with life in this world, as opposed to **spiritual power**, which has to do with eternal or spiritual things

## Dates to Remember

**524:** Boethius' death and the *Consolation of Philosophy*
**529:** St. Benedict's founding of Monte Cassino
**533:** publication of the *Codex Justinianus*
**535–554:** the Gothic Wars
**565:** death of Justinian
**590–604:** St. Gregory's papacy
**663:** the Synod of Whitby

## Central Characters

**Justinian I (483–565):** "the Great," emperor of the Eastern Roman Empire and lawgiver

**Theodora (d. 548):** wife of Justinian, co-empress with her husband

**Belisarius (505–565):** Justinian's general and conqueror of the Vandals and the Ostrogoths

**St. Patrick (5th century):** missionary to the Irish

**Boethius (480–524):** statesman, philosopher, author of textbooks on ancient learning

**St. Benedict of Nursia (480–543):** founder of Western monasticism and author of the *Rule*

**St. Gregory the Great (407–604):** pope; rebuilder of Italy after the devastation of the Gothic Wars

**St. Augustine of Canterbury (d. 604):** missionary to the Saxons of England

## Questions for Review

1. Why is the *Codex Justinianus* so important to history?
2. What was Justinian's great dream? In what ways was he successful? In what ways did he fail to achieve his dream?
3. What were Boethius' great contributions to the generations to come?
4. From what land did St. Patrick come? How did he first come to Ireland? Why did he return there?
5. What things made the Irish Church different from the Roman Church? Why is there today no separate Irish Church with different customs from the Roman Church?
6. What does the *Rule of St. Benedict* prescribe for the life of monks? What, according to the *Rule*, were monks to do to help people outside the monastery?
7. What is the difference between temporal power and spiritual power? Give examples of temporal power and spiritual power.
8. Pope Gregory the Great took on more temporal power than the popes had before him. What events forced him to take on so much temporal power?

## Ideas in Action

1. Study a Byzantine icon. What makes it different from other kinds of religious pictures? Why do you think Byzantine artists have made icons in this way? Iconographers are said to "write" their icons, not paint or draw them. Why do you think this is?
2. Describe how the life of a Benedictine monk differs from the life of a layperson. What can laypeople learn from the Benedictine monastic life?
3. Where are the missionary lands of our day? Is it possible for every Catholic to be a missionary? If so, how?
4. Learn as a class to sing one Gregorian chant, perhaps the *Pater Noster* or the *Salve Regina*.

# Highways and Byways

### St. Patrick's Dreams

The pagan Gaels who inhabited Ireland were not kind to slaves. They especially scorned the Gaels in Britain for accepting the "weak" religion of Christianity. Patrick was sold into the interior of Ireland to a farmer who was himself the servant of an Irish clan chief. To break his young slave's spirit, the farmer beat and tortured him. Patrick was forced to herd the pigs and find his own food from their trough scraps and from wild plants. He later wrote that only his faith in Christ kept him alive.

While a captive, God sent Patrick several dreams that kept his hope alive. One day, he received a most vivid dream of a ship waiting for him on the coast and a voice warning him to be ready for a brave try at freedom. He knew he must run away and get to that ship—or be a slave forever. After six years of captivity, Patrick escaped. He left in the night, traveled some 200 miles as a hunted fugitive, and reached the ship that he had seen in his dream.

# Chapter 7: The Rise of Islam —A.D. 624–800

Islamic geometric design

When Pope Gregory the Great died in 604, the largest and most powerful state in the Mediterranean world was the Byzantine Empire—the Roman Empire of the East. The Byzantine Empire held sway over Greece and the Balkans, Asia Minor, Syria, and the valleys of Mesopotamia as far as the Caucasus and Zagros mountains to the north and east. It ruled Egypt, nearly the entire North African coast, Sicily, southern Italy, Sardinia, and several cities along the coast of Spain.

Since Western Europe had fallen into little, quarreling states, the Byzantine Empire thought of itself as the only civilized land left in the world. After all, Constantinople, the richest and most beautiful city in the world, was its capital; it was the Nova Roma. And this New Rome had the promise of Christian faith and the Roman law. It was civilization for the Mediterranean world.

How was it then possible that within 10 years of Pope Gregory's death, the Byzantine Romans were fighting for their lives and for the very existence of their Christian Faith? The Germanic nations had in the fifth century swept away the imperial Roman government in the West; but the Germans, in turn, had become Christian and were slowly adopting much of Roman civilization. But two threats to Roman order in the seventh century, more serious than even the Germanic invasions had been, took the civilized world by complete surprise. The second of these threats would prove to be a grave danger not only to the Eastern Empire but to the entire Christian world.

# Persia Threatens Byzantium

The Colossus of Barletta, in Barletta, Italy: a statue of a Byzantine emperor, possibly Heraclius I

Though united politically under the emperor in Constantinople, the people of the Byzantine Empire were deeply divided. The Emperor Justinian had taxed his provinces to their limit to pay for his wars, as did his successors to pay for the defense of the borders against the German tribes and the Persian armies. Overtaxed city folk in places like Syria and Egypt did not see why they should pay for fighting that was occurring as far away from them as the Danube valley or the Mesopotamian frontier.

The Byzantine army had not made itself popular with the peoples of the eastern provinces, where the imperial army was used to strike at the emperor's political opponents and punish heretics and rioters in the cities. Christian heretics were treated as enemies of the state. Full of resentment, unhappy people joined the heretical Christian sects just because the government opposed them. Heresies and strange cults sprang up all over Syria and Egypt. Fighting between Jews and Christians, and between orthodox Christians and Christian sects, troubled the cities of the East.

The people of the eastern provinces of the empire began to think of the Eastern Roman Empire as their oppressor, not their defender. Little revolts broke out, and general hostility to Constantinople smoldered among the population.

It was against this divided empire that the Persian king struck. King Chosroes II had united the Persian tribes and cities. He had formed a new and deadly army that, beginning in 602, swept across

Chapter 7   The Rise of Islam—A.D. 624–800   **169**

### The True Cross

Among the treasures the Byzantine Emperor Heraclius recovered from the Persians was the True Cross, the relic of the cross on which Christ died.

Over 300 years earlier, the Emperor Constantine's mother, St. Helena, had discovered the cross of Christ in Jerusalem and had it placed in the Basilica of the Holy Sepulchre, a church built by Constantine over the site of Christ's tomb. When they sacked Jerusalem, the Persians had taken the True Cross from the burning city and kept it for 14 years. After his final defeat, Chosroes returned the True Cross to Heraclius.

After recovering the relic, Heraclius took it to Constantinople. Then, in 629, he embarked for Jerusalem, to return the True Cross to the Holy Sepulchre. According to tradition, the emperor, dressed in gold and gems, thought to carry the relic in its silver case to the Holy Places. However, when he tried to pass through the gate that led to Mt. Calvary, where Christ was crucified, he found he could not move forward. No matter how he tried, he could not pass through the gate.

Seeing the emperor's plight, Zacharias, the patriarch (bishop) of Jerusalem, said the emperor's rich dress did not match the humble garments of Jesus as he carried his cross to Calvary. "You, O emperor," said the bishop, "walk in royal robes while he was poorly clad. On your head is a rich crown, while on his head was a crown of thorns. You walk with shoes on, while he walked barefoot." Then Heraclius, casting away his rich garments, dressed in common clothes and went barefoot; only then was he able to enter the Holy Places and return the True Cross to its shrine in the Holy Sepulchre.

Church of the Holy Sepulchre, Jerusalem

Mesopotamia and into Syria and Palestine. The Persians even took Jerusalem from the Byzantine Empire.

The Byzantine emperor at this critical moment was Heraclius (ca. 575–641), a career soldier and wise ruler. To drive back the Persian invasion that had penetrated all the way to Chalcedon, a city in Asia Minor near Constantinople, Heraclius recruited and trained a new army. For 10 years of hard fighting, Heraclius led the armies of the Byzantine Romans against the Persians. He finally forced Chosroes to surrender in 628. The Persian king gave up all the lands he had seized from the Byzantine Empire.

Heraclius was a military genius of the old Roman model. His men called him the "New Scipio" after the Roman general who had defeated Carthage during the Punic Wars hundreds of years before. Heraclius' defeat of Chosroes, it appeared, had saved the empire from its greatest foe. Today, we might think of Heraclius as a great general—the equal of Julius Caesar or Constantine, perhaps—if it had not been for the foe who faced him in the last years of his life.

Heraclius was 60 when news of an invader, appearing totally unexpectedly out of the Arabian Desert, reached him in Constantinople. Sick and dying, Heraclius sent his brother Theodorus with the same veteran army that had defeated the Persians, to put an end to this troublesome annoyance on the Syrian border.

# The Deserts of Arabia

In the 500s, the wars between the Byzantine Empire and Persia closed off the old trade routes through the Persian Gulf by which goods came from India through Mesopotamia to Syria. Because the Gulf was infested with pirates and Persian warships, merchants began shipping their goods overland through Arabia to Mesopotamia and Syria. Huge caravans of hundreds of heavy-laden camels began to make the trip from Yemen in the south of the Arabian Peninsula overland to Damascus in Syria.

The caravans were owned by families or clans in the little cities of the western Arabian mountains. Caravan owners often hired members of nomad tribes, called the Bedouin, to guard and drive the caravans, for the Bedouin were expert at handling camels. The Bedouin were also fierce warriors. Armed bands of tribesmen had long fought for water rights in the parched desert.

The Bedouin worshiped nature spirits and saw these spirits, called djinns, in every strange corner of the land. The most important sanctuary for this nature worship was the shrine around which Mecca, the principal town of the Arabian caravan route, had been built. The shrine, called the Kaaba, was built of stone and was nearly the shape of a perfect cube.

The Kaaba housed a sacred black stone, a meteorite, said to have magical powers. The chief god of the Meccans was thought to reside in the stone. The Kaaba housed, as well, the statues of some 360 lesser Arabian gods.

Chapter 7   The Rise of Islam—A.D. 624–800   **171**

**Map of Arabian Peninsula in the days of Muhammad**

**An Arab caravan resting at an oasis**

Both the Byzantines and Persians despised the Arabs. They thought of these wandering tribes as little more than nuisances. The Arabs, though, only needed to be united under a strong ideal to become the terrible threat they became to the Byzantine Empire—and eventually to all of Christendom.

# The Prophet Muhammad

The man who united the Arabs began his life in poverty. Muhammad was an orphan who belonged to the Quraish, an ancient and powerful clan or tribe of the city of Mecca. As a young man, Muhammad was a manager of caravans, bringing the spices of southern Arabia into Damascus and the cities of Syria. An older lady of Mecca, named Khadija, married him and gave him command of her large caravan business.

On his travels, Muhammad made contact with Christians and Jews, from whom he learned about the One True God. He became a convinced **monotheist** and was determined that the God of Abraham must become the God of his people.

In his late thirties, Muhammad began to have trances in which he seemed to hear divine voices. He would go alone to a cave on the slopes of Mount Hira near Mecca to pray. One night in 610, in the month of Ramadan, he heard a tinkling of bells and a voice saying with authority, "recite!"

"What shall I recite?" the terrified Muhammad replied.

"In the name of thy Lord the Creator, who created mankind from a drop of blood, recite!" The voice went on to describe and recount the acts of **Allah** and speak of his nature. Muhammad memorized and recited every word the voice spoke to him.

Muhammad thought that an angel had told him to proclaim a new revelation to his countrymen and to the world. Men were to turn from idolatry to the worship of one god, from hatred of one another to brotherly love. All men must submit to Allah's will. This "submission" was called Islam (in Arabic), and those who submitted were called Muslims.

## Flight to Medina

Muhammad found many converts among his own family and his wife's relatives. But the elders of Mecca resented his attack on their many gods. In 622, they drove him from Mecca, and Muhammad and his followers fled to the neighboring city of Medina. Muslims call this year the year of

**monotheist:** one who believes in one God (from Greek monos, meaning "one," and theos, "god")

**Allah:** the Arabic word for God

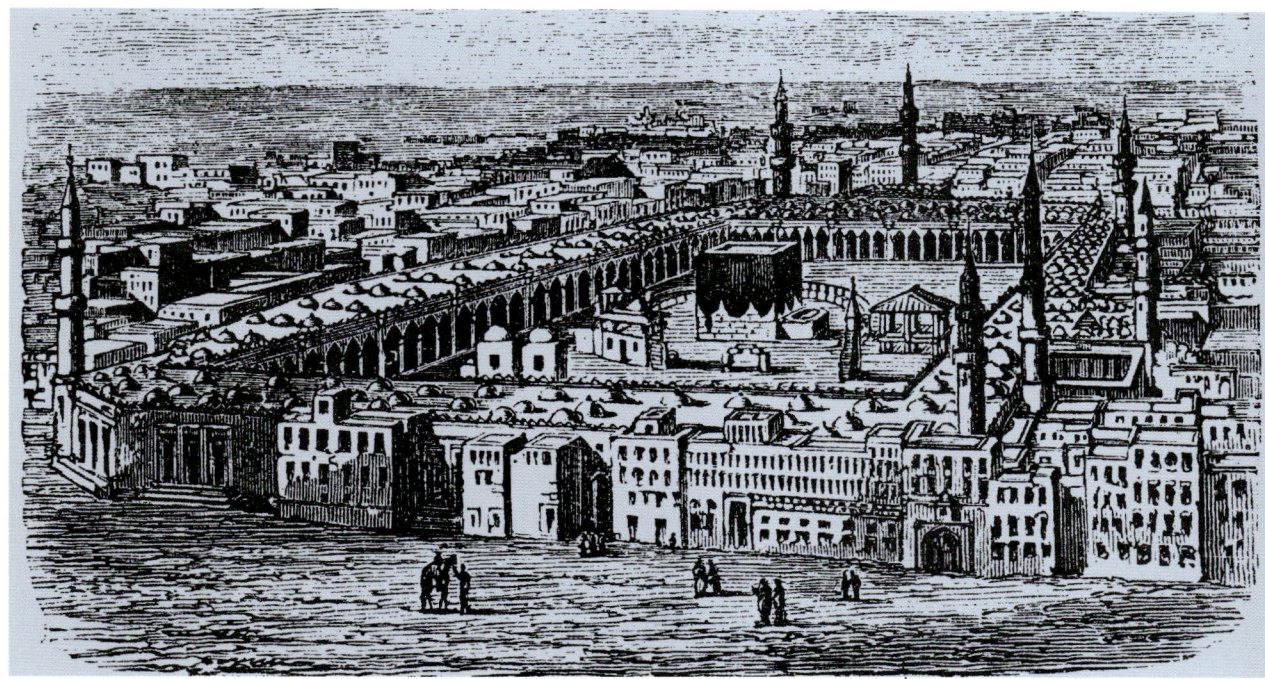

View across Mecca. The building at the center of the great walled rectangular space is the Kaaba.

the "flight," or Hejra (Hegira in Latin). In their calendar ever afterward, it has been known as Year One.

Muhammad's wife and followers wrote down the messages delivered to him in his trances. Each of these messages is called in Arabic a sura, meaning "a row." The suras were collected after his death and arranged in one collection called the Quran, or Koran. The Koran is the sacred book of Islam.

The Koran contains a mixture of profound insights and strangely ignoble elements of cruelty, lust, and ignorance. Muslims believe that every word and every letter of the Koran is divinely inspired. Therefore Muslims do not believe that the Koran can be translated. Every faithful Muslim attempts to learn the whole collection of suras by heart in the original Arabic.

Because Muslims need to learn Arabic to read the Koran, Islam was instrumental in making Arabic the language of the Middle East.

## Jihad

When the elders of Mecca refused to allow his followers to remain in their city, Muhammad received a message from his "angelic voices" tell-

**An ancient Koran**

ing him to impose Islam on all the world by means of the sword. This effort he called jihad—a "struggle" Allah asked of his faithful. Though jihad had at first meant an inner struggle in each believer to submit fully to God's will, it came to mean, as well, a holy war against unbelievers.

Muhammad's first jihad was against Mecca. His followers met the tribesmen of Mecca at the Battle of Bedr in 624 and conquered them. Six years later, Mecca surrendered to Muhammad without more fighting and accepted conversion to the new religion.

After the surrender of Mecca, Muhammad returned with his lieutenants to Medina, which he made his capital. To the end of his life in 632, he went forth conquering the tribes of Arabia until he had built up a small kingdom of the "faithful" on the desert peninsula.

## The Teaching of Muhammad

Muhammad's teaching contains many things borrowed from both the Christian and Jewish religions. Though he taught that Jesus was not the Son of God, Muhammad gave great honor to him, calling Jesus the last and greatest of the Hebrew prophets, which included Moses and Abraham. Muhammad claimed that he himself was the last and greatest of all prophets.

The message of Muhammad was simple: The faithful are always to act with justice toward their fellows, to care for the poor, to show mercy to the repentant, and to bring unbelievers to submission to God's will. Muslims are forbidden to drink alcohol in any form. They may not eat the flesh of swine or the blood of animals or the flesh of any animal dedicated to a pagan god. Following the Law of Moses, Muhammad forbade the making and worship of images. (Muslim art developed geometric design and an elegant **calligraphy** of the Arabic script to replace images.)

Muhammad preached a faith that raised the people of Arabia out of a paganism that practiced human sacrifice, infanticide, legal robbery, and

**calligraphy:** beautiful and ornate handwriting

drunkenness. His message of brotherhood and surrender to God was a "light" compared to the darkness of the old religion of the tribes.

But Muhammad lost the purity of his original vision. His triumphs had come by bloody means. He took revenge against his opponents and enemies and was suspicious and cunning in his dealings with his first lieutenants. To pacify the elders of Mecca, Muhammad did not destroy the ancient shrine of the Kaaba. Though the idols of the many gods were destroyed, the sacred black stone, where human sacrifice had once taken place, was now said to be a shrine set up by Abraham for his son Ishmael, father of the Arab peoples. The shrine of the Kaaba became the holiest site in Islam.

Muhammad claimed that the Arabs replaced the Jews and Christians as the Chosen Race of God. He allowed his followers to plunder the goods of their enemies and promised them a heaven of sensual pleasures after death—especially for those who died in battle for the sake of the new faith.

Muhammad mixed compassion with violence in his message. He made a special effort to improve the lot of the poor, of women, and of slaves. To relieve the suffering of the very poor, Muhammad established a tax on all believers and required them to give alms to the degree they were able. However, the poor tax also funded troops and other projects the administration of Islam required.

A woman had had no rights at all in Arabian tribal society. She was merely the property of her husband and could be divorced at her husband's pleasure. Muhammad tried to ease women's burdens by limiting **polygamy** and regulating divorce, but he did not abolish polygamy and the mistreatment of women. A devout Muslim may have only four legal wives at one time but as many **concubines** as he can afford.

**The Kaaba stone shrine**

**polygamy:** having two or more wives
**concubine:** a woman who is not legally married to a man but who is treated by him as a wife

## The Five Pillars of Islam

Muhammad left five commands to his followers that every devout Muslim is obligated to observe. They are called the Five Pillars of Islam.

1. shehada—acknowledgment that there is no god but God (Allah) and Muhammad is his prophet

2. salat—prayer five times a day facing toward Mecca and the Kaaba

3. sawn—a fast from food and drink during the daylight hours for the whole month of Ramadan

4. zakal—giving alms and paying the poor tax for the relief of the unfortunate

5. hajj—making a pilgrimage to Mecca at least once in one's life

---

Slavery was acceptable to all ancient cultures, and the Roman world had always depended on it. Islam did not abolish slavery but tried to control it by limiting the power owners had over their slaves and spelling out the rights of slaves. But since Muslim armies were allowed to exact hideous cruelties on the populations that opposed them or to massacre whole towns and cities that refused to surrender, the conquered often preferred slavery. The African slave trade continues to this day in many Muslim countries.

## A Simple Religion

Islam was attractive because it taught a simple monotheism and an uncomplicated morality. Islam teaches that God is one being and not a trinity. Muslims believe that everyone owes Allah unconditional obedience and worship, and his commandments are easy to understand.

Unlike the Christian Faith, Islam has no sacraments, no ordained priesthood, and no official theology. Anyone may convert to Islam simply by declaring solemnly before any Muslim this sentence: "I testify: There is no god but Allah, and Muhammad is his Prophet." The declaration is for life, and anyone who abandons Islam can be punished with death.

# The Prophet's Successors

After conquering Mecca, Muhammad set up both a religious and political government over his followers. His system was a complete **theocracy**—Muhammad was not only a religious leader, but the supreme lawgiver and commander of the armies.

When Muhammad died on June 8, 632, Islam was left leaderless. His young lieutenants were ready to spread his religion by the sword beyond the limits of Arabia, but they had no leader. Muhammad had left the leadership of public prayer to his old friend, Abu Bakr, who had been one of

**theocracy:** a government carried out directly by God or by one who is considered to be directly guided by God

**A Persian depiction of Muhammad destroying idols**

his first followers. But he had chosen no one to succeed him as judge and ruler of the faithful, or as supreme commander of the armies.

Two factions fought for the leadership of Islam. On the one hand were the native Medina families, especially Muhammad's own Quraish clan, and on the other were Muhammad's relatives from Mecca, led by his nephew, Ali. The factions compromised by electing the pious, gentle, and wise Abu Bakr. Abu Bakr became the first caliph ("successor") to the Prophet.

Caliph Abu Bakr recognized that certain religious teachers and students of Muhammad's message had the authority to preach and conduct prayer. They were called mullahs. Another religious leader, called an imam, has religious authority over a local place of Muslim worship, called a mosque, or over a particular territory. The armies were put under the authority of emirs—the fiercest, most dedicated warriors Muhammad had gathered around him. Later the emir would also be the governor of a conquered territory.

Islam had one great and fearful advantage over its enemies—the power to turn its followers into wild fanatics, careless of life or death on the battlefield. Life meant for them the duty to smite the infidel; victory, the promise of despoiling him of his worldly goods; death, the joys of a paradise of sensual delights. The infidel were pagans, Christians, and Jews.

Abu Bakr waged a three-year war against his opponents and subdued the entire Arabian Peninsula. Abu Bakr waged a three-year war against Arabian tribes who had refused to obey him as the Prophet's successor. Led by Khalid ibn al-Walid (called the "Sword of Allah"), the Muslims subdued the entire Arabian Peninsula. For the first time in its history, Arabia was united under one rule of religion and government. Thus united, the Arabs could now direct their zeal toward the conquest of the civilized world.

# Islam Expands Beyond Arabia

Abu Bakr assembled all the tribesmen of the peninsula under the green banners of the Prophet. He then dispatched four armies of the fiercest Bedouin warriors to ride out of the desert and bring Muhammad's message to the infidels. The first army was sent against the Persians, striking at the heart of Persian royal power in the cities of the upper Euphrates and Tigris valleys. The other armies rode directly into Syria and threatened Damascus.

Faced with the Arab threat, the governors of Syria and Palestine begged the emperor for help. Heeding their call, Emperor Heraclius dispatched his brother Theodorus with his veterans against the Arabs, expecting a quick victory over the wild barbarians. Meanwhile, Abu Bakr, to strengthen his Syrian invasion, sent part of the force that had invaded Persia to Syria. The leader of this new Arab force, Khalid ibn al-Walid, took command from Obeida and in July 634 badly defeated Theodorus and the imperial army in Palestine.

**The Ummayad Mosque, built on the site of a former Roman temple and the Church of Saint John the Baptist in Damascus**

In 635 Damascus, the greatest city of eastern Syria, fell to the Arab Muslims. With the fall of Damascus, Jerusalem was defenseless. In alarm, Heraclius poured in reinforcements. Some 80,000 Byzantine troops, mostly untested raw recruits, met the enemy in late summer of 636 on the banks of the little river Hieromax—or, in Arabic, Yarmouk—in what is now Jordan. The Muslims numbered less than 25,000. The battle, fateful for civilization, is known by the name Yarmouk.

That day, August 20, 636, the Arabs threw themselves against the imperial legions while the winds blew the desert sands into blinding storm. The Arabs pushed the exhausted Byzantines back in wild disorder and panic; soldiers were cut down by Arab swords or leapt from the precipices of the river bank, falling into ravines and crevasses of the desert plateau in their panic to escape. This panic killed thousands without the stroke of a sword. The imperial commander, Theodorus, fell in the onslaught.

On that late-summer afternoon in August, 636, the Arabs wiped out the Byzantine army of the East. No other force could be collected in time. Nothing stood in the way of Khalid's Bedouins and the cities of Syria and Palestine.

## Conquest of the East and Africa

After the defeat at Yarmouk, city after city fell to the Muslims. In 636, broken by disease, the emperor paid a hasty visit to Jerusalem and removed the True Cross, which he had replaced there in triumph only six years before. He took the holy relic with him and sailed for Constantinople. In 637, Antioch fell—the capital of northern Syria and one of the five chief centers of the Church, where believers were first called Christians. After taking Antioch, Khalid overwhelmed Jerusalem.

The Caliph Omar crossed the desert in person to receive the surrender of Jerusalem, which Muhammad had proclaimed, after Mecca, as the second most holy city in the world. Omar left the Christians all their churches but built for himself a great mosque on the site of Solomon's temple, on a high rock hill overlooking the city. Called the Dome of the Rock, the mosque stands there to this day.

While Syria was falling to the Arabs, Persia had met a swifter end. Khalid and his armies sacked and destroyed the Persian capital, Ctesiphon, and drove the last Persian king into exile and death. Then the Arabs turned

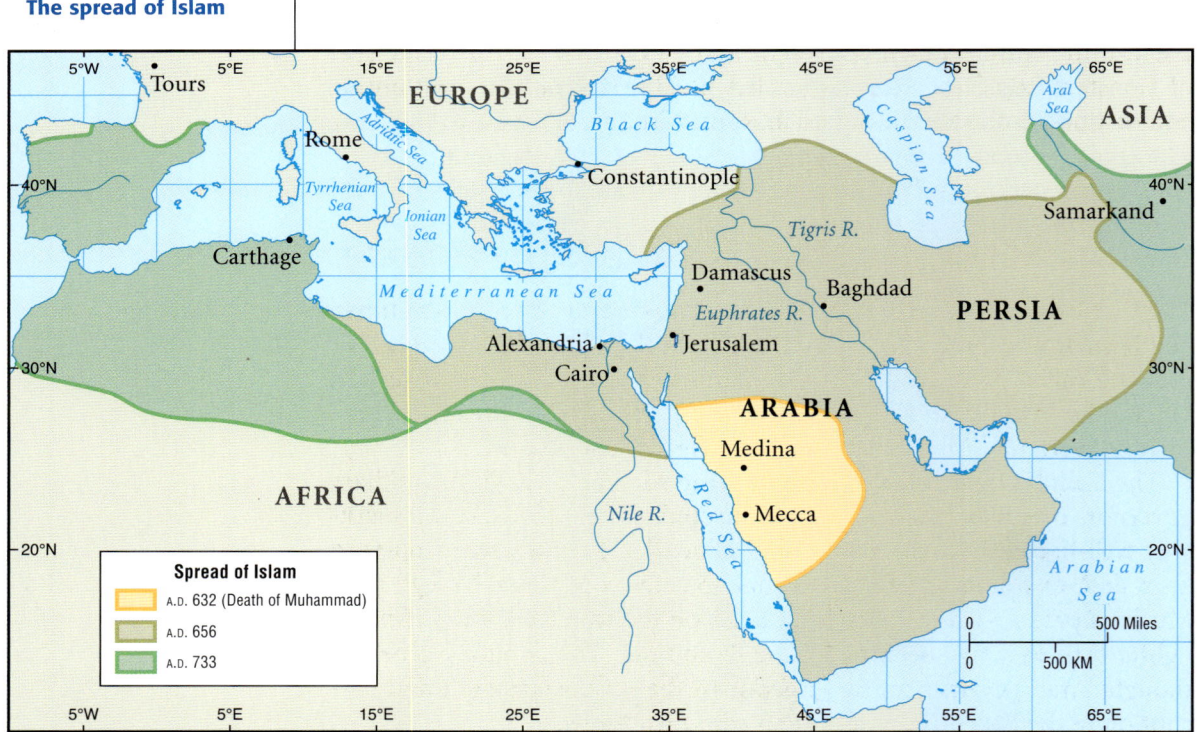

The spread of Islam

back south and drove the Eastern Romans out of Mesopotamia entirely. The entire Middle East except for Asia Minor was in the caliph's hands.

In 639, the Arabs fell upon Egypt. They easily routed the dispirited Roman army, captured Memphis and all of Upper Egypt, and settled down to besiege Alexandria. Egypt's heretical Christians received the Muslims as liberators from orthodox oppression. Only in orthodox Alexandria was there any serious resistance to the Muslims. The great seaport city—one of the most important in Christendom, and the home of the first fathers of Christian thought—was still in Christian Roman hands when the Emperor Heraclius died of heart failure on February 10, 641, at 66 years of age.

In 642, Alexandria finally fell to the Arabs. Irritated by the city's long resistance, the Muslim general, Amr, put to death many of its inhabitants and pulled down its walls. For another 50 years, the Romans held out in Carthage. Then that city, too, fell to the Arabs, and all of North Africa was added to the lands of the caliph.

By the end of the seventh century, nearly all the old civilized lands of Asia and Africa were under Muslim control: Persia, Mesopotamia, Syria, Palestine, Egypt, and North Africa. Of the five greatest Christian churches, the Muslims ruled Antioch, Jerusalem, and Alexandria; only the major sees of Constantinople and Rome were left in Christian hands. Constantine and Justinian's dream of a Christian Roman Empire was ended.

# The Struggle for the Caliphate

The first four caliphs were men who had known and served Muhammad and been among his earliest converts. These "Rightly Guided Caliphs," as they are called, were Abu Bakr, Muhammad's friend and father-in-law; Omar, the Prophet's most trusted adviser; Othman, a wealthy, young, early convert; and Ali, Muhammad's cousin and son-in-law.

The Caliph Omar ruled his empire from Medina through his military governors or emirs. His troops were unsophisticated, pious, and remarkably well-behaved young men. Omar allowed the conquered peoples to keep their own laws and forced no one to convert to Islam, though non-Muslims paid a high extra tax. But taxes on the whole were significantly lighter than they had been under the Byzantines. The populace generally thought Arab government far superior to the mismanagement and corruption of the Byzantine and Persian administrations.

**Cairo, Egypt, in the 19th century**

## Succession through Murder

In 644, the Caliph Omar was stabbed with a poisoned dagger while he was preparing to lead the morning prayers in the Medina mosque. On his deathbed Omar chose Othman as his successor. Othman belonged to the house of the Umayyads, a powerful Meccan noble family. Caliph Othman carried Islam eastward into Armenia, the first kingdom that ever had become Christian, and completed the conquest of Persia and Bactria.

Under Othman, however, the vast wealth coming from the conquered lands to Arabia began to change the Arabs. The sturdy desert warriors met luxuries and vices they had never even imagined. Their garrison towns on the edge of the cities of Syria and Egypt grew from tent villages to brick cities, with their own mosques, shops, artisan districts, and entertainment quarters. Mecca and Medina grew prosperous. The simple piety of early Islam began to slide away. Omar had lived in a plain brick compound in Medina, sleeping on a bed of rushes like his ancestors and eating the common fare of Arabian Desert dwellers—dry bread and goat's milk, dates, and an occasional roast goat. Othman's first concern, on the other hand, was increasing his already considerable wealth.

Caliph Othman appointed his Umayyad relatives to important posts. As governors of the principal cities—Damascus, Jerusalem, Antioch, and Alexandria—the Umayyad family grew rich overnight. The tribal warriors, with no further conquests to achieve, grew impatient, and revolts erupted among garrisons across the caliphate. A delegation from the armies in Egypt arrived at Othman's palace, demanding his resignation. He refused. That night, they stormed the palace and cut Othman down as he was reading the Koran in his evening meditation.

## Caliph Ali

The next caliph after the death of Othman was Muhammad's cousin, Ali, who was married to the Prophet's daughter, Fatima. All admired Ali for his generosity and eloquence, and for his military skills. Since he was the nearest male relative to Muhammad, Ali's followers felt he should have been the first caliph, rather than the fourth.

But some were not happy with Ali's rise to power. The Umayyads, for one, feared they would lose their own power and privileges. On becoming caliph, Ali had removed some of Othman's Umayyad relatives from important positions and governorships and replaced them with his own men. But the powerful Umayyad governor of Damascus, Mu'awiya, refused to step aside. He accused Ali of being behind the murder of Othman and demanded that Ali produce Othman's killers and punish them.

When Ali did nothing to punish the killers of Othman, Mu'awiya accused Ali of himself being one of the murderers. In Damascus Mu'awiya displayed the bloodstained robe of Othman and called for vengeance.

Finally Ali was forced to lead his warriors against Mu'awiya and his alliance. Ali's forces met Mu'awiya's army on the banks of the upper Euphrates. At first, Ali's men were prevailing in the battle; but then Amr ibn al-As, Mu'awiya's general, ordered his men to stick pages from their Korans on their spear points. The troops loyal to Ali would not fight against the sacred word of Allah, and the battle came to a halt. Ali agreed to hold discussions with Mu'awiya and submit to a judgment of umpires representing both him and the Umayyad governor.

Ali's spokesmen were no match for the cunning Amr, who represented Mu'awiya. Both sides argued for six months as their troops slowly drifted away. Finally they announced their decision: both men, Ali and Mu'awiya, should resign their offices, and a new governor and a new caliph would be chosen. Both men resigned, as agreed; but after Ali stepped down from being caliph, Amr loudly declared that Mu'awiya should be the new caliph.

Ali refused to submit to this trickery, but many of his followers abandoned him. He had violated God's will, they said, by agreeing at all to a judgment between himself, the caliph, and Mu'awiya. A large number of his former followers, called the Kharijites, or "seceders," threatened Ali with armed resistance.

The Kharijites became such a threat that Ali had to fight them before going after his greater foe, Mu'awiya. But the fight with these former supporters left Ali so weakened that he could not meet Mu'awiya's forces directly. Ali had to accept Mu'awiya's independence. Mu'awiya ruled his province as a separate caliphate, adding Egypt to his control and raiding Ali's lands in Mesopotamia in the name of "True Islam."

Three years after defeating the Kharijites, Ali was entering the mosque at Kufa to pray when a Kharijite leaped from hiding and plunged a dagger into the caliph's heart, killing him instantly. Ali's followers proclaimed his son, Hasan, the next caliph. But Hasan had no wish to continue the quarrel and turned over the office of caliph to Mu'awiya and the Umayyads in Damascus.

## Shiites and Sunnis

In 680, Ali's second son Husayn, Muhammad's only living grandson, rode to join a rebel party in Iraq. He and his men were waylaid by a larger Umayyad force and cut down to the last man. Husayn's head was sent to Damascus as a trophy.

For many Muslims, this incident became a symbol of heroic opposition. A political movement dedicated to restoring Ali's line to the office of caliph took shape. It called itself the Shiat Ali, the "Party of Ali." Its members were called Shiites. Shiite groups sprang up throughout the Muslim world, particularly in the eastern provinces, in Mesopotamia and Persia. The site of the massacre of Husayn near the city of Najaf in modern Iraq became a Shiite pilgrimage site. Shiites came to hold several different beliefs from most Muslims. Islam was thus divided between two groups or sects, the Shiites and the majority, who were called Sunnis. (Shiite means "partisan," and Sunni means "legitimate, loyal, traditional.")

# Umayyad Caliphate

The Umayyad caliphs moved their capital from mud-brick Medina in the desert to the ancient and wealthy city of Damascus. Mu'awiya made arrangements to name his son Yazid his heir, ensuring that the caliphate would pass through inheritance to the heirs of his line. Fourteen Umayyad caliphs ruled from Damascus from 661 to 750.

Under the Umayyads, a distinctive Islamic culture took shape. The new Arab masters sought out the scholars and teachers of their new lands. The Umayyads even began to search for the works of the pagan writers. Works that had not been seen for generations were brought forward and translated into Arabic. Libraries of thousands of books, pagan and Christian, became the pride of Umayyad princes and statesmen. The respect of Muslims for the achievements of the classical Greek and Roman past helped preserve the artistic and scientific traditions of the Greek Christian civilization.

Under the Umayyads, exquisite mosques were erected everywhere, employing the finest Christian and Muslim architects and craftsmen of the eastern world. A few of the greatest Christian churches were converted to mosques, but most churches were left in the hands of the Church—though Christians were not allowed to build new sanctuaries. The Great Mosque of Damascus is a wonder of the artistry and architecture of its day, domed like Hagia Sophia and resplendent with the gold of the new empire.

The Umayyads led Islam's second great wave of conquests. Muslim armies went as far to the east as the Indus valley in India and into the regions beyond Persia inhabited by the nomadic Turk and Khazar tribes.

The huge port of Carthage in North Africa had remained an important naval base of the Byzantine navy, allowing the Eastern Romans access to Western Europe and southern Italy. But then Mu'awiya built a fleet of ships that were swifter and lighter than Byzantine galleys. His ships met the Byzantine fleet off the Carthaginian coast and demolished it. Carthage soon opened its gates to the Arabs.

A tower rises above the arcaded exterior of the Umayyad Mosque, in Damascus, Syria

**A depiction of the ruined Roman Grand Aqueduct in Carthage**

## The Rock of Gibraltar

For centuries, the narrow strait through which ships passed from the Mediterranean Sea into the Atlantic Ocean beyond was called the Pillars of Hercules. This name comes from two great rocks that stand, one on the northern and the other on the southern side of the strait. After Tarik's conquest of Spain, however, the great rock on the northern side of the strait became known as Jibr al-Tarik, the "Rock of Tarik." From this Arabic phrase comes the name Gibraltar, today the name of both the rock and the strait it guards.

In 711, Emir Tarik, the caliph's governor-general of the west, invaded the Iberian Peninsula across the Gibraltar Strait. Within seven years, almost all of Visigothic Spain had fallen into Tarik's hands; only the mountainous northwest remained in Christian hands.

# The Rise of the Abbasids

Even though they had conquered new lands for Islam, the Umayyads had many powerful enemies. With the support of the Shiites and other groups, the Abbasid family in Persia and Mesopotamia proclaimed that the Umayyads had never been true caliphs. The Umayyads, said their enemies, lived worldly and decadent lives and had murdered the last of the legitimate heirs of the Prophet. Because they were blood relatives of Muhammad, the Abbasids claimed they were the true heirs of the Rightly Guided Caliphs. They declared they would restore Islam to its original purity.

In 747, the Abbasid revolt became a serious threat to the Umayyads. Led by a brilliant Persian general, the Abbasids swept away Umayyad resistance and defeated the Umayyad caliph Marwan II at the Great Zab River, a branch of the Tigris River on the eastern side of Mesopotamia. Marwan fled for his life, but was caught in Egypt and killed. His head was sent to the new caliph as a present.

This new caliph was an Abbasid, called Al-Saffah, "the Bloodspiller." He ordered all surviving members of the Umayyad family executed. Al-Saffah invited 80 Umayyad men to a "peace banquet" and there had them murdered and beheaded in one monstrous slaughter. The headless corpses were covered, and the rest of the dinner party, terrified,

A late 19th century photograph of the tombs of the Abbasid Caliphs in Cairo, Egypt

resumed their meal. The one surviving Umayyad, Abd-ar-Rahman, fled to Spain and declared himself the true caliph.

The Abbasids tried to eliminate everyone who might undermine their rule, even their former supporters, including the Shiites. A Persian general who led Al-Saffah's armies was hacked to death while meeting with the caliph, and his head was thrown out of the window to his men below.

## Baghdad, Islam's "Byzantium"

In 762, Al-Saffah's heir chose a new site for his capital, to be near to his frontiers. Constructed in the valley of the Tigris River in Mesopotamia, Baghdad was designed to be an impregnable fortress as well as a rationally planned city. It was built with three concentric walls, rising 90 feet above the Mesopotamian plain and pierced by four huge gateways. At the center of the new city, the royal palace had a beautiful dome, covered with green tiles, rising 130 feet above the city walls.

Around the caliph's palace and its outbuildings were army barracks, mosques, and the palaces of high officials and princes. A system of sewers and water cisterns, like those built in Constantinople, ran under the city streets. Water fountains fed by wells and aqueducts from the mountains gave a fantasy of water sculptures to the hot valley. Baghdad's luxury was a far cry from the mud-brick dwellings of Mecca and Medina in Arabia.

A depiction of Baghdad, from 1808

Baghdad became a great center of trade and commerce. Caravans and sailing ships brought gold from Nubia and linen from Egypt, carpets from Armenia and the Persian city Esfahan, rubies and emeralds from India, and spices from as far away as the Indies. From China came silk and felt, brocades, drugs, and that new wonder of the age, paper. From the far north came amber and furs of fox and martin, ermine and beaver—and golden-haired slaves.

The intellectual awakening begun in Damascus rose to its highest pitch in Baghdad. The poets and philosophers of the Abbasid court were the best minds in the world, and the city became a center of thought. The caliphs **patronized** medicine, mathematics, and astronomy. The law courts developed the Sharia, the system of Islamic law derived from the Koran.

The Abbasid line lasted 500 years. Its caliphs were not all so bloodthirsty and treacherous as Al-Saffah. Still, they guarded their power with ruthless cunning.

> **patronize:** to support, guard, or protect arts, learning, music, and so forth, usually with wealth and influence. One who patronizes is a patron.

# The Continuing Muslim Threat

With the fall of the Christian East, Christian Europe, unprepared and disunited, alone stood against its Muslim foe. In the West, Visigothic Spain had fallen to the Muslims, who now held a caliphate on European soil. In the East, the Roman-Byzantine Empire controlled only Asia Minor and the often-plundered European provinces of Dacia, Thrace, and Greece. Constantinople maintained the only bulwark against the Muslim threat. In one century, Islam had swept over the birthplace of the Christian Faith and almost obliterated the heritage of the martyrs. As the eighth century began amid fire and steel, the future looked grim for Christendom.

# Chapter Review

### Summary
- Because the Byzantine Roman emperors taxed the people of the empire heavily and punished heretics, many in the empire became discontent with Byzantine rule.
- The Persians invaded the Byzantine Empire, sacking Jerusalem and going as far as Chalcedon in Asia Minor. After 10 years of war, the Emperor Heraclius forced the Persian king Chosroes to surrender in 628.

- Muhammad began his life in poverty but became a wealthy owner of caravans. In his late thirties, he began to have dreams in which he said he heard divine voices. Muhammad believed he was given a new revelation that he was to be the prophet of Allah. This new revelation he called Islam, meaning "submission."
- Muhammad's revelations were collected into the Islamic holy book, called the Koran.
- Angry at Muhammad for attacking the worship of their many gods and making converts to Islam, the elders of Mecca drove Muhammad from their city in 622. The "Prophet" fled to the neighboring city of Medina.
- Muhammad called for a jihad or "holy war" against Mecca. In 624, his followers conquered the Meccans at the Battle of Bedr. The conquered city agreed to accept Islam and put away its ancient gods.
- Islam is a simple religion, calling only for worship of Allah as the only god and acknowledgment of Muhammad as his prophet. Those who submit to God are called Muslims. In some ways, Islam was an improvement over the ancient pagan religions of Arabia. Islam preached a universal brotherhood of all believers in Allah, but it also had many cruel and barbaric elements. The Muslim heaven is a paradise of sensual delights.
- After Muhammad's death in 632, his followers struggled over who should be his caliph (successor). The struggle between Muhammad's followers and their successors was often bloody.
- Under Caliph Omar, Islam began its violent expansion beyond the borders of Arabia. Over the next 100 years, Muslim armies conquered Persia, Syria, Palestine, Egypt, North Africa, and the Iberian Peninsula.
- The assassination of Caliph Ali and his son Husayn was the origin of a political and religious movement called the Shiat Ali. Ever since, Islam has been split between the "legitimate, loyal," and "traditional" believers, called Sunnis, and "partisans," the Shiites, the descendents of Ali's followers.
- The Umayyad caliphs oversaw a flowering of Islamic culture, drawn from Greek and Christian traditions. This flowering was continued and intensified under the Abbasid caliphs, who built their beautiful capital, Baghdad, in Mesopotamia.

### Key Concepts
**Allah:** Arabic for God
**Kaaba:** the shrine at the center of Mecca and Islam's holiest place

**Hegira:** Muhammad's flight from Mecca and the beginning of the Muslim count of years
**Islam:** "submission" to Allah and the name of the religion founded by Muhammad
**Koran:** or Qur'an, the scripture of Islam containing the record of Muhammad's prophecies and commands
**Jihad:** interior "struggle" to submit one's will to Allah as well as a holy war against the unbelievers
**Five Pillars of Islam:** the central tenets of the Islamic faith
**caliph:** "successor" to the Prophet Muhammad and the spiritual and military leader of Islam
**emir:** the Muslim governor of a province
**Shiite and Sunni:** the two major divisions of Islam. Shiite means "partisan," and Sunni means "legitimate, loyal, and traditional."

## Dates to Remember
**622:** the Hegira (Muslim Year One). Muhammad and his followers flee Mecca for Medina.
**632:** death of Muhammad
**636:** Battle of Yarmouk. The Arabs defeat the Imperial legions.
**762:** founding of Baghdad

## Central Characters
**Heraclius (575–641):** the Byzantine emperor who defeated the Persians and lost to the Arabs
**Muhammad (d. 632):** founder and Prophet of the Islamic religion
**Abu Bakr (ca. 573–634):** Muhammad's father-in-law and the first caliph
**Omar (ca. 581–644):** second caliph whose armies conquered Mesopotamia, Persia, and Egypt
**Othman (d. 656):** third caliph, founder of the Umayyad dynasty of caliphs.
**Ali (600–661):** fourth caliph, Muhammad's son-in-law

## Questions for Review
1. Why did Emperor Heraclius' army lose the Battle of the Yarmouk? Why is this battle so important to history?
2. How did Muhammad first receive his "messages" from Allah?
3. What is the name of Muhammad's religion? What does that word mean in English?
4. How was the Koran written? Why do Muslims believe it cannot be translated?

5. What are the two meanings of the word jihad?
6. Why is Islam called a simple religion?
7. What is a caliph?
8. Where does the name Shiite come from? How do Shiites differ from other Muslims?
9. Who built Baghdad? What city was it intended to rival?

**Ideas in Action**
1. Discuss the Five Pillars of Islam. Which pillars might be acceptable to Christians and which might be unacceptable? Why?
2. Draw a map of the extent of Muslim expansion over the world since the founding of Islam. Color each conquered land a different color to show when the Muslims conquered it.

# Highways and Byways

### The Poetry and Mathematics of Araby

The Abbasid Caliph Harun al-Rashid presided over the world's most sophisticated and advanced culture from 786 to 809, the brief golden age of Islamic learning and culture. This golden age is fondly recalled in that great medieval collection of tales, The Thousand and One Nights—or as it is better known, The Arabian Nights.

In The Nights, the Princess Scheherazad tells one tale each night to her brother-in-law, the caliph, to save her sister, his wife, from death. Each morning the caliph puts off the threatened execution, and over the thousand and one days he comes to love Scheherazad herself and finally takes her as his wife alongside her sister, whom Scheherazad has saved from death. The Thousand and One Nights was the first collection of short tales linked together by one plot. It inspired medieval authors to make similar collections, such as Chaucer's Canterbury Tales, or Boccacio's Decameron.

The mathematicians of Baghdad learned from the Hindu mathematicians a number system that we use today and call "Arabic." And they learned about algebra, the way to find unknown quantities in an equation. The Muslims passed algebra along with the Arabic numbering system to the West.

Besides "algebra" (from the Arabic word al-jabr), our mathematics took many names and terms from Arabic. For instance, the word algorithm is derived from the name of an Arabic mathematician, al-Khwarasmi, who gave the Arabic number system to Europe.

# Chapter 8: The Defense and the Building of Christendom

In the wake of the Muslim conquests in the East, the future of the Byzantine Empire looked grim. It appeared that the power of the East Romans to defend themselves had evaporated. During the late 7th and early 8th centuries, the armies of Islam burst through the boundaries of the Eastern Roman Empire at every point. On the eastern border of Asia Minor, the Muslims crossed the Taurus Mountains and sacked the cities of Asia Minor.

The Caliph Suleiman resolved to collect a force against Constantinople so large that it could not be resisted. He gathered a fleet of one thousand ships from the ports of Syria and Egypt. Additionally, by land from Tarsus, on the coast of Asia Minor, he sent an army of 100,000 men to advance on Constantinople. Leading this vast host was the caliph's own brother, Maslama.

A detail of an icon of the Dormition (falling asleep) of the Virgin Mary. Mary's soul is depicted as a child in Christ's arms.

## Leo Saves the East

To prove his valor, Maslama attacked the strong fortress city of Amorium, the chief stronghold of Phrygia and gateway to Constantinople. Here the Muslim host met its first difficulty.

This difficulty was Leo, the Byzantine governor of Anatolia in Asia Minor. Under his leadership, the Byzantine forces routed the caliph's **vanguard** and lifted the siege of Amorium. Then, to Maslama's surprise and delight, Leo came to him with a proposal: If Maslama would halt his advance, Leo himself would march on the capital to overthrow the

**vanguard:** troops moving at the head of an army

193

**194** LIGHT TO THE NATIONS: The History of Christian Civilization

> **Orthodox:** as defined in a previous chapter, means "right teaching"; capitalized, the word *Orthodox* came to refer to the Eastern branch of Christianity. Likewise, "Catholic," came to refer to the Western branch of Christianity.

emperor. Maslama was completely fooled by Leo's daring ruse. In 717, he allowed Leo to take the Byzantine throne, thinking he would be a puppet of the caliph. Leo, however, had other plans. His ruse, in addition to saving his forces, bought him more time.

Born to wealthy landowners in Asia Minor, in the border province of Isauria, Leo had risen fast in the army while still a very young man. Leo's Isaurian roots gave him connections with the men of that mountainous land—free, proud of their **Orthodox** faith, and ruggedly honest. He had formed himself by imitating their brave and independent ways.

When Leo moved on Constantinople, the unfortunate Emperor Theodosius III abdicated in his favor, recognizing and honoring Leo's superior military abilities. Leo, now the Emperor Leo III, at once set about readying the city for the coming siege.

Leo had only five months to prepare. He spent the time accumulating vast stores of food and weapons, recruiting men from all over Asia Minor to garrison the city, and strengthening the fortifications and the ships of the fleet. On August 15, the Feast of the Dormition of the Virgin (Assumption of the Blessed Virgin in the Roman tradition), Maslama appeared on the Asian side of the Bosporus (the strait of water that separates Constantinople in Europe from Asia) with an army of 80,000. A few days later, the huge Muslim fleet appeared offshore to take the army across to the European side. The Muslim troops at once

**Map of the eastern Mediterranean, showing the Bosporus Strait**

Chapter 8   The Defense and the Building of Christendom   195

began a blockade of the city from the landward side. Constantinople was under siege.

Leo, however, was not content to remain within the city's walls and wait out a siege. His first blow was to send his fleet out of the **Golden Horn** without warning while the Muslim fleet was divided and somewhat in disorder. The Byzantine galleys and fire ships, shooting the deadly **Greek fire** at their enemies, burned 20 Muslim ships of war.

Maslama sent for reinforcements, and a second army marched up from Baghdad. A great fleet drawn from Africa and Egypt joined the Muslim squadron and moored on the opposite shore beside the second army. Maslama hoped to stop Constantinople's grain shipments from the Black Sea and so starve out the city.

Again Leo dashed from the Golden Horn with his galleys, each armed with Greek fire blowers, and fell on the enemy fleet while it was beached on the shore. Many crewmen of the Muslim ships were Christians, forced to man the caliph's ships. Now they deserted to the imperial ships or fled overboard and ran into the hills. Unable to maneuver or escape, the Muslim sailors were caught at anchor. The Byzantines burned the enemy's ships or towed them back to the city. Leo then landed a force on the Asian shore and drove off the Muslim troops that were encamped there, capturing their tents, supplies, and treasure. The terrified men fled in disorder.

Maslama and his army were left in Thrace, cut off from Asia. Whatever food and supplies the troops could scavenge from the emptied lands had been exhausted. Many men had died of cold and starvation. Then Maslama heard of a great Bulgarian army of Christian warriors heading toward him. Maslama's army tried to hold back the Bulgars. But near Adrianople, north of Byzantium, the barbarian host fell on the Muslims and cut them to pieces. Twenty thousand fell on that day.

> **Golden Horn:** the great natural harbor of Constantinople through which the city became rich and powerful
>
> **Greek fire:** a mixture of chemicals not exactly known to modern science. Greek fire was shot as a liquid out of a pumped cannon and caught fire as soon as it was wetted.

**A view of the Golden Horn from Suleiman's Mosque, Istanbul (Constantinople)**

In autumn 717, Maslama abandoned the siege of Constantinople. His remaining fleet picked up the surviving troops and sailed back to Tarsus. Of the 100,000 who had left on the invasion, only some 30,000 returned.

If Constantinople had fallen, the pagan tribes of Eastern Europe would probably have become subjects of the caliph and followers of Muhammad. The Western European Germanic kingdoms might not have been able to stand attack on two fronts—from the East and from North Africa and Spain. Leo is to be remembered as among the saviors of Europe.

## Iconoclasts and Iconodules

Leo instituted many beneficial reforms for the empire; his mistake was that he chose to undertake a reform of the Church as well. Leo's homeland, Isauria, was on the border of the Muslim lands. Though strongly orthodox, the Isaurians had been influenced by the Muslims and thought sacred images, or icons, of Christ emphasized his humanity over his divinity. For this reason, Leo forbade the veneration of icons, and he became the first of the *iconoclast* (meaning "icon-breaker") emperors.

Leo began his campaign against the veneration of icons in 726, eight years after his great victory over the Muslims. His edicts ordered the removal of all holy statues and images from churches and the whitewashing of all holy pictures on church walls. The beautiful mosaics of Hagia Sophia were plastered over and painted white. All over the empire, clergy and especially monks called *iconodules* ("those who serve images") condemned the emperor and began to preach **sedition** and rebellion among the people. The emperor in turn bitterly persecuted the iconodules, even threatening to imprison Pope Gregory II if he refused to destroy Rome's sacred images. The pope, however, refused to obey Leo.

Even though the boundaries of the empire were safer, the population larger, and wealthier, and the armies more efficient and better motivated than they had been, **Iconoclasm** had created a dangerous rift in the empire. Leo had checked the Muslim advance on the eastern edge of Europe, but his attack on the icons had divided and weakened the Christian community of the East.

**Byzantine icon of the Theotokos (meaning "Godbearer")**

**sedition:** encouraging resistance to or an uprising against the government or other lawful authority

**iconoclasm:** "image-breaking," the rejection of the use of images depicting holy people and things as idolatry

## Triumph of Orthodoxy

Persecution of iconodules continued under Leo III's successors, Constantine V and Leo IV. When Leo IV died, in 780, his wife, the Empress Irene, ruled as regent for her underage son, Constantine VI. Irene had been a secret iconodule and, as regent, she ordered the restoration of images to the churches.

Irene asked the reigning pope, Adrian I, to send representatives to Constantinople for a synod of bishops that became the Seventh Ecumenical Council. The council, which ended up meeting in Nicaea (the site of the first ecumenical council in 325), declared that honoring sacred images is not idolatry, as the iconoclasts had claimed. Images, however, said the council, were not to be worshiped as if they were divine, but given honor only for the sake of the persons they represent—whether God himself or the saints.

The ecumenical council did not end iconoclasm in the Byzantine Empire. An iconoclastic emperor, Leo V, ordered the removal of sacred images from churches only 27 years after the council and persecuted the iconodules. The persecution ended, however, with another empress, Theodora. As regent for her son, Michael III, Empress Theodora ordered the restoration of icons to the churches. On the first Sunday of Lent, February 19, 842, solemn processions carried the icons to the churches. Forever after, the Churches of the East have kept the first Sunday of Lent as a special feast marking the restoration of the icons. They call it the "Triumph of Orthodoxy."

# The Muslim Conquest of Spain

The battle that won Spain for the Muslims took place at La Janda, or Guadalete, near the southern tip of the Iberian Peninsula. In this week-long battle, fought in July 711, fell Roderick, the last king of the Visigoths. The Emir Tarik, the victorious Muslim general, then swept over southern Spain and entered Toledo, the Visigothic capital, unopposed. His army plundered the city and sent lists of the treasures they amassed to the caliph in Damascus.

From Toledo, the victorious Muslims overran nearly all of the lands of Spain. They found little resistance among the remaining quarrelsome Visigothic lords. Some of these lords made peace and gave oaths of allegiance to the caliph's emir; some fled to the mountains. The towns and people were helpless. They accepted the Arabs as just another foreign master like the Visigoths, likely to tax and oppress them with the same injustice. The inhabitants of Spain called their Muslim conquerors *Moros*, Spanish for "deadly ones." From this word comes the name Moors.

However, in their haste, Tarik's forces bypassed some small areas in the mountains of northern Spain. In these hard-to-reach areas of Asturias, resistance to Islamic rule began to take shape.

Holy cave of Covadonga

## Beginnings of the *Reconquista*

The first Hispanic leader of the Christian resistance to the Muslims was a Visigoth named Pelagius in Latin but remembered, in Spanish, as Don Pelayo. Don Pelayo is said to have been a nobleman and a member of Roderick's royal guard. After La Janda, Don Pelayo was made a prisoner of war; but, eventually, he managed to make his way north to mountainous Asturias. He helped other refugees regroup and join forces with the local mountaineers. In Visigothic fashion, they elected Don Pelayo their king.

Determined to resist being conquered by the Muslims, Don Pelayo and his little band of Christians prepared to fight to the end. They took refuge in a cave named Cova Dominica (after *Domina nostra*, "Our Lady"). The place eventually became known as Covadonga.

It was in a small battle at Covadonga in around 718 that Don Pelayo forced the Muslim army to retreat. The battle was only a small skirmish, but it was the first Christian victory over the Muslims in the Iberian Peninsula. The Battle of Covadonga lifted the morale of the beleaguered Christians and inspired them to further resistance.

Don Pelayo reigned as king until 737, setting the foundations of the little kingdom of Asturias that was to play an important role in Spanish history.

The Battle of Covadonga was the first battle in what became known as the *reconquista*, the "reconquest" of the Iberian Peninsula by the ancestors of the Christian Spaniards and Portuguese—a struggle that lasted almost 800 years. The Christians of the Iberian Peninsula fought for political freedom, for possession of land and economic prosperity, for the preservation of their culture and lifestyle, and for their Catholic Faith. They wanted their Catholic Church and their own political institutions with a legal system rooted in Roman law, not Islam and Muslim rule. In essence, they fought to remain a part of Western Civilization, to practice their religion, and to organize their society following Christian principles.

## The Deeds of Charles the "Hammer"

A medieval depiction of Charles Martel in battle before the gates of Rousillon

The next Christian lands to face the Muslim threat were the realms of Gaul, north of the Pyrenees Mountains. The greatest of these realms, the kingdoms of the Franks, were under the rule of the Carolingian Mayors of the Palace. The Meroving kings, as we saw in Chapter 5, still sat on the throne but were powerless—their mayors handled all the tasks of government. When Tarik was invading Spain, the Frankish kingdoms, Neustria (northern France) and Austrasia (the old Frankish homeland along the Rhine River Valley), were united under the rule of Charles Martel, a strong Mayor of the Palace from Austrasia.

The Frankish realm found itself surrounded by enemies. On the south were the Moors, the Muslims of Iberia. On the northeast were the pagan Frisians and Saxons. To the southeast were the Arian Christian Bavarians and Hessians. Across the Alps in Italy, the pope was calling for aid against the Germanic Lombards, who were harrying the towns of central Italy. Charles was aware of the threat from the Moors, but he chose to deal first with the pagan Germans across the Rhine. It was for his lightning-like campaigns against the pagan Germans that Charles gained the nickname *Martellus* or *Martel*—"hammer."

## Conversion of the Pagan Germans

Charles encouraged Bishop Willibrord of Utrecht to send missionaries over all the Frisian land, in what is now the Netherlands. In one generation, the missionaries would convert the Frisian people to the Faith. The Saxons could not be evangelized as yet, but Charles drove them back over the Weser and Ruhr Rivers to their home territory along the northern German coast. He dealt with the Arian Christian Bavarians as he had the pagan Saxons, driving them from his borders and forcing them to give him hostages in return for peace.

Only when he had **pacified** the Saxons and Bavarians did Charles think it safe to encourage missionary activity among the Bavarians. For aid, he turned to St. Boniface, a great preacher and evangelist of the Frisians.

Boniface was born in England. He had become a Benedictine monk and was well known for his learning and understanding of the Scriptures. In 716, he began his missionary work among the Frisians. Two years later, Boniface visited Pope Gregory II in Rome. There, the pope appointed him a missionary to the heathens in Germany. For about four years, Boniface did missionary work in Germany. In 722, he again met with the pope, who consecrated him a bishop.

Returning to Germany, Boniface preached in the region called Hesse. He then undertook the renewed conversion of the Bavarians, most of whom were already Christian but who had fallen into heresy. For the next 31 years he walked the roads and trails of southern Germany, bringing all of Bavaria and Thuringia solidly into the Church. Everywhere he went, Boniface founded churches, monasteries, and abbeys.

Boniface is called the "Apostle of Germany" because of his immense work and its success. As an old man he returned to Frisia, where he made many converts. In 755, a band of heathen Frisians fell on Boniface and 52 companions, killing them all. When some Christians found Boniface's body, beside it was a bloodstained copy of a book. It was the *Advantage of Death*, written by St. Ambrose of Milan.

**pacify:** to restore to a peaceful state; to subdue

## Invasion from Spain

With the borders of his land secure from the Saxons and Bavarians, Charles Martel could turn his attention south to the growing danger beyond the Pyrenees—Islamic Spain.

The Muslims had conquered Spain but had not pushed farther into Europe because of the violent bickering among Muslim lieutenants and generals. Not until 732 did the Emir Abd-ar-Rahman, who ruled in Spain as **viceroy** of the caliph in Damascus, gather a force large enough to move against the dukes of Aquitaine (in southern Gaul). Abd-ar-Rahman assembled an enormous army—80,000 mounted men along with reinforcements from North Africa, Egypt, and the Abbasid caliph in Syria. Abd-ar-Rahman had siege engines to batter the walls of the Aquitainian cities, Toulouse and Bordeaux. He had oxcarts loaded with food, wine, and tents for an army camp that extended for miles along the Mediterranean shore.

**viceroy:** a governor who rules in place of a king

In the early spring of 732, Abd-ar-Rahman and his huge army crossed the Pyrenees. Eudo, the duke of Aquitaine, tried to hold the Muslims at the Garonne River in southern Gaul, but his troops failed him. Eudo escaped north to join Charles Martel, leaving his people to face the wrath of the invaders. Meanwhile, Abd-ar-Rahman broke through the walls of Bordeaux and allowed his men to loot and terrorize the city.

Charles Martel wasted no time. Relying mostly on his own troops from Austrasia, Charles crossed the Loire River and advanced south to meet the Muslim threat.

### Caliph and Emir

Though they shared the same name, the Emir Abd ar-Rahman and the Caliph Abd-ar-Rahman were not the same man. The caliph was the last Umayyad caliph in Damascus who fled (as we saw in Chapter 7) to Spain and set up the caliphate of Cordoba not many years after the Battle of Tours.

## The Battle of Tours

The armies met on a battlefield near Tours, the last fortress of Aquitaine. For seven days the Muslims and Christians faced each other across the open fields, neither side daring to advance, each side taunting the other and trembling with fear at the appearance of its enemy.

The Muslim army was three times larger than that of the Franks. Charles had at his command no more than 30,000 men—armed peasants and freemen on foot; Frankish nobles and their cavalry on horseback.

History has preserved few details of the great struggle. But we know that the Muslim horsemen surged in vain around the impenetrable lines of the Frankish infantry. The Austrasians, Martel's countrymen from the Rhine Valley, were at the forefront of the battle, fighting long and fiercely around their leader, Charles. Martel drew up his men to form the Frankish shield wall, a line of interlocked shields behind which the warriors could strike with spear and sword at

**Battle of Tours, 732 A.D.**

**The Battle of Tours in 732, when Charles Martel defeated the Moors, thus preserving Christianity in Europe**

the attacking enemy. It was the spearmen of the shield wall who slew the Muslim chief, Emir Abd-ar-Rahman, as he charged their wall.

The fighting went on until night fell, when it was no longer possible to tell friend from foe. The Moors withdrew, the survivors straggling off toward the south and the passes of the Pyrenees. Abd-ar-Rahman himself lay slain on the field; many more thousands of bodies were piled up in front of the exhausted Frankish line. In the darkness, the Muslim commanders ordered the whole army to leave its camp and retreat for the coast.

In this fateful year, 732, the Franks were victorious. They had halted the Muslim advance into Northern Europe.

# The Splendor of Al-Andalus

The Muslims of Spain, torn by civil wars after Abd ar-Rahman's death at Tours, could make no further attempts to conquer Gaul. We hear of no further Moorish invasions of Gaul but, hereafter, of Frankish invasions of Spain.

Yet, despite their inability to extend their conquests north of the Pyrenees, the Muslims in Spain were wonderfully prosperous. The Muslims called the land they had conquered by the Arabic name, *Al-Andalus*. Established at the time when the Islamic rulers of the Middle East were patronizing learning and art, Al-Andalus was a shining example of the lasting civilization of antiquity. The Umayyad caliphs of Cordoba, who came to rule Al-Andalus, spent their great wealth on a glittering court of poets and scholars and on the collection of a library greater than any other in Europe. Al-Andalus was the envy of its Christian neighbors, not only for its beautiful cities and just law courts, but for its booming commerce, and luxurious lifestyle.

Arcades in the Great Mosque at Cordoba, now part of a Catholic cathedral

Being able to trade with the prosperous Muslim lands to the East, and with India beyond, Al-Andalus was much more prosperous than the small, independent Christian kingdoms in the northern parts of the peninsula.

### The Peoples of Al-Andalus

Many different groups of people who originated in Europe, Africa, and Asia lived in Al-Andalus. At times they had friendly relations with one another; but more often, open animosity led to persecutions, rebellions, and wars. These groups included the descendents of Hispano-Romans and Visigoths, of African Berbers and Arabian Bedouins and Syrians. There were Sephardic (or Hispanic) Jews. Many Andalusis were bilingual, speaking Arabic as well as the language of their particular community or ancestors. These diverse peoples belonged to one of the three great monotheistic religions: Judaism, Christianity, and Islam.

Christians who lived in Arabian-controlled territories were known as *Mozarabes*. Christians and Jews in Islamic territory paid special taxes for the privilege of practicing their faith and operating a few churches and synagogues. These taxes were not small, and they helped drive most non-Muslims into poverty. Over the centuries, the Christian and Jewish communities dwindled to small, impoverished, and proud minorities that struggled to keep the faith and liturgy of their ancestors in adverse circumstances.

This uneasy assemblage of cultures and peoples made Al-Andalus prosperous but also unruly with quarreling divisions. The various Arabic princes found little allegiance from their populace, nor could they trust their fellow princes and emirs. Civilized and cultured Al-Andalus was a patchwork of rival territories, asking for trouble.

# Springtime of Learning in the British Isles

The islands of Britain and Ireland escaped the troubles of Muslim invasion from the south. Instead, in these lands, English nobles vied with one another to endow new monasteries. The kings of Mercia and Kent gave lands and moneys to their bishops, but no kingdom was so generous to the monasteries as Northumbria. The monks and learned men of England would be responsible for a revival of learning in all Europe, called the

Carolingian Renaissance after its patron, the Frankish king and emperor Charles the Great—Charlemagne.

The monasteries founded by Gaelic monks in Britain continued after the Synod of Whitby forced them to accept Roman customs, including the *Rule of St. Benedict*. These monasteries founded daughter houses throughout the formerly pagan Anglo-Saxon lands of Northumbria. The monks of Northumbria, Gaelic and Saxon alike, brought a new love of learning and teaching to Britain. They sent for books from Italy and Gaul and raised a generation of scholars from a people who could not even write their own language 100 years before.

Much of the written work of the ancient world has survived because monks put a high priority on preserving the many surviving classical Latin texts. Copying them required much physical and intellectual effort. Most men believed that intellectual life would not improve unless the wisdom of the classical poets, philosophers, and early Christian theologians was preserved. So it was that the monks recopied all the ancient texts many times, sending them off to daughter monasteries hundreds of miles apart. In this way, the ancient texts were preserved.

The period of peace that allowed the growth of a lettered culture in the northern lands was brief, a mere 100 years—from the founding of the monastery of Jarrow in 681 to 793. In that last dreadful year of peace, northern invaders, called the Vikings, sacked and burned the monastery on the Holy Isle of Lindesfarne off the northeast coast of England, beginning their raids on the riches of the south.

## St. Bede the Venerable, Historian and Teacher

A man who was said to be the most learned man of his time was a monk who rarely left his monastery—St. Bede, the Venerable. In 679, when Bede was seven years old, his well-to-do parents entrusted him to the care of Ceolfrith, co-abbot of Jarrow Abbey in Northumbria. The boy had a talent for language and words, a fine appreciation of poetry and music, as well as a prodigious memory. Bede spent the rest of his life in the confines of Jarrow, free to study and ponder the works in the large monastic library.

**Medieval engraving of Saint Bede the Venerable**

Bede is mostly remembered today for his *Ecclesiastical History of the English People,* a history of England from the landing of Julius Caesar to Bede's own times. But Bede was more than just a historian. He wrote on many subjects, including grammar, music, and natural science. He was also a poet and a composer of hymns.

Bede said he undertook all his studies to enable him better to understand Sacred Scripture. He thought the many commentaries he wrote on the scriptures were his most important work.

## The Franks Found an Empire

After his death, Charles Martel's two sons divided the Frankish kingdom between them. Unlike brothers among the Meroving kings, Charles Martel's two sons—Pepin, called the "Short," and Carloman—were not rivals for power but regarded each other with great affection. As mayors of the palace, Pepin and Carloman each ruled over one-half the Frankish kingdom. But when he saw that his Austrasian lands were in order, Carloman gave up his office, presenting his lands to Pepin. Carloman left Austrasia for Italy and there built himself a hermitage cell on Mount Soracte.

An illustration depicting a friar cutting the hair of Childerich III, a Merovingian king, deposed by Pepin and confined to a monastery

Pepin had difficulty bringing all of his brother's lands into union with his own. Since he was only a mayor of the palace and not the king, he had no legitimate claim on the allegiance of his many lords. His grandfather, Pepin, and his father, Charles Martel, had not dared to claim the title of king. After all, they were not descended from a legendary hero like Merovech, as the Merovings claimed to be.

Still, the mayors of the palace had done all the practical work of ruling while the Merovings merely held the title of king. What's more, the last male of that line, Childerich III, was an imbecile, unable even to dress himself. So it was that Pepin was able to convince the Frankish Great Council to crown him king of the Franks in place of Childerich, who was sent to live in a monastery.

In November 751, Pepin was acclaimed king by voice vote of the tribal assembly and then lifted on a shield, after the ancient Germanic custom. The great missionary bishop, St. Boniface himself, as the pope's representative, anointed and crowned Pepin as a Christian king.

Pepin, a powerful and successful king, extended his power outside his own lands, protecting the pope from the troublesome Lombards in Italy. When he died, Pepin left his two sons a peaceful realm and a crown recognized as legitimate by pope, Eastern Roman emperor, and Muslim caliph.

But Pepin's sons, Charles and Carloman, were not like their father and his brother. They began at once to quarrel, and only their mother Berthe kept them from open war. Different bishops separately crowned the brothers in 768. Although Charles had several reasons for attacking his brother, he did not. Then, in 771, Carloman died a natural death, and the whole Frankish realm was left to Charles.

## The Christian Empire of the West

Pepin's son Charles was the king his grandfather Charles Martel would have hoped for. Later generations called him *Carolus Magnus*, "Charles the Great"—from which came the French name, Charlemagne, by which he is chiefly remembered. The achievements of his age and the dynasty are called "Carolingian," from his Latin name, Carolus.

Because so much was written of Charles the Great in his own time, we know a great deal about his appearance and his daily life. He was a robust and active man, strong of body and quick of mind. He loved swimming, and plunged into a cold pool virtually every day of his long life. He is said to have chosen Aachen, a city on the Rhine, for his capital because it had preserved the large Roman baths he liked for his swimming. He was tall for a man of that period—about six feet. He ate heartily, preferring roasted meats to vegetable dishes. Church fasts, he said, were bad for his health. Hating drunkenness, he restricted himself to three flagons of wine per day. His manner was open and friendly, but his voice (always surprising to strangers because of his physical size) was high-pitched and very loud.

Charles could read, write, and speak his Germanic mother tongue as well as Latin. He also spoke Saxon and Greek, though less fluently. He prayed in both Latin and Frankish, and he took great care that the liturgy be conducted in Latin with solemnity, beauty, and reverence.

**Charlemagne, by Albrecht Dürer**

At meals, Charles employed readers and singers to read to him from histories, sing ancestral tales, and recite the works of the ancients. He called often for the works of St. Augustine of Hippo, especially the *City of God*.

Charles inherited from his father and grandfather the duty that they had undertaken of protecting Christian Europe from the Muslim, the pagan Slav, and the heathen Saxon. Yet not only did he want to subdue these nations, he desired to convert them, and so Charles sent missionaries among the Saxons and Slavs. Because he knew the Muslims could not be converted, he wanted to expel them from the continent. But that task would have to wait on a more pressing one—the struggle against the pagan Saxons.

## Protector of the Church

Like his father Pepin before him, Charles had to deal with the Germanic Saxons. The Saxon lands lay to the northeast of the Frankish lands, in Frisia and what is now northern Germany. The Saxons were a fierce,

**Map showing the development and extent of Charlemagne's empire**

pagan people who sacrificed to a sacred tree, called Irminsul. Sometimes the victims were human. The Saxons also slew Christian missionaries and constantly raided Frankish lands.

To deal with the threat of the Saxons, Charles led an expedition against them. He entered their land, forcing them to give him hostages. He also cut down Irminsul. Charles, however, had to cut short his war against the Saxons. The new pope, Adrian I, needed his aid.

As we saw in Chapter 6, the popes had begun taking on temporal as well as spiritual power after the Gothic wars that had laid waste to Italy. By the time of Pepin, the popes controlled lands, called the Patrimony of St. Peter, in central Italy. In 772, when Charles was fighting the Saxons, the Lombards seized three cities belonging to the pope and were threatening the life of Pope Adrian I himself.

Charles's father, Pepin, had already overcome the Lombards and secured papal power over central Italy. In return, the pope recognized the Frankish king as his protector. Like his father, Charles led his armies into Italy and by June 774 had driven the Lombard king out of Italy and crowned himself king of the Lombards. Charles recognized the pope's rule over central Italy, and the pope consecrated the Frankish king as the protector of the Catholic Church. Like Pepin, Charles received the title "Patrician of Rome."

With the defeat of the Lombards, the Frankish realm included, besides northern Italy, all of Gaul to the Pyrenees; the entire Rhine Valley; Burgundy; the Frisian **duchy** (today the Netherlands); and central and southern Germany, including Swabia and Bavaria. To the east were the Slavs, Bohemians, and Moravians; to the north, in Germany, the ever-hostile Saxons.

**duchy:** lands ruled by a duke

## The Saxon Wars

While Charles was still in Italy, the Saxons again began attacking Frankish lands, burning many churches. Returning to his own lands, the king was determined once and for all to end the Saxon threat.

In 775 Charles resumed his conquest of the pagan Saxons, tribe by tribe. Saxony, their country, was a land of forests, open heath, and swamps, where the Saxons lived in villages and on isolated farmsteads. When attacked, they abandoned their thatch dwellings and melted into the trees and swamps. When Charles's armies had gone, the Saxons came out again and resumed their raids into Frankish lands.

The Saxon lands were without roads, and the heavy horse and wagon trains of the Franks had trouble pursuing the vanishing warriors. If the

Franks surrounded them and forced them to submit, the Saxons gave hostages and paid great fines in cattle and livestock. But they took arms again when the army had gone.

By 777 Charles had forced some three-fourths of the Saxon tribes to submit to him. Swearing oaths of allegiance, the Saxon chieftains allowed their people to be baptized. In a mass baptism, thousands of Saxons converted. But the greatest of the Saxon chieftains, Wittekind, escaped.

## The Iberian Expedition

In 777 some ambassadors from Spain, sent by rebel Muslim lords in the north of Spain, offered homage to Charles if he would protect them from the Umayyad caliph of Cordoba, Abd ar-Rahman II. Though still fighting the Saxons, Charles accepted their offer and undertook to extend his lands south over the Pyrenees.

In 778, Charles led his first great expedition into Spain, marching against Saragossa. But Saragossa did not fall to Charles. Because the rebel Muslim lords proved as faithless to Charles as they had been to their own overlord, the expedition achieved almost nothing except to hold for the Frankish kingdom a narrow strip along the coast as far as Barcelona.

Seeing that his expedition against the Muslims was a failure, Charles lost patience and in 778 returned to Aquitaine by the way he had come. He stormed the city of Pamplona on his retreat, and the Basques and Navarrese in the Pyrenees Mountains surrendered and swore oaths of loyalty to Charles. But as he crossed over the Pyrenees, the Basques and Navarrese attacked his rear guard. The ambush in the mountain pass of Roncesvalles was later recalled in a great medieval epic, the *Song of Roland*.

## Saxony Again

While Charles was fighting in Spain, the Saxon chieftain Wittekind returned to Saxony. With Danish allies, Wittekind and the Saxons rose up against Charles's governors, killing Christian priests and burning churches. In 779, Charles came back in overwhelming force and defeated Wittekind's forces. In 781, Charles decreed that all the Saxons not only had to convert to the Catholic Faith but pay tithes to the Church as well.

But Wittekind would not give up his dream of independence or his paganism. Gathering the Saxons around him once again, he defeated a Frankish army at Suntal on the Weser River. Charles returned to Saxony and forced the Saxons to surrender. In 782, at Verden, Charles ordered

**Chapter 8** The Defense and the Building of Christendom  **211**

**Wittekind surrenders to Charlemagne at Paderborn**

the beheading of the Saxons most involved in killing priests and burning churches—about 4,500 Saxon prisoners died.

This "Massacre of Verden" only hardened the Saxons against the Franks. For another two years, Charles remained fighting in Saxony, reducing the land to misery. Finally, after suffering two defeats to Charles's forces, Wittekind surrendered. Acknowledging that Christ was more powerful than his own god, Odin, Wittekind agreed to be baptized. In 785, the Saxon chieftain received baptism, with Charles the Great himself as his godfather.

The surrender and conversion of Wittekind, however, did not end the Saxon wars. Charles continued fighting this warlike people until 799. Only in 804 were the Saxons completely subdued.

## Reforming the Empire

Charles was more than a conqueror; he was a great organizer and reformer. He divided his realm into counties, each with a *comes* (Latin for companion), or "count," to rule it. To keep an eye on his subordinates, the king himself throughout his life made trips to all parts of his realm, arriving with little or no warning. He also sent out emissaries, called *missi dominici*, to travel a regular circuit and report to him on the state of his provinces and the needs of his subjects. These royal legates, who traveled in pairs—one a count, the other a bishop—were appointed for a year's duty over a certain number of counties. Complaints against a local count or his administrators were brought before the emissaries, and they would send the complaints up to the king.

Among the reports brought back to Charles by his *missi dominici* were letters from provincial bishops. Because Charles saw how badly these letters were written, he began to fear that his clergy did not have enough Latin to understand the Scriptures. He thus established schools in every monastery and cathedral for the perfect teaching of the Latin tongue. The English scholar, Alcuin, who headed the school in Charles's palace, called the "palace school", was commanded to staff and oversee these many schools. Scholars from the British monasteries were brought over to Charles's kingdom to train new teachers. Thus Charles brought the Anglo-Saxon renaissance of learning to the continent.

We today owe the care and preservation of virtually all of the classical authors to Charles the Great. He financed the copying of all the classical works, "almost worn out by the carelessness of our ancestors," he said. Charles devoted much attention to religious books, and his desire was to have the entire body of Frankish epic poetry written down and copied out for future generations. But this library of pagan poetry was later destroyed by Charles's son, King Louis.

## The Emperor of the Romans

Charles faced other enemies besides the Saxons and the Muslims in Spain. When a duke in Bavaria rebelled, Charles had to force him to submit fully to his rule. The Lombards, too, briefly revolted, only to be subdued by the king. Then, in 791, he had to deal with a pagan tribe, the Avars, whom he also defeated.

In the last years of his reign, Charles had once again to defend the pope. Leo III, who had become pope in 795, faced powerful enemies in Rome. Four years later, Leo fled Rome, seeking protection from Charles. The king was determined to seat the pope once more in his own city; so, in late 800, Charles and his troops crossed the Alps and headed swiftly to Rome. There he held a synod, reestablished Leo on the papal throne, and executed or imprisoned the pope's enemies.

A few days after proclaiming the pope's innocence, Charles—with the royal and papal courtiers—thronged St. Peter's for the festival of Christmas. When Mass was ended, Charles remained kneeling at the altar. Leo advanced with a crown.

He placed it on the bowed head of the king and cried, "God grant life and victory to Charles, Augustus, crowned by God, great and **pacific** Emperor of the Romans." All present joined in the cry, *Vivat!* Then all there—Frankish nobles, Lombards, Roman senators and citizens, Italian clergy, even the pope himself—knelt before Charles and saluted him with the reverence paid to the ancient emperors.

Charles later said that the pope crowned him emperor without his prior consent and that he would never have entered St. Peter's on that day if he had known what the pope had planned to do. But Charles did not refuse the crown. In return for the ceremony of coronation, Charles confirmed papal control of central Italy.

**Charlemagne bust reliquary**

**pacific:** peaceful

Charles made all his subjects swear allegiance to him a second time, not as king of the Franks and Lombards, but as emperor of the Romans. The clergy warned the people that they were not merely promising obedience to Charles, but to God and his law. The new empire thus was to be a close union of Church and state. From then on, this empire was to be the embodiment of "Christendom," a Christian society,

## The Passing of Charlemagne

In 806, Charles decided to divide his empire among his three sons: Charles, Pepin, and Louis. The eldest, Charles, would be emperor. The other sons would reign as kings under him. But when Pepin and Charles died, only Louis was left to carry on the imperial name. Grieving for his sons, and suffering from sickness, Charles retired to his palace at Aachen and its baths. He died January 28, 814.

Charles had changed the world. Once again in Western Europe, people could look to an emperor and to the reestablishment of the peace, order, and law of the old Roman empire. But this empire would be **Christendom**, a Christian society supported by its workers, protected by its emperor and his lords, guided by the pope and bishops. The nations had their schools and the Church its protector and master. Civilization was saved, and the Dark Ages could be less dark in deed as they were in spirit. The Emperor Charles was, indeed, "the Great."

**Christendom:** the society and culture of Europe, formed and founded on the Christian Faith

# Chapter Review

### Summary
- Caliph Suleiman sent an army of 100,000 under his brother Maslama to attack Constantinople. Leo, the governor of Anatolia, convinced Maslama to stop his advance. When the reigning emperor abdicated in his favor, Leo himself became emperor. Though Maslama laid siege to Constantinople, the Emperor Leo ultimately broke the siege, forcing the Muslim force to withdraw.
- Though Leo had saved the Church in Constantinople, he subsequently supported the heretical and unpopular cause of iconoclasm, ordering the destruction of holy pictures of the saints, Our Lady, and Christ.
- In 711, Muslim forces under Tarik defeated Christian forces at La Janda, near the southern tip of Iberia. The Muslim forces conquered

most of the Iberian Peninsula, except for Asturias, where a small Christian kingdom continued its resistance to Islam. This resistance marked the beginning of the *reconquista*, the Christian reconquest of Spain, that would last almost 800 years.
- Though surrounded by heathens and Muslims, the Frankish kingdom had an able leader in Charles Martel. Charles sent missionaries to convert the pagan Germans to the east. St. Boniface established churches, monastic communities, and abbeys throughout southern Germany.
- In 732, an enormous Muslim force crossed into the Frankish lands. They were defeated by Charles Martel and his outnumbered army at the Battle of Tours.
- A rich and beautiful culture grew up in Al-Andalus, as Islamic Iberia was called. Though its peoples were often divided by strife, Al-Andalus became the envy of its less civilized and wealthy Christian neighbors.
- Monasteries in Britain and Ireland preserved the learning of the ancient world and the writings of the Church fathers. Notable among the scholars of these lands were St. Bede the Venerable and Alcuin, who founded a school in the court of the Emperor Charlemagne.
- After deposing the last Merovingian king, Pepin the Short, son of Charles Martel, was crowned king of the Franks by St. Boniface, as the pope's representative.
- Charles the Great (Charlemagne) succeeded his father Pepin as king of the Franks. Charles fought many wars, including a 32-year war against the Saxons, another against the Lombards in Italy, and a brief war against the Muslims in northern Spain. But Charles was not just a warrior; he was a great political reformer who brought peace, learning, and prosperity to his vast domains.
- Charles was also a protector of the Church. Pope Leo III crowned Charles emperor of the Romans on Christmas Day, 800. This marked the establishment of Christendom in the West.

## Key Concepts

**Golden Horn:** the great natural harbor of Constantinople through which the city became rich and powerful

**iconoclasm:** "image-breaking," the rejection of the use of images depicting holy people and things as idolatry as well as the destruction of such images

**Orthodox:** "right teaching"; capitalized, the word *Orthodox* came to refer to the Eastern branch of Christianity

**Al-Andalus:** the Arabic name for Spain or Iberia

**Emperor of the Romans:** title given to Charlemagne by the pope on Christmas Day, 800

**count:** an official appointed by Charlemagne as the governor of a province or region (from Latin *comes*, meaning "companion")

## Dates to Remember

**711:** Tarik conquers the Visigoths of Spain at La Janda.
**ca. 718:** the Battle of Covadonga, where Don Pelayo and the Asturians defeat the Muslims for the first time in Iberia
**717–718:** Leo the Isaurian delivers Constantinople from the Muslims.
**732:** the Battle of Tours, where Charles Martel stops the Muslim invasion of Gaul
**800:** Christmas Day, Pope Leo crowns Charlemagne Emperor of the Romans.

## Central Characters

**St. Bede the Venerable (673–735):** monk of the Abbey of Jarrow in northern England, author of *The Ecclesiastical History of the English People*
**Leo III the Isaurian (ca. 680–741):** eastern Roman emperor who defeated the Muslims and stopped their advance into Europe. Leo became an advocate of a heresy called iconoclasm.
**Tarik (died ca. 720):** Arabic Muslim conqueror of Iberia
**Don Pelayo (died 737):** first king of Asturias, commander of Christian resistance against the Muslim conquerors
**Charles Martel (688–741):** "Charles the Hammer," mayor of the palace, victor at Tours
**Pepin the Short (714–768):** son of Charles Martel, first Carolingian king of the Franks
**St. Boniface (d. 754):** Apostle to the Germans, crowned Pepin king of the Franks
**Charles the Great (742–814):** "Charlemagne," son of Pepin the Short, king of the Franks and Emperor of the Romans
**Alcuin (735–804):** English monk and scholar, Charlemagne's supervisor of schools and teacher at the royal court

## Questions for Review

1. Why did Leo make an alliance with the sultan of the Muslims? How did Leo save Christendom?

2. What technological invention saved the Byzantine Christian fleet from the Muslim ships?
3. What happened at Covadonga? Why was it important?
4. Who was the victor in the Battle of Tours in 732? Why was that battle important?
5. Why did Pepin the Short ask to be crowned king of the Franks?
6. How did the Irish and British monasteries help to preserve civilization?
7. Why did Charlemagne start schools across Frankish lands?
8. Why was the crowning of Charlemagne as Roman emperor so important to history?

## Ideas in Action

1. Discuss why those who know the Ten Commandments might reject the use of images. Can images be used in worship if the Old Testament forbids anyone to make images or bow down before them? Do Catholics worship images? How is reverence different from worship? Is iconoclasm still with us?
2. Like a medieval monk, copy a page from your Bible in your best handwriting (suggestions: the Twenty-Third Psalm, the opening paragraphs of the Gospel of John, or some other familiar passage). Decorate it with illustrations and ornaments. How is copying a text both a good exercise in memorization and a method of focusing on the text? Why would the old monasteries make copying a discipline of spiritual growth?
3. Find and copy out a Carolingian alphabet. Try to make the letters in the Carolingian form. Compare it to another style of making the letters, such as our own.
4. Make a map of Charlemagne's empire. How much of Europe did it cover?

# Highways and Byways

## St. Boniface and the Oak of Woden

As a missionary to the pagan Germans in Hesse, St. Boniface preached to people who were sternly faithful to their gods. To show the heathens how powerless were their gods, Boniface took an axe to an oak tree sacred to the god Thor, the god of thunder, who in Germany was pictured as wielding a giant hammer. The pagans believed that Thor was a stout and fierce god.

  The heathens were certain that Thor would strike Boniface down with thunder, but when he had felled the tree and no thunderbolt had struck him dead, many of the heathens, astonished, converted to the Faith. From the wood of the felled tree, Boniface built and dedicated a church to St. Peter.

Chapter 9 # The Achievements of Feudalism: A.D. 800–1000

## Age of Invasions

One night in 793, the old, rich monastery of Lindisfarne on the Holy Isle off the coast of Northumbria was sacked and burned to the ground. The invaders were "Northmen," wild Germanic barbarians from the Scandinavian north. They burned the buildings, killed the abbot and many of the monks, seized the monastery's treasures, and carried off the surviving monks to be sold as slaves. Then, in 794, another group of Northmen ravaged the great monastery of Iona off the west coast of Scotland.

For two centuries thereafter, invasions of Northmen terrorized England and the continent of Europe. Many a mother closed down her household at night in fear of fire and sword, praying, "from the fury of the Northmen, Good Lord, deliver us."

### The Vikings

Unlike the Germanic tribes of the fourth and fifth centuries, which had entered the Roman Empire in search of new homes, security, and the benefits of Roman civilization, the Germanic invaders from Scandinavia in the ninth century came only to plunder, enslave, and destroy. They were the terrible Vikings. *Viking* is the name they gave

**A stone from 8th-9th century Sweden depicting a woman offering a drink to a Viking**

**The Vikings besiege Paris**

themselves when traveling or sailing from their northern lands into the greater world. It means "sailor," or just "traveler."

The Vikings, or Northmen, were still pagan. Christian forgiveness was not their way. They had no reverence for Christian holy places. They looked on monks and clerics as less than men because they did not fight. Vikings thought of Christian communities as treasure troves of plunder. The Viking method was to sail in and take a village by surprise, killing all the leaders and seizing men and women to be carried off to slavery. They would then bring their treasures north to enrich the poor homesteads where their wives and children waited.

The Vikings sailed far and wide in search of plunder. In the middle of the ninth century, Viking raiders sacked Nantes in Gaul. They then sailed up the Garonne River as far as Toulouse, pillaging the lands along both banks of the river. In another foray, a fleet of 100 ships entered the River Seine, ravaged the villages along the banks, and, in 845, reached Paris without meeting any resistance. But the Parisians fought back and saved their city, though not their fields and farms. Farther south, the Northmen raided all the coasts of Gaul and Spain, entered the Mediterranean, and sailed 150 miles up the Rhône River. In some 100 years, the Vikings' annual summer raids managed to destroy the flourishing culture of Ireland, devastate the English province of Northumbria, disrupt all life in Frisia (the present Netherlands), and set back the economy and agriculture of France, Italy, and Moorish Spain for decades.

Some Viking groups, however, did not just make raids but settled lands and established kingdoms. The Viking Danes seized Northumbria and brought it under the control of the king of the Danes. In Gaul, the king of the Franks made peace with a powerful Danish Viking chief, Hrolf (Rollo), giving him the lands at the mouth of the Seine. In return Hrolf agreed to protect France from his fellow Northmen. Hrolf's warriors brought their families to settle on the rich river valley plains and thus mixed with the Frankish inhabitants. This region, named for the Northmen, is still known as Normandy.

Another nation of Northmen, the Swedes, headed east and south into the forests of Russia and beyond. A band of Swedish Northmen under their chief, Rurik, sailed south along rivers into the heart of Russia and founded a kingdom at Novgorod. Later, Rurik's descendents mingled with their Slavic subjects and made a kingdom on the banks of the River Dnieper at Kiev. These Northmen were called *Rus*, "red-haired," by their Slavic subjects, from which came Russia, the name of the Northmen's kingdom.

The Swedish adventurers, however, were not content with their lands around Kiev. Called Varangians by the Byzantines, the Swedes greedily desired the riches of the Eastern Romans. They sailed down the rivers to the Black Sea and laid siege to Constantinople itself. The Eastern emperors bought them off with gold and hired many of them for a new personal, imperial army, called the Varangian Guard.

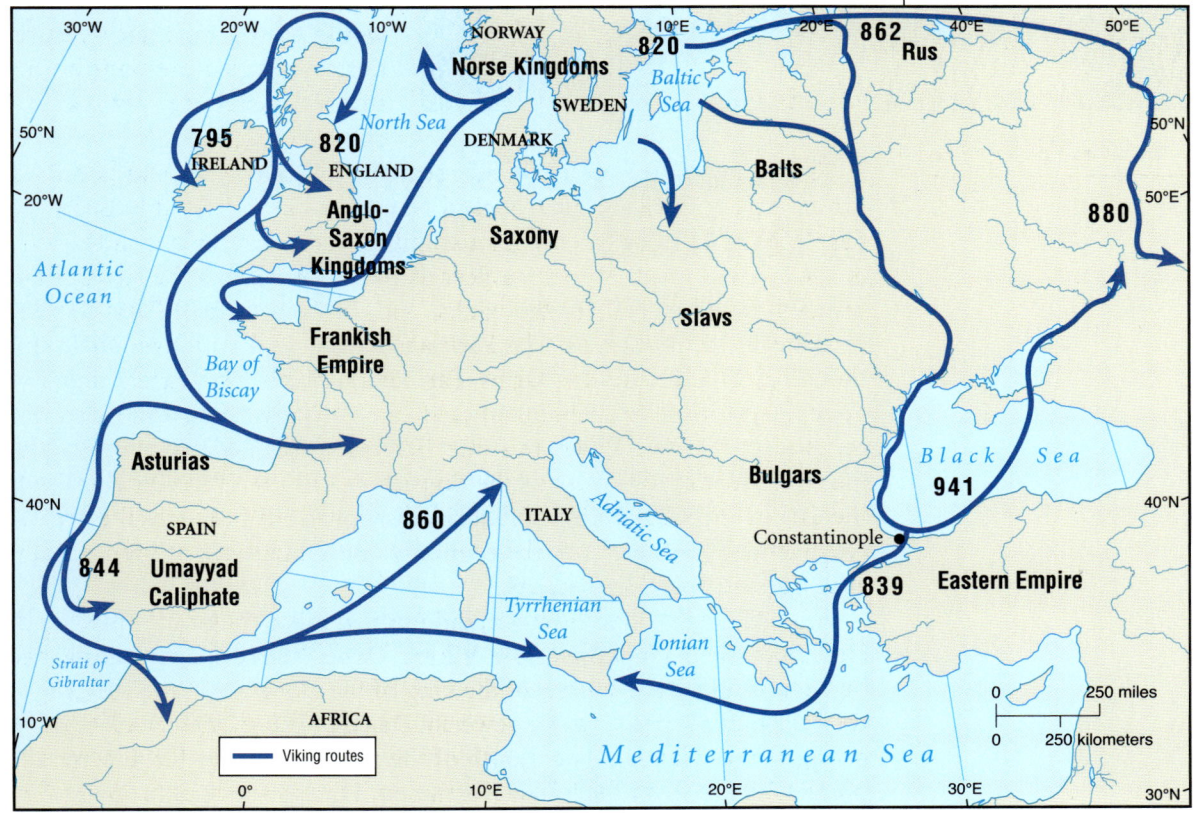

Viking routes from the 8th to the 11th centuries

### Saracens and Magyars

The divided Frankish Empire suffered not only from the Northmen. From the south sailed the Muslim "Saracens," as the Franks called them. From the east rode the pagan Magyars.

The Saracens from North Africa were skillful seamen and pirates. But when piracy failed to satisfy them, they, in 809 and 810, attacked and conquered Sardinia and Corsica. Later, in 827, they began a conquest of the rich island of Sicily that continued until they entirely drove out the Byzantines in 941. From these new bases, Saracen raiders attacked the southern coasts of Gaul and terrorized the whole Italian peninsula. In early 846, like the Goths and Vandals two centuries before them, the Saracens plundered Rome.

In the east, another barbarian people rode out of the steppes of Asia, as had the Huns before them. The Magyars were highly skilled horsemen and fierce warriors. They took control of the Danube plain and raided all the way into the northern fields of Italy. For over 50 years the Germans and Italians suffered from surprise attacks by these wild horsemen.

The Magyars resisted all attempts at evangelization and remained pagan. They settled in the Hungarian plain along the Danube and cut off travel and trade on the river for 100 years.

# Charlemagne's Empire Is Divided

After the death of Charlemagne in 814, the Frankish-Roman Empire could do little to protect its peoples from invasions of Viking, Magyar, and Saracen. Louis the Pious, who became emperor after Charles' death, was not the ruler his father had been.

When he was 43, Louis was injured when a wooden bridge on which he and his courtiers were passing from the palace to the cathedral at Aachen collapsed. Certain he was going to die of his injuries, Louis followed Frankish custom and divided his kingdom among his three sons.

In 817, in an edict called the **Partition** of Aachen, Louis made Lothair, his eldest son, co-emperor and joint ruler of all the empire. After the death of Louis, Lothair was to have control of Rome, Lombardy, and all the old Frankish lands, including Neustria in northern Gaul and Austrasia along the banks of the Rhine River. Louis gave Pepin, his second son, the lands of southwestern Gaul, called Aquitaine, while to Louis, the third son, went Bavaria and the **marches** of the east.

**partition:** the act of dividing into parts or shares

**march:** a province on the boundaries of a kingdom. In German, *Mark*. The ruler of a march is a *Markgraf* ("march count") or, in English, margrave; in French, marquis

Louis the Pious, however, did not die. When his wife, the mother of Lothair, Pepin, and Louis, died in 818, the king married a woman named Judith. After four years, Judith gave birth to a son, named Charles. Judith wanted her son to share in the division of the kingdom, so Emperor Louis, having no more lands to leave young Charles, carved out a realm for him from the lands he had given to Lothair. Lothair and his two brothers were not happy with this new arrangement and rose in armed rebellion against their father.

Repeated rebellions by his sons marred the last years of Emperor Louis's life. After the emperor's death, his sons continued to fight among themselves. So it was that the empire, divided by bickering brothers and their descendents, was too weak to resist the assault of the Vikings.

## No Hope in the King

The weakening of the empire meant that the people could find little help from the government in times of crisis. The fate of Paris is a good example.

In 886, the Northmen unexpectedly attacked Paris. Charles the Fat, emperor at the time, was at Metz in northeastern France, too far away to help immediately. So it was that Odo, the count of Paris, led the defense of his city. The bishop of Paris and the abbot of Saint Germain, a monastery close to Paris, were on the walls of the city, leading the citizens in a desperate attempt to hurl rocks, arrows, and boiling oil on the attacking Vikings.

The siege of Paris was finally lifted by the approach of Charles the Fat and his army. But instead of taking revenge on the Vikings, Charles paid their chiefs 700 pounds of silver and gave them the country around Sens in central Gaul to plunder. Such an act did little to inspire the people of Paris, or Sens, with confidence in the king. They, and the people of France and Italy in general, by necessity had to look to their local bishop, abbot, or count for leadership. If no leadership was forthcoming, the people turned to whoever was willing and able to defend them. This state of things led necessarily to a system which historians have called *feudalism*.

# The Emergence of Feudalism

The words *feudalism* and *feudal* come from the old German word, *feod*, which means "fee" or "payment." In the years after the death of Charlemagne, powerful men granted land as a *feod* or *fief* to those who

**224** LIGHT TO THE NATIONS: The History of Christian Civilization

**The ruins of Spišsky Hrad castle in Slovakia**

swore an oath of loyalty to them and promised to serve them as warriors. Those who swore this oath were called vassals (from the Celtic word *vassa*, meaning "servant"). Those who accepted the oaths from their vassals were called lieges (from the German word *lige*, meaning "sworn-man").

In return for his vassals' service, the liege promised them aid and protection. Sometimes to gain protection from a powerful lord, another lord would hand over his lands to him and receive them back as a fief after swearing an oath of loyalty. Fiefs were not private property as we understand it. A liege lord could in theory take back a fief from a vassal who did not fulfill his oath of loyalty—though oftentimes, a vassal was powerful enough to resist his lord. No written laws governed the relationship between liege and vassal, only custom.

Feudal relationships can be pictured simply as a pyramid. At the top of the pyramid stood the king, the supreme liege lord. Under him were the great lords of the realm (called dukes, from the Latin *dux*, meaning "leader"), who were his vassals and held their lands as fiefs from the king and, in return, swore oaths of loyalty to him. These king's vassals, however, were in turn liege lords to other vassals, who held lands from *them* as fiefs. These vassals, too, could be liege lords to still other vassals. Under the king, vassals formed the ruling class in medieval society.

Though it appears simple, feudalism could get quite complicated at times. For instance, one vassal could hold separate fiefs from different liege lords—and when these lords went to war with each other, it could be unclear to which lord the vassal was to show his loyalty. A king, too, though the liege lord in his own realm, could be the vassal of a lord in another realm. The relationship between vassal and liege was an agreement between equals. It was no disgrace to be a vassal—as is clear from the fact that even kings could be vassals of other lords or kings.

Those vassals who held their lands directly from the king were the greatest lords in the realm. In France they held the titles of duke, marquis (commander of the "mark," or border), and count. In England the name used in place of

### The Castle

To protect their people against enemy marauders, lords built forts, or castles. Early castles were often little more than wooden stockades with an occasional tower to which the people of the district could come for safety. Villages tended to cluster outside these strong places.

In the 10th and 11th centuries, castles became more complex and stronger. Wood gave way to stone in the construction of walls and towers. A castle typically consisted of a central tower—called the keep, or *dongeon*—for final defense if the enemy broke through the walls. A castle also had outbuildings, barracks, and stables. All these were surrounded by a defensive wall, called a "curtain," with smaller towers and a fortified gate. The gate was itself defended by a portcullis, an iron or wood grill that could be raised and lowered to allow people to pass through. The gatehouse itself, which defended the gate passage, was composed of two towers, placed side by side. Some gate passages had "murder holes" through which archers might shoot attackers or drop stones and hot oil on them.

The wall surrounding the castle had screens, such as battlements, behind which defenders might shelter as they shot or dropped things on those below. Around these walls rose another, outer wall with its own gate, overlooking a ditch—or moat—that might be filled with water but was deep enough, even without water, to make climbing the wall difficult. Over the moat, a drawbridge, which could be drawn up from inside or swiveled away from the gate, allowed entry over the moat.

Castles were often built near water, on hilltops, or on easily defended **promontories**. Since having enough drinking water was a major problem for the castle, rainwater cisterns were built to collect rainfall, or deep wells were dug within the walls.

**promontory:** a high rise of land extending out into a body of water

"count" was "earl" (from the Saxon *jarl*). Below the counts in rank were the viscounts, the barons, and finally the simple knights, the lowest title on the ladder of feudalism. All those involved in feudal relationships came to be considered nobles.

Feudalism was "do-it-yourself" government, made necessary because kings and great lords were either too weak or too far away to defend local areas. Feudalism filled the gap. First and foremost, it was local government, providing ways of dealing with local conditions and mobilizing local manpower for defense against enemies. Whoever was able to provide military leadership was looked to for protection. Whoever could solve the problems of local justice and administration was welcomed as lord and master.

## Knighthood

The members of the medieval nobility, lords and vassals alike, all belonged to the order of knighthood. Knights were men who fought on horseback.

On reaching manhood, every feudal nobleman was knighted by his lord, receiving his sword in a religious ceremony attended by all the lord's vassals. A young man was knighted only after he had spent his childhood and adolescence being trained in the physical skills of a warrior, enduring hours of weightlifting and sword practice.

**Medieval knights in the heat of battle**

The knight's sword was the long and very heavy broadsword, tiring to the arm and exhausting to the body after hours of fighting. A boy had to master that weapon or forfeit his claim to knighthood. A knight also had to carry the heavy armor of the battlefield—a *cuirass*, a leather chest and back protector; a *hauberk*, a long shirt of chain mail, with a hood; a *helmet* of iron worn over a leather cap; and boots of leather. The heavy iron plate armor familiar to us through paintings and movie images was not developed until the late 15th century (the end of the Middle Ages), but the cuirass, hauberk, and iron helmet were heavy enough, rather like a professional football player's complete equipment.

Before the king knighted him, a young man made a nightlong vigil before a church or chapel altar and pledged to God or to Our Lady the strength of his sword, promising to use it for holy causes and to protect women and the helpless from evil. After his vigil, he received the blessing of his priest or bishop and knelt before his liege lord, who presented him with his sword. The lord then performed the knight's "dubbing"—a tap on his shoulders with the sword, representing the danger he would face as a knight even to the point, if necessary, of sacrificing his life.

When a father died, a son, in order to inherit his father's fief, had to go through a ceremony in which he received the fief from his lord. Kneeling in the presence of the other vassals and placing his hands between the lord's hands, he made the act of homage (that is, becoming the lord's *homme*, or "man"). He also swore an oath of fealty, or loyalty, promising to keep faith with his lord, to render all due services, and to be the friend of his lord's friends and the enemy of his enemies. The lord then confirmed the young heir by giving over to him, or *investing* him with, his lands. In this last element of the triple ceremony, the lord symbolically handed to the vassal something that represented the fief—a box of earth, a cup of earth, or a bough from a tree.

## Chivalry, the Last Development of Feudalism

Over the centuries following the Viking invasions, feudalism produced one of the most important advances in civilization—the concept of chivalry. Although chivalry did not achieve its highest form or general acceptance until the 12th century, the Church had planted in the European mind the concept of fair play and respect for others. Jesus' parable of the Good Samaritan can be said to be the first story of chivalry in our tradition.

The code of chivalry (the behavior of a knight) assumed that warfare should be conducted under certain rules of conduct, that the question of fair play must be considered even in matters of life and death, and that both public and private actions were religious. Chivalry spread through all Christian lands. Fair play became the duty of a Christian knight, as did the protection of women and the poor. A knight's honor was held as sacred as his life. Keeping his word, doing what he promised, was the foundation of personal honor for a knight. Lying or cheating or refusing his promised aid besmirched a knight's honor and brought him public disgrace or loss of reputation.

## Our Lady and the Image of Women

Amid the assaults on civilized life in Europe, the strength of the Catholic religion held communities together. Belief in the power of the Blessed Mother Mary to help people in need brought medieval men and women an inner courage and conviction that allowed them to withstand trials. Villages and cities showed their gratitude for Our Lady's help by dedicating churches and shrines to her. Lords and kings built great cathedrals to her glory.

The image of God's merciful and mild mother began to change the ideas men had about women. Women were treated with a new respect.

A medieval knight was supposed to treat women with great respect; valor in defense of the lady became an idealized topic in literature and painting for many centuries.

## The Feudal Manor

The number of people who made up the feudal nobility—the king, his dukes, the counts, barons, and knights—was small; only about 5 percent of the population. The rest of the population, the commoners or peasants, were the farmers and craftsmen who supported the warriors in return for their protection. These farmers and, in the early Middle Ages, most of the craftsmen, lived on a manor and supported the landowner by their labor.

The center of life on a manor was the village—a cluster of huts or houses for 20 to 50 families, centering on a church and located near the manor house, where the lord lived. Sometimes the farmers' cottages were situated alongside a lane with their vegetable gardens at the back. The village might have a mill, a blacksmith's shop, a common oven or bakery to save on fuel, and a harness-maker's shop. The manor house might be nearby on higher ground to make it easier to defend against attack.

The manorial village provided for most of the needs of those who lived there. Transportation during the early Middle Ages, especially, was very difficult. Roads were few and in bad repair. The manor had to be self-sufficient in case it was cut off from neighbors by weather or invaders.

Throughout the ninth and tenth centuries, farmers often were serfs, bound to the land on which they were born and subject to its lord's will. Serfs were not slaves, for they could not be sold away from the manor, and their lord could not (as could a Roman slave owner) put them to death without a legal trial. Being bound to the manor where they were born was a protection for the serfs, for the lord could not force them off their land or put them out on the roads to beg or starve. Serfs could count on the production of the manor to support them and their families. Many needed the lord's consent to leave the manor, to marry, or to perform several other specified actions, but they were allowed to accumulate property, to own land, and to buy their freedom in time if they worked hard and saved their money.

**Medieval peasants working in the fields, from the *Les Très Riches Heures du duc de Berry***

Although the serf lacked some personal rights, he was guaranteed the lifetime use of certain pieces of land (which his children could inherit)—provided he kept up the payments and services he owed to the lord. The peasant farmer could keep everything he produced over and above the part that had to be deducted for these payments and for the tithe—the tax paid to support the church.

However, in the early Middle Ages, farmworkers were never far from famine. Until changes occurred in agricultural techniques, the yield of a farmer's land remained small and chancy. At best, in good years, farmers were able to put away only small reserves for use in a future time of scarcity. No one needed much money, for most transactions were conducted by barter—the exchange of goods and services for other goods and services.

The ancient rights of farmworkers to the produce of the land encouraged self-sufficiency. Farmers had the right to wood from the forest and the "common lands" that lay around the village. This wood they used for most of their tools and household articles as well as for building materials and fuel. They also had the right to pasture their animals on the common meadow. Pigs were turned loose in the woodland, while sheep, cattle, and horses grazed together on the common.

Under the best of circumstances, the farmer's life was a hard one. He toiled from dawn to dusk and enjoyed few comforts. Some lords were kindly while others treated their servants and serfs with rough justice, thinking of them as little better than livestock and less valuable than cattle and warhorses. But the efforts of the Church, which insisted on justice and the enforcement of customary rights, slowly improved conditions. (For instance, the church won for serfs the right to marry whomever they wanted to—even if they lived on different manors.) There are records of many serfs buying their freedom and becoming men of substance and influence in their communities. Many important figures of medieval history, particularly clergy, were the children of serfs. Pope Sylvester II came from serf origins and was trained and schooled by the monks of a neighboring monastic house.

## Medieval Farm Life

Feudalism provided the essentials of law and order that allowed conditions of life to begin to get better. The population grew, and agriculture greatly improved.

Farming in the Middle Ages was a community activity. All the workers worked the manor's farmland together. Each family, whether they were serf or free, worked its own plot of land, arranged in long, narrow strips. The lord's holdings were interspersed with those of his tenant farmers, and the result was a beautiful patchwork quilt of various crops.

From the eighth century on, a new method of crop planting began to spread through Europe, north of the Alps. In the "open-field" system, the manor's farmlands were divided into three great sections, or fields, with only two of these fields actually planted in crops in any one year. The third field (a different one every year) was left "open," to "lie fallow" (left unplowed or unsown) so that it might recover some part of its fertility. This discovery did not appear during the long period of Roman farming, but only when it was necessary to grow enough food locally to supply the surrounding area. The fallow or open field seemed a simple solution to the overuse of fields and the overproduction of crops that could not be either stored or transported for sale elsewhere. The idea spread over Western Europe within a few years, through word of mouth among farmers and localities.

The manor had to produce enough food to feed and house its farmers, with a surplus to equip the manor's lord to defend the manor's inhabitants. Because it was far more efficient to work the land together, the community as a whole decided on how the land would be divided and what farming methods to follow. Village councils of elders, acting under the supervision of the lord's agent, who was called the bailiff, usually represented the people in such decisions. The village council divided farm plots among the various families so that all had a share in the land.

## Medieval Inventions

The Middle Ages developed important inventions that helped in the development of civilization and allowed the population of Europe to grow. In particular, those inventions that aided farming helped bring about what historians have called the Second Agricultural Revolution—a "revolution" as important as the First Agricultural Revolution, the discovery of agriculture during the New Stone Age.

Among the most important of these inventions was a heavy, wheeled plow with a "moldboard" plowshare—a large blade like a great axe that was bent or tilted to raise the earth as it dug a trench through the field. Unlike the metal-tipped tooth plow of ancient Rome, which merely scratched or stirred the soil, the medieval moldboard plow not only dug a trench, but actually lifted and turned the earth over completely, making it possible to bury the sod and expose the loose dirt underneath for follow-up planting. The moldboard plow made it possible to farm the heavy, rich bottomlands of central and western Europe.

Pulling this new plow through heavy soils required a larger and stronger horse or ox, and so breeders produced both a heavy ox, suitable for team plowing, and the heavy farm horse. These heavy horses (from which come our Percherons and Clydesdales) allowed farmers to bring unused land into cultivation, so increasing crop yields. The heavy farm horse was also

A farmer (above) plows the fields with a moldboard plow. (right) A moldboard plow

useful as a battle steed, since it could carry a fully armed man as well pull a plow. When used as a warhorse, the heavy horse was called a destrier.

Another important medieval invention was the horse stirrup, invented in Byzantium or brought from China to Constantinople. This invention allowed a man in heavy armor to stay balanced in the saddle. It also gave the rider greater control over his horse. Another invention perhaps even more significant, dating from the late ninth century, was the iron horseshoe, designed to protect the horse's hooves from injury from stones in the moist and sticky soil of the north.

A still more important invention was the padded horse collar. Before the padded horse collar, people attached their horses to wagons or plows with yokes. If a horse tried to pull a heavy load, the two straps holding the yoke pressed tightly against the horse's neck, thus interfering with the horse's breathing. With the new horse collar, the animal could push with his whole strength against a pad that rested on his shoulders. The collar did not interfere with breathing, nor did it cut into the horse's hide.

Chapter 9   The Achievements of Feudalism: A.D. 800–1000   **233**

**Padded horse collars**

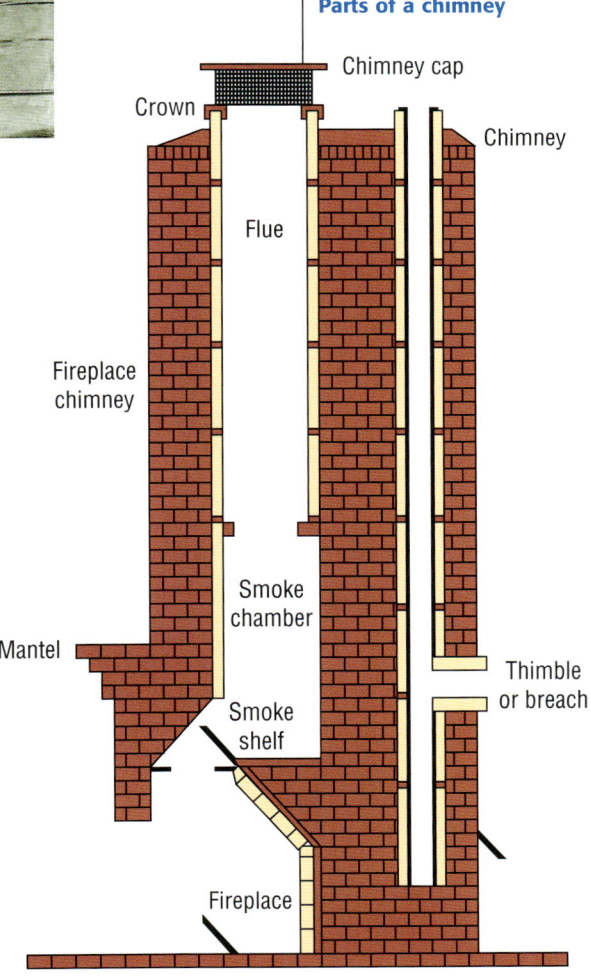

**Parts of a chimney**

With the new plow and the use of iron-shod horse teams, Europeans started thinking about draining wetlands, such as swamps, to increase farm acreage. To accomplish this, the windmill was invented. The windmill was a huge wheel with sails that were turned by the wind. It generated power for operating a pump to clear away excess water into drainage ditches and for milling the grain of the village at the same time.

The final invention to make itself common property throughout Europe was the chimney and fireplace flue. Ancient buildings had only a hole in the roof to take off the smoke of fires within a building. At some time in the seventh or eighth century, a brilliant but unknown inventor made the first fireplace and with it a chimney to carry off the smoke. The fireplace not only heated the rooms of the house, but allowed for cooking to be done indoors.

To keep the winds above the house from coming down the chimney and putting out the fire, medieval craftsmen developed a bend or turn in the chimney, called the smoke shelf.

**Windmills**

Smoke rises into the chimney and curls around the smoke shelf so that it does not turn back into the room below.

Improved agricultural methods and inventions led to an increase in the amount of available food, which allowed the population of Europe to increase. Some manors found that they had a surplus of workers for the first time. Lords released workers from the land or sent them into towns where they could make use of their skills or crafts to benefit the lord. Thus the improvements of the medieval "agricultural revolution" encouraged the growth of towns.

## The Drive to the East

Europe's growing population created a need to clear new lands and settle vast areas previously uninhabited or only sparsely populated. One such area was the eastern frontier of Germany, which was conquered by lords determined to make new estates for themselves. And to open these new lands, lords attracted farm workers from the more settled regions by offers of freedom and pay and other benefits common folk could not get elsewhere in Europe. Serfdom was practically unknown in these newer communities. These settlers formed new communities, driving the less-civilized pagan tribes—the Wends, Prussians, Letts, and Slavs—east beyond the River Elbe.

This greater freedom on the frontier attracted so many workers that lords of manors in the older lands of France and Germany were in danger of losing their labor force. To keep their workers from running away, lords had to make the lives of the tenant farmers easier. So it was in Europe that the number of freer and more prosperous men grew larger year by year.

## Growth of Towns

Trade between different regions of Europe grew slowly during the early Middle Ages. There had been towns during this period; but, except in Italy, they had ceased to be centers of trade. But when the manorial villages began to produce surplus crops, they began to trade with areas where

Venice was a properous and wealthy maritime city.

these crops were scarce. Merchants who traded grain and cattle formed trading communities in many towns of the early 11th century.

In Italy, the city of Venice began a trade with inland districts near the city and with Constantinople and other populous cities of the Byzantine Empire. Venice became the wealthiest and most powerful of the Italian **maritime** cities. Other cities followed Venice's example. Genoa and Pisa grew wealthy by carrying on trade between the eastern Mediterranean and North Africa on the one hand and the European markets on the other.

Cities in the interior of northern Italy also grew more prosperous through trade. Regions such as Lombardy and Tuscany saw the growth of important cities like Milan, Florence, Lucca, and Piacenza. These cities became market centers for their surrounding agricultural districts, and they developed industrial specialties such as the manufacture of woolen cloth.

In the north, trade in agricultural products and woolen cloth began to thrive in the Low Countries, especially in Flanders. This Flemish wool industry was the first one to exist north of the Alps. By the 12th century, Flemish cloth was being shipped in large quantities to more fertile regions in exchange for farm produce. Cloth was also sent to the more distant northern lands of the Baltic in exchange for lumber, furs, and metals.

**maritime:** located on or near the sea; concerned with shipping or navigation

**Weaving of cloth became so popular that sheep needed to be imported from other countries.**

Flemish cloth was eventually exported to the Mediterranean, and Genoa began sending it to the Near East and North Africa.

Trade centers also arose in the Rhineland, the Paris region, some of the Baltic and North Sea towns, and England. Trade centers were most likely to prosper and grow if they were located at the junction of two or more river valleys or near a rich and densely populated farming region. Seaport cities were also likely to prosper.

Throughout France and Italy, and sometimes in England, medieval towns developed on the sites of former Roman towns. Others (especially in France and Germany) grew up around some of the many fortresses constructed during the ninth and tenth centuries.

## The Government of the Town

It was highly important for a rising town to receive protection from some strong local authority against the lawless elements in feudal society. The great feudal lords were often eager to sell to the citizens of towns charters that allowed great freedom, including a good degree of self-government. Great lords sometimes deliberately created towns, which often then developed into important cities.

Townsmen received a grant or purchased a charter from the king or lord of the territory to protect them from interference by feudal lords. Lords could not seize their runaway serfs who fled to the cities after the serf had lived there for a "year and a day."

Under their charters, cities developed their own governments. Most medieval towns were directed by the wealthiest citizens. Some towns allowed nearly all householders or regularly employed men to vote in their popular assemblies, though a small council usually made the day-to-day decisions of government.

## The Guilds

Organizations called *guilds* developed in medieval towns as a means of protecting, promoting, and regulating the economic activities of their members. Guild members were the merchants or craftsmen who owned their own enterprises.

To protect their interests, the guilds of either merchants or master craftsmen (such as butchers, bakers, tailors, shoemakers, and the like) aimed at restricting competition both from outside and within the town. Craft guilds regulated prices, controlled how goods were manufactured and sold, and set high quality standards for what their members produced. The members of a craft guild were organized under the protection of a patron saint. The guilds carried on religious observances and looked after the welfare of members and their families.

Though all craftsmen in a given trade were under the guild, only the masters managed the guild's affairs. Besides the masters there were journeymen, who worked for wages, and apprentices, who were young lads living in the home of a master to learn the trade. Apprenticeship lasted anywhere from 3 to 12 years depending on the craft and the locality. During this time, the master paid the young man no wages, but gave him food and lodging and was responsible for his religious education. Usually a master had two or three apprentices to help him in his work. If he needed additional labor, he hired a journeyman.

The journeyman was a man who had served his apprenticeship but had not yet raised enough money to purchase his own tools or rent a shop. To become a master, the journeyman had to demonstrate his skill before a jury of experienced craftsmen, usually by presenting a "masterpiece" that he had made. As time went on, masters limited the number of workshops, and they sought to pass on their businesses to sons or other relatives. It then grew more and more difficult for journeymen to qualify as masters.

**Scene of the professions from the fifteenth century Lombard manuscript *De Sphaera***

## Markets and Fairs

Every town held its local market, to which the nearby farming population brought its produce. But alongside the local markets were the fairs that were held usually once a year. These fairs took place in all parts of Europe, often growing up near a famous shrine. Craftsmen and dealers in raw material might place their stalls next to local farmers or wandering food vendors. The grunting of pigs mingled with the sizzle of cook-pots and the bargaining of clothing sellers. Wandering minstrels and jugglers might be seen entertaining the crowd while children played through the stalls and tents. A fair could last from three days to six weeks.

Market day in the French medieval city of Villefranche-de-Rouergue. Such markets were typical in medieval cities.

Eventually, journeymen formed their own guilds to force masters to pay higher wages. These were the first true labor unions; and though they were declared illegal, they were occasionally able to improve the journeyman's lot.

# Chapter Review

### Summary
- The Viking invasions from Scandinavia terrorized Europe from Spain to Russia during the ninth century. The Vikings, also called Northmen, pillaged and destroyed villages, cities, and monasteries, enslaving the inhabitants. The invasions set back the economy and agriculture of France, Italy, and Moorish Spain for decades. In Russia, England, and northern France (Normandy), Vikings set up permanent settlements.

- A barbarian people from the East, the Magyars, were fierce warriors and skilled horsemen. They settled the Hungarian plain, raiding Germany and northern Italy.
- Charlemagne's son, King Louis the Pious, divided the Frankish Empire between his three sons. Later, when another son, Charles, was born to the king, Louis cut out a domain for him from the lands he had already partitioned out to his other sons. This led Louis's three older sons to rebel against their father. Rebellions and rivalries between his sons lasted until the end of Louis's life.
- Because kings could not protect their subjects, the people began to seek aid from local lords. This was the beginning of feudalism, a customary network of local military leaders, who swore by oath to come to each other's defense.
- Under feudalism, men called vassals swore oaths of allegiance to lords, called lieges, promising to aid them in time of war. In return, the vassals received grants of land from their lords. Feudal lords were military men, called knights, who fought on horseback to defend their people.
- A feudal manor provided everything needed for daily life. Farmers on the manor were usually serfs—not slaves, but men bound to the soil they worked. Serfs were guaranteed the lifelong use of certain pieces of land, which their children could inherit. A serf could keep all his produce, except for what he owed in taxes to his lord or in tithes to the Church. Through hard work a serf could eventually buy his freedom.
- The code of chivalry laid out ideals for the behavior of knights, such as justice in war, fair play, protection of women and the poor, as well as behavior regulated by religious principles.
- During the medieval period, the veneration of Mary, the Mother of God, brought inner courage to the European peoples and inspired them with a new respect for women.
- Improvements in agricultural technology and techniques during the Middle Ages allowed for larger crop yields with less labor. This period has been called the "Second Agricultural Revolution." Among the important advances were the open field system, the moldboard plow, the breeding of the heavy farm horse, the horse stirrup, the padded horse collar, and the windmill.
- As the population of Western Europe grew, new lands were opened up for settlement in the East. Lords conquered lands held by pagan nations and invited peasants to settle them.
- The Middle Ages witnessed the growth of new towns and the renewal of old ones. Italian cities such as Venice, Genoa, and Pisa grew wealthy

and powerful by carrying on trade between the eastern Mediterranean and North Africa, on the one hand, and the markets in Europe, on the other. In Lombardy and Tuscany, cities developed industrial specialties. In northern Europe, cities grew up around trade centers. Cities in the Low Countries thrived by manufacturing and trading in woolen cloth.
- Cities received charters that made them largely independent of local lords. Under these charters, cities established their own governments.
- In the cities, merchant and craft guilds developed as means of protecting, promoting, and regulating the economic activities of their members. The trade guilds were governed by master craftsmen, who were independent owners of their businesses under the guilds. These guilds included apprentices and journeymen who could, eventually, become masters themselves.

## Key Concepts

**Vikings:** wandering raiders from Scandinavia

**feudalism:** the system of local authority by which strong or powerful men were given control of a region by its inhabitants in return for protection and loyalty; a system dependent on oaths and loyalty for its continuation

**vassal:** one who swears an oath of loyalty and support to a lord

**liege:** one who takes an oath from another and gives him protection and gifts in return

**fief:** the land granted to a vassal in return for his service

**knight:** a man admitted to the fighting class as a mounted master of arms

**manor:** the house and farm of a landlord and the center of a medieval community

**guild:** an organization of merchants or craftsmen, formed to protect their craft or business

**serf:** a servant bound to the place of his birth and obligated to work for the landowner

## Dates to Remember

**795:** Vikings sack the monastery of Lindisfarne on England's east coast: The first Viking raid.

**817:** the "Partition of Aachen." Louis I divides his empire among his sons.

**886:** the Vikings besiege Paris. Hrolf (Rollo) is given Normandy by Charles the Fat.

## Central Characters
**Louis I, the Pious (778–840):** Charlemagne's only surviving son, who divided the Frankish Empire between his four sons, thus causing civil war between himself and his sons

**Hrolf (ca. 911):** (Rollo) the Norwegian Viking who received Normandy from the king of the Franks in Gaul

**Rurik (ca. 968):** Swedish Viking who settled in Russia and founded a kingdom around Novgorod

## Questions for Review
1. Why did the empire of Charlemagne break apart?
2. Where did the Vikings come from? Where did they settle in civilized Europe?
3. What sort of government is feudalism? Why is it a local organization rather than a national one?
4. What duties did a liege owe to a vassal? What duties did a vassal owe to a liege?
5. What is chivalry? What are its ideals?
6. How did serfdom differ from slavery? What advantages did serfs have?
7. Why was the open-field system needed? What advantages did it bring?
8. How did the increase in food production affect the population of Europe?
9. Why did the western European nations expand to the east? How was that done? Why did the new landowners not carry serfdom with them?
10. What were the functions of the medieval guilds? What was an apprentice? A journeyman? How might one become a master in a guild?

## Ideas in Action
1. Read the Old English poem, "The Battle of Maldon." Dramatize the fight and the raid by Vikings on this Saxon English town. How did the defenders show heroism?
2. Find a picture of a moldboard plow. What does it look like? How do you think it was discovered by its unknown inventor?
3. Look carefully at a fireplace and chimney. What is the smoke shelf, and where is it? How is it operated today? Why was the chimney an improvement over an open hole in the roof?

4. Find out why a horse will tolerate an iron shoe nailed to its hoof. What does the shoe do for the horse? How does it keep the horse's hoof from damage?
5. What advantages and disadvantages did medieval people get for living in a city or town? Why did so many people not leave the country and go to the towns? What do you think was attractive about farm life? Is it still attractive? Why or why not?

# Highways and Byways

### Place Names from Danish and Saxon Settlers

During the ninth and tenth centuries, England was overrun by Viking Danes who conquered and then settled on the almost empty lands of northern England. Today there are many English and American names, of both places and families, that came from the names of English villages and towns. The endings of these names indicate whether they were originally Saxon, Danish, or Gaelic.

The ending *–ham* indicates the Old English name for settlement, or village. It is like the word *home*, and is used in Durham, Birmingham, Brigham, and Walsingham. All have the meaning of a settlement by a tribe or family. The ending *–ing* indicates a family or "the child of." The ending *–ton* indicates a town, a village surrounded by a fence or wall. Add *–ton* to *–ing* and then the name of a man or tribe, and the result is something like "Washington." The endings *–stowe*, or *–stead*, indicate a Saxon farm manor, as in Barstowe or Winstead. The ending *–y*, as in Derry or Rushy, is a Gaelic ending, meaning "place of."

Then there are the Viking place names, indicated with *–by*, as in Derby, Willoughby, and Whitby, the site of the famous Synod of Whitby that determined the fate of the medieval English church. The ending *–by* meant a farm barn or "byre" in Danish. Likewise *–thorpe* is a Danish ending, meaning "a plot of land marked out as a claim," as in the name of the state of Georgia's founder, Oglethorpe. Sometimes we see the ending *–scale*, meaning a hut or temporary shelter, as in Windscale.

Saxon and Dane lived side by side in medieval England. We know this because the towns of Allingham and Thoresby both appear less than five miles apart, and they are near Grainsthorpe in the same county.

# Chapter 10: The Medieval Reformation

The Church underwent one of the darkest periods of her history in the 9th and 10th centuries. Feudalism, though it helped save Europe, was destroying the Church. While the power of pope and emperor grew ever weaker, the power of local lords and kings grew ever stronger until they began to see themselves as the masters of their local Churches and all that they possessed.

Throughout western Europe, and particularly in Germany, bishops and abbots of monasteries came to control large tracts of land. Because of this, kings and feudal lords began to treat churchmen just like they treated their secular vassals. And just like vassals, bishops came to possess not only lands and castles, but the right to tax and the authority to administer law. Bishops were not just spiritual but **secular** lords. And since they had to answer only to the king, they became more and more independent of the pope.

Because bishops and abbots became so powerful, the king took great interest in who should be elected to those offices. Unlike secular lords, who married and had children, churchmen were celibate and so could not pass their lands down to sons. The clergy and the people elected their bishop, while the king only gave his approval to the election.

But, in the ninth century, kings and princes wanted to make sure that only men who were faithful to them and their interests would become bishops. They did this by investing the man elected bishop with the symbols of his office—a ring (symbolizing the bishop's marriage with his church) and the crosier (a shepherd's crook, symbolizing that he was a spiritual shepherd).

> **secular:** having to do with worldly or temporal matters, not spiritual

**A medieval wall painting of a bishop**

243

**benefice:** lands and the wealth they produce given as a grant by a secular lord to a member of the clergy; a fief (from Latin *beneficium*, meaning "favor," "privilege," "right")

**lay investiture:** the practice by lay rulers of granting the symbols of spiritual authority to churchmen, such as bishops and abbots

**simony:** the buying and selling of Church offices or privileges for money (named after Simon Magus, who, in the Acts of the Apostles, tried to buy the power of granting the Holy Spirit from Peter and John—see Acts 8: 9–24)

Because this was done before the man was consecrated bishop, it looked as if a bishop received his authority to rule his diocese from his temporal lord, not the Church. By investing the bishop-elect, the king was granting him a **benefice**—the land of the diocese and the wealth it produced. Since no one could be consecrated bishop except those whom the king or lord wanted to invest, secular rulers came to control who would be bishops. This practice, called **lay investiture**, led to a serious conflict between Church and state later on in the Middle Ages.

Because kings and princes were often more concerned about temporal power than the spiritual good of the Church, they did not always choose worthy men to fill high Church offices. They wanted bishops who would be faithful to them first, not the Church. They wanted bishops who were good vassals, not holy shepherds. This meant that many bishops had very little interest in spiritual things and desired wealth and power for themselves. At times, kings and princes outright sold a diocese or abbey to the man who could pay the most for it. This led to the widespread practice of **simony**, the buying and selling of Church offices or privileges for money.

These evils affected not just the bishops, but their priests as well. Priests, too, received benefices and were not always chosen for their spiritual qualifications. In some cases, lords themselves controlled the parish and its benefice, and they exercised absolute power over it and the priest who received it. This state of things affected the moral lives of priests and bishops, and many of them openly lived with women and had families.

The pope himself did not escape the evils of the time. As we shall see, for a time popes became the servants, first of the temporal lords of Rome and then of the emperor himself. By the end of the 10th century, it looked as if the Church was becoming a part of the feudal kingdoms, the servant of the temporal lords. The Church desperately needed reform, but how would it come?

# Reform Begins in the Monasteries

One feudal lord of the 10th century did not seek to use the Church to increase his wealth and political power. He was William, called "the Pious," the duke of Aquitaine in France. In 910, William established a Benedictine monastery at Cluny and made it entirely independent of his authority. William specifically forbade any temporal lord, including his own son, to exercise feudal control over the monastery or appoint its abbot. Instead, he allowed the monks to elect the head of their monastic family, as Benedictine monks had always done. The Cluny monastery owned its land outright and did not hold it as a fief from the duke. On this land Cluny flourished materially and spiritually and became an example to all those wishing to reform monastic life.

The monks at Cluny strove to return to the strict observance of St. Benedict's *Rule*, except in a few particulars. As the *Rule* taught, the monks of Cluny led a regular life of prayer and study, but they departed from Benedict's vision by doing less physical labor. The monastery had the wealth to hire farmworkers. Instead of physical labor, a Cluniac monk was expected to dedicate himself to a deeper study of the truths of Scripture and pass on the learning of the Christian past, and even pagan learning, for the renewal of civil and societal life.

Monasteries formed from Cluny, or those that came under it, eventually spread across western Europe. Like a feudal lord, the abbot of Cluny ruled over each of these far-flung monastic houses. Traditionally, each Benedictine monastery had been independent. Each had its own abbot, who was elected by the community. The Cluniac monasteries, however, were all under the authority of the abbot of Cluny. Each monastery was headed by a **prior**, who was appointed by the abbot of Cluny. Thus, every Cluniac monastery was like a fief of the motherhouse at Cluny.

Cluny not only worked to reform monasticism, but to renew society—for instance, by trying to limit the frequent warfare between feudal lords. Odilo, who became abbot of Cluny in 994, introduced something called the Truce of God into France, and from there it spread throughout Europe. Under the Truce, councils of reform-minded bishops and abbots forbade armed conflict from Wednesday evening until Monday morning and during the whole week for some four months out of the year. But the Truce was not as successful as another approach preached by Cluniac

**The Abbey of Cluny**

**prior:** a superior in a monastery or religious house; second in authority to the abbot

**The gallery of the library at the Abbey of Cîteaux**

monks, called the Peace of God. The Peace was an attempt to preserve certain groups from the horrors of war. Knights were not to harm clergy, monks and nuns, the poor, pilgrims, or even merchants. The Peace represented a Christianization of feudalism and is one of the origins of the code of chivalry.

Cluny worked to reform the spiritual life of the Church by demanding that the clergy be celibate, in keeping with the ideals of the ancient Church. Cluny also preached against all forms of simony and encouraged kings and lords to protect the Church from corrupt clerics who practiced simony. Since civil rulers are the temporal arm of Christendom, said the monks, they have the responsibility to preserve the purity of the clergy and the safety of the ordinary faithful.

Many pious noblemen donated land to Cluny or asked that Cluny send some of its members to reform the monasteries subject to these noblemen. Eventually, some two thousand new monasteries throughout Europe were associated with the abbey of Cluny.

Some feudal lords began to look to Cluny for virtuous and learned men to appoint as bishops. Thus what began as a monastic reform became a way to restore the entire Church to its original purity.

## Cluny's Reform Sparks New Monastic Orders

Cluny was not the only reform movement in the Church of the 9th and 10th centuries. Another movement, the Cistercians, founded at the abbey of Cîteaux in 1098, dedicated themselves to a revival of the strict Benedictine Rule. Due to the influence of St. Bernard of Clairvaux (Clairvaux was a daughter house of Cîteaux), the order grew rapidly during Bernard's lifetime and after. New monastic houses sprang up all over France and Germany.

In company with the monks of Cluny, the Abbey of Cîteaux carried the reform movement beyond France into Spain, Italy, Germany, Hungary, and England. In Spain, the Cistercians started schools, brought wilderness into cultivation, and began to evangelize the lands only recently retaken from the Muslims of Al-Andalus.

Reform also embraced clergymen called "canons." A *canon* was originally any clergyman attached to a church in which there were several clerics. The name comes from the list or canon of a church to which a clergyman signed his name. As part of the reform movement of the 11th and 12th centuries, many groups or chapters of canons adopted a rule (in Latin, *regula*) and were thus called "regular" canons. Most chapters adopted the *Rule of St. Augustine*, which was based on instructions the great St. Augustine of Hippo gave to his clergy.

A reforming canon, St. Norbert, founded a new house of regular canons at Premontre near Laon in France. The life there attracted so many that new foundations and houses were needed. To maintain the ideals of the original establishment, Norbert gave his followers a set of statutes that united the several houses, thus creating an order—the Praemonstratensian order (so called from the Latin word for *Premontre*) or Norbertines. Many Premonstratensian foundations (particularly those in France) became monasteries devoted to prayer, while others (especially those in Germany) became centers for priests who devoted themselves to preaching and the care of souls.

At the Cathedral School of Reims in France, an early reform center for the Church, a certain star pupil was introduced to all the power and luxury that the medieval church could give. Bruno of Cologne rose quickly in the church. Though lords and bishops of France honored him as a scholar and writer and counselor, Bruno decided to abandon the comfortable life he could have had and retired to a hermitage.

St. Hugh, the bishop of Grenoble, gave Bruno a piece of land in the "Desert" of Chartreuse, a high, mountainous valley in the French Alps. There Bruno lived with six companions and built hermit cells. His order remained dedicated to poverty and hard work, farming their poor and unproductive mountain retreat and making their income from the copying of books. The order is now called the Carthusian Order after Chartreuse, the place of its founding. St. Bruno died in 1101 while serving as adviser to Pope Urban II in Rome.

**Saint Bernard of Clairvaux (1090–1153)**

# Rebirth of the Empire

Though the Christian empire founded by Charlemagne decayed under subsequent Frankish kings, it never died out as an ideal. Ironically, it revived under the rule of a duke of the Saxons, the people who were Charlemagne's great enemy.

In the 9th and 10th centuries, the duke of the Saxons was only one of the great powers ruling over the lands that made up Germany. The others were the dukes of Bavaria, Franconia, Frisia, Swabia, and Upper and Lower Lotharingia (Lorraine). Feudalism was not common in Germany, except along its western border with France. The manorial system, too, had not yet spread far into Germany. Most German peasants were free men and small landowners.

Germany did not suffer from Saracen invasions, for the Alps proved too difficult an obstacle for the Muslim armies to cross. And while the Vikings did sail up German rivers to plunder and destroy, Germany did not suffer greatly at their hands, nor did Norse settlements become established in Germany. Too, since Germany was not as ancient a civilization or as wealthy as Gaul, Spain, and Italy, it did not tempt the Vikings as much as those lands did. Moreover, unlike the farmers of Gaul, who had long since ceased to be warriors and were helpless when the government failed to defend them, German society was still largely tribal. Every man and boy was trained in the use of spears, swords, and battle-axes. The Vikings faced a more formidable reception when they disembarked in Germany than when they raided Gaul or Italy.

The "Magdeburg Rider" statute, thought to be of Otto I

But the Germans did suffer from the Magyars, who swept up the Danube Valley and into Germany at the end of the ninth century. For over 50 years, Germans underwent surprise attacks of these wild and swift horsemen.

The German warriors fought these barbarians with little success. The Magyars appeared from nowhere, struck swiftly from horseback, and used their arrows to deadly effect. First, the German kings constructed a line of frontier forts to protect against attack. Then they used heavy, armored cavalry against the lighter horses and less well-armed invaders.

The decisive victory against the Magyars occurred near the city of Augsburg in Bavaria in 955. There—on a field near the river Lech—Otto, the duke of Saxony, was joined by the forces of the dukes of Bavaria, Franconia, Lotharingia, and Swabia and the king of Bohemia. Though outnumbered by the Magyars, the Germans under Otto routed their enemy. The Magyars would never invade Germany again. On the field of battle, called Lechfeld, the German lords raised Otto on their shields according to the ancient German custom and proclaimed him emperor.

## Otto I, King and Emperor

The lords of Germany had elected Otto king of Germany in 936, nineteen years before the Battle of Lechfeld. Otto had succeeded his father, Henry the "Fowler," who had been elected king of Germany before him.

Since becoming king, Otto—taking Charlemagne as his ideal—had worked to unite all of Germany under his rule. To provide justice to the vast German territories, Otto needed local administrators. The German dukes and counts, however, resisted his attempts to bring them firmly under his control. Otto attempted to overcome their opposition by installing members of his family, especially his sons and sons-in-law, as dukes. But even they quickly became more concerned about their local concerns than about the unity of the German kingdom.

Otto's solution was to prune back the power of the great feudal lords, the dukes and counts, by making the bishops independent of the temporal lords. To do this, Otto gave the bishops royal lands that were not in use. The Church thus came to own one-third of the farmland of Germany and so could control the wealth of the kingdom. The bishops and abbots saw to it that the lay lords continued to serve a united kingdom. This reduced the power of the lay lords, leaving them less capable of rebellion.

The bishops proved more loyal to the king than the dukes and counts had been. When a duke or count died, his son inherited his office. Since the son owed his position to his birth, not to the king, he was not necessarily loyal to the king. A bishop, however, was unmarried by Church law and so had no legitimate heir to whom he could give his lands. It was the king who appointed the new bishops and abbots—and he made sure to appoint only men who were loyal to him.

Unlike other kings and lords, however, Otto was concerned for the spiritual good of the Church. He wanted not only loyal bishops, but holy bishops who were committed to Church reform and to rooting out simony and the other evils that had corrupted the Church. Yet, Otto treated the Church as if it were subject to the king. He looked upon himself as the supreme head of everything in Germany, including the Church. The king, he thought, was supreme lord of all things temporal and spiritual.

# 250 LIGHT TO THE NATIONS: The History of Christian Civilization

The Empire of Otto I the Great, ca. 963. The empire included Germany as well as Slavic lands to the east and disputed regions such as Lorraine to the west.

## The Pope and the Emperor

Early in his reign, Otto I was forced to deal with an international scandal involving the pope. This scandal was much more serious than the sins of some local bishop in Germany, since it had to do with the spiritual head of Christendom. Otto had to clean it up, or else forfeit the reform he was promoting in the Church in his homeland.

The pope, who was the feudal lord of central Italy, held a position of great political power. For this reason the great families, who were powerful vassals of the pope, coveted the papal office for their sons. As a result, intrigue, treachery, and murder came to surround the see of Peter. From 896 to 904 there was, on the average, one pope a year. The 10th century saw worse, and it has been called "the iron age of the papacy." For several decades Rome was controlled by two women, Theodora and her daughter Marozia, who succeeded in placing Marozia's corrupt and worldly son in the papal office as Pope John XI (reigned 931–936).

Otto I brought all this scandal and corruption to a halt. In 962, the unworthy Pope John XII (reigned 955–964) invited Otto to come to Italy to bring peace and unity to that troubled land. Otto fulfilled the pope's wish, and John crowned him Emperor of the Romans on February 2, 962. As emperor, Otto declared himself a successor of Charlemagne and combined his German territories with the lands and cities of northern Italy. Thus was born the Roman Empire of the Germans.

The result was only partially what Pope John expected. Otto ruled Italy by the same means he used in Germany—he appointed loyal, virtuous, and learned men as bishops in his new lands. This included popes. When John eventually turned against Otto, joining forces with the emperor's enemies, Otto deposed him and made Leo VIII pope in his place. When Leo died, Otto chose John XIII as his successor. Otto came to control the papacy just as he did the Church in Germany.

Otto's many accomplishments were remarkable. He rivaled his predecessor, Charlemagne, in making his empire Christian, civilized, and prosperous. He showed that political power is based on a leader's ability and willingness to provide protection and justice for his people. He established a fair and just system of law courts and appointed royal judges to preside over them. Otto had to deal with troublesome neighbors to the east—the Wends, Poles, and Magyars—and sent missionaries to convert them. He kept the new churches in Poland and Hungary (the land of the Magyars) under the supervision of German archbishops to ensure that the new churches helped to control their countrymen.

Otto did much to reform and strengthen the Church, but at a great price. Making the bishops and the popes basically servants of the

## Two Women Poets Who Influenced the Middle Ages

The brilliance of Otto's Roman Empire of the Germans owed much to several great women. In medieval Germany, women's monastic schools achieved a high level of learning and were the equals of the monastic schools for men. Women's monastic schools produced several great women poets and scholars who helped bring about a revival of art and learning, called the Ottonian Renaissance, after the Emperor Otto I.

The first recorded European playwright after Roman times was a woman poet of medieval Germany. Hroswitha of Gandersheim (ca. 935–ca. 1002) came from a noble family. Like many parents of the time, Hroswitha's mother and father sent her to a monastery while she was still a child. At the height of her poetical powers, she turned to writing plays with Christian themes, especially of miraculous occurrences in history.

Later in life Hroswitha devoted herself to history, celebrating the triumphs of Otto I in her *Deeds of Otto* (967) and telling in verse the history of her own monastery, in the *Origin of the Abbey of Gandersheim*. Hroswitha died peacefully in 1002 at her monastery in Gandersheim.

A century later, Hroswitha's example and poetic creation were matched by another poetess—the saintly abbess named Hildegard of Bingen. Like Hroswitha, St. Hildegard (born in 1098) entered religious life as a child of eight years. She lived at the house of a holy nun, Blessed Jutta. Little Hildegard was so sickly she could barely walk, and her eyes were so poor that she had difficulty reading and writing. Yet despite her disabilities, Hildegard learned to read the Roman classics in Latin and mastered the rudiments of musical notation.

**Hroswitha**

Hildegard was not only a major poet of her time, but a mathematician, musician, medical scholar, and monastic reformer. Hildegard received visions, which were recorded by secretaries at the command of her bishop and Pope Eugenius II. Considered a seer and prophetess, Hildegard was called the Sybil of the Rhine. As a scholar and political thinker, Hildegard was sought out by the major leaders of Church and state for her advice and analysis of events. Theologians consulted Hildegard on difficult issues of doctrine. St. Bernard of Clairvaux is said to have introduced her to the pope as a "prophetess of God."

Hildegard met with leaders of the German Church and with princes, admonishing and encouraging them to rise to the highest of Christian ideals. She died peacefully in September of 1179. The emperor and many other heads of church and state honored her at her death. She was never formally canonized a saint, but her name is recorded in the Roman Martyrology as if she were. Her feast day is September 17. She is honored with pilgrimages to her shrine and tomb to this day.

**Hildegard**

emperor would have dangerous results in the not too distant future.

## The Second Otto

Otto II was only 18 years old when his father's death left him sole ruler of the Roman Empire of the Germans. Otto II, however, cared less than his father had for his German territories. The new emperor was Burgundian and Italian on his mother's side, and his wife, Theophano, was the daughter of the Byzantine emperor. Through his wife's influence, Otto II came to think of his role as emperor as being more important than his role as king of the Germans.

With the help of the German bishops, Otto II was able to make his German lands safe and secure from rebellions. The bishops helped stem invasions from the East by converting the Slavic peoples to Christianity and introducing them to civilization.

With Germany secure, Otto II turned his attention to Italy. He began a campaign to sweep the Muslims once and for all out of the Italian "boot." In 981 and 982, he carried on a successful war in southern Italy, taking the cities of Salerno, Bari, and Taranto. But in the summer of 982, a traitorous alliance of Byzantine Greeks and Sicilian Muslims defeated Otto at Crotona. In returning from that battle, Otto was ambushed on a narrow road and, only by sheer luck, escaped with his life. His whole army was almost destroyed.

After the defeat at Crotona, the powerful **magnates** of both Germany and Italy met at a **diet**, or assembly, in Verona and resolved on a holy war against the Muslims. The lords chose Otto's 3-year-old son (also named Otto) to be their king in case the German emperor died in the war.

Though Otto II assembled a mighty force to attack the Muslims in Sicily, he was unable to carry out his war. The lords of Venice, joining with the Muslims and the Byzantines, refused to ship the emperor's army to Sicily. (Venice carried on a good deal of trade with the Muslims and did not want to anger them.) Then other troubles interrupted the war. A rebellion in Poland forced Otto to send troops back to Germany. While in Rome, where he chose a new pope to succeed the deceased Benedict VII, the emperor caught a deadly fever and died on December 7, 983. He was only 28 years old. His son and heir, Otto III, was not quite 4.

Coronation of St. Stephen

**magnate:** one who has rank, power, or influence; a prince, duke, count, margrave, etc.

**diet:** an assembly of princes gathered to make laws or decide on measures a government should take

## Otto III, Emperor and Reformer

When his mother, the Princess Theophano of Byzantium, died in 991, Otto III was only 12. Two churchmen, the bishops of Mainz and Hildesheim, took control of the young king's education. Otto was educated in Roman history and literature and raised even less in the German way than his father had been.

Young Otto was deeply influenced by the Cluniac reform movement. He became enthusiastically religious, seeking out holy places and inspired hermits. The state of the Church during his time seemed to him to call for a champion and house cleaner. Further, from his mother's teaching Otto had inherited the Byzantine ideas of the sacredness of the empire. The young king's mind was filled with glowing images of a kingdom of God on earth, in which pope and emperor ruled in harmony over a world of peace and prosperity. His ideals were generous, noble, and unselfish, even if they were impractical for so troubled an age.

When Otto III was old enough to rule on his own, he crossed the Alps to be crowned emperor at Rome. As he entered the Lombard plain, a delegation of Roman nobles met him with news that the see of Rome was vacant. They begged Otto to appoint a new pope. The young king at once chose his cousin Bruno, who was 24 years old and a zealous champion of the Cluniac reforms.

Bruno took the name of Gregory V. On May 21, 996, he crowned Otto as the Roman emperor. Gregory V, however, died soon after, leaving the city again without a pope. Otto then raised Gerbert of Aurillac to the papal throne. In Gerbert, Otto found the man who could understand his dream of a sacred empire and help him bring it to reality.

**A depiction of Otto III from his prayer book. A monk presents the prayer book to the emperor.**

## The Second Pope Sylvester

Gerbert of Aurillac had been Otto III's tutor. The boy and the adult scholar had become fast friends and shared an enthusiasm for reform of Church and state.

Gerbert of Aurillac was born in about 945 to a poor farm family in southern France. After his parents' death, Gerbert went to live with the monks of Aurillac. There he received an excellent education in Latin and the literature of classical antiquity. After spending some time in Muslim Spain, where he studied mathematics and natural science, Gerbert went to Rome. Pope John XIII introduced him to Otto I, who sent him to study philosophy at the cathedral school at Reims, where Gerbert soon became a teacher. After serving as archbishop of Reims, Gerbert went to the imperial court as Otto III's teacher.

When he was elected pope, Gerbert took the name of Sylvester II. He did so in memory of Pope St. Sylvester, who according to legend had baptized the Emperor Constantine. With his friend, Emperor Otto III, Sylvester II labored to reform the Church and to renew Christian society everywhere.

Pope Sylvester and Otto III dreamed of a Europe united not by power but by the Christian Faith. Indeed, Otto often referred to himself as "the Servant of Jesus Christ." In the winter of 999–1000, Otto entered the newly formed nation of Poland—not at the head of a conquering army but as a simple pilgrim to the shrine of the martyr, St. Adalbert of Prague, who had been a missionary to Poland.

Otto brought to Poland a document from Pope Sylvester II establishing an archbishopric at the Polish city of Gnesen. By this act Otto made the Polish Church independent of the German Church. Otto treated the Polish ruler as his "brother and co-ruler" rather than as his vassal. The fact that Otto III recognized the independence of Poland troubled the German princes. The first two Ottos had sought to extend German control over the eastern lands of Poland, and now Otto III was seemingly destroying everything his father and grandfather had worked for.

**St. Stephen I, from a medieval chronicle**

Otto III and Sylvester II also helped make Hungary, the land of the Magyars, an independent Christian kingdom. The pope organized a Hungarian Church, free of German control. And both pope and emperor recognized the Christian Magyar chieftain, Stephen, as king of Hungary. Pope Sylvester sent to King Stephen I the gift of a royal crown that Hungary reveres to this day as "St. Stephen's Crown."

But Otto's imperial dreams ended with his early death at the age of 22. In 1002, he died, some say, from malaria. Pope Sylvester II died a year later.

The Ottos ruled Germany and the Roman Empire for 66 years. After the death of Otto III, Henry, the son of the duke of Bavaria, became emperor. Henry II favored the reforms of the Church begun by the Cluniac monks and helped bring about reforms in the German Church as well as encouraging missionary work in the Slavic lands. The Catholic Church recognizes Henry and his wife, Kunigunde, as saints.

# The Investiture Conflict: Second Stage of Church Reform

The German emperors of the 10th and 11th centuries supported the reform movement by appointing capable and pious abbots, bishops, and even popes. During this period, Church and state worked together to reform the Church. The chief power to push reform, however, was the emperor, who continued to insist on absolute loyalty from bishops and popes.

Emperor Henry III (1017–1056), like his predecessors, enthusiastically supported the reform movement while continuing to hold complete control over the Church. For instance, in 1046, when three men in Rome each claimed to be pope, Henry marched his army to Italy and at the Council of Sutri deposed all three. He then appointed one of his own reform bishops as pope. In this way, the reform movement was established in Rome. Yet the danger continued that a less reform-minded emperor than Henry III might appoint an unworthy man as pope.

Pope Urban II (left), surrounded by cardinals, consecrates the church of Cluny.

## The Pope's New Electors—the College of Cardinals

To make the appointment of an unworthy pope impossible, the reformers tried to improve the method for choosing a new pope. In 1059, Pope Nicholas II issued a Papal Election Decree that basically was a declaration of independence of the Church from the state.

The election decree said that, as in the early Church, the clergy and people were to elect the pope. Nicholas appointed 7 bishops of the Roman suburbs, the 28 pastors of the most important parishes in Rome, and 18 deacons who assisted the pope in governing the

Church, to be representatives of the clergy. These chief, or "cardinal," clergy were to choose the next bishop of Rome and then seek the approval of the rest of the clergy and people of the city. This was the beginning of the College of Cardinals, which continues to elect popes to this day.

Pope Nicholas allowed the emperor the right to approve the election of a pope. But this was a favor granted by the pope. It showed that the pope, not the emperor, was to decide how papal elections would go.

## Pope Hildebrand

Freed themselves from lay control, the popes now tried to free the rest of the Church from lay control. The Church's champion in this struggle was Hildebrand, archdeacon of Rome and advocate of the Cluniac reforms. Hildebrand was elected pope in 1073 as Gregory VII.

To reform the rest of the Church, Gregory VII sent out **legates**, who encouraged local Church councils to attack abuses and appoint only men of virtue and learning as clergymen. Like the popes before him, Gregory also forbade the practice of simony.

**legate:** an official representative or emissary

Simony, however, was just what Emperor Henry IV, the son of Henry III, was practicing. Henry IV not only appointed bishops, but he sold the appointments. As kings and lords had been doing for two centuries, Henry invested new bishops-elect with the symbols of their office, the ring and crosier. Pope Gregory, however, declared that this practice of lay investiture must stop. Only the Church, said the pope, had the right to invest bishops because a bishop's authority comes not from kings and emperors, but from God through the Church.

In 1075, Gregory forbade any layman from investing bishops or clergy of any sort. Any who did so, he said, would be excommunicated—cast out from the Church. Henry IV, however, had no intention of obeying the pope. He continued to practice lay investiture and to recognize as bishops those who had been excommunicated for having bought their office from him. Henry told the pope that the emperor receives his right to rule from God—something no one in those days, including Gregory, would have

**Woodcut of Pope Gregory VII (Hildebrand): (1020–1085)**

**Henry IV, king of Germany and Holy Roman emperor, 1050–1106. Copper engraving**

denied. But Henry claimed much more. He insisted that no one could judge him or his actions, since he was God's representative on Earth.

Henry believed it was the king's duty, not the pope's, to reform the Church. Priests, bishops, and even the pope, he thought, had to obey him in all matters except prayer for the world. Henry's position had centuries of custom on its side. Even many reformers did not fully agree with Gregory that kings could not control bishops. They remembered the good things the emperors from Otto I to Henry III had done for the Church.

There was, of course, another reason that Henry resisted Gregory's attempt to eliminate lay investiture. To Gregory it meant freedom for the Church, but to the emperor it meant destruction for the empire. The emperor needed his bishops and abbots to help him govern the empire. If he did not appoint these churchmen, he could not be sure that new bishops and abbots would be loyal to him. For Gregory, however, the Church's freedom was more important than the good of the empire.

On January 24, 1076, Henry declared that "Hildebrand," as he insultingly called Gregory, was no longer the pope. Hildebrand, however, would not back down. In February 1076, the pope excommunicated and deposed Henry, releasing his subjects from their oaths of allegiance to him. The lords of Germany rebelled against Henry. At the Diet of Tribur in October 1076, the lords decided that a council headed by Gregory would judge whether Henry should remain emperor. If Henry remained excommunicated for more than a year, the diet said it would elect a new king.

Gregory did not claim he had the right to choose whomever he wished as emperor. That was the function of the German princes. Gregory thought his own function was to rule on the moral question of whether the ruler was providing justice. According to the reformers, the clergy could judge the ruler only in moral questions. And such a question had arisen when the king interfered with the spiritual welfare of others, as Gregory thought Henry had done by appointing unqualified bishops and by selling Church offices.

## The Emperor in the Snow

Henry IV, however, scored a diplomatic victory over Pope Gregory and the German rebels. In 1077, Henry evaded the ambushes of his rebellious subjects and crossed the Alps to Italy, where the pope was staying at the castle of Canossa. For three days, Henry stood barefoot in the snow and cold outside the castle. He was a touching figure, pleading for repentance and begging the pope to absolve him. Finally Gregory, moved by sympathy, absolved Henry. Forgiven by the pope, Henry reclaimed his powers as emperor. The German lords could not refuse to obey him without risking excommunication themselves. They would be sinning if they refused to give their allegiance to the emperor, now that the pope had forgiven him.

Henry IV, excommunicated by Pope Gregory VII in 1076, is seen in this contemporary manuscript illumination at St. Nicholas's Chapel at Canossa in 1077 asking Matilda of Tuscany and the Abbot of Cluny to intercede for him with the pope.

**antipope:** one who claims to be pope while the true pope is ruling

But Henry returned to his practice of simony and lay investiture. When Gregory sent word of a second excommunication, Henry led an army into Italy. After a three-week siege, Rome fell to Henry, who set up an **antipope** in place of Gregory. Gregory fled to the Castel Sant'Angelo, where the emperor almost took him prisoner. But the pope's vassal Robert Guiscard, leading an army of Normans, rescued the pope and took him to their lands in southern Italy.

At Salerno in southern Italy, Pope St. Gregory died on May 25, 1085. His last words were a sad rephrasing of a verse from Psalm 44 (in the Vulgate): "I have loved justice and hated iniquity, and so I die in exile."

# The Concordat of Worms: Final Stage of Church Reform

The cause of Church reform, however, did not end with the death of Gregory VII. The popes after him continued to fight over lay investiture and simony against Henry IV and his son, Henry V. One pope, Paschal II, even said the Church should give up all her temporal possessions and live off the donations of the faithful. In that way, kings and lords would have no reason to want to control the Church. But this plan, even if noble, was impractical. The Church without possessions would have been left at the complete mercy of the state.

Like his father, Henry V defied the popes. He even took Paschal II prisoner and forced Paschal's successor, Pope Gelasius II, to flee to Cluny while the emperor set up an antipope in his place. The next pope, Calixtus II, excommunicated Henry and said his subjects no longer had to obey him. Threatened by rebellions in both Italy and Germany, Henry had to come to an agreement with the pope.

**canon lawyer:** an expert in canon (or Church) law

The agreement was a compromise between Church and empire. Since the death of Gregory VII, theologians and **canon lawyers** had come to the conclusion that, since bishops and abbots were spiritual *and* temporal rulers, both the Church and the emperor had an interest in choosing who should fill these offices. This being the case, said these theologians, a Church official should bestow on bishops the ring and crosier (as symbols of the spiritual authority), while the temporal ruler should bestow the symbols and powers of temporal administration.

These ideas became the basis for a kind of treaty signed in 1122 by pope and emperor. The treaty was called the Concordat of Worms (Worms being a city in Germany). The **concordat** provided for two methods of selecting a bishop in the empire. In Germany there was to be a free election of the candidate (the goal of the reformers), to be held in the presence of the emperor or of his representative (to recognize the rights of the temporal ruler). After the election, the ruler was to give the bishop-elect the symbols of his office as an imperial administrator. Only then was another bishop to consecrate the bishop-elect and invest him with the ring and crosier. Thus in Germany the emperor could not appoint bishops, but he could veto the election of a man whom he did not wish to have as an imperial administrator.

> **concordat:** an agreement, compact, or covenant

In Italy, said the concordat, a bishop was to be consecrated after a free election. Within six months of the election, the emperor was to give him the symbols of temporal authority. The emperor, however, had no right to veto the election of a bishop in Italy. This meant he could not ensure that men who were loyal to him would be bishops there. Without loyal bishops in Italy, the emperor's power there would grow weaker. As in Germany, the emperor had controlled Italy by controlling its bishops.

# Frederick Barbarossa

In Germany, the Church remained free for almost half a century after the Concordat of Worms. The two emperors following Henry V generally did not veto the election of bishops. With Frederick I —usually called Barbarossa ("Red Beard")—things were different. His reign of 38 years (1152–1190) was one of almost continual warfare with the pope. He led invasions of Italy, installed anti-popes, and appointed bishops who would do what he wanted them to do.

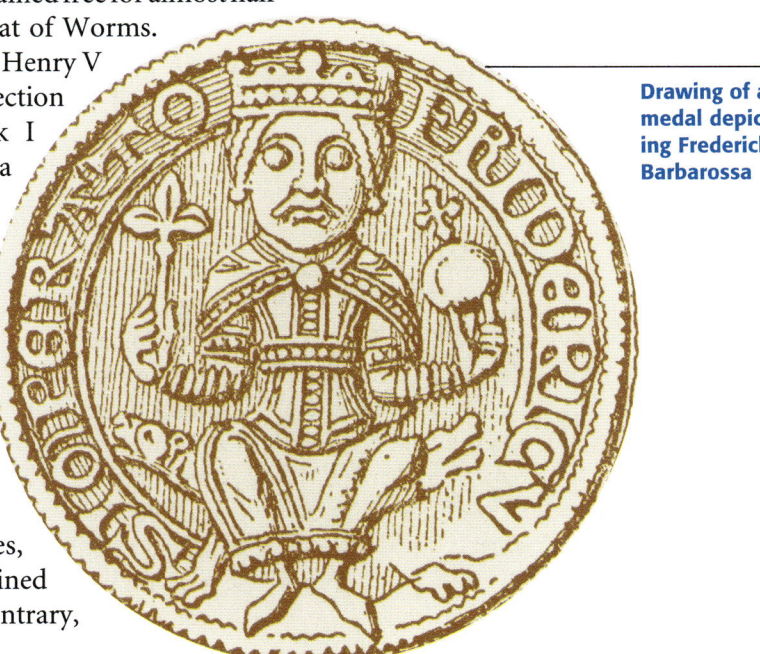

Drawing of a gold medal depicting Frederick Barbarossa

Yet, despite appearances, Frederick I was not a determined foe of the Church. On the contrary, he was a sincerely religious man who was to die en route to the Holy Land while trying to recapture it for Christendom. His reign illustrates well that the Investiture Conflict was a battle between Christians who disagreed on how Church and state should be governed.

Frederick attempted to reestablish the power of the empire over Italy. When the city of Milan resisted him, he leveled it to the ground. Because of this, many northern Italian cities became allies of the papacy against the emperor and eventually defeated the imperial army at Legnano in 1176. After Legnano, Frederick made peace with the pope. At St. Mark's Cathedral in Venice, the emperor humbly knelt at the feet of Pope Alexander III and begged his forgiveness.

In 1186 Frederick arranged the marriage of his son Henry to Constance, heiress of the kingdom of Sicily, which included southern Italy as well as the island of Sicily itself. This was a clever move, for it meant that the Papal States would be surrounded by lands controlled by Henry when he became emperor. Southern Italy once provided a refuge for the popes when the emperor threatened them. But with Henry controlling the kingdom of Sicily, the popes had nowhere to flee if they were in danger.

The papacy, however, survived the short reign of Henry VI (1190–1197). When he died, struggles in Germany over who should be the next emperor gave the Church a welcome breathing space during which those who favored Church reform could enjoy further triumphs.

# Chapter Review

## Summary

- The period from about 1000 to 1300 has been called the "Medieval Reformation." Reformers wanted to purify the lives of the clergy and to end abuses, such as simony and lay investiture.
- Reform of the Church began at the Benedictine monastery of Cluny, founded in 910. Daughter houses of Cluny spread all over Europe. Cluniac monks wanted to eliminate simony and encourage clerical celibacy. They also promoted measures to limit feudal warfare: the Peace of God and the Truce of God.
- Other reforming monastic orders inspired by Cluny were the Cistercians, Carthusians, and the Praemonstratensians or Norbertines.
- Otto I, king of Germany, defeated the Magyars at the battle of Lechfeld in 955. Otto used the Church to unite his kingdom and appointed

bishops. But he was careful to appoint only good, reform-minded men as bishops in the German Church.
- Otto I helped reform the papacy. The election of pope had been under the control of noble families in Rome, who did not appoint worthy men to head the Church. After Pope John XII crowned him emperor of the Romans, Otto undertook to reform the Roman Church. He appointed worthy men to the office of pope.
- Otto I had made the Roman Empire of the Germans a prosperous, united empire. His son, Otto II, was instrumental in converting the Slavic peoples to the Christian Faith.
- Emperor Otto III worked with Pope Sylvester II to reform the Church and society. Both Otto and Sylvester made the Churches in Poland and Hungary independent from the German Church and supported the crowning of Stephen I as king of Hungary.
- After the Ottos, the Church sought to gain greater independence from temporal rulers. In 1059, Pope Nicholas II established the College of Cardinals as a means of freeing the Church from lay control. Pope Gregory VII sought to free the Church entirely from the control of lay lords by fighting against simony and by forbidding the practice of lay investiture.
- Emperor Henry IV resisted Pope Gregory VII's attempts to end lay investiture. After the pope excommunicated the emperor twice, Henry marched into Italy and forced Gregory into exile in southern Italy, where he died.
- The Investiture Conflict ended in a compromise, called the Concordat of Worms. The concordat decreed that the emperor would give up investing bishops with the symbols of spiritual authority. He could continue to invest bishops with the symbols of temporal authority, but only after they had been elected by the Church. In Germany, but not in the lands south of the Alps, the emperor or his representative would be present at the election of bishops.
- The emperors Frederick I ("Barbarossa") and Henry VI renewed conflict with the Church. In trying to control Italy, Frederick was opposed by the pope as well as by the northern Italian city-states.

## Key Concepts

**Roman Empire of the Germans:** the German kingdom raised by the pope to the imperial title once held by Charlemagne

**benefice:** lands and the wealth they produce, given as a grant by a secular lord to a member of the clergy; a fief
**investiture:** the granting of the symbols of spiritual and temporal authority to a bishop
**lay investiture:** the practice by lay rulers of granting the symbols of spiritual authority to churchmen, such as bishops and abbots
**secular:** having to do with worldly or temporal matters, not spiritual
**simony:** the buying and selling of Church offices or privileges for money
**Cluniac reform:** the beginning of the medieval reformation
**College of Cardinals:** the electors of a pope, established by Pope Nicholas II
**antipope:** one who claims to be pope while the true pope is ruling

## Dates to Remember
**910:** founding of the Abbey of Cluny
**955:** Battle of Lechfeld, where Otto I defeated the Magyars
**1059:** College of Cardinals established by Pope Nicholas II
**1077:** Emperor Henry IV's penance in the snow before Pope Gregory VII at Canossa
**1122:** Concordat of Worms

## Central Characters
**Otto I (936–973):** first Roman Emperor of the Germans
**Otto II (955–983):** second Roman Emperor of the Germans
**Otto III (971–1002):** third and last of the Ottos; reform emperor
**Sylvester II (945–1003):** Gerbert of Aurillac; pope, scholar, reformer
**Gregory VII (1020–1085):** Hildebrand; pope and reformer
**Henry IV (1050–1106):** the German Roman emperor who fought Gregory VII over the right of investiture

## Questions for Review
1. What problems in the Church did the medieval reformation seek to correct?
2. How was the Abbey of Cluny different from other abbeys and monasteries at the time it was founded?
3. What were the ways Cluny sought to reform Church and society?
4. What new orders besides Cluny came out of the medieval reform?
5. Why did the Emperor Otto I give the bishops in Germany royal lands?
6. What was Otto III's great dream for the empire?
7. Why did Pope Nicholas II establish the College of Cardinals?

8. What was the Investiture Conflict? Why did kings and emperors want to have control of their bishops? Why did the pope want that right?
9. What was the Concordat of Worms? What problem did it solve and how?

**Ideas in Action**
1. Make a map of medieval Germany. Show the Empire and the several duchies that were part of it.
2. Why should it make so much difference who invests a bishop with the symbols of his office? Think about the appointment of a class president—who should give him his authority, the teacher or the parish minister? Consider the appointment of a new school principal—should the school board or the mayor of the city appoint her? Why does it matter?
3. Report on one of the existing reform orders today: Cistercian, Carthusian, or Norbertine. What is its way of life, its dress (habit)? What makes it different from other orders?

# Highways and Byways

### A Medieval Mathematician
He had come to the monastery of Aurillac as a penniless orphan. Even so, the monks soon recognized young Gerbert's exceptional abilities.

The abbot of Aurillac decided to send his brilliant young monk to school in Muslim Spain, to a city now called Barcelona. From the advanced schools of the Muslims, Gerbert could acquire a deeper and more current knowledge of mathematics and science (especially astronomy) than the French schools of the time could offer.

Gerbert was especially fascinated by scientific learning. On returning to Christian lands, he brought with him an abacus for calculation and a globe for studying astronomy. These two tools were unknown to his students and colleagues, and some began to think they had magical powers.

Emperor Otto I gave Gerbert permission to study philosophy at the cathedral school at Reims in France. There Gerbert became headmaster of the school, where he initiated the study of what scholars of his time called "arithmetic"—the philosophic meanings of numbers and the four functions of adding, subtracting, multiplying, and dividing. Medieval arithmetic had not yet become purely a method of calculating sums, and the philosophical study of numbers brought Gerbert and his students to explore other aspects of God's creation as well as numbers. Gerbert trained his students to use the abacus.

When he became Pope Sylvester II, the scholar and scientist never forgot the sciences. He supported the young scholars and mathematicians who flocked to Rome to be his students.

Chapter 11

# The New Nations: Spain, England, and France

After the Muslim conquest of Iberia in 711, the kings of the little Christian kingdom of Asturias, in the mountainous northwest part of Spain, continued to defend their lands against Moorish conquest. By the time Don Pelayo's great-grandson, Alfonso II "the Chaste," ascended the throne in 791, the people of Asturias had a clear sense of identity and purpose. They knew they were Christian, and that their goals were to reconquer the entire Iberian Peninsula and recreate the united kingdom of their forefathers.

And God seemed to favor their goal of reconquest by sending them—as a heavenly *conquistador*—the Apostle, St. James.

A Spanish legend says that after James the Apostle, the brother of John, was beheaded in the Holy Land in A.D. 44, a group of his disciples took his casket by sea to Hispania for burial. They built a small mausoleum for his remains in the northwest, in Galicia. As time passed, people gradually ceased visiting the holy site. It deteriorated and eventually was forgotten.

The tomb of St. James (or *Santiago* in Spanish) was rediscovered in 813 in Galicia, when Alfonso II ruled Asturias. The Christian fighters in northern Spain thought the discovery that one of the Twelve Apostles was buried among them was a sign that God fought on their side against Islam. St. James, they believed, would help them turn back the infidels who had taken the land of their ancestors. Alfonso II built the first medieval church over the ruins of the first-century tomb. Around the church he founded, there arose the town now called Santiago de Compostella.

According to Spanish tradition, Santiago appeared personally in numerous battles in support of the Christians as they faced the Muslims. A Spanish image of Santiago, mounted on a white horse and brandishing a sword, is called *Santiago Matamoros*, or "St. James the Moorslayer."

**A statue of St. James the Apostle at the Cathedral of Santiago de Compostela, Galicia, Spain**

267

# Beginnings of the Reconquest

The late ninth century, when Alfonso III "The Great" was king in Asturias, was a time of great turmoil in Al-Andalus. The Muslim lands were a mixture of racial and religious groups. There were Arabs and Syrians from Asia and Berbers from North Africa. There were Muwalladun, the descendents of Latin and Visigothic Christians who had converted to Islam. Also living among the Muslims were the Christians—called Mozarabs—who had kept their religion, as well as a small Jewish population called the **Sephardim**. These different groups fought frequently with each other. Alfonso III welcomed their bickering, which brought disunity to Al-Andalus. The king aided rebellions in Al-Andalus and welcomed the Mozarabs, who fled to Asturias.

Alfonso III sent these fugitives from Muslim Spain to settle the frontiers of his kingdom. The frontier southeast of Asturias soon had so many new forts, strongholds, and small castles that the Moors called this region Castile—"land of castles."

Colonizing new lands between Christendom and the Muslim parts of Spain was dangerous. People living in the areas along the border, exposed as they were to enemy raids, developed a unique culture. These Spanish frontiersmen were extraordinarily religious, independent, and self-reliant. They tended to take the law into their own hands and to count on their neighbors rather than the king for defense and support. Their Catholic religion was simple and fervent. They were loyal to the Catholic clergy they had come to trust and to the Faith that had sustained them and their ancestors since the Moorish conquest in the eighth century.

After Alfonso III's death in the early 10th century, the Christians pushed the frontier southward. It became clear to them that the capital of the realm needed to be closer to the border. After the king moved his capital from Oviedo in Asturias to León further south, the kingdom of Asturias became the kingdom of León.

Christian Spain, however, was soon divided among different realms—and despite the Moslem threat, they were rivals of each other. León formed one kingdom; Castile, another. Then there was the

**Sephardim:** European Jews who originally settled in Spain and Portugal and later spread to other parts of the world. *Sephardim* is the plural of *Sephardi*.

The Tajo River, near Toledo, in La Mancha, Spain

**Map of medieval Spain**

Kingdom of León
Kingdom of Navarre
Kingdom of Castile
Kingdom of Almohades
Kingdom of Portugal
Kingdom of Aragon

**Entrance to a church in Zamora, Spain**

Basque kingdom of Navarre to the north and the kingdom of Aragon to the east. Finally, however, King Alfonso VI (1065–1109) was able to unite León, Castile, and Navarre under his rule. Thus began a new era in Spanish history.

## Reconquest of Toledo

During Alfonso VI's reign, Al-Qadir—the Muslim ruler of Toledo, the ancient Visigothic capital on the Tagus River in central Spain—was threatened

Spanish city of Toledo

by enemies within his own kingdom. Al-Qadir asked Alfonso for help, and in 1079 the king sent a Christian army to Toledo. When Muslims in Toledo saw Alfonso's Christian soldiers stationed in their land, they deposed Al-Qadir and installed another monarch.

The deposed Al-Qadir appealed to Alfonso again. The king agreed to help him regain his throne, but for a stiff payment. Once returned to his throne, Al-Qadir had to give Alfonso a large portion of the kingdom of Toledo. Al-Qadir would continue to rule the kingdom, yet Toledo would become a **tributary** to Alfonso's larger realm of Castile.

Al-Qadir feared that his enemies would accuse him of cowardice for handing Toledo over to Alfonso without a fight. Along with his supporters, he asked the king to let them act as if they were putting up an energetic defense against the Christians. Alfonso agreed to this plan—but only until the end of the war, when Al-Qadir would hand the city over to him.

For four more years, Alfonso left some troops to besiege Toledo while he led other troops in campaigns elsewhere. Finally, though, Alfonso demanded the surrender of Toledo. On May 25, 1085, the 48-year-old Alfonso rode through a gate in the walls on the north side of the city. After almost 375 years, Toledo was again part of Christendom.

> **tributary:** an independent kingdom or state that pays another kingdom or state to remain independent

## Invasion of the Almoravids

At the time of Alfonso's reconquest of Toledo, Al-Andalus was divided between more than 20 small states whose Muslim rulers often fought among themselves. At times, these rulers joined even with Christian kings like Alfonso VI against the other Muslim states. After the fall of Toledo, however, these Muslim lords united in seeking aid from the Almoravids. The Almoravids were a zealous Muslim religious group that had established a military empire in North Africa. Led by their fierce sultan, they moved their armies into Spain the year after Alfonso recovered Toledo.

In October 1086, the Almoravid sultan won a spectacular victory over Alfonso VI. But these conquerors proved they were no friends to the Muslim rulers who had invited them to Spain. During the next few years the Almoravids conquered Muslim Al-Andalus piece by piece, removing the native Muslim rulers. Alfonso spent the rest of his life keeping the Almoravids from overrunning the Christian parts of the Iberian Peninsula as well. The Almoravids were much more formidable enemies to the Christians than the old Muslim rulers of Al-Andalus had been, but they failed to regain Toledo for Islam.

Instead, Toledo became a permanent part of the Christian kingdom of Castile and León. The capture of Toledo allowed Christians to push south of the Douro River in Portugal and to reconquer the cities of Segovia and Avila as well as cities along the Tagus River. With the reconquest of these towns, the Tagus became the new dividing line between Christian and Muslim Spain.

## El Cid Campeador

Alfonso VI's fame was surpassed only by one other man of his time, whom Spanish legend presents as a loyal soldier and vassal. He was Rodrigo Díaz, called *El Cid Campeador*, meaning, "the Lord, Master of the Battlefield."

When the Cid was in his thirties, he had helped Alfonso's brother—Sancho, then the king of Castile —to seize León, which belonged to Alfonso. When Sancho was slain, Alfonso, who became king of both Castile and León, held a grudge against the Cid. In 1081 the monarch banished the Cid, forcing him to earn a living in foreign lands.

The Cid and a few followers who went into exile with him became full-time, professional soldiers—mercenaries who hired themselves out to any lord, Christian or Muslim, who would pay them. The Cid and his men fought Al-Andalus Muslims, African Almoravids, and occasionally fellow Christians.

During the approximately 15 years the Cid spent in exile in the eastern part of the Iberian Peninsula, he remained faithful to Alfonso. When the king was tightening his grip on Toledo, the Cid was in the service of the Muslim ruler of Saragossa. The loyal Castilian exile made sure his employer never sent aid to Toledo and stayed away from Castile.

In 1092, the Cid besieged the rich Muslim-held city of Valencia on the east coast of Spain. For 20 months, the Cid fended off various armies, kept supplies from reaching Valencia by land or sea, and maintained the siege. The city finally surrendered on June 15, 1094, and the famous Castilian warrior entered the city in triumph. The reconquest of Valencia was the Cid's greatest military accomplishment. He held Valencia until his death in 1099.

**Equestrian statue of El Cid Campeador**

The Cid's contemporaries were amazed because he did not set himself up as an independent ruler in Valencia. Instead, El Cid Campeador ruled Valencia as a vassal of Alfonso VI and Castile. Alfonso's misjudgment and mistreatment of the Cid were a blotch on his successful reign of over 44 years. On the other hand, the Campeador's loyalty to his unsympathetic sovereign enhanced his reputation as a great man and an ideal knight. At his death, the Cid was still the governor of Valencia and the loyal subject of Alfonso VI of Castile.

After the Cid's death, the Almoravids pressed in against Valencia and the Christians were unable to defend it. Retreating from the city, the Cid's widow, Jimena, and his close companions took their beloved leader's remains with them for reburial in Castile. To this day, thousands of Spaniards every year visit the tombs of Rodrigo Díaz and Jimena in the cathedral of Burgos.

# Growth of the English Monarchy

Early in 1066, the childless old Saxon king of England, Edward the Confessor, died without settling the question of who should inherit his throne. Two men claimed the crown of England. One was Edward's nephew, Harold. The other was William, the duke of Normandy in northern France.

Fearing Duke William, the Saxon nobles of England elected the Saxon prince Harold as king. Refusing to give up his claim to the English throne, William set out with all his forces, sailed across the channel separating England from France, and landed near the town of Hastings. The new Saxon king, Harold, and his major nobles and warriors were in the north near York, putting down a rebellion and repelling an invading force of Danes. After defeating the invaders and putting down the rebellion, Harold and his men turned south to meet William. Fifteen days later, they reached the channel coast and Hastings.

**Saxon King Harold on the Bayeux Tapestry, which depicts the story of William the Conqueror**

After arriving too late in the day on October 13, 1066, to begin battle with the Normans, the Saxons drew up the shield-wall and waited until morning. The next day Harold's men, exhausted by their battles in the North and the forced march to Hastings, fought off several attacks by William's archers and repeated charges of the Norman armored horsemen. But in the end Harold's men were worn down by the Normans' persistence. In late afternoon, Harold's brothers were both killed. The royal guard surrounded the king and tried to protect him from his enemies, but King Harold was struck down as night fell over the field. Many of the nobility of Saxon England died along with their king at Hastings. The English surrendered at last, on October 14, 1066.

William moved quickly against all possible resistance in England and to prevent the English council from electing another king. William had himself crowned king of England in Westminster Abbey in London on Christmas Day, 1066.

## William the Conqueror

We remember William as "the Conqueror" because, as England's king, he was a harsh and unbending ruler. He ruthlessly stamped out all resistance to his rule and built castles at strategic points to overawe the population. King William claimed all land in England for himself. Half of the land he gave to his Norman barons in return for their oaths of allegiance. Of the remaining land, he gave about a third to its former holders (including the Church), who became the king's sworn vassals. He kept a sixth part for himself as his royal domain.

William not only made his vassals swear allegiance to him but also required *their* vassals to swear allegiance to him. The king claimed the right to enter any castle, no matter whose, at any time. He said that no castle could be built without his consent. He prohibited private warfare and allowed no one but himself to coin money. William kept in place the 34 shires (counties) into which the Saxons had divided England and continued to govern them through officials called sheriffs (from "shire reeves").

England's new Norman rulers spoke Old French, while the conquered peoples of the land spoke Anglo-Saxon, or Old English. Over time, everyone in England came to speak a mix of French and Saxon that became our English language.

William carried out a reform of the English church, favoring clergy who were influenced by the Cluniac reform movement. Among the churchmen William brought to England was Lanfranc, abbot of the monastery of Bec in Normandy. Born in Pavia, Italy, around 1005, Lanfranc had studied in Italian schools. He had become a respected theologian, teacher, and founder of schools.

Archbishop Lanfranc embarked on a successful reform of the English Church. With the king's backing, he worked to replace native English

Ruins of a Norman castle

bishops with educated Normans who would carry out a reform of the English Church. Still, William did not adopt all of the Cluniac reform. He insisted that the English Church was not subject to Rome, but to the king. He asserted that no papal decrees had any effect in England unless the king himself approved them.

William instituted a royal judicial system, with judges traveling a circuit to hear cases several times a year. William chose his judges based on their honesty and knowledge of the law. Norman law was written law—not customary law, as the English law had been. But the Norman law courts tried to unite the French written law with the Saxon customary law, and they gained a reputation for justice.

Though king of England, William remained duke of Normandy in France. In 1087, he led an invasion of a region in France in response to raids made on his territory. Following a battle on the Normandy border, William the Conqueror was injured. He died on September 9, 1087, of an infection arising from the treatment of his wound. He was buried in St. Stephen's Church in Caen, Normandy.

## William "Rufus" and Anselm

The reign of the Conqueror's son, William II "Rufus" (1087–1100), was the beginning of troubles between the crown and the English nobles and of controversy between king and Church. The nobles resented the king's harsh and arrogant rule. At the same time, the Church resisted the king's attempt to force the election of his own men to Church offices. The battle between Church and king came to a head when William II banished Anselm, the learned and respected archbishop of Canterbury, from England.

St. Anselm was already well known as a theologian before he became archbishop of Canterbury in 1093. Born in Italy, Anselm as a young man went to study with Lanfranc at the monastic school of Bec in Normandy. Three years later, in 1060, Anselm took monastic vows and later was elected prior of Bec. When Lanfranc went to England, Anselm was elected the monastery's abbot.

William the Conqueror had granted lands both in England and Normandy to the monastery of Bec, so Anselm made three visits to England to view these lands and to found a priory at Chester. In 1093, during one of these visits, William II Rufus named Anselm archbishop

**Painting of St. Anselm in the Church of San Anselmo in Bomarzo, Italy**

of Canterbury to succeed Lanfranc, who had died in 1089. In 1094, Anselm accepted the see reluctantly but with the king's promise that he might continue the reform of the English Church.

But trouble arose between the king and Anselm. As a favor to the crown, William demanded a sum of money from the treasury of Canterbury. But Anselm refused to pay it, thinking that such a payment looked too much like simony. William then refused to allow Anselm to go to Rome to receive the *pallium*—the mantle given to archbishops as a symbol that the pope approved of their election. The reigning pope, Urban II, was being opposed by an antipope. William said that until he himself decided who the real pope was, Anselm could not receive the pallium from Urban. Anselm, however, said the king had no right to interfere in a matter that concerned the Church alone. After another controversy with the king in 1097, Anselm left England and went into exile on the continent. In Rome, he completed one of his most famous works, *Cur Deus Homo* ("Why did God become Man?")

In 1100, William Rufus died in a mysterious hunting accident. His younger brother, Henry, seized the Anglo-Norman throne and removed his eldest brother Robert from the duchy of Normandy. As king, Henry I recalled Anselm to England; but Anselm fell into a serious disagreement with the young king because Henry insisted on investing Anselm and the other English bishops with the symbols of spiritual authority. Anselm took the matter to the pope, who decided that Henry had no right to practice lay investiture.

**A 13th century miniature painting of King Henry I of England**

When Anselm threatened to excommunicate Henry in 1105, the king decided to reconcile with his archbishop. In 1107, Henry agreed to give up lay investiture. From that time on, the clergy belonging to cathedrals were to elect bishops freely. Even so, they were to consult the king about the suitability of candidates for the office of bishop. A synod of bishops at Westminster, however, agreed that, after his election, a new bishop had to pledge his loyalty to the king. In this way, the king gained what he wanted—the obedience of his bishops in temporal affairs—while the Church was freed from lay investiture.

Anselm spent the last two years of his life in peace. He died in April 1109.

## The Reign of Henry and Eleanor

At Henry I's death, civil war engulfed England. Neither the Norman nor the English barons wanted King Henry's chosen heir to be their king. This heir was Henry Plantagenet, the son of Matilda (King Henry I's daughter) and Count Geoffrey Plantagenet. From Geoffrey, Henry Plantagenet inherited the French fiefs of Anjou, Touraine, and Maine, as well as Normandy. After the civil war in England ended, Henry came into his inheritance there as King Henry II. (From Henry's family name, we call his line of English kings the *Plantagenets*.)

He controlled not only England and a large portion of northern France, but much of southern France as well. As lord of the four French fiefs, Henry II controlled a large section of France. Before becoming king he had, in 1152, married Eleanor of Aquitaine—heiress to the French provinces of Poitou, Guienne, Gascony, and most of southern France. This marriage made Henry the most powerful man in western Europe.

Eleanor of Aquitaine, born about 1122, was one of the wealthiest and most intelligent women of the age. She had been queen of France as wife of Louis VII and had borne him two daughters. She had also traveled to the Holy Land with Louis and made his court a center of literature and music. But Louis claimed the marriage was invalid since he and Eleanor were close relations. (Eleanor had also not given him a male heir.) A council of French bishops agreed with Louis, and they annulled the marriage. Six weeks later, Eleanor married Henry Plantagenet, then just the count of Anjou—for love as well as for a political alliance. She was 11 years older than Henry.

Eleanor's father, William X of Aquitaine, was both a duke and a leading poet of medieval France. Lord over more land and more wealth than the king of France, William was a patron of the leading poets of France. Eleanor had grown up in the company of poets and musicians. She made the duke's court in Poitiers a center of culture. In England, too, she became the patroness of poets and judge of artistic quality. She was responsible for the development of troubadour poetry as well as for the writing of songs and poems about King Arthur, the legendary king of England, that became the basis of the medieval **romances** about Arthur and his Knights of the Round Table.

Eleanor was an extremely capable woman. When Henry was absent from England, Eleanor served as his regent there. She administered her own extensive lands in France. During the conflict of Henry with Thomas

**Effigy of Eleanor of Aquitaine, from her tomb of Fontevraud Abbey, France**

**romance:** a tale of chivalric love and adventure based on legend

Becket, archbishop of Canterbury, Eleanor tried to find common ground for both men and to resolve their quarrel. The strong-willed, intelligent woman finally came into conflict with her husband for personal as well as political reasons.

Eleanor and Henry had five sons—William (who died in childhood), Henry, Richard, Geoffrey, and John. King Henry, however, was unfaithful to Eleanor. In 1173, she encouraged her sons to rebel against their father. For this rebellion, Henry placed her under house arrest and even briefly imprisoned her. She remained under house arrest until King Henry died, 16 years later.

In 1200, when she was nearly 80 years old, Eleanor helped defend Anjou and Aquitaine against her rebel grandson, Arthur of Brittany. After King Henry's death, Eleanor served as regent of England and her French provinces while her son, King Richard the Lion-Heart, was away at the Crusades. She finally retired to the monastery of Fontevrault in Anjou, where she died on April 1, 1204. Her death was mourned by poets and princes throughout England and France. All knew they had lost in her both a patron and an inspiration—a truly great woman.

## The King and the Archbishop

Like the Norman kings before him, Henry II wanted to make England a united nation under the strong rule of the king. Henry made the barons destroy the castles they had built without royal permission, and he recovered the royal lands they had seized. Henry also greatly increased the role of the royal traveling judges. One of his methods was to order 16 men from each locality to appear before his judges to declare what crimes had been committed in their district and to name the suspected culprits. This is the origin of our grand jury system. A little later, Henry ordered that a jury of 12 men be present at trials as witnesses and to decide upon the guilt or innocence of the accused.

Henry, however, wanted to extend his power over the Church in England. The Church had established its own law courts at least as early as the days of William the Conqueror. In these courts, clergy were tried and, if guilty, punished. Unlike the royal courts, however, Church courts could not inflict the death penalty. Because of this, Henry wanted clergy who were proven guilty of certain crimes to be given over to the royal courts, where they would be given harsher punishments than what they would receive in Church courts.

But Henry wanted to control the Church in more ways than through the courts. To make sure the Church would approve his plans, the king

## The New Poetry of Romance

The songs William of Aquitaine sang told of the devotion of a knight to a distant lady—a lady he called his "lord and master." Though the poet praises his lady's beauty, her elegant manners, and perhaps her wit, she wants nothing to do with him. She is always too good for him.

The theme of William's songs became that of the poets called *troubadours*, as they were called in the southern French dialect, Provençal. Those writing in northern French were called *trouvères*. Under the patronage of Eleanor of Aquitaine, the taste for the troubadour style spread throughout France and later England.

The troubadour's repertoire could include songs of the Crusades, songs that celebrated love from afar, or songs lamenting humdrum life and poverty. However, it was Chrétien de Troyes, the court poet of Eleanor's daughter, Marie de Champagne, who began to write long stories that were both adventure and romance—tales about King Arthur and his knights.

Among other works, Chrétien de Troyes wrote the romances, *Erec and Enide*, *Yvain* (or "Knight of the Lion"), *Lancelot* (or "Knight of the Cart"), and *Perceval* (or "Story of the Holy Grail"). Many claim that Chrétien was responsible for the invention of the modern novel.

**Walter von der Vogelweide**

The influence of the French troubadours and trouvères spread to the courts of Germany in the 1100s. German troubadours were called "minnesingers," from *minne*, the German word for courtly love. The minnesingers produced two important poets: Walter von der Vogelweide, the most important German lyric poet of the Middle Ages, and Wolfram von Eschenbach of Bavaria.

Wolfram is the most interesting of the minnesingers. His epic, *Parzifal*, written around 1210, completed Chrétien de Troyes's unfinished *Perceval*. *Perceval* simply retells an old folk tale of an innocent youth named *Perceval* who finds a great treasure, the Grail (the chalice of Christ used at the Last Supper). Wolfram's *Parzifal* tells the same story—the hero progresses from a simple dunce to seeing the precious and hidden Holy Grail, and then to becoming, in his turn, the Grail's wise and responsible keeper. But Wolfram, unlike Chrétien, emphasizes the religious and mystical aspects of the story.

The troubadour tradition, imported to other lands from Provençal France, had great and creative results in the German minnesingers. It created a strong German poetic language that survived into modern times. The stories of King Arthur, spread by the troubadours, have significantly influenced European literature.

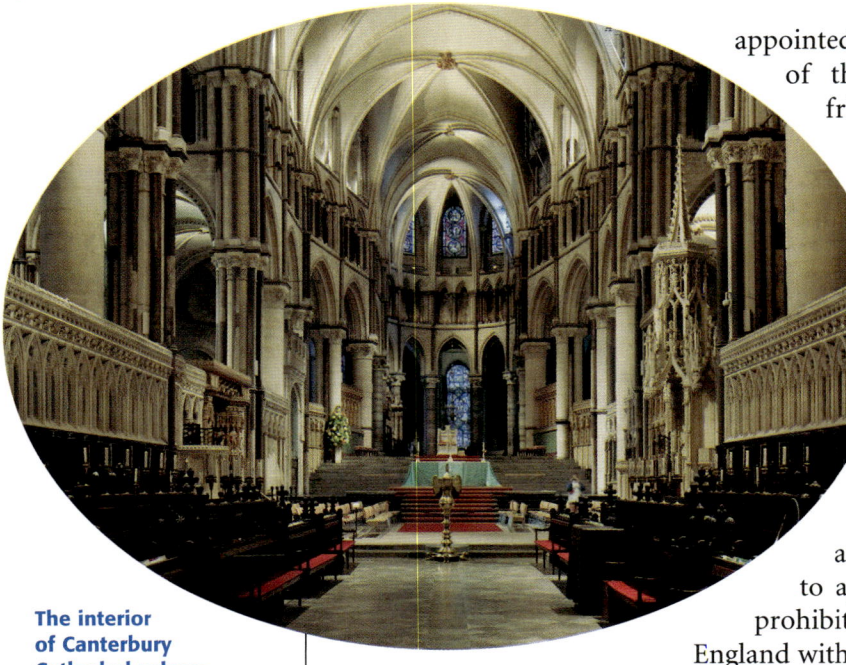

The interior of Canterbury Cathedral, where Thomas Becket was martyred

appointed Thomas Becket—chancellor of the kingdom and his close friend—as archbishop of Canterbury. But, much to the king's surprise and annoyance, Becket, as soon as he became archbishop, stood up for the rights of the Church and opposed the king's plans.

In 1164 Henry issued the Constitutions of Clarendon. These royal decrees limited the jurisdiction of Church courts and forbade anyone in England to appeal to the pope. They also prohibited the bishops from leaving England without the king's permission and allowed the bishops to excommunicate the king's subjects only with the king's approval.

Though his fellow English bishops did not resist the Constitutions of Clarendon, Thomas Becket did. Henry was furious with his old friend, and in 1164 Thomas saw he had little choice but to flee to France. But nearly six years later, Thomas, who had won the pope's support, returned with the king's permission to England and Canterbury. On Christmas Day 1170, Thomas publicly excommunicated all those, including some bishops, who had supported the king against the Church.

When Henry heard of this excommunication, he flew into a rage and exclaimed, "Will no one rid me of this contentious priest?" Four of the king's knights interpreted his rashly spoken words as a command and set off for Canterbury. On December 29, 1170, they appeared before Thomas and demanded that he remove the excommunications. Thomas refused. Later that day, the knights returned with armed men and entered the archbishop's cathedral while he was leading **Vespers**. "Where is the traitor?" they cried, to which Thomas replied, "Here I am, not traitor, but archbishop and priest of God." The knights slew Thomas before the altar, scattering his brains on the pavement.

**Vespers:** the evening prayer of the Church's Divine Office

Thomas gained more by his martyrdom than by his opposition to the king. After the archbishop's murder, the people rose up and forced

Henry to give up much of what he had gained. Thomas Becket's tomb at Canterbury became the site of constant pilgrimages for miraculous healing through the following centuries, until it was destroyed by Protestant zealots in the 16th century.

The English barons used the martyrdom of Thomas Becket as an excuse to rebel against the king. But Henry had built up his own army, paying for it with money he had gotten over the years from the very nobles who were rebelling against him. With this army Henry was able to stop the rebellion, bring the king of Scotland to swear fealty to him, and invade Ireland. But in the 19 years following the death of St. Thomas Becket, Henry faced the rebellion of his own sons, who were encouraged by their mother, Eleanor of Aquitaine. The king died in 1189, abandoned and broken-hearted, separated from the wife he had once loved and from his sons and family.

## The Sons of Henry II

Of all Henry's sons, only two became king after his death. Henry's second son, Richard I, called *Cœur de Lion*, or "Lion=Heart," came to the throne peacefully at his father's death. Though Richard was rarely in England, the monarchy under him was so strong that it could still demand respect.

Richard the Lion-Heart led the crusading armies of the Third Crusade in the siege of Acre in Palestine (which you will learn of in Chapter 12). On the way home, he was imprisoned by the duke of Austria. Richard was forced to pay a large ransom, which his mother, Eleanor of Aquitaine, collected from his reluctant English subjects. To pay for his crusading activities, for his ransom, and for his wars in France, Richard forced his English subjects to accept new taxes. He died childless, shot by an arrow from the wall of a little French castle he was besieging to force funds from its inhabitants.

**King John of England (1167–1216), also called John Lackland**

With Richard's death in 1199, John—the youngest son of Henry and Eleanor of Aquitaine—came to the throne. The new king had little money and faced much ill will from the people and the barons. He made matters

> **Magna Carta:** the document, signed by King John of England, expressing the medieval idea that kings do not stand above the laws and customs of their lands, but are subject to them
>
> **prelate:** a churchman of high rank, such as a bishop, archbishop, or abbot

**A copy of the Magna Carta**

worse for himself by losing most of his family's possessions in France (for which he was nicknamed "Lackland") and by quarrelling with the Church.

The English barons were angry over what they thought were the loss of their rights and the high taxes the Plantagenet kings had made them pay. Under the leadership of Simon de Montfort, the Earl of Leicester, the barons rebelled. In 1215 they forced John to sign a document called the **Magna Carta**, which spelled out in writing the barons' traditional rights that the king could not violate. The Magna Carta, or "The Big Charter," is so called because of the length of the scroll it was written on. It expressed the medieval idea that kings do not stand above the laws and customs of their lands, but are subject to them.

When John died in 1216, his son, King Henry III, found the barons more determined to resist the crown. Henry was an inept ruler who spent money extravagantly on various schemes, including trying to regain the Plantagenet lands in France. The barons refused to agree to the new taxes Henry requested from them. Finally the barons, under the leadership of Simon de Montfort, rose up in rebellion against the king. In 1265 the barons captured the king in battle, and Simon de Montfort governed England in his place.

The same year, Simon de Montfort called on every shire in England, directing them to elect two knights, who would serve as their representatives in a great council that would include the barons and **prelates**. In addition, De Montfort asked each town (borough) to choose two citizens (burgesses) as their representatives to this council. This assembly was the seed of what grew to be an important institution: the English Parliament.

## King Longshanks

King Henry III's son, Edward I, became king after his father's death in 1272. Edward, called "Longshanks," was moody, bad tempered, and treacherous. He was, however, an able and far-sighted king.

Edward wanted to make the king in England so powerful that none could stand against him. His idea of kingship differed from the ideal of the medieval king. As we have seen, a king in the Middle Ages was one lord among many. Though his vassals honored him and pledged fealty to him, the medieval king did not think he was above the rules of custom or law. But Edward, ignoring feudal custom, demanded obedience from his vassals and built up a strong army to enforce whatever demands he made of them.

Edward completed what previous English kings had attempted—the conquest of Wales. The Welsh were a Celtic or Gaelic people, the descendents of the original Britons whom the Anglo-Saxons had conquered in England. In 1277, Edward forced the great Welsh chieftain, Llewelyn ab Gruffyd, to surrender. The king then worked to establish an English form of government in the areas of Wales he had conquered. Edward proclaimed his own baby son "Prince of Wales," which has been the title of the firstborn son of every king of England since.

One of Edward's goals was to bring Scotland under his power. In 1295, however, this goal was hampered when he declared war on France in order to gain back lands he had lost to the French king, Philip the Fair. But just then, the Scots rose up against Edward, and he faced enemies to the north and south of his lands. To meet this emergency, Edward called together a parliament, inviting representatives of the shires and the towns to join with representatives of the Church and the barons. The king wanted to get the support of all the English people for his plans. This "Model Parliament," as it has been called (because it became the model of all future English parliaments), gave Edward its full support against the French and the Scots.

**King Edward I of England**

With the support of his subjects, Edward invaded and conquered Scotland in 1296. But in 1297, the Scottish baron William Wallace led a bloody war against Edward that lasted until 1303. Edward finally trapped Wallace by treachery and then had him convicted of "treason" and executed. Scotland, however, remained rebellious. The cause of Scottish freedom was taken up by Robert I ("the Bruce"), who defeated Edward's son, Edward II, at Bannockburn in 1314, twelve years after the death of Longshanks.

Edward I had forced the English people to think of themselves as a united people—as Englishmen. He had achieved what we call a **nation-state**—the unification of people sharing a common language and culture under one government. To achieve this, however, Edward brought pov-

**nation-state:** a grouping under one government of people sharing a common language and culture

erty to conquered Wales and stirred up Scotland against England. While on his way to conquer Scotland a second time, Edward died at Burgh-by-the Sands near Carlisle on July 7, 1302.

Though Longshanks' son, Edward II, was an inept ruler, his grandson, Edward III (reigned 1327–1377), had a long and prosperous reign. Under Edward III, England began a prolonged war with France (the "Hundred Years War") that forged the English people more firmly into a nation. Edward III completed the work of Edward I—and, really, of William the Conqueror—to make one English nation of peoples who came from the very different Saxon and Norman traditions.

# The Growth of the French Monarchy

The crowning of Hugh Capet as king of France at Reims in 987

When Duke William of Normandy led his army across the English Channel in 1066, France was hardly more than a name. France had a king, but he controlled only the "Île de France"—a few counties clustered around Paris. The rest of France was under the power of various powerful nobles.

In 987, almost 70 years before William conquered Saxon England, the great French feudal lords elected Count Hugh Capet of Paris to be king of France—mainly because he was too weak to threaten their power. To get the support of the great nobles, Hugh and the French kings after him had to give up claims they had to wider lands and more extensive powers. Even in the king's own territories, the lesser nobility built castles as they pleased and often defied him. Only the Church (which was interested in reducing feudal warfare) wished to maintain any royal authority at all. The ideas of the Cluniac reform would help strengthen royal power in France, just as they had done in England and Germany.

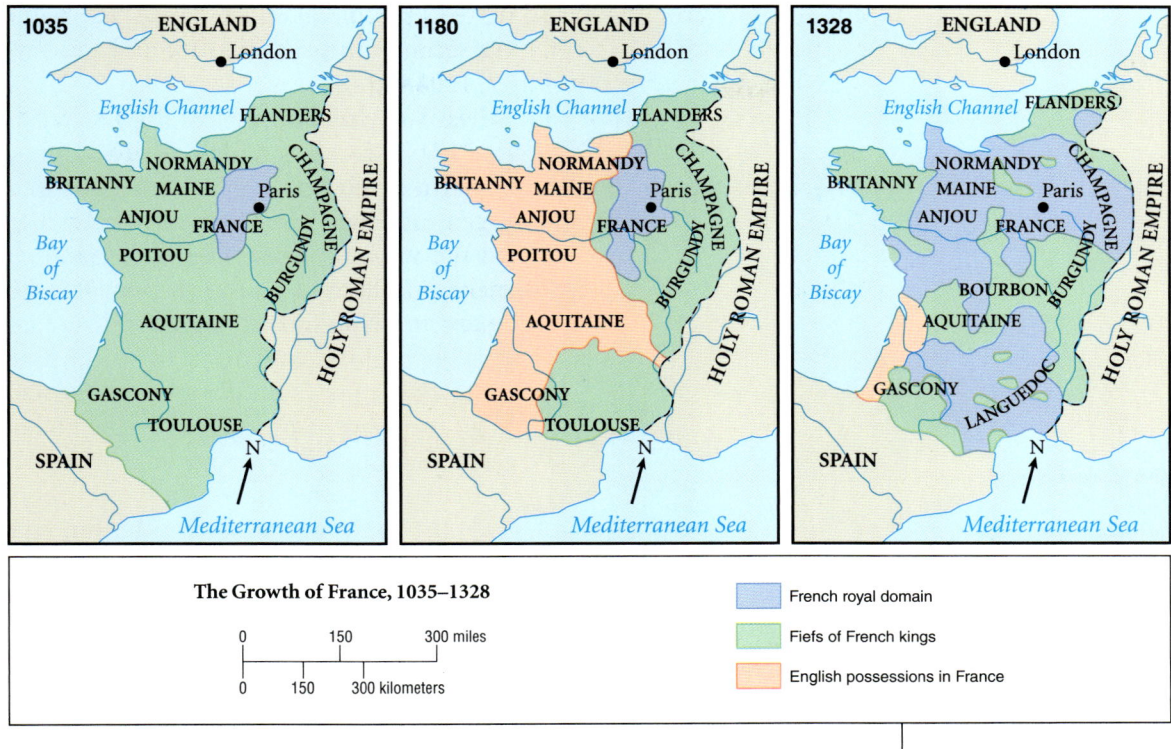

Growth of France and the French monarchy from the 10th to the 13th century

## The Abbot Who Helped Build France

The man who helped strengthen the power of the French king in the 12th century was himself neither a king nor a noble, but a churchman. He was Suger, abbot of the important monastery of Saint-Denis near Paris. During the reigns of the Capetian kings, Louis VI (1108–1137) and Louis VII (1137–1180), Suger worked to bring the nobles more firmly under the authority of the king—but not just for political purposes. Abbot Suger saw a strong monarchy as a way to make France a more Christian kingdom.

Suger was born a peasant near Paris, probably in 1081. Seeing he was an intelligent boy, his parents entrusted him to the care of the monks of the abbey of Saint-Denis, a monastery with close ties to the royal family. At the abbey's monastic school, he became friends with a boy his own age who shared Suger's quiet and thoughtful temperament. This boy was Louis Capet, the future King Louis VI.

At the age of 25, Suger became secretary to the abbot of St. Denis. When the abbot sent him on a mission to Normandy. Suger was impressed by

**Cathedral of Saint-Denis: tombs of the kings and queens of France**

**beachhead:** an area along an enemy's shore from which an army can land more troops and supplies

the orderly government of the Normans and wanted to bring that kind of government to France.

The French honored the Abbey of Saint-Denis because it was the shrine of St. Denis, the patron saint of France. Suger saw that if he stressed the idea that the French kings were the vassals of St. Denis, the feuding nobles could more easily be brought to respect royal authority. Suger also saw that the king could be, and ought to be, the protector of the poor and the town craftsmen. In all this, Suger was inspired by the political ideas of the Cluniac reform.

But Suger's interests were not only political. In 1122, when his brother monks elected him abbot of Saint-Denis, he set about guiding the monks of the monastery back to a disciplined and ascetic life, as called for by the Cluniac reform. Suger made friends with St. Bernard, the famous abbot of Clairvaux. With Bernard's help and support, Suger oversaw the construction of a rebuilt abbey church designed by the finest French architects. This church was the first gothic-style church in Europe. His friendship with the king gave Suger the authority to encourage reform in both Church and state.

In working to reform Church and state, Suger had the support of his friend, King Louis VI, whom he served as adviser. After the king's death in 1137, his son, the new king (Louis VII), rejected Suger as his adviser and dismissed his father's entire council. But in 1142, in an act that led to civil war, Louis seized lands belonging to his most powerful feudal vassal—Thibaut, count of Champagne. Suger knew that what the king had done was foolish; Louis VII needed Thibaut as a friend, not an enemy. Suger stepped in—invited or not, as he had always done with Louis's father—and made peace between the two lords.

Feeling remorse for the lives he had taken in the civil war, Louis decided to do penance by joining in the Second Crusade against the Muslims in the Holy Land. The Christian kingdom of Jerusalem had just fallen to the Muslims, and St. Bernard of Clairvaux was organizing a relief force to defend the last Christian **beachheads** left in the East. In 1147, the young king sailed for the Holy Land with eager hope. But sickness and poor supplies forced the French army to return home after two years without accomplishing anything.

Suger served as Louis's regent while the king was on the crusade. The king even gave his crown to Suger for safekeeping. As regent, Suger ruled France wisely. The abbot overcame the difficulties the kingdom faced and used the opportunity he had as regent to enact Church reform in France. He devised new taxes that were fairer than the old ones and brought in more revenue because they did not discourage enterprise and industry. He gave orders to stop the deforestation of the last woodlands of France, commissioning foresters to care for the trees and game in the royal preserves.

Suger's critics thought he would not return the crown to Louis. When the king returned to France, however, Suger had the crown presented to Louis in a ceremony at Saint-Denis. Louis himself bestowed on the abbot the title, "Father of the Country."

Suger did not long survive Louis's return to France. In 1150, the old abbot fell sick with malaria. He died in January of 1151.

## A Saint for France and Europe

Perhaps no one man has had such great influence on his age as St. Bernard of Clairvaux (1090–1153), a monk of the Cistercian Order. Bernard's preaching and example gave religious direction to the French nation and all of Western Christendom.

**Gothic-style cathedral at Reims, France**

The sons of a Burgundian lord, Bernard and his five brothers had been well educated in Latin, verse making, and feats of arms. But Bernard abandoned the life of the nobility. In 1113, he entered the monastery at Cîteaux only a few years after it was founded. He even persuaded four of his brothers and an uncle to join him. In all, Bernard persuaded 31 friends to follow him to Cîteaux.

After Bernard had been at Cîteaux three years, the abbot ordered him and 12 monks to found a new house in a place called the Valley of Wormwood, a wilderness surrounded by forest. The 13 young monks scratched a meager living out of the hostile and poor soil. The monks lived a life of hardship, but the reputation of the house and of the holiness of its young abbot soon grew so great that 130 monks joined the initial 13.

Bernard changed the valley's name from Wormwood to Clairvaux (*Clara Vallis*, meaning "Bright Valley"), because it looked directly at the dawning sun.

Bernard was a monk, a man dedicated to God alone; yet he was the leader of Christendom in the 12th century. So influential was he that when, in 1130, two men—Anacletus and Innocent III—each claimed to be pope, Bernard backed Innocent and convinced most of Europe to support him as well.

Bernard showed his leadership by arousing Europe to fight the Second Crusade. Bernard convinced whole nations—the Saxons, Danes, and Moravians—to aid the crusading armies. Moreover, he was able to bring an unwilling Emperor Conrad II into the ranks of the crusading host.

Bernard was the counselor for cardinals, archbishops, bishops, abbots, and popes. He wrote letters of praise or admonishment to lay rulers as well. Whether churchmen or laymen, Bernard told them they were to lead lives of Christian virtue and to rule as Christian leaders.

Bernard died on August 20, 1153, at the age of 63. He had been abbot of Clairvaux for 38 years.

**Portrait of St. Bernard of Clairvaux**

## Philip Augustus

Philip II "Augustus," the son of Louis VII, became king when his father died in 1180. Philip was a ruler of tremendous energy who devoted himself to strengthening royal power by any means he could, whether they were moral or not. He won great popularity with most of his subjects because he protected them from the power of their local lords, who were often tyrannical.

Philip encouraged the sons of Henry II of England to rebel against

**A 13th-century statue of Philip Augustus at Reims Cathedral, France**

their father. After Henry's death, Philip took Richard the Lion-Heart's French lands by force when the English king was on crusade. Then, in 1221, Philip defeated the forces of England's King John and those of the Emperor Frederick II, adding John's French lands to the French kingdom. The English king went from holding about one-third of France to controlling only a few coastal port cities and their surrounding territories. In a crusade (1209–1218) against a heretical group (the Albigensians) in the South of France, Philip Augustus defeated those lords who supported or sheltered heretics and so won for himself all of southern France—a region called Languedoc. Philip extended the power of the royal courts and was a clever ruler. By the time he died in 1223, no French lord was so powerful as the king.

## St. Louis of France

Louis IX, Philip Augustus's grandson, further strengthened the French monarchy when he became king in 1226, for he was a wise and efficient ruler.

Louis established the *Parlement de Paris*, a supreme court of appeal for the entire kingdom. He virtually abolished private warfare among his subjects, thus bringing about a peace that allowed the kingdom to prosper. While remaining the head of a feudal system of government, Louis created the beginning of a new governing system that in the long run replaced feudalism in France.

Louis was not only a statesman and wise administrator, but so good and holy a man that the Church declared him a saint barely 30 years after his death. He was pious, kind, honest, and dutiful. Louis IX combined in his person the medieval ideals of a just ruler, a gallant knight, and a humane gentleman.

Louis built many fine churches, of which the most beautiful was the Sainte-Chapelle—a glowing jewel box enclosed by richly colored stained glass windows—near Notre Dame Cathedral in Paris. Louis died in Tunis in 1270 while leading a crusade. He left to his successor a powerful and well-ordered state whose people were loyal to the crown.

A 15th-century depiction of King Louis IX of France

Louis fit the Church reformers' ideal of a Christian ruler. He brought French law into line with Christian morality and united the great vassals of France under him as their king. During Louis's reign, France became a united kingdom under the rule of a monarch who was admired and respected for his nobility and justice.

# Chapter Review

## Summary

- The kingdom of Asturias was able to hold its own against the Muslim kingdoms of Al-Andalus and was able to expand. The rediscovery of the tomb of St. James the Apostle in Galicia gave Christian warriors the confidence that God fought on their side.
- King Alfonso III found settlers to repopulate lands along the frontier, southeast of Asturias. This region, for its many castles, became known as Castile.
- Alfonso VI made the Muslim kingdom of Toledo tributary to his kingdoms of León and Castile. Because of this, the Almoravids of North Africa invaded the Iberian Peninsula, defeating Alfonso in battle and overrunning all of Muslim Al-Andalus.
- One of Alfonso VI's Castilian vassals, Rodrigo Díaz—nicknamed *El Cid Campeador*—had several disagreements with the king and so was forced into exile. Though the Cid served Muslim lords in Al-Andalus, he remained faithful to Alfonso. In 1094, the Cid reconquered Valencia for King Alfonso VI.
- Both the Saxon Harold and William, duke of Normandy, claimed the throne of England after the death of its king, Edward the Confessor. William invaded England and, in 1066, defeated Harold at the Battle of Hastings. William the Conqueror became king of England, ruthlessly stamping out all opposition and establishing a government centralized under him as king. William put Norman reformist clerics in control of the English Church.
- William II made St. Anselm archbishop of Canterbury but sent him into exile when Anselm insisted on the rights of the Church. Anselm is one of the great theologians of the Middle Ages.
- King Henry I settled the crown's controversy with the Church by allowing for the free election of bishops but said bishops had to swear an oath of loyalty to the king.

- King Henry II ruled not only England, but the French lands of Normandy, Anjou, and Touraine. By his marriage to Eleanor of Aquitaine, he gained Aquitaine and other French territories.
- Eleanor of Aquitaine introduced a rich cultural life into the English court. In 1173 she encouraged her sons to rebel against their father, King Henry II, for which she was kept under house arrest until Henry's death. After his death, Eleanor reigned as regent while her son, King Richard the Lion-Heart, was on crusade.
- King Henry II appointed his close friend Thomas Becket as archbishop of Canterbury. Archbishop Thomas resisted the king, standing for the freedom of the Church. For this he was sent into exile and, finally, martyred.
- Henry II's sons, King Richard and King John, succeeded to the throne after their father. Richard spent much of his reign on crusade in the Holy Land and then in captivity to the duke of Austria. After Richard's death, John succeeded him. He quarreled with the Church and with his barons, who forced him to sign the Magna Carta in 1215. Under John's son, Henry III, England saw the beginning of Parliament.
- King Edward I ("Longshanks") completed the formation of England into a nation-state. Edward conquered Wales and invaded Scotland, where he met resistance under William Wallace. Scotland secured its freedom under King Robert I ("the Bruce"), who defeated Edward II at Bannockburn.
- The Capetian kings of France were weak. But beginning in the 12th century, the French king's power began to grow. Under Kings Louis VI and Louis VII, Abbot Suger established the beginnings of a royal court. Suger strengthened the French monarchy by his wise stewardship of the kingdom.
- St. Bernard, founder of the monastery of Clairvaux, was the leader of Christendom in the 12th century.
- King Philip Augustus was ruthless in strengthening the power of the crown. He became very popular, however, with most of his subjects.
- King Louis IX gave France an efficient administration and a supreme court of appeal, the *Parlement de Paris*, for the entire kingdom. Louis, who was later canonized, was pious, kind, honest, and dutiful.

## Key Concepts

**monarch/king:** Kings were the feudal leaders of European nations, one among fellow noble equals. Monarchs assumed complete power over the nation-state and ruled alone.

**Magna Carta:** the document, signed by King John of England, expressing the medieval idea that kings do not stand above the laws and customs of their lands, but are subject to them
**Parliament:** the English representational assembly; begun as a council of barons, churchmen, and representatives of the shires and towns
**nation-state:** a grouping under one government of people sharing a common language and culture
*Parlement de Paris:* the supreme court of France

### Dates to Remember
**813:** discovery of tomb of St. James by Alfonso II
**1085:** reconquest of Toledo by Alfonso III
**1066:** Battle of Hastings
**1170:** death of St. Thomas Becket of Canterbury
**1215:** signing of the Magna Carta

### Central Characters
**Santiago:** St. James the Apostle, patron of Spain. Also called *Santiago Matamoros* ("Moorslayer")
**Alfonso III (r. 866–914):** called "the Great," king of Asturias who encouraged the resettlement of abandoned lands on the kingdom's border with Muslim territory
**Alfonso VI (1040–1109):** the king of Castile and León who liberated Toledo
**El Cid (ca. 1043–1099):** Rodrigo Díaz, *El Cid Campeador*; the Castilian hero of legendary exploits who took Valencia and gave it to the Castilian crown
**William the Conqueror (1027–1087):** duke of Normandy and king of England who defeated Harold at the Battle of Hastings in 1066 and made England a Norman realm
**Henry II (1133–1189):** Henry Plantagenet, descendent of William the Conqueror, king of England
**Eleanor of Aquitaine (1122–1204):** daughter of the troubadour Duke William of Aquitaine, queen of France and England, mother of Richard the Lion-Heart and John Lackland
**St. Thomas Becket (1118–1170):** Henry II's chancellor, whom the king appointed to be archbishop of Canterbury; martyred before his altar in the cathedral of Canterbury
**John "Lackland" (1167–1216):** king of England, forced to sign the Magna Carta

**Edward I (1239–1307):** the English king who conquered Wales and Scotland and made the English monarchy into a nation-state
**Abbot Suger (1081–1151):** abbot of Saint-Denis, adviser to the French kings, reformer of church and state
**St. Bernard of Clairvaux (1090–1153):** Cistercian monk who was the most influential man in 12th-century Europe
**Philip II, "Augustus" (1165–1223):** king of France who added to France most of England's lands on the continent
**St. Louis IX (1214–1270):** the French king who brought order to the French realm and gave it a law court system that survived for centuries

## Questions for Review
1. When was the tomb of St. James rediscovered, and by whom? Why was the discovery of St. James's tomb important for Christians in Spain?
2. What did El Cid accomplish? Is the retaking of Valencia sufficient reason to see him as a hero, or was his character the real reason to hold him up as an example and model for centuries?
3. What did William the Conqueror accomplish in England? How did his government differ from that of the Saxons?
4. Who was Eleanor of Aquitaine? What did she do in history (besides marry two powerful men) to make her so remembered and revered?
5. How was St. Thomas of Canterbury martyred? Why was he martyred?
6. How did St. Bernard affect his own time?
7. What did Louis IX accomplish as king?

## Ideas in Action
1. Draw a picture from a photograph of a castle from Castile. What is the distinguishing mark of these castles? Against what enemy were they constructed? When?
2. Discuss the Magna Carta in class. How is it different from what we moderns would expect in a constitution? What rights and powers did it give the people? The barons? The king? How does the Magna Carta limit government's powers to this day?
3. William Wallace of Scotland has achieved heroic stature in our time. His fight against Edward I is remembered as a crusade for freedom. Look up the history of Wallace and his campaign against the English. Who had the better right to the title of hero, Wallace or Edward Longshanks? What sort of freedom did Wallace fight for?

4. Find a life of Eleanor of Aquitaine, and research her patronage of the great poets of the time. What poets did she or her daughter, Marie de Champagne, make well known? How did the Arthurian romances affect European manners and imagination?
5. Draw up a time line of the events of nation-forming in Spain, England, France, and Germany. Illustrate the main events.

# Highways and Byways

### The Legends of Robin Hood

The reigns of Richard the Lion-Heart and his brother, John Lackland, are the background for the many stories and legends of the outlaw champion of the poor, Robin Hood. Robin Hood was—according to the stories—a minor lord, Robert of Locksley, who incurred the enmity of Prince John while King Richard was away at the Crusade. Robin took to the forest with a band of fellow outlaws. Together they robbed rich clerics and nobles and gave the proceeds to the impoverished poor of the countryside.

The Robin Hood stories take place in the shire of Nottingham, in what was then the great royal forest of Sherwood. Robin's chief enemy is the Sheriff of Nottingham, presented in the stories as a thoroughly bad man and a fool as well. Robin and his Merry Men escape into the depths of the dark forest and make sport of the sheriff.

Robin's exploits were celebrated in many popular ballads—songs sung among the country folk. These ballads are political in their denunciation of official abuse of the poor and comic at the expense of pompous and self-satisfied officials and clerics. Later medieval ballads made more of the comic aspect of the stories and less of the political. All of them relate the tragic end of the hero—murdered by a trusted abbess, his cousin, who bleeds him to death when he goes to her for help. The image of a "Robin Hood," one who takes from the rich and gives to the poor, has fixed itself in the English-speaking imagination as that of a hero and a moral example.

# CHAPTER 12  The Crusades

Pope Urban II (reigned 1088–1099) was troubled at the growing power of Islam in the East. The Arabic rulers of Baghdad and the Muslim caliphs of Egypt had surrendered to a new and fiercer Muslim people, the Seljuk Turks. Fresh from the Asian grasslands, the Seljuks—under the command of their leaders, called **sultans**—soon had all the Middle East in their hands. The Seljuks were not as tolerant of other faiths as the former Arab rulers had been. Seljuk edicts, for instance, forbade Christian pilgrims from entering shrines, such as the Holy Sepulchre in Jerusalem.

The whole of Asia Minor up to the Bosporus soon fell under Turkish Muslim control. Seeing the Turkish threat, the Eastern Roman emperor at Constantinople asked the pope for a contingent of knights to help the Byzantine armies hold back the Seljuks from overrunning the Eastern Empire.

**sultan:** a king or ruler of the Turks

A 15th century depiction of Pope Urban II summoning the whole of Christiandom to arms on November 27, 1095.

## God Wills It!

Pope Urban II believed the recovery of the lands where Our Lord had walked and died was an act of piety and love, so he did not send just a

295

contingent of knights to rescue the Eastern Empire, but a whole army. In 1095, at a Church council in Clermont, France, Pope Urban called on the great lords of the Western lands to mobilize their forces to take back the holy places for Christendom. The assembly of clerics and nobles from all of France, stirred by the pope's call to arms, answered with the shout, *Deus lo volt!*—"God wills it!"

## The Peasants' Crusade

Pope Urban's appeal for the relief of the Christian holy places, however, did not inspire only kings and nobles. A preacher called Peter the Hermit wandered about Europe, calling on all Christians to join in the pious cause of freeing the Holy Land from the Muslim Turks. Moved by Peter's preaching, a virtually leaderless mass of thousands of peasants (including small children) set out for the Holy Land. This "Peasants' Crusade," as it has been called, got under way in 1096 without plan or preparation. Since most of the force had never traveled far from their homes, they had no concept of the distances they had to cross to reach Constantinople. The motley force, however, gathered at Cologne on the Rhine, set off for Mainz in April of 1096, and traveled up the Rhine, down the Danube, and across the Balkans to Asia Minor.

**Peter the Hermit preaching the First Crusade**

Already a huge mob, the peasants' "army" collected numbers of zealous folk as it moved eastward. They lived on what they could seize and left a trail of destruction across the Balkans to Constantinople. The Byzantine emperor fed and sheltered the large host—but safely, miles away from the city—and then transported it over the Bosporus into Muslim-held Asia Minor. Harried by Turkish forces, the remnant of the great unorganized force finally took shelter in a hill fort, where they were besieged. At last they surrendered to the Turks, who sold them into slavery.

## The First Crusade

Meanwhile, a more organized force was gathering for the long march to the Holy Land. Thousands of warriors and their leaders had made a solemn vow to fight until Jerusalem was taken. Sewing a red cross to the front of their cloaks, these warriors came to be called "crusaders" (from the Latin word *crux*, meaning "cross.") They were engaged, they believed, in a holy task. They were "taking up the cross."

Three crusader armies eventually converged on Constantinople: the men of the Rhineland under Godfrey of Bouillon and his brother Baldwin; the men of southern France under Bishop Adhemar of Le Puy and Count Raymond of Toulouse; and the men of northern Europe, joining the Normans of the heel of Italy, led by Count Bohemond of Taranto.

The Christian forces seemed formidable to their Turkish foes. The knights wore steel helmets and covered themselves in long coats of chain mail. An Arab or Turkish warrior wore a tunic of mail, but only a soft head covering and leather leggings. The Christian warriors were trained to make massed charges with their heavy cavalry. They advanced like a huge wall of iron with lances at rest and supported by infantry. But Arabic and Turkish warriors excelled as light cavalry; they were mobile and deadly in a cut-and-turn technique.

After receiving oaths of loyalty from the crusader leaders, the Byzantine emperor hastily sent the "Frankish" force (as the Byzantines called them) off to Asia Minor, where they were lucky enough to find the Muslims so distracted by local rivalries and religious differences that they were unable to resist the invaders effectively. After taking the great city of Antioch in Syria, the crusaders moved against Jerusalem. In June 1099, after three years on their armed pilgrimage, the crusaders finally came in sight of the towers of Jerusalem. Only one in five of their number had survived the trip. Beholding the holy city, the crusaders knelt and wept.

*Four Leaders of the First Crusade* by Gustave Doré

**Godfrey of Bouillon made lord of Jerusalem**

On June 7, 1099, the crusaders laid siege to Jerusalem, a major fortress defended by walls and towers. The final assault broke through the defenses on July 15, and the army poured into the city. In the frenzy of attack, the crusaders slaughtered defenders and ordinary citizens alike. At dawn, having conquered the city, the crusaders wept with gratitude for survival—and with shame for their atrocities. The next day, July 16, 1099, the exhausted crusaders trooped into the Church of the Holy Sepulchre to give thanks to God for their victory and pray forgiveness for their sins.

The victorious crusaders, amid great rejoicing, set up a Christian feudal kingdom in Jerusalem. They offered the crown first to Raymond of Toulouse, who had commanded the siege of Jerusalem, but he refused to be "a king in Christ's kingdom." Godfrey of Bouillon accepted the crown but asked to be called Prince of Jerusalem and Duke of the Holy Sepulchre, not king.

Godfrey fell ill and died in 1100, after reigning only a few months. His brother, Baldwin, count of Edessa and ruler of Syria (two lands the crusaders had conquered on their way to Jerusalem), was asked to take his brother's throne in Jerusalem. Baldwin did not share his brother's humility and was crowned king, not prince, of Jerusalem in 1100. Under his 18-year rule, the kingdom was secure and prosperous.

# The Crusader Kingdoms of Outremer

In their march to Jerusalem, the crusaders had conquered large portions of Syria. A group of crusaders had even marched east, to the Euphrates River, conquering a land called Edessa. Out of all the conquered lands, the crusaders formed four states: Jerusalem, Tripoli (on the Syrian coast), Antioch (on the northern border of Syria near the sea), and Edessa. The lands of the crusader lords stretched in a narrow line from the Euphrates to the desert of Sinai—some 600 miles. In some places the Christian territory was only 10 miles wide.

The Holy Land was under the control of crusader lords for about 100 years. During this time, Christians resumed making pilgrimages to the holy places, and trade was established between Europe and the Holy Land, which Europeans began to call *Outremer* (meaning "over-the-sea"). Pilgrims, colonists, and more warriors swelled the number of Western settlers until they reached about 140,000 people.

The original inhabitants of Palestine and Syria included many Christians as well as Muslims. The crusaders, however, had no respect for these "foreign" Christians because they spoke the same language and wore the same dress as their Muslim neighbors. Native Palestinians, both Christian and Muslim, became second-class subjects of the new lords and paid high taxes to support their feudal states. Local Christians, orthodox or not, were excluded from government along with Muslims. This inspired bitter feelings among local Christians, both for the crusaders and for the Western Catholic Church they represented.

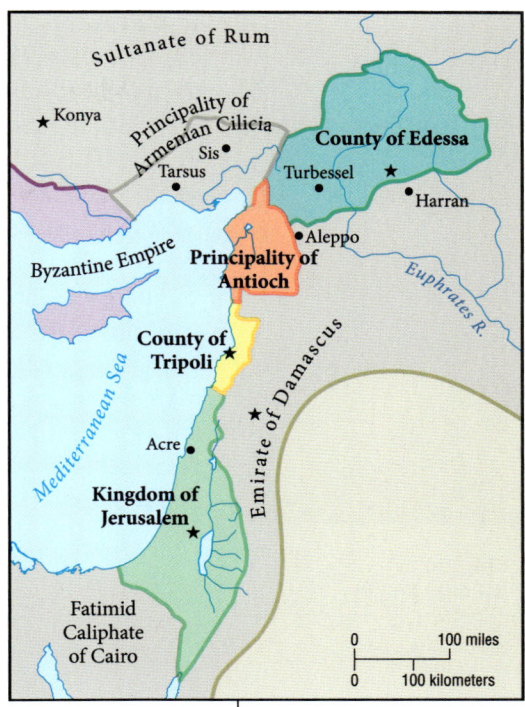

**Crusader kingdoms of Jerusalem, Antioch, Edessa, and Tripoli**

## Templars and Hospitallers

In the early years of the Latin kingdom, a knight of Burgundy, Hugh de Payens, formed a group of companions to protect pilgrims coming to Jerusalem. The king of Jerusalem granted them a house next to the ruined temple in Jerusalem, from which they received their name, Knights Templar. The Templars took the threefold monastic vow of poverty, chastity, and obedience. But they were still soldiers, keeping their weapons and martial organization as protectors of the pilgrimage routes from the coast of Palestine to Jerusalem.

It was not long before the Templars went from their main business of protecting pilgrims to engaging in a general war against the Muslims. Templar heroism and **austerity** attracted new members to their order from western Europe. Nobles and ordinary citizens gave them huge gifts,

**austerity:** the quality of being ascetic, unadorned, severe (adj., *austere*)

**Effigy of a Templar Knight**

so that within 100 years the Templars were the wealthiest order in western Europe, with recruiting centers in major cities and their own fleets to transport troops to Outremer from the north and south of France.

Before the crusaders' conquest of the Holy Land, the citizens of Amalfi in Italy had set up a hospital in Jerusalem for poor pilgrims, dedicating it to St. John the Baptist. After the conquest of Jerusalem, the pope permitted this charitable institution to become a military order of knights, like the Templars.

These Knights of St. John, known as the Hospitallers, became as strong and almost as wealthy as the Templars. Across Europe, the houses of both orders became recruiting centers, pouring more and more armed men into Outremer. These recruits kept alive the forces of the Latin kingdom. Huge fortresses, like the magnificent Krak des Chevaliers of the Hospitallers, east of the Jordan River on the desert's edge, defended the kingdom's most perilous borders.

**Crusader castle Krak des Chevaliers (1140–1260), Syria**

The fighting monks formed their own states within the feudal state, and they were often at odds with the king of Jerusalem and each other. Nevertheless, the two orders were the most indestructible military force in the kingdom. Their well-drilled units allowed the crusader kingdom to hold its own against Arab and Turk.

## The Second Crusade

The Christian crusader states, however, suffered weaknesses. After the First Crusade, many crusaders returned home, leaving too few men to guard the newly conquered lands. Reinforcements from Europe came from time to time, but they were never enough. The crusader states, too, did not work together and at times quarreled amongst themselves. As long as the Turks themselves were divided, the crusader states could hold their own against them.

The first crusader state to fall to the Muslims was Edessa in 1144. Though the Muslims had not yet become strong enough to threaten the other crusader states seriously, the loss of Edessa caused alarm in Europe. In 1145, St. Bernard of Clairvaux preached a second crusade and moved King Louis VII of France to take up the cross. Though he was at first reluctant to join the crusade, Germany's Emperor Conrad III cast in his lot with Louis, and the two rulers led a splendid army to Constantinople.

Moving into Asia Minor, the crusaders met their first disaster. The Turks defeated Conrad III of Germany on the mountain roads of Asia Minor, and the emperor escaped with a few companions to the French camp at Nicaea. Louis VII of France, meanwhile, followed the coastal road south and reached Antioch. But instead of reinforcing Jerusalem,

**Raymond of Poitiers welcomes Louis VII to Antioch**

Louis and Conrad attacked the rich city of Damascus. This assault was an utter failure, and Conrad and Louis went home, leaving Outremer to defend itself.

For the next 30 years after this Second Crusade, the Latin kingdoms prospered, though the Latin princes quarreled among themselves. After Baldwin no strong king ruled Jerusalem, and corruption and selfishness replaced the religious zeal of the First Crusade. Outremer had to rely more and more on the Templars and Hospitallers to defend it.

## Saladin, the Conqueror

Then, in 1169, a strong Muslim leader named Saladin came to power in Egypt. Over the next two years, Saladin took complete control of that land and then moved against the Muslim city of Damascus. After seizing control there, he marched his forces into Mesopotamia, conquering most of that ancient land between the Tigris and Euphrates Rivers. For the first time, a united and powerful Muslim kingdom, ruled by a generous and crafty sultan, surrounded the Christian states of Outremer.

Saladin next turned his attention to the Kingdom of Jerusalem. On July 4, 1187, the Christian forces under Guy of Lusignan, king of Jerusalem, met Saladin in battle on the shores of the Sea of Tiberias (or Galilee). The Muslim leader destroyed the Christian army, took Guy of Lusignan prisoner, and seized the relic of the True Cross that King Guy had taken with him into battle. Saladin then moved against Jerusalem itself, which fell to the Muslims on October 2, 1187. Saladin showed mercy to the Christians in the Holy City. He allowed them the use of their holy places, though they had to pay a heavy tax for this favor.

After the fall of Jerusalem, only Tyre, Tripoli, and Antioch remained in Christian hands.

## The Third Crusade

News of Saladin's conquest of Jerusalem spread alarm throughout Christian Europe. No great preacher needed to move Christian princes to take up the cross. Emperor Frederick Barbarossa, King Philip Augustus of France, and England's King Richard the Lion-Heart assembled a very large host and, in 1189, set off for the Holy Land. Frederick led his forces by land through Constantinople and Asia Minor, while the kings of France and England advanced by sea from Italy.

Meanwhile, Saladin had released King Guy, sending him on his way to his cousins in Tripoli. But Guy surprised Saladin. Taking with him a small party of knights, the king of Jerusalem rode instead to Saladin's port city and fortress of Acre and laid siege to it. When the first ships from Europe arrived, they sent ashore their crusader troops, who dug trenches and fortifications around the city.

When the crusaders were in place, Saladin and his troops arrived, trapping the Christian army between the Muslim host and the city. The crusaders besieging the city were themselves now under siege, fighting on two sides. At last the two kings, Philip and Richard, landed with their troops to bolster the besieged crusaders. The fighting was unbroken. The siege lasted for 683 days. At last the second wave of crusaders broke into the city, the first attackers led by Richard himself. The city surrendered in July 1191, and Saladin's army withdrew to the hills of Judea.

**A 16th century depiction of Saladin**

Satisfied with capturing Acre, Philip returned to France. Richard the Lion-Heart, left in sole command, marched his force to Jaffa, a city on the route to Jerusalem. Richard was a careful and wise **tactician**. His spies had told him that Saladin had laid an ambush on the route, at a place called Arsuf. Richard sent forward his spearmen, while his crossbowmen and longbow archers remained behind. When Saladin attacked, Richard's archers and crossbowmen rained a terrible hail of steel on the Muslims. Richard then brought up his rear guard of heavy horse, crushing the lighter-armed Turks between spear and lance. After Arsuf, no Muslim army dared face Richard again.

Richard then looked to conquer Jerusalem, but Saladin had no intention of giving up the Holy City. Saladin's troops laid waste to the lands between the coast and the city, poisoning the wells in that dry country and destroying everything that could not be carried into Jerusalem. Judea became an artificial desert.

Richard knew too well the costs of war. He saw no way for the crusaders to hold Jerusalem, even if they should take it. So he arranged a truce and a treaty with Saladin to save whatever he could of Christian Outremer.

**tactician:** one who is an expert in coming up with sound *tactics*—on the battlefield, the arrangement of troops and the directing of how the battle should go

**Richard the Lion-Heart at Arsuf**

In the autumn of 1192, Richard and Saladin signed a treaty, leaving the crusaders in possession of their coastal cities, ensuring the return of the True Cross relic, and guaranteeing safe passage for pilgrims to the holy shrines in Jerusalem. The treaty did not satisfy the knights, who had come to the Holy Land to regain Jerusalem; but it was the best that could be won. Richard, as the final commander, received the blame for the failure of the Third Crusade.

# The Failure of the Fourth Crusade

Innocent III's goal, when he became pope in 1198, was to continue the reform of the Church as begun by his predecessors on the Throne of Peter. But the failure of the Third Crusade to recover Jerusalem made another crusade to the Holy Land the pope's first priority. In the very year he became pope, Innocent ordered another crusade. Knights from France and Germany, led by Boniface, marquis of Montferrat, pledged to take up the cross.

The crusaders' goal was first to conquer Egypt, the center of Turkish Muslim power, and from there to move against Jerusalem. The crusader leaders came to an agreement with the Italian city-state of Venice to transport their army by ship to Egypt. The crusaders, however, could not pay the entire amount the Venetians demanded. Seeing an opportunity, the Venetians said they would forgive the amount

## The Noble Infidel

Dying only five months after his treaty with Richard the Lion-Heart, Saladin lived on in the history and the legends of western Europe. Europeans remembered their Muslim foe as gallant, noble, and courteous—a **paragon** of chivalry. So courteous was Saladin that once, when King Richard the Lion-Heart was unhorsed at Jaffa, the sultan sent him a fresh mount. Later, when Richard fell ill with a fever, Saladin had snow brought from the Syrian mountains to cool him.

**paragon:** a model of excellence or perfection

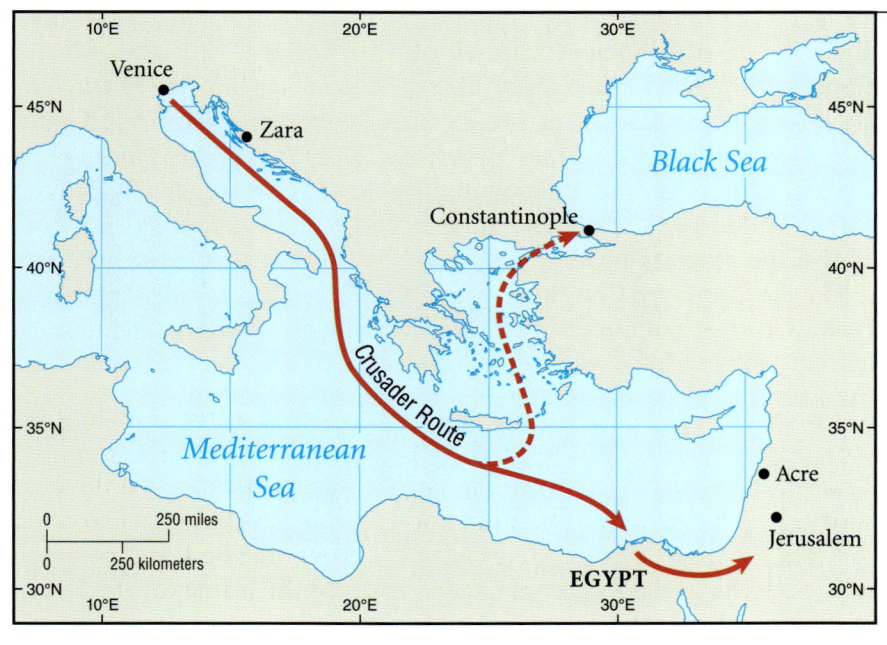

Proposed route for the Fourth Crusade from Venice to Egypt (solid line). Actual route (dotted line)

the crusaders still owed—if they helped Venice attack the Christian city of Zara, in Dalmatia, across the Adriatic Sea from Venice. The crusaders agreed and, in November 1202, Zara fell to the combined crusader and Venetian force. Sorrowful at the news of the fall of Zara, Pope Innocent excommunicated the leaders of the crusade for turning their arms against fellow Christians.

In the end, Innocent absolved the crusaders and urged them to set out for Palestine. But the army, instead, sailed toward Constantinople. Alexius—son of the deposed Byzantine emperor, Isaac Angelus—promised them that if they helped him regain the imperial throne, he would aid them in the crusade. The crusaders and the Venetians reached Constantinople in 1203. The **usurper** emperor, who had deposed Isaac, fled the city. The crusading army placed Alexius and his father on the imperial throne.

**usurper:** one who seizes power or authority without any right to them

Alexius, however, was slow in keeping his promises to the crusaders—and only seven months after he gained the throne, a revolution deposed both him and his father. The crusaders and the Venetians then laid siege to Constantinople. The nobles of Byzantium closed the great gates of the city to these threatening foreigners. The Byzantine army, under the new emperor, put up a strong resistance to the crusaders.

A Byzantine traitor, however, opened the sea-gates to the enemy. The host of crusaders and Venetians slipped into the city, storming it on April 12, 1204. For three days, the crusaders and Venetians looted and burned the ancient capital of the Eastern Christian world. Constantinople held the masterpieces of the ancient world. The invaders smashed the statues of the classical heroes and pagan gods and melted down bronze statues to make coins. They even pillaged the city's churches, loading mules with the gold and jewels that adorned the sacred buildings. The plunder of the civilized world's richest city was almost too much to believe.

Having conquered Constantinople, the leaders of the crusade claimed the Eastern Roman Empire for their own. Fanning out from Constantinople, crusader forces looted and burned the cities of Greece, confiscated land from ancient families, and allotted territories to individual crusader leaders. Amid the ruins of Constantinople the crusaders established a French feudal state and imposed Latin Christianity on the Greeks. Baldwin, count of Flanders, was chosen as emperor of the Romans.

Innocent III was appalled at the result of his call to crusade. Instead of delivering Jerusalem from the Muslims, the crusaders had conquered

St. Mark's cathedral in Venice, enriched by spoils taken from Constantinople

and plundered a Christian people. The papacy had, it was true, control of the Church of Constantinople, which had been in schism with the pope since 1054. But the conquest only turned the Greek people against everything having to do with Catholic western Europe, including the papacy. The Fourth Crusade made the schism of 1054 a permanent division, not only between the churches of Rome and Constantinople, but between the Catholic Church and the Orthodox churches in Greece, the eastern Mediterranean, Russia, and eastern Europe.

## The Schism of 1054

Since the end of the Western Roman Empire in 476, the Churches of the Christian East and the Western Church under the pope gradually grew further and further apart. They remained, for most of the period between 476 and 1054, in union with each other. They held the same Faith, but differences in culture, language, and the ways they expressed certain mysteries of the Faith led to misunderstandings. The West, for instance, used unleavened bread in the celebration of the Eucharist, while the East used leavened bread. The Eastern Churches maintained the original words of the Nicene Creed, where it reads "I believe in the Holy Spirit . . . who proceeds from the Father." In its Mass liturgy, however, the West added the words, "and the Son" to this phrase, and some in the East thought this addition was heretical.

Another problem was that the leaders of the Church of Constantinople, called "patriarchs," began to insist that they were at least second in honor to the pope, the bishop of Rome. After all, was not Constantinople "New Rome"? Was not the Patriarch of Constantinople the bishop of the imperial city? Controversy between Rome and Constantinople grew more intense when the popes, in their attempts to reform the Church, insisted more and more on the authority given them as the successors of St. Peter. At the same time, some patriarchs of Constantinople wanted to increase their power and authority in the Eastern Church and resented any "meddling" on the part of the bishop of "Old Rome."

A serious schism between Constantinople and Rome occurred in the ninth century, but the churches were finally reconciled. Less than 200 years later, however, controversy broke out between the pope and the ambitious patriarch of Constantinople, Michael Kerullarios. In 1053, Michael closed the Latin churches in Constantinople and condemned Latin customs. The pope demanded that Michael recognize his authority. But when the patriarch refused, in 1054 the pope's representative in Constantinople presented Michael with a document from the pope, excommunicating him. In turn, Michael excommunicated the pope.

**Hagia Sophia, 1852**

Though the pope had only excommunicated Michael—and Michael, the pope—the excommunications led to a split between the Churches of Rome and Constantinople. Eventually, the other great Churches of the East—Antioch, Jerusalem, and Alexandria—joined Constantinople in a permanent schism with the Catholic Church. The churches in Russia and eastern Europe that had been founded by Constantinople also went into schism. With the older Eastern Churches, they formed what today we call the Eastern Orthodox Church.

The mutual excommunication between the pope and the patriarch of Constantinople stood for 911 years. On December 7, 1965, however, Pope Paul VI and Patriarch Athenagoras I each read a formal statement lifting the excommunications against one another.

# The Iberian Crusade

Normally, when we think of the Crusades, our minds turn to the wars fought to recover the Holy Land from the Turks. But the Middle Ages had other crusades. Some were fought against pagans, others against heretics, and still others against Muslims for other reasons than the recapturing of Jerusalem.

The wars for the reconquest of Spain from the Muslims were true crusades, even if not called for by popes. From the 8th to the 12th centuries, the small Christian states had expanded and held their own against the Muslims. But, in the late 12th century, the Christian kingdoms of Portugal, León, Castile, Navarre, and Aragon faced a new Muslim threat. The Almohads had replaced the Almoravids as the greatest power in North Africa. Crossing into Spain, the Almohads drove out the Almoravids and added Al-Andalus to their empire.

After conquering Muslim Spain, the Almohads repeatedly attacked the Christian borderlands, killing defenders, enslaving captives, carrying off booty, and burning crops. The Almohads took many forts and castles. Christian rulers in Spain could not stop them, because the Christians

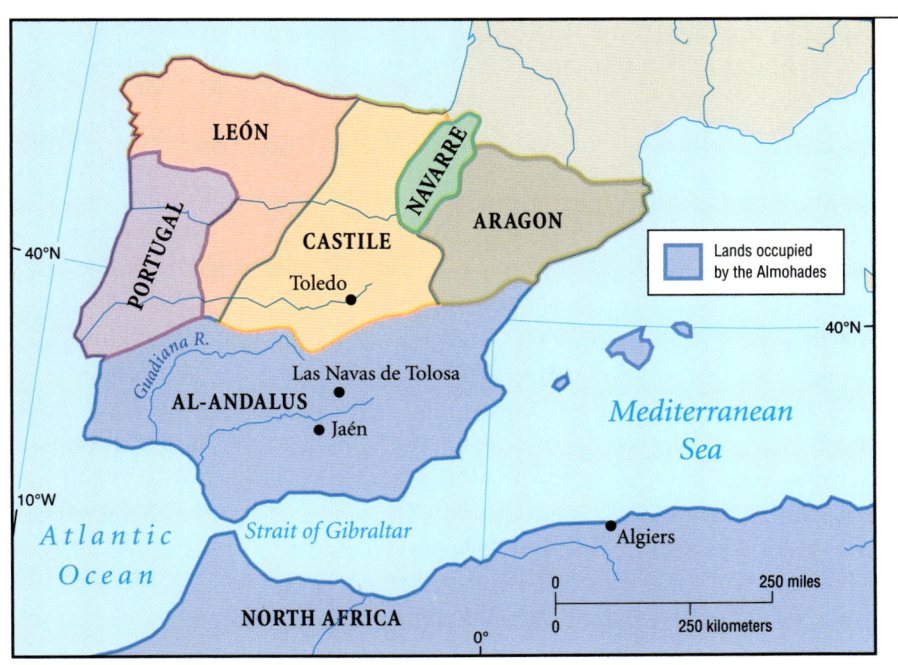

Iberia in the early 13th century

rarely put aside their own disagreements to coordinate their military campaigns against the common enemy.

Church leaders worked to get the Christian monarchs of Spain to join forces against the common enemy. Several popes urged the kings to cooperate. Finally, Pope Innocent III, understanding the danger facing the Christian kingdoms of Spain, called for a crusade against the Almohads. He exhorted Christians all over Europe to take up the cross and head for the Iberian Peninsula.

With the aid of the crusade, King Alfonso VIII of Castile vowed to break the Almohad power. He made peace with his Christian neighbors and announced his intention of marching deep into Al-Andalus to confront its fierce Almohad overlords. He invited volunteers to meet him in Toledo on Pentecost Sunday, 1212. Gallant King Peter II of Aragon and gigantic Sancho VII of Navarre also made preparations for the great campaign.

## Las Navas de Tolosa

The Almohad emir had a long name—Abu Abd Allah Muhammad Al-Nasir—but Spanish-speaking peoples called him simply Miramamolin. The emir was bent upon conquering Al-Andalus. He had gathered such a large army in North Africa that it took almost three months to ferry his troops across the Straits of Gibraltar in the spring of 1211.

As Alfonso VIII had asked, a large international army of crusaders mustered at Toledo during the week before Pentecost Sunday in 1212. Meanwhile, prayers for a successful venture were being said in all the churches of Rome. The crusaders left Toledo on June 20 and headed south through La Mancha. They took the fortress of Malagon on June 24 and Calatrava Castle on the 30th. From Calatrava, Alfonso pushed south and took several other castles. Peter II stayed at Calatrava, waiting for the seven-foot- tall Sancho VII, who arrived on July 7 with a modest force. Joining their forces, the three monarchs crossed the mountains of the Sierra Morena on July 14 and sighted the bulk of the enemy forces encamped below.

The Muslim army covered several low hills and promontories, though most of it gathered on a hill named Cerro de los Olivares. Some of the Muslims tied themselves together in pairs by the legs so they could not abandon their stations; behind them, a circle of slaves (blacks from central Africa and Hispanic Europeans), chained together, formed a ring around Miramamolin's red silk tent, perched on top of the hill. The 31-year-old emir, wearing a black cape and a magnificent turban, stood before his tent,

A depiction of the Battle of Las Navas de Tolosa

brandishing a sword in one hand and holding the Koran aloft in the other. His forces were twice the size of the Christian army.

Before sunrise on the morning of July 16, the Catholics were absolved of their sins, heard Mass, and formed ranks. In the summer heat, the Christians, encased in metal armor, struggled up the Cerro de los Olivares. In the thick of the battle, the forces of Peter and Sancho encircled the Africans. Alfonso rushed forward, breaching the enemy lines. Then Sancho drove into the main body of the adversary, breaking the circle of chained slaves guarding Miramamolin.

Defile of Despenaperros, Spain; its name means, "where dogs are thrown over", and refers to the "infidel hounds" overthrown in the battle at Las Navas de Tolosa

The Almohad emir panicked. So hastily did he flee that he lost his bejeweled turban. Miramamolin did not stop riding until he reached Jaen at nightfall. Left behind on the field of battle, the Muslim troops now saw, atop the Cerro de los Olivares, not their emir but Christian crosses, banners with images of the Blessed Virgin and Santiago, and Sancho VII, the tall king of Navarre. Dismayed, the Muslim army broke ranks and dissolved. The Muslim troops untied their legs and disbanded; and the crusaders routed them. Because they were chained together, many African slaves were killed that day. Indeed, so many men were slain that they could not all be buried.

The Christian triumph at Las Navas de Tolosa destroyed Almohad power and pushed the frontier in central Spain as far south as the Guadiana River.

# The Albigensian Crusade

By the end of the 12th century, southern France was the center of a vibrant and flourishing culture. It was there that the poetry of the troubadours was born—those poets whose songs, praising fair ladies and knightly deeds, had spread to all of Europe. This region of France was known as Languedoc (meaning the "language of Oc") because its people, who spoke a different dialect of French from those in the north, said *Oc* for yes. Those in the north said *Oui*—so those lands were called "Languedoui" (meaning the "language of Oui").

Yet, despite its glittering culture, Languedoc at the end of the 12th century had become the stronghold of a terrible heresy. This heresy was called the Albigensian or Cathar movement. It spread quickly over southern France and claimed the allegiance of many nobles and townsmen there.

The preachers of this heresy lived lives of rigorous self-denial and asceticism, and were thus called *Cathari*, meaning "the purified." They were also called Albigenses after the southern French district of Albi, where they were first identified. The Albigenses established communities in every town and city of Languedoc, preaching against the luxury of the noble courts and the greed of the Catholic clergy. Because many of the Catholic clergy of southern France lived immoral lives, the Cathars could claim they themselves were reformers of Christianity.

But the Albigenses were anything but Christian. Like the Manicheans, they believed and taught that there are two gods, one good and the other evil. The evil god, said the Albigenses, is the creator of this physical world and, particularly, of the human body. Albigenses thought the soul, created by the good god, is imprisoned in the material world and is to be freed only through denying all pleasures of the flesh. They also despised marriage (since it produces new physical life) and praised suicide, since it freed the soul from the body. The Albigensian teachings threatened not only the Church but human society by undermining marriage and the family and creating a culture that despised life itself. But the Albigenses were popular because they preached against the corrupt clergy, whom even the common people had come to despise.

St. Dominic subjects both Albigensian and Catholic books to a trial by fire. The flames reject the Catholic books but burn the Albigensian books.

For 30 years, beginning in the mid-12th century, the Church had tried to meet the threat of the Albigenses by peaceful means—sending preachers, such as St. Bernard of Clairvaux himself, to Languedoc. The Albigenses themselves, however, became violent and plundered the regions in and around Albi and Toulouse. In 1198, Pope Innocent III called on the Cistercians to re-evangelize Languedoc. The two Cistercian preachers sent to the south of France had the help of a young, charismatic Spaniard named Dominic de Guzman. Their preaching, however, had little impact on the heretics or their followers.

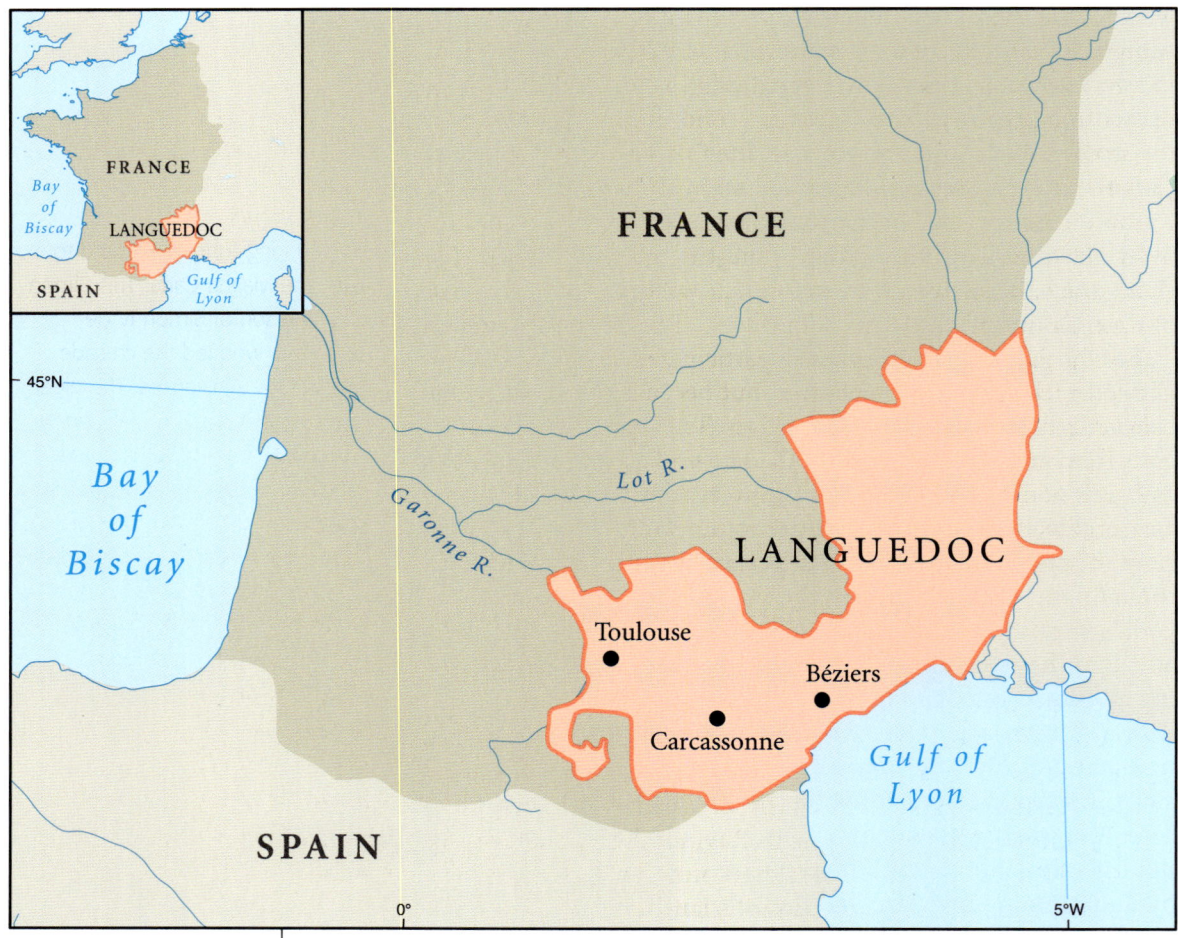

Map of Languedoc in the early 13th century

## The Murder That Brought on War

The Albigenses had the support of a powerful lord of Languedoc—Count Raymond VI of Toulouse. Great-grandson of that Raymond of Toulouse who had been a hero of the First Crusade, Raymond VI ruled Toulouse, the largest portion of Languedoc. The first cousin of the French king, Philip Augustus, and brother-in-law of King Richard the Lion-Heart and King John of England, Raymond VI was indeed a powerful lord.

Count Raymond, however, was an enemy of the Catholic clergy. Though not a Cathar himself, he protected the heretics against any attempts to stamp them out. In 1207 Pope Innocent III's legate, Peter of Castelnau, excommunicated the count because he had not restored to the Church certain churches that he had seized for himself. In a fit of anger, Raymond spoke wrathfully against "meddlesome priests"—and on January 15, 1208, one of his knights murdered the papal legate. Innocent III then deposed Raymond and preached a crusade against him and all his Albigensian subjects, whom the pope called "worse than Saracens."

In 1209, even though Philip Augustus did not himself join the crusade, a host of northern French warriors took the cross against Raymond and the Albigenses. The greatest families, including the duke of Burgundy, participated in the crusade—not so much for religious reasons, but because they wanted the rich lands of Languedoc for themselves. The leader of the expedition, however, was a man of unbending will and fierce religious zeal. His name was Simon de Montfort, a baron of Normandy. His son was that Simon de Montfort of England who forced King John to sign the Magna Carta and called the first parliament.

## The Assault on Languedoc

Confronted with so fearsome a host of northern warriors, Raymond of Toulouse was terrified. He promised the new papal legate that he would punish the Albigenses. But Raymond's vassal—Raymond Roger, viscount of Béziers—refused to submit to the crusaders. They, together with Raymond of Toulouse, laid siege to Raymond Roger's fortresses of Béziers and Carcassonne, slew the inhabitants, and laid waste to the viscount's lands.

With the defeat of Raymond Roger, Simon de Montfort gained control of Béziers and most of the crusaders returned home. But the defeated southerners again found courage, and Simon found he had to defend Béziers and Carcassonne against the forces of Languedoc. Raymond of Toulouse again took arms in defense of his own lands and people.

Once again, in 1212, the northern French invaded southern France and Languedoc was awash in blood. Raymond's brother-in-law, Peter II of Aragon, hero of Las Navas de Tolosa, attempted to make peace. Innocent III was willing to accept his offer, but the northern lords insisted on continuing their "crusade," which had turned into a war for plunder. Peter took the field on the side of Raymond, but Simon de Montfort met his army at the battle of Muret, 1213, and broke it. Peter of Aragon himself was killed in the battle.

### Two Simons

In Chapter 11, you read of a Simon de Montfort who led a rebellion in England that, in 1215, forced King John of England to sign the Magna Carta. This Simon was the son of Simon IV de Montfort, who led the crusade against the Albigenses. The elder Simon participated in the Fourth Crusade and vigorously opposed attacking Constantinople. Though a Frenchman, Simon IV inherited the earldom of Leicester in England, which he passed down to his youngest son, Simon V de Montfort, the hero of the Magna Carta.

**316** LIGHT TO THE NATIONS: The History of Christian Civilization

Carcassonne is a fortified French town, in the former province of Languedoc.

This defeat settled the fate of Languedoc. Raymond abandoned Toulouse, and Simon de Montfort became lord of the city and all the southern lands. He divided his new territories between the northern lords, hungry only for land and booty, who had fought beside him. Pope Innocent III gave a fragment of Toulouse to Raymond VII, the son of Raymond VI.

Map of the eastern Mediterranean lands at the time of the last crusades

## The Medieval Inquisition

The Albigensian Crusade did not destroy Albigensianism, as Pope Innocent III had hoped it would. The heresy still had a strong hold in Languedoc, though it went underground. To ferret out the secret Albigenses and destroy the heresy once and for all, Pope Gregory IX in 1231 instituted a tribunal, called the Inquisition. In establishing the Inquisition, the pope had two aims—to crush the heresy and to replace violence with the rule of law. An office of the Holy See, the Inquisition spread to all of Europe.

Under the Inquisition, the pope appointed judges to seek out and reconcile the remaining Albigenses to the Church. The judges were generally Franciscans or Dominicans because they were the best-educated members of the clergy and, the popes thought, they were less likely to be influenced by worldly motives.

Under the Inquisition, judges would come to a town and preach a sermon on the basic doctrines of Christianity. They would then urge the Albigenses to come forward and be reconciled. If any did so, they were given a mild penance and accepted back into the Church. If the evidence was strong that a person was a member of the Albigenses but refused to admit it, the judges would gather together a jury of local clergy and laymen. The jury would examine the witnesses for and against the accused, determine whether witnesses were telling the truth, and decide if the accused was guilty or innocent.

The accused had certain safeguards to protect him: He could reject a judge whom he considered personally prejudiced against him, and if convicted of heresy, the accused could appeal the case to a higher court. However, those accused of heresy were not allowed to confront the witnesses against them, though they could draw up a list of their known enemies, who were then disqualified from testifying. The Inquisition used torture as a means of bringing the guilty to confess the truth. But it must be remembered that all the tribunals of Europe used torture; the Inquisition did not invent torture but in fact carefully limited it.

The Inquisition punished those guilty of heresy, meting out sterner punishments to those with greater guilt and milder punishments to those with less. A repentant heretic was given a relatively mild penance, while those who pretended to repent and were later convicted of **perjury** were imprisoned so that they would not corrupt others. Convicted heretics who, after repentance, returned to their old beliefs and heretical practices, were turned over to the state for execution.

**perjury:** saying what is false, as in court, when under oath to tell only what is true

# The Last Crusades in Outremer

Though he was disappointed in the results of the Fourth Crusade, Pope Innocent III continued to cherish plans for a crusade to free the Holy Land. In 1207, he decided to organize a new crusade to retake Jerusalem, but his plans were interrupted by the need to do something about the Albigenses and then the Almohads in Spain.

Finally, in 1213, Innocent ordered a crusade to regain Jerusalem to be preached throughout Europe. In 1215, at the tomb of Charlemagne

**Aachen cathedral in Germany, where Charlemagne's tomb is located**

in Aachen, the German Emperor Frederick II vowed to lead the crusade. In 1216, Pope Innocent died, thinking his hoped-for crusade was finally under way.

### The Fifth and Sixth Crusades

But Innocent was deceived. Only six months after the pope died, Frederick received permission from Pope Honorius III to delay entering the crusade. Without Frederick, King Andrew II of Hungary and Duke Casimir of Pomerania sailed to Acre in 1217.

But the main action of this, the Fifth Crusade, was led by the King of Jerusalem, John of Brienne, and the pope's legate. With a force of German crusaders, King John assaulted Egypt, the center and stronghold of Muslim rule in Middle East. They took the fortress of Damietta on the mouth of the Nile in November 1218. The crusade, however, ended in failure when a Muslim army defeated the Christians on July 24, 1221, and forced John of Brienne to surrender Damietta.

Though he had officially been the leader of the Fifth Crusade, Emperor Frederick II had remained in Europe. He finally set sail for Outremer in June 1228, but only after Pope Gregory IX had excommunicated him for failing to set sail the previous year. The pope's opposition to Frederick undermined this, the Sixth Crusade, and many of Frederick's troops abandoned it. So, instead of waging war, the emperor began negotiations with the sultan of Egypt. In 1229, the sultan gave control of Acre, Bethlehem, and Jerusalem to Frederick, who had proclaimed himself king of Jerusalem.

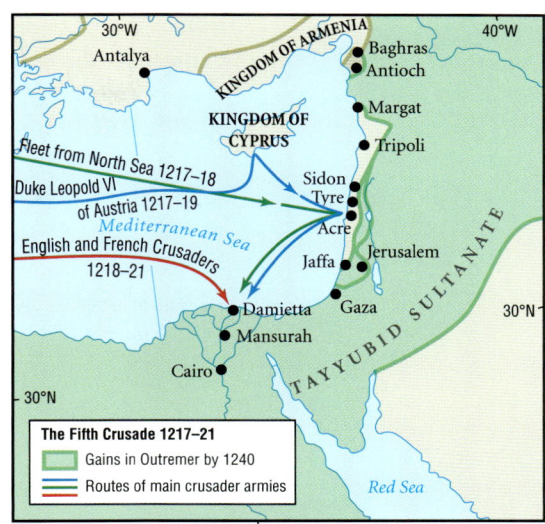

**Map of medieval Egypt and Palestine**

The return of Jerusalem to Christian hands after 40 years was the last real triumph of the Crusades. But the lands of Jerusalem were not easy to defend, and Frederick could not command the allegiance of the crusader lords of Syria. Frederick eventually returned to Italy, and the Christian lands in Outremer fell into disorder and civil war.

In 1244 a new Turkish people, the Khwarazmians, swooped down on Jerusalem and retook it, slaughtering Christian and Muslim inhabitants. Never again would Christians hold Jerusalem. Only a few coastal cities in Outremer remained in Christian hands.

## The Crusades of St. Louis of France

When the Holy City was lost a second time, only one monarch in Christendom could be roused to take up the cross. In the summer of 1248 the saintly king of France, Louis IX, sailed for Cyprus, where a large host of fellow Frenchmen joined him.

Louis and his lords were persuaded to follow the strategy of the Fifth Crusade and invade Egypt, the center of Muslim power, rather than land on the Syrian coast. Landing in Egypt, Louis took the fortress of Damietta—the key to the Egyptian coast—on June 7, 1249. Yet, despite this victory, the Seventh Crusade did not succeed. The heavily armed horses and knights of Europe sank in the Nile mud; disease and heat exhausted the soldiers; and the waters of the Nile, muddy and contaminated, were not suitable for drinking.

When Louis finally ordered his dispirited and sickly men back to the coast, the Muslims threw themselves on the retreating host. Louis fought valiantly in the rear guard in defense of his men, but he was taken prisoner at last. The whole French army, weakened by plague and thirst, surrendered; but they were put to the sword. To obtain his freedom, Louis agreed to pay his Muslim captors an enormous sum of money and to abandon the fortress of Damietta.

Freed by his captors, King Louis went to Palestine. He remained there until 1254, working to restore the Christian fortresses and cities. At last, upon hearing that his mother—who had been acting as his regent in France—had died, Louis returned to France.

Beginning in 1263, a series of disasters befell the remaining Christian states in Outremer. That year, the Muslims destroyed the Christian church at Nazareth. Two years later, they conquered the coastal cities of Caesarea and Jaffa. In 1268, the city of Antioch fell to the Muslims.

Most monarchs in Christendom had come to care little for what happened to Outremer—unless, of course, going on crusade was in their personal interest. King Louis IX, however, did care. On March 24, 1267, he and his three sons took up the cross and began preparing a new crusade.

**King Louis IX of France**

This time, Louis decided to direct his attack against Tunis, which lay on the North African coast to the west of Egypt. Landing in North Africa, however, Louis soon found himself blockaded in his camp, among the ruins of ancient Carthage. Both the king and his men suffered bitterly from heat and plague; and on August 25, 1270, Louis himself died. The grieving crusaders took the body of their king back to France.

The last of the seven crusades ended in the sands of North Africa. The Christian kingdoms in Palestine and Syria did not long survive it. In 1289, Tripoli fell to the Muslims. In 1291, Acre, the capital of the Latin East, surrendered. Henceforth, only the Hospitallers' stronghold on the island of Rhodes and Guy de Lusignan's "Kingdom of Jerusalem" in Cyprus remained in Christian hands. The commercial wealth of Cyprus and Rhodes made the "Kingdom of Jerusalem" a rich jewel of Greco-Frankish castles and European courts. The music of Cyprus, moreover, was acknowledged as the height of European composition in the late 14th century. But of the Christian realms in Syria and the Holy Land, not one remained.

## Effects of the Crusades

Judging them simply by their religious and political goals, the Crusades to reconquer Jerusalem and the Holy Land were a failure. The Christian kingdom of Jerusalem lasted less than a century. The Muslims again came

A picture by Gustav Dore, depicting a battle of the First Crusade

to dominate the Holy City and all of Palestine. And, because of the Fourth Crusade and the crusaders' mistreatment of native Christians in the East, the split between the Catholic and Orthodox churches widened, ending in a schism that continues to this day.

The Crusades were far more successful in reducing feudal warfare in Europe because they gave feudal lords the opportunity of fighting a common enemy rather than feuding among themselves. The Italian cities, particularly Venice, reaped great benefits. The Crusades kept the Mediterranean from being completely controlled by the Muslims, thus permitting Italy to engage in a profitable trade with the East. More importantly, though, the Crusades pushed back the Muslim advance against eastern Europe, allowing the peoples there to develop Christian rather than Muslim cultures and so keeping them as members of Christendom.

Perhaps the most impressive feature of the crusading movement was the tremendous response of everyone—from emperor to noble to peasant—to the Church's call for action. One distinguished medieval historian has said that nothing shows more clearly than the Crusades the strength of medieval Europe's religious faith or the effectiveness of the Church's leadership in those far-off times.

# Chapter Review

## Summary

- The Seljuk Turks conquered the Middle East, threatened the Eastern Empire, and forbade Christians from making pilgrimages to holy places in Jerusalem. The Eastern Roman emperor asked the pope for aid against this new threat.
- Pope Urban II called the First Crusade to recover the Holy Land for Christendom. Europeans, both lords and peasants, responded enthusiastically to the pope's call. The main host conquered Antioch and then Jerusalem in 1099. A feudal kingdom was established in Jerusalem, along with others in Antioch, Tripoli, and Edessa.
- These crusader kingdoms lasted for about 100 years. Two military religious orders, the Knights Templar and Knights Hospitaller, were established to protect the Holy Land.
- Quarrels among the crusader kingdoms allowed the reunited Turks to take Edessa. This inspired the unsuccessful Second Crusade in 1145.

- Under their great leader, Saladin, the Turks were able to overthrow most of the Christian kingdoms and take Jerusalem itself in 1187. Only three coastal cities in Palestine and Syria remained in Christian hands.
- This disaster led to the Third Crusade. Under the leadership of King Richard the Lion-Heart of England and King Philip of France, the crusaders took the coastal city of Acre in 1189. Philip then returned home, leaving Richard to face Saladin. Though he defeated the great Turkish leader in battle, Richard knew he could not hold Jerusalem, even if he succeeded in taking it. He thus signed a treaty in 1192 that opened Jerusalem to Christian pilgrims.
- The last four crusades to the Holy Land were not successful. The Fourth Crusade ended in the Latin conquest of Constantinople. The Fifth Crusade was an unsuccessful assault on Egypt. In the Sixth Crusade, the Emperor Frederick II won Jerusalem by negotiation, but it was again conquered by the Turks. The Seventh Crusade ended ingloriously on the northwest coast of Africa.
- In the late 12th century, the Muslim Almohads conquered Muslim Iberia and attacked the borderlands of the Christian kingdoms there. The kings of Castile, Aragon, and Navarre joined forces in a crusade to defeat the new Muslim threat. The crusaders crushed the Almohad power at Las Navas de Tolosa in 1212.
- Adherents of the dangerous Albigensian heresy had the protection of Raymond VI of Toulouse, the powerful lord of Languedoc in southern France. Pope Innocent III called a crusade against Raymond and his heretical subjects. Lords of northern France, however, joined the crusade—not for religious reasons, but to conquer and divide the rich lands of the south.
- To deal with the Albigensian threat that remained after the crusade against them, Pope Gregory IX established a tribunal called the Inquisition. It was an attempt to curtail violence and to reconcile the Albigenses to the Church.

## Key Concepts

**crusade:** a war fought in defense of Christianity, named from the cross (Latin: *crux*) worn by the first crusaders

**Holy Land:** Palestine, called *Outremer* by the crusaders

**Templars:** the Knights of the Temple; crusader military order of knights, organized like a monastic order

**Hospitallers:** the Knights of St. John of the Hospital; crusader military order
**sultan:** the king or ruler of the Turks
**Albigensian/Cathar:** the name for someone who held to the heresy asserting that material existence is evil
**The Inquisition:** ecclesiastical court created after the Albigensian Crusade to deal with the threat of heresy

## Dates to Remember
**1054:** the pope and the patriarch of Constantinople excommunicate one another, leading to a schism between the Eastern and Western Churches
**July 150, 1099:** fall of Jerusalem to the crusaders
**1187:** Jerusalem reconquered by the Muslims under Saladin
**1204:** sack of Constantinople in the Fourth Crusade
**1209–1218:** the Albigensian Crusade
**1212:** Battle of Las Navas de Tolosa
**1231:** Pope Gregory IX institutes the Inquisition
**1291:** Fall of Acre to the Muslims

## Central Characters
**Urban II (1042–1099):** the pope who called the First Crusade
**Godfrey of Bouillon (1061–1100):** French leader of the First Crusade
**Richard I, Lion-Heart (1157–1199):** king of England and leader of Third Crusade
**Saladin (1138–1193):** the Turkish sultan of Egypt and Syria who reconquered Jerusalem from the Christians
**Innocent III (1160–1216):** the pope who called the Iberian and Albigensian crusades, as well as the failed Fourth Crusade.

## Questions for Review
1. Why were the wars against the Turks in the Holy Land called "crusades"?
2. Why did Pope Urban II call for a crusade in 1095?
3. When did Jerusalem fall to the crusaders? Who refused to take the title of king of Jerusalem? Why?
4. Describe what the Templars and the Hospitallers were. Why were they so called?
5. Why did the crusaders not gain the help and affection of the Christians they had liberated in the Holy Land?
6. When did crusader control of Jerusalem end? Who ended it?

7. Why did the Fourth Crusade attack Christian Constantinople?
8. Why did Pope Innocent III call for a crusade in Iberia? What were the results of this crusade?
9. Why did the pope call for a crusade in the south of France? Was the crusade successful? Please explain.
10. What was the purpose of the medieval Inquisition?

## Ideas in Action

1. Discuss: What is a crusade? For what other causes, besides military ones, do we now use the term? Why do we call these causes "crusades"?
2. Make a map of the kingdom of Jerusalem and the other three crusader principalities of the Middle East. Make another map of the final coastal cities held by the crusading armies.
3. Find Languedoc on a map. Draw your own map showing the principal lands and cities of Languedoc: Toulouse, Carcassonne, Beziers, Marseilles, Avignon, and Albi.
4. Find a photo of the surviving walls of Carcassonne. Draw a picture of that fortress city and then write reports on its fortifications, its location in the countryside, and the great sieges it endured.
5. Find photos of the treasures of the Iberian Crusade: the tent of Miramamolin and the other relics and objects kept in Spain from that event. Find Las Navas de Tolosa on a map.
6. Report on the facts about Saladin. Was he the chivalrous gentleman that Western tradition has remembered?

# Highways and Byways

## The Bells of Cordoba

One achievement of the Iberian Crusade against the Almohads was the king of Castile's conquest of the old Muslim capital of Cordoba. The victorious Castilians crowded into the spectacular city's Great Mosque, which had been hurriedly consecrated as a Christian church, and prepared for a solemn Mass. But King Alfonso VIII's first command after taking possession of Cordoba was that the bells of the Cathedral of Santiago de Compostela be taken down from the mosque and sent back where they belonged, to Compostela.

The bells had been taken as war trophies by a great Islamic warrior, Al-Mansour, when he raided Santiago in 997. Christian prisoners had been forced to carry the bells hundreds of miles across the Iberian Peninsula. Then the bells, whose sound the Muslims hated, were turned upside down to be used as oil lamps.

Hispanic Christians had never forgotten the insult inflicted on their patron, Santiago. Recovered by Alfonso, the great bells were rehung in the cathedral of Santiago de Compostela. There, in 1492, they tolled for the capture of Granada, the last Muslim stronghold in Spain. The next year, 1493, the bells rang to commemorate another great event—Christopher Columbus's successful voyage to the New World.

# Chapter 13  The Great Century

More than at any other time in the history of Western civilization, the Middle Ages triumphantly affirmed that God is good and everything he creates is good. Medieval Christians believed that they must make a basic choice: to live with God or without him. If one lives with God, then God's love is poured into all other loves—friendship, family, marriage, nature, art, and work—and life is happy, full, and complete. But if one turns away from God, not even the good things of this world can bring happiness, nor can any good thing long survive the destruction of sin.

Because they believed life and the world are basically good, medieval Christians tried to express the truths of the Faith in art using the familiar sights of nature, including human and animal life. The medieval reform movement that began at Cluny in the 10th century had encouraged the arts because its leaders wanted to use art to restore holiness to monastic life. They also wanted to use it to connect the daily life of laymen with the very thing that gave it meaning—salvation in Christ. Moreover, the reformers encouraged the building of new churches and the restoration of old ones. They hired the best artists and architects to build to the glory of God and the edification

**Medieval stained-glass window, Notre Dame Cathedral, Paris**

327

of the people. During the period called the High Middle Ages (the 13th and early 14th centuries), the efforts of Cluniac and Cistercian reformers resulted in the flowering of the arts and creativity.

# The Flowering of Medieval Creativity

In the Middle Ages the general populace learned their philosophy, theology, and science through great public arts, especially architecture, painting, and sculpture. As the minds of people today are formed by what they see on television and in the cinema, the minds of medieval people were formed and inspired by the art and architecture they saw daily—in great cathedrals as well as humble village churches. These church buildings gathered under their roofs all the arts that adorned divine worship—sculpture, painting, weaving (used in tapestries and vestments), and music (the chant and, later, sacred **polyphony**).

**polyphony:** a musical style in which two or more voice parts sound against one another

## The New Church Architecture

Medieval churches were built as magnificent tributes to God and as a means of bringing the people closer to him. The great cathedrals have been called "sermons in stone" because their every detail was intended to teach a Gospel truth. The church, and the liturgy within, was to be an image of the heavenly Jerusalem above. Painting and sculpture told Bible stories or depicted holy saints and heroes of the Faith.

Churches along the main highways leading to the great pilgrimage points of Europe—Rome, Saint James at Compostela in Spain, Laon and Saint-Denis near Paris, Glastonbury, Walsingham,

**Rose window at Reims Cathedral**

and later, Canterbury in England—had to accommodate large numbers of Christians who wished to visit the holy places. Because of this, architects developed new engineering techniques and designed new styles that would allow for big buildings and large, open spaces under a roof.

Medieval cathedrals of the 11th and 12th centuries were built in two basic styles: Romanesque and Gothic. The two styles seem to have developed in France in the 11th and 12th centuries. French architects brought both styles to other countries in western Europe.

Romanesque churches were built in the period from roughly 1000 to 1250. Most Romanesque churches are characterized by their use of round Roman arches, which support a high, barrel-vaulted ceiling, arching high over the heads of worshippers below. This high barrel ceiling, along with thick walls and heavy pillars, gives Romanesque churches a feeling of solid, comforting strength.

Gothic churches were built from roughly 1150 to about 1550 and are best known for their pointed arches, which seem to draw the eye upward toward heaven. Saint-Denis Abbey near Paris, built by Abbot Suger, is the earliest Gothic structure. Suger wanted every detail of his church—particularly the pointed arches—to lift the eyes of worshippers to heaven and to explain the teachings of the Catholic Faith in visual images.

Gothic churches allow plenty of space for large windows of either stained or clear glass. The stained glass taught the people by picturing biblical stories, saints, and symbols of the mysteries of the Catholic

## Old-Fashioned and Crude

The Romanesque and Gothic styles of architecture were not called *Gothic* and *Romanesque* in the 12th and 13th centuries. They received their names from 15th-century scholars and critics who called the nearly one-thousand-year period from the 5th to the 14th century the "Dark Ages." These critics and scholars thought these medieval architectural styles were old-fashioned and crude—and so they called them Romanesque, or "imitation Roman," and Gothic, or "barbaric," like the Goths who had overrun Rome.

**Interior of the Romanesque church of the Abbey of St. Foy, Conques, France**

**Vaulted ceilings of the inside of Cologne Cathedral, Cologne, Germany**

Faith. It also threw softly colored light over the interior of the church. It is hard to imagine today the full effect Gothic churches had on those who saw them in the Middle Ages, but they must have been wondrous to behold. The church walls, its vault, pillars and statues, were painted in rich colors, including shimmering gold. And all this, together with the colored light passing through the stained glass window, made the cathedral a festival of light and tint.

## The Rise of Universities

One of the crowning glories of the Middle Ages was the founding of institutions of learning that remain an important aspect of our Western civilization. These institutions, called "universities," have been vital to forming the intellectual life of Western peoples.

**Notre Dame Cathedral, in Paris, France**

## Veneration of the Blessed Virgin

The names of many of the great medieval cathedrals—Notre Dame (Our Lady) de Paris, Notre Dame de Chartres, the Cathedral of Saint Peter and Mary in Cologne, among others—refer to one of the chief inspirations of medieval Catholic culture—the veneration of the Blessed Virgin Mary.

Throughout the Middle Ages, Christians repeated the *Ave Maria* (Hail Mary), a prayer begging the Virgin's help in times of need. In the 11th century, Christians recited "aves" (pronounced *AH-vays*) using strings of beads. Beginning in the 13th century, Christians in France began saying their aves in 15 groups of 10 prayers each ("decades") while meditating on the events of Jesus' life. This is the origin of the rosary as we know it today.

The veneration of Mary greatly affected popular culture and imagination. With the recognition of the Virgin's purity and mercy, women achieved a new and exalted status. Europeans came to see motherhood as a spiritual gift to women, and they saw women themselves as equal companions with men in the journey to heaven.

The image of the Virgin and Mother—her purity and compassion—affected people's behavior. The influence of the Blessed Virgin was felt especially in the development of the codes of chivalry. The chivalrous man was expected to be not only a great warrior and champion but also a man of his word, unfailingly courteous to ladies, and a protector of the weak and unfortunate. Before going into battle, knights often dedicated their lives and actions to the Blessed Virgin.

**A medieval depiction of Mary and the crucified Christ**

**At the medieval University of Paris, a teacher leads fellow scholars in discussion. All students wore scholars' caps and gowns.**

During the 12th century monastery schools, such as those begun by the reformers in Cluniac communities, were gradually being replaced by cathedral schools as the most vibrant centers of study. Influential cathedral schools grew up at Paris, Bec, London, Laon, Chartres, and Canterbury. The English word "school" derives from *schola*, the Latin word for *choir*—the place in the cathedral or abbey where the students would sit to hear and talk with the master of studies. From *schola* also comes the name of the philosophy that came to characterize the Christian Middle Ages—scholasticism.

Eventually, various cathedral schools began joining in associations among themselves to form larger institutions, called universities. Though, in a university, the individual schools retained most of their independence, they were united under a common system that set up a standard curriculum, made sure textbooks were available in acceptable and university-authorized copies, organized public examinations, and conferred bachelor's, master's, and doctor's degrees.

Medieval universities were divided into four faculties or colleges (though not every university had all four). These were the colleges of arts, medicine, law, and theology. Study at the arts faculty embraced the Seven Liberal Arts: grammar, rhetoric, and logic (the *trivium*), and arithmetic, geometry, music, and astronomy (the *quadrivium*).

Many aspects of the medieval university continue even in our time. Universities are still divided into faculties; they are self-governing institutions; they still grant bachelor's, master's, and doctor's degrees, and their professors at times even wear old-fashioned gowns, the design of which dates back to medieval times. The university is one of the lasting, crucial contributions the Middle Ages made to the Western intellectual tradition.

At the beginning of the 13th century, five prominent university centers existed in Europe, each with its own specialty. Italy's University of Bologna specialized in law; Montpellier in France and Salerno in Sicily were famous for the study of medicine, while Oxford in England and Paris in France were known for the study of philosophy and theology. Other universities arose over time throughout Europe, making their contributions to Europe's fund of knowledge.

The medieval imagination fed from both cathedral and university. One could find Truth in worship and study. Through cathedral and university, the medieval mind raised Christian civilization to new heights of beauty and understanding.

> **Lectures and Disputations**
>
> Since books had to be copied out by hand in the Middle Ages—a painstaking and time-consuming process—scholars had few books to work from. The masters possessed the necessary books; students, however, had to rely on the masters' lectures and public readings, which students copied down in notes and memorized on hearing. Education in the Middle Ages began with the cultivation of memory in early childhood and continued throughout life. What a medieval scholar could and did remember is astounding to us, who rely on the written word as an aid to memory.
>
> Along with lectures, public disputations or debates formed an important part of the intellectual life at the cathedral schools and, later, the universities. These disputations explored difficult questions in such subjects as philosophy or theology in light of the different ideas presented in the great texts or defended by those engaged in a debate. Medieval scholars looked for truth by seeking to understand different arguments and weighing them against what they knew by the light of reason and divine revelation.

# The Age of Innocent III

The 13th century has been called the "Great Century," for it saw the full flowering not only of medieval art and architecture, but of medieval thought, especially in philosophy and theology. The Great Century revealed how Catholic culture could find new ways of expressing itself and renewing the life of Christian people.

The 13th century began under a pope who saw the reform of the Church and Christian society as his divine mission. When he became pope in 1198, Innocent III was only 37. You have read of him as the pope who called two crusades to free Jerusalem, as well as crusades against the Albigenses and the Almohads. But these religious wars were just a part of what Innocent did as pope. Though he thought his crusades very important, he had much farther-reaching goals than regaining Jerusalem or even protecting Christendom from Muslims and heretics.

**Pope Innocent III with Saint Benedict, from a 13th century fresco**

As pope, Innocent's goal was to reform society completely. The Church, he thought, must take an active role in bringing about social justice as well as ensuring that all believers grow in faith and holiness. Innocent and his fellow clergy wanted nothing less than a perfect Christian society. However, they did not expect to establish heaven on Earth, for they believed that human weakness and the tendency toward sin would always be present in this world, requiring continual reform of Church and society.

Like the popes before him, Innocent took an active role in the political life of Europe, both to protect the rights of the Church and to make sure Christian rulers ruled justly, as Christians should. But, as with his crusades, Innocent was not always successful in dealing with kings and emperors. For instance, his attempt to reform the German empire to make it truly what it was supposed to be—the defender of the Church and the secular leader of Christendom—did not succeed as he wished. In 1201, when the nobles of Germany were divided over who should be the next emperor, Innocent backed Otto IV, one of three candidates, for the imperial throne and tried to influence the election in favor of his candidate. But when he became emperor, Otto went back on promises he had made to Innocent and began seizing Church land in Italy. Otto invaded the kingdom of Sicily, whose king—Frederick II—was under the pope's protection. The German nobles then rejected Otto as emperor and elected Frederick in his place.

Innocent constantly intervened in the internal disputes of every country in Europe—which did not necessarily make him popular with their rulers. For instance, he placed León under **interdict** because King Alfonso IX had broken Church law by marrying his cousin, Berengaria of Castile. Innocent lifted the interdict when Berengaria voluntarily separated from the king. Innocent placed France under an interdict when King Philip Augustus dismissed his wife, Ingeborg of Denmark, and took another

**interdict:** a sanction or punishment placed by the Church on a city or region. When a land is under interdict, no public rites of the Church, including public Masses, may lawfully be said. Priests, however, may privately administer necessary sacraments.

woman as his wife. When that woman died, Philip agreed to be reconciled to Ingeborg, and Innocent lifted the interdict.

Innocent placed England under an interdict when King John refused to allow the pope's chosen man, Stephen Langton, to become archbishop of Canterbury. Angered at the interdict, John persecuted a group of monks, driving them from their monastery—for which Innocent excommunicated the king.

John, however, was faced with an invasion from France led by King Philip and by rebellion from his own barons. He found he had no other choice than make peace with Innocent. John begged Innocent's forgiveness and made himself, and all future English kings, the pope's vassals. But this move brought John no peace. The English barons, refusing to pay the tribute John owed as a vassal to the pope, rose in an armed rebellion that ended in John's signing of the Magna Carta in 1215.

Pope Innocent objected to the Magna Carta because the barons had used violence to get the king to sign it. But, despite the pope's protests, the Magna Carta remained law in England.

The church of St. John Lateran in Rome, where the Fourth Lateran Council was held

## The Fourth Lateran Council

Innocent III's greatest triumph as pope was not political, nor was it a crusade. Rather, it was a council he called to bring about a more perfect reform of the Church.

This council, the Fourth Lateran Council, is perhaps most famous for using the word *transubstantiation* for the first time. It was used to describe how the elements of the Mass, the bread and the cup, can be called the Body and Blood of Christ. The council fathers declared that while the "appearances" of bread and wine remain, the bread and wine change substance. That is, the elements still look, smell, taste, and have the effects of bread and wine, but they change from having the substance of bread and wine (from *being* bread and wine) to becoming the substance of Christ—body, blood, soul, and divinity. This transubstantiation occurs when the priest says the words of consecration: "This is my body"; "This is my blood."

Because fewer and fewer Christians were receiving communion frequently, and some not at all, the council declared that every Christian had to go to confession if aware of committing a serious sin and to receive the Eucharist at least once a year. Further, it forbade priests to accept money for administering the Sacraments. The council directed bishops to maintain schools and to give teaching sermons when they presided at Mass. The council ordered bishops and priests to refuse to pay taxes on church property.

Many of the Lateran Council's reforms did not continue beyond Innocent's death. Powerful kings continued to demand a portion of the wealth of the Church in their countries and to violate the Church's independence when it came in conflict with their political aims. But the council's teaching on the Eucharist, as well as the word *transubstantiation*, have continued to our day to nourish the reverence of Catholics for the presence of Jesus in the Sacrament.

In the months following the close of the Fourth Lateran Council, Pope Innocent worked to push forward preparations for another crusade to retake Jerusalem. He wanted the crusade to be under way in 1217. But in the summer of 1216, Innocent died at only 56 years of age. He did not achieve all his goals, and he saw many of his plans stray from their course. Still, Innocent was one of the greatest men to hold the see of Rome, and he may have been the most powerful of all the medieval popes. For nearly 20 years, he shaped the history of all of Europe.

**Medieval depiction of St. Francis of Assisi**

# Mendicant Friars and New Orders

The young Francesco Bernadone liked nothing better than revels, feasting, fine clothes, and the companionship of his friends. The son of a rich cloth merchant of the town of Assisi in Italy, and rather spoiled, Francesco—or Francis—had plenty of money, which he spent lavishly on himself and his companions. A merry young man, Francis enjoyed music—especially the new troubadour songs that had made their way into Italy from Languedoc in southern France.

When he was about 20 years old, Francis joined his townsmen in a battle with a neighboring city. After being taken prisoner, Francis fell sick; and while convalescing, he began thinking about God and eternity. He did not change his way of life immediately, however. After returning to Assisi, he was filled with dreams of becoming a soldier and winning great honor and renown. But when he was stricken with a second illness in 1205, Francis began turning from his former way of life to embrace a life of poverty for the love of God.

## St. Francis of Assisi and the Friars Minor

Even before his change of life, Francis had been generous to the poor. After his "conversion," he was even embracing lepers, kissing their hands and giving them alms. He began visiting hospitals and, on a pilgrimage to Rome, he left all the money he had with him at the tomb of St. Peter. As he left the church, Francis gave his clothes to a poor beggar, dressed himself in the poor man's rags, and began begging for alms.

One day, while praying before a crucifix in the ruined church of San Damiano near Assisi, Francis heard a voice from heaven saying, "Go, Francis, and rebuild my Church, which you see is falling in ruins." He thought the voice meant the ruined San Damiano (though the voice was speaking of the Catholic Church itself). To purchase building materials, Francis took and sold some of his father's cloth stocks. Pietro Bernadone, angry with his son for his strange behavior, grew even angrier when he heard about his lost cloth stocks. Accusing Francis of theft, Pietro brought him before the bishop. There, Francis stripped off all his clothes and renounced his inheritance so he would owe nothing to his family. To Pietro he said, "Until now I have called you my father on earth; henceforth, I desire only to say, 'Our Father who art in Heaven.'" The astonished bishop handed his own cloak to Francis to cover his nakedness.

Separated from his family and alone, Francis set to work replacing the stones and roof of the little ruined chapel of San Damiano. He lived a life of prayer, poverty, and service to others, even attending to the poor, homeless lepers. Having cast aside his rich clothing, he donned the gray, undyed tunic worn by farmers. Some townspeople thought Francis was half crazy, but others recognized his authentic holiness. Others began to gather around him, joining in his prayers and labors.

When Francis had gathered 11 followers around him, he wrote a short rule of life for them. According to this rule they would live in poverty, owning no possessions, and rely on the alms given them by the people or by working at trades and manual labor. Going out two by two (as the disciples did in the Gospels), Francis and his followers were to preach to the people about the Kingdom of God and the call to repentance.

**Pope Innocent III approves Franciscan rule.**

**mendicant:** one who lives by the gifts or alms given him for preaching or teaching and not by his own labor (from the Latin *mendicare*, "to beg")

**convent:** a local community or the house of a religious order, commonly of religious sisters, but also of religious brothers and fathers

Francis called himself and his followers the *Fratres Minores* ("Friars Minor"—"Little Brothers"). In 1209, Francis went to Rome to seek the pope's approval for his little community of wandering preachers and evangelists. The pope, Innocent III, was reluctant to approve a group that was not bound to one house or place. But that very night, God spoke to him in a dream. In his dream, the pope seemed to see the Church of St. John Lateran in Rome begin to fall all around him—when, suddenly, a little man in a gray smock came and held up the walls and roof, keeping them from collapsing. On waking, Pope Innocent realized that the little gray-clad man of his dream was the one who had approached him the day before. The pope sent for Francis and in 1209 approved his brotherhood—the Friars Minor. The brothers returned to build lodgings in the town of Assisi.

St. Francis's Friars Minor represented a new kind of religious life. Like monks or canons regular, friars take vows and live according to a rule. But unlike Benedictine monks, for instance, friars do not earn their living by the work of their hands but by alms of food and money they receive from the faithful. So it was that friars were called **mendicants**—beggars. Friars, too, work outside their houses, or **convents**. They are to go wherever they are needed, to preach, teach, and minister to the spiritual needs of Christians. As preachers and missionaries, the friars had to be well trained; and so, as the order grew and became more established, they began not only to attend the new universities, but to become professors in them as well.

Francis did not attract only men to his fellowship of little brothers. During Lent of 1212, a young woman came to him, wanting to embrace his way of life. She was Clare, the 18-year-old daughter of one of Assisi's wealthiest leading families. Clare's parents objected, but one night after Palm Sunday in 1212, she slipped out of her house. Francis and a procession of friars received her by torchlight. Because there was no place to house her properly, Francis took her to the local Benedictine nuns, with whom she lived for a while. Clare's personal holiness drew other women of the region to her. Francis gave the women their own rule; they became the Poor Ladies, known to us now as the Poor Clares.

Francis had a burning desire to convert the Muslims to the Christian Faith. In 1219, he accompanied the Fifth Crusade to the shores of Egypt.

Chapter 13   The Great Century   **339**

There he gained an audience with the sultan of Egypt himself. His attempt to convert the ruler of the Muslims was unsuccessful, but his manner and fervor so impressed the sultan—and made him fear that the little poor man might convert even the Muslims—that he sent Francis back unhurt and with a safe conduct to the Christian lines.

Francis's life was not without sorrow. As his order grew, many of its members began demanding that it should be more like existing religious orders, with permanent houses and churches of its own. Francis resisted such changes. But in the end, he gave into some of them, which he humbly accepted were for the good of the order.

After resigning as head of the Friars Minor in 1224, Francis, with his closest brothers, went into the Apennine Mountains, where he built a hut of branches for his lodging. There, fearful for the future of his order (he worried it would lose its devotion to poverty) and after spending a night in prayer, Francis had a vision of a winged seraph, nailed to a cross. Seeing it flying toward him, Francis felt stabs of pain in his hands, feet, and side. When the vision was gone, Francis saw he had received the *stigmata*, the visible wounds of Christ, on his hands and feet. These he kept hidden from others until his death, only two years later, in 1226.

The Franciscan order multiplied rapidly after Francis's death. The appeal of the life of poverty and

### Carols and Crèches

Among Francis's many contributions to the Faith, none is better known or loved than his Christmas celebration. Francis staged actors in costume in a church as representations of the Christmas Nativity scene. That performance led to the making of figurines of Mary, Joseph, the Child Jesus, and shepherds—the Christmas crèche—to keep the Nativity in every house. Francis composed and collected songs in honor of the newborn Christ child, which led to the tradition of Christmas carols.

*Saint Francis Receiving the Stigmata*

*Saint Dominic* by Giovanni Bellini

**parchment:** the skin of a sheep or goat prepared for writing on, as we use paper today

preaching drew hundreds to the order, especially when the friars were sent to study at the universities. The Little Brothers used the universities to evangelize the world.

## Hounds of the Lord

"I could not bear to prize dead skins while living skins were starving and in need." So said the young Dominic de Guzmán, who would give his life to help "living skins"—his Christian brothers and sisters. Dominic, a canon of the cathedral church of Osma in León, had sold his prized collection of **parchment** religious books ("dead skins") and given the money to the poor.

Dominic was born in the Castilian province of Burgos to a devout family of the lesser nobility. Dedicated by his parents to the Church, Dominic had become a canon while still a student, and he was ordained a priest in 1195. So strictly did he live his religious life and love solitude and prayer that his fellow canons regarded him as the holiest among them. Eventually, he became prior of the chapter of canons in the city of Osma.

In 1203, Diego d'Azevado, the bishop of Osma, asked Dominic to accompany him on a journey to northern Europe on behalf of King Alfonso IX of León. Passing through Languedoc, they stayed at an inn, where Dominic spent the entire night in discussion with the innkeeper, who was an Albigensian. After their conversation, in which Dominic convinced the innkeeper to abandon his heresy, Dominic himself became convinced that he was not called to live a life of secluded contemplation but one of public preaching and teaching.

Following a second journey to France, Dominic and Bishop Diego went to Rome to ask the pope, Innocent III, to send them to preach the Gospel to the Muslims in the East. Innocent, however, asked them instead to go to Languedoc to preach against the Albigenses.

The priest and bishop, with monks from St. Bernard's Abbey of Cîteaux, spent several years in Languedoc, trying to convert the Albigenses. They made some conversions, but they were not very successful in stopping the heresy. Dominic continued to preach while the Albigensian crusade raged around him—once saving the life of a young man who was to be burned at the stake for being a heretic. The man later became Catholic and joined Dominic's band of preachers. Dominic ministered as well to the crusaders, whom he found to be ignorant of the Faith and living immoral lives. Once he rebuked the bishop of Toulouse, who went about accompanied by soldiers and servants. "The enemies of the Faith cannot be overcome in this manner," Dominic told the bishop. "Arm yourself with prayer instead of a sword; be clothed with humility instead of fine clothing."

Dominic thought the time in which he lived needed a new kind of preacher, one who would have the theological education and training in public speaking necessary to debate with the most learned of the Albigensian leaders. Dominic himself lived an austere life of poverty, and he wished his "preachers" to do the same. Unlike older orders of monks and canons regular that lived in independent monasteries, Dominic's preachers, wherever they were, would be directed by a centralized head, called the master general. Like the Franciscans, they would live by the alms given them by the faithful.

**Painting of a scene from the life of Saint Dominic**

Dominic sought approval of his "Order of Preachers" from Pope Innocent III. The pope at first hesitated. But then he was inspired, it is said, by a dream—much like the one he had concerning Francis of Assisi—and approved the order. Innocent's successor, Pope Honorius III, formally approved Dominic's order in 1216.

Dominic's Order of Preachers, also called Friars Preachers, became known as the "Hounds of the Lord"—in Latin, *Domini canes* ("the Lord's dogs"). This is a pun on *another* name they have as the followers of Dominic—the "Dominicans." Dominic unleashed these "hounds" across

Christendom, as well as into the universities and schools of Europe, to evangelize and teach as they did among the heretics of southern France.

Dominic sent friars to study and preach at the University of Bologna, in the Papal States, and at the University of Paris. The Dominicans started priories in those cities. Bologna became Dominic's headquarters, although he traveled constantly. The lean Spaniard was a familiar figure along the major thoroughfares of France and Italy. Dominic wore a threadbare habit, he carried a bag of books, and he usually slept, without any bedding, on the stone floor of a church. He preached on street corners just as happily as he disputed with learned theologians in academic circles or discussed grave matters with popes, rulers, and other religious leaders.

St. Dominic de Guzmán died after a short sickness in 1221, at his priory in Bologna. He was only 51. The saint who practiced the poverty he preached expired in a borrowed bed because he did not have one of his own.

The orders founded by Dominic and Francis helped renew and reform the Church in the 14th century. In lands where bishops and priests had grown corrupt or just lazy—where the Church was collapsing, like the church St. Francis saw in his dream—the friars' ascetic lives and zeal inspired many with love for Christ and the Church. But their influence was not just spiritual. In the coming years, they would bring about a flowering of learning in Europe's great universities.

# Struggles on Christendom's Borders

In 1240, eastern Europe was invaded by the armies of the Mongol horde, ferocious warriors on horseback from Central Asia. A warrior named Temujin (born around 1160) had formed the Mongol tribes into a powerful nation. When he was 45, he became Genghis Khan, (*khan* means "ruler") of the several Mongol tribes of the Asian steppes.

## Mongol Invasions

In 1215, Genghis Khan and the Mongols swept down on China and conquered the valleys of the Yellow and Yangtze rivers, all the way to the Pacific coastlands. In 1217 his armies moved west to Samarkand and the kingdom of Persia. The Mongol horde that conquered Samarkand celebrated the victory by slaughtering the inhabitants—thus showing

Chapter 13   The Great Century   343

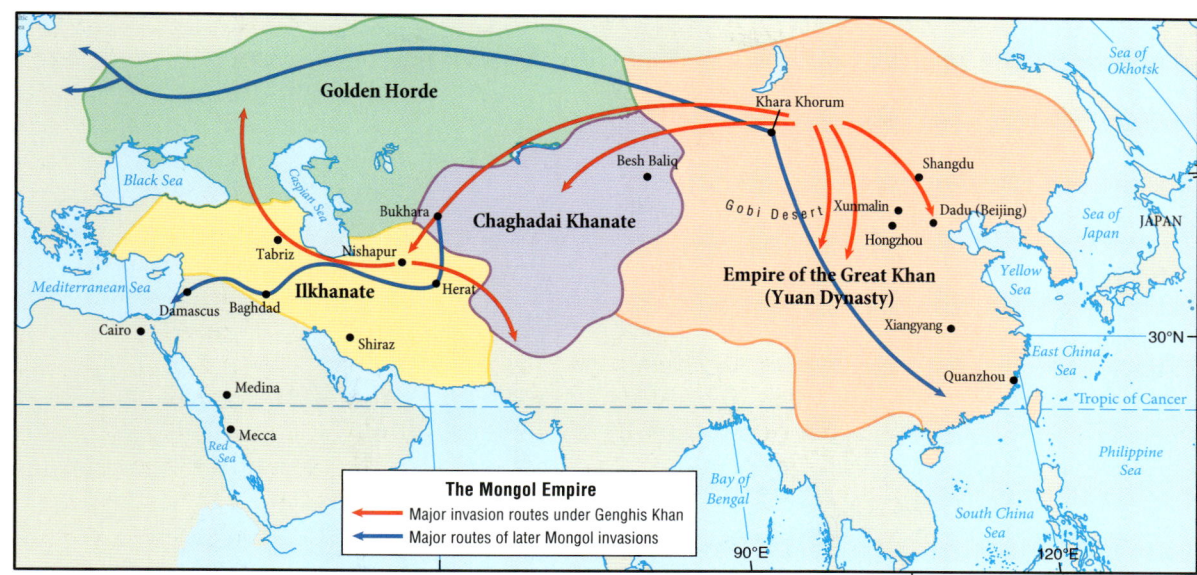

**Major routes of Mongol invasions**

the peoples of other lands what would happen to them if they refused to submit.

In 1227, Genghis was struck by a fever and died. His son, Ogodei, succeeded him as khan. Ogodei turned the Mongol horde toward the lands west of the Volga River and subdued the Russians of Novgorod and Kiev. The army moved farther west under the command of Batu, who was Genghis' leading general. Meanwhile, Ogodei Khan returned to his tent capital at Khara Khorum, in Mongolia. Batu overran Poland in April 1240 while a portion of the army—under Batu's grandfather, Subedei—swept

**Movie extras as Mongolian warriors on horseback during a scene from the 2004 film *Genghis Khan***

## Marco Polo's Travels

The court of Kublai Khan in China in 1275 was the subject of the most famous travel book in history: *A Description of the World*, written by a young Venetian named Marco Polo. Polo was impressed by the beauty and opulence of Kublai's way of life. Sweet soap, fireworks, gunpowder (used by the Chinese not in guns, but in fireworks), fine porcelain, asbestos, and coal fires were all unknown in Europe but were found in Kublai Khan's China. Marco Polo described the convenience of Chinese paper money as compared with gold and silver coins (as used in Europe). He described the marvels of Chinese paper, also little known in the West, where people still wrote on parchment. In the 13th century the West had only a very crude paper, the manufacture of which Europeans had learned from the Muslims, who had learned of it from the Chinese.

Polo's account of the marvels of the Far East and China caught the interest of some merchants. Most Europeans, however, dismissed it as a fantasy.

**The Polo brothers arrive at Bukhara**

into Hungary and defeated the heavily armored, mounted Hungarian knights in one horrible battle. Europeans to the west of Poland heard reports of the savagery of these Mongols and trembled.

Then, in December of 1241, when the princes of Germany were sending tribute to Batu and Subedei, Ogodei Khan died. The Mongol commanders returned to Kara Khorum in Mongolia for the election of the next khan. Subedei and Batu and all their warriors suddenly and mysteriously disappeared from Poland and Hungary. In Christian Europe, their disappearance seemed a miracle, the answer to many prayers.

## Fernando III, "the Saint"

Fernando III became king of Castile in 1217, at the age of 19, one year after the death of Pope Innocent III and five years after the Iberian Crusade. Thirteen years later, he inherited the crown of León. King Fernando III was a great war leader. Never once in his 35-year reign did he lose a battle against the Moors. But Fernando was more than a great warrior; he was a devout Catholic who fasted, did penances, and sometimes spent whole nights in prayer. It is for this he is remembered in Spain as San Fernando—St. Fernando.

King Fernando was also a just ruler. It is said of him that he was careful not to overtax his subjects, saying he feared the curse of one poor woman more than an army of Moors.

Fernando was at war with the Moors throughout his reign. One of his greatest triumphs was recovering the fabled city of Córdoba, the former seat of the caliphs of Al-Andalus. Córdoba had been the capital of the Islamic West, fabled for its wealth, its scholars, and the caliph's huge library of some 400,000 books.

The reconquest of Córdoba began in an unexpected way. On their own initiative a small group of young Castilians, who lived in Ubeda on the Christian borderlands, attacked the great city in the off-season for war. Disguised as Moors, the men, led by a young knight named Domingo Muñoz, scaled the walls of Córdoba in the midst of a storm and took the city by surprise on the night of January 7, 1236. After gaining control of a major suburb, the intrepid group sent a messenger to the Castilian king. They would try to hold their precarious position, they told the king, until he could arrive with an army.

In mid-January—in the town of Benavente, in León—the king was just sitting down to dinner when a messenger arrived with the astounding news that a handful of Christians had gained control of part of the grand capital of western Islam. Fernando got up from the table without eating a morsel. He immediately began dictating letters and issuing orders; within a few hours he was on his way south, to Córdoba, accompanied by one of his brothers and an escort of some 100 men. The weather was awful. The royal party had to ford swollen rivers and cross through mountain passes almost entirely blocked by snow. King Fernando arrived at Córdoba on February 7, after a three-week journey. The band of Christian frontiersmen in the city had been able to hold out for a month because several Castilian bishops had sent them reinforcements.

**Statues of King Fernando and his wife, Beatriz**

As more troops came together, the Christians closed in on the city. No help from other Islamic kingdoms in Al-Andalus or from North Africa arrived to save the former Muslim capital. Córdoba surrendered on the Feast of Sts. Peter and Paul, June 29, 1236. King Fernando and his army staff entered the city triumphantly a few days later. They crowded into the spectacular Great Mosque there, which had been hurriedly consecrated as a Christian church, and prepared for a solemn Mass in thanksgiving for their victory.

King Fernando did not rest long after redeeming Córdoba from Islam. He next set his eyes on Jaén, a well-fortified city dominated by a great castle on a hill. Fernando laid siege to Jaén for six months. Finally, the city's people, compelled by hunger, surrendered to him in April 1246.

Fernando then turned his attention toward Seville, the largest city in Al-Andalus. Surrounded by many castles and fortified towns, Seville was

Cities of Córdoba, Jaén & Seville in Spain

hard to take. Fernando needed a fleet of ships to blockade the city, which sat on the right bank of the Guadalquivir River. He thus ordered his Basque subjects on the northern coast of the Iberian Peninsula to assemble a squadron of ships and sail it all the way to the mouth of the Guadalquivir.

On November 23, 1248, Seville surrendered—537 years after it had fallen to the Muslims. King Fernando gave the inhabitants who chose to migrate to Muslim lands 30 days to depart. The king, as was his custom, allowed them to take their valuables with them. He also gave them safe-conduct protection and beasts of burden as far as the seaport of Cádiz. On December 22, 1248, King Fernando made his triumphal entry into Seville.

**Cathedral of Seville, Spain**

The pious ruler of Castile and León focused on re-evangelizing the areas regained from Islam. Fernando helped the new bishops in these regions reorganize ancient diocesan sees and institutions that had all but disappeared under centuries of Muslim rule. He endowed the Church with crown lands and revenues, besides the contributions from his private fortune. Fernando built men's and women's monasteries and parish churches. The king is well known for having begun construction of three of the finest Gothic cathedrals in southern Europe at Burgos, Toledo, and Seville.

Fernando III died of sickness and fatigue at the age of 54. Four hundred years later, in 1671, he was canonized by Pope Clement X. However, Spaniards had venerated their holy monarch long before his canonization. When he rode into combat, the king always hooked a small ivory statue of Our Lady onto his saddle—the Virgin of Battles. St. Fernando's statue, his sword, "Lobera," and his body (showing no signs of decay), encased in a glass and silver urn, can be found to this day in the Royal Chapel at the Cathedral of Seville.

# The Achievement of Scholasticism

At the beginning of the Middle Ages, learning in Christian Europe was far inferior to learning in Islamic countries. When the Arabs conquered such ancient centers as Antioch in Syria and Alexandria in Egypt, they found in them vigorous communities of scholars and thinkers. Continuing the intellectual traditions they found in these places, scholars in the Arab and Persian cities not only possessed the complete texts of Aristotle and other classics of ancient Greece and Rome, but they were busily engaged in adding to this learning by commentary and further investigation.

In the 8th through the 10th centuries, the great works of Greek science and Aristotelian philosophy were translated into Arabic at cultural centers like Baghdad. Through contact with Muslim scholars in Al-Andalus, western European Christians discovered the ancient works—most importantly, the works of the Greek philosopher, Aristotle. The gigantic task of translating the ancient texts into Latin occurred in the 12th and 13th centuries.

A medieval *magister* (teacher) reading a text to his students

The philosophy of Aristotle took Europe by storm in the late 12th century. Scholars in the universities thought Aristotle offered a better explanation of the natural world than did the Platonic philosophy that had dominated the schools until then. But adopting Aristotle's philosophy was not without some problems. Some Christian thinkers adopted Aristotelian ideas that were contrary to the Catholic Faith. For instance, Aristotle taught that the material universe was eternal, having no beginning or end. This concept went against the Church's teaching that the universe had a beginning, at Creation. Other thinkers, however, found in Aristotle's philosophy an effective tool to better understand Divine Revelation.

Accompanying the rediscovery of Aristotle was a method of philosophical inquiry called Scholasticism—the method of the *schola*, or "school." Scholastic philosophers and theologians developed a special kind of argumentation by which they found the truth in a given subject. A scholastic argument might go something like this. A question would be asked—for instance, "Is the human soul immortal?" Various objections or arguments against the soul being immortal would then be considered, followed by an argument (called a *responsum*) proving that the soul is immortal. Then would follow replies to the objections, solving their difficulties, based on the *responsum*.

Scholasticism caught on among the new orders of friars. The Dominicans and Franciscans provided well-trained scholars whose ideal of learning was much more like that of ancient times than any that western Europe had known in over 500 years. Among these friar scholars were two great lights of learning: one was St. Bonaventure (1221–1274), a Franciscan; the other was St. Thomas Aquinas (1225–1274), a Dominican.

*St. Bonaventure* by Antonio Begarelli

## "O, Good Fortune!"

According to an old tradition, in 1221 an infant boy named Giovanni, suffering from a dangerous illness, was brought to St. Francis of Assisi. Upon seeing the child, Francis exclaimed, *O buona ventura!* ("Oh, good fortune!"), and after that, the child became known as Bonaventure. Later in life, this same Bonaventure said that the saint's prayers had saved him from death (though it is unclear whether he actually was brought to Francis while the saint was alive). For the rest of his life, Bonaventure had a great devotion to St. Francis—so great that when he was a young man, Bonaventure entered the Order of Friars Minor.

Little is known about Bonaventure's life as a boy or a young man. Around 1243, after joining the Franciscans, he left his native Italy to study at the University of Paris, where he received his master's degree.

Bonaventure was a great scholar. He became the greatest of the Franciscan scholastic philosophers and theologians of his day. He wrote about all the great questions in philosophy and theology that the scholastics explored. In some areas he disagreed with Thomas Aquinas, though they remained close friends and admired one another's learning and holiness. Bonaventure saw the pursuit of truth as a road to God. He was a faithful student of the writings of St. Augustine of Hippo; though, unlike other Augustinian thinkers of his time, he did not reject Aristotle but drew on the philosopher's insights in his own works.

Bonaventure was elected by the Franciscan order as its minister general at a time when the Little Brothers were divided by two groups with different views about how Franciscans should live their profession. Bonaventure worked to restore unity within the order by undertaking exhausting travels to visit each province of the order. He restored the Franciscan ideal, preached the Gospel constantly, and focused on the importance of the spiritual life.

According to a story, Thomas Aquinas once visited Bonaventure's cell in Paris while the latter was writing a life of St. Francis. Thomas found his friend in ecstasy, unaware of his visitor. Withdrawing quietly, Thomas said, "Let us leave a saint to work for a saint."

Bonaventure resigned his post as minister general in 1274 to take part in a Church council held in Lyons, France, where he served as director of the council at the pope's request. He was responsible for the council's temporary reconciliation of the Eastern Orthodox churches and the Western Church. Bonaventure died during the council on July 15, 1274, and was buried the next evening. His funeral was splendid—attended by the pope, the king of Aragon, cardinals, and other members of the council. It was not until 248 years later, in 1482, that Pope Sixtus IV declared Bonaventure a saint. He was declared a Doctor of the Church in 1588.

## Dumb Ox

"He will enter the Order of Friars Preachers and so great will be his learning and sanctity that in his day no one will be found to equal him." So a hermit told Theodora, the countess of Teano (in Italy), of the child she carried in her womb. The child, whom they named Thomas, was born in 1225 (some accounts say 1227) to the countess and her husband, Landulph, count of Aquino (for which Thomas has been called "Aquinas"). Thomas Aquinas lived to fulfill this prophecy—despite, as it turned out, his family's opposition.

Thomas's parents had their own plans for his future. When he was five years old, they sent him to the Benedictine monks at Monte Cassino, whose abbot was Thomas's uncle. The education he would receive from the monks could have been the beginning of an illustrious career in the Church—as an abbot, perhaps, or a bishop. At the monastery school, Thomas was known to be an unusually bright and

St. Thomas Aquinas, painting attributed to Botticelli

thoughtful student who loved meditation and prayer. He surprised his teachers by asking frequently, "What is God?"

So brilliant was young Thomas that the abbot insisted that he be sent to the University of Naples. So, to Naples he went—when he was only 10 or 11 years old. There he studied the liberal arts and astounded his teachers by his deep and clear understanding. In Naples, Thomas met members of the new Dominican order. So impressed was he by their life and dedication to study that he desired to join them. However, the Dominican prior in Naples told the young man—then 16 years old—to wait three years before entering the order. The prior knew Thomas's parents would likely oppose their son's decision.

Thomas's parents were rich and powerful. Related, as they were, to the Emperors Henry VI and Frederick II, as well as to the kings of France, Aragon, and Castile, they would not like the thought of Thomas entering an order of mendicants—religious beggars! So it was that, when they heard about Thomas becoming a Dominican in 1244, his parents were quite upset. The countess tried to persuade her son to change his mind. She even asked the archbishop of Naples and the pope himself to force Thomas to leave the Dominicans. But when these measures did not work, and Thomas refused to change his mind, his parents took more drastic steps.

At their mother's insistence, Thomas's two brothers, who were knights, kidnapped him and put him in a fortress belonging to their father at Rocca Secca. There Thomas remained, imprisoned by his own family, for three years. During that time his parents, brothers, and sisters tried by various means to force him to change his mind and abandon the Dominicans. Seeing they could not shake his resolve and that even Pope Innocent IV and the Emperor Frederick II were opposed to their treatment of Thomas, the family at long last let him go free.

Thomas returned to Naples, where he made his final profession as a Dominican. From Naples, his superiors sent him to the University of Paris. On the way he traveled to Cologne in Germany to study with the celebrated teacher, Albert the Great (or Albertus Magnus). The German Albert, a fellow Dominican, was one of the most brilliant scholars of his time, a man who was interested in many areas of learning, including the study of the natural world. While in Cologne, Thomas spoke little—which his fellow students thought was because of dullness and stupidity. And because Thomas was a large man, they called him the "dumb ox." But the great Albert came to see that behind Thomas's humble silence lay a great intellect. Once, after Thomas defended a difficult **thesis**, Albert exclaimed,

**thesis:** an idea or proposition that someone puts forward to defend with a reasoned argument

"we call this young man a dumb ox, but the bellowing of that ox will one day resound through the whole world."

In time, Thomas received his doctorate in theology at Paris and taught there in the Dominican faculty. Young Dominicans from all over Europe eagerly attended his lectures because of the power and clearness of his thought. He had achieved complete mastery of Aristotle's philosophy, and he showed how it could be used in leading one to a deeper understanding of Divine Revelation.

Thomas brought Aristotle's thought together with Divine Revelation in a great work of theology, called the *Summa Theologica* (Theological Summary). Thomas began his *Summa* as an attempt to write a textbook in theology for his brother Dominicans. The work grew to encompass almost all the questions asked by medieval theologians.

Thomas Aquinas's teachings were at first accepted only by his own Dominicans. Indeed, many of his ideas were hotly disputed for centuries. But his theological writings have exerted great influence on the teachings of the Catholic Church, and he has given his name to a still influential philosophy that is called "Thomism" after him.

Thomas traveled across Europe several times during his life, typically on a donkey's back. After spending some years in Paris, teaching his fellow Dominicans, he went to Orvieto in Italy to teach at the papal court. He taught there from 1259 to 1269, while also writing a treatise on the Blessed Sacrament. In a chapel one night, as Thomas knelt in prayer before the altar, he heard a voice that seemed to come from the crucifix: "Thou hast written well of me, what reward wouldst thou have?" To which Thomas said, "Nothing but thyself, Lord."

Thomas returned to Paris, where he taught for a few more years. In

**Albertus Magnus, German scholastic philosopher, theologian, scientist, and writer. Fresco by Tommaso da Modena**

1272, he went to Naples to form a Dominican House of Studies at the university there. In Naples, however, he ceased work on his *Summa*, leaving it unfinished. He had received a vision of God. To one of his brother Dominicans, he said, "the end of my labors is come. All that I have written seems to me so much straw after the things that have been revealed to me." This was in 1273.

The next year, an ailing Thomas began his final journey. He went to attend the general council at Lyons in France. On his way north, however, his illness forced him to stop at the Cistercian monastery of Fossanova, south of Rome. At that monastery Thomas made his final profession of faith, just before he received the **viaticum** for the dying. "I receive Thee," he prayed, "the price of my redemption, for whose love I have watched, studied, and labored. Thee have I preached; thee have I taught. Never have I said anything against thee. If anything was not well said, that is to be attributed to my ignorance."

Thomas Aquinas died at Fossanova on March 7, 1274. His remains were solemnly transported to the Dominican church at Toulouse, France, in 1367. The Church observes St. Thomas's feast on January 28.

The Church canonized Thomas as a saint in 1323 and named him a Doctor of the Church in 1567. In 1880, Pope Leo XIII declared Thomas's work the foundation of Catholic thought and accorded him the title *Doctor Angelicus*. He is the patron of all Catholic universities, colleges, academies, and schools throughout the world.

**Saint Thomas Aquinas**

**viaticum:** Holy Communion given to a person in danger of death (The Latin word signifies what one takes on a journey.)

### Pange Lingua

Besides being a theologian, St. Thomas Aquinas was a poet and the author of several Latin hymns. His hymns followed the new model of verse in his day—created by the troubadours, having meter and end rhyme. The best known to us of Thomas's hymns is the *Pange Lingua*, sung during the procession to the Altar of Repose on Maundy Thursday. The last two stanzas are used in Adoration and the Benediction of the Blessed Sacrament:

*Tantum ergo sacramentum*
*Veneremur cernui,*
*Et antiquum documentum*
*Novo cedat ritui:*
*Praestet fides supplementum*
*Sensuum defectui.*

Therefore we, before Him bending,
This great sacrament revere,
Types and shadows have their ending
For the newer rite is here;
Faith, our outward sense befriending,
Makes our inward vision clear.

*Genitori, Genitoque,*
*Laus et jubilatio;*
*Salus, honor, virtus quoque*
*Sit et benedictio:*
*Procedenti ab utroque*
*Compar sit laudatio.*

To the Father and the Son,
Glory, praise and joy we sing,
Salvation, honor, power in one,
To them both, our blessings ring;
Each from each proceeding One,
Equal laud and reverencing.

# Chapter Review

## Summary

- Medieval architects raised cathedrals that were tributes to God. The cathedrals of the 11th and 12th centuries were built in two basic styles: Romanesque and Gothic.
- Veneration of the Blessed Virgin Mary affected all aspects of life in Middle Ages, especially influencing attitudes toward women.
- During the late 12th century, cathedral schools replaced monastery schools as the most vibrant centers of study. Some cathedral schools began to associate with one another to form universities. The universities were divided into four faculties or colleges: arts, medicine, law, and

- theology. The predominant university centers at the beginning of the 13th century were at Bologna, Montpellier, Salerno, Oxford, and Paris.
- Pope Innocent III affected the life of Europe profoundly in the 13th century. His goal as pope was to reform society and the Church to make them truly Christian. He exercised great authority, even over kings.
- Pope Innocent's great triumph was the Fourth Lateran Council, which enacted many reform measures for the Church. However, the council is most significant for defining the doctrine of Transubstantiation.
- Two new orders, the Franciscans and Dominicans, arose during the reign of Pope Innocent III. St. Francis of Assisi formed the Order of Friars Minor, men who were to be wandering preachers and evangelists living a life of strict poverty. St. Dominic de Guzmán formed the Order of Preachers, who would be learned enough to debate with learned Albigensians. These Dominicans, as they came to be called, began to teach in the schools and universities of Europe, as did the Franciscans.
- Fierce Mongol hordes invaded eastern Europe in the mid-13th century. Under their leader Ogodei Khan (son of Genghis Khan) and under the generalship of Batu, they swept into Hungary, defeating the Hungarian knights. But the death of Ogodei Khan turned back the invasion before it reached as far as Poland or Germany.
- King Fernando of Castile and León fought Islam for over a quarter of a century without losing a battle. In the territories he reconquered from the Moors, he restored Catholic dioceses and institutions.
- A method of study, called scholasticism, was developed in the medieval universities. The Dominicans and Franciscans, especially, contributed to the development of this method.
- Foremost among Franciscan scholars was St. Bonaventure, who saw the pursuit of truth as a road to God and used Aristotelian logic in his writings. From the Dominicans came St. Thomas Aquinas, who is famous for having constructed a vast synthesis of Aristotelian and Christian thought that he called the *Summa Theologica* (Theological Summary).

## Key Concepts

**Romanesque:** architectural style characterized by its use of the Roman arch

**Gothic:** architectural style characterized by its pointed arches

**cathedral schools:** schools that followed the monastic schools of the earliest Middle Ages and from which universities were formed

**universities:** larger unions of small colleges and schools
**Seven Liberal Arts:** grammar, logic, rhetoric, arithmetic, geometry, astronomy, and music
**friar:** "brother," the name given to members of the Franciscan and Dominican orders and eventually to members of other orders
**Franciscans:** the Order of Little Brothers, founded by St. Francis of Assisi
**Dominicans:** the Order of Preachers, founded by St. Dominic de Guzmán
**Aristotelianism:** the philosophy derived from the works of the Greek philosopher Aristotle
**transubstantiation:** the doctrine of the change in substance (essence) of the elements of the Mass, the bread and wine, into the body and blood of Christ.

### Dates to Remember
**1198–1216:** Innocent III's reign as pope
**1215:** the Fourth Lateran Council
**1236:** King Fernando's reconquest of Córdoba
**1248:** King Fernando's reconquest of Seville
**1274:** the death of St. Thomas Aquinas and St. Bonaventure

### Central Characters
**Innocent III (1160–1216):** most influential pope of the Middle Ages
**King St. Fernando III (1201–1256):** king of Castile-León
**St. Francis of Assisi (1182–1226):** founder of the Friars Minor
**St. Dominic (1170–1221):** founder of the Order of Preachers (Dominicans)
**St. Bonaventure (1221–1274):** Franciscan superior general; theologian
**St. Thomas Aquinas (1225–1274):** Dominican friar; theologian and author of the *Summa Theologica*

### Questions for Review
1. What were the two architectural styles developed in the medieval centuries? What characterizes each style?
2. When did Pope Innocent hold the papal office? Why was his reign as pope so important?
3. How does the Fourth Lateran Council still influence the Church today?
4. What did St. Francis want his order to be and do? What did he call it? Why?

5. What sort of order did St. Dominic want to form? What kind of work did they end up doing?
6. What is the *Summa Theologica*? What did St. Thomas want it to be used for?

## Ideas in Action

1. Photocopy from books, or cut from magazines, pictures of Gothic and Romanesque cathedrals. Mount them on separate boards, one for Gothic and the other for Romanesque. Indicate when the churches were built and where. Discuss how the Gothic and Romanesque churches differ and how particular Gothic churches differ from other Gothic churches and Romanesque churches from other Romanesque churches. Are there any examples of Gothic or Romanesque architecture near where you live?
2. Pope Innocent III believed it was his duty to influence the social and political life of the world. The popes of our day continue in this tradition. Collect news stories that describe various things the pope, the Holy See, and the bishops do and say to influence the social and political life of our time. How do the Church's actions today in this regard differ from those of Pope Innocent III? Why do they differ in these ways?
3. Discuss how a modern St. Francis might live. How would he dress? Where would he live? What might you think of him if you saw him? Do you think he would attract many followers in our day? Why or why not? Discuss where a modern St. Thomas might live and where he would work.
4. Learn one of St. Thomas's hymns and prepare to sing it with your class. Consult a hymnal.

# Highways and Byways

## St. Francis the Poet

St. Francis has been remembered for his affection for the natural world, and for his sense that all creatures, great and small, are God's children and emissaries of His will. Legends persist about his sermons to the birds and forest creatures. And statues of St. Francis have become garden ornaments in many Catholic countries. His great hymn to God the Creator is now sung as a hymn in Catholic and Protestant lands. The following translation of St. Francis's "Canticle of the Sun" is a familiar hymn in many churches today.

## "All Creatures of Our God and King"

All creatures of our God and King
Lift up your voice and with us sing,
Alleluia! Alleluia!
Thou burning sun with golden beam,
Thou silver moon with softer gleam!

*Refrain*
*O praise Him! O praise Him!*
*Alleluia! Alleluia! Alleluia!*

Thou rushing wind that art so strong
Ye clouds that sail in Heaven along,
O praise Him! Alleluia!
Thou rising moon, in praise rejoice,
Ye lights of evening, find a voice!

*Refrain*

Thou flowing water, pure and clear,
Make music for thy Lord to hear,
O praise Him! Alleluia!
Thou fire so masterful and bright,
That givest man both warmth and light.

*Refrain*

Dear mother earth, who day by day
Unfoldest blessings on our way,
O praise Him! Alleluia!
The flowers and fruits that in thee grow,
Let them His glory also show.

*Refrain*

And all ye men of tender heart,
Forgiving others, take your part,
O sing ye! Alleluia!
Ye who long pain and sorrow bear,
Praise God and on Him cast your care!

*Refrain*

And thou most kind and gentle Death,
Waiting to hush our latest breath,
O praise Him! Alleluia!
Thou leadest home the child of God,
And Christ our Lord the way hath trod.

*Refrain*

Let all things their Creator bless,
And worship Him in humbleness,
O praise Him! Alleluia!
Praise, praise the Father, praise the Son,
And praise the Spirit, Three in One!

*Refrain*

This translation into English by William H. Draper first appeared in the *Public School Hymn Book*, 1919. It was composed for a children's Whitsuntide (Pentecost) festival in Leeds, England.

# Chapter 14: Decline and Decay of the Middle Ages

King Philip IV "the Fair" of France (reigned 1285–1314) did not appear to be an enemy of religion. He attended Mass daily and wore a **hair shirt** as a penitential act. He was charitable and kindly toward the poor and counted himself a loyal son of the Church. Nor was Pope Boniface VIII (reigned 1294–1303) anti-French; on the contrary, his policies as pope often favored France. Boniface and Philip should have been on friendly terms with each other. Instead, they came into serious conflict. The pope and the king had very different views of the nature of Church and the state and how they relate to one another.

**hair shirt:** a rough shirt or girdle made from goat's hair and worn as a means of doing penance and of resisting temptations of the flesh

## The Wounded Authority of the Church

The quarrel between Philip the Fair and Pope Boniface arose because the king needed money for a war with England and decided to tax the French clergy to get it. The French bishops did not protest against the tax, but the lower clergy appealed to the pope for help. In 1296,

**Pope Boniface VIII**

**bull:** a papal statement, sealed with the official seal called *bulla* in Latin

Boniface replied by issuing an official statement or **bull**, called *Clericis Laicos*, in which he excommunicated any king or prince who taxed the clergy without the pope's permission. Philip retaliated by forbidding any gold or silver to leave France, thus cutting off a large part of the wealth the pope received from France. The English King Edward I took similar measures in his domains. Confronted with so much resistance, Pope Boniface was forced to allow that kings, in times of necessity, may tax the clergy of the realm without approval from Rome.

What brought about the final break between Boniface and Philip was the king's arrest of the bishop of Palmiers on a rather flimsy charge of treason. Boniface had sent the bishop to Philip to protest against the king's continued oppression of the clergy and to remind him of his promise to lead a crusade to retake Jerusalem.

After Philip had arrested the bishop, Boniface summoned the bishops of France to a council in Rome. He sent a letter to King Philip urging him to do justice to his subjects. But Philip's counselors arranged a clever lie. They burned the pope's letter and circulated a false letter in which Boniface was made to say that the king was subject to the pope in all spiritual and temporal matters. This **forgery** provoked the French people to outrage against the pope. But Boniface did not back down. In 1302, he issued another bull, *Unam Sanctam*. In that bull he reasserted his authority, as the spiritual leader of Christendom, to correct what was morally wrong—even in the conduct of kings. The bull ends with these words: "We declare, say, define, and pronounce that it is necessary for salvation for every human creature to be subject to the Roman Pontiff."

**forgery:** a false document

The following year, Philip answered the pope's challenge by calling a council of the French Church. The council, meeting in June 1303, declared

### The Naming of Bulls

The names of documents issued by popes, such as bulls and, later, encyclical letters, get their names from the opening words of the texts. Thus, the bull *Unam Sanctam* is so called because the first line of the bull reads, in Latin, *"Unam sanctam Ecclesiam catholicam et ipsam apostolicam urgente fide credere cogimur et tenere."* In English, this means "Urged by faith, we are compelled to believe and hold that the Church is one, holy, and apostolic." The words *Unam Sanctam* mean "one holy."

Pope Boniface guilty of heresy, blasphemy, simony, gross and unnatural immorality, magic, and murder. Five French archbishops and 21 bishops sided with King Philip, who also sent his agents throughout the kingdom to force monasteries, cathedral chapters, and cities to sign a document condemning the pope. Finally, Philip sent his right-hand man, Guillaume de Nogaret, to Italy to kidnap the pope and bring him back to France as a prisoner.

## "At Least I Shall Die as Pope"

On the night of September 7, 1303, a force of 600 cavalry and 1,500 infantry, under Nogaret's command, attacked the sleepy little Italian town of Anagni (Boniface VIII's ancestral home, where he was then residing). The town gates had been opened through treachery; the soldiers entered and pillaged the town. When Boniface saw it was useless to resist the French, he declared, "Since I am betrayed like the Savior, and my end is nigh, at least I shall die as pope."

His assailants found Boniface in his palace, clad in his papal robes, seated on his throne. Seeing Nogaret before him, the pope said, "Here is my head,

Western Europe in the late 13th, early 14th centuries

## Dante Alighieri, Chief Poet of Medieval Europe

*I see the flower-de-luce Anagni enter,
And Christ in his own Vicar captive made;
I see him yet another time derided;
I see renewed the vinegar and gall,
And between living thieves I see him slain.*

So wrote a poet of Florence, Italy, about the treatment Pope Boniface VIII received at the hands of the French (the "flower-de-luce" is the symbol of the French kings). Ironically, Dante Alighieri (1265–1321), the poet who wrote these lines, was a bitter critic of Boniface. It was not that Dante was not a faithful Catholic; he simply did not approve of this pope's interference in political affairs. Like other medieval Catholics, Dante respected the papal office even if he thought little of the man who held it. Even a bad pope was seen as the "Vicar of Christ." To insult him was to insult Christ Himself.

Dante was one of the greatest poets of the Middle Ages. He wrote many of his poems (in Italian) about a lady he called Beatrice. This Beatrice was a real woman Dante once had known, but she was no longer alive. Dante, however, used her in his poems as an ideal of spiritual virtue. Her name, Beatrice, means "she who leads to blessedness."

Dante belonged to the Ghibelline faction, which believed that Italy needed to be united under the authority of the emperor. Opposed to the Ghibellines were the Guelfs, who favored the independence of the Italian cities. The pope, always fearing to lose his independence to the emperor, was an ally of the Guelfs. Dante became an important man in the government of Florence. But in 1302, when he was 37, his political enemies banished him from the city—to which he never returned. While in exile, Dante

**Portrait of Dante Alighieri**

brooded on his misfortune, consoled himself by reading philosophy, and considered how political government could be improved.

The year he died, Dante completed his last and greatest poem, the *Divine Comedy*, which he had begun about 20 years earlier. It is a long narrative poem in Italian about an extraordinary, imagined journey he says he made at the age of 35. To Dante and all medieval writers, a comedy meant not a funny story, but a story that begins badly for the chief character and ends happily. The *Divine Comedy* begins badly because, in the opening lines of the poem, the poet says he was lost in a symbolic "dark woods":

> *In the middle of the journey of our life*
> *I found myself lost in dark woods,*
> *For I had lost the straight path.*
>
> To help him escape the "dark woods" (which symbolize the life of sin), Lady Beatrice in heaven asks the Roman poet Virgil to guide Dante through hell and purgatory. Virgil wrote the *Aeneid*, an epic poem Dante had read and studied in Latin. Virgil, who met Dante in the "dark woods," dwelt in Limbo, where the souls of unbaptized infants and the souls of the just pagans (including Saladin) spend their eternity. They suffer no punishment but are sad, for they will never see God.
>
> As he travels with Virgil into hell, Dante learns about the many forms of sin. In the poem, hell is imagined as a pit of nine circles deep under the earth. The pit is shaped like a cone with its endpoint at the center of the earth. At the tip of the cone of hell is a pit of ice where a raging Satan, the bottom half of his body encased in ice, chews Judas Iscariot and claws his body.
>
> The *Divine Comedy* describes Purgatory as a mountain island in the sea, on the opposite side of the world from Italy. Climbing Mt. Purgatory with Virgil, Dante learns how the souls who have repented of their sins in life are purified. At the summit of the mountain sits the Garden of Eden, where Virgil leaves Dante. From Eden, Beatrice (representing Divine Revelation) is Dante's guide.
>
> It is Beatrice who takes Dante into paradise. The woman who once inspired Dante's early poetry appears now as his saintly guide to the kingdom of God. She leads him up through the heavens to the abode of the blessed. In the final part of the poem, Dante is allowed to see God himself. Dante imagines God as a tricolor light that causes love in those who see it. In the final lines, Dante says that he feels present within him the divine love "that moves the sun and other stars."

here is my neck; I will patiently bear that I, a Catholic and lawful pontiff and Vicar of Christ, be condemned and deposed . . . I desire to die for Christ's faith and His Church." Boniface's kidnappers handled him roughly, but they were unable to abduct him to France. They were stopped by the citizens of Anagni, who rose up against Nogaret and his French soldiers and forced them to flee the city. Boniface himself returned to Rome. Three weeks later, overcome by the shock of the attack made against him, he died.

Boniface's fall was much more than a personal misfortune. It symbolized the downfall of the medieval reform movement and of the pope's influence in Europe. Bishops of Rome had suffered insults and even martyrdom before, but never—not, at least, in the High Middle Ages—had a king so insulted a pope in the name of "Christian" principles. Because Christendom had cared little about, or even approved of, the events at Anagni, a new attitude seemed to be arising in Europe. Kings, not churchmen, were becoming the leaders of Christendom. For Western people, it meant the things of this world were growing more important than the things of the Faith.

## The "Babylonian Captivity" of the Papacy

Boniface VIII's successor, Benedict XI, made peace with King Philip the Fair. Philip had sent messages to Benedict, congratulating him on his election and promising to be obedient in the future. In turn, Benedict **absolved** Philip of the penalties Boniface had placed on him. Benedict was a saintly man who might have strengthened the papacy if he had lived longer. But he died in 1304 after reigning as pope for only eight months.

The next pope—Clement V—was a Frenchman whom the cardinals, it seems, elected to please King Philip. Instead of being crowned pope in Rome, Clement insisted that the ceremony be held in France; and it was, in the presence of Philip. Clement remained in France after his coronation, appointing mostly French clergymen to be cardinals.

Philip tried to force Clement to stage a trial of the deceased Boniface VIII, whom the king accused of heresy and other crimes. Clement did not refuse, but he delayed calling a trial. Finally, at the king's insistence, Clement set a date for the trial. In the end, however, Philip called the trial off, allowing it to wait for an ecumenical council. The king even withdrew his charges against Boniface, declaring that his motives in attacking the dead pope had been only the purest.

**absolve:** to free from an obligation or from sin

The coronation of Pope Clement V, inaugurating the "Babylonian Captivity" of the popes in Southern France. Miniature from the "Cronaca Villani."

View of the papal palace at Avignon

Pope Clement lived in various places throughout France. He finally settled in Avignon, a town that was part of the Roman Empire of the Germans but lay directly across the Rhône River from French territory. Clement V and the eight popes who followed him remained in Avignon, where they built a huge palace and installed an elaborate court. Being so close to France, these popes were heavily influenced by the French king.

The popes reigned from France and Avignon from 1305 to 1377, a 72-year period called the "Babylonian Captivity" of the popes—a reference to the 70-year exile of the Jews in Babylon in the sixth century B.C. The popes' "captivity" weakened the respect Christians had for the papacy—to the Germans, Englishmen, Italians, and all the European nations, it appeared that the popes worked only for France's benefit. Another development that lost the Avignon popes the respect of many throughout Europe was their practice of **nepotism**—the granting of high church offices to relations.

**nepotism:** favoritism shown to relatives, especially in granting appointments to offices or jobs (from the Latin *nepos*, meaning "nephew")

Though not wicked men, the Avignon popes often seemed to be more concerned with the worldly aspects of the Church than with its spiritual welfare. They set up a large bureaucracy to govern the Church. To pay for the many bureaucrats as well as for the luxurious court life at the papal palace, the Avignon popes levied new taxes and established an army of papal tax collectors to gather the money. For instance, before they could become bishops, those elected to the office had to pay a special tax; and the pope claimed the right to take for himself the treasury, library, and furniture of a bishop who died. The taxes levied by the popes in Avignon affected even common priests, who sometimes cut back on their charitable and educational work or charged fees for baptisms, weddings, funerals, and other services in order to pay the taxes.

One of the worst abuses, however, was the granting of more than one benefice to a cardinal or member of the papal court. One man could become the bishop of two or more dioceses, even in countries where he did not live and would never visit. The Avignon popes often chose bishops or other high-ranking churchmen who were not native to the country in which their dioceses lay, but who could pay the high costs of their office. Such bishops had little knowledge of local problems or customs. All too often, these appointments went to those self-serving men who had won favor by their service at the papal court. These men were frequently disliked for their foreign ways when they arrived as bishops, abbots, or canons in Spain, England, or Germany.

### The English Heretics

Edward III, the king of England, could not have been pleased that his enemy, the king of France, had gained so much influence over the pope. Nor was he pleased when, in 1366, Pope Urban V (who lived in Avignon) demanded that Edward pay the annual tribute to the papal court. England's kings had owed the pope this tribute since the days of King John, when he became Pope Innocent III's vassal, but no English king had paid the tribute for more than 30 years. John of Gaunt, Edward's son and the duke of Lancaster, suggested that his father continue the tradition and not pay the tribute. Parliament agreed with John, and no tribute was paid.

In refusing to pay the tribute, Parliament, John of Gaunt, and King Edward had the support of a leading preacher of the time. The preacher was John Wycliffe (1324–1384), who was also an Oxford University scholar. Wycliffe had come up with what, in the Middle Ages, were rather radical ideas. He held that only righteous clergymen had any authority from God. This meant that unrighteous clergy had no authority to administer the sacraments, nor could they own property. Basically, according to Wycliffe, if the pope and his cardinals were not righteous, the king had no duty to pay tribute to them. Furthermore, if the king determined that churchmen were not living according to Christian morality, he could seize their property, said Wycliffe.

Over time, Wycliffe's teachings became more and more heretical. In 1380, he wrote a treatise denying the doctrine of transubstantiation. The bread and wine in the Eucharist, he said, do not become the Body and Blood of Christ but remain bread and wine. Wycliffe believed in the Real Presence, but said Christ is only present in the bread and the wine. Wycliffe came to teach that the bishops and the pope were not the real Church but that the Church was invisible, made up only of true believers. He eventually rejected most of the sacraments and taught that the Bible alone is the only true source of doctrine—not tradition or the Church. Wycliffe and his followers translated the Bible into English, and he sent men, whom he called his "poor priests," to preach his doctrines throughout England. Catholics called these poor priests "Lollards," from the Dutch word meaning "to mutter."

**John Wycliffe**

In 1381, a peasants' revolt erupted in England. An army of peasants marched on London, where they killed the archbishop of Canterbury. Thinking Wycliffe was responsible for the revolt, a synod of English bishops condemned him. They forbade him to teach and ordered him to retire to his benefice at Lutterworth. Wycliffe remained there until his death in 1384, writing his most important works, the *Trialogus* and *Opus Evangelicum*, unhindered by the English Church and government.

After Wycliffe's death, King Henry IV and his son, Henry V, persecuted the Lollards. But Wycliffe's ideas did not die. When, later, England's King Richard II married the daughter of the king of Bohemia, students from Oxford went to study at that kingdom's chief university in Prague. With them the students brought Wycliffe's teachings, which influenced a popular preacher and professor there—a priest named John Hus.

## Return from Captivity

During their stay in Avignon, the popes had not utterly forgotten their Italian lands, nor did they intend to stay in Avignon forever. One problem they faced was that Italy, particularly its papal states, was torn by struggles between rival lords. The Avignon popes thought it would be too dangerous for them to return to Rome.

One pope, Urban V (who became pope in 1362), did return to Rome. But faced with threats of revolution and overcome with fear, he changed his mind. Though the Romans begged him to remain, he returned to Avignon, where he died, three months later, in 1370. The next pope, Gregory XI, was determined to return to Rome. But when warfare again erupted in Italy, he remained at Avignon.

Living in war-torn Italy at the time was a woman named Catherine, of the city of Siena. Catherine was known far and wide as a holy woman. She lived a life of poverty as a lay Dominican and tended the sick and the poor. She attracted even the pope's attention. In letters to Gregory, she begged him to return to Rome, calling the city "a garden watered with the blood of the martyrs, which is still boiling and calling for others to follow in their footsteps." By returning to Rome, she insisted, the pope could bring peace to Italy.

**Statue of Saint Catherine of Siena**

Moved by Catherine's urgings and prayers, Gregory XI did return to Rome, entering the city on January 17, 1377. After nearly 75 years, the pope reigned again in the Eternal City. The long "Babylonian Captivity" was over. But all was not well with the Church; new and greater evils were soon to follow.

# The Great Schism

The cardinals who met to decide who should be pope after Pope Gregory XI's death in 1378 could not agree on a candidate. Should they choose a Frenchman or an Italian? The people of Rome, however, were clear on what *they* wanted. They wanted a Roman, and they made it clear to the cardinals that they would accept no one else but a Roman. Knowing that the Roman mob would tear them to pieces if they elected a Frenchman, the cardinals were forced to compromise. In the end, they chose an Italian who was not a cardinal. He was Bartholomew Prignano, the archbishop of Bari, who took on the name Urban VI.

## The Father of English Poetry

During the period when the popes first stayed at Avignon until they returned to Rome, there lived a man we now call the "Father of English Poetry." Geoffrey Chaucer of London, the first to write great poetry in the common English language, was born about 1344. The son of a wealthy wine merchant, Chaucer grew up among the courtiers and prominent men surrounding King Edward III. He held several public offices during the middle years of his life, and he wrote and published many works that achieved fame not only in England, but throughout Europe.

For some 13 years (1387–1400), Chaucer worked on *The Canterbury Tales*, a collection of tales in verse. The collection, left unfinished at the time of Chaucer's death, is presented as the stories told by a group of pilgrims. They have started out from an inn across the river from London and are heading for the shrine of the martyr St. Thomas Becket at Canterbury, 25 miles southeast of London. Many different kinds of men and women are among this group—from a noble knight crusader to a slimy pardoner (a seller of false relics). *The Canterbury Tales* presents Chaucer's image of the people who made up English society during his time.

**Portrait print of Geoffrey Chaucer**

The leading cardinals had thought they would be able to control the new pope. But to everyone's surprise, Urban turned out to be a strong pope who was determined to reform the Church and the College of Cardinals itself. Urban energetically began setting things to rights by correcting abuses—starting with the cardinals, the papal court, and the bishops.

The new pope, however, could be quite rude and so made many important enemies. The French cardinals, in particular, were none too happy with Urban—and they left Rome, claiming the Roman people had forced them to elect this pope. Since papal elections had to be free in order to be valid, the French cardinals declared that Urban was not a true pope. After leaving Rome, the French cardinals elected an antipope who called himself

Clement VII and set up his court in Avignon. Pope Urban, of course, excommunicated Clement; and Clement excommunicated Urban. But this new schism did not end. For some 40 years afterward, two lines of men—one at Rome and the other at Avignon—claimed to be pope.

The split between the pope at Rome and his rival in Avignon spread to all of Christendom. During this "Great Schism," as it has been called, no one could be completely certain who the legitimate pope was. Even those whom the Church acknowledges as saints were divided. St. Catherine of Siena, for instance, sided with Rome, while St. Vincent Ferrer went with Avignon. All over Christendom, bishop rose up against bishop, abbot against abbot, and priest against priest. France acknowledged the pope in Avignon. England, which was at war with France, sided with Rome. Scotland, often at odds with England, chose Avignon—as did Spain and southern Italy, while central and northern Italy opted for Rome. But in deciding which pope to follow, kings and lords put their political and national interests before the welfare of Christendom as a whole.

In the end, the real winners in the struggle between the rival popes were the temporal rulers. The Great Schism allowed kings, princes, and dukes to seize ever-increasing power over the Church in their domains.

## Calls for a Council

How to heal the Great Schism was the most important question of the time, but no one could come up with a solution. Finally, in 1394, the theology faculty at the University of Paris came up with one—have both popes resign and a new pope elected in their place. The university actually demanded that both popes resign, and the clergy of France, Bohemia, Hungary, and Navarre said they would not obey the Avignon pope until the Church was reunited. These efforts, however, came to nothing, since neither pope was willing to step down.

With the failure of the first attempt to heal the schism, churchmen throughout Europe came up with another solution. A general council should be called, they said, one that would if necessary depose both popes and replace them with a new pope. Just such a council met at Pisa in northern Italy in March 1409, and the 300 or so clergymen who met for the council voted to depose both popes and then elected Alexander V in their place. Alexander died the next year and was succeeded by the antipope John XXIII.

**Statue of Antipope John XXIII**

"Oh, happy choice! Peace has been restored! Oh, pacific union!" So rejoiced the University of Paris. The problem was, however, that according to Church teaching, no one—not even a council—has the authority to depose a pope. So it was that the pope in Rome and his rival in Avignon condemned the council and refused to step down. Instead of two contending popes, there were now three.

The confusion of the time gave rise to a new theory about how the Church should be governed. The theory said that a general council, not the pope, is the highest authority in the Church. This theory, called the "**conciliar theory**," became popular among many churchmen, who saw in it a way to heal once and for all the schism and other ills affecting the Church.

**conciliar theory:** the idea that Church councils have the highest authority in the Church, superior even to that of the pope

The conciliar theory had a great influence at another council, called by the German emperor Sigismund. In 1414, churchmen representing the three factions in the Church and coming from all parts of Western Christendom streamed toward the little southern German town of Constance, where the council was to be held. Thousands—bishops, professors, royal ambassadors, and their staff and followers—were eventually crowded together in the little town, and each nobleman and prelate was escorted by a train of servants.

Gathered in Constance, the council fathers heard a list of accusations against the pope of Pisa, John XXIII. John, who was present at the council, feared what might happen to him if the fathers decided he deserved punishment. He declared under oath that he would resign as pope; but then, in disguise, he fled from Constance—thinking that without him, the council would disband. But instead of ending the council, the fathers deposed John XXIII on March 29, 1415. A few weeks later, John agreed to the council's action. One of the three popes was thus gotten out of the way.

Upon learning that the pope in Rome, Gregory XII, had decided to **abdicate**, the council's next task was to deal with Benedict XIII, the pope in Avignon. Benedict acted as if he were willing to resign; but in the end, he refused. Abandoned by all his supporters (even by St. Vincent Ferrer, who had been one of his staunchest defenders), Benedict fled to an impregnable fortress on the coast of Valencia. There he died in 1423, still claiming to be pope. The council, however, after several months of deliberation, voted on July 26, 1417, to depose Benedict, saying he was guilty of perjury (for failing to abdicate when he claimed he would) as well as schism and heresy.

**abdicate:** to renounce or give up a high office, dignity, or function

With the three rival popes out of the way, the Council of Constance was free to elect a new pope. On November 11, 1417, the council fathers chose

Pope Martin V

Cardinal Otto Colonna, who took the name of Martin V. The election of Pope Martin marked the end of the Great Schism.

## The Church: United but Sick

The Council of Constance had reunited the Church. But the 19 years of schism, following nearly 75 years of the "Babylonian Captivity" of the popes in Avignon, had seriously damaged the unity of the Church and Christendom. With Martin V, the Church once again had a pope everyone recognized—and he did not go to live in Avignon, but reigned in his city of Rome. However, outside the papal states in Italy, the pope's authority had been greatly weakened. During the nearly 100 years of confusion in the Church, kings and temporal lords had cut away at the power of the Church courts in their dominions, had seized the wealth of the clergy, and had taxed the Church. Temporal rulers became, for all practical purposes, the rulers of the Church in their lands. They were forming national churches that tore at the unity of the Catholic Church.

Since the papacy had lost much of the respect Christians formerly had for it, the popes could not effectively work to reform the Church of the many abuses that had grown up in it during the Avignon years. Indeed, some popes who reigned after Martin V were not interested in reforming the Church. They were more concerned with political power (to keep the Church independent from temporal lords) or in cultivating the arts.

Temporal lords were too interested in power and wealth to concern themselves with the religious life of their subjects. The Church still had its reformers, but these reformers tended to stress individual or private devotion rather than the reform of Church and state, which the medieval reformers had wanted to achieve. In the 15th century, the Church entered an age in which reform was desperately needed but seemingly impossible to achieve. This state of things would make some Christians so desperate

## Wycliffe Comes to Bohemia

Though ending the Great Schism was the most important question facing the Council of Constance, the fathers considered other matters. They tried to tackle the reform of the Church as a whole—and failed. Then, they had to deal with a particularly troublesome priest who was causing problems in the kingdom of Bohemia.

This priest was John Hus (1369–1415), a famous preacher from the city of Prague in Bohemia. Hus also was a professor, and twice the rector, at the University of Prague. He was among those who had learned of John Wycliffe and his teachings from students who had come to Prague from the University of Oxford. Hus himself became a zealous promoter of the teachings of Wycliffe—so much so that, when the archbishop of Prague in 1410 ordered the burning of all Wycliffe's books, he excommunicated Hus as well.

Hus, however, had become extremely popular in Prague. He ignored the archbishop and continued preaching. He had little to worry about from the archbishop, for Hus had the support of Bohemia's King Wenzel. Because of Hus and his preaching, John XXIII, the pope of Pisa, placed Prague under an interdict in 1411. Yet, despite this, Hus went on preaching. In the end, however, he lost the support of the theologians at the university. At the king's request, he left Prague for the small town of Krakowitz in Bohemia.

In 1414, the fathers of the Council of Constance ordered Hus to appear before them. The German emperor, Sigismund, promised him "safe conduct" to and from Constance—which meant that whatever the council decided concerning him, Hus would be free to return unharmed to Bohemia.

Trusting in the emperor's promise, Hus appeared before the council. In June 1415, the council condemned many of his teachings and demanded that he **recant** them. Though the council ruled that he had denied the doctrine of Transubstantiation, Hus insisted that he accepted it. But he said he would not reject his other teachings that the council declared heretical—including his belief that Peter was not the head of the Church. Hus said the council had to prove from Scripture that his teachings were false. Finally, on July 6, 1415, despite Sigismund's promise of safe conduct, the council condemned Hus to death as a heretic. John Hus was burned at the stake. Enveloped by the smoke and flames, he cried out, "Christ, Son of the Living God, have mercy on us!" Then, he expired.

John Hus

The execution of Hus ignited a brutal series of wars in Bohemia between his followers and the supporters of Pope Martin V and Emperor Sigismund. The Hussites denied that the pope is head of the Church; they taught that only Scripture and the law of Christ are the sources of Christian teaching, and that temporal rulers have authority only if they are in a state of grace. The wars raged for 17 years, devastating whole regions in Bohemia. In the end, the Catholic side could not crush the Hussites, who have continued to this day to exist in Bohemia as a distinct religious group.

> **recant:** to publicly and formally withdraw a statement or belief

## The Scourge of the Black Death

It was a bitter, horrible way to die.

In 1347, a plague worse than any people of the time could recall spread across Europe and killed millions of people. Those struck by the disease saw, first, egg-sized black swellings, called buboes (from whence it was called the bubonic plague), on their neck and in their armpits and groin. This stage was followed by high fever and delirium. Near the end, the buboes burst, causing excruciating pain. Then came death. Because the bodies of those with the plague turned black from bleeding under the skin, the disease came to be known as the Black Plague.

Before arriving in Europe, the plague had already struck the Mongols and China in the Far East. Thousands died in the great cities of China. It may be that the plague came to Europe in a shipload of furs and silks sent from China and carried by a Venetian merchant ship into the West. The Venetians unloaded their cargo in Italy, and the infected merchandise began its travels through the peninsula.

The disease spread most rapidly in the crowded, dirty European towns and the more prosperous, more heavily populated rural areas. Beginning with the Mediterranean lands in 1347, the plague spread northward to France, Spain, the British Isles, and Scandinavia. It then moved eastward to Germany, Poland, and Russia. In northern Europe the plague raged for three years, killing nearly half of the population. Pockets of infection lingered on for many years and brought on at least five smaller outbreaks of the disease between 1350 and 1400. Sporadic recurrences of the plague continued into the early 18th century, especially in cities.

**Death as depicted on a medieval grave marker**

The plague did much to change the economic and social life of Europe. Because so many laborers died during the plague, those workers who survived could demand higher wages than before. Peasants went to work for landlords who could offer them higher pay, and serfs could win freedom from their lords and obtain wages in return for their labor. Kings and lords made laws to keep wages and the prices of goods low, and in so doing they caused widespread anger and peasant revolts. A new class of freedmen in Western Europe arose from the serfs who had left their bondage and added to the growing population of towns and tradesmen.

The plague affected religion as well. People became less respectful of the clergy, for some clerics had fled from their duties—such as caring for the sick—during the crisis. Of the many good priests who had sacrificed themselves to tend the sick, almost all had died. Their loss was one reason for the sad state of the Church in the 14th and 15th centuries. To fill their ranks, the Church had to accept less worthy men into the priesthood. While the personal faith of many Christians grew stronger in the face of suffering and the threat of death, others fell into despair, which they tried to escape by overindulging in pleasures. The Black Plague was a tragedy that had lasting effects on European civilization and helped bring an end to the great cultural and religious achievements of the High Middle Ages.

that, in a few decades, their descendents would willingly accept even revolutionary methods to reform and renew Christendom.

# The Empire and France

Not only was the papacy weakened in the late Middle Ages, but so was the Western Roman Empire. The people of the Middle Ages had thought of the pope as the spiritual and moral leader of Christendom. But, as we have seen in previous chapters, the emperor, too, was seen to have an important role. To people in the Middle Ages, the German "Roman" emperor was not only the protector of the Church, but the supreme temporal lord of Christendom. Under him were united all the various kingdoms, duchies, principalities, and even republics.

As we have seen, the empire, however, failed to fulfill its high calling. The last truly powerful emperor was Frederick Barbarossa, founder of the Hohenstaufen line of emperors. But his grandson, Frederick II, failed to be the same strong monarch Barbarossa had been—in fact, Frederick II cared more for his domains in southern Italy and Sicily than he did for his German lands.

When the Hohenstaufen line died out in 1254, the German princes elected William of Holland (who died in 1256) and then two non-German princes, who reigned at the same time but did not even visit Germany. During this time Germany was basically left without an emperor, so the German princes became more and more independent. By the end of the 13th century, Germany was divided into many duchies and little principalities that were powerful enough to resist the emperor if they needed or wanted to. There were indeed emperors in the 14th and 15th centuries, but as their authority and power weakened, the power of the German princes grew ever stronger. What's more, these emperors no longer tried to control Italy, and so the empire became merely a German thing. It was no longer regarded as an authority for all of Europe.

France, on the other hand, became a more centralized kingdom during the High Middle Ages. From a loose collection of nearly independent feudal principalities, France had become a powerful state by the time of Louis IX (St. Louis, reigned 1226–1270). Only 15 years after the death of Louis, his grandson Philip IV "the Fair" ascended the throne and occupied it for nearly 30 years (1285–1314). (This was the same Philip who opposed Pope Boniface VIII and under whom the popes came to Avignon.) Philip got his way by lies, trickery, and brute force. In this way he gave the French monarchy a reputation for unscrupulousness and injustice.

**Effigy of Philip IV in the necropolis of the church of Saint Denis, France**

After Philip's death, the great lords of France tried to regain much of the power they had lost to the king. They formed provincial leagues to protect their traditional rights, and they forced Philip's son, King Louis X (reigned 1314–1316), to issue a series of charters confirming these rights.

Louis X died without a male heir; so, first one of his brothers (Philip V) and then the other (Charles IV) became king after him. Like Louis, Philip and Charles had no male heirs. When the last brother died, the Capetian line of kings, who had ruled France since Hugh Capet became king in 987, came to an end. In 1328, Philip—the count of Valois, a cousin of the last Capetian kings—succeeded to the throne as Philip VI. He founded a new dynasty, the Valois dynasty, that lasted until 1589. Under the Valois kings, France would fight a war for its independence against English kings who sought to unite the two kingdoms—France and England—under their rule.

# Chapter Review

### Summary

- When King Philip the Fair of France decided to tax the clergy of his realm, Pope Boniface VIII protested. Boniface issued the famous bull, *Unam Sanctam*, in which he reasserted his moral authority over church and state. King Philip's response was to send henchmen to mistreat and insult the pope at Anagni.
- Pope Clement V, made pope in France, was a weak man who did what King Philip the Fair wanted him to do. Clement established an elaborate papal court at Avignon, from where Clement and several of his successors ruled the Church. This period has been called the "Babylonian Captivity" of the papacy.
- The Avignon papacy resorted to many new and ingenious devices to raise the money to support the growing papal government. This, along with the fact that the Avignon popes were seen as servants of the French king, led to much resentment in the rest of Europe toward the papacy.
- Under King Edward III, England proposed withholding tithes from the Avignon popes. This policy of the king and his son, John of Gaunt,

- was supported by a preacher at Oxford, John Wycliffe, who promoted heretical teachings on the Eucharist and the authority of priests and bishops.
- In 1377, Pope Gregory XI returned the papal court to Rome. The French cardinals, however, were dissatisfied with Urban VI, his successor. They elected an antipope, Clement VII, who established himself at Avignon. For 40 years, there were two lines of claimants to the papacy, one at Rome and the other at Avignon. In 1409, a council at Pisa voted to depose both popes and elected another, Alexander V. But when the two other popes refused to abdicate, the Church was further split between three rival claimants to the papal throne. This "Great Schism" was ended by the Council of Constance, which elected Martin V as pope.
- Beginning in 1347, the bubonic plague—called the Black Death—swept across Europe and killed vast numbers of people. The plague had devastating effects on both Church and state in Europe.
- With the end of the Hohenstaufen line in the Western Roman Empire, Germany went from a united state to a collection of small, rival states. The empire remained, but the influence of the emperor was diminished. France, on the other hand, under Philip the Fair, became more united. Under the reigns of Philip's two sons, however, the great lords of France forced the monarchy to recognize their traditional rights. After the death of Philip's sons, the crown passed to their cousin, Philip of Valois—thus ending the Capetian line of kings and establishing the house of Valois.

## Key Concepts
**bull:** (from Latin *bulla*, "seal") a decree or law sealed with a heavy official seal and its ribbon
**Lollards:** the followers of John Wycliffe's ideas
**conciliar theory:** the idea that Church councils have the highest authority in the Church, superior even to that of the pope
**Black Death:** the bubonic plague, a terrible disease that ravaged Europe for some 60 years and killed nearly half the population

## Dates to Remember
**1303:** Boniface VIII assailed at Anagni
**1305–1377:** the "Babylonian Captivity" of the popes
**1378–1417:** the Great Schism
**1414:** Council of Constance
**1347–1400:** the Black Death

## Central Characters

**Boniface VIII (r. 1294–1303):** the pope who fought the attempt of the French king to usurp the authority of the Church

**Dante Alighieri (1265–1321):** Italian poet and author of the *Divine Comedy*

**Clement V (r. 1305–1314 ):** the pope who removed the papal court to Avignon

**John Wycliffe (1324–1384):** English theologian who promoted heretical ideas and translated the Bible into English

**Geoffrey Chaucer (1344–1400):** English poet and author of *The Canterbury Tales*

**John Hus (1369–1415):** Bohemian preacher, professor, and follower of John Wycliffe; executed as a heretic by the Council of Constance

## Questions for Review

1. Why did King Philip the Fair of France and Pope Boniface VIII quarrel? What resulted from their quarrel?
2. Why is Dante's great poem about a journey through hell and purgatory and into paradise called a "comedy"?
3. Who was John Wycliffe? What were his teachings?
4. How many men claimed to be pope during the Great Schism? How did having more than one man claiming to be pope divide and weaken the Church?
5. What was the conciliar theory? How does it differ from Church teaching about the authority of the pope?
6. What was the Black Death, and what were its consequences?

## Ideas in Action

1. Report on Dante's *Divine Comedy*. Take a small passage or section from the poem, read it, and discuss its imagery and what it represents. How, for instance, do the punishments described in the *Inferno* and the *Purgatorio* fit the sins of those who are punished?
2. Read in class "The Nun's Priest's Tale" from *The Canterbury Tales*, and discuss the characters (Chanticleer and his wife) and the human situation the tale describes.

# Highways and Byways

## The Gate of Hell

In *L'Inferno* (the "Underworld"), the first part of the *Divine Comedy*, Dante writes of his imaginary descent into hell. He and the poet Virgil pass through the infernal gates, which bear mysterious inscriptions. Here is a passage of the poem in the translation of the 19th-century American poet William Wadsworth Longfellow.

*Through me the way is to the city dolent;*
*Through me the way is to eternal dole;*
*Through me the way among the people lost.*

*Justice incited my sublime Creator;*
*Created me divine Omnipotence,*
*The highest Wisdom and the primal Love.*

*Before me there were no created things,*
*Only eterne, and I eternal last.*
*All hope abandon, ye who enter in!*

*These words in sombre colour I beheld*
*Written upon the summit of a gate;*
*Whence I: "Their sense is, Master, hard to me!"*

*And he to me, as one experienced:*
*"Here all suspicion needs must be abandoned,*
*All cowardice must needs be here extinct.*

*"We to the place have come, where I have told thee*
*Thou shalt behold the people dolorous*
*Who have foregone the good of intellect."*

*And after he had laid his hand on mine*
*With joyful mien, whence I was comforted,*
*He led me in among the secret things.*

*There sighs, complaints, and ululations loud
Resounded through the air without a star,
Whence I, at the beginning, wept thereat.

Languages diverse, horrible dialects,
Accents of anger, words of agony,
And voices high and hoarse, with sound of hands

Made up a tumult that goes whirling on
Forever in that air forever black,
Even as the sand doth, when the whirlwind breathes.*

# Chapter 15  Two Centuries of Conflict

Thus far in our story, we have focused almost entirely on western Europe. Yet, to the east, stretching from the Baltic Sea in the north to the Black Sea in the south, across dense forest lands and the grassy **steppe**, from the borders of Poland to the Ural Mountains—the very edge of Europe—another great European people was taking shape. Unlike the lands we have been discussing—Spain, France, England, and Germany—this people did not belong to the Western Christian tradition. Its religious traditions were indeed Christian, and very rich and beautiful, but they came from Constantinople, the capital of the Byzantine Empire. The people whose history we now turn to are the Russians.

The founding of Russia, like that of Spain, is a story of reconquest. The enemy invaders of Russia were not Muslims, however. They were the Mongols, those nomadic tribes organized by Genghis Khan that in the early 1200s set out to conquer Asia and the lands to the west. No mountain ranges rise to stop the movement of hostile invading peoples entering Russia from the east over the vast flat land.

The forests became the refuge of the Russian people. Like the little refugee bands of Hispanic Christians in the mountains of Asturias, holding off the Islamic conqueror, the Russian Christians withdrew into their forests and moved out against their Mongol oppressors during 300 years of steady reconquest of the Russian soil.

**steppe:** a vast and usually level and treeless tract of land, found in southeastern Europe and Asia

**A view of the Dnieper River**

# The Kingdom of Rus

In the ninth century, when the raids of the Northmen were terrorizing western Europe, a Viking chief, Rurik, and his warriors settled in the vast plains of what is today northern Russia. Rurik's warriors were called the *Rus*—meaning "red-haired"—from which Russia takes its name. These "red-haired" men were traders, and the richer trade lay with Constantinople far to the south. So it was that one of Rurik's companions, Oleg, moved southward to the Dnieper River, which flows into the Black Sea and gave easier access to Byzantium. On the banks of the Dnieper, Oleg founded the settlement of Kiev.

Though the Rus were Scandinavian, the tribes of the lands where they settled were Slavs. The Slavs of Novgorod and Kiev were pagans who worshipped many gods. Their kin, the Slavs of Moravia, however, had become Christians. About the same time Rurik settled at Novgorod, two Greek brothers, Sts. Cyril and Methodius, had been preaching the Gospel in Moravia. Coming as they did from Constantinople, the brothers translated the Greek form of the liturgy into Slavonic and spread the religious traditions of Byzantium among the Slavs. In translating the Scriptures into Slavonic, the brothers developed a new alphabet based on Greek, the alphabet has come to be called *Cyrillic* script. The Christian faith spread gradually

**Depiction of Rurik on a memorial in Novgorod celebrating the millennium of his arrival there**

toward Russia—but if there were Christians in the land of the Rus, they were secret ones.

In 972, the pagan ruler of the Rus divided his kingdom (which included Novgorod, Kiev, and the lands lying between them) among his three sons. The youngest son, Vladimir, was given Novgorod. In 980, after a series of wars fought with his brothers, Vladimir became the ruler, called the Grand Prince, of all the kingdoms of the Rus. He made Kiev his capital.

Though his grandmother, St. Olga, had been Christian, Vladimir was a pagan and lived like one. He had five wives, erected shrines to the Slavic gods in Kiev, and conquered the tribes and lands all the way to the Black Sea. Eyeing rich lands of the Byzantine Empire, Vladimir demanded that Emperor Basil II marry him to Anna, the emperor's sister, or else face an invasion. Basil, however, said that Anna could not marry a pagan. Vladimir would have to become a Christian first. To this Vladimir readily agreed.

It is told in an ancient chronicle that Vladimir had been thinking of becoming Christian even before Basil suggested it. In 987, Vladimir had sent emissaries to the Jewish Khazars, the Muslim Bulgarians, the Latin Catholic Germans, and the Greek Church in Constantinople with orders to find out about each religion so that he might discover if he wanted to adopt one of them. Of all these groups, the emissaries were most impressed by the Greek Church. The splendor of Constantinople, its great churches, the beauty of the Byzantine liturgy—its jeweled vestments, its choirs, the colorful icons of Christ and the saints—enchanted the emissaries. In describing all this to Vladimir, they said with wonder, "We knew not whether we were in heaven or on earth."

**Mosaic of Saint Vladimir in Sevastopol, Ukraine**

In the city of Kherson on the Black Sea, in the year 988, Vladimir was baptized. Returning to Kiev, he ordered the destruction of the statues of the pagan gods. Seeing that their gods were helpless before the Christian Vladimir, the Slavic people of Kiev converted in great numbers. At first Vladimir threatened to punish those who did not become Christian. But he later adopted milder methods of converting his people —and was even reluctant to punish criminals. Though his conversion at first seemed purely political, Vladimir became a zealous and fervent Christian. The Russian and Ukrainian Orthodox and Catholic Churches to this day remember him as St. Vladimir, and call him *Ravnoapostol*—"Equal to the Apostles."

What the culture of ancient Rome had done for the western barbarians, the culture of New Rome—Constantinople—did for the Russian Slavs. Byzantine culture influenced Russia's political and social life, its arts, and its religion. Russia adopted the Byzantine rite of the liturgy as translated into Slavonic by Cyril and Methodius. Russian artists imitated Byzantine icon painting, liturgical music, church mosaics, and church architecture—giving them, in time, a distinctively Russian flavor. Vladimir's city, Kiev, grew rich and famous. It came to be known as "Kiev the Golden" for its many churches with **gilded**, onion-shaped domes that glittered in the sunlight.

**gilded:** overlaid with gold

As the Merovingian and Carolingian kings had done with their kingdoms, Vladimir divided his realm among his sons. When Vladimir died in 1015, war broke out among these sons—and there were many of them (12 in all)—from Vladimir's many wives (before his conversion) and from the Byzantine princess Anna. Inspired by Christ's words, "resist not evil with evil," Anna's two sons, the princes Boris and Gleb, refused to fight their kindred. They surrendered to their brother Svyatopolk, who murdered them. Both the Catholic and Orthodox Churches remember Boris and Gleb today as saints and martyrs. Warfare between the remaining brothers ended in 1036 when Vladimir's son, Yaroslav, became ruler of all Russia.

*The Baptism of Saint Prince Vladimir,* by Viktor Vasnetsov (1890)

Yaroslav has been remembered as the "Wise." He crushed the power of the Pechenegs, one of the nomadic tribes of the steppe who continually troubled Kievan Russia throughout its history. He married his family members into the ruling families of western Europe. During Yaroslav's reign, Kiev became famous from Constantinople to France as a center of culture. The prince himself, imitating the Byzantine emperors, even built a great cathedral in Kiev, calling it Holy Wisdom (after Hagia Sophia in Constantinople).

Yaroslav's attempt to create an orderly method for passing the office of Grand Prince to his successors failed, and Russia suffered from struggles between heirs to

Russia in the 12th and 13th centuries

the throne as well as from poor rulers after Yaroslav's death. During this period, Russia was governed not only by the Grand Prince, but by a council of advisors, called the *duma*. The duma was made up of wealthy landowners, called *boyars*. Towns, however, each had an assembly, called a *veche*, which all freemen could attend. In the countryside, the common farmer, unlike those in western Europe, was not a serf but a free property holder.

Probably the last great ruler of Kievan Russia was Vladimir II, "Monomakh." In 1101, 1103, and 1111, he led victorious campaigns against the newest threat from the steppe, the savage Polovtsy tribesmen. During Monomakh's time and afterward, bold Russian warriors fought valiant and chivalrous battles against invaders. In the process, these warriors saved western European countries from many invasions. The Russian struggle, however, was hopeless, for the invaders were numberless. Kiev began to decline in the 11th and 12th centuries, and Russia became divided into smaller and smaller princedoms. These realms could not unite to drive out the new and more terrible threat that was coming—the Mongols.

# The "Golden Horde"

As we have already read, the invading Mongols under Genghis Khan struck terror into western European lands. But the Mongol invasions had little lasting effect on the history of western Christendom. The case was different for Russia, for the Mongol invasions changed Russian history forever.

The Mongols invaded Russia by passing onto the steppe through the Caucasus Mountains in the south. They first attacked the Polovtsy, who begged the Russians for help. The Russians assembled the greatest force they could find from peasants and nobles of the realm to stop the Mongols. In 1223, the Russians and Polovtsy met the Mongols in battle on the Kalka River. At a critical moment of the battle, the Polovtsy fled, and the Mongol horsemen overwhelmed and destroyed the Russian forces. After the battle, the Mongols forced several Russian princes and knights to lie on the ground. Over them, the Mongols built a platform, on which the victors held a feast as their weight crushed the Russians to death.

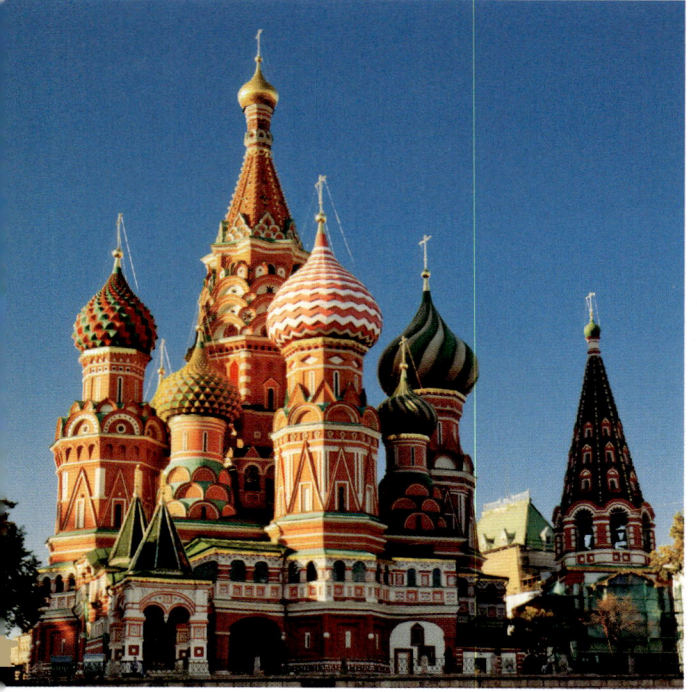

**Cathedral of St. Basil the Blessed in Moscow**

After the Battle of Kalka, the Mongols went on a spree of murder and pillage, destroying Russian lands all the way to the Dnieper River. They laid waste to "Kiev the Golden" itself, until barely 200 houses remained standing in the city. The Mongol horde, however, then withdrew to the east. Fourteen years later, in 1237, the Mongols returned under Batu Khan, leader of a third of the Mongol horde.

Within three years, Batu conquered all of Kievan Russia, except Novgorod in the cold, forested northlands. From his encampment on the steppe, called the "Golden Horde" (*horde*, from the Mongolian word meaning "camp"), Batu forced the conquered lands to pay him tribute. Batu's demands for tribute and his slave raids reduced the Russian people to abject poverty and despair; their children were taken for the slave markets of Persia and

Baghdad, their crops destroyed, and their churches looted and burned. The Mongols allowed the Russian principalities and cities to keep their governments and permitted the Church to exist, but they were cruel overlords. They are also known as Tatars and, sometimes, Tartars—a name reminiscent of the place from where they were thought to have sprung—*Tartarus*, a name for hell.

The Mongol conquest cut Russia off from Byzantium and the West for two centuries. The Mongols forced the Russians to devote all their resources to defending themselves and paying tribute to them. The poor Russian peasants sought help from the boyars, trading their freedom for boyar defense and security.

Many peasants, however, escaped both the Mongols and the boyars. They fled into the forested lands farther north, or farther south into the broad river valleys of the Dnieper and Volga. These peasants became frontiersmen, called *Cossacks*—a name meaning "adventurers" or "pioneers." Soon large communities of Cossacks were found along the Dnieper River, in the heart of Ukraine, and along the eastern and southern borders of Russia. They spread into the steppe with their horse herds, or they cleared forest lands for their farms.

One institution that survived from Kievan Russia and continued to hold Russia together was the Russian Church. Like the Church in Spain, which inspired the struggle against the Muslim invader, the Russian Church became identified with the people's struggle against the Mongol.

## Lord Novgorod the Great

The northern city of Novgorod—called by its citizens, "Lord Novgorod the Great"—had escaped the Mongols only to find itself threatened by enemies to the west. Novgorod was no backwater city, but the center of a huge and rich territory spreading from the Baltic Sea to the Urals. So it was a tempting morsel for its neighbors—including the Swedes, who in 1240 tried to cut off Novgorod's access to the Baltic Sea by blockading the mouth of the Neva River. But the Swedes were defeated when Alexander, the prince of Novgorod, crushed them in battle. For this victory, Alexander became known as "Nevski," a name meaning "of the Neva."

Alexander Nevski, however, soon had to face another threat: the Teutonic Knights. Though originally a crusading order, the Knights had established a powerful realm along the Baltic coast, stretching eastward from Germany. The grand master of the Knights had taken on the power and trappings of a feudal king among his military knights and fellow conquerors. In 1242, the

A medieval depiction of Alexander Nevsky

Teutonic Knights decided they needed to "Christianize" Russia—for Russia's Orthodox Church had followed Constantinople into schism with the pope in 1054—and marched against Novgorod. Not far from the city, at Lake Peipus, Alexander Nevski met the Knights in battle and routed them. Pursued by the Russians, the Knights fled over the ice of the lake. It was spring, and the thawing ice broke under the weight of the heavily armored horsemen. Hundreds of them drowned in the lake's icy waters.

Faced with western Christian enemies, however, Alexander Nevski was forced to make peace with the Mongols. In 1242, he appeared before Batu Khan and acknowledged the Mongol chief as Novgorod's overlord. In return for payments of tribute, Batu gave Nevski the title "Grand Prince of All Russia." Alexander's people, however, were not pleased with what he had done—but what choice did he have, faced with enemies to the west as well as to the east? In 1263, Novgorod was threatened with Mongol invasion because some Russian towns refused to pay tribute to the khan. Alexander appeared before the Mongol lord, begging for the khan's mercy on his people and their city. He obtained it; but on his journey home, Alexander Nevski died.

## The Rise of Moscow

At his death, Alexander Nevski left to his youngest son, Daniel, the small city of Moscow as his inheritance. Situated where the Moska and the Yauza rivers join, Moscow was not one of the Russian centers of power, as were the cities of Rostov, Riazan, Vladimir, and Tver. It was, in fact, quite unimportant—which is probably why Alexander left it to his youngest son.

Like his father, Daniel was of an active turn of mind. By conquest and inheritance, he expanded Moscow's territory. One of Daniel's descendants, Ivan I, worked closely with the Mongols and so received the title of Grand Prince and the right to collect taxes. By taking more in taxes than what the Mongols demanded—for which the people called him "Money Bag"—Ivan soon gained extra wealth. He bought more land with the money, until Moscow's territory was five times larger than what it had been under Daniel. Moscow attracted many settlers and thus grew in population. In 1328, the **metropolitan** archbishop of Russia—the chief bishop of the land—moved his seat from Vladimir to Moscow, making the city the head of all the churches in Russia. The presence of the Russian metropolitan greatly added to Moscow's prestige.

**metropolitan:** an archbishop, the chief bishop of a region

In 1378, Moscow's Grand Prince Dmitri refused to pay tribute to the Mongols. Two years later, forming an alliance with the powerful Catholic Christian kingdom of Lithuania, the Mongols led 200,000 warriors north to punish Moscow. Seeing the threat, the Russian Church called on all Russians to come to the aid of Moscow and Dmitri in this struggle against the enemy of Russia and the Orthodox faith. Russian princes gathered their forces in support of the great cause, giving Dmitri an army 150,000 strong.

If he hoped for any victory, Dmitri had to engage the Mongols in battle before they could join forces with the Lithuanians. He did so at a place called Kulikovo Pole ("sniper's field"), where the Don and Nepryavda Rivers meet. In the bloody battle that followed, the Russians lost over 100,000 men, and Dmitri was seriously wounded. But, despite these losses, Dmitri and his army routed the Mongols, who fled back to the Golden Horde. For this victory, Russians gave Dmitri the name "Donskoi," meaning "of the Don."

The victory at Kulikovo Pole, however, was short-lived. In 1382, the Mongols sacked Moscow, slaughtering 24,000 of its citizens. But Dmitri Donskoi's victory two years earlier showed Russians that the Mongols could indeed be defeated. Donskoi was a hero to all Russians. In the coming years, his Moscow became the leading principality of all Russia.

# The Hundred Years' War

When, in 1328, the last Capetian king of France died without a son to succeed him, the throne of France passed to Philip of Valois, who was crowned King Philip VI. Philip succeeded to the throne, though he was not the closest male relative of his Capetian cousins. Actually, the closest male relative was Edward III, king of England—the son of Isabelle, daughter of King Philip the Fair. Edward was thus Philip the Fair's grandson, while Philip of Valois was only the king's nephew.

Still, the French rejected Edward as king. They said French law did not allow the royal line to pass through a woman, and Edward could claim the French throne only through his mother. Edward still claimed to be the rightful king of France, but he did nothing about it—for a while.

France and England had long been rivals and, at times, open enemies. The English Plantagenet kings had once held vast territories in France. By the end of the 14th century these territories had shrunk to include only Guienne and Gascony in southern France, which the English kings held

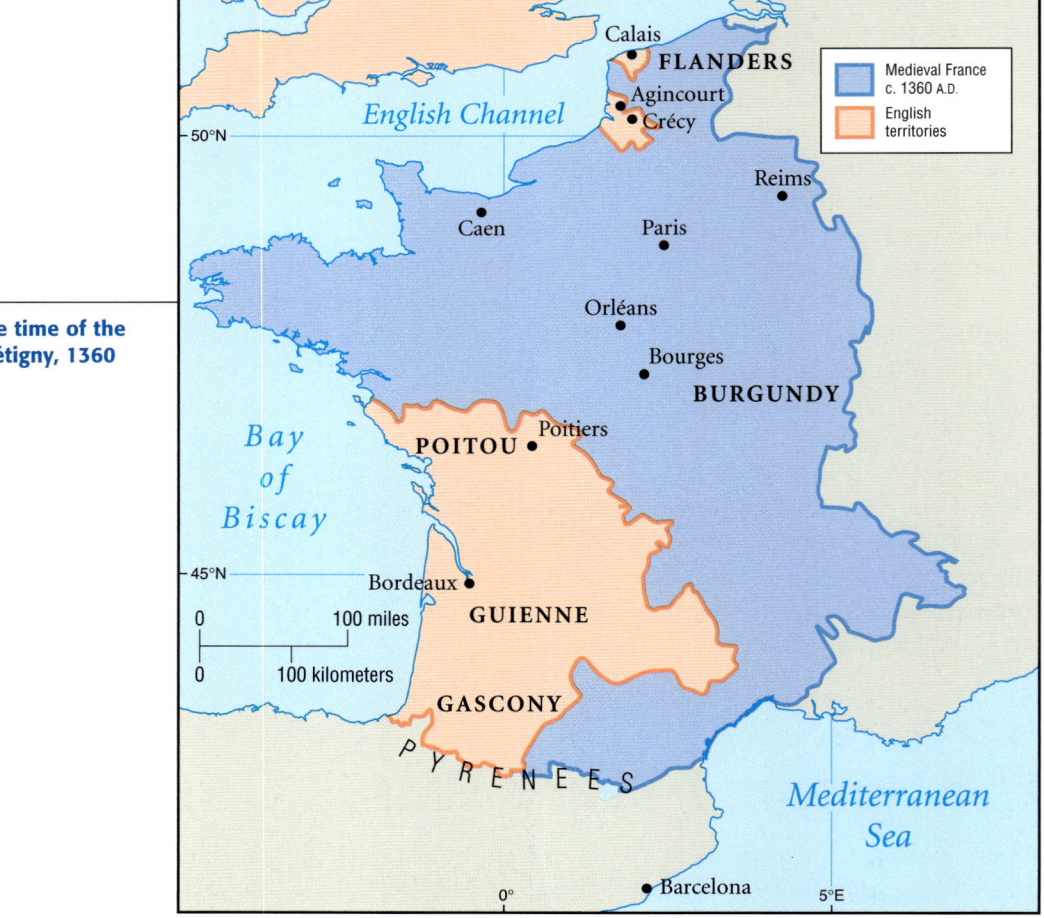

France at the time of the Treaty of Brétigny, 1360

as fiefs from the French king. The French kings were not happy with this arrangement, since it prevented them from bringing all of France firmly under their control.

The French and English had other disputes as well. Both Philip the Fair and Philip VI had long been trying to bring the wealthy territory of Flanders under their control, but England's King Edward III aided the Flemish (as the people of Flanders are called) in resisting France. On the other hand, the French had an alliance with England's enemy, Scotland. Yet, despite these problems, France and England remained at peace with each other for the first 12 years of Philip VI's reign.

Matters came to a head, however, in 1337. The Flemish had rebelled against the French and made an open alliance with England. With the Flemish naval fleet on his side, Edward III claimed his supposed right—to be king of France. Edward, though liege lord of England, held Guienne and Gascony as a vassal of the French king, Philip VI. In proclaiming himself king of France, Edward broke his oath of fealty, in Philip's view. So, the French king responded to Edward's claim by declaring the **forfeiture** of Edward's French territories. In 1340, Philip sent the French naval fleet against the combined English and Flemish fleet in the English Channel. But, in a battle fought at Sluys, the English and the Flemish roundly defeated the French fleet.

**forfeiture:** the loss of a right to something on account of a crime or some offense. Under feudalism, a liege could declare the forfeiture of a vassal's lands—that is, take back the lands from the vassal—if the vassal had broken his oath of fealty to his lord.

**King John II of France surrenders to Edward the Black Prince of England in 1356 at the Battle of Poitiers during the Hundred Years' War.**

So began what has been called the Hundred Years' War. Despite its name, however, the war did not go on continuously for 100 years. It was really a series of three wars, the first fought from 1340 to 1360; the second, from 1369 to 1389; and the third, from 1415 to 1453. Even during these periods of conflict, fighting was not continuous. Yet, the Hundred Years' War was a bitterly destructive struggle, at least for France. And it had important effects on the history not only of France and England, but of all Europe.

## Victories of the Longbow

For another six years after the Battle of Sluys, the English and French fought no important battles. In 1346, however, Edward III crossed the English Channel with 15,000 men and captured the city of Caen in Normandy. The English then moved east, pillaging the country as they went. Philip, with an army of about 20,000 men, moved north. On August 26, 1346, the English and the French met at Crécy, near the Flemish border.

At Crécy, Edward III's army used a new weapon, the cannon. The cannon used by the English, however, was not the powerful weapon it would become. It was a crude, smooth-bore gun capable of only short-range firing of two- to three-pound iron balls. But Edward's cannon caused panic in the French cavalry lines, scaring and crippling horses and men with bouncing blows.

A more effective English weapon was the longbow, a five-foot-long bow of seasoned yew that could fire a deadly rain of arrows in half the time it took to load, crank, and fire a crossbow. At Crécy, rain and damp spoiled the bowstrings of the French crossbowmen while the English longbowmen kept theirs dry by rolling them up under their helmets. The French cavalry milled around, unable to move in unity against the English lines, because the English longbowmen sent barrage after barrage of arrows against them, hitting horses as well as men. The horses panicked and fell back, crushing the foot soldiers behind them and leaving the troops open to the English assault. Because of the longbow, Crécy was a resounding English victory.

In the ten years after the Battle of Crécy, the English and French engaged in a few skirmishes but no great battles. In 1356 Edward III's son, Edward the "Black Prince" (so named for the color of his armor), led a small

### A New Weapon

The cannon is said to have been invented by a German monk, Bernhard Schwartz, using gunpowder brought to Europe from China by Marco Polo. The cannon, however, was an unpredictable weapon in the 14th century, because gunpowder was unstable and easily ruined by weather. The development of the cannon as well as other firearms in the coming years helped bring an end to the effectiveness of warfare by mounted knights—and to the culture of chivalry as well.

force from Guienne in the south of France and met the French in battle at Poitiers. Again, the longbow gave the victory to the English, who captured John II "the Good," who had become king of France in 1350.

With King John a prisoner in England, his son Charles, the **Dauphin**, took over the government of France. Charles was an able and courageous leader who successfully resisted the English. In 1360, King Edward III and Charles signed the Treaty of Brétigny, in which Charles gave Edward the French territories of Aquitaine, Calais, and Ponthieu. In return, Edward gave up all claims to the French crown. The treaty said King John was to be ransomed. But when the French could not pay the required ransom, the chivalrous old French king, whom the English had freed in order to raise the needed funds for his release, voluntarily returned to England. He had made an oath that he would not try to escape, and he kept it. King John died in London in April 1364.

**Dauphin:** title given to the firstborn son of the king of France, from the province of Dauphiné in southeastern France

After the death of John the Good, the Dauphin became king as Charles V. The new king was an able ruler who, despite the peace treaty, continued the war with England. With the help of his commander in chief, Bertrand du Guesclin, Charles was able to take back many of the territories he had given to England in the Treaty of Brétigny. By 1380, the English held only the coastal towns of Bordeaux, Bayonne, and Calais.

When both Charles V and Guesclin died in 1380, France faced an uncertain future. The new king, Charles VI, was weak and mentally unstable. Furthermore, instead of having a strong advisor like Guesclin to guide him, the king was surrounded by men interested only in their personal advantage. Under Charles VI, France was thus not prepared to resist the energetic kings who soon would sit on the English throne.

The Battle of Crécy, 1346

## The Road to Agincourt

In the years following Edward III's death in 1377, matters did not look too good for England either. The new king, Richard II, was only 10 years old when he ascended the throne. (Richard was the son of Edward the "Black Prince," who had died some years earlier.) For a time, all went well for England under Richard, who had his uncle—John of Gaunt, the duke of Lancaster—to guide him. But, eventually, the young king replaced Gaunt with a group of self-interested nobles, of whom the barons did not approve. Finally, Richard was forced to submit to the barons and dismiss his friends. Several years passed until, in 1397, Richard was able to overcome his enemies and rule with nearly absolute power in England.

**Death of Richard II**

But Richard exercised this power foolishly and made powerful enemies.

Richard II in the end had so little support that he could not defend himself when his cousin, Henry Hereford, led a rebellion against him in 1399. Henry was John of Gaunt's son who, when his father died, was supposed to inherit the duchy of Lancaster. Instead, fearing Henry as a rival, Richard had sent him into exile. Returning from exile, Henry Hereford faced little opposition and forced Richard to surrender to him. The king was arrested and most probably murdered in prison. Hereford took the throne as Henry IV, thus establishing a new ruling house—the House of Lancaster. Richard II was the last of the Plantagenet kings of England.

Henry IV was an able and energetic king. In 1413, his equally able and energetic son, Henry V, succeeded him as king. At the same time, in France, Charles VI had grown insane. He could do nothing as his kingdom was torn by civil war between the supporters of the duke of Burgundy and the "Armagnacs," supporters of the duke of Orléans. In 1415, Henry V took advantage of the civil unrest in France and landed an army at Calais. On October 25, 1415, at Agincourt in northern France, Henry's outnumbered forces defeated the heavy armored French cavalry, slaughtering many of the leading nobility of France. As at Crécy and Poitiers, so at Agincourt; it was the longbow that gave the English the victory over French chivalry.

After Agincourt, Henry V remained in France, conquering all of Normandy while the Armagnacs and the Burgundians fought among themselves. Finally, the Burgundians abandoned the French king and joined the English. Opposed by so strong an alliance, the French made peace with the English. In the Treaty of Troyes in 1420, Charles VI agreed not only to give his daughter in marriage to Henry V but also to name him the next king of France. Henry V, it appeared, would fulfill the dream of Edward III and unite the thrones of England and France.

But Henry V never became king of France, for he and Charles VI both died in 1422, and the French king's son, Charles the Dauphin, refused to accept the Treaty of Troyes. Calling himself King Charles VII, he set up his capital at Bourges in central France. In England, Henry V's infant son, Henry VI, became king of England—and of France, at least in English eyes. But the French themselves were not happy with English rule. They especially disliked Henry VI's governor in France, the duke of Bedford—not because he was a bad governor, but because he was not French. Treaty or no treaty, the French people were not ready to accept a foreign monarch as their king.

**Battle of Agincourt**

## *La Pucelle*

Three years before the English victory at Agincourt, an obscure maiden was born in the small village of Domrémy, in Cham-pagne. The daughter of the peasant farmer, Jacques d'Arc, this young girl was named Jehanne (Joan, in English). Like other peasant girls, Joan helped out on the family farm. She was skilled at sewing and spinning, but she could not read. Yet, Joan was unusual; years later, those who had known her testified that she was often at prayer in the village church and showed a tender love for the poor.

In 1425, when she was only 13, Joan began hearing "voices," as she called them. Later she came to know these voices as those of St. Michael the Archangel, St. Catherine, St. Margaret, and other saints. Over time she said her voices told her that she was to help King Charles VII in his struggle against the English invader.

The cause of Charles VII in his war against the English and Burgundians had grown more desperate. In October 1428, when the

English were laying siege to the city of Orléans, Joan's voices told her to present herself to Robert Baudricourt, Charles VII's commander in the neighboring town of Vaucouleurs. Joan had presented herself to Baudricourt once before; then he had told Joan's cousin, who had brought her to Vaucouleurs, "Take her home to her father and give her a good whipping." During her second visit to him, Baudricourt became more kindly disposed toward Joan. On February 17, 1429, after she told him of a defeat of the king's army outside of Orléans (a fact Baudricourt learned a few days later and something that Joan could not possibly have known by herself), he allowed Joan to visit the king.

Traveling to the royal court at Chinon through dangerous lands, Joan wore male attire for disguise and safety. News of Joan had reached the king. To test her, Charles disguised himself to see if she could recognize him—and through a secret sign given her by her voices, Joan recognized Charles. But when she took the king aside and told him of a secret he had hidden in the depths of his own heart, he began to believe that, perhaps, God had indeed sent the maid to him. Before she would be allowed to lead the forces of France, she was examined in Poitiers by a committee of bishops and theologians. After questioning her for three weeks about her voices, the committee ruled that they found nothing heretical in what she said. The king, said the committee, could use Joan in his service, if he wished.

**Entry of Joan of Arc into Orleans, by J. J. Scherrer**

Joan told the king that she would force the English to abandon their siege of Orléans. She told him that, in the battle before the city, she would be wounded by an arrow. She also told Charles that, like the kings of France before him, he would be crowned king the following summer in Reims.

Led by Joan, the French army appeared before Orléans in April 1429. Joan was clad in white armor and bore a banner bearing the words "Jesus: Maria" and an image of two kneeling angels presenting the Eternal Father with a **fleur-de-lis**. After commanding the English to withdraw, she entered the city. Their hearts lifted by *La Pucelle*—the "Maid"—as they called her, the French forces in Orléans by May 8 had taken all the English forts surrounding the city and forced the English to withdraw. But as she had foretold, Joan was wounded by an arrow on May 7.

Though she herself never fought, Joan next led a short campaign along the Loire River, accompanied by one of her best friends and admirers, the duke of Alençon. The campaign was a stunning success, and the English suffered a crushing defeat at Patay.

After the battle at Patay, Joan urged Charles to go to Reims for his coronation, saying that was the mission she had originally been sent to accomplish. Charles and his nobles, reluctantly, consented to follow her to the city. On July 17, 1429, Charles VII was anointed king in Reims cathedral with the oils used by every French king, it was said, since Clovis. By Charles's side stood Joan, holding her banner. "As it has shared in the toil," she said, "it was just that it would share in the victory."

Yet, this great victory was spoiled by the unwillingness of the king and his counselors to fight. On September 8, after an unsuccessful attempt to take Paris (during which Joan was injured by a crossbow bolt), Charles signed a temporary truce with the duke of Burgundy. For the next several months, Joan remained with the court, awaiting the end of the truce.

When the truce expired in the spring of 1430, Joan was in the city of Compiègne to defend it against a Burgundian attack. On the evening of May 24, she led a **sortie** out of the gates but was driven back. Before she could reenter the town, someone within the city lifted the drawbridge (whether by accident or intention is not known), trapping her and her men outside the city. The jubilant Burgundians dragged Joan from her horse and made her a prisoner. From then until late autumn, she was a prisoner of the duke of Burgundy. Though Charles VII could have tried to rescue or ransom the Maid, he did nothing in her behalf, nor did any of his subjects.

**Execution of Joan of Arc**

**fleur-de-lis:** the "flower de luce," a stylized lily that is the symbol of the French kings

**sortie:** a sudden issuing of troops from a defensive position (such as a fortress or walled city) against the enemy

The English offered to buy Joan from the Burgundians, who sold her to them for a large sum of money. Though they could not condemn her to death simply for defeating them in battle, the English commanders could have her sentenced as a sorceress and heretic. During six public and nine private sessions, the judges—theologians led by Pierre Cauchon, the bishop of Beauvais, an ally of the Burgundians—cross-examined Joan about her voices and visions, her male dress, her faith, and her willingness to submit to the Church. When the sessions ended, the judges declared her revelations to have been diabolical. Joan refused to deny that God had given her the mission to save France, and she was handed over to the secular authorities for execution as a heretic.

On Wednesday morning, May 30, 1431, Joan was burned at the stake in Rouen's marketplace. She was not yet 20 years old. Her ashes were cast into the Seine River to prevent her followers from recovering them as relics.

In 1456, twenty-three years after the Maid's death, Pope Callistus III appointed a commission that declared the trial of Joan and its verdict null and void. Then, 450 years later—on May 16, 1920—Pope Benedict XV canonized her as St. Joan of Arc. The French throne and land she had fought for and given her life to save remembered Joan with gratitude in later centuries, though they had scorned and abandoned her in this life.

## The End of the Hundred Years' War

Joan of Arc helped the French cause, not so much because of the battles she won but because she enkindled a new spirit in the heart of the French people. Believing they were led by a saint, the French were filled with new hope that the English could be driven from France. God, it appeared, was fighting for France in the person of a "Maid from heaven."

After Joan's death, Charles VII threw off his lethargic and hesitant ways and began to act the part of a king. In 1435, he convinced the duke of Burgundy to break his alliance with the English. Charles enlarged his army, even building up an artillery force using those crude new inventions called cannons. King Charles led the French forces to new victories against the English, driving them from Normandy and forcing them, in 1453, to abandon Bordeaux, their last possession in southern France. The Hundred Years' War ended with the English controlling only the city of Calais on the northern coast of France.

From the days of William the Conqueror, the kings of England had held vast territories in France. The Hundred Years' War ended this situation forever. Henceforth, England and France were clearly and definitely two separate kingdoms. This was one great result of the war. Another was that it inspired in the French and English a sense of patriotism for their countries. Frenchmen and Englishmen thought of themselves not simply as belonging to a region, such as Champagne or Sussex, but as members of a nation that was larger than any local loyalty. This was the spirit of **nationalism**—devotion to a people or nation based on a shared language, history, and customs.

The spirit of nationalism, however, indicated that the people of Europe were thinking of themselves less and less as belonging to one Christian society—Christendom. National interests, not the good of all Christian peoples, were becoming the most important concerns for Europeans.

At the end of the Hundred Years' War, the French king still had as his rival the powerful duke of Burgundy. Both Duke Philip "the Good" (reigned 1419–1467) and Duke Charles "the Rash" (reigned 1467–1477) tried to make Burgundy an independent kingdom. But they were no match for Charles VII's son, Louis XI, who became king of France in 1461. Louis was called "the Spider King" because he was intelligent and crafty—and not above using underhanded and dishonest means to extend his power. Yet, he was very successful in strengthening the royal power in France. The Spider King restored the French state to the strength it had under King Philip the Fair, 100 years earlier.

> **nationalism:** devotion to a group, sharing a common language, history, and customs. At times, nationalism includes a sense that one's nation is superior to or more important than all other nations.

**Louis XI of France**

# Civil War in England

The French victory over England in the Hundred Years' War strengthened the power of the king in France. The war, however, did not have the same effect on England. The war to capture the French crown was expensive, and King Edward III and his successors needed the money to wage it. To get the needed funds, Edward had to turn to Parliament, the advisory body formed under King Edward Longshanks over a century before.

Since its founding, Parliament had been divided into two groups or "houses." The "upper" house, known as the House of Lords, included the great lords and bishops of the realm, who were called "lords temporal" and "lords spiritual." The "lower" house, known as the House of Commons, included the knights and barons (representing the rural shires or counties) and the burgesses (representing towns or boroughs).

Portrait of King Edward III

**impeach:** to charge (a public official) with a crime
**indict:** to charge with an offense

The kings before Edward III had used Parliament as a means of influencing public opinion. They had also used Parliament to obtain financial support for wars against Philip the Fair as well as to gain approval for royal actions against the pope and for control of the English Church. But, while they might back the king in putting down violence at home, members of Parliament were not always willing to support a foreign war. So, when Edward III asked Parliament for money to wage war against France, Parliament asked favors from the king in return. In 1340, Parliament forced Edward to agree that he would not create any new taxes without Parliament's approval. Parliament gained, too, some part in making laws—it could petition the king to issue statutes, for instance. Another power Parliament gained was the authority to **impeach** and try royal officials; the House of Commons would **indict** an official, and the House of Lords would try him.

Parliament, however, gained even more influence when it became a king maker. Opposition by the barons in Parliament led to the revolt that toppled Richard II from the throne in 1399—and Parliament chose Henry IV of Lancaster as Richard's successor. Under the kings of the House of Lancaster, Parliament became a powerful force in English government.

## The Wars of the Roses: 1455–1485

When only an infant, King Henry VI of England had inherited England and France from his conquering father, Henry V. Henry VI might have been a good ruler in more peaceful times. He grew up to be a sincere, honest, and faithful man. He was pious and devout. He was also a patron of learning, as seen by his funding of Eton and King's Colleges at Cambridge University. But Henry VI was not shrewd enough to handle the increasingly powerful Parliament, nor did he have the best advisors to help him to do this.

Henry VI's difficulties stemmed from the Hundred Years' War. When the king came of age to rule by himself, he supported a peace plan with France. The plan stated that England could at least keep Gascony and Guienne, though it had to give up the French crown. Among those opposed to this plan was the ambitious Richard, Duke of York, the next in line to the throne after Henry VI. As we have seen, England ended up losing nearly all its territories in France—and one reason for this was that the governor King Henry appointed after the death of the duke of Bedford was incompetent.

But the trouble really began in 1453, when King Henry became mentally deranged. Seeing an opportunity to seize control of the government, Richard of York was able to get Parliament to appoint him protector of the kingdom—which meant he basically ruled England. Richard, however, had a powerful rival—Henry's queen, Margaret of Anjou. In 1454, Henry regained his sanity, and Margaret and Edmund Beaufort, the duke of Somerset, replaced Richard of York as the real rulers of England.

Henry VI, king of England

Unwilling to accept his loss of power, Richard gathered an army of his supporters and rose in rebellion against the king. On May 22, 1455, Richard's army defeated the king's army at St. Alban's, outside London. This battle was the beginning of a series of civil wars, fought between the Houses of Lancaster and of York over which should control the kingship. The wars are known as the "Wars of the Roses," because the members of each faction took either a red or a white rose as its emblem. Those supporting the House of York took the white rose, while the House of Lancaster and its supporters took the red.

The adherents of York and the followers of Lancaster fought a war of mutual extermination for no higher aim than power and spoils. The Wars of the Roses destroyed a significant part of England's feudal nobility by wiping out whole families, whose male heirs had been killed in war. At first, the Yorkists had the advantage. When Richard of York was executed after being captured in battle, his son, Edward, was victorious against the Lancastrians. In 1461,

402 LIGHT TO THE NATIONS: The History of Christian Civilization

**England during the Wars of the Roses**

he became king as Edward IV. The unfortunate Henry VI fled England for Scotland. But he was captured in 1471 and murdered in the Tower of London, where he had been imprisoned. Henry's executioner was probably Edward IV's brother Richard, Duke of Gloucester.

It was this same duke of Gloucester who became king after Edward's death in 1483—but by dishonorable means. After his brother's death,

Richard had become the "protector" of Edward's young son, now King Edward V, and his brother. Richard, however, immediately began plotting against his nephew. Edward V had been king only two months when voices were raised against him, saying he was not Edward IV's legitimate son. A session of Parliament was called, and on June 25 it was declared that since he was not the former king's legitimate son, Edward was not the rightful king. Parliament then offered the crown to Richard, who pretended to take it reluctantly. Edward V and his brother were placed in the Tower of London, where they were murdered—some say by Richard's orders.

Whether Richard murdered his nephews or not, many Englishmen believed he did. Their hearts turned against the new king. Richard III had reigned for about two years when rebellion broke out against him. The leader of this rebellion was Henry Tudor, a grandson of John of Gaunt and thus a **scion** of the House of Lancaster. Henry had the support of many nobles, including some Yorkists, as well as the king of France.

**scion:** a descendent or child of a family (pronounced *SIGH-un*)

Setting sail from Brittany, where he had been taken as a child during the reign of Edward IV, Henry Tudor landed his forces at Milford Haven on the coast of Wales. On August 22, 1485, the army of Henry Tudor, the champion of the House of Lancaster, met the army of Richard III, the Yorkist king, at Bosworth Field. Though outnumbered, Henry's army defeated Richard's. Richard III himself, fighting bravely to the end, was slain in the battle.

The Battle of Bosworth Field ended the Wars of the Roses. The following October, Henry Tudor was crowned king at Westminster Abbey in London. Before his coronation, he had promised his Yorkist allies that he would marry Elizabeth, Edward IV's daughter and heir. In this way, the House of Tudor, the line of the new king, Henry VII, united the Houses of Lancaster and York. The Red Rose of Lancaster was joined, through matrimony, with its rival the White Rose of York. And peace came to England at last.

# The New Muslim Threat to Christendom

While Western Christendom was absorbed by its own problems—the Great Schism, the Black Plague, and the **fratricidal** wars between Christian kingdoms—a new threat was building in the East. This new threat was the Ottoman Turks, who—driven westward from the plains of central Asia by

**fratricidal:** referring to an act of *fratricide,* the killing of a brother or sister

**404** LIGHT TO THE NATIONS: The History of Christian Civilization

**The ruins of the Ottoman fortress at the top of Kekova Island along the Aegean coast of Turkey**

the Mongols—had settled Anatolia in Asia Minor. They were soon poised for an invasion of Europe.

The Ottomans, who had become Muslim, had a fierce devotion to their religion. The Ottomans interpreted the Muslim concept of Holy War—*jihad*—as not only allowing the conquest of "infidel" lands, but as blessing the capture and enslavement all those "infidels" taken in battle.

The first to suffer from this new Muslim threat was Constantinople, the **bastion** of Christendom in the east. In 1261, the Greeks had driven out the Latin-French emperors from Constantinople and reestablished a Greek emperor there. But, the restored Greek emperors could not revive the former strength of the Byzantine Empire. Not only did they have the Muslims to contend with, but the empire faced the hostility of its Christian neighbors in Serbia, Bulgaria, and the Republic of Venice. The Byzantine emperors could expect little aid from the Christian monarchies of western and central Europe, who were too busy with their own conflicts or too weakened by the ravages of plague and unrest to worry about Constantinople. To defend his lands, the Byzantine emperor drained Anatolia of its best troops—and in 1337, Orkhan, the Ottoman sultan, took advantage of this opportunity. His troops attacked the Byzantine fortress of Nicomedia on the coast of Asia Minor.

**bastion:** a stronghold or fortification

Byzantium sent an army of only two thousand to defend Nicomedia. The mighty Byzantine state had been broken by Western occupation after the Fourth Crusade in 1204 and then by plague and civil wars. It no longer had the men or finances to mount a more determined defense. In the battle that followed, the Ottomans broke the Byzantine line and scattered the Greek army.

Orkhan did not have to force his way into Europe. John Cantacuzene, the guardian of the young emperor, John V Palaiologos, proclaimed himself emperor in Thrace in 1341. In search of military support, Cantacuzene appealed to Orkhan for aid, and offered his daughter in marriage to the Turk. In 1356, Orkhan with six thousand troops crossed the Dardanelles,

**The Ottoman Empire**

a strait separating Europe from Asia and forced the Byzantine Senate to proclaim Cantacuzene as co-emperor with John V.

With a foothold now in Europe, Orkhan's forces poured into Greece. Under Orkhan's son, Murad, the Ottomans conquered Adrianople. When Murad became sultan in 1359, he made Adrianople his capital. Sultan Murad then led his victorious armies into the Balkans and conquered Bulgaria.

The once great Byzantine Empire had lost nearly all its territory to the Ottomans; its emperor now reigned over little more than the city of Constantinople itself. The Christian capital of the East was henceforth like an island surrounded by an ever-rising Muslim sea.

The conquest of Bulgaria struck alarm into the neighboring kingdom of Serbia. To halt the Ottoman advance against his land, King Lazar of Serbia gathered the Serbian nobility and their armies. They met Murad's army on the plain of Kosovo on June 15, 1389.

The Serbians fought bravely against the Ottomans, and at first they had the advantage. But at a critical moment in the battle, one of Lazar's nobles fled the field with 12,000 men. The Serbian lines dissolved, Prince Lazar was killed, and the Christian forces were captured or slaughtered. Though at first the Ottomans had to withdraw from Kosovo because they had lost so many men in the battle, they later forced Serbia to become a vassal state to the sultan.

But Murad himself lost his life at Kosovo. A legend says that before the battle, King Lazar had accused his son-in-law of treachery. To prove

### The Dreaded Janissaries

Sultan Murad conceived a plan that would supply Ottoman armies for centuries. He placed a tax on every Christian family—but not a tax of money or produce. Murad's tax was far more brutal, for he demanded that every fifth Christian boy child be taken from his family and given to the sultan's service. The boys so taken were raised as Muslims and trained to be warriors.

These once-Christian boys were called "slaves of the port," because, in theory, they would always stand ready at the door (the port) of the sultan's tent. When these boys were old enough to fight, they were organized as an infantry corps, called the *Yeni Ceri*, or "New Force"—or "Janissaries," as Europeans called them. These Janissaries were the best trained of the sultan's armies, and he used them to great effect in fighting against Christian forces.

his innocence, this son-in-law pretended to be a deserter and entered the sultan's camp. Once there, he killed Murad—and then, in his turn, was cut down by the sultan's men. All of Europe celebrated Murad's death as a gift from God. It was a victory, indeed, but a short-lived one. The Ottoman threat did not end with the death of the sultan. Indeed, it had only just begun.

# Chapter Review

## Summary
- The Rus, under their chief, Rurik, founded Novgorod in what is now northern Russia. One of Rurik's companions, Oleg, founded Kiev on the Dnieper River.
- Two brothers, Cyril and Methodius, preached the Gospel to the Slavs in Moravia, translating the liturgy into Slavonic. They translated the Scriptures into Slavonic, developing an alphabet based on Greek and called Cyrillic script.
- Vladimir, who became Grand Prince of Kiev in 980, accepted the Christian Faith from Constantinople. Vladimir was baptized in 988 and immediately set about converting the people of Russia to the Christian religion.
- During the reign of Grand Prince Yaroslav, Kiev became famous as a center of culture. So beautiful was the city that it became known as "Kiev the Golden."
- Kievan Russia had to face many invaders from across the steppe. In the early 13th century the Mongols, under Batu Khan, conquered all of Kievan Russia. The khan, from his encampment called the Golden Horde, forced the Russian princes to pay tribute.
- The city and realm of Novgorod had to contend not only with the Mongols, but with Christian powers to the west. For his victory over the Swedes at the Neva River, Prince Alexander of Novgorod received the name "Nevski." Alexander Nevski was able to defeat the invading Teutonic Knights. However, because of these Christian enemies, Alexander was forced to make peace with the Mongols. In return, the Mongols named him Grand Prince of all Russia.
- Under Ivan I ("Money Bag"), the formerly insignificant city of Moscow began to become an important power in Russia, and the ruler of Russia began to be called "Grand Prince." In 1328, the city became the seat of the metropolitan archbishop of all Russia. In 1380,

Moscow's Grand Prince Dmitri Donskoi defeated the Mongols at Kulikovo Pole. This victory showed Russians that the Mongols were not invincible.
- A dynastic struggle called the Hundred Years' War began when England's King Edward III claimed the throne of France. English troops landed in France in 1339. Using the longbow and a new invention, the cannon, the English won great victories over the French at Crécy (1346) and at Poitiers (1356).
- Joan of Arc, the daughter of peasants, heard heavenly voices calling on her to rise in defense of the French kingdom against the invading English. Winning the confidence of Charles VII, the uncrowned king of France, Joan led troops to the besieged city of Orléans, capturing the English forts around the city and lifting the siege. After a stunning success in a short campaign along the Loire River, Joan accompanied Charles VII to Reims, where he was crowned king on July 17, 1429. Almost a year later, Joan was captured by the Burgundians, who turned her over to the English. After being tried by English judges as a sorceress and a heretic, Joan was burned at the stake on May 30, 1431.
- The Hundred Years' War ended with England losing all its French possessions except for the channel port of Calais. Under King Louis XI, the French state became as strong as it was under Philip the Fair 100 years earlier.
- King Richard II succeeded his grandfather, Edward III, as king of England. He was overthrown by his cousin, who became king as Henry IV, establishing the House of Lancaster on the English throne. Henry IV's son, Henry V, reasserted his claims to the French throne, winning an important victory against the French at Agincourt in 1415.
- During the 14th and 15th centuries, the English Parliament gained more and more power and authority over the English kings. Parliament's approval became essential for every important change in law or policy.
- After the death of King Henry V, England was torn by a series of civil wars. Called the "Wars of the Roses," they pitted the House of York against the House of Lancaster for control of the English crown. In 1485 Henry Tudor, a Welsh prince and last surviving member of the House of Lancaster, defeated King Richard III and the Yorkists at the Battle of Bosworth Field. Henry Tudor became king as King Henry VII.
- The Muslim Ottoman Turks threatened Christian civilization in the 15th century. In 1337, the Ottoman sultan Orkhan conquered Nicomedia, the last Byzantine stronghold in Asia. Osman's successor,

Orkhan, invaded Europe. Orkhan's son, Murad, took the old city of Adrianople—which he made the chief Ottoman base in Europe—thus opening up the Balkans for Muslim conquest.
- To supply his armies, Murad demanded that Christian villagers give up their young boys to him. These boys were indoctrinated in Islamic beliefs and as young men were organized in an infantry corps that became known as the "New Force," or Janissaries.
- Seeing the Balkans fall to Murad's armies, Prince Lazar of Serbia brought together Christian Serbian princes to drive the Turks out. At Kosovo in 1389, however, the Ottomans destroyed the Serbian army, and Prince Lazar was killed.

## Key Concepts
**Ottomans:** Turkish Muslim people organized by Sultan Osman
**Hundred Years' War:** war between England and France over the right to the crown of France
**nationalism:** devotion to a group, sharing a common language, history, and customs. At times, nationalism includes a sense that one's nation is superior to or more important than all other nations.
**Parliament:** the representative assembly of England
**House of Lords:** the upper house of Parliament, comprised of the feudal aristocracy
**House of Commons:** the lower house of Parliament, comprised of the knights, burgesses, and lesser nobility
**Wars of the Roses:** civil war between the Houses of Lancaster and of York for possession of the English crown

## Dates to Remember
**988:** baptism of Vladimir, grand prince of Kiev
**1223:** Mongols defeat the Russians at the Battle of Kalka River
**1337–1453:** the Hundred Years' War
**1346:** the Battle of Crécy
**1356:** invasion of Europe by Sultan Orkhan and the Ottoman armies
**1380:** Dmitri Donskoi defeats the Mongols at Kalikovo Pole
**1389:** the Battle of Kosovo in Serbia
**1415:** the Battle of Agincourt
**1431:** execution of St. Joan of Arc
**1455–1485:** the Wars of the Roses

## Central Characters

**St. Vladimir (956–1015):** grand prince of Kiev; he converted Russia to the Christian Faith

**Alexander Nevski (1220?–1263):** grand prince of Novgorod; he saved Novgorod from the Swedes and the Teutonic Knights

**Orkhan (flourished 1341):** Osman's son, the sultan who brought the Ottoman armies into Europe

**Dmitri Donskoi (1350–1389):** grand prince of Moscow; he defeated the Mongols in 1380

**St. Joan of Arc (1412–1431):** French heroine and warrior who fought to drive the English from France and bring the young king of France to his throne; executed as a sorceress and heretic

**Edward III (1312–1377):** king of England; he started the Hundred Years' War

**Henry Tudor (1457–1509):** king of England; he won the Battle of Bosworth Field and started the Tudor line of monarchs as King Henry VII

**Louis XI (reigned 1461–1483):** French king called the "Spider King" for the cunning and often unscrupulous ways he sought to strengthen his power

## Questions for Review

1. Why did Vladimir decide to receive the Christian Faith from the Church in Constantinople?
2. What effects did the Mongol conquest have on Russia?
3. Why was the Hundred Years' War fought?
4. When did the Battle of Crécy occur? What new weapons, used in this battle, changed the nature of warfare in Europe?
5. How did the Hundred Years' War change France? How did it change England?
6. What changes in English government came about because of the Hundred Years' War? Why did Edward III have to give Parliament more power?
7. What did St. Joan of Arc see as the purpose of her mission? Was she successful? Please explain.
8. Who were the combatants in the Wars of the Roses? Why are these wars called the Wars of the Roses? What were results of these wars?
9. What is nationalism? What effect did the spirit of nationalism have on Christendom?
10. What new threat to Europe arose in the East during the 14th century? What parts of Europe were threatened?

## Ideas in Action

1. Learn as a class the English medieval song, "Our King Went Forth to Normandy."
2. Study the battles of Crécy and Poitiers. What happened? What were their results? Who led the English? Who led the French?
3. Read the young people's novel, *The Black Arrow* (by Robert Louis Stevenson), set during the Wars of the Roses. What does such a novel teach about history?
4. Watch a dramatization of Shakespeare's play, *Richard III*. A good version is one by Sir Laurence Olivier. Discuss what Shakespeare's drama depicts about history.
5. As a class, study the life of St. Joan of Arc. Why would God choose a young girl like Joan to save France?

# Highways and Byways

## The Twilight of Arthur

In the 1400s, at the end of the medieval period, when the world of chivalry and knights was passing away, an English author attempted to collect the tales of Arthur and his court into one continuous story. This writer was Sir Thomas Malory (died 1471), a knight on the Yorkist side in England's Wars of the Roses. Captured by his enemies, Malory was held for ransom for years and charged with heinous crimes he may or may not have committed. As he sat in prison awaiting his ransom, release, or death, he began writing his version of the epic of Arthur, called *Le Morte D'Arthur*, "The Death of Arthur"—not in verse, as were earlier versions, but in a stately prose.

As Malory told it (thinking about the ruin of the civil wars of his own time), Arthur tried to create a kingdom of justice and nobility out of the warring tribes of Britain. The attempt, however, failed on account of human weakness and, ultimately, treachery. In the following passage, Malory tells of the death of Arthur at the hands of his illegitimate son, Mordred. The author likely drew his imagery from battles in which he himself fought:

> And never was there seen a more dolefuller battle in no Christian land; for there was but rushing and riding, foining and striking, and many a grim word was there spoken either to other, and many a deadly

*stroke. But ever King Arthur rode throughout the battle of Sir Mordred many times, and did full nobly as a noble king should, and at all times he fainted never; and Sir Mordred that day put him in devoir, and in great peril. And thus they fought all the long day, and never stinted till the noble knights were laid to the cold earth; and ever they fought still till it was near night, and by that time was there an hundred thousand laid dead upon the down. Then was Arthur wood wroth out of measure, when he saw his people so slain from him. . . .*

*Then the king gat his spear in both his hands, and ran toward Sir Mordred, crying: Traitor, now is thy death day come. And when Mordred heard Sir Arthur, he ran until him with his sword drawn in his hand. And there King Arthur smote Sir Mordred under the shield, with a foin of his spear, throughout the body, more than a fathom. And when Sir Mordred felt that he had his death wound he thrust himself with the might that he had up to the bur of King Arthur's spear. And right so he smote his father Arthur, with his sword holden in both his hands, on the side of the head, that the sword pierced the helmet and the brain-pan, and therewithal Sir Mordred fell stark dead to the earth; and the noble Arthur fell in a swoon to the earth, and there he swooned ofttimes.*

Chapter 16 # The Birth of a New World

**Detail of the head of a man, from a Romanesque church on the pilgrimage route to Santiago de Compostela in Spain**

The Middle Ages were a time very different from our own. In our modern world, God and religion are not particularly important—at least, compared to their importance in the Middle Ages. There are today many religious people, to be sure, who take the worship of God and the teachings of their religion very seriously. But our society, as a whole, draws a bright line between religion and politics, for instance, or religion and science. At best, religion is seen as just a part of life in our day. It is thought to be good, but a private good—something that gives people comfort and meaning in their individual lives. It is not seen as something that speaks to all of human life.

During the Middle Ages, however, everything in art, politics, poetry, religion, and everyday life reflected the belief that God exists and that man has a unique dignity among all the creatures of the world. From this vision came Romanesque and Gothic architecture, the poetry of the *troubadours* and minnesingers, and the epic vision of Dante Alighieri. The fervor of St. Francis and St. Dominic and their followers, and the theology and philosophy of St. Bonaventure and St. Thomas Aquinas, all show the power of the Christian faith in the medieval world.

For medieval people, the idea that one could even think of nature and life apart from God would have been considered nonsense. The entire structure of medieval life was built upon the belief that God was involved in human life and history. Belief in the Incarnation—that God had become man in Jesus Christ—caused medieval people to think of all life as reflecting God and his will, as we learn of it through the Church. Everything was to be done for the greater glory of God and to fulfill the purpose of human existence—eternal life with God.

Thus, for medievals, society's institutions, laws, and customs were to be directed to the goals of the Christian life and to inspire people to live it. The Church—the community of faithful Christians, ruled by the bishops and the pope—was therefore seen as the center of life. And the worship of God in the Church was the very thing for which everything else in life was done.

This medieval world gave way to what has become known as the Renaissance.

What was the Renaissance?

"Renaissance" is the name that later generations gave to the period of history when Europeans developed a renewed respect for the literature, architecture, and art of ancient Rome and Greece. The word *renaissance* means, simply, "rebirth." To later generations, the Renaissance was the time when the creativity and spirit of the classical ages were reborn in the arts and philosophy.

The Renaissance marks the time when Europeans began to turn away from the ideals of the Middle Ages. Indeed, the Renaissance marks the beginning of our own modern world.

# Renaissance Humanism

The Renaissance did not wholly destroy the beliefs of the Middle Ages, but it gave rise to new doubts about those beliefs. We give the name "**Humanism**" to the philosophy, or way of looking at the world, that developed during the Renaissance. Humanism tended to see man, not God, as the center of the world. Human ideas and ideals, it was thought, were what should guide the life of people and human society—not the ideals of the Gospel or divine revelation or the Church. Renaissance thinkers began emphasizing the importance of life in this world and focused less on the life of the world to come. Because of Humanism, Europeans began to emphasize secular over spiritual goods.

Renaissance Humanism, at first, was not contrary to Christian beliefs; early Humanists wanted to encourage virtue and a virtuous society. Humanist philosophers in mid-15th-century Italy and France thought

> **Humanism:** the philosophy of the Renaissance that tended to see man, not God, as the center of the world and held that human ideas and ideals, not the Church, should guide the life of people and human society

*The School of Athens,* by Italian Renaissance painter Raphael

Humanism offered a broader understanding of what it means to be truly human. The ideal of the Renaissance man was of someone who perfected himself in all areas of life—in scholarship, the arts, statesmanship, the life of moral virtue, and in bodily health and strength.

Humanists looked to the writers and thinkers of classical Greece and Rome for inspiration. They preferred the texts of ancient Roman and Greek authors to the works of medieval authors and theologians. Humanists modeled their prose writing after the Latin works of the Roman orator Cicero and their poetry after the verses of the Roman poets Seneca, Horace, and Virgil. Humanists viewed the literary works of the Middle Ages as barbaric, because these works did not fit classical Greek and Roman styles. Humanists despised the scholastic philosophy and theology of their day, which often was occupied with useless questions—or "logic chopping," as the Humanists called it. But the Humanists also rejected the serious and important scholastic thought of the High Middle Ages, such as the works of St. Thomas Aquinas.

For the Humanists, the study of the Greek and Roman classics was the only proper training for the mind. It was the Humanists who first spoke of the centuries between their time and the end of the Western Roman Empire in 476 as the "Middle Ages." Humanists gave the name "gothic" to medieval architecture, because they thought it was as barbaric as something made by the ancient Goths.

# Humanism and the Christian Faith

Francesco Petrarca (1304–1374), Italian poet and humanist. Fresco by Andrea del Castagno

In the beginning, Humanists were not at all anti-Christian. Francesco Petrarca (1304–1374), called the "father of Humanism," was a member of the clergy and a reasonably devout Catholic. Petrarca, or Petrarch, collected the works of ancient writers like Cicero, which he found in monastic libraries, and he published classical works that had been forgotten over the centuries. Petrarch thought the Latin prose of his day was barbaric, and so he began to model his Latin writings after the style of Cicero. Many other writers began to follow his example. Petrarch wrote prose works, poems, and epics in Latin; but, perhaps, his greatest poetry was written in Italian, not Latin.

Along with Petrarch were other Catholic leaders and intellectuals who thought that classical learning and Christian spirituality benefited each other. In the early 15th century, some Greeks came to Italy and revived the study of Greek and the Greek classics, especially the philosophy of Plato. One of these was Bessarion, who attended the Council of Florence, which had put a temporary end to the schism between the pope and the Church of Constantinople. Bessarion, a great scholar, stayed in Italy and eventually became a cardinal of the Church of Rome.

But, even though many Humanists were serious and devout Catholics, other Humanists became so fond of the pagan spirit of the ancient classical world that they began to ignore the Christian religion. They had the very Catholic desire to experience the joys and beauty of the world, but they shied away from ascetic and penitential practices. It was not long before their love of beauty became mere **sensualism**. Many Humanists no longer wanted to follow the narrow way of the Gospel, but the broad road of earthly pleasure. So it was that Humanism grew more pagan and increasingly less Christian in its spirit.

One of the **maxims** of Humanism was: "Man is the measure of all things." This maxim basically says that man is the center of the world, the one for whose benefit everything created exists. Such an idea is not necessarily contrary to the Christian faith, which holds that God

**sensualism:** an excessive love of the pleasures gotten through the senses—what one sees, hears, and touches
**maxim:** a saying that expresses a key idea; a proverb

did create the world for the sake of man. But when this idea is separated from the notion that man is created for the sake of God—to worship and enjoy Him forever—it can lead to anti-Christian conclusions. And it did. Severed from Christian teaching, Humanism offered something quite different than the splendid, beautiful, and virtuous human being so idealized by the Renaissance.

Niccolò Machiavelli of Florence (1469–1527) is an example of a Humanist who came to non-Christian conclusions about human society. Machiavelli was an elegant and famous Humanist writer and thinker, but he tried to think about history and human events apart from morality. He wrote a famous book about power and society, called *The Prince*. In this work, Machiavelli claimed that the best ruler—the "prince"—makes his decisions based only on what benefits himself and his realm. Such a "successful" ruler does not consider moral principles but uses fear, bullying, and even terror to subject others to his will. Of course, such an **unscrupulous** ruler would become a monster of a human being. Those who use such tactics have been called "machiavel" ever since.

Humanists, like Machiavelli, did not consider God when they thought about how people should live. They desired a world without God's presence or intervention. Because of this, we call such Humanism atheistic—not because all these Humanists did not believe in God, but because they basically ignored him. Nothing in the history of Christendom, except for, maybe, Albigensianism, was as **corrosive** to the Faith as atheist Humanism was. Instead of promoting the dignity of man, as the original Humanists desired, atheistic Humanism degraded human life and morals. The spread of atheistic Humanism threatened the unity of Christendom, for it undermined the Catholic religion, which fostered and preserved that unity.

In the end, because of Humanism, the Renaissance was not simply an artistic and scholarly movement. It was something that came to eat away at political and social life. Because religion began to be seen as less important to everyday life, people began more and more to rebel against the idea of Christian-inspired medieval institutions controlling everything from art to business to politics.

The medieval guild, for instance, tried to make sure that sellers and buyers, employers and employees, and master craftsmen and their rivals

**Detail from the Sistine Chapel, by Michelangelo. This, the figure of Adam, represents what the artist saw to be the ideal human form.**

**unscrupulous:** without principles or morals
**corrosive:** from the verb *corrode*, meaning "to destroy something by gradually weakening it"

**Niccolò Machiavelli, detail from a painting by Santi di Tito**

**autocracy:** rule by one having absolute or unrestricted power; a ruler in an autocracy is called an *autocrat*

in business treated each other with justice. They did this because the Christian faith demanded such justice. But during the Renaissance, people began to demand the removal of such restrictions on their activities. Merchants and craftsmen did not want to obey guild rules that told them how much they could charge for their services or goods. They wanted to be able to compete with their business rivals with greater freedom.

During the Middle Ages, the king was not the absolute power in his kingdom; he had to share power with his lords as well as the communes, cities, and the Church. During the Renaissance, however, kings and lords both no longer wanted to cooperate with feudal vassals. Kings, in particular, sought to gain sole power over their vassals and subjects. Renaissance rulers strove to establish an **autocracy,** where they would have sole and unrestricted power over their subjects and the Church itself.

The ideals of Humanism led to a new awakening for the mind of Europe—and, coming after the misfortunes and disappointments of the late Middle Ages, this new awakening seemed to offer great benefits. But, separated from God, the teachings of the Church, and morality, Humanism ultimately dealt Christendom a serious wound from which it has never recovered.

# The Wellspring of the Renaissance

The Renaissance spread to all of Europe, but it began in Italy. This is not surprising, for Italy had been the center of the Roman Empire, and so it had more reminders of classical civilization than any other country in western Europe. Roman roads, aqueducts, ruined temples of the pagan gods, and ancient temples converted into Christian churches could be found throughout Italy. They served as reminders of the civilization that existed before the "barbaric" Middle Ages.

The first great center of the Italian Renaissance was the city of Dante—Florence. Situated on the Arno River just north of Rome, in central Italy, Florence had become an important trade center. Those who entered Italy from the north, or who crossed to the north from Italy, passed through Florence. Products arriving in Venice on the east coast of Italy and in Genoa on the west coast came to and passed through Florence. The city was also a center of the wool-dyeing trade and banking. If "all roads lead to Rome," those same roads passed, first and last, through Florence.

Though Florence was a republic with a strong democratic character, its government, beginning in the 15th century, was under the control of the Medici family. A merchant family, the Medicis built their fortune through the silk trade and banking. They gradually became as powerful and rich as any monarch of Europe. Several of the family's sons entered religious life, and some even became popes.

The Medicis collected beautiful things for their own enjoyment. They commissioned glorious paintings and sculptures for the enjoyment of themselves and of all in Florence. They were the patrons of writers and philosophers, artists and architects. They founded schools, built magnificent public buildings, and added to the incredibly beautiful cathedral in Florence. They delighted and entertained the populace of Florence by holding balls, pageants, and banquets.

Many great scholars, artists, architects, philosophers, and poets came from all over Italy and the rest of Europe to Florence. The Medicis sponsored archeological digs to recover classical statues and ancient architectural forms so sculptors could imitate them in their own work. The most famous of the Medici family was Lorenzo (1449–1492), who became known as "the Magnificent" for his generosity and patronage of the arts

**Florence in the 16th century**

and learning that made Florence glorious—the richest cultural and artistic center in Europe.

## The Renaissance in Rome

In the early 16th century, the center of the Italian art world moved from Florence to Rome, where the popes patronized the arts. At first, the popes had looked on the Renaissance with suspicion. But this view changed when, in 1447, a Humanist scholar ascended the throne of Peter. This was Tommaso Parentucelli, who took the name Nicholas V.

**Pope Nicholas V, by Peter Paul Rubens**

As pope, Nicholas worked to root out abuses in the Church and to restore papal authority throughout Europe; but he had other goals as well. The pope wanted Rome to become the center of art and literature. He welcomed Humanist scholars to the city—and patronized them. He established a center for the translation of ancient Greek texts in the city. He worked to rebuild the Vatican, including the Basilica of St. Peter, built by the Emperor Constantine over 1,000 years earlier. Pope Nicholas planned the demolition of the ancient church—and even had part of it pulled down—because, he said, it was falling into ruin. The current St. Peter's Basilica in Rome does not date from the time of Nicholas V, but he began the process that resulted in the raising of the structure. Nicholas V's greatest cultural achievement is probably the founding of the Vatican Library, which over the centuries has preserved ancient works that otherwise might have been lost.

Even after Nicholas V's death in 1455, Rome continued to draw people to it, and they were not only Renaissance thinkers and artists. Though the painter Botticelli (1444–1510) spent nearly all his life in Florence, he visited Rome in 1481–1482, where he painted **frescoes** on the walls of the Vatican's Sistine Chapel. But the painter and inventor Leonardo da Vinci and the painter/sculptor Michelangelo, along with many other artists and scholars who had their beginnings in Florence, ended up living permanently in Rome.

**fresco:** a painting done on moist lime plaster

## Renaissance Artists

Like the Humanists, Renaissance painters, sculptors, and architects were inspired by classical civilization. Medieval art had tried to represent the spiritual world that lay behind and gave meaning to the physical world. Classical Greek and Roman art, on the other hand, sought to portray the world realistically as it is experienced through the senses. Studying ancient artworks, Renaissance artists strove to make paintings and sculptures that faithfully represented the physical world. They wanted to imitate in their art what they saw with their eyes, but in a way that brought out the beauty of what they saw. They tried to portray beautiful figures that represented the created world as God had meant it to be. Adam and Eve, the first parents in their glory before the fall—this was the ideal for Renaissance artists, who tried to capture that glory in human form in whatever they painted or designed.

One of the most famous Renaissance artists, Leonardo da Vinci (1452–1519), was also an inventor. Born and trained in Florence, Leonardo made his reputation in Rome and Milan. In his old age, he moved to France as a guest of the French king. There Leonardo died.

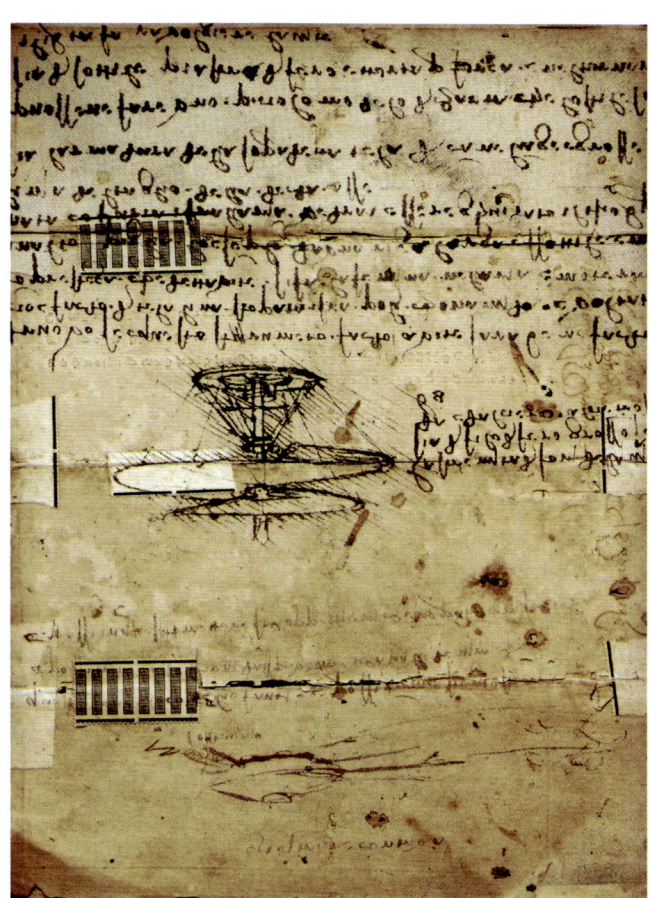

**Da Vinci's design for a helicopter and a lifting wing**

As a painter, Leonardo's most famous works are the *Mona Lisa* and the *Last Supper* fresco. But throughout his life, Leonardo also explored the way the world works. He invented or imagined machines and devices that might allow men to fly, or let them travel beneath the sea. He also studied perspective in painting, the art by which some figures in a painting (such as a background mountain range) are made to appear farther away than other figures—just as, in real life, things farther away appear smaller than things closer by. The Italian painter Filippo Brunelleschi (1377–1446) is believed to have developed the use of perspective. It is one of the most distinguishing characteristics of Renaissance art in contrast to medieval art, which did not use perspective.

**Detail from Michelangelo's *David***

One of the most famous Renaissance artists was Michelangelo di Buonarroti (1475–1564). Though Michelangelo thought of himself primarily as a sculptor, he was also a master of painting, poetry, and architecture.

Michelangelo's most famous works are the paintings in the Vatican's Sistine Chapel. Michelangelo's depictions of the human body on the ceiling of the Sistine Chapel are models of scientific accuracy. His most famous sculptures include *Moses*, *David*, and the *Pietá*. Michelangelo's masterpieces were made possible by his intense study of human anatomy and proportion.

Another great artist of the period was Raphael Santi (1483–1520). Raphael worked both in Florence (1504–1508) and in Rome (1508–1520). His portraits of the female form and face—especially in his Madonna paintings—made Renaissance beauty the model not only for other painters but also for stylish ladies. Raphael found a realism that depicted the tenderness and warmth of the human face.

***Madonna*, by Raphael**

# The Fall of Constantinople

Just as the Humanist movement was beginning in Italy and France, Christendom suffered its greatest shock since the sack of Rome by the Goths in 410—the fall of Constantinople to the Muslim Ottoman Turks. Like ancient Rome, the city of Constantinople was thought to be eternal. It was the "Second Rome," the greatest Christian capital of the world, and the strong, ancient bastion of Christendom in the East. Its fall was a catastrophe of indescribable magnitude.

How did the great city of Constantinople, surrounded by a series of seemingly **impregnable** walls, fall to its Muslim conquerors? As with many other world-shaking events, the source could be traced to something quite small—to pride or treachery. Constantinople's fall was brought about by both.

**impregnable:** unconquerable

## Union and a Failed Crusade

The death of Murad I at the Battle of Kosovo in 1389 did not end the Ottoman threat to Europe. Constantinople, completely surrounded by Muslim territory, stood in most danger of Turkish conquest. But the conquest of the Balkans showed that the Ottomans were a threat to western Christendom as well. To combat the Ottoman threat—the common enemy—the Catholic West and the Orthodox East had to join forces.

Benozzo Gozzoli's *Journey of the Magi,* inspired by the international character of the participants of the Council of Florence

Yet, though both called on the name of Christ, the Catholics and the Orthodox believers were separated by religious and cultural differences. To bridge the gap between them, the emperor of Constantinople, John VIII Palaiologos (reigned 1425–1448), traveled in splendid attire to Italy with a delegation of nobles, bishops, and military men. The emperor's plan was to meet with representatives of the pope to solve the theological differences separating the two branches of Christianity. If this old schism could be ended, it would make for a strong and united front of Christian nations against the invading Turks.

The "Greek" and "Latin" bishops, along with Emperor John VIII and Pope Eugenius IV, gathered for an ecumenical council that met in Florence in 1439. This council, it was hoped, would end the schism. Yet, though the council fathers discussed the theological differences between the Eastern and Western Churches, in the end they could not agree. Finally, reminded that the Turks were growing stronger while the bishops and theologians wrangled and fought, both sides signed a declaration of union (on July 5, 1439). In signing the declaration, the Orthodox, among other things, acknowledged the pope as head of the Church. After the solemn reading of the declaration in

Greek and Latin, Emperor John first, and then all the Greeks in succession, genuflected before Pope Eugenius and kissed his hand.

With union restored (or so it seemed) between the churches of Rome and Constantinople, Pope Eugenius IV asked for a crusade against the Turks. A crusading army, led by Hungary's King Ladislaus, Albania's Prince Scandenberg, and John Hunyadi, the "White Knight of Wallachia," defeated the Turks at Nissa in Serbia. Emboldened by this victory, Hunyadi invaded Bulgaria in 1444—but upon meeting a Turkish force three times larger than his own, he was defeated. Four years later, at Kosovo, a Turkish army 40,000 strong wiped out Hunyadi's force of 17,000.

The defeat at Kosovo ended whatever hope the besieged Greeks in Constantinople had in the crusade or the Western Christian powers. Indeed, except for this crusade—which was fought more to protect Christian Balkan lands—the Western powers showed little interest in coming to the aid of Constantinople; they were too involved in their own affairs. In Constantinople itself, the Greek bishops—pressured by the people, the clergy, and the monks—rejected the union that had been forged at the Council of Florence.

The new emperor, Constantine XI Palaiologos, however, still hoped to bring about an alliance with the West. He begged Pope Nicholas V to send theologians to Constantinople, to convince the people and clergy there to accept the union. The pope did send a mission to the emperor, and the result was that the union between the Churches of Rome and Constantinople was solemnly proclaimed on December 12, 1452 in the cathedral of Hagia Sophia—the great church built by Justinian eight centuries before.

**Byzantine fresco (14th century) of Christ delivering Adam and Eve from Hades**

But this union, like the one in Florence, was doomed to failure. Most of the Greek priests, the monks, and the people (remembering, perhaps, the sack of Constantinople by the soldiers of the Fourth Crusade) opposed union with the "heretics" and "schismatics" in the West. The pope's delegates tried to persuade the Greeks that union was necessary, but the people only replied, "Better the turban than the tiara!"—better to be ruled by the sultan than the pope. Sadly, they would all too soon see their wish fulfilled.

## The Last Emperor

Scarcely four months passed after the proclamation of union between the Churches, when the Turks, under their new sultan Mahomet II, a great-great-grandson of Othman, laid siege to Constantinople. So great was the Turkish host that it surrounded the city by land and sea. Mahomet, too, had weapons Constantine could not match—enormous bronze cannons that hurled stones at the walls of the city, battering the defenses, so old that they could not long withstand such an assault. Within the city, the Greeks and their few Venetian allies fought bravely; but they battled against overwhelming odds.

A painting by the Greek folk artist, Theopholis Hatzimihail, of the battle inside the walls of Constantinople. The figure on the white horse is Constantine XI Palaiologos.

The siege continued from early April to late May 1453. Day in and day out, the citizens of Constantinople—men, women, children, priests, monks, and nuns—repaired the walls that had been breached by the cannons. Finally, hearing rumors of a Christian fleet coming to aid the city, Mahomet II planned a general assault on Constantinople. On May 28, the day before the assault, Constantine ordered processions along the city walls to beg God's mercy, to turn away what he called the "just punishment sent by God" because of the city's sins.

On the evening of the same day, Constantine and all his court attended a Divine Liturgy (Mass) in the Cathedral of Hagia Sophia. Also present were the patriarch and the Latin Cardinal Isidore, churchmen representing both the Latins and the Greeks, and the nobility of the city, along with Venetians and Genoese. The differences between Catholics and Orthodox disappeared in the face of the common danger both faced. In this, the last Divine Liturgy offered in Hagia Sophia, Latins and Greeks together partook of "the undefiled and divine mysteries." Many worshippers were openly crying and asking each other's forgiveness.

In the early morning hours of May 29, 1453, Mahomet unleashed his assault on the city, attacking it from three sides. The defenders repulsed

## The Heroic Charge of St. John Capistrano

With Constantinople in Turkish hands, the West prepared for another invasion by Mahomet II, the conqueror of Constantinople. The king of Hungary knew that his kingdom would suffer first from a Turkish invasion. He appointed John Hunyadi as the governor of the fortress city of Belgrade, which, sitting on the Danube River, was the defense of the Hungarian kingdom. An elderly Franciscan priest and statesman, John Capistrano, organized an army of peasants from Hungary to go to the relief of the city and hold the line against the Turk.

In July 1456, the Turks laid siege to Belgrade. They encircled the city, and they blocked the Danube River with Turkish ships. The garrison at Belgrade had only 6,000 soldiers, who faced between 100,000 and 300,000 Turks. But though he was outnumbered, and not fully prepared for battle, Hunyadi successfully broke the naval blockade and brought food and troops up the river into the city.

At sundown on July 21, Mahomet II ordered the assault on Belgrade, which continued through the night. This time, however, the Christian defenders drove the sultan's Janissaries back. On the third day of the siege, July 23, some of the Christians went outside the city's fortifications. There they began jeering and shooting arrows at the Turkish soldiers nearest them. More crusaders came out to join the hecklers, and the incident exploded into a violent skirmish.

Though he was 70 years old, the priest, John Capistrano, rallied the Christians and then led them in a furious charge against the Turks. Calling out to the crusaders, he said, "The Lord has made the beginning and will take care of the finish!" John Hunyadi's army soon reinforced Capistrano's men. United and furious, they forced the Turks to retreat and abandon the siege. Belgrade was saved.

**The conquests of the Ottoman Sultan Mahomet II at the time of the siege of Belgrade, 1456**

---

two of the attacks; but the last attack overwhelmed them. Mahomet repeatedly threw his Janissaries, 12,000 of them, against the city's high and strong surrounding walls. A small side door in the wall seems to have been only partly closed, whether by treachery or the defenders' battle haste is unknown. After the attacking Janissaries forced the door open, the Turks poured through it and into the city. The emperor, his guards, and several nobles moved out against the invading Janissaries, but they were soon trapped as a fresh onslaught by the Janissaries broke through the city wall.

Despairing of victory for his city, the Emperor Constantine threw off his imperial insignia, which would have revealed who he was to the Ottomans. With seven other noblemen of the city, he plunged into the onrushing invaders. He was never seen again.

Chapter 16   The Birth of a New World   427

**The Ottoman Empire**
Mahomet II's conquests during the siege of Belgrade in 1456

By mid-morning, the streets of the city ran with blood as the invading Turks pillaged and destroyed. Men, women, and children were slaughtered in the great cathedral of Hagia Sophia, where many had taken refuge. For three days, the Turks rampaged through Constantinople, murdering its citizens, pillaging private homes, desecrating churches, destroying icons, burning priceless works of theology, philosophy, and literature.

Sometime during the course of these three days of slaughter and mayhem, Mahomet II himself entered the city. Going into Hagia Sophia, he offered there a Muslim prayer. From thenceforth, the great cathedral (at the completion of which the Emperor Justinian had cried, "I have outdone you, Solomon!") would be a Muslim mosque, and Constantinople (called

Istanbul by the Turks) became the capital of the Muslim Ottoman empire. The Byzantine, Eastern Roman Empire was no more.

# Moscow: The "Third Rome"

The power and influence of Moscow in Russia grew in the years following the Battle of Kalikovo Pole, where Dmitri Donskoi defeated the Mongols. Moscow had become so powerful that Vasili I—who became grand prince of Moscow after the death of his father, Dmitri Donskoi, in 1389—stopped paying the full tribute the **Muscovite** princes had paid to the Mongols, in 1378. It was during Vasili's reign (1389–1425) that the Golden Horde began to break up into smaller **khanates**.

Much had changed in Russia during the 250 years of Mongol dominion. Kievan Russia had had mild laws and local governments in which even the common people could participate. The Mongol invasions had put an end to this. Instead, Russian rulers tended to imitate the khans' harsh and cruel rule. An example of such a ruler was Dmitri Donskoi's great-grandson, who became grand prince of Moscow in 1462—Ivan III, remembered in history as "the Great."

**Muscovite:** an inhabitant of the city or principality of Moscow, called *Muscovy*

**khanate:** a region ruled by a Mongol ruler, called a khan

**Ivan III destroys Novgorod's assembly, the *veche***

## The Empire of Muscovy

By shrewdness and by ruthlessness, by forced purchases of lands and by war, Ivan the Great extended the territory controlled by Moscow. The greatest addition to Muscovy during Ivan's reign was Lord Novgorod the Great, including both the city and its wide territory stretching from the Baltic Sea eastward across the cold, forested lands north of Moscow.

The wild lands of Novgorod had long been settled by colonists from Muscovy. The first to wander into the forests north of Moscow were St. Sergius of Radonezh and his monks, who founded the monastery of the Holy Trinity-St. Sergius in the days of Dmitri Donskoi. From this monastery, other monks went into the wild lands controlled by Novgorod.

The expansion of Muscovy under Ivan the Great

Hardy settlers followed in the monks' wake. These men and women were as freedom loving and independent as those pioneers who, in two more centuries, would colonize the West of North America.

Since they were from Muscovy, these settlers had more fidelity to Moscow than to Novgorod. Ivan wanted Novgorod, but not because of its Muscovite settlers, whom he probably would find hard to govern anyhow. He wanted Novgorod because through it he could get access to the Baltic Sea and the sea trade with western Europe. Ivan wanted as well the control of Novgorod's rich trade in furs. Ivan's conquest of the great northern state was swift. Novgorod surrendered its independence to Moscow in 1478, and Ivan abolished the city's assembly (the *veche*) and its elected mayor. Ivan said no one but he himself would rule Novgorod.

Ivan conquered other parts of Russia, adding to Muscovy the principality of Tver as well as the old Kievan lands of Chernigov, Polotsk, and Smolensk. In 1480, when he refused to pay tribute to the Mongols, the Grand Khan Ahmad could do nothing about it, for the once mighty Golden Horde was torn by wars between the khanates. In 1487, Ivan forced the khanate of Kazan to become his vassal. From then on, the Mongols were no longer a serious threat to Russia.

The Kremlin. Annunciation Cathedral rises on the right

## The First Tsar

Ivan III desired not only a large realm and great power. He longed for glory—to be recognized as an equal by the monarchs of western Europe. And he gained this glory (or so he thought) through marriage. In 1472, Ivan was wed to Sophia Palaiologos—the niece of Constantine XI, the last Byzantine emperor, who died at Constantinople nearly 20 years earlier.

Ivan declared that his marriage to Sophia made him the rightful heir to the Eastern Roman Empire. He thus called himself the tsar (sometimes spelled czar, a form of Caesar) of the East. He added the Byzantine double-headed eagle to his family crest and, like the Byzantine emperors, called himself "autocrat." He not only called himself autocrat, but was able to make himself sole ruler of the land by reducing the power of the boyars (the Russian nobles), who once had been a powerful force in Muscovy.

The Russian Orthodox clergy and theologians helped Ivan further the glory of Moscow. They created a doctrine that Moscow had become the "Third Rome." The first Rome—Rome in Italy—had fallen to the barbarians, said these theologians, because of heresy. The second Rome, Constantinople, had fallen to the infidels because its people had lived luxuriously. As for Moscow, "The Third Rome will stand!" they declared. "And a fourth there will not be."

Under the influence of the Tsarina Sophia, Ivan established a court ritual that imitated the ritual of the imperial court in Constantinople. Ivan, too, brought Italian architects to Moscow to build a grand palace for him. In the Kremlin, the fortress of the tsar in Moscow, Ivan ordered the building of three stone cathedrals that stand there today—the churches of the Archangel, the Assumption, and the Annunciation.

Ivan held his divided realm together by his authority and personality. But his son, Vasili III, was not as lucky, or as charming, as his father. The

## A Technological Revolution: The Printing Press

In 1454, one year after the fall of Constantinople, Johannes Gutenberg, a German, produced a *Türkenkalender* (Turk calendar) as one of the first works on his invention, the printing press. The Turk calendar warned of the impending danger of invasion by the Ottoman Turks. It chronicled the progress of Turkish conquest across Europe and made a fortune for Gutenberg, its publisher. The money he earned from the *Türkenkalender* allowed him to print the most significant book of the age, the Bible.

Gutenberg had invented a printing press using movable type that allowed individual characters—for instance, letters—to be arranged into words. The characters were made of metal that was melted and cast in a mold. Gutenberg used his press to print a Latin Bible, the first full book ever to be set into print.

Gutenburg's printing press made the Bible—and, soon, other books and pamphlets—affordable to ordinary people, rather than only the wealthiest and greatest churches. While the initial typesetting for a printing press required much work and time, the printed book could be printed and reprinted in large numbers. The only books before the printing press had been hand-copied texts, which were rare and expensive, requiring many months of preparation and careful artistry.

**A model of the original Gutenberg press**

boyars had him poisoned, or so the charge ran, and named his boyar-born wife regent for Vasili's little son, Ivan. That little boy grew to be Tsar Ivan IV, remembered more commonly as Ivan the "Terrible."

# End of the Reconquest and Beyond

One of the greatest, most revolutionary changes not only for Europe but for all the world occurred in the late 15th century in that western outpost of Europe, the Iberian Peninsula. The little Christian kingdoms of that land—Castile, León, Aragon, and Navarre—had not been at the center of learning and culture, like France. They had not given birth to the Renaissance or been the seat of the Church, like Italy. None of these Iberian states had served as the great political arm of the Church, like Germany. For over 700 years, the Iberian Peninsula had been divided between Christian and Muslim realms, which had been locked in the struggle called the Reconquest. That struggle, in the late 15th century, was about to end and a new task to open for the Christian powers of Iberia.

**Christopher Columbus shows his project, the "Enterprise of the Indies," to the Council of Salamanca**

When Enrique IV, king of Castile and León, died in 1474, the crown went to his sister, Isabel. Enrique IV had been a weak king, and during his reign the Castilian nobles had ignored his authority. Castile was torn by many factions, and when Isabel became queen, she faced a war with Portugal. That country's king, Alfonso V, was betrothed to Enrique IV's daughter Juana and claimed the Castilian throne for her. The war ended in 1479, and in 1480 Juana entered a monastery. From thenceforth, Isabel I was the unquestioned queen of Castile and León.

In 1469, Isabel had married Fernando, who became king of Aragon in 1479. Though the two kingdoms, Castile-León and Aragon, would remain separate, Isabel

The Iberian Peninsula under Queen Isabel and King Fernando

and Fernando agreed that they would rule them together as if they were one kingdom. Fernando also was lord over Barcelona and Valencia. Thus, all of the Iberian Peninsula, except for Portugal and Navarre and the Moorish kingdom of Granada in the south, came under the rule of the two monarchs. Thus began the united kingdom of Spain, which Isabel and Fernando (to whom Pope Alexander VI gave the title the "Catholic Monarchs") ruled wisely and well.

## The Reconquest of Granada

Not long after Isabel had secured her queenship, however, the Moors of Granada seized the city of Zahara, which belonged to the "Catholic Monarchs." This was a declaration of war that Isabel and Fernando could

**Surrender of Granada in 1492 to Fernando and Isabel**

not ignore—and it gave them the pretext of ending Muslim rule in Iberia once and for all.

In 1482, Fernando and Isabel's forces took the Muslim city of Alhama. So began the last war of the Reconquest, which had begun in the eighth century. Isabel raised funds for the war, recruited armies, provisioned troops, and organized what are said to be the first field hospitals in European history. Fernando directed his and Isabel's armies, as well as the strategy of the war.

Not all, however, went well for the Catholic Monarchs. The Christian forces suffered two serious defeats, but they did not give up the struggle. In 1489 Isabel even pawned the crown jewels of Castile to raise cash for the war. For 10 years, the Spanish forces fought, conquering Granada city by city. Finally, in 1491, Fernando and his army laid siege to the beautiful Islamic city of Granada, after which the Moorish kingdom was named.

The siege of Granada lasted nearly two years. Finally, though, the Moorish power was spent. On November 25, 1491, the last Islamic ruler of Al-Andalus, Muhammad XI (known by his nickname, "Boabdil") surrendered. The gates of Granada were thrown open to receive the city's new Christian rulers on January 2, 1492. The long Reconquest of the Iberian Peninsula was at an end.

## Portugal Reaches India

The conquest of Constantinople by the Ottoman Turks had made trade between Europe and the Far East—India, China, and Cipangu (Japan)—more difficult. To obtain the luxury products produced by these lands—silks and spices—European merchants could not cross through the Ottoman-held lands. They were forced to trade with the Muslims, who obtained these goods from the Far East. This, of course, added to the cost of the products. Europeans thus began to consider how they themselves could reach the Far East—the "Indies"—and bypass the Muslims altogether.

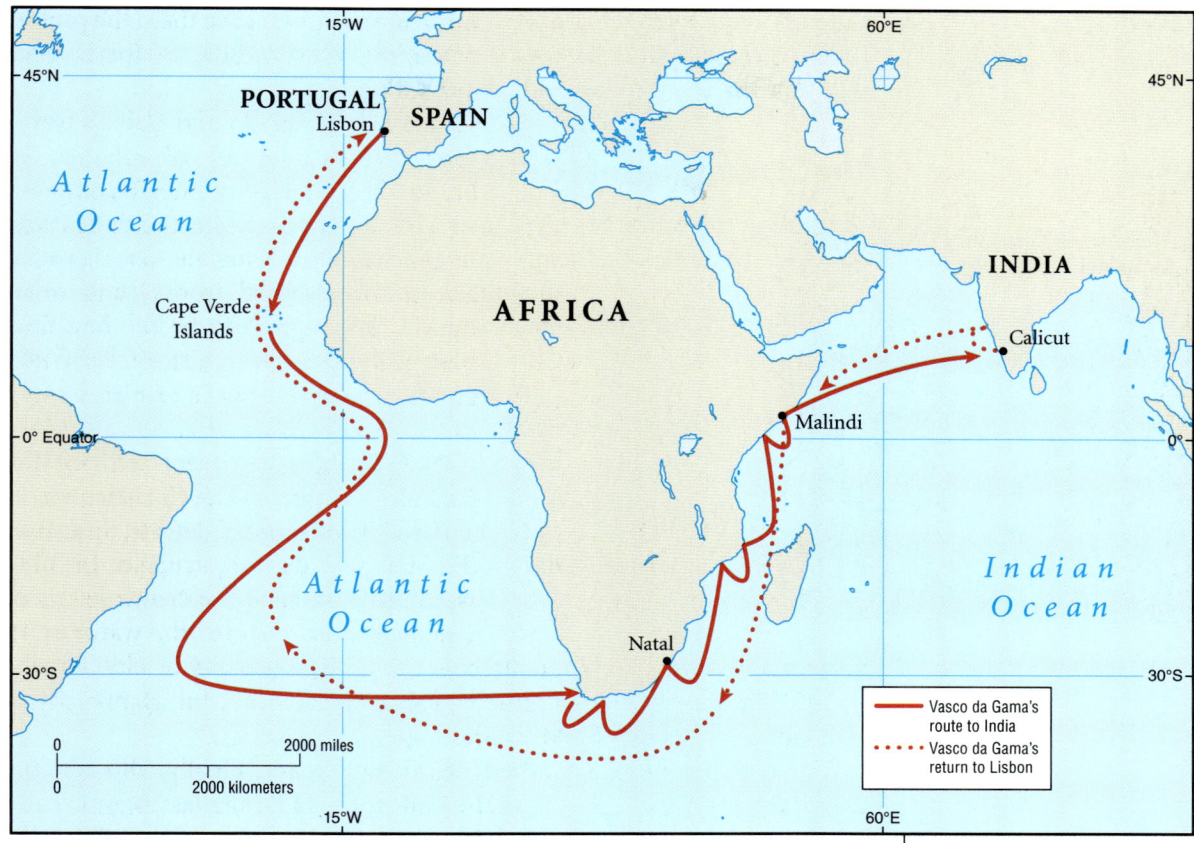

**Vasco de Gama's route to and from India**

It was the small kingdom of Portugal that began the search for a new route to the Indies—by sea rather than by land. Portugal's Prince Henry the Navigator began this task by sending out expeditions from Portugal to explore the west coast of Africa. One goal of these expeditions was the spreading of the Gospel to the coastal Africans. But the main object was finding a sea route to the Indies and, in the meantime, obtaining the ivory and gold to be found on the African coast.

In 1497, the Portuguese captain Vasco da Gama set sail on an expedition down the west African coast. Starting in July, da Gama's four ships followed the African coast. On the voyage they met terrible hardships, and for three months they were out of sight of land. In December they rounded the southern tip of Africa, going farther than any Europeans had traveled by sea before. For the next five months, the Portuguese ships sailed up the east coast of Africa, and then they set out eastward across the

Indian Ocean. On May 20, 1498, the fleet sailed into the port of Calicut in India. Vasco da Gama had discovered a sea route to the Indies, opening a rich trade between those lands and the kingdom of Portugal.

## The "Enterprise of the Indies"

Trade with the Indies brought great wealth to Portugal. But was the route discovered by da Gama the only way to reach those far-off lands? One man thought there was another, and better, way to reach India, China, and Japan. His name was Christopher Columbus.

*Christopher Columbus, by Rafael Atche*

Columbus, who was born in the little maritime city-state of Genoa in Italy in 1451, thought it was possible to reach the Orient by sailing westward across the ocean. He would cross the Atlantic, pass Japan, and so approach the Indies. His plan was actually impossible for the small ships of his day, for the distances across the ocean from Europe to Asia were far greater than he thought they were. Too, he did not know that a vast continent lay between him and his goal.

In 1484, when he was 32 years old, Columbus began to seek funding for his plan, which he called the "enterprise of the Indies." He took his idea first to the king of Portugal, who showed little interest in it. After being rejected by Portugal, Columbus in 1485 went to Castile to seek the backing of Queen Isabel. During the war with Granada, the queen could not spare funds for any risky ventures. But Columbus did not give up. He persevered for seven years until Granada was conquered. Because the war had ended, the queen could no longer use it as an excuse to dismiss Columbus's request. Isabel provided funds for chartering three small, privately owned ships, salaries for the crew, and provisions. The names of the vessels were the *Niña*, the *Pinta*, and the *Santa María*.

Columbus was the captain-general of the fleet and personally commanded the **flagship**, the *Santa María*. His flagship was the largest of the vessels, yet she was only 77 feet long. She carried 40 men, while the other two ships carried fewer.

**flagship:** the ship that carries the commander of a fleet

Chapter 16  The Birth of a New World  437

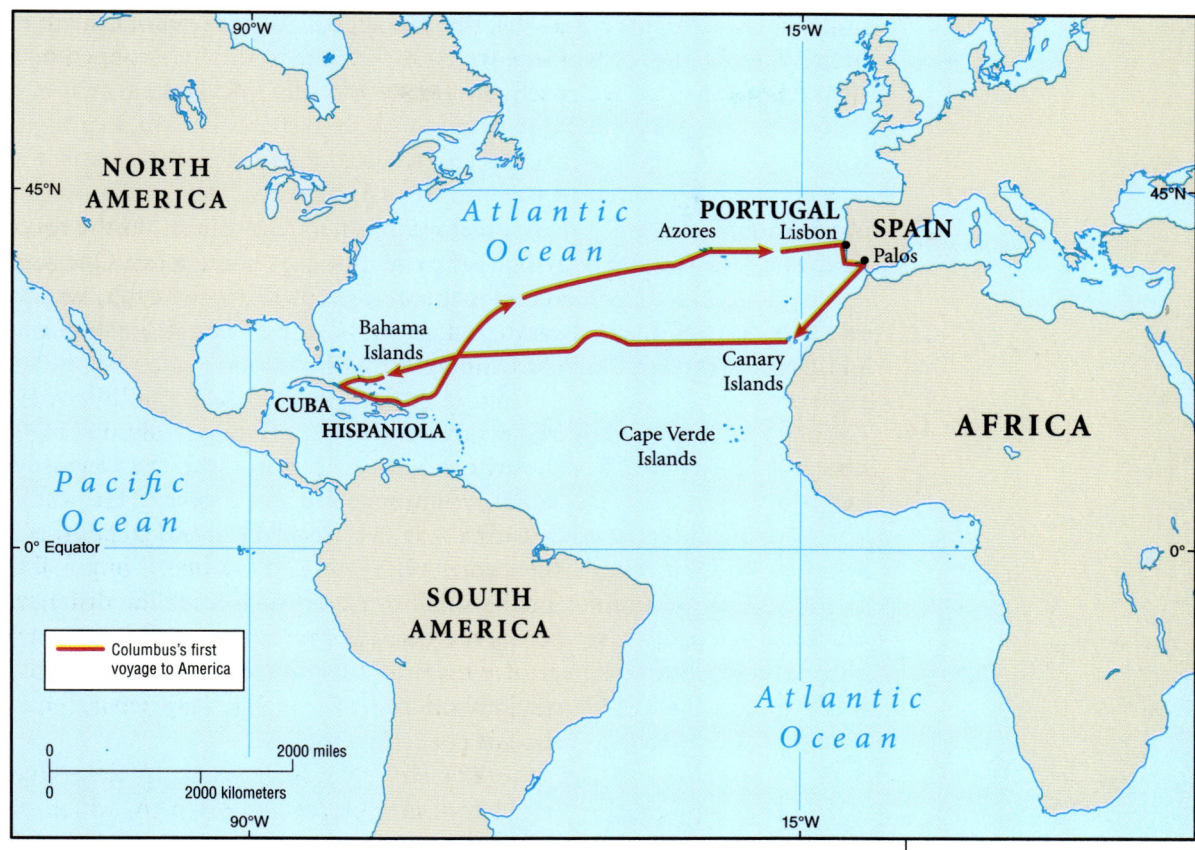

Columbus's first voyage to the New World

A sea captain from the Spanish town of Palos, Martín Alonso Pinzón, was the second in command on the voyage of discovery. Pinzón convinced some 90 men—his relatives and neighbors from his village and several other towns along the coast—to join this expedition led by an Italian foreigner.

In Columbus's day, ships rarely ventured out of sight of land for more than a few days; yet, for 33 days (September 9–October 11, 1492) Columbus, the Pinzón brothers, and their men saw nothing but water and sky. After sailing away from the known world for two weeks, the sailors wanted to turn back because food was getting scarce.

Columbus was able to steady the emotions of his men, boost their morale, and keep them moving toward his goal. In the twilight of dawn on the morning of October 12, 1492, there appeared, out of the mists ahead, the shape of a mountain. The lookout shouted, "Land! Land!" and the little ships sailed into a bay, shrouded in mist. Columbus and his men thought they had reached their goal; they thought they had reached the Indies.

After sunrise the fleet anchored in the bay of a small island that was called *Guanahani* by the Taino natives who lived there. The three captains (Christopher Columbus and the two oldest Pinzón brothers) and the queen's two representatives were the first to go ashore. The five Europeans carried the white-and-green standard of their expedition, the flag of Castile, and a Christian cross. Hiding in the lush undergrowth, dozens of naked Taino natives watched in amazement as Christopher Columbus and the Pinzóns planted banners and the Cross of Christ in the sand and claimed the land for the Church and the Catholic Monarchs, Isabel and Fernando.

The expedition, of course, had not reached the Indies. Columbus and his crew had arrived at the outer islands of a vast continent unknown to Europeans. Yet, Christopher Columbus and his men had made the most significant geographical discovery ever recorded—though they did not then know it. They had begun the meeting of two worlds, the "old world" of Europe and the "new world" of what would be called America. They had opened the first chapter of a new story that would tie Europe ultimately to all the peoples of the world. Columbus's discovery on that autumn morning in 1492 changed the course of global history more profoundly than any other event except the Incarnation of Our Lord.

# Chapter Review

### Summary
- "Renaissance" is the name that later generations gave to the period of history when Europeans developed a renewed respect for the literature, architecture, and art of ancient Rome and Greece. The Renaissance began in Italy and then spread to the rest of Europe.
- Humanism, the philosophy of the Renaissance, tended to see man, not God, as the center of the world. Human ideas and ideals, it was thought, should be the guides of human society.
- Francesco Petrarca (Petrarch), called the "father of Humanism," collected and published classical works and began modeling his Latin prose after the style of Cicero and other ancient Roman authors. Others soon followed his example.

- The Humanists at first thought Humanism and the Christian Faith complemented each other. Soon, however, a pagan spirit began to characterize Humanism.
- The first center of the Renaissance was Florence. In the 16th century, Rome became the center of the Renaissance.
- The first pope to patronize Renaissance artists and Humanist thinkers was Nicholas V. He planned the demolition and rebuilding of St. Peter's Basilica in Rome and founded the Vatican Library.
- At the Council of Florence in 1439, representatives of the Orthodox Church of Constantinople and the pope signed a declaration of union, ending the schism that had begun in 1054. The union between the churches, however, did not last.
- The Ottoman sultan, Mahomet II, laid siege to Constantinople in April 1453. On May 29, 1453, the Turks broke through the walls and took the city. Thenceforth, Constantinople was a Muslim city and the capital of the Ottoman Empire.
- John Hunyadi, with the help of the Franciscan priest, St. John Capistrano, broke the Turkish siege of Belgrade, Hungary, in 1456.
- Ivan the Great, the grand prince of Moscow, expanded his power over neighboring principalities, such as Novgorod, Tver, and lands once belonging to Kiev. Ivan ended all tribute payments to the Mongol khan.
- In 1472, Ivan the Great married the niece of the last Byzantine emperor. On account of this marriage, Ivan proclaimed himself tsar and autocrat of the East—the successor to the Byzantine emperors. The Russian Orthodox leaders followed along with Ivan's plan and proclaimed Moscow the Third Rome.
- Johannes Gutenberg invented the printing press in 1453. His first full book using the invention was a Latin Bible.
- The "Catholic Monarchs" of Spain, Fernando and Isabel, began a war against Granada, the last Muslim kingdom in Iberia, in 1481. The war ended when the Spanish rulers took the city of Granada on January 2, 1492, thus ending the 800-year Reconquest of the Iberian Peninsula.
- Portugal began to search for a sea route to the Indies. On May 28, 1498, the Portuguese captain, Vasco da Gama, reached Calicut, India, after a voyage around the southern tip of Africa.
- Following the conquest of Granada, the mariner Christopher Columbus received Queen Isabel's backing for a sea voyage to discover the Indies by sailing westward across the ocean. On October 12, 1492, Columbus and his crew landed on an island lying off the coast of a

continent they had not known existed. They had discovered North America.

## Key Concepts
**Renaissance:** a word meaning "rebirth" and the name later generations gave to the period of history when Europeans developed a renewed respect for the literature, architecture, and art of ancient Rome and Greece
**Humanism:** the philosophy of the Renaissance, which tended to see man, not God, as the center of the world and held that human ideas and ideals, not the Church, should guide the life of people and human society
**autocracy:** rule by one having absolute or unrestricted power; a ruler in an autocracy is called an *autocrat*
**Third Rome:** Russian Orthodox theological claim that Moscow had succeeded Rome and Constantinople as the chief center of Christendom

## Dates to Remember
**1374:** death of Francesco Petrarca (Petrarch), the "father of Humanism"
**1439:** Council of Florence
**1447:** the Humanist Tommaso Parentucelli becomes pope as Nicholas V (reigned until 1455)
**1453:** the fall of Constantinople
**1455:** printing of the Gutenberg Bible
**1456:** the siege of Belgrade
**1462:** Ivan III "the Great" becomes grand prince of Moscow (reigned until 1505)
**1472:** Ivan III names himself first tsar of Russia
**1492:** the fall of Granada to Isabel and Fernando
**1492:** Columbus lands in the Americas

## Central Characters
**Lorenzo di Medici (1449–1492):** Florentine Renaissance prince and patron of the arts
**Leonardo da Vinci (1452–1519):** Florentine artist and inventor, painter of the *Mona Lisa* and the *Last Supper*
**Michelangelo di Buonarotti (1475–1564):** Florentine artist who painted the Sistine Chapel and made the sculptures, *Moses* and *David*
**Raphael di Santi (1483–1520):** Florentine artist, famous for portraits of women
**Mahomet II (1432–1481):** Ottoman Turkish sultan and conqueror of Constantinople
**Johannes Gutenberg (ca. 1400–1468):** inventor of movable-type printing.

**St. John Capistrano (1386–1456):** leader of the resistance at the siege of Belgrade
**Isabel I (1474–1504):** queen of Castile, married to Fernando of Aragon; both were the conquerors of Granada and patrons of Columbus's expedition
**Fernando II (1452–1516):** king of Aragon, married Isabel I of Castile
**Christopher Columbus (1451–1506):** discoverer of America
**Ivan III, the Great (1440–1505):** first tsar of Muscovy and Russia

## Questions for Review
1. What was thought to be "reborn" in the Renaissance?
2. How did Renaissance Humanism's way of looking at God, man, and the world differ from the way medieval people looked at these things?
3. What role did the Medici family play in the development of the Florentine Renaissance?
4. What sort of man made a good ruler, according to Machiavelli's *The Prince?* What did this work reveal about the character of the Renaissance?
5. When did Constantinople fall to the Turks? Why did the attempt to reunite the Churches of Rome and Constantinople fail?
6. Why did Ivan III think he was the successor of the Byzantine emperors?
7. What was the idea of the "Third Rome"? Who developed the idea, and why?
8. Who invented the printing press? What have been its effects on civilization?
9. Who were Fernando and Isabel? When did the last Moorish city fall to Fernando and Isabel?
10. What did Columbus seek to do in sailing west across the ocean? What did Columbus really find or sail to in his first voyage? What lands did he think he had found?

## Ideas in Action
1. Discuss in class what the highest ideals of human behavior and creativity might be. Do we, in our time, achieve these ideals? Why or why not?
2. Write out a timeline of the Reconquest of Spain from its beginning to the fall of Granada in 1492. Include the most important events.
3. (a) Write a character description of Queen Isabel from the encyclopedia or another source. Or (b) Compose for class performance a little

dramatization of Columbus asking Isabel for her aid in getting the "enterprise of the Indies" under way. Who would be the characters? What could Columbus say that would persuade the queen to invest so much money in this gamble of an exploration?

4. Make a wall map of the Old World of Europe and the New World of America. Show the lands that Spain, Russia, and the Ottoman Empire came to own. Why would the Ottoman Empire have been a threat to Christian Europe? To Spanish territories? To Russian territories?

# Highways and Byways

### Moscow's Cathedral of St. Basil

St. Basil's Cathedral in Moscow (see picture, Chapter 15, p. 386) was built by Ivan the Terrible and completed in 1561. Its original name was the Cathedral of Intercession of the Virgin on the Moat; but a very popular saint, Basil the Fool for Christ, was buried there. The people, remembering this saint, the only man Ivan the Terrible feared, called the cathedral by his name—the name it is called to this day.

Like all Russian churches of its time, St. Basil's is brightly painted and built in a cluster of chapels, each with its own distinctive onion-shaped dome, tapering into a point topped by a cross. The largest dome represents Christ; the smaller domes, the apostles or saints. St. Basil's has nine chapels, each one dedicated to a saint upon whose feast day Ivan had won a battle. The cathedral was built to commemorate Ivan's victory in 1552 over the khanate of Kazan, one of the Muslim offshoots of the Golden Horde.

St. Basil's Cathedral was situated in Moscow to represent symbolically the unique placement of Russia between Europe and Asia. According to legend, after the magnificent cathedral was built, Ivan the Terrible ordered the architect, Postnick Yakovlev, to be blinded so that he could never design another church more beautiful than St. Basil's.

# Chapter 17: The Protestant Reformation

On April 18, 1506, Pope Julius II laid the cornerstone for a new basilica church over the burial place of St. Peter the Apostle in the Vatican. A great lover of the arts and patron of artists, Pope Julius hoped to accomplish what Pope Nicholas V had begun, 50 years before: to replace the aging St. Peter's Basilica (built by the Emperor Constantine) with a new church that would shine with all the splendor with which Renaissance architecture and art could adorn it.

A year later, Pope Julius proclaimed a jubilee indulgence to fund this great project. An **indulgence** is a full or partial remittance by the Church of the temporal punishment for sins (such as one suffers in Purgatory) following the forgiveness offered in the Sacrament of Penance. Julius's indulgence did not differ from indulgences issued by earlier popes. To obtain the indulgence, one had to be truly repentant, receive the Sacrament of Penance, and perform a good work. In the case of the jubilee indulgence, the good work was contributing money to the building of St. Peter's Basilica. It was not unusual for the Church to issue indulgences for the funding of churches—which was considered a very holy work. Yet, this jubilee indulgence, in a few short years, would have tragic results that no one, including the pope, could foresee in 1507.

Pope Julius II was a bundle of contradictions. Taking his duties as the head of the Church seriously, he fought against abuses, like simony and nepotism, even calling the Fifth Lateran Council in 1512 to reform

**indulgence:** a full or partial remittance by the Church of the temporal punishment for sins (such as one suffers in Purgatory)

*Pope Julius II*, by Raphael

443

the Church. All the same, before becoming pope, Julius had engaged in bribery to make sure he became pope—and, when he became pope, he personally led armies in battle to protect and extend the political power of the Papal States.

Pope Julius II focused more on the temporal than the spiritual good of the Church—a problem that had been afflicting the entire Church since the days of the Avignon popes. By the 16th century, too many churchmen seemed to have forgotten their spiritual offices in their pursuit of political power and wealth. Benefices did not go to the holiest or even the most learned men, but to the wealthiest and most powerful. Bishops, therefore, often cared little for the spiritual good of those entrusted to them. Too many of their priests were little better—and many were, moreover, ignorant and immoral. Even many monks and friars were living lax lives of pleasure and self-indulgence.

Far worse was that the Roman **curia** and the popes themselves were in large part the cause of the ills of the time. To become a bishop, for instance, one had often to pay a large sum of money to Rome—which meant only the richest (or those with the richest friends) would be made bishops. The pope, too, often allowed one man to be the bishop of more than one see—something forbidden by Church law—or to be bishop of a see in a country he would never visit. Churchmen at all levels practiced nepotism and simony. In Rome itself, cardinals openly lived immoral lives, while the popes spent their energies in extending their political power or patronizing the arts.

In those days, one still could find holy priests, conscientious bishops, and strict monasteries. But the Church as a whole was sick. The laity suffered from ignorance and immorality. Some humanist scholars, particularly in Germany, openly mocked the Church and churchmen. Kings and princes thought chiefly of their personal power and wealth and making themselves almost the absolute lords over the Church in their regions.

Many believers, both lay and clergy, believed that a reform of the Church was necessary. They sought a reformation, like the great medieval reformation. But who would lead such a reform movement? Though Pope Julius II called strongly for reform, he died in 1513, four years before the reform council he had called ended. Julius's successor, Pope Leo X (a Medici), was too taken up by the arts and pleasure seeking to pay attention to the spiritual good of the Church. (It was told that when

**curia:** the congregations, offices, and tribunals, made up usually of cardinals, by which the pope governs the Church

*Pope Leo X (Giovanni de Medici) and His Cardinal Nephews,* **by Raphael**

he became pope, Leo said, "Let us enjoy the papacy, since God has given it to us.") Though there were many critics of the Church, nowhere in Europe could be found a king, a bishop, or a religious order to lead in the reform of the Church.

But Christendom was waiting for a reformer—and when he came, he would find a host of people to follow him, wherever he might lead.

## The Spark That Set the World on Fire

The year 1517 witnessed the end of the Fifth Lateran Council. This council made decrees that, if they had only been followed, could have begun the long-awaited reformation of the Church. Near the end of the council, a layman, Gianfrancesco Pico della Mirandola, told the council fathers that if churchmen did not begin to lead moral lives, then all was lost. If Pope Leo X, said Mirandola, did not punish the immoral clergy, God himself would cut off those rotten limbs and burn them in fire. Leo, however, did nothing.

Instead, the same year, Pope Leo made a deal with a wealthy German churchman, Albert of Brandenburg. Though he was already the archbishop of Magdeburg in Germany, Albert wanted to be archbishop of the German city of Mainz as well. To do this, however, Albert had to pay an enormous sum of money to the Roman curia. To help Albert come up with the money, Leo allowed him to take one-half of the funds raised in the indulgence for St. Peter's Basilica and use it to pay off his debt to the curia.

Typically, in those days, preachers were sent throughout Europe to offer the indulgence to rich and poor alike. Though these preachers were supposed to tell people that they needed to repent of their sins and go to confession before the indulgence could do them any good, they often did not do so. Instead, they emphasized how much people needed to pay—the wealthy

**A woodcut of Johann Tetzel**

more, the poor, less, while some only had to promise prayers—and spoke as if the simple payment of money alone could win the indulgence for people or for family members who were in Purgatory. This was the case with the indulgence Albert of Brandenburg (with the pope's blessing) ordered to be preached in Germany. The Dominican preacher, Johann Tetzel, who preached this indulgence, used this rhyme to convince people to offer their money: "When copper coin in coffer rings / The soul from Purgatory springs."

In 1517, word came that one of the indulgence preachers was coming to Wittenberg, a city in German Saxony. When the Augustinian priest Martin Luther, head of the theology faculty at the new University of Wittenberg, came to hear of it, he resolved to do something about it. Luther, like other theologians, had come to the conclusion that the way indulgences were being preached led people away from a true understanding of the forgiveness of sins offered by Christ. But Luther went even further, for he began to doubt that the pope had the power of issuing indulgences at all. On October 31—the eve of the feast of All Saints—in 1517, Luther posted his Ninety-five Theses (questions for debate) on the door of the Castle Church in Wittenberg, announcing a public lecture and debate on indulgences and other matters.

**Martin Luther fastening his Ninety-five Theses on the door of the Castle Church, Wittenberg, on Oct. 31, 1517**

Martin Luther was a persuasive preacher and popular university lecturer. He had entered the Augustinian order and become a priest against his father's wishes. To prove to his father and himself that he could be a priest, Luther tried to observe religious life perfectly. But though he took on severe penances and piled on many good works, he felt he could not earn God's favor. Even though his confessor spoke to him about God's mercy, offered through the crucified Christ, Luther still feared God terribly.

While still a young man, Luther had been appointed a professor of theology at the University of Wittenberg. Studying St. Paul's epistles, Luther slowly came to the conclusion that God offered salvation to those who simply believed and trusted in his mercy. Luther came to think that salvation came by God's Grace through the gift of faith—which the Catholic

Church taught. Yet, Luther went on to deny that good works count for anything, even for those who have the Grace of God within them.

It was partly on account of this belief that Luther objected to indulgences —for how, he said, can any good work we do remove any of the punishments for sin? In his Ninety-five Theses, Luther also complained that so much money, taken through the indulgence, was passing from Germany to Rome. Luther said that if the pope knew how poor the German people were, he would not take their hard-earned money even to build that new basilica over St. Peter's tomb.

The point about the money appealed to Germans, who for years had been taxed heavily by Rome. Luther did not stop with just posting his theses for debate; he had them translated into German from Latin and printed on that new invention, the printing press, and they were distributed throughout Germany. The theses quickly became very popular among Germans of all classes. It was not long before Luther's name

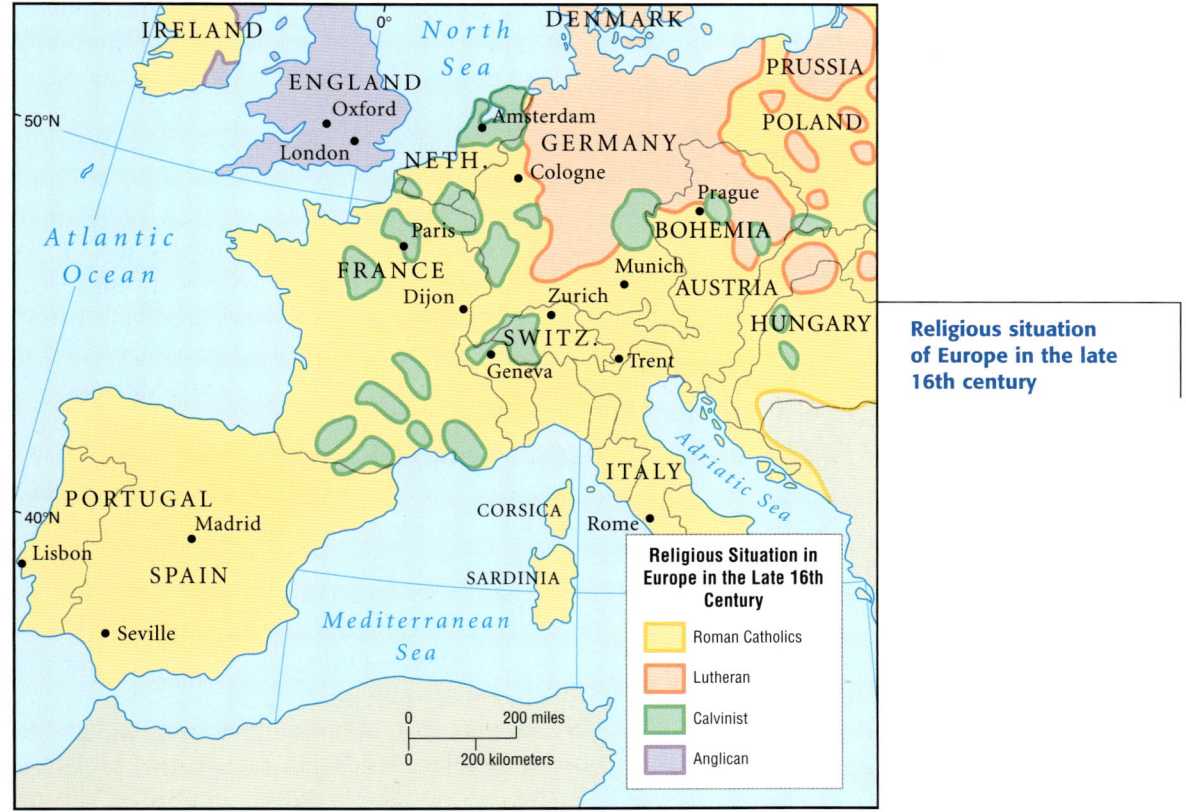

Religious situation of Europe in the late 16th century

became well known throughout Germany and even reached the pope in Rome. In 1518, the curia began the process that would end in the condemnation of Luther.

Pope Leo, however, did not want to move too quickly against Luther, for the priest had a powerful protector—Frederick III, the **prince elector** of Saxony. The pope needed Frederick's friendship for political reasons and did not want to anger him. In the autumn of 1518, the learned Cardinal Cajetan met with Luther to try to convince him to recant his teachings. Luther, however, appealed to a general council—basically saying such a council had more authority than the pope.

It was in July 1519, in a debate with the theologian Johannes Eck, that Luther made an important discovery. During the debate, Eck had accused Luther of being a follower of John Wycliffe and the Bohemian John Hus. Like others of his time, Luther had thought Hus a heretic. Eck's accusation, however, led Luther to look into Hus's ideas and Luther discovered that he agreed with the Bohemian preacher in many areas. Returning to the debate, Luther told Eck that not only did he find much good in Hus but that he had reached another conclusion—that not only the pope, but even ecumenical councils could be in error.

**prince elector:** One of the seven German princes who elected the emperor. The electors were drawn from both lay princes and prince archbishops.

*Statue of Martin Luther outside St. Mary's Church, Berlin*

Luther had gone from being what many thought him—a reformer of the Church—to denying not only the pope's authority, but the authority of ecumenical councils as well. Basically, Luther now denied the authority of the Catholic Church. That he had come to that conclusion was as much a surprise to him as to those who heard him. But now that he had reached that conclusion, he would not turn back from it.

## Luther's Disagreements with the Church

Martin Luther did not intend to destroy the Catholic Church, nor did he intend to start a separate church. Luther wanted to reform the Church, to bring it back to what it was meant to be—the pure Bride of Christ.

Luther was not alone in wanting to reform the Church. Catholic humanists like Desiderius Erasmus of Holland, Thomas More of England, and the Cardinal Francisco Jiménez of Castile protested as loudly as Luther did against the problems in the Church. Even Cardinal Cajetan, who confronted Luther at Augsburg in 1518, carried on the same fight in the Roman curia. Unlike Luther, however, these reformers did not promote teachings that directly undermined the teaching authority of the Church.

Luther advocated several doctrines that were contrary to the Catholic Faith. His foremost idea was that salvation comes by faith only (*sola fide*) and not by any good works. Against the Catholic teaching that human nature, though fallen, is essentially good, Luther taught that human nature is wholly corrupt because of Original Sin. Since human nature is corrupt, only by God's Grace (*sola gratia*), working through faith, can one be saved from eternal punishment. For Luther, however, Grace does not remove human sinfulness but only covers a person's sins.

Luther rejected the Church's teaching that what God has revealed to us can be known in two ways—Holy Scripture and Sacred Tradition. For Luther, Scripture alone (*sola scriptura*) is the source of divine revelation. Since Luther also rejected the authority of the pope and Church councils, he said that every Christian has the ability (by God's Grace) to understand Scripture. Even the simplest believer, said Luther, has as much divine help to interpret Scripture as any pope or council.

These three ideas—*sola fide*, "by faith alone"; *sola scriptura*, "by Scripture alone"; and *sola gratia*, "by Grace alone"—were the foundations of Luther's teaching. But they were not all he taught.

Like Wycliffe, Luther threw out the Catholic teaching on the Mass. Luther defended the real presence of Christ in Communion, but he rejected transubstantiation. The bread and wine, he said, do not change their nature to become the Body and Blood of Christ. Believers, he said, receive the Body and Blood of Christ in, with, and under the bread and the wine. Furthermore, Luther taught that the Mass is only a banquet, not a sacrifice—and since it is not a sacrifice, there is no need for a special priesthood. All believers are equally priests, declared Luther.

Luther taught that such things as **sacramentals**, pilgrimages, private devotions, sacrifices, and almsgiving do not bring Grace to the soul. This led him to conclude that religious life in monasteries and convents is opposed to the Gospel, and that all believers are to live as laity. In the parts of Germany that ultimately followed Luther, monasteries and convents were closed and ransacked, and the monks and nuns were turned out into the streets. Luther himself eventually ceased to live like an Augustinian and later married a former nun who, hidden in a herring barrel, had escaped from her convent.

> **sacramental:** a thing or an action (such as a blessing or an object such as holy water) that brings Grace to the soul. Sacramentals differ from Sacraments, which—established by Christ—bring Grace simply by the fact that they are performed. (Baptism, for instance, removes Original Sin and makes one a member of the Church, even if the recipient does not understand the Sacrament or the minister does not believe in its power.) Sacramentals, however, require faith on the part of those who use them or administer them in order to be of any effect.

## Excommunication

After his debate with Eck, Luther's attacks on the pope became more and more violent. Luther had a powerful and moving prose style, and he used it to his advantage. In 1520, he published in German a revolutionary treatise, called *An Appeal to the German Nobility*, in which he used a popular style that was charged with eloquence. In this *Appeal*, Luther called on the German princes to reform the German Church. They did not have to wait on the clergy, said Luther, since all Christians are priests—not just the pope and the bishops. On account of the printing press, the *Appeal* and the many other tracts written by Luther spread quickly throughout Germany, and many Germans began to see in Luther the great reformer and German patriot they had been waiting for.

Title page of Leo X's "Bull Against the Errors of Martin Luther and Followers," published in Rome in 1520

It was not until the summer of 1520 that Pope Leo X took any action against Luther. In June, the pope issued the bull *Exsurge Domine* ("Rise, O Lord"), condemning many of Luther's teachings and giving him 60 days after he received the bull to recant his errors or face excommunication. Luther received a copy of the bull on October 10. Would he recant? He gave his answer two months later.

On December 10, 1520, the deadline for Luther's recantation, students and professors of the University of Wittenberg gathered around Luther at a city gate. Because Luther's books had been burned in other cities, Luther and his friends built a fire into which they cast works of scholastic theology. Finally, Luther took the pope's bull and threw it into the flames. This was his answer to Leo. Luther would not recant.

## The Diet of Worms

Being excommunicated, Luther was given over to the temporal power for punishment. But Luther's prince, the Elector Frederick, had become his protector. The task of bringing Luther to justice fell, therefore, to the newly crowned German emperor, Charles V.

Charles von Habsburg had become the most powerful ruler in Europe. The son of Juana, a daughter of Isabel and Fernando of Spain, Charles had become king of Spain when Fernando died in 1516. Charles, too, had inherited Flanders from his father, Prince Philip I (the "Handsome"). When Charles's grandfather, Emperor Maximilian I von Habsburg, died in 1519, Charles was elected German emperor—even though he was not in Germany at that time. Charles V's first journey to Germany did not occur until 1521, when he was to meet with the Imperial Diet at the city of Worms on the Rhine River.

Charles had many questions of imperial importance to address at Worms. The most important had become deciding what to do about the troublesome Augustinian monk, Martin Luther. Elector Frederick persuaded the emperor to summon Luther to Worms under a safe-conduct, for Frederick did not want Charles to condemn Luther unheard.

Luther defends himself before Holy Roman Emperor Charles V at the Diet of Worms.

Luther's friends tried to dissuade him from attending the Imperial Diet. Luther, however, insisted that he had to defend himself in person before the emperor. On Luther's journey to Worms, a crowd of university friends and a contingent of German knights accompanied him and when he reached Worms, crowds thronged the streets to greet him as a popular hero. What the authorities intended to be the treatment of a condemned heretic had become a triumphal procession.

Luther appeared before the diet on April 17, 1521. He was unusually quiet and appeared timid; he asked for another day to consider his reply. The next day, however, Luther stood boldly before the emperor and the assembled princes. Asked to recant his errors, Luther replied, in German, "I neither can nor will recant anything, for it is neither safe nor right to act against one's conscience." According to an old tradition, he then added, *"Hier steh ich; ich kann nicht anders. Gott helfe mir. Amen!"* ("Here I stand, I can do no other. God help me. Amen.") Luther repeated his statement in Latin. Then, throwing up his arms like a victorious knight, he left the hall.

The next day, Charles V declared that he would not depart from the traditions of his forebears, the kings of Spain, Burgundy, and Germany who "were all faithful to the death to the Church of Rome, defending the Catholic Faith and the honor of God. A single friar who runs counter to all Christianity for a thousand years must be wrong." The young emperor condemned Luther; but, true to his word, Charles allowed him to leave Worms in peace.

Luther left the diet on April 26, his safe-conduct good for 21 more days. On May 8, a minority of those who had attended the diet approved the Edict of Worms, which condemned Luther's heresy and declared him an outlaw under sentence of death. Luther was to be arrested as soon as his safe-conduct expired. But the Elector Frederick intervened. By his order, a party of soldiers ambushed Luther's party on the night of May 4. They took Luther to a castle called the Wartburg, where he went into hiding, disguised as a knight.

Martin Luther's study at the Wartburg

At the Wartburg, Luther, left to himself, underwent terrible doubts and struggles—was he alone right and the generations of Catholics wrong? He composed bitter attacks against his enemies, especially the papacy, which by then he was calling the Antichrist. Yet, in the course of the year 1522, Luther translated the whole of the New Testament into a forceful, spoken German. (He later translated the Old Testament, as well. The entire German Bible was published in 1534.) Luther's German Bible became an important tool for carrying his reform forward among the common German people. It also became the basis for the modern German language.

### The Protestant Revolt

We give the name "Protestant" to those churches that arose during what has been called the Reformation of the 16th century. The name was first given to Luther's followers, who published a pamphlet called The *Protest of Speier* after a German Imperial Diet held in Speier, Germany, in 1529 condemned Luther's teachings. *Protest* at that time meant a "witness" *for* something; it did not have the modern sense of opposition and protest *against* something. Voicing support for the Catholic Church could just as accurately have been called the "protest" of Rome. So it was that those who *protested* against the Diet of Speier and *for* their own beliefs became known as Protestants.

# The Radical Reformers

While Luther was in the Wartburg, the city of Wittenberg was in a religious uproar. Inspired by Luther's ideas, priests married, monks and friars abandoned their cloisters, a mob of students destroyed altars and smashed stained-glass windows at the city's Franciscan convent, and general religious mayhem erupted. On Christmas Day, 1521, one of Luther's associates, Karlstadt, in street clothes and wearing no vestments, said Mass in German, and he invited all who attended to take the bread in their hands and drink from the cup. Two days later, the "prophets" from the nearby town of Zwickau arrived. They claimed that God spoke to them directly and that no Christian should own private property, but that all believers should hold property in common.

From the Wartburg, Luther applauded most of these events—and even approved of Karlstadt's marriage to a young woman. Yet, in March 1522, Luther, dressed again in his monastic habit, suddenly returned to Wittenberg and preached a series of sermons against what had been occurring there. With Luther's return, Mass again was sung in Latin, priests returned to wearing vestments, and adoration of the Eucharist was restored. Why Luther changed his mind about the radical events occurring in Wittenberg is unclear, but his actions upon his return stopped his reform from becoming too revolutionary.

Elsewhere, however, other reformers took Luther's idea that every individual Christian could interpret the Bible as well as the pope and Church councils, and they ran with it. These reformers went farther in "reforming" the Church than Luther thought wise or right—and earned Luther's bitter condemnation for it. Since Luther and his followers accepted no authority, tradition, or teaching authority outside the Bible, disputes arose among them over how to interpret Scripture, and these disputes became very bitter. The consequence of these warring doctrines

**The Castle Church (Schlosskirche) at Wittenberg, Germany**

was the splintering of Protestantism, right from its beginning, into dozens of factions.

In comparison with the newer reformers, Luther was almost traditional. Unlike the more radical reformers, Luther taught that the Eucharist and Baptism are Sacraments. Lutheran churches kept images, Catholic liturgical forms (though, for the Mass, he did replace Latin with German), and singing—especially singing, for Luther was a great lover of music. He himself wrote hymns; his most famous being *Ein Feste Burg*—"A Mighty Fortress." Yet, many of the newer reformers thought music in church services was **papistical**—and, even, diabolic—and they banned all religious singing.

One of these newer reformers was Ulrich Zwingli, a priest and humanist scholar. In 1518, Zwingli became the preacher at the cathedral in the Swiss town of Zürich, where, a year later, he condemned the selling of indulgences. By 1522, Zwingli was preaching doctrines similar to Karlstadt's, condemning the Mass, the doctrine of Purgatory, prayers to the saints, monasteries, relics, and the use of images in churches.

Zwingli disagreed with Luther on many points. Zwingli denied the real presence of Christ in the Eucharist, and he denied that even Communion and Baptism were Sacraments. Like Luther, however, he held that the individual believer could interpret the Scriptures for himself. In

**papistical:** from *papist*; a disparaging term referring to anything having to do with the pope or the Catholic Faith

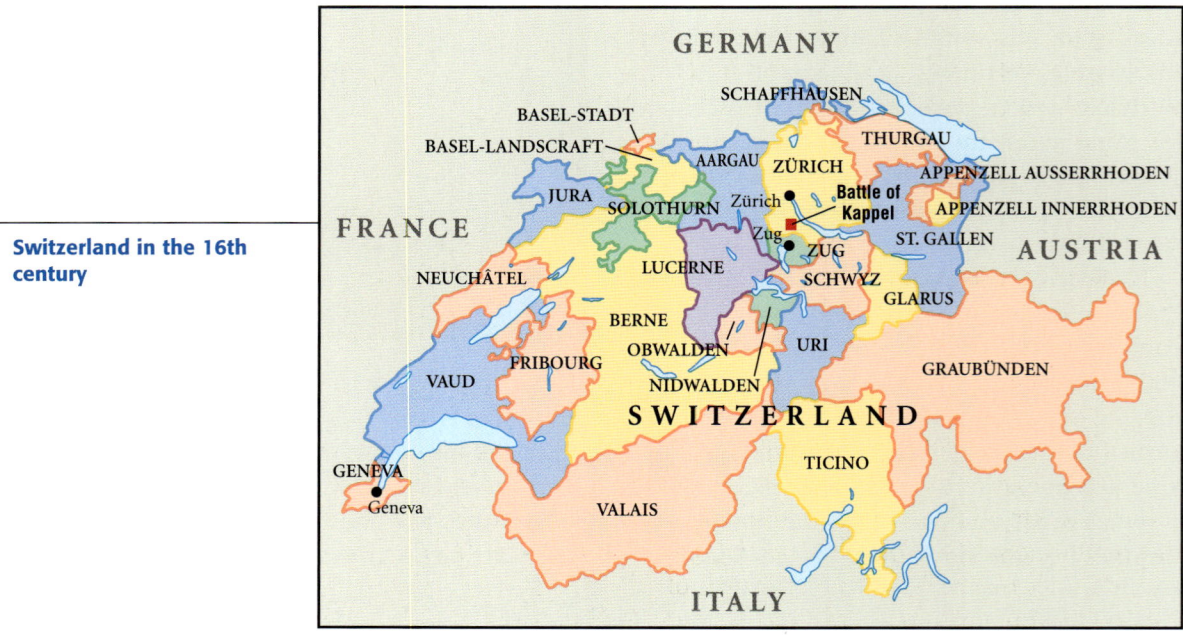

**Switzerland in the 16th century**

September 1523, after the Zürich town council put Zwingli in charge of the city's cathedral, he ordered the destruction of all church decorations and religious art in the city. In December, under Zwingli's direction, Zürich forbade monasteries and convents to accept new members. Finally, during Holy Week of 1525, the town abolished the Mass in favor of a simple communion service.

Zwingli used politics and war to spread his doctrines. Several Swiss towns followed his lead and adopted his reforms. The Swiss cantons (states) of Uri, Schwyz, Unterwalden, Lucerne, Zug, and Fribourg remained faithful to the Catholic Church. To force these regions to accept his doctrines, Zwingli planned a war against them in 1529. The fighting did not begin until 1531, when the Catholic cantons attacked Zürich and its allies. At the battle of Kappel on October 11, 1531, the Catholic forces defeated Zwingli's army, and the reformer himself was killed.

More radical than Zwingli or Karlstadt were the Anabaptists. Their name means "rebaptizer," because they rejected infant baptism and insisted that everyone who had been baptized as an infant had to be rebaptized as an adult. The Anabaptists differed among themselves and had no unified church structure. Some were communistic, holding all their possessions in common. Some were peaceful, believing that no follower of Christ must shed blood. Others were violent, like a group in the lower Rhine region of Germany who rose in revolt against the empire, seized the city of Münster, and proclaimed their leader king of the "New Sion."

Whether they were peaceful or violent, the Anabaptists were seen by Catholics, Lutherans, and Zwinglians as a threat to the peace of society. All religious factions persecuted them. Luther himself bitterly denounced them and called for their extermination.

Anabaptist groups survived the persecutions of the 16th and 17th centuries. The Men-nonites, founded by the Dutch preacher Menno Simons (who had been a Catholic priest), exist today, particularly in North America. One of their sects is the Old Order Mennonites, called more commonly the Amish. These people maintain a distinctive mode of life in tight-knit farming communities that reject the use of much of modern technology, such as automobiles

**The burning of the 16th-century Dutch Anabaptist, Anneken Hendriks**

and tractors. Some Mennonite groups today are known for their work for peace in a violent world.

## John Calvin of Geneva

A man who would become as important to Protestantism as Luther himself was only eight years old when Luther nailed his Ninety-five Theses to the Wittenberg church door. This eight-year-old was John Calvin, who was born to a middle-class family of Noyon, France, in 1509. The Calvin family had connections to the Church, and when John was only 12, he received a church benefice. Though he never became a priest, he was made the curé (pastor) of two parish churches before his 18th year.

John Calvin, French theologian

John Calvin was a brilliant young man who had basically finished his studies at the University of Paris when he was 18 years old. In Paris he had come under the influence of Humanist scholars and men who had been influenced by Luther's ideas. By 1529, Calvin was a firmly convinced reformer.

It was dangerous to be a reformer in France in those days, for the king, Francis I, was persecuting those who promoted Lutheran, Zwinglian, and other reformed heresies. Calvin himself finally fled France to the German city of Strasburg, which was then under the control of the reformer, Martin Bucer. There, in 1536, Calvin came out with the first edition of his *Institutes of the Christian Religion*, the great theological work that would shape and form one of the great divisions of Protestantism besides Lutheranism.

In July 1536, Calvin made his way to the Swiss city of Geneva, which had become Protestant less than two months before he arrived. The city government had abolished the Mass, ordered the destruction of altars and images, and been imprisoning priests. Calvin settled in Geneva as a teacher of theology and became a powerful force. He influenced the city council to pass laws that governed the personal moral lives of citizens according to his own ideas. Though the Geneva city council exiled Calvin in 1538, he returned in 1541 and took over the city government.

Calvin's government in Geneva was grim and showed little mercy. The city issued laws that governed in detail the personal lives of the citizens, punishing such acts as wild dancing or singing filthy songs. In 1552, the city council decreed that Calvin's *Institutes* were a "holy doctrine which no man might speak against." Those who did speak against the "holy doctrine" could face prison, exile, or even death. In the first five years of his "rule" of Geneva, Calvin condemned 76 people to exile and 58 to death. Many others languished in prison.

Calvin's teachings were similar to Luther's. He taught *sola scriptura* and, like Luther, insisted that Grace came to believers through faith alone. Like Luther, too, Calvin taught that human nature has been totally corrupted by Original Sin. But Calvin differed from Luther by saying that Baptism and the Eucharist are not Sacraments, and by teaching that in Communion the bread and wine only represent the Body and Blood of Christ. Calvin's most famous teaching, however, is that God predestines—or has chosen before all time—who will go to heaven and who to hell.

Calvin was only 54 when he died on May 27, 1564. But his influence and teachings formed Protestant thought in English and French lands for centuries. From Geneva, preachers spread Calvin's teachings to France, Holland, England, and Scotland. In France, Calvin's followers, called Huguenots, became a powerful political party that threatened civil war in the kingdom. In Scotland and England, Calvinists were called Presbyterians because of Calvin's teaching that the Church was not to be ruled by bishops but by a council of elders, or "presbyters." Today, the German Reformed, the Dutch Reformed, and the Presbyterian Church are descended from the churches founded by Calvin's followers.

**Charles V, Roman emperor and king of Spain as Charles I**

# Charles the Emperor

The Emperor Charles V did not remain long in Germany after the Diet of Worms ended in 1525. The 25-year-old emperor faced a rebellion in Spain, where he was not very well liked. To strengthen his position in Spain, Charles was forced to remain there until 1529.

During the emperor's absence, the Protestant cause in Germany gained more and more strength. German princes, who saw the reform as a way of increasing their power against the emperor—and as an excuse for seizing Church and monastic wealth—proclaimed themselves and their territories "reformed." They abolished the Mass, destroyed monasteries (whose wealth they seized), and established a new "reformed" clergy. Not all the princes, of course, took up Luther's cause; but enough did to make Protestantism a mighty force in Germany.

## Renewed Threat in the East

**Suleiman the Magnificent, sultan of the Ottoman Empire, 1520–1566**

Even had Charles been in Germany, he would have found it difficult to deal effectively with the German Lutheran princes, for they were not the only problem he faced. There were, of course, his difficulties in ruling Spain, which now included the vast new territories Spain had come to hold in North and South America since Columbus had discovered this "New World" in 1492. But in Europe itself, Charles faced two persistent enemies besides the troublesome German Protestant princes—Francis I, the king of France, and the new Ottoman sultan, Suleiman I.

Since becoming sultan in 1520, Suleiman I, called the "Magnificent," sought to spread Islam further into Europe. Turkish forces moved against Poland–Lithuania and clashed with the Christian defenders across the plains of Ukraine. Then, in 1521, Suleiman attacked Belgrade, the great Christian fortress on the Danube River in Hungary. In 1456, Belgrade had stood firm against Suleiman's grandfather, Mahomet II. But in August 1521, with only a few hundred defenders, the city fell to the sultan. The capture of Belgrade opened up Hungary and Austria to a Turkish invasion. Its loss was a great blow to Christendom.

Suleiman, however, did not immediately push farther into Europe. Instead, he turned his attention to the sea fortress of Rhodes, an island in the eastern Mediterranean. Held by the Christian Knights Hospitaller, Rhodes was one serious obstacle to the Turks' complete control of the Mediterranean. The Hospitallers had acquired Rhodes in 1309 and ruled it as an independent state. For more than two centuries, the Knights on Rhodes had blocked Muslim expansion into the Aegean Sea.

In 1522, Suleiman I laid siege to Rhodes. For six months, the island fortress held out until the 7,000 Hospitallers defending it could no longer withstand the Turkish force of 200,000 men and 400 ships. On Christmas Eve, 1522, Suleiman took Rhodes. With the island in his possession, the sultan could now turn his attention once again to Europe.

## His Most Christian Majesty vs. the Most Holy Emperor

If Charles V could not expect help from the French king, Francis I, against the German Lutheran princes, it seems he at least could expect Francis to stand with the empire against the Turks. After all, the Turks threatened the freedom of all Christendom. But instead of helping Charles defend Christendom against the Lutherans and the Turks, Francis aided both in their struggles against Charles. Why Francis aided Christendom's enemies is not fully known. He may have thought he was helping France against her Habsburg enemies, for Charles V's territories surrounded France on three sides. Charles seemed too powerful to Francis; so the French king

In the Battle of Mohács, forces of the kingdom of Hungary, led by King Louis II, were defeated by forces of the Ottoman Empire, led by Sultan Suleiman the Magnificent.

sacrificed the good of all Christendom for the good of France—an attitude that had left Europe in such peril before.

War broke out between the French king and the German emperor in 1521. After some fighting in southern France, Francis invaded northern Italy and, in October 1524, laid siege to the imperial city of Pavia. Charles sent an imperial army to defend the city.

During the Battle of Pavia, fought in February 1525, the French troops panicked in the face of the fire from a new weapon called the harquebus, one of the earliest handheld guns. Only the Swiss mercenaries and the Spaniards, who both fought for Charles, had mastered this weapon. Terrified by these new guns, the French ran—right into a unit of Swiss pikemen. In the confusion, King Francis himself was captured and taken a prisoner to Madrid, where he was confined in a castle until he and Charles could agree to a treaty. This treaty, the Peace of Madrid, was signed by both monarchs in December 1526 and brought an end to their war—for a time.

Charles hoped that the Peace of Madrid would allow him to turn his attention to dealing with the Turks and the German Protestant princes. He was wrong. Not a year had passed since the signing of the peace when Francis I made a pact with England, Milan, and Florence against the emperor. Even Clement VII, who had become pope in 1523, joined this pact, called the Holy League of Cognac. The pope, too, wanted to see Charles's power in Italy weakened. For nearly a year, Clement pretended to make peace with Charles, only to join again with the emperor's enemies.

Meanwhile, Suleiman II had returned to eastern Europe with 100,000 Turkish troops and was threatening Hungary. In that summer of 1526, the 20-year-old king of Hungary, Louis II Jagiello, had only a token army of 20,000 to face the might of the Turk. On August 29, 1526, the Turks annihilated the Hungarian army on the field of Mohács (pronounced *MOH-hatch*) beside the Danube River.

Following this victory, Suleiman entered the Hungarian capital of Buda unopposed. From that city he led away 100,000 Christian captives to be sold in the Turkish slave markets. Hungary became a Turkish province. The Turks now stood less than 150 miles from Vienna, the heart of Europe.

### From the Sack of Rome to the Peace of Nuremberg

Charles V could do little about the Turks in Hungary, for he was too busy fighting Francis I in Italy. Pope Clement VII, however, soon paid for his treachery to the emperor and Christendom. To fight Francis, the emperor had brought a large force of mercenaries to Italy. By the spring of

Pope Clement VII (left) and King Francis I (right)

1527, these mercenaries were suffering from a lack of provisions and pay. Learning that the pope had not paid a sum of money he had promised to the emperor, the mercenary army mutinied and marched against Rome.

On May 6, 1527, the emperor's mercenaries, many of whom were Lutheran, attacked and sacked Rome. While Clement VII was holed up in Castel Sant'Angelo, the soldiers pillaged Rome, desecrating churches and plundering the great city's wealth. Thousands of people died in the city. Charles himself was not responsible for the violence, though he saw in it God's just punishment of Pope Clement.

The second war between Charles V and Francis I continued until 1529. Again, Francis was forced to surrender to the emperor. Pope Clement, too, made peace with Charles—and on February 24, 1530, crowned him Roman emperor.

The year 1529 witnessed the Turks' first attempt to take Vienna. Leading his army across the Hungarian border and up the Danube River, Suleiman the Magnificent laid siege to Vienna in the fall of the year. Against Suleiman's 120,000 Turks stood only 12,000 defenders in the city, under the command of Count Nicholas von Salm, a mercenary. Suleiman proclaimed that he would not rest until the Muslim call to prayer was heard from the tower of St. Stephen's Cathedral in Vienna.

For three weeks the Turks assaulted Vienna, but the Count von Salm's German and Spanish mercenaries withstood the attacks. After three weeks of fierce fighting, the sultan ordered the retreat and removal of his remaining forces. It was late October, and Suleiman knew that the winter

A painting depicting the 1529 Siege of Vienna

snows would trap his army. The remnants of the huge Muslim army stumbled back down the long, muddy roads to Belgrade. Christian Europe was saved.

With the Turks at least temporarily turned back and peace achieved with France, Charles decided to make one last attempt to restore the unity of Christendom. He invited the Lutherans to present a statement of their beliefs at the Imperial Diet of Augsburg, to be held in June 1530. At the diet, the Lutherans presented their statement of belief, called "the Augsburg Confession" and written by Luther's close associate, Philip Melancthon. Catholic theologians, in turn, wrote up a refutation of the confession, and debates between the two sides went on for many days. It was obvious almost from the beginning that the two sides could not be reconciled.

The Diet of Augsburg closed with Charles reaffirming his intention to defend the Church and to stand by the Edict of Worms. The Protestant princes, for their part, formed a defensive league that they called the Schmalkaldic League (after the town of Schmalkald in eastern Germany, where they met). Discussion between the two sides had failed to unite them. It was now, it seemed, time for the sword.

Religious war, however, had to wait. In the summer of 1532, Charles learned that a quarter of a million Turks under Sultan Suleiman were once again marching toward Christian Europe. Expecting no help from France, Charles could not risk a war with the Protestants; so the emperor proclaimed the "Peace of Nuremberg," by which he suspended all laws against the Protestants. At least until the Church called another ecumenical council, Charles said, he would tolerate the practice of the Lutheran churches. In response, the Protestant princes contributed thousands of soldiers to Charles's army of 80,000, which he marched to Vienna in September. Faced with such a formidable force, Suleiman did not attack Vienna but withdrew yet again to Belgrade.

## The Beginning of Catholic Reform

The necessity of a true reform and renewal of the Catholic Church had long been recognized by faithful Catholics. Cardinal Francisco Jiménez, regent of Spain after Fernando's death, had set about restoring the Church in Castile and Aragon to spiritual purity even before Luther posted his Ninety-five Theses. The humanist writers Erasmus of Rotterdam and Thomas More of England had called for a renewed attention to Catholic principles, and Emperor Charles himself had repeatedly asked the pope to convene a general council for the reform of the Church.

Paul III, who became pope after the death of Clement VII in 1534, recognized the importance of holding a council that would clearly uphold and explain the doctrines the Protestants were attacking, make necessary reforms, and attempt to restore Christian unity. Pope Paul called for the meeting of such a council on May 23, 1537. He ordered all bishops, abbots, and heads of religious orders to attend, and he urged the kings of Christian Europe to attend or send representatives.

Too many obstacles, however, stood in the way of the council. It did not meet on the date the pope had proposed. Perhaps the most important obstacle to the council was Francis I's continuing plots against Charles V.

The French king was negotiating an alliance with the Lutherans against the emperor, aiding the Turks, and sending no fewer than six armies of his own against Charles in what is called the Fourth Italian War. But in September 1544, Charles's army won a series of victories against the French and marched as far as Paris. Francis offered peace, and Charles accepted.

Since peace with France was at last a reality, Charles's longed-for council could meet. The council fathers first convened at the little city of Tridente (Trent) in the Italian Alps on March 15, 1545, eight years after the pope had wanted them to meet. We shall discuss this council, one of the most important in Church history, in the next chapter.

While an ecumenical council could bring reform to the Church, it was doubtful that it could reconcile the Protestants—either the Lutherans, Calvinists, or other groups—to the Church. Luther and his followers refused to attend any council the pope called. Instead, in March 1545, one year before his death, Luther published his last pamphlet, "Against the Papacy at Rome, Founded by the Devil." In this pamphlet, Luther referred to the popes as "a set of desperate, thoroughgoing arch-villains, murderers, traitors, liars, and the most utterly debased and depraved beings on earth."

Luther had spent the years after his return to Wittenberg in 1522 organizing what amounted to his new church. Abandoning his monastic habit, he married a nun, Katrina von Bora, in 1525. Together they had a large and, by all accounts, happy family. But as the years passed, Luther grew more bitter against the pope and the Catholic Church. His writings, too, grew nastier—and in blasts of ill temper he struck out not only at Catholics, but at the Protestants who refused to agree with his own interpretation of Scripture. Although at the beginning of his "reform" Luther had condemned punishing anyone simply on account of his beliefs, at the end of his life Luther called on the civil government to punish all heretics—that is, all those who disagreed with him. Luther's last published work was a series of coarse drawings of the popes by the artist Lucas Cranach, with verses by Luther.

**Martin Luther**

Not long after the publication of these drawings, Luther died at his home in Eisleben on February 18, 1546. His body was taken to Wittenberg, where it was buried in the Castle Church. Luther was gone, but the deep division of Christendom he had initiated remained. It is with us to this day.

### Cuius regio, eius religio

Charles V's last years were spent trying to break the power of the Schmalkaldic League of Protestant German princes while protecting the eastern borders of the empire against the Turks. In 1544, he was forced to grant religious rights to the Protestant princes in return for their aid against Suleiman. In 1546, however, the emperor opened a war against the Schmalkaldic League. Over the next year, he conquered southern Germany and then moved into Saxony. In 1547 he imprisoned Philip of Hesse, one of the most powerful Lutheran princes.

Charles had humbled the Protestant princes, but they were still powerful. In 1551 the new king of France, Henry II, made a new alliance with the German Protestant princes. The following year, King Henry invaded territories in the western part of the empire. Though Charles signed a treaty with the Protestant princes, for the next three years, three of them waged a war of plunder in Germany. Finally, in 1554, a tired Charles left the reins of the empire to his brother Ferdinand, the archduke of Austria.

To bring peace to divided Germany, Ferdinand called a meeting of the Imperial Diet at Augsburg. On Septem-ber 25, 1555, the diet proclaimed the "Religious Peace of Augsburg." The peace laid down the principle *cuius regio, eius religio* ("whose region, his religion"), meaning that every prince was to decide what religion—Catholic or Lutheran—his lands would follow. Those who were not willing to accept their sovereign's religion could sell their property and leave the state. Those who remained had to follow the religion chosen by their lord.

Charles never officially ratified the peace, nor did the pope, but it was followed throughout Germany. The Peace of Augsburg made the religious division of Germany permanent. All hope of reconciliation between Lutherans and Catholics was ended.

**An anti-Luther cartoon depicting Luther as a seven-headed monster**

In 1556 Charles, exhausted from overwork and disappointed by his failure to preserve the unity of Christendom or the peace of his empire, abdicated, giving the imperial title to his brother Ferdinand and the crown of Spain to his son, Philip II. Charles retired to the monastery of Yuste (St. Just) in Spain. Surrounded by works of art and music, for which he had a great love, and living a life of study, Charles died peacefully in 1558 at the age of 58.

# The Reformation in England

Protestantism, which began by dividing Germany and Switzerland, soon spread to other parts of Europe. Only a few years after Luther began his reformation, his followers—and later, those of Calvin—could be found in

Italy, Spain, France, England, and Scandinavia. The religious division soon became political as well, with some monarchs embracing Protestantism while others remained faithful to the Catholic Church. Among those remaining Catholic were the Italian states, Spain, and France, though France had a large population of Calvinists. Scotland, the northern half of the Netherlands (Holland), Scandinavia, and Denmark, however, became Protestant.

But what of England? At first, it looked as if it would remain Catholic. But a strange course of events determined otherwise. England, too, became "reformed," and one of the most powerful and influential Protestant powers in Europe.

## A Fateful Marriage

As we saw in Chapter 15, King Henry VII, who ended the Wars of the Roses, established a new ruling house, the House of Tudor, in England. Henry was an astute and ruthless monarch who brought order to a land torn by civil war and lawlessness, and he was even able to bring Parliament under his control. Henry had an uncertain claim to the English throne, but the monarchs of Europe respected him enough to marry their children to his heirs.

Even the powerful Fernando and Isabel of Spain agreed to marry their daughter, Catherine of Aragon, to Henry's eldest son, Arthur. The wedding took place in November 1501, when Arthur was 16 and Catherine, 14. Arthur, however, was sickly. He died on April 2, 1502, leaving Catherine a widow after less than six months of marriage.

After Arthur's death, Henry wanted to keep Catherine—and her plump **dowry**—in England. He therefore proposed to Fernando and Isabel that Catherine marry his younger son, Henry. The Catholic Monarchs agreed, and Catherine remained in England until Henry, who was only 11, was old enough to marry. During the next few years, the young Henry came to know and love the beautiful and intelligent Catherine (she was one of the few women of her time schooled in philosophy

**Catherine of Aragon, first wife of King Henry VIII of England**

**dowry:** money or goods a woman brings to her husband when they are married

and theology). When Henry VII died in 1509, and his son became King Henry VIII of England, one of the new king's first official acts was to marry Catherine.

Henry and Catherine seemed to be a happy and fortunate match, but for one thing. Catherine miscarried almost all of the children she conceived; and those who survived to birth did not thrive. Only one lived beyond infancy—a daughter, named Mary, born in 1516.

As time went by, the fact that his only heir was a female worried Henry. England had never before acknowledged a queen as sole ruler; and if Henry had no male heirs, would his Tudor line survive? Since Catherine was not giving him any sons, Henry began to consider if he could divorce her and marry another woman who could give him a male heir.

**King Henry VIII of England**

But divorce would mean a break with the Church, and Henry had proven himself a faithful son of the Church. He had opposed the spread of Lutheran teachings in England and, in 1521, had published a book, *In Defense of the Seven Sacraments*, defending Catholic teaching against Protestantism. (For this, Pope Leo X had given Henry the title "Defender of the Faith," still held by the monarchs of England.) To avoid the split with the Church that a divorce would cause, Henry thought he might end his marriage by **annulment** instead.

Henry claimed that his marriage to Catherine had been invalid because, against the teachings of Scripture, he had married his brother's widow—something Church law forbade. Yet, the Church could give permission, called a "dispensation," for such marriages, and Henry had received a dispensation for his marriage from Pope Leo X. Henry, however, wanted the reigning pope, Clement VII, to declare that the dispensation itself had been invalid.

In 1526, Henry sent his chancellor, Cardinal Wolsey, to Rome to persuade the pope to agree to an annulment. About the same time, Henry had found another reason to desire an annulment. He had fallen in love with a young woman named Anne Boleyn.

**annulment:** a decree by the Church court that a marriage is invalid; that is, has never existed. It differs from a divorce, which is the splitting of a valid and existing marriage.

## Supreme Over the Church of England

Pope Clement VII received the annulment request at the very time he was holed up in Castel Sant'Angelo to escape the emperor's marauding mercenaries, who were sacking Rome. The annulment request presented the weak Clement with difficulties. Catherine was Charles V's aunt, and the pope was not willing to anger Charles V further; at the same time, he wanted to keep good relations with Henry VIII. What was Clement to do about the annulment?

The pope's solution was not to do anything right away. At first, he was willing to let Cardinal Wolsey and another cardinal look into the annulment. But in 1529, when he was making up with Charles V, Clement decided that the annulment case had to be tried in Rome, not England. Not until 1531 did Clement take any action, and that was only to tell Henry he could not marry Anne Boleyn until the Roman court had made a decision about the annulment.

Finally, Henry took matters into his own hands. When the reigning archbishop of Canterbury died in 1532, Henry nominated Thomas Cranmer to be made archbishop. Cranmer was a Lutheran and a strong supporter of the king against the pope. And, as archbishop, Cranmer did the king's will. In May 1533, Archbishop Cranmer gave the king the annulment he had wanted, declaring that his marriage to Catherine was "null and void." Only five days after this declaration, Cranmer blessed Henry's marriage to Anne Boleyn. (They had been secretly "married" in 1533.) In July, Pope Clement responded by declaring Henry's marriage to Anne null and void and excommunicating the king.

Henry answered Clement by declaring that the king, not the pope, was the head of the Church of England. In March 1534, Parliament followed suit by passing the first Act of Supremacy, which declared the king supreme head over the English Church, the pope having no say over it all. Parliament said further that every English subject had to take an "Oath of Succession," recognizing that the rightful queen of England after Henry's death would be Henry and Anne's infant daughter, Elizabeth, rather than Henry and Catherine's daughter, Mary. In taking this oath, English subjects were agreeing that Henry and Anne's marriage was valid and not null and void, as the pope had declared. Parliament then

**Anne Boleyn, second wife of King Henry VIII of England**

passed laws that said anyone who acknowledged the authority of the pope over the English Church was a traitor to the king.

Nearly all the clergy, bishops and priests alike, took the Oath of Supremacy and followed the king into schism. But John Fisher, bishop of Rochester, stood firm for the pope. "If I were to consent that the king is the head of the English church," he said, "I would be guilty of tearing the seamless garment of Christ, the *one* Catholic Church." Fisher was imprisoned in the Tower of London and beheaded.

St. Thomas More. English author, statesman, and martyr

A layman named Thomas More—Henry's friend, whom he had made chancellor of the kingdom in 1529—also refused to take the Oath of Supremacy. Instead, More resigned his office and retired to his home. Yet, though More took no public stand against the king, his refusal to recognize Henry publicly as head of the English Church was enough to condemn him in the king's eyes. Like Fisher, More was imprisoned in the Tower of London.

Eventually, More was tried for treason before a court of Anne Boleyn's relatives. Although during the trial More refused to say whether he did or did not accept the supremacy of the king over the Church, the court sentenced him to death. Finally, on July 6, 1535, More suffered death by beheading. His last words were, "I die the King's good servant, but God's first."

Saints Thomas More and John Fisher were not the only ones to suffer martyrdom under Henry VIII. Some members of the Carthusian, Brigittine, and Franciscan religious orders died for their faith the same year as More and Fisher.

## The Dissolution of the Monasteries

After making himself supreme over the English Church, Henry next turned to the English monasteries, whose lands and wealth he coveted. Under Henry's chief minister, Thomas Cromwell—who, with Thomas Cranmer, had suggested that the king make himself head of the English Church—"visitors" inspected the English monasteries and afterward reported that monks were living lives of gross immorality. The charges, undoubtedly true in some instances, were greatly exaggerated.

Based on the visitors' report, Parliament in February 1536 ordered the **dissolution** of the smaller monasteries, handing over their wealth to

**dissolution:** in law, the ending or closing down of any institution or community; the institution that is closed down is said to have been "dissolved"

the king. This strike against the monasteries spurred a revolt, called the Pilgrimage of Grace, among the common people of northern England. The rebellion, however, was dispersed, and the king and Cromwell turned their attention to the larger monasteries.

Over the next four years, Henry dissolved the larger monasteries, seizing their property and wealth. More than 8,000 monks and 1,500 nuns were driven from these houses to find secular livings. Some 18 abbots and all the superiors of the largest houses were executed under trumped-up charges of treason. The lands went to the king, who gave much of the property to Cromwell and his friends, thus creating a new and powerful class of wealthy men who were dependent on the king and Cromwell. The poor who had depended on the monasteries for livelihood and charity could no longer receive it and formed a new class of beggars.

### Schism, Not Heresy

King Henry VIII thus took the Church of England into schism with little opposition from the clergy and the people. The bishops easily succumbed to the king's pressure because, for many years, most of them had not lived as serious and devout churchmen. Even before the schism, these bishops had been more servants of the king than shepherds of the Church. Since the 14th century, too, the English kings had exercised a great deal of control over the Church in their realm, treating it as a national Church rather than as a part of the universal Church.

*Thomas Cranmer,* by Gerlach Flicke

As far the English people were concerned, except for the dissolution of the monasteries, they saw little change in the English Church. Masses continued to be said in Latin, Communion was given only under the species of bread, priests did not marry as they did in Germany, and all the Sacraments remained in place. Henry might admit that he was a schismatic, but he denied being a heretic. In fact, he cruelly punished anyone who denied the old Catholic teachings. Though Thomas Cranmer was a Lutheran, he was a secret one. Protestants did not fare well in Henry's church.

Henry was no more faithful to Anne Boleyn than he had been to Catherine. In 1536, he accused Anne of infidelity and ordered her to be beheaded. He then married an even younger bride, Jane Seymour. Queen Jane gave birth to a son, Edward, and Henry at last had a male heir. Jane died in childbirth, and after her Henry had three more wives. One annulled her marriage with the king, another he had beheaded for treason, and the last outlived him.

Henry VIII himself died on January 28, 1547, at the age of 55. In his last will and testament he requested that Masses be said for the repose of his soul.

## The Church of England Becomes Protestant

Henry's son, the 10-year-old Edward VI, became king after his father's death. During Edward's reign of six years, Protestants took control of the Church of England and began making drastic changes in its doctrine and worship.

Under Edward, Archbishop Cranmer composed the *Book of Common Prayer*, which included a new liturgy in English and a daily office of Morning and Evening Prayer. A talented poet and musician, Cranmer translated the old prayers into an elegant and poetic English. His style of prayer suggested the ancient Latin and echoed many of the Latin phrases and figures of speech. The *Book of Common Prayer* has influenced English literature and speech ever since. Edward ordered the prayer book to be used in all English churches—and as a result ignited a peasants' rebellion, in the west of England in 1549, that was crushed by an army of mercenaries.

Under Edward, too, the Church of England adopted a confession of faith that drew from the theology of John Calvin. The Church of England's reformers adopted new rites for consecrating bishops, priests, and all members of the clergy. Since that time, the Church of England has not performed valid ordinations, because it has considered its clergy to be ministers of the word only, not priests who offer the sacrifice of the Mass.

It looked, however, as if all the efforts to make the Church of England Protestant would come to nothing when Edward VI died in 1553. The throne passed to his older half-sister, Mary, the daughter of Catherine of Aragon. Mary was a Catholic.

## The Catholic Queen

When Mary came to the throne in 1553, she declared her resolve to remain faithful to the Catholic Church. Further, she said, it was her

**Queen Mary I of England,** by Antonio Moro

"fervent prayer" that the English people would embrace the same religion "in all peace and charity." Mary immediately suppressed all the Protestant changes made under Edward VI and restored the Mass and Catholic customs. On November 30, 1554, Cardinal Reginald Pole, representing the pope, solemnly restored the Church of England to full communion with Rome.

Queen Mary might have kept England in the Catholic Faith, if she had remained prudent and cautious. But she made mistakes. Her first mistake was marrying Philip II, son of Emperor Charles V and heir to the Spanish throne. The English thought Philip too fanatical a Catholic. Philip and Mary were strangers to each other, and he only briefly visited his wife in England.

Yet, Mary's biggest mistake was her decision to persecute the Protestants in her kingdom. The most famous of these was Thomas Cranmer, the man who had aided Henry VIII in annulling his marriage to Mary's mother, Catherine. Mary ordered Cranmer and two other Protestant bishops to be imprisoned in the Tower of London for heresy. Cranmer's two companions refused to recant, were condemned by a Church court, and were handed over to the state for execution. Cranmer was also condemned; but he renounced his Protestant beliefs. Yet, on March 21, 1556, when standing before the people gathered to hear his public recantation, Cranmer declared his earlier denials of Protestantism were false. Like his fellow Protestant bishops, he was burned at the stake.

Mary imprisoned and executed 277 Protestants. These men were a threat to her throne, and if she had executed them as traitors, public opinion might not have turned against her. But Mary executed them as heretics, making them appear as martyrs and, therefore, heroes to many in England.

Mary was not in good health. She died in 1558, after reigning only five years. She had been childless, and the only surviving Tudor was Anne Boleyn's daughter, Elizabeth, who succeeded Mary as queen.

During her reign, Elizabeth executed thousands of Catholics—many more than Mary's 277 Protestants. Yet, Elizabeth is remembered as "Good Queen Bess" while Mary has gone down in history with the unflattering name, "Bloody Mary."

## The Reign of Elizabeth I

Elizabeth had promised the dying Queen Mary to keep England Catholic after her death. Upon becoming queen, however, Elizabeth broke her word and took England, once again, into schism. This brought her into conflict with Philip II, who as king of Spain was the most powerful monarch in Europe. Spain and England, once allied against France, now became mortal enemies.

Elizabeth continued the work of Protestantizing the Church of England that her half-brother, Edward VI, had begun. By her order, Parliament passed the Act of **Uniformity,** which abolished the Mass and decreed that all public worship had to follow the *Book of Common Prayer*. Every English subject had to attend Church of England services or pay a fine. Unlike the clergy in the time of Henry VIII, however, nearly all the Catholic bishops refused to renounce their faith and were removed from their sees, along with about 400 priests.

**uniformity:** the legal demand that all the citizens of a country adhere to the official religion.

During the first 10 years of her reign, Elizabeth was relatively gentle in her treatment of Catholics; they suffered only from fines, loss of property, and imprisonment. Elizabeth earned the affection of the English people by her moderation in religious matters. Though a declared Protestant, to the end of her life she kept a Latin Mass for her own chapel and promoted Catholic musicians for her personal worship.

But, in 1570, Pope Pius V issued a bull excommunicating Elizabeth and declaring that her subjects were not bound to obey her. Ever after, Elizabeth became a bitter persecutor of the Catholics in her realm.

All Catholics suffered under Elizabeth, but none more than the priests. With the financial assistance of Philip II, a seminary for English priests had been set up, first in Douai, Belgium, and then at Reims, France. The priests ordained at Douai crossed the Channel into England, risking their lives to bring the Sacraments to the English Catholics. Elizabeth's ministers used "priest hunters" to track them down. Captured priests were usually given the chance to take the Oath of Supremacy; if they refused, they were accused of treason and then tortured and executed. The common method of execution was to be hanged, drawn, and quartered. The priests would be hanged by the neck, but then cut down while still alive. They were then disemboweled (drawn) and cut into four pieces (quartered).

**Elizabeth I, Queen of England and Ireland**

### An English Bible

The English Catholic seminary at Douai, and then at Reims, was responsible for translating the Scriptures from Latin into English. This Bible became known as the *Douai-Reims* version (1582). It was preceded by the *Bishops' Bible* (1568) in England and the *Geneva Bible* (1560), which were the two most popular English versions of the Bible available to English readers at the time.

The Douai-Reims Bible came out 25 years before the well-known *Authorized Version*, also called the *King James Bible* (1611). In fact, the Catholic translation influenced the way the *Authorized Version* itself was translated. The Douai-Reims Bible was the one English translation read by English-speaking Catholics until the mid-20th century.

### Death of the Queen of Scots

Elizabeth's one serious rival for the English throne was her cousin, Mary Stuart, queen of Scotland. In 1559, Mary, then only 16 years old, had been married to Francis II, the king of France. When Francis died in 1560, Mary returned to Scotland. Mary was Catholic, but the situation in Scotland

The execution of Mary, Queen of Scots, at Fotheringhay Castle on February 8, 1587

when she returned did not favor the Catholic Faith. The year before her return, John Knox, a follower of John Calvin, had convinced the Scottish parliament to abolish the Mass and organize the Scottish Church according to Calvinist beliefs. This, the Presbyterian Church, became the state or **established church** of Scotland, as the Church of England (also called the Anglican Church) had become the established church of England.

Needing support to keep her throne, Mary married Henry Stuart, Lord Darnley. But Darnley demanded from Mary the powers of a king—something he did not have simply by being married to her. In 1567, Darnley was murdered; shortly afterward, Mary married the man who was accused of murdering him. This marriage angered her chief supporters as well as the Presbyterian clergy of Scotland. Her life was threatened in Scotland, so Mary fled to England and sought protection from Elizabeth. Mary left behind the son she had with Darnley—James, who was raised a Protestant. He became King James VI of Scotland.

Instead of protecting Mary when she arrived in England, Elizabeth had her arrested in 1568. Mary remained under house arrest in England for the next 19 years.

Philip II was determined to rescue Mary Stuart if he could, and Elizabeth's fears of a Spanish invasion may have decided Mary's fate. Mary was condemned to be executed as a traitor to the English crown. Throughout the night before her execution, with the hammering on the scaffold in the background, Mary prayed, "Even as Thy arms, O Jesus, were spread here upon the cross, so receive me into Thine arms of mercy, and forgive me all my sins." She went to the place of execution carrying a crucifix and a prayer book. She was executed by beheading on February 8, 1587. She was 44 years old.

> **established church:** a church declared (or "established") by a government to be the official church of a state. An established church is often supported by taxes, and a government may declare it to be the only legal religion in the state.

## The Last Tudor

Though Queen Elizabeth had many male friends and admirers during the course of her long reign of over 40 years, she never married. For this, the English remembered her not only as "Good Queen Bess," but as the "Virgin Queen." Because she never married, however, Elizabeth had no heir. Her death spelled the end of the House of Tudor. Elizabeth's throne passed to Mary Stuart's son, King James V of Scotland, who in 1603 became King James I of England.

Elizabeth I has been remembered as the greatest Tudor monarch and an English heroine. During her long reign, England was prosperous and began its rise to become one of the greatest powers in Europe. Elizabeth's reign saw the writing of some of the greatest English—and European—

## The Spanish Armada (1588)

Philip II of Spain had been preparing an invasion of England since 1585; but when word reached him of the execution of Mary Queen of Scots, he ordered the immediate preparation of a huge fleet that would carry his invasion force to the island kingdom. Philip appointed Admiral Santa Cruz, the greatest Spanish seaman of the age, to command this fleet. It is remembered as the Spanish **Armada**, and it numbered 130 ships.

The Spanish Armada set sail on May 28, 1588, carrying nearly 30,000 men. On June 19, the Armada ran into a terrible storm that scattered the ships. It took almost a month before the fleet was reassembled, the damage repaired, and more supplies obtained. The regrouped Armada set sail again and, on July 29, was in sight of the English coast.

Francis Drake commanded the English fleet that opposed the Armada. During the first five days of August, the English ships successfully kept the Spanish ships from getting close to shore. Spanish supplies of food, water, powder, and shot became dangerously low.

The Spanish were outgunned and outmaneuvered by the smaller English ships and their captains, who were more familiar than the Spaniards were with the waters of the English Channel. Finally, after losing a large number of ships, the Armada was forced to withdraw. Its surviving ships tried to sail for home by going north around the whole of the British Isles. But off the western coast of Scotland, the Spanish fleet encountered fierce storms, and many ships were wrecked and sank. Only a few ships and a fourth of the original men aboard reached Spanish ports. English Protestants saw the Armada's defeat as an act of God protecting the English Protestant Church and its head, Queen Elizabeth.

**armada:** a large fleet of ships

The Spanish Armada

works of literature, composed by such masters as Edmund Spenser, Ben Jonson, and William Shakespeare. Under Elizabeth, England made its first attempts to establish settlements in North America, in the region the English named "Virginia" in honor of the "Virgin Queen."

Elizabeth, however, was a lonely woman. She was the product of a cruel father by whose order her own mother, Anne Boleyn, had been killed. After Anne's death, Elizabeth had suffered the shame of being declared illegitimate. Her own cruelty can be seen as a reflection of the cruelty she had suffered at the hands of Henry VIII, who had led the Church of England into schism.

Shortly before she died in 1603, Elizabeth was unquiet, refusing to sleep because she was afraid of nightmares. For days she stood bolt upright or was propped up in a semi-standing position. She refused to lie down. Once she said to her maid of honor, "I saw one night my own body, exceedingly lean and fearful, in a light of fire." She rejected the Church of England clergyman who was sent to give her last rites, calling him a "hedge priest"—a false priest. "There are no more priests in England," she said. "I have killed them all!" She finally collapsed and was carried to bed, where she died in silence.

# Chapter Review

## Summary

- In 1507 Pope Julius II issued a jubilee indulgence to fund the rebuilding of St. Peter's Basilica in the Vatican.
- Martin Luther nailed his Ninety-five Theses on the door of the Castle Church in Wittenberg on the eve of All Saints Day, 1517, the traditional beginning of the Protestant Reformation.
- Luther debated the Catholic theologian, Johannes Eck, in 1519. During this debate, Luther discovered that he agreed with John Hus on many points and declared that the pope as well as the ecumenical councils could be in error.
- In 1520 Pope Leo X issued the bull, *Exsurge Domine*, condemning Martin Luther's teachings and threatening to excommunicate him if he did not recant. On December 10, 1520, Luther answered the pope's challenge by publicly burning the bull.
- Luther appeared before the Imperial Diet in Worms in 1521, defending himself and his teachings before the Emperor Charles V and the assembled princes. The diet condemned Luther in the Edict of Worms.

- Luther's reform early on splintered into several different groups. Among these were the followers of the Swiss reformer Ulrich Zwingli, the French reformer John Calvin, and the Anabaptists.
- John Calvin came out with his *Institutes of the Christian Religion* in 1536. Calvin and his teachings became the foundations of the Reformed tradition, one of the great branches of Protestantism besides Lutheranism.
- The Ottoman Turks again became a danger to Christendom under their new sultan, Suleiman I. In 1521, Suleiman took the important fortress city of Belgrade; the following year, he took the island of Rhodes in the eastern Mediterranean.
- War between Emperor Charles V and King Francis I of France lasted on and off from 1521 to 1544. Francis allied himself with the German Protestant princes, Pope Clement VII, and the Ottoman Turks against the emperor. Charles was ultimately successful against Francis.
- Charles V's troops in Italy mutinied in the spring of 1527 and marched on Rome. While Pope Clement VII was holed up in Castel Sant'Angelo, the imperial troops pillaged Rome.
- In 1529, the Turks under Suleiman I laid siege to Vienna. After an assault of three weeks, the Turks withdrew.
- At an Imperial Diet held in Augsburg in 1530, the German Lutheran princes presented a confession of faith, called the Augsburg Confession, to the emperor. Charles V pledged to enforce the Edict of Worms against the Protestants; but needing the help of the Lutheran princes against Suleiman, Charles proclaimed the Peace of Nuremberg by which he suspended all laws against the Lutherans.
- Pope Paul III called for a meeting in 1537 of an ecumenical council at Trent. Because of Francis I's continued plots against Charles V, however, the council was not able to meet until 1545.
- War between the Lutheran princes of Germany and the emperor began in 1546. It continued until 1555, when an Imperial Diet proclaimed the "Religious Peace of Augsburg." The Peace gave every prince the right to choose what religion he and his subjects would follow in his territory.
- When his wife, Catherine of Aragon, did not give birth to any sons, England's King Henry VIII wanted his marriage to her annulled. When, after several years, the pope rendered no decision about the annulment, Henry took matters into his own hands. His newly appointed archbishop of Canterbury, Thomas Cranmer, annulled Henry's marriage to Catherine and blessed his marriage to Anne Boleyn.

- Parliament decreed that Henry VIII was head of the Church of England. Anyone who refused to acknowledge that the king was supreme over the English Church was accused of treason. Bishop St. John Fisher and St. Thomas More were executed for remaining faithful to the pope.
- Beginning in 1536, King Henry VIII ordered the dissolution of the monasteries in England. The wealth from the monasteries went to the king and his supporters, forming a new class of powerful and wealthy men.
- Under Queen Mary I, the Church of England was restored to communion with the pope. However, Mary's hundreds of executions of Protestants made her unpopular and brought the Catholic Church into disrepute.
- Queen Elizabeth I continued the Protestantizing of the Church of England, which had begun during the reign of her half-brother, Edward VI.
- Elizabeth required all her subjects to attend Church of England services. At first she was relatively gentle toward Catholics; but after Pope Pius V excommunicated Elizabeth, she began a bitter persecution of Catholics, in which thousands died.

## Key Concepts

**indulgence:** a full or partial remittance by the Church of the temporal punishment for sins (such as one suffers in Purgatory)

**Protestant:** one who "witnesses" (protests) to the complaints against the Church; one of the reforming theologians of the 16th century or a follower of the reformers

*sola fides, sola gratia:* Luther's doctrine that only by God's Grace, through faith alone, may one be saved

*sola scriptura:* Luther's teaching that divine revelation comes through the Scriptures alone

**annulment:** a decree by the Church court that a marriage is invalid; that is, has never existed. It differs from a divorce, which is the splitting of a valid and existing marriage.

**uniformity:** the legal demand that all the citizens of a country adhere to the official religion.

## Dates to Remember

**1509:** the marriage of Henry VIII and Catherine of Aragon
**1517:** Luther posts his Ninety-five Theses

**1521:** the Diet of Worms condemns Luther
**1527:** the sack of Rome
**1529:** the Protest of Speier
**1533:** Archbishop Cranmer annuls Henry VIII's marriage to Catherine of Aragon
**1534:** the Act of Supremacy is issued in England
**1536:** John Calvin comes out with the first edition of his *Institutes of the Christian Religion*
**1536:** dissolution of the monasteries of England
**1545:** the Council of Trent begins
**1554:** Cardinal Pole reconciles the Church of England to Rome
**1555:** the Peace of Augsburg
**1570:** Pius V excommunicates Elizabeth
**1588:** the English defeat the Spanish Armada

## Central Characters

**Leo X (r. 1513–1521):** pope who excommunicated Luther
**Martin Luther (1483–1546):** German Protestant reformer: began the Protestant Reformation
**Charles V (1500–1558):** the king of Spain and emperor of Germany
**Ulrich Zwingli (1484–1531):** Swiss Protestant reformer
**John Calvin (1509–1564):** French Protestant reformer; author of the *Institutes of the Christian Religion*
**Henry VIII (1491–1537):** the king of England, who declared himself head of the Church in England
**Catherine of Aragon (1485–1536):** Henry VIII's first wife, daughter of Isabel of Castile and Fernando of Aragon
**Anne Boleyn (ca. 1507–1536):** Henry VIII's second wife; mother of Queen Elizabeth I
**Thomas Cranmer (1489–1556):** archbishop of Canterbury, author of the *Book of Common Prayer*
**Mary I Tudor (1516–1558):** daughter of Henry VIII by Catherine of Aragon; the English queen who restored the Church of England to the Catholic Church
**Elizabeth I (1533–1603):** daughter of Henry VIII and the English queen who protestantized the Church of England

## Questions for Review

1. What was Luther objecting to in the Ninety-five Theses?
2. What was the Edict of Worms? Why was Emperor Charles V not able to enforce it?

3. What did Luther mean by *sola fide*? What did he mean by *sola scriptura* and *sola gratia*?
4. What is Calvinism? How does it differ from Lutheranism? What did Calvin mean by predestination?
5. Why did Henry want a divorce from Catherine? Why could he not get an annulment from the pope? What was his solution?
6. Who was Henry VIII's heir? What important English book was written during his reign?
7. What was the effect of the dissolution of the monasteries of England?
8. What did the Peace of Augsburg accomplish? How did it perpetuate the religious division in Germany?
9. What did King Philip II of Spain hope to accomplish with the Spanish Armada?
10. Why did Pope Pius V's excommunication of Elizabeth turn her against her Catholic subjects?
11. What poets and great men made Elizabeth's reign famous in English history?

## Ideas in Action

1. Make a map showing the divisions of Europe between Protestant and Catholic after the Lutheran revolt.
2. Read a passage from the Douai-Reims Bible and then read the same one from the King James Bible. What differences, if any, do you spot?
3. Discuss in class the splintering effect of Luther's revolt on the body of Christendom.
4. Discuss with your teacher and the class: "How does the Protestant Reformation still affect us even today?"

# Highways and Byways

### Cardinal Reginald Pole (1500–1558)

Reginald Pole, whose mother was Margaret, a niece of King Edward IV, was a cousin of King Henry VIII. An English Renaissance scholar and a friend of the humanists Erasmus and Thomas More, Pole also enjoyed the favor of the king. Henry paid for Pole's studies in Padua and Paris and granted him a Church benefice.

Pole could not agree with Henry's plan to annul his marriage to Catherine of Aragon—and he forcefully told the king this to his face. Despite Pole's forthrightness, in 1532, Henry allowed him to return to

Padua to study. In 1536, Pole sent Henry a treatise in which he argued that Henry's marriage to Catherine was indeed valid. Henry ordered Pole to return to England. Instead Pole went to Rome, where Pope Paul III soon made him a cardinal. As a cardinal, Pole went on diplomatic missions to Europe's Catholic monarchs, urging them to form a league in support of the pope against Henry. In revenge, Henry executed Pole's mother and his brother, Richard, Lord Montague.

In 1542, Cardinal Pole was appointed papal legate to the Council of Trent and presided over the council's opening session. After Henry's death, Pope Julius III sent Pole to England in 1553 as legate to the court of Queen Mary. Pole not only received the Church of England back into the Catholic fold, but began to reestablish the dissolved monasteries and assembled a synod to institute many Church reforms.

Pole was made archbishop of Canterbury in 1557. Although he was not responsible for the burnings of Protestants that marred Mary's reign, he did nothing to stop them—though he himself spared three heretics who had appealed to him. Pole fell out of favor with Pope Paul IV, who succeeded Paul III in 1555. Paul IV had a political quarrel with Spain's king, Philip II, who supported Pole; and the pope falsely suspected Pole of heresy. The pope ordered Pole to return to Rome, but he was spared further humiliation. The cardinal, who had done so much to reconcile Christendom, fell sick and died only a few hours after the death of Queen Mary.

# Chapter 18: Catholic Renewal and Religious War

*Laetare Jerusalem*—"Rejoice, O Jerusalem"—was the title of Pope Paul III's bull that called for the **convoking** of an ecumenical council at Trent in northern Italy on March 15, 1545. The council had been a long time in coming, and many had awaited it eagerly.

**convoke:** to call together for a meeting or assembly

Talk of an ecumenical council to correct abuses in the Church and address the Protestant challenge had been ongoing since 1529. But it had faced many obstacles. Controversy had erupted, for instance, over where

**Council of Trent**

483

**venue:** the place or locale of a gathering

to hold the council. The Lutheran princes in Germany demanded that it be held on German soil, while Pope Clement VII was in favor of an Italian **venue**. The pope demanded that, in order to attend the council, the Protestants had to acknowledge the teaching authority of the Church. This they refused to do.

Another problem was His Most Christian Majesty, Francis I, king of France, who kept interfering with the council preparations. He used the excuse of his war with Emperor Charles V to forbid the French bishops to attend the first scheduled meeting of the council (at Mantua, in Italy) in 1536. For this and other reasons, the meeting of the council was delayed to May 1538, then to Easter 1539, then to All Saints Day 1542. On this last date, the council fathers were to meet at Trent; but the meeting was not held. The Protestants voiced their violent opposition to the council—and their ally, Francis I, would not allow the bull convoking the council to be published in France.

So it was that the council was again delayed until 1543—but war between Francis and Charles, and bad relations between Pope Paul III and Charles, forced another delay. Even the date of March 15, 1545, called for by the bull *Laetare Jerusalem*, came and went without a council. But at long last the council did meet, on December 13, 1545. A Mass of the Holy Spirit opened the long-awaited assembly that would, it was hoped, bring true reform and renewal to the Catholic Church—and perhaps reunite divided Christendom.

# The Trials of the Council of Trent

Great hopes were held for the Council of Trent, but the fulfillment of those hopes had to wait a long time. Once it had come together, the council was not free from controversy or the opposition of monarchs. Altogether, the council met on and off for 18 years, from December 1545 to December of 1563. At times it looked as if it might fail to achieve its goals.

For many years, Charles V had pushed for a council. But it became clear after the council met that he had his own ideas about the sort of council he wanted. Always hoping to reconcile the Protestants to the Church and so have a united empire, Charles did not want the council to address the doctrinal questions that divided the Protestants from the pope—such as whether Scripture alone is the source of doctrine, or Scripture and

Chapter 18   Catholic Renewal and Religious War    485

Tradition; or whether Christians are saved by faith alone, or by faith and works. Instead, Charles wanted the council to address questions of Church reform—such as whether one bishop should be allowed to hold two sees, or whether the Mass should be said in a language other than Latin, or whether laymen could receive both the bread and the cup in Communion. The emperor hoped that if the Protestants saw the Church reforming its behavior, they would agree to come back into the fold, even if they continued to hold to heretical doctrines.

The council fathers, however, insisted that they would address doctrinal and disciplinary questions together. During the council's first session that began in December 1545, the fathers tackled some important issues and **promulgated** decrees on justification (how God saves or justifies men) and the Sacraments, as well as decrees on Church reform. This session of the council lasted until March 1547. Then, because of an outbreak of disease in Trent, the council fathers voted to move to Bologna in northern Italy.

**promulgate:** to make public, proclaim

Charles V was opposed to moving the council to Bologna; so, even though most of the council fathers went there, Charles (since he was king of Spain) would not allow the Spanish bishops to leave Trent. Seeing he could not convince the emperor to change his mind, Pope Paul III suspended the council on September 17, 1547.

Pope Paul died in November 1549, and the new pope, Julius III, was not elected until February 1550. Julius called for the council to resume at Trent in May 1551. This time the council met opposition from the Protestant German princes, who insisted that Lutheran theologians have a vote in the council. The princes demanded, too, that neither the pope nor his representatives lead the council. King

Map of Italy ca. 1600

Henry II of France was a source of trouble as well. He was allied with the Protestant princes against the emperor and refused to send French bishops to the council. Still, the council met eight times, promulgating important doctrinal and reform decrees. In April 1552—after learning that the Lutheran prince, Mauritz of Saxony, was leading an army toward Trent—the council adjourned to meet at a later time.

It was nine years, however, before the council could meet again. Julius III died in 1555. He was succeeded by Pope Marcellus II, who reigned only

**Pope Julius III**

22 days. The next pope, Paul IV, wanted to avoid difficulties with the emperor, the French king, and the German princes, and so decided he would not resume the council. Paul wanted to reform the Church by himself, without the aid of a council.

It was Pius IV, after becoming pope in 1559, who called the council together for what would be its final session. But though Pius called for the council to meet in 1561, the council fathers did not gather again in Trent until January 1562. During this session, the pope and his supporters (called the **Ultramontanes**) were opposed by the French bishops, who wanted to weaken the pope's authority in the Church in favor of the bishops. Under the control of the French king, these bishops pushed the idea that national Churches should be fairly independent of the pope. They wanted a **Gallican** Church that, while in communion with the Church of Rome, was mostly under the king's direction.

At the council, however, the pope had a strong champion—his nephew, Cardinal Charles Borromeo. Under Charles's leadership, the council was able to complete its work. It promulgated new decrees and voted to approve the decrees from previous meetings. On December 4, 1563, the council **adjourned**, finishing its part in the reform of the Church. On January 26, 1564, Pope Pius IV issued the bull *Benedictus Deus*, in which he approved all the council's acts. The pope drew up the Profession of Faith of the Council of Trent, which he ordered all bishops and university professors to sign. So ended the Council of Trent, one of the most important councils in the history of the Church.

**Ultramontane:** the name given to those who favored strong papal control over national churches (from *ultra*, meaning "beyond" or "on the other side," and *mons, montes*, meaning "mountains"—"on the other side of the mountains" or the Alps)

**Gallican:** having to do with *Gallicanism*, a position held by many French churchmen that the French Church should be in most respects independent of the pope while remaining in communion with him (from the Latin, *Gallia*, or Gaul)

**adjourn:** to bring to an end or conclusion

## The Triumph of Trent

For 18 years, the Council of Trent promulgated decrees that addressed the challenges laid down by the Protestant reformers. It also corrected abuses in the Church. Among the council's many important decrees were the following:

1. *The equal authority of Scripture and Tradition.* The council fathers acknowledged that the Church's tradition was just as much a source of Church teaching as the Sacred Scriptures.

2. *Man is not totally depraved.* The council condemned Luther and Calvin's teaching that man was totally corrupted by Original Sin. Even without Grace, people are capable of doing good works.
3. *Not faith alone, but faith, hope, and charity are necessary for salvation. All are gifts of God's Grace.* The council asserted that faith is necessary for justification; but without hope and charity, faith is dead. Faith, hope, and charity, too, said the fathers, must be manifested in works. These works, in turn, are God's gifts.
4. *The Eucharist is truly the Body, Blood, Soul, and Divinity of Christ.* The council reaffirmed Transubstantiation and taught that the Eucharist should be worshipped.
5. *There are seven, and only seven, Sacraments.* The council condemned Luther's teaching that only Baptism and Communion are Sacraments, as well as Calvin's teaching that there are no Sacraments. In accord with Church tradition, the council said that only Baptism, Confirmation, the Eucharist, Penance (reconciliation), Extreme Unction (anointing), Holy Orders, and Marriage are Sacraments.
6. *All the books found in the Latin Vulgate are inspired.* Luther said several books found in the Catholic Old Testament are not inspired. The council said these books are truly the word of God.
7. *The pope is the head of the Church.* Against the reformers and those who said an ecumenical council stands above the pope, the council taught that the pope, as the successor of St. Peter, is the supreme head of the Church.
8. *Bishops must be fit for their office.* The council said only good and learned men should be bishops. They must live in their dioceses and may not have more than one diocese at one time.
9. *Priests must be worthy of their calling.* The council said all men who became priests must remain celibate and undergo training in the doctrines and liturgy of the Church. For the first time, the Church required all candidates for the priesthood to undergo training in schools called *seminaries*.
10. *The liturgy must be reformed.* The council decreed that the rites of the Mass and other liturgical functions had to undergo a revision, to remove rites and practices that were not reverent, not in full accord with Catholic teaching, or not very ancient. Though some

**Pope Pius IV**

council fathers wanted to allow celebrations of the liturgy in the vernacular, the council decreed that the language of the Roman Rite would continue to be Latin.
11. *Abuses must be suppressed.* The council forbade such practices as simony and the offering of money for indulgences, though it affirmed that the pope had the power to grant indulgences.

> **Anglican:** the name given to the Protestant Church of England: the Anglican Church

In one sense, the Council of Trent was an utter failure. It did not bring the Protestants—whether Lutheran, Calvinist, Anabaptist, or **Anglican**—back into the Church. The council, too, did not immediately reform the Church. The king of France, for one, refused to allow the council's decrees to be published in France. Yet, though the council faced opposition in parts of Europe for decades, it was a triumph. It clearly spelled out Catholic teaching on several points the Protestants had challenged. It set in motion a true reform of the Church's life, and it inspired Catholics with a renewed sense of what it means to be Catholic.

The period of Church history following the council has been called the *Counter-Reformation*, but this is really not a good name. A better name for the period is the "Catholic Reformation." The council did not just stand *against* the Protestant reformers; it also began a positive renewal of the life of the Church. The renewal of Church life that the council inspired halted further Protestant advances into Catholic Europe, and it allowed Catholic Europe to regain some of the lands that it had lost to the Protestants. The Church could now face the future with new confidence.

# The Age of Catholic Renewal: The "Counter-Reformation"

The task of reforming the Catholic Church met opposition right from the beginning. Many bishops, priests, and members of the nobility liked things as they had been for over a century. They enjoyed the revenues they received from possessing or controlling Church offices. Princes and kings did not want to sacrifice the power and wealth they had obtained by controlling the Church in their domains. Indeed, they exercised as much control over their national Churches as Henry VIII did over the Church of England—though, without going into schism. Only Portugal, Poland, and Austria fully accepted the reform called for by the Council of Trent. France at first opposed it, and Spain, the kingdom of Philip II, reluctantly accepted reform only after several years.

Reform of the Church by the popes had begun even before the council ended. In 1542, Pope Paul III established what was called the Congregation of the **Holy Office**, or the "Inquisition." Its purpose was not the same as that of the medieval inquisition—it did not send out inquisitors to investigate and try accused heretics. The Holy Office (today called the Congregation for the Doctrine of the Faith) issued doctrinal teachings in what are called "decrees" and condemned heretical teachings. Its task was, and is, to protect the purity of the Catholic Faith.

The same pope initiated the ***Index librorum prohibitorum*** **(Index of Forbidden Books)**, a list of books the faithful were forbidden to read. No earlier age had needed such a list of books; but because the printing press had made available all kinds of books—both instructive and destructive books—the council fathers thought a list of the dangerous books was necessary to protect the faithful from error.

St. Pius V worked zealously to make the **Tridentine** reforms a reality. He strove to eradicate simony and the holding of multiple benefices by one man, and he took precautions to assure that only worthy men would become bishops. To make sure that priests were fit to teach the faithful, Pius published the *Catechism of the Council of Trent*, which laid out the teachings of the council in a simplified way. This was the first catechism written for the entire Church.

Pius V, however, is most famous for his reform of the liturgy. With all the changes and abuses of the liturgy made by Lutherans, Anglicans, and others, it was necessary to establish one, uniform liturgy for the Latin Rite of the Church. Though the pope allowed some dioceses and orders to continue using a few of the most ancient Latin rites of the Mass and the liturgy, he commanded all others to use his reformed Roman Rite. This rite is commonly known as the **Tridentine Rite**.

The popes had help from bishops in carrying out the Tridentine reforms. Among these bishops was St. Charles Borromeo. His uncle, Pope Pius IV, had appointed him a cardinal and the administrator of the archdiocese of Milan in Italy when Charles, though a member of the clergy, was not a priest. When Charles's brother, an Italian count, died in 1562, many—including the pope—urged him to marry. Charles, however, had himself secretly ordained a priest in 1563. In the same year, he was consecrated bishop.

> **Holy Office:** the "Inquisition," a congregation of the curia that issued doctrinal decrees and condemned heretical teachings. Its purpose was to protect the purity of the Catholic Faith.
>
> **Index of Forbidden Books:** the list of those books the Church considered dangerous to the Catholic Faith and forbade Catholics to read
>
> **Tridentine:** (adj.) related to the Council of Trent

> **Tridentine Rite:** a name given to the reform of the Roman rite carried out under Pope Pius V after the Council of Trent

**Pope St. Pius V**

**Mass as said at the time of the Council of Trent**

**St. Charles Borromeo**

Now, Charles Borromeo was not merely the administrator but the archbishop of Milan. In 1565, he left Rome for Milan, where he immediately began reforming the archdiocese. He founded a congregation of priests who were to teach the doctrines of the faith, work as the spiritual directors of nuns, and run colleges and seminaries. He thought seminaries were central to reforming the clergy. During his time in Milan, he founded three theological seminaries, three preparatory seminaries (for those too young to enter a theological seminary), as well as a college for priests from Switzerland. Pope Pius V appointed Borromeo to visit other dioceses and help them in their own reforms.

St. Charles Borromeo was also known for his great charity. When plague struck Milan in 1576, he turned his episcopal palace into a hospital. He himself helped nurse the sick, heard their confessions, and gave them last rites. He died in 1584, when he was only 46. When news of Charles's death reached Pope Gregory XIII, the pontiff reportedly said, "A light has been extinguished in Israel."

# An "Army" for the Reform

As a young courtier, serving one of King Fernando and Queen Isabel's provincial governors, Iñigo de Loyola was like other courtiers his age. The handsome young man from the Basque region of Spain enjoyed all the pleasures of court life, living in laxity and self-indulgence. Above all, though, Iñigo longed for the glory that can only be won in battle. Like the medieval knights, he sought honor and fame—the praise of men and the regard of ladies.

In 1517, Iñigo entered the army and spent the next few years fighting the French on the northern borders of Spain. But Iñigo's life was not to follow the course he had mapped out for it. In 1521, while he was leading the defense of Pamplona against the attacking French, a cannon ball smashed into his right shin, breaking it. The French took Iñigo to his father's castle of Loyola, where he had been born. There he had to undergo the pain of having his leg rebroken and set, as well as having a protruding bone sawed off. He endured all this without uttering a cry of pain.

After this operation, Iñigo was confined to bed. Bored, he requested a book—the kind of book that delighted him most, a tale of knightly adventures. When such a book could not be found in the castle, he had to content himself with reading a book about the lives of saints and their miracles—a medieval work called the *Golden Legend*—and another about the life of Christ. At first these works pleased him little; but gradually they inspired him with a desire for a glory different from the sort he had longed for before. Iñigo began to dream of the glory won by the saints in service of Christ.

Engraving of St. Ignatius of Loyola

Abbey of Montserrat near Barcelona, Spain

Iñigo began to lead a life of penance. As the faithful had done for centuries, he went on pilgrimage, to the Benedictine abbey of Montserrat. There, abandoning his sword (and all his dreams of military glory) at the altar, he donned sackcloth—the poor dress of a pilgrim. A few miles from the abbey, near the town of Manresa, Iñigo found a cave. He remained there, living a life of prayer, for nearly the entire year of 1522.

The next year, calling himself now Ignatius, the soldier-turned-penitent set off on a pilgrimage to the Holy Land. He remained there, suffering many trials, until 1524. Upon returning to Spain, Ignatius felt the need for education. He went to Latin school in Barcelona, where he was the only adult among the children. From there he attended the University of Alcalá, near Madrid. At Alcalá, Ignatius was imprisoned for six weeks for teaching the Faith to children without permission. At the University of Salamanca, where he went after Alcalá, he was imprisoned again because he was suspected of holding heretical ideas. After being declared innocent and released from prison, Ignatius left Spain in 1528 and journeyed to what was then the greatest university in Europe—the University of Paris.

At Paris, besides studying philosophy, Ignatius spent time in prayer and in doing works of charity. He persuaded some of his fellow students to do the same. These young men were inspired by Ignatius's dream of going to the Holy Land after their studies were completed and living as Christ did. On August 15, 1534, Ignatius and his companions took vows of poverty and chastity. They pledged to go to the Holy Land after they had finished their studies.

In 1537, Ignatius and his companions met in Venice to begin their journey to Palestine. However, they were unable to continue their journey because of a war that was then being fought against the Turks. Instead they journeyed to Rome, where eventually all were ordained priests. There they awaited an opportunity to take ship to the Holy Land.

## The Society of Jesus

A year later, upon finding that they still could not go to Palestine, Ignatius and his companions decided to offer their services to the pope. They called themselves the Company of Jesus—for, like a company of soldiers, they wanted to fight heresy and battle the spirit of immorality and laxity. Pope Paul III accepted the services of these zealous men. Some he appointed as teachers, to others he gave different tasks. Ignatius himself, the pope decided, was to work on a series of meditations he had begun years earlier to help people come to a deeper love for God. These meditations, called

**Pope Paul III formally recognizes the Society of Jesus (St. Ignatius of Loyola kneels before the pope).**

the *Spiritual Exercises*, would be instrumental in renewing a true Christian spirit among many in Europe.

Pope Paul wanted to send Ignatius and his companions as missionaries to different parts of Europe. To carry on this work more perfectly, and to continue their ideals after their deaths, the Company of Jesus decided to form a religious order. According to the rules, or constitutions, it adopted, the Company would function like an army. At its head would be a superior general to whom every member vowed absolute, unquestioning obedience—just like soldiers do their commanders. The superior general was to be subject to no one but the pope. And the company added a further vow—that they would go wherever the pope sent them. The pope would be their "king," and they would be his "army."

Pope Paul III formally recognized the new order on March 14, 1543—though he called it not the Company, but the Society of Jesus. On September 27, Ignatius's companions chose him as their first superior general —which he accepted only when his confessor ordered him to. Critics of the newly formed Society of Jesus called its members "Jesuits"—a name that was then considered an insult. It has, however, become the most common name for members of the Society.

The Jesuits seemed ready-made for the Tridentine reform. Since they were not required to live in community like other religious orders, the members could easily go wherever they were needed. Even during

St. Francis Xavier

Ignatius's lifetime, Jesuits were found throughout Europe. They worked in Catholic lands, such as Spain and Portugal, teaching Catholic doctrine and striving to inspire the faithful with love for Christ and His Church. In many places, Jesuits founded schools and colleges or were asked by rulers to staff existing institutions of learning.

The Jesuits are especially remembered for braving torture and death to minister to Catholics in Queen Elizabeth's England as well as in Scotland. And many Jesuits suffered fearful martyrdoms at the hands of English Protestants. Jesuits went as well into other parts of Protestant Europe to minister to the Catholics living in those lands.

Jesuits went outside the borders of Europe—to Muslim Morocco in North Africa, to minister to enslaved Christians; to Ethiopia and the Congo, as missionaries; to the Spanish and Portuguese lands in Mexico and South America. In 1542, St. Francisco (or Francis) Xavier, one of Ignatius's first companions, landed at the Portuguese stronghold of Goa on the west coast of India. For the next 10 years, Francis—with only his Mass kit, his breviary, and an umbrella to shield him from the tropical sun—traveled through many towns of India, preaching, teaching, and baptizing. In 1547 he went to Japan, where, despite opposition from the Buddhist monks, he baptized many of the people. Francis then decided he must go to China; but he died on December 2, 1552, before accomplishing his plan.

When St. Ignatius of Loyola died in Rome in 1556, the Jesuits numbered some 13,000 men. His Society was the most effective force the Church had at the time to carry on the reforms called for by the Council of Trent. The success of the Catholic Reformation was in large part due to these zealous and courageous soldiers of Christ.

# The Turks Halted

The Council of Trent had been called to deal with a threat—Protestantism—that had arisen from within Christendom. Yet, throughout the 18 years of the council, all Christendom continued to face the common threat of the

## "Hammer of the Heretic"

Because of Luther's revolt, much of Germany had become Protestant; and even in regions that had remained Catholic, Protestantism was making inroads. Beginning in the 1550s, however, the Catholic Faith in Germany began a period of renewal that was largely due to the work of a Jesuit priest, St. Peter Canisius, who has been called the "Second Apostle of Germany."

Peter was born in 1521 in Nijmegen in the Netherlands. Although he later accused himself of having wasted his time as a boy, Peter received his Master of Arts degree at Cologne University when he was only 19. During his time at Cologne University, Peter decided he would become a priest. After following the *Spiritual Exercises* under the direction of Blessed Peter Faber, an early follower of St. Ignatius, Canisius vowed to become a Jesuit.

After making his solemn profession as a Jesuit in Rome in 1549, Peter was sent to Germany. In Bavaria, Peter reformed a university. By his inspired preaching, by catechizing, and by a campaign against the sale of immoral and heretical books, he brought about a religious revival among the people. Peter's main work was education. He knew that the Protestants had drawn away many people because they had been ignorant of the Faith. Peter did everything he could to see that Catholics learned the doctrines of the Church.

In 1552, Ignatius sent Peter to Vienna, Austria, where for 20 years no priest had been ordained and only about 10 percent of the people were still practicing Catholics. At first Peter preached to almost empty churches. Then a plague broke out, and Peter tirelessly ministered to the sick and the dying. Seeing his devotion and charity, the Viennese began coming to church to hear his sermons. Though he has been called the "Hammer of the Heretic" for his work in turning many from Protestantism, Peter was never rude with his opponents. He always addressed them with charity and gentleness.

Peter wrote several **catechisms**. The first, published in 1555 and called the *Summary of Christian Doctrine*, was nicknamed the "Short Catechism." After publishing this catechism, he saw the people needed an even simpler one, so he wrote the *Shorter Cate-chism*, and then the *Shortest Catechism*. The catechisms were eventually translated into 25 languages, including English, Hindustani, and Japanese.

Peter helped to found a Jesuit college in Prague, and it was so successful that even Protestants sent their sons there. In Switzerland in 1580 his preaching helped to keep the city of Fribourg Catholic. By his preaching, writing, and work in education—but most of all by his charity—Peter Canisius kept Catholic Germany from becoming Protestant. Indeed, he brought some Germans who had wandered into Protestantism back into the Catholic fold. In 1591 Peter had a stroke that left him partially paralyzed; but he recovered enough to continue writing until his death on November 21, 1597.

**catechism:** an explanation of the doctrines of the Faith

Ottoman Turks. Though the Ottoman Turks had been prevented from conquering Vienna, they had not gone away. That even Protestants felt this threat is indicated in the first lines of a "children's song" by Martin Luther:

*Lord, keep us in Thy Word and work,*
*Restrain the murderous pope and Turk,*
*Who fain would tear from off Thy throne*
*Christ Jesus, Thy beloved Son.*

It was Catholic and Orthodox Europe, however, that continued to bear the brunt of Turkish attack. When the Ottoman sultan Suleiman the Magnificent died in 1566, he was succeeded by his son, Selim II. Wanting to imitate his father's conquests, Sultan Selim began in 1570 to launch ambitious plans to expand the Turkish Empire across Europe. By 1571, Ottoman forces had conquered the Orthodox island of Cyprus, where they killed thousands of Cypriot Christians and sold many of the women and young men into slavery.

**The Battle of Lepanto**

The same year he conquered Cyprus, Selim II plotted another invasion, this time of Italy. The sultan began to assemble a large fleet that, when launched, would carry an invading force of nearly 50,000 soldiers and sailors.

In response to the gathering threat, Pope Pius V sent out an appeal to Europe's monarchs to unite in a Holy League against the Turks. But of all the Christian kingdoms, only Genoa, Venice, and Spain responded with ships and men. These, joined with ships from the Papal States, were placed under the supreme command of Don Juan of Austria, the half-brother of King Philip II of Spain. Don Juan received from the pope's representative a huge banner bearing the figure of Christ Crucified, to unfurl on the day of the battle. The pope asked all of Christian Europe to pray the rosary for victory. When the assembled fleet sailed from Messina harbor (on the northern tip of Sicily) on September 16, sailors and soldiers alike carried rosaries.

On October 7, 1571, the Christian and Turkish fleets clashed in a great sea battle on the western coast of Greece, near the Gulf of Corinth, then called Lepanto. The Turkish ships sailed in a crescent formation in hopes of flanking the Christian fleet. However, the Christian admirals at Lepanto, seeing this maneuver, avoided the trap.

Even though the Christian ships were outnumbered by the Turkish fleet, they were much more heavily armed with cannon and musketry. As the Turkish ships approached, they met a hailstorm of cannon fire and musket volleys. On board the Christian ships, priests said Mass and gave general absolution. Don Juan went from ship to ship holding a crucifix and telling the men, "Live or die, we are here to conquer or to die, as heaven chooses." Then he hung the crucifix on the mast of his flagship, the *Ciudad Real*.

**Map of the Battle of Lepanto**

**galley:** a ship or boat propelled solely or chiefly by oars

The Turks held hundreds of Christian captives chained to the oars of their **galleys** in a horrible and terrifying captivity. When a galley went down, the chained slaves went down with it. It appears that at Lepanto, the galley slaves helped prevent their Turkish masters from attaining the speed they needed to ram the Christian ships; the slaves rowed only half-heartedly and fouled the oars as much as they could get away with.

These captive Christians could hear the sounds of the chanted rosary coming across the water, for the crews of the Christian ships sang as they fought. It was said that a vision of the Blessed Virgin appeared above the Turkish fleet as the Christians drew close to it. Inspired by this vision, the Christian mariners charged over the rails against the foe.

Don Juan's ship sailed straight toward the *Sultana*, the flagship of the Muslim commander, Ali Pasha. The *Sultana* was the first to be boarded after the two ships collided, and a two-hour struggle began. On decks awash with blood, the Spanish sailors and marines pushed the surviving Turks over the ship's rails and then raised the banner of Christ Crucified on the *Sultana*'s mast.

The Battle of Lepanto ended at 4 p.m. when what remained of the Turkish fleet sailed away toward Istanbul (Constantinople). The Christians, who had lost only 17 ships, captured 177 Turkish ships and destroyed 15 others. Twelve thousand Christian galley slaves were liberated; many more may have been lost to the seas as their ships sank.

Don Juan of Austria's fleet had won a great victory against the Turks and halted their invasion of Europe. The Turkish fleet was not destroyed at Lepanto, but thereafter it was no longer the threat it had been. Europe had once more been saved from Ottoman conquest.

## Religious War in France

Catherine de Medici

By 1589, France had undergone over 40 years of religious struggle and war. Though its people were mostly Catholic, France also had a large population of Protestants who were followers of John Calvin. Many Frenchmen had gone to Calvin in Geneva, in the French-speaking region of Switzerland. From Geneva, the French Calvinists had returned to France to spread their "reformed" religion.

The kings of France had made it difficult, however, for Protestantism to spread in the kingdom. Though King Francis I (Emperor Charles V's old enemy) supported the Lutheran princes in Germany, he was vigorous in trying to stamp out Calvinism in France. Francis's son, King Henry II, had carried on his father's work. Throughout France the king was aided by magistrates who tried those teaching heretical doctrines and sentenced those convicted of heresy to be burned at the stake.

Yet, despite the efforts against them, the French Protestants increased in number and in power. Beginning in 1547, they began organizing churches in the major French cities, including Paris. It was in Paris in 1559 that Protestant French ministers formed a national church based on the teachings of John Calvin. These French Calvinists, called Huguenots, attracted members of the nobility—including Jeanne d'Albret, the queen of Navarre, and her husband, Antoine de Bourbon. The Huguenots thus had the backing of men of wealth and power.

Attempts to crush Protestantism in France ended when Francis II died in 1560. His younger brother, Charles IX, was only 10 years old when he became king; so the boy's mother, Catherine de Medici, ruled as regent. In an attempt to weaken the Guises, a powerful Catholic noble family, Catherine tried to gain the favor of the powerful Huguenot families. Yet, though she issued edicts granting freedom of religion to the Huguenots, they demanded more favors. At Montpellier, Huguenots rose and massacred about 30 people on October 20, 1561, and committed several other murders besides. Catholics under the Duke of Guise retaliated by slaying 23 Huguenots and wounding more than 100 others at Vassy on March 1, 1562. These slayings marked the beginning of all-out religious war.

16th century map of France

Wars, known as the "Wars of Religion," between the Huguenot and Catholic forces continued until 1563. The conflict broke out again in 1567 and continued to 1570, when Catherine again allowed the Huguenots freedom to practice their religion in certain cities and other locations in France. She even married her daughter to a prominent Huguenot named Henry de Bourbon, who became king of Navarre in 1572. Catherine, however, tried to have the Huguenot leader, Admiral de Coligny, assassinated—and when that failed, she ordered a mass killing of the Huguenot leaders on the Feast of St. Bartholomew, August 24, 1572. The ringing of church bells was the signal for the massacre, in which Coligny and his followers were slaughtered. Henry de Bourbon escaped their fate by promising to become Catholic. Like a wave, the massacre spread from Paris (where about 2,000 Huguenots had been killed by mobs) to other French cities and towns, where thousands more were slain. But instead of weakening the Huguenots, these massacres only stiffened their resolve to resist.

When Charles IX died in 1576, his brother, Henry III, became king. Like his mother Catherine had done, Henry granted favors to the Huguenots—including the right to hold public office. In response, Catholics, led by Henry de Guise, formed the Catholic League to defend the Faith. Warfare broke out between the League and the Huguenots, led by Henry de Bourbon, who had again become Protestant. Conflict ended in 1580, leaving the Huguenots with the same freedoms they had before.

St. Bartholomew's Day Massacre

Though he made himself head of the Catholic League, Henry III at times favored the Protestants because he feared the power and influence of the Guise family. When the king in 1588 assassinated Henry de Guise, the people of Paris became so enraged that they drove the king from the city. Fleeing south to Chartres, Henry III made an alliance with Henry de Bourbon. But before the two Henrys could march on Paris, the king was killed by a mad Dominican monk named Jacques Clément. Henry III's death brought to an end the House of Valois, which had ruled France since 1328.

## The Bourbons and the Edict of Nantes

Clément murdered Henry III because he believed the king was an enemy of the Catholic Faith. Yet, the next in line to the throne was none other than the Huguenot king of Navarre, Henry de Bourbon. The Catholic League refused to acknowledge Henry de Bourbon—now Henry IV—as king, and for four years civil war again bloodied France. Finally, seeing he could not rule France and remain a Protestant, Henry IV renounced his heresy before the archbishop of Bourges at the basilica of St. Denis in Paris on July 25, 1593. In this way, Henry firmly established his new dynasty, the House of Bourbon, over France.

The Huguenot threat did not disappear when Henry IV became Catholic. Indeed, the Huguenots had regrouped and were set to establish a republic in the heart of the kingdom of France. But instead of trying to crush this conspiracy with war, Henry IV came to an agreement with the Huguenots in what is called the Edict of Nantes. Upon being signed in 1598, the Edict of Nantes granted Protestants the freedom to hold their religious beliefs and the right to worship in the places where they had been worshipping up to 1597, as well as at other specified locations. The edict granted Protestants equal rights with Catholics in holding public offices, and turned 100 fortresses over to them for a period of eight years. Public tax money went to pay the soldiers who manned these fortresses. Neither Catholics nor Huguenots were entirely satisfied with the Edict of Nantes, but it stopped for a time the religious violence that had afflicted France.

When Henry IV was assassinated in 1610, his eight-year-old son, Louis XIII, became king. During the early years of Louis's reign, the Huguenots—dissatisfied with the Edict of Nantes and fearing an alliance between the king and Catholic Spain—again rose in rebellion. The king's forces were able to seize several rebellious towns but could not conquer the Huguenot city of Montauban in southwestern France. In 1622 the king signed a treaty that renewed the Edict of Nantes and gave the Huguenots complete control of Montauban and La Rochelle, a port city on the western coast of France.

Henry IV

## The Rise of Richelieu

As long as the Huguenots held political and military power in France, they remained a real threat to the peace and unity of the kingdom. No one, king or Catholic nobleman, had found a solution to the Huguenot problem. In 1624, however, the king appointed Cardinal Richelieu to be prime minister. It was the able and energetic Richelieu who finally ended the religious wars in France and set the stage for the establishment of a strong French kingdom, united under its sovereign.

*Armand-Jean du Plessis, Cardinal and Duke of Richelieu, by Philippe de Champaign*

Armand-Jean du Plessis de Richelieu was born September 9, 1585, the third son of a minor nobleman. When Armand was only five, his father died, leaving his estates nearly bankrupt. Through Armand-Jean's mother's influence, in 1605 King Henry IV named the young Richelieu bishop of Luçon, a diocese near La Rochelle that was controlled by the Richelieu family. Richelieu was both pious and ambitious. Intent on making his diocese both holy and orderly, he was the first bishop in France to implement the reforms of Trent. But Richelieu was ruthless and single-minded in the pursuit of his policies, and he believed intensely not only in God, but France.

As prime minister, Richelieu (who had been made a cardinal in 1622) worked tirelessly to make the king the absolute power in the state. Because Cardinal Richelieu believed that "the king receives his crown and his temporal power from God alone," he viewed all disobedience to the king as sin. In time, Richelieu even came to hold that the Church in France was subject to the king in all areas except doctrine. The pope had the authority, Richelieu thought, to make laws for the entire Church; but the king could force the Church in France to pay taxes and could even take Church lands. Richelieu, thus, became a defender of Gallicanism.

The Huguenots were the first obstacle to the king's power, and Richelieu soon found an occasion to crush them. In the south of France, the Huguenots again rose in rebellion; and in 1627, an English fleet with 10,000 men attempted to land at the Huguenot city of La Rochelle to aid the Protestants. Acting quickly, Richelieu and Louis XIII led a force to La Rochelle, drove off the English, and laid siege to the city. Unable to receive aid from the English or its Huguenot allies, La Rochelle surrendered to the cardinal. Richelieu granted the Huguenots in the city complete religious freedom but forced them to give up their political and military power.

Richelieu's war with the Huguenots lasted another two years after the fall of La Rochelle. Finally, in 1629, both sides signed the Peace of Alais. The Peace granted the Huguenots full religious and civil liberty but forbade them to control towns or fortresses or hold political assemblies. Basically, the Peace of Alais ended the political power of the Huguenots in France. Never again would they be a threat to the peace of the kingdom.

# A Tragedy for Europe

Cardinal Richelieu wanted not only to make his king all-powerful in France, but to make France the supreme nation in Europe. To do this, Richelieu had to weaken the power of the Habsburgs, the most powerful ruling family in Europe.

Indeed, the Habsburgs were most powerful. The Habsburg archduke of Austria was king over Bohemia and Hungary, as well as the emperor ruling, in title at least, over all Germany. His cousin, the Habsburg king of Spain, ruled the Netherlands, northern Italy, Naples, and the vast Spanish dominions in North and South America, rich with gold and silver. Habsburg lands surrounded France to the west and the south, and Spanish fleets could attack France at any port on its long Atlantic coastline.

So powerful were the Habsburgs, so completely did they surround France, that Richelieu could not simply declare war on them. But he could

Map of Habsburg domains at the beginning of the Thirty Years' War

take advantage of Habsburg troubles and use them to weaken Habsburg power. And the Austrian Habsburgs soon had plenty of trouble. It all began with a revolt in Bohemia.

Bohemia had long been among the most important, and troublesome, states of the German Roman Empire. Centered on the city of Prague, Bohemia was the empire's wealthiest and most productive region. Its agriculture and mines produced the wealth that paid for most of the imperial expenses. Bohemia—the home of John Hus—had, however, experienced a good deal of unrest. Even into the 17th century, many Hussites still lived there, and Protestantism had made many inroads among both the German- and Czech-speaking populations. For this reason, many in Bohemia wanted nothing to do with the Catholic Habsburgs. They wanted a Protestant king.

In 1612 Matthias von Habsburg, the archduke of Austria, became both Roman emperor and king of Bohemia. The old and sickly Matthias, however, had no children and so named his cousin, Ferdinand von Habsburg, to succeed him as emperor as well as king of Bohemia. It was important, if he were to become emperor, that Ferdinand become king of Bohemia, for the Bohemian king was one of the seven imperial prince electors. Of these electors, three were Catholic and three were Protestant. As the seventh elector, the king of Bohemia would cast the deciding vote for emperor. If the king of Bohemia were a Protestant, the electors might end up choosing a Protestant—and a non-Habsburg—as emperor.

Though the Protestant Bohemian nobles at first accepted Ferdinand as their future king, in May 1618, they rose in revolt against him and Emperor Matthias. Instead of Ferdinand, the Bohemian nobles wanted for their king Frederick, the elector of the Palatinate (a principality on the Rhine River). Frederick was a Calvinist; his father had been the founder of the union of Protestant German princes, called the League of Evangelical Union. Since Frederick was already elector of the Palatinate, by becoming king and elector of Bohemia, he could cast two votes for emperor.

## The Defenestration of Prague

Elector Frederick, however, did not have even the support of his fellow Protestant princes. They backed Ferdinand's claim to Bohemia, for they feared Frederick might become too powerful if he held Bohemia as well as the Palatinate. Yet, though Ferdinand became king of Bohemia, the Bohemian Protestant nobles still supported Elector Frederick. In May 1618, they gathered in a great assembly in Prague. King Ferdinand, who was absent from Prague, sent two of his counselors, Wilhelm Slavata and

and Jaroslav Borsita von Martinitz, as his representatives to the assembly.

Feeling against Ferdinand was strong in Prague. On May 23, 1618, an angry crowd of Protestants gathered at a rally in Prague. Thousands attended, and the rally grew violent. Calling for the death of Ferdinand's two representatives, the Protestants rushed to the royal castle in Prague, where the Habsburg governing council was meeting.

After storming the castle, the mob grabbed Slavata and Martinitz and dragged them toward a high window overlooking a moat 50 feet below. The king's counselors struggled for their lives, praying aloud to the Mother of God. According to one account of the event, as the mob pushed Ferdinand's counselors out the window, someone taunted, "We will see if your Mary can help you!" A few seconds later, another exclaimed, "By God, his Mary has helped!" The two councilors had fallen on top of a thick pile of manure. Martinitz was unhurt, except for his dignity; Slavata was knocked unconscious but recovered.

The Defenestration of Prague

This peculiar event, called the "**Defenestration** of Prague," marked the beginning of a long and bitter conflict. Known as the Thirty Years' War, this conflict was one of the greatest tragedies in European history.

**defenestration:** from *to defenestrate*, meaning "to throw from a window" (from the Latin *de*, meaning "from," and *fenestra*, meaning "window")

## The Bohemian Revolt

Following the defenestration of the king's counselors, Protestant Bohemian nobles rose in revolt against Ferdinand and Emperor Matthias. When Matthias died in March 1619, the Hungarians and Moravians joined the Bohemian revolt and advanced on Vienna, the Habsburg capital. When, however, the Austrians would not join the rebels, the invaders withdrew to Bohemia. There, the Protestant Bohemian nobles elected Elector Frederick as their king.

Despite the rebellion, Ferdinand was elected emperor on August 28, 1619. The new emperor's first task was to deal with the Bohemian rebellion. Ferdinand II received the powerful support of Bavaria's Catholic king, Maximilian, the leader of the Catholic League of German princes. Polish forces and Spanish armies from Ferdinand's Habsburg cousin, King Philip IV of Spain, joined in the war against Bohemia, as did the Protestant

**Johannes Tserclaes, Count von Tilly,** by Sir Anthony Van Dyck

joined the Bohemians. Imperial forces kept these princes from joining with Frederick in Bohemia, and Catholic League troops, under the command of Johannes Tserclaes, Count von Tilly, a Bavarian nobleman and military leader, advanced into Bohemia. In 1620, at White Mountain, near Prague, Tilly defeated the Protestant Bohemian army. Emperor Ferdinand II confiscated the estates of the rebellious Bohemian noblemen and distributed them among Catholic lords. Elector Frederick, called the "Winter King" because of his short reign over Bohemia, fled to the Palatinate.

From Bohemia, the fighting then turned to the Rhine River Valley and northern Germany. Here the war raged until June 1622, when Tilly and the forces of the Catholic League almost destroyed the Protestant army at Höchst. His army defeated, Frederick the Winter King went into exile. Emperor Ferdinand gave the Palatinate to King Maximilian of Bavaria and made him a prince elector. By the fall of 1623, the Bohemian revolt was finally crushed, and Tilly was victorious in northern Germany. The war, too, should have ended at that point. But it did not.

**Count Albrecht von Wallenstein**

## Foreign Powers Intervene

The war did not end, because foreign powers got involved. France's prime minister, Cardinal Richelieu, saw the war in Germany as an opportunity to weaken the Habsburgs. He began negotiating with Protestant German princes and with the Lutheran king of Denmark, Christian IV (who was also the count of Holstein in northern Germany and thus a prince of the empire). England, too, encouraged Christian IV to invade Germany on the Protestant side and thus continue the war. Christian IV took command of the Protestant forces and invaded Germany in 1625.

Emperor Ferdinand knew King Maximilian's Catholic League forces were not strong enough to withstand Denmark and the Protestant princes together. He needed to raise a second army. At this point, a Catholic Bohemian nobleman, Albrecht von Wallenstein, stepped forward. He offered to raise troops for the emperor and support them at his own expense. The desperate Ferdinand accepted Wallenstein's offer.

Both Wallenstein's army and that of his opponent, the Protestant commander, Ernst von Mansfeld, were made up of mercenaries—soldiers who fought for pay, not patriotism. Mansfeld had earlier raised a force of 50,000 mercenaries, and now Wallenstein did the same. Neither the Protestant nor Catholic mercenary armies carried enough food to support themselves. Instead, they lived off the countryside—by **plundering** and **pillaging**, taking food from the farms and people. By the end of the war, the armies' policy of living off the land had left Germany in ruins. Its people could not replant their crops or rebuild their herds, their houses had been burned, and their villages were destroyed.

**Germany and Bohemia during the Thirty Years' War**

While Tilly marched his forces against King Christian, Wallenstein faced off with Mansfeld. On April 25, 1626, Mansfeld was defeated as he attacked Wallenstein at Dessau on the Elbe River. Four months later, Tilly defeated Christian IV in a 10-day battle at Lütter-am-Barenberge in the northern German state of Brunswick. In that battle, Christian IV lost more than half his army. After Tilly again defeated Christian IV in another battle, the Danish king abandoned the war. The emperor and the Catholic League were again victorious.

## The Edict of Restitution

After 11 years of fighting, it seemed the war was over. The Protestants had been decisively defeated. Ferdinand II now thought he could force the Protestant princes to return lands that had been seized from the

**plunder:** taking the goods and food of a place
**pillage:** to plunder ruthlessly

Church over a period of nearly 75 years. The seizing of these lands had been illegal, for it violated the Peace of Augsburg, which the emperor and the German princes had signed in 1555. Confident in his victory over his enemies, Ferdinand on March 6, 1629 issued the Edict of Restitution, which required the Protestants to return all of the Church lands they had taken since the Peace of Augsburg.

Not surprisingly, the Protestant princes opposed Ferdinand's edict. The edict threatened the economic and social order across Germany. Lands and property held by Protestants for over half a century were taken from their owners, many of whom thus faced financial ruin. The edict, too, weakened the emperor's cause. Because of the edict, some Protestant princes who had supported Ferdinand up until 1629 now joined his enemies. The edict, though just, was not wise. Its effect was to undermine the gains Ferdinand had thus far made in the war.

### Sweden Renews the War

By 1629, it appeared that Emperor Ferdinand and the Catholic League had broken the power of the German Protestant princes. But once again, foreign powers interfered. Fearing the possible destruction of the Protestant cause in Germany and hoping to seize some of the northern German states

**Gustavus II Adolphus, at the Battle of Breitenfeld**

for himself, the Lutheran king of Sweden, Gustavus II Adolphus, decided to enter the war.

France had been encouraging Gustavus Adolphus to join the German Protestant cause. Cardinal Richelieu thought that if the king of Sweden were successful against the emperor, the Protestant German states could separate from Austria and its Habsburg rulers. The empire then would be permanently divided and the Habsburg power weakened. At the same time he was trying to undermine the emperor, Richelieu made a treaty with the Protestant Netherlands, whose people were revolting against their overlord, the Habsburg king of Spain.

Gustavus Adolphus was a valuable ally to the Protestant German princes. He had equipped a new army of soldiers who were trained to use the most modern firearms and rapid horse-cavalry attacks. In June 1630, Gustavus's army landed in Germany. To resist the Swedish king, Emperor Ferdinand needed the aid of the German princes—but even the Catholic princes had grown dissatisfied with Ferdinand. In particular they feared that, with Wallenstein and his powerful mercenary army, the emperor could become all-powerful in Germany. To enlist the princes' support, Ferdinand agreed to dismiss Wallenstein. The command of the imperial and Catholic League forces went to Tilly, now an old and sickly man. In August 1630, the German electors agreed to support the emperor. Later, however, the Protestant electors, including the powerful elector of Saxony, withdrew their pledge and joined forces with the Swedes.

In January 1631, Cardinal Richelieu agreed to fund Gustavus Adolphus if he pledged to carry on war against Ferdinand for a period of four years. But, at first, Gustavus Adolphus would not join battle with Tilly; so, instead of fighting the Swedes, Tilly laid siege to the important city and fortress of Magdeburg. On May 20, 1631, as Tilly stormed Magdeburg, the city went up in flames, possibly as a result of arson. The city's destruction was so great that Tilly had no base and no food supply for his army, and he retreated toward southern Germany. Protestants blamed the fire on Tilly, who became known in central Germany as "the Butcher of Magdeburg."

It was not until September 1631 that Tilly met Gustavus Adolphus on the field of battle, at Breitenfeld in Saxony. The combined armies of Gustavus Adolphus and the elector of Saxony destroyed Tilly's army, opening the way for an invasion of Bavaria. After Tilly's defeat, Ferdinand once again appointed Wallenstein as commander of the imperial army, leaving the Catholic League forces under Tilly's command. But Wallenstein did nothing as Gustavus Adolphus's rapidly moving army marched south toward Bavaria. The Swedish army drove Tilly's forces

**Magdeburg as it appeared in the 17th century**

from the field in a battle on the Lech River in Bavaria on April 15, 1632, and Tilly was mortally wounded.

After Tilly's death, Wallenstein alone was left to defend the imperial cause. But Wallenstein avoided fighting Gustavus Adolphus. It was not until November 16, 1632, that the Swedish king forced Wallenstein into battle at Lützen in Saxony. The fight, however, went against the Swedes. Shortly before noon that day, Gustavus Adolphus himself was struck in the arm by a musket ball as he led a cavalry charge. He fell to the ground—his men fled—and he was left on the field. The young king may have bled to death as he lay wounded, or he may have been killed by an enemy foot soldier. Only on the day following the battle did the Swedish army learn that Gustavus Adolphus had died. The Swedish king, who had become known for his gallantry and mercy to captives, had achieved the legend of a hero in his short lifetime. Catholic and Protestant Europe alike fondly remembered the dashing young king, mounted on his horse at the head of a cavalry charge.

The death of Gustavus Adolphus did not end the war. Swedish troops under a new commander remained in Germany and threatened Bavaria and Austria. Meanwhile, Wallenstein was carrying on secret negotiations with the Swedes and did little fighting. Reports reached the emperor that Wallenstein was plotting with his enemies. When presented with evidence of Wallenstein's treason, Ferdinand openly considered assassinating the general. Whether by Ferdinand's order or due to some private feud with one of his own officers, Wallenstein was murdered on February 24, 1634, while lying ill in bed.

After Wallenstein's death, the Catholic League and imperial armies fought on under the duke of Lorraine and the emperor's son, Ferdinand III. On September 6, 1634, they met the Swedes in battle at Nördlingen and soundly defeated them. The finely trained Swedish army was destroyed. Swedish troops remained in Germany, but never again were they the fighting force they had been under Gustavus Adolphus.

Yet, despite the imperial victory at Nördlingen, the war did not end. Once again Cardinal Richelieu interfered. But this time, Richelieu would not rely on other nations in his attempt to shatter the Habsburg power. Instead, on May 19, 1635, France itself declared war on the emperor and on the emperor's ally and cousin, Philip IV of Spain.

## Richelieu Unleashes Destruction

The threat of France entering the war convinced the elector of Saxony to make peace with the emperor. Ferdinand II tried to get other Protestant princes to follow the elector's example, and in the Treaty of Prague, he granted amnesty to all princes who consented to sign it. The treaty was an attempt to unite Germany against the French foe—and several Protestant princes did indeed sign it on May 30, 1635. But other Protestant princes decided to continue supporting the Swedes and their ally, Cardinal Richelieu.

Richelieu's strategy was twofold. France would help fund the Swedes and the Protestant princes in their war against Ferdinand in Germany, while France itself would attack the territories of Habsburg Spain. Thus, while France's allies continued fighting in Germany, French armies moved against the Spanish-controlled Netherlands (or the "Spanish Netherlands" —the southern Netherlands, modern-day Belgium), Franche Comté (a territory of Burgundy in France), and northern Italy as well as Spain itself. So violent were the French attacks that eventually, King Philip IV of Spain could no longer send troops to help the emperor against the German Protestants—which was just what Richelieu wanted to happen.

At first, the Spanish had a far superior army and were victorious against the French. In 1636, a large Spanish force invaded northern France and nearly captured Paris itself. The following year, a Spanish army crossed the Pyrenees Mountains and invaded southern France.

Gradually, however, the French began to score victories against the Spanish. France defeated Spain's armies in the Netherlands because the Spanish had little local support there. (Ten provinces in the northern

**King Philip IV of Spain**

Netherlands had already declared themselves independent of Spain under their prince, William II of Orange.) By 1640, Philip IV was in deep trouble. Portugal, which Philip II had made part of Spain, revolted, as did Aragon and Naples in southern Italy. Philip IV was able to crush all these rebellions except the one in Portugal, and he even held on to the Belgian Netherlands. But in 1643, a French army destroyed the Spanish army at Rocroi in the Netherlands. By 1646, the Spanish held only a few large cities in the Belgian Netherlands.

In Germany, the emperor and his allies had been able to hold off the Swedes and the Protestant princes. But the weakening of Spain allowed Richelieu to send more and more French forces into Germany. The war in Germany now grew especially violent and lost any religious character it may have had. It had become a political struggle, with Protestants fighting with the emperor and Catholics fighting on the side of the Protestants. Neither side showed any Christian charity to the civilian population, which was caught between the contending armies. French, Swedish, and Protestant armies on the one hand, and the imperial and Catholic League armies on the other, ravaged Germany. They burned houses, massacred inhabitants, destroyed livestock, and ruined crops. Both sides said such destruction was the necessary consequence of the "religious" disagreement. The "enemy" was expected to suffer and pay for his "opposition to the Truth."

Richelieu did not live to see the results of the warfare he had unleashed. In the fall of 1642 the cardinal, who had always been sickly, fell seriously ill. The elderly King Louis XIII, who had feared Richelieu and done his bidding, now personally attended the sick man, feeding him egg yolks from the royal spoon because the cardinal could not digest solid food. On December 4, 1642, Richelieu died after passing on his office to Cardinal Jules Mazarin—a man as committed as Richelieu had been to making France supreme in Europe.

With Mazarin as prime minister of France, the war continued. Yet, only a year after Richelieu's death, the first moves toward peace were made. Emperor Ferdinand II, who had died in 1637, had been succeeded by his son, Ferdinand III. The German states desired peace, and in 1643 they convinced Ferdinand III to open peace talks with the French and Swedes.

The talks, however, did not begin until late 1644, and it was August 1645 before Spain and the Netherlands joined in.

For the next three years peace talks continued, but so did the war. In 1646, the Swedes and the French occupied Bavaria, forcing Elector Maximilian to sign a treaty with Sweden. By 1647 the French and the Swedes controlled the entire empire, except for the Habsburg lands of Austria, Bohemia, and Hungary. Ferdinand wanted to make a separate peace with Sweden so he could continue to aid his cousin Philip IV in his war against France; but Sweden refused to agree to a peace treaty without France. Left with the choice of continuing the war or making peace with France and thus abandoning Spain, Ferdinand chose peace. Philip IV of Spain would have to fight on against France without help from his Austrian Habsburg cousin.

## The Peace of Westphalia

The Thirty Years' War finally ended with the Peace of Westphalia, which was signed after long negotiations on October 24, 1648. Under the

**The swearing of the oath to ratify the final treaty of the Peace of Westphalia**

agreement, though Ferdinand III still held the title of emperor, the German states became practically independent of his power. Ferdinand, however, still held control of Austria, Bohemia, and Hungary, which, in the future, would form a strong Habsburg-controlled state. But the German empire, from then on, would be an empire only in name.

More important and lasting than the parts of the Peace having to do with the empire were those that touched on religion. For the first time, the empire was forced to recognize Calvinism alongside Lutheranism and the Catholic Church as an official religion. But more significant than this was the provision stating that all states that had been Protestant in 1624 would remain Protestant, and all states then Catholic would remain Catholic. This provision made the religious division of Germany permanent and signified that any hope of reuniting Christendom had been openly abandoned.

The Thirty Years' War was thus a great tragedy for Europe as a whole and Germany in particular. That land was devastated. Whole provinces were left uninhabitable wastelands, and almost half of the population of Germany had been killed. It took nearly 150 years for Germany to recover economically to the level of prosperity it had enjoyed before the conflict.

France's war with Spain continued until 1659. Abandoned by Ferdinand III, his cousin for whom he had sacrificed so much, Philip IV, with the Spanish, fought bravely on. The Spanish cause, however, was hopeless. Portugal and England joined France against Spain. The Spanish treasury was empty, and vast numbers of Spanish soldiers had been killed in the long war. When the war ended in 1659, Spain, once the richest and strongest state in Europe, had become one of the poorest and weakest.

Richelieu's supreme goal had been achieved, though he did not live to enjoy his victory. France came out of the Thirty Years' War the most powerful nation in Europe. But to achieve this, France had forced Europe to pay an enormous price—the permanent dismemberment of Christendom into Protestant and Catholic states.

# Chapter Review

### Summary
- The Council of Trent met on and off from 1545 to 1563. The council addressed both doctrinal issues and Church reform.
- The Council of Trent began a movement of Church reform and renewal that has been called the Counter-Reformation, or, better, the Catholic Reformation.

- Reform of the Church began before, and continued during and after, the council. The reform was carried through by the pope, bishops, and by religious orders, particularly the Society of Jesus.
- Ignatius de Loyola had dreamed only of military glory; but, after being injured in battle, he began to dream of serving Christ. At the University of Paris, he inspired other young men to follow his example. In Rome, they offered their services to the pope and formed a new religious order called the Society of Jesus, or the Jesuits. The Jesuits were an important force in carrying the Catholic Reformation forward.
- By his preaching, writing, and work in education—but most of all by his charity—St. Peter Canisius saved Catholic Germany from Protestantism and brought many Protestant Germans back into the Church.
- By 1571, the Ottoman sultan Selim II had conquered the island of Cyprus and launched a large fleet for an invasion of Italy. A Christian fleet under Don Juan of Austria defeated the Turkish fleet at the Battle of Lepanto on October 7, 1571.
- Religious civil war between Calvinists (called Huguenots) and Catholics troubled France from 1547 to 1597. In 1598, the first Bourbon king of France, Henry IV, issued the Edict of Nantes, granting religious and political liberty to the Huguenots. The Huguenots continued to threaten the unity of France until 1629, when, after the capture of La Rochelle, King Louis XIII and Cardinal Richelieu signed the Peace of Alais with the Huguenots. In the Peace of Alais, Louis XIII and Richelieu gave the Huguenots full religious liberty but ended their political and military power.
- The Protestant nobles of Bohemia did not want Ferdinand von Habsburg as their king. Choosing, instead, the Calvinist Frederick, elector of the Palatinate, the nobles revolted against Ferdinand, who in 1619 became the German emperor. With the aid of King Maximilian of Bavaria and the army of the Catholic League, Ferdinand II defeated Frederick and the Bohemians at the Battle of White Mountain in 1620. The Bohemian revolt finally ended in 1623.
- With the encouragement of England and France, King Christian IV of Denmark invaded Germany in 1625, joining forces with the Protestant German princes against the emperor and the Catholic League. Albrecht von Wallenstein's mercenary army and the Catholic League army under Tilly defeated the Protestant and Danish forces. In 1626, Christian IV withdrew from the war.

- After the defeat of Christian IV and his Protestant allies, Emperor Ferdinand issued the Edict of Restitution, which said that the Protestant princes had to return all the lands they had seized from the Church since 1555. The edict weakened the emperor's cause, for it turned many of the Protestant princes who had supported him against him.
- In 1631, King Gustavus II Adolphus of Sweden began his war of conquest in Germany. In 1632 he defeated Count Tilly's Catholic League forces, but Gustavus himself was defeated by Wallenstein at the Battle of Lützen. The Swedish king died in this battle. In 1634, the combined imperial and Catholic League forces defeated the Swedes at Nördlingen.
- In 1635, France under Cardinal Richelieu declared war on the Habsburg emperor and his cousin, King Philip IV of Spain. At first the Spanish scored victories against the French, but gradually Spain lost its advantage. Aided by rebellions in Spain and Naples, the French began defeating Spanish armies. French forces began pouring into Germany to aid the Protestant princes and the Swedes. By 1647 the entire empire, except for the Habsburg lands, was under the control of the Swedes and the French.
- The Peace of Westphalia, signed October 24, 1648, made the German princes practically independent of the emperor. More importantly, however, the Peace made the religious division of Christendom into Protestant and Catholic camps permanent.
- The war between France and Spain continued until 1659. At war's end, the Spanish power had been crushed. France became the most powerful nation in Europe.

### Key Concepts

**Counter-Reformation:** the common name for the Catholic Renewal and Reform of the 16th and 17th centuries

**Ultramontane:** the name given to those who favored strong papal control over national churches (from *ultra*, meaning "beyond" or "on the other side," and *mons, montes*, meaning "mountains"—"on the other side of the mountains" or the Alps)

**Holy Office:** the "Inquisition," a congregation of the curia that issued doctrinal decrees and condemned heretical teachings. Its purpose was to protect the purity of the Catholic Faith.

**Index of Forbidden Books (*Index librorum prohibitorum*):** the list of those books the Church considered dangerous to the Catholic Faith and forbade Catholics to read

**catechism:** an explanation of the doctrines of the Faith
**Tridentine Rite:** a name given to the reform of the Roman rite carried out under Pope Pius V after the Council of Trent
**Society of Jesus:** the order founded by St. Ignatius of Loyola, whose members are called Jesuits
**Huguenots:** French Calvinists
**Edict of Nantes:** issued by King Henry IV of France in 1597, the Edict gave the Huguenots freedom of religion and worship, and granted them political and military power. It was later modified by the Peace of Alais, which assured the Huguenots freedom of religion and worship but removed their political and military power.
**Peace of Westphalia:** the 1648 treaty ending the Thirty Years' War; the Peace made the religious division of Germany permanent and indicated that any hope of reuniting Christendom had been openly abandoned.

## Dates to Remember
**1540:** Pope Paul III approves the Society of Jesus
**1545–1563:** the meeting of the Council of Trent
**1559:** French Protestant Huguenots form a national church in France.
**1562:** beginning of all-out war between Huguenots and Catholics in France
**1571:** the Battle of Lepanto
**1589:** Henry de Bourbon becomes king of France.
**1598:** the Edict of Nantes
**1618–1648:** the Thirty Years' War
**1624:** Cardinal Richelieu becomes prime minister of France
**1629:** the Edict of Restitution
**1629:** Peace of Alais ends the Huguenots' political power.
**1632:** Battle of Lützen and the death of Gustavus Adolphus
**1648:** the Peace of Westphalia
**1659:** end of the war between France and Spain

## Central Characters
**Paul III (1468–1549):** the pope who convened the Council of Trent
**Pius IV (1499–1565):** the pope who carried the Council through to its end
**St. Charles Borromeo (1538–1584):** nephew of Pope Pius IV and the reforming archbishop of Milan
**St. Pius V (1504–1572):** the pope who called on European powers to resist the Turkish invasion of Italy that led to the Christian victory at Lepanto in 1571; responsible for reform of the liturgy after the Council of Trent
**St. Ignatius of Loyola (1491–1556):** founder of the Jesuits

**St. Peter Canisius (1521–1597):** Jesuit priest, known as the Second Apostle of Germany for his work in renewing the life of the Catholic Church in Germany

**Don Juan of Austria (1547–1578):** son of King Philip II of Spain and commander of the fleet at Lepanto

**Henry IV (r. 1589–1610):** first Bourbon king of France; issued the Edict of Nantes

**Cardinal Armand-Jean de Richelieu (1585–1642):** prime minister of France whose policies crushed the power of the Huguenots in France and brought about the victory of France over the Habsburgs in the Thirty Years' War

**Ferdinand II (r. 1619–1637):** Habsburg archduke of Austria, king of Hungary and Bohemia, and German emperor who led the Catholic forces in the Thirty Years' War

**Johannes Tserclaes, Count von Tilly (1559–1632):** Catholic League general who fought on the imperial side during the Thirty Years' War

**Albrecht von Wallenstein (1583–1634):** Bohemian nobleman and mercenary general who led the imperial troops in the Thirty Years' War until his assassination in 1634

**Gustavus II Adolphus (r. 1611–1632):** king of Sweden who invaded Germany on the side of the Protestant princes during the Thirty Years' War

## Questions for Review

1. When did the Council of Trent begin? When did it end? How many years were there between Luther's posting of the *Ninety-five Theses* and the close of the council?
2. What sort of questions did Trent consider?
3. What doctrines did the Council of Trent affirm? What reforms did it call for?
4. How did the order founded by St. Ignatius de Loyola help the cause of Catholic reform?
5. Who fought at Lepanto? Why was it an important battle?
6. What was the Edict of Nantes? What did it give the Huguenots? How was it later changed?
7. Who was Cardinal Richelieu? What were his goals for France? Why did he support the Protestant side in the Thirty Years' War?
8. Was Emperor Ferdinand II's issuing of the Edict of Restitution wise or foolish? Why?
9. How did the Peace of Westphalia affect the German Roman Empire? How did it affect Christendom?

## Ideas in Action

1. Find a copy of the *Catechism of the Council of Trent* in English. Read a short portion of it—for instance, on Transubstantiation or Baptism or one of the other Sacraments. Read a similar section from the modern *Catechism of the Catholic Church.* How are they alike? How do they differ?
2. Read G. K. Chesterton's poem, "Lepanto." What can be learned from this poem about the battle?
3. Discuss what sort of books might be put on an *Index* today. Why? Should Catholics be forbidden to read certain books? Why or why not?
4. Make a list of modern Protestant and Catholic countries. Are they the same countries that were Catholic or Protestant in the 17th century? (For non-European countries, indicate what European countries founded them.)

# Highway and Byways

### Krakow Cathedral Serves an Astronomer

While Europe was being torn by the Protestant Reformation, a Polish astronomer, Nicholas Copernicus (1473–1543), was at work changing the science of the West. Copernicus was a member of the clergy and a devout Catholic. He studied at the University of Krakow as well as at the University of Bologna in Italy and taught in Rome. In 1497, he made his first observations of motions of the stars and the planets from atop the tower of the cathedral in Krakow.

Up to Copernicus's time, astronomers followed the theories of the Greek astronomer Ptolemy, who said that the universe is a great sphere. At the center of this sphere, said Ptolemy, is the earth, around which revolve the sun, the planets, and the stars. Copernicus came to think that Ptolemy's explanations of the movements of the planets and the stars were too complicated. Reading the Greek scientist Aristarchus, Copernicus discovered that if it was assumed that the sun, not the earth, was the center of the universe, it was possible to come up with simpler explanations for the movements of the heavenly bodies. Instead of Ptolemy's *geocentric* (earth as center) theory of the universe, Copernicus proposed a *heliocentric* (sun as center) theory. Copernicus's theory was the beginning of modern astronomy.

It was not until 1543, at the urging of two bishops, that Copernicus allowed his completed heliocentric theory of the universe to be published in the work, *On the Revolution of the Heavenly Spheres*. Copernicus presented this work to Pope Paul III, who received it cordially.

Copernicus never knew what a storm his work would eventually raise in the West, or that he would revolutionize the way the world looked at the universe and man's place in it.

Chapter 19  # Europe Before the Flood

While the nations on the European continent battled each other with fratricidal hatred during the Thirty Years' War, the island kingdom of England was engaged in a struggle of its own. It was not so much a religious struggle, though it was inspired partly by religion. England's struggle was the continuation of the old rivalry between the king and Parliament.

The Tudor monarchs, Henry VIII and Elizabeth I, had been able to make Parliament do their bidding. But, beginning with the first Stuart king of England, James I, Parliament began to insist that its authority was superior to the king's. The king resisted Parliament's attempts to weaken his power, which led to a struggle that ended in **regicide**—the killing of a king. In the 17th century, regicide was shocking and unthinkable. To many in Britain and on the Continent, Catholic and Protestant alike, England's killing of its king seemed a rejection of civilization itself.

What events led up to this terrible act?

**regicide:** the killing or assassination of a king

## James I and the Divine Right of Kings

James I became king of England in 1603—when he was already James VI, king of Scotland. As king of England, James's goal was to strengthen the royal power—and, if he had been more like Elizabeth I or her father, he might have been able to keep the royal power as strong as they had.

**James I of England**

The Tudors had strengthened their power over Parliament by not depending on it for money. The Plantagenet and Lancastrian kings had been forced to allow Parliament more powers, so that it would vote to give them the money they needed to carry on their wars. But the Tudors had raised the money they needed without asking Parliament for it—by confiscating Church lands, for instance, and by being thrifty.

James Stuart, however, was anything but thrifty. Often in need of money, he was forced to ask Parliament for it. Parliament, however, did not always grant James the money he asked for; and when this happened, the king had to raise it himself by placing taxes on trade and using other measures. Such methods of raising money displeased Parliament, which protested against what its members thought were the king's high-handed measures. In carrying them out, the members said, James I was ignoring Parliament. Thus the king and Parliament became rivals and, finally, enemies.

King James felt justified in ignoring Parliament because he held to a rather revolutionary doctrine that he had learned from his Scottish Calvinist teachers—the "divine right of kings." This doctrine held that God had placed kings on their thrones and given them the right to exercise absolute power in their kingdoms. According to his divine right, the king is not subject to any earthly authority, but to God alone. God has made the king the "father" of the kingdom, and his subjects are his "children," who must obey him. To resist the king is to disobey God, who gave the king his authority.

James I's notion of the divine right of kings came up against the old English idea of government, rooted in the Middle Ages and represented by the *Magna Carta*. In signing this document in 1215, King John had recognized the customary rights of barons. The Magna Carta had said that the king was subject to the customary laws of England and, thus, did not have absolute power.

Despite the Tudors, Parliament had not forgotten its old rights. So it was that Parliament objected to James I's attempts to make himself absolute lord over England. Parliament would have nothing do with the supposed divine right of kings.

Among all the factions in Parliament, King James I earned the special hatred of the **Puritans**.

Puritans, like the Scottish Presbyterians, were Calvinists, and being Calvinists, were a rather **dour** and cheerless folk. They despised **carnal** entertainment of every sort—dancing and music, theater and festival celebrations. They even disapproved of celebrating Holy Days, like Christmas and Easter. Yet, despite its rather dreary aspects, Puritanism appealed to the young intellectuals of the 17th century, because it seemed to them heroic. Puritans were generally well educated and wealthy; they filled the law profession and staffed the universities.

Because King James came from Presbyterian Scotland, Puritan members of Parliament at first hoped he would make the Church of England more Presbyterian and less **episcopal**. But James believed almost as much in the divine right of bishops as he did in the divine right of kings—and those who objected to being ruled by bishops, he said, had better accept it or be driven out of England.

It was not long before the Puritans in Parliament and in all England began to suspect that James was a secret Catholic. Of course, he was not. But his mother—Mary, Queen of Scots—had been Catholic, and James was far easier on English Catholics than Elizabeth had been. Then there was James's support for Catholic Spain, which he had even backed against the "Protestant side" in the Thirty Years' War. Spain had been England's great enemy under Elizabeth, and Puritan merchants had grown rich on the gold and silver taken from Spanish ships by English "privateers"—who were really pirates that had the backing of the queen. James's friendliness toward Spain threatened to deprive the Puritan merchants of a **lucrative** source of wealth.

So it was that King James I and Parliament were always at odds with each other. And when James died on March 27, 1625, his son, Charles I, inherited a group of powerful enemies as well as a kingdom.

> **Puritans:** Calvinist reform party in England. They were called "Puritans" because they wanted to purify the Church of England of the traditional traces of Catholicism
> **dour:** stern, harsh, gloomy
> **carnal:** having to do with bodily passions; worldly
> **episcopal:** having to do with bishops or government of a church by bishops (from Greek *episcopos*, "bishop")
>
> **lucrative:** profitable

# The Road to Regicide

At first, even the Puritans liked King Charles I. He was courteous and had (unlike his father) the reputation of being virtuous. Unlike the very Scottish James I, Charles was dashing and every inch an Englishman. And Charles was an avowed enemy of Spain. Moreover, even though he had married

Henrietta Marie, the daughter of King Louis XIII of France and a Catholic, Charles promised Parliament that he would show no tolerance toward the English Catholics. He appeared, at first, to be a quite tolerable king.

But Charles believed as much as his father had in the divine right of kings. Despite his promise to Parliament to deal roughly with Catholics, Charles allowed his queen to practice her religion and was quite gentle toward the Catholics of England.

**Charles I, king of England, Scotland, and Ireland. Triple portrait by Sir Anthony Van Dyck**

The king's tolerance of Catholics, of course, did not please the Puritans. Neither did the fact that in carrying on a war against Spain, he seemed to waste the money Parliament had voted him. Because of this, Parliament grew more and more unwilling to grant the king money.

To get the money he needed, Charles in 1628 signed the Petition of Right, in which he promised that he would not **levy** taxes without Parliament's consent. Being so beholden to Parliament did not sit well with Charles, believing as he did in his divine right as king to rule as he saw fit. Parliament's continued opposition to him finally so angered Charles that in 1629 he dissolved it. Parliament could not meet again unless the king summoned it—and Charles did not summon it again for another 11 years. Instead, Charles tried to rule England by himself, without Parliament.

**levy:** to collect (for instance, a tax) by legal authority

## The "High Church" King

With or without Parliament, King Charles I still needed money. Despite his belief in his divine right to rule, however, he did not ignore the law to get money. At least, he did not ignore the letter of the law. As he had promised in the Petition of Right, Charles did not levy new taxes without Parliament's consent. Instead, he revived old laws from feudal times—and when anyone broke these laws, he punished them by forcing them to pay fines. Charles angered seaport towns in 1634 by forcing them to pay "ship money"—basically an old tax that had been used to support the navy. He eventually forced inland towns and counties to pay this ship money, which earned him the opposition of many who lived in the parts of England where Puritanism was strongest.

Charles further angered the Puritans by making William Laud archbishop of Canterbury. Laud was **High Church**—that is, he favored many Catholic teachings and the reintroduction of Catholic practices into the Church of England's worship. Even worse (as far as the Puritans were concerned), Laud allowed people to dance and shoot at targets on the Sabbath—practices the Puritans thought abominable. Worse still, Charles did not enforce laws against Catholics and began enforcing laws against Puritans, especially those Puritans called "Separatists" and "Independents" because they refused to worship in Anglican churches and formed their own groups. Because of the king's preference for Catholics, Puritans and Separatists began fleeing England, going to the Netherlands and America. In 1620, one group of Separatists founded a colony at Plymouth in what is now New England. They are remembered in American history as the "Pilgrims." Later, in 1628, some Puritans settled in the town of Salem in the Massachusetts Bay Colony.

**High Church:** in Protestantism, favoring practices and ritual that are liturgical, traditional, and Catholic. Those favoring a simpler, less ritualistic worship are called *Low Church*.

## Revolt in Scotland

Charles I, like his father, was king in both England and Scotland. But, even though these two realms were united under the same king, they were separate kingdoms. Because of this, Archbishop Laud's church reforms did not affect the Scottish Presbyterian Church.

But as king of Scotland and England, Charles I wanted to unite the Churches of England and Scotland and bring religious unity to the two realms. To do this, in 1637 he forced the Scottish churches to use the English *Book of Common Prayer*. He also appointed bishops over the old dioceses of Scotland. The problem was that the Scots were predominantly Calvinist and Low Church. As Presbyterians, they would have nothing to do with bishops, and they opposed the rather "Catholic" form of English worship.

William Laud, archbishop of Canterbury

When the Scottish Calvinist leaders heard about this plan to impose bishops and the Prayer Book on them, they were furious. In 1638, they formed a group called the "Covenanters," from the covenant (agreement) of mutual defense and protection they made with each other to protect Calvinist worship in Scotland.

**Covenanter flag**

**standing army:** a permanent army, as opposed to a levy of militia

**militia:** traditionally, the group of male citizens of a region who have the legal right to bear arms and who can be called upon for military service

**armistice:** temporary end to fighting; a truce

They prepared their congregations to resist the prayer book the king wanted to force on them and deposed the bishops he had set over the Church of Scotland.

Charles decided he had to use force against the Covenanters. England, however, had no **standing army**, just local **militias**; so Charles had to rely on the nobility to provide him with the men he needed. His main support came from Catholics, but they were handicapped because they had been forbidden for years to own weapons. The Scots Catholics were better prepared militarily because the clans in the Scottish Highlands, many of them still loyal Catholics, were used to fighting—often with each other.

Fighting broke out in December 1638. By the time the king was able to get an army to the Scottish border, the Covenanters had seized Edinburgh Castle. After two dismal defeats at the hands of the Scots, Charles signed the Pacification of Berwick, which ended the fighting—for a time, at least—in June 1639.

## Charles Summons Parliament

Charles did not abandon his hopes of finally subduing the Covenanters. But to do this, he needed to raise a larger army. The problem was, neither his extraordinary ways of getting money nor the ship money gave him enough funds to do this. Since he could not levy taxes without Parliament's approval, Charles was forced to summon it for the first time since 1629.

Charles's enemies, the Puritans, controlled Parliament when it met on April 13, 1640. Headed by the radical country gentleman, John Pym, the Puritans said they would vote the king funds if he first gave Parliament greater powers. This Charles refused to do; and in frustration, he dissolved Parliament on May 5. Because it was in session for less than a month, it became known as the Short Parliament.

But then, in August 1640, the Covenanters crossed the Scottish border and invaded the northern counties of England. The army Charles sent to meet the invaders was defeated. In October Charles had to agree to an **armistice**, leaving the Scots in control of six counties in England.

To drive the Scots from England, Charles needed money to form an army. Once again, he had no choice but to summon Parliament. This

Chapter 19   Europe Before the Flood   527

**Map of England and Scotland in the mid-17th century**

Parliament, which assembled on November 3, 1640, continued to meet for the next 13 years—for that reason, it has been called the Long Parliament.

Puritans dominated the Long Parliament as they had the Short Parliament, and John Pym was again their leader. In Parliament, Pym openly declared not only that Parliament was supreme even over the king, but that the House of Commons could ignore the acts of the House of Lords. Claiming the power to impeach even the king's ministers, the House of Commons sent Archbishop Laud and Thomas Wentworth—earl of Strafford, the king's most faithful minister—to the Tower of London.

Charles attempted to save his friend Strafford's life. He appealed to the House of Lords and even tried to seize the Tower of London by force. But on May 10, 1641, with a mob at the doors of his London palace, Charles signed Strafford's death warrant. "If my own person only were in danger, I would gladly venture it to save my Lord Strafford's life," Charles said.

**rue:** to regret, feel remorse for

"But seeing my wife, children, and all my kingdom are concerned in it, I am forced to give way unto it." Charles ever after **rued** his betrayal of Strafford, who shortly afterward was beheaded. Archbishop Laud was executed four years later.

To gain their support, Charles gave in to the Puritans' demands. He agreed to give up the right to dissolve Parliament without its consent and said he would no longer raise money through such measures as ship money. He even made a show of turning against Catholics by collecting fines for failure to attend Anglican services, and he dismissed Catholic officials. But none of these measures earned the Puritans' favor. Instead they pushed even harder against the king.

On November 23, 1641, Parliament approved a document called the Grand Remonstrance, which was a defense of Parliament and a condemnation of the king. Then, in December, the Puritans introduced into Parliament a bill to impeach Queen Henrietta Marie for treason. Enraged, Charles sent troops to Parliament to arrest Pym and four other Puritan leaders; but after being forewarned, the five escaped. The House of Commons now openly turned on the king, and since London was filled with Puritans and their supporters, Charles and the royal family had to flee the city for their own safety.

## The Great Rebellion

Charles I fled north into Nottinghamshire and there began organizing an army. Among those who flocked to the king's standard were most of the nobles, country squires, High Church Anglicans, and Catholics. Parliament, too, raised an army; it was composed of Puritan small landowners, merchants, mechanics, and shopkeepers, drawn mostly from London and towns in the southern and eastern sections of England. The Puritan army was nicknamed the Roundheads, because they wore their hair close-cropped to their heads. The king's supporters—many of whom, unlike the Puritans, wore their hair long—were called the **Cavaliers**, because so many of them were knights.

In their first battle with the Cavaliers at Edgehill in 1642, the Roundheads were unprepared to meet the king's forces, and expert cavalry charges against the Roundheads gave the victory to the Cavaliers. Parliament then made common cause with the Covenanters. In 1643, both groups signed a "solemn league and covenant" in which they pledged to impose Presbyterianism on the Church of England and in

**cavalier:** a word derived from the French word *chevalier*, signifying a horseman or knight

Ireland. Early in 1644, the Covenanters invaded northern England, while the Parliamentarian army marched north to York. On July 2, 1644, the Parliamentarian and Covenanter army defeated the royalist army at Marston Moor, near the city of York.

Among the leaders of the Parliamentarian forces at Marston Moor was Oliver Cromwell. Cromwell was an "Independent," the most radical group of Puritans in Parliament. Since the royalists were not destroyed after Marston Moor, Cromwell became highly critical of the leadership of the Parliamentarian army. In 1645, he was given command of the army, now called the "New Model" army. Being a most stern Puritan, Cromwell enforced a strict morality among his troops. They were, for instance, fined if they were caught swearing. But Cromwell did more than this. He trained the Parliamentarian cavalry after the model of Gustavus Adolphus's army and began winning battles. On June 14, 1645, Cromwell's army, nicknamed the "Ironsides," met and destroyed the royalist army at Naseby in Northamptonshire. The following year, King Charles, realizing that he had little hope of overcoming Cromwell and his Ironsides, surrendered himself to his enemies.

Oliver Cromwell

In 1647 King Charles was able to escape from his imprisonment. The king came to an agreement with Scottish leaders; and, in 1648, a Scottish army invaded England. Cromwell, in command of the Parliamentary army, marched north, put down a rebellion of royalists in Wales, and then met the royalist Scottish army at Preston in August. Though outnumbered two to one, Cromwell's army defeated the royalists. Charles, now left without any support, again surrendered himself to Parliament.

## Trial and Execution

The English Puritans in Parliament had long been split into factions. The largest faction, and the most moderate one, was the Presbyterians. Though Charles was completely in Parliament's power, the Presbyterians wanted to negotiate an agreement with him. But Cromwell's faction, the Independents, wanted the king executed.

The problem for the Independents was that, since the Presbyterians outnumbered them in Parliament, the Independents could not hope to get a majority of Parliament members to condemn the king. This problem was

**Execution of Charles I, January 30, 1649. Contemporary painting by 'Weesop'**

solved in December 1648 when armed men entered Parliament, prevented the Presbyterian members from taking their seats, and ejected them. The remaining 60 members, all Independents, were called "the Rump," or the remainder. And the Rump voted to bring the king to trial.

Charles I's trial began on January 20, 1649, before a court set up by the Rump Parliament. The charges were read to Charles—he had waged war against the people and was thus a tyrant, traitor, murderer, and public enemy. He was called the "Grand Delinquent" and the "Man of Blood." When the king asked by what authority he was being tried, he was told it was by the authority of the English people, who had *elected* him king. Charles replied he had not been elected king but had inherited his crown, as had all the English kings before him. As for being a tyrant, Charles declared that he had fought not for himself, but for the liberty of the English people. As he was led from the hall, many of the people who had gathered to watch this unthinkable thing, the trial of a king, cried, "God save the king!"

On January 27, the final day of the king's trial, the president of the court silenced Charles as he tried to answer the charges against him. The court then read off the sentence: "that the said Charles Stuart, as a Tyrant, Traitor, Murderer and a Public Enemy, shall be put to death, by the severing of his head from his body." As soldiers removed him from the court,

Charles protested, "I am not suffered to speak. Expect what justice other people will have."

Now that the trial was over, it was time to sign the death warrant. The commissioners were reluctant to become regicides, for all Christians looked on kings as God's anointed. Finally, the relentless Oliver Cromwell took the warrant and signed his own name to it in large letters. Following his example, 58 other members of Parliament eventually signed. The execution was set for January 30, 1649.

King Charles I showed great dignity as he was led to his execution. In his speech on the scaffold, Charles said he had only wanted to secure the freedom and liberty of the English people. Even at the threshold of death, he declared his belief in the king's divine right. The people's "liberty and freedom," he said, "consists in having government. . . . It is not in their having a share in the government; that is nothing appertaining unto them. A subject and a sovereign are clean different things." Charles forgave everyone. Almost his last words were, "I go from a corruptible to an incorruptible Crown, where no disturbance can be, no disturbance in the world."

# The Protectorate

After the death of King Charles I, the Rump Parliament and Oliver Cromwell ruled England. Representing as they did only a small portion of the English people, the Independents were not necessarily popular, but they were powerful. Cromwell's army was seemingly invincible; at least, the remaining royalist forces could not stand up to it.

And royalist forces there still were. Ireland, the island of Jersey, and Scotland had acknowledged the dead king's eldest son, Charles II, as king. Anglicans, Catholics, and even Presbyterians joined the young king's cause. But on September 3, 1651, Cromwell's army defeated the king's mostly Scottish forces at Worcester, and Charles himself was almost captured. Hidden by Catholic families in the area, Charles, with the help of a Catholic priest named Father John Huddleston, was able to escape to France.

After the Battle of Worcester, Cromwell grew annoyed with the Rump Parliament because its members seemed interested only in enriching themselves by selling royalist lands. Finally, in 1653, upon declaring, "Your hour is come, the Lord hath done with you," Cromwell disbanded the Rump Parliament and set up a new legislature, which was dubbed "Barebone's Parliament" (after a Puritan member named Praisegod

Durham Cathedral, England

Barebone.) But soon after, becoming disappointed with Barebone's Parliament, Cromwell dissolved it. Cromwell's friends then set up the "Protectorate," with Cromwell serving in the king's place as "Lord Protector."

Though Cromwell was to rule with the aid of Parliament, he again dissolved that body in 1655. From then on, until his death in 1658, he ruled England as its dictator. Cromwell did not take the title of king, but he ruled as an absolute monarch. Like the Stuarts, he saw his authority to rule as coming from God.

Cromwell sought to enforce Puritan religion and morality in England, Scotland, and Ireland. He granted religious liberty to all Protestant sects, but he kept the laws against Catholics on the books. Cromwell outlawed all the traditional Christian holidays, including Christmas and Easter, which Puritans thought of as mere vanities and papist idolatry. In the name of purging England of anything Catholic, Cromwell's armed men desecrated churches and cathedrals throughout the land, beheading and smashing statues. (They shot at the beautiful stained-glass windows at Salisbury Cathedral for target practice.) At Durham Cathedral, Cromwell's men demolished and desecrated the ancient tombs of Sts. Cuthbert and Bede the Venerable.

When Oliver Cromwell died on September 3, 1658, his son Richard succeeded him as the new Lord Protector. But the younger Cromwell could not control the army. Finally, Richard Cromwell stepped down as Lord

Engraving of Charles II

## Cromwell Destroys Ireland

In 1649, the same year Charles I was executed, royalists in Ireland took up arms on behalf of Charles's son, Charles II. In response, Oliver Cromwell brought his army to Ireland and ruthlessly suppressed the uprising. The massacres at the towns of Drogheda on September 11, 1649, and at Wexford a month later were particularly brutal. Cromwell took Drogheda and ordered it burned to the ground. All the survivors were killed or sold into slavery in the West Indies.

To further punish the Irish for their resistance to his "godly" rule, Cromwell ordered all Irish men of fighting age to leave the country on pain of death. Then he confiscated almost all Irish land, except for some in the far west province of Connaught, and distributed it to Protestant landlords of his own choosing. As he had done with the survivors of Drogheda, Cromwell ordered his forces to capture Connaught's orphaned children and sell them into slavery.

**Massacre at Drogheda**

Protector. Army officers restored the Rump Parliament, forcing it to recall all the members of the Long Parliament, which had been disbanded in 1648. Tired of Cromwell's dour Puritan dictatorship and with Parliament restored, England was now set for the return of her king.

# The Restoration

While Parliament was being restored, an English general named George Monck approached Charles II, who was an exile in France. Monck offered Charles the crown if he, in turn, promised to guarantee religious toleration and grant amnesty to those who had rebelled against his father. Charles agreed and swore to respect the Magna Carta and the rights of Parliament—and not to raise illegal taxes. After returning to England, Charles II was crowned king of England and Ireland on April 23, 1661.

Charles had two goals when he returned to England. One was to stay on the throne; the other was to ensure that the Stuart family would keep the throne. To achieve these goals, King Charles was willing to make almost any compromise. For example, in 1661 Parliament enacted the Clarendon Code, which placed penalties on anyone who refused to worship in the Church of England. Charles was not pleased with this code, but he was not going to object to it because he did not want to endanger his throne.

On May 21, 1662, Charles married Catherine of Braganza, a Portuguese princess, first in a secret Catholic ceremony and then in a public Protestant one. Catherine, a deeply devout Catholic, was also charming and good-natured. Charles permitted her to have a Catholic chaplain and private Masses in her apartments. But Charles was not a faithful spouse, and Catherine suffered greatly on account of the king's infidelity. Still, she was faithful and devoted to him.

Queen Catherine, however, could bear no children for Charles. With no son to succeed him, Charles II's heir was his brother, James, the duke of York. James's first wife, Anne Hyde (who was the mother of his two daughters, Mary and Anne), had become a Catholic shortly before dying of cancer —and, not long after her death in 1671, James himself entered the Catholic Church. This conversion would make it difficult for James to become king after his brother's death, since many in England were opposed to having a Catholic king.

Queen Catherine, wife of Charles II

## Struggles with Parliament

No matter how careful he was, King Charles II inevitably came into conflict with Parliament. In 1672, he issued the Declaration of Indulgence in which he suspended Parliamentary laws against Catholics and Protestant dissenters from the Church of England. Parliament objected, saying the king did not have the authority to suspend parliamentary laws. Charles again compromised and withdrew the Declaration of Indulgence.

The following year, the king meekly agreed to Parliament's enactment of the Test Act, which required every holder of office to take communion publicly in the Church of England. Charles suggested to James that he take communion even though he was a Catholic. James refused and had to resign his office as Lord High Admiral, through which he had done much to build up the British navy. In the same year, James married his second wife—Mary

Beatrice d'Este, the Catholic princess of Modena, Italy— a move that only increased public hostility toward him.

Charles, however, refused to make two compromises that Parliament demanded of him. He would not divorce Catherine and marry a Protestant wife to produce an heir. And in 1679 he rejected the Exclusion Act, which would have barred all Catholics, including his brother James, from the throne.

Controversy over the Exclusion Act led to a split in Parliament itself. Those who supported the act (they were backed by Puritans and other dissenters) came to be called "Whig"—a popular insult given to radical Protestants. Those opposing the act were supporters of the Church of England and of the royal power. They became known as "Tory"—the name for a Catholic outlaw in Ireland. These two parties not only represented religious differences. The Tories included the old landed families, while the Whigs represented the newer wealth of the merchant class and the lesser gentry of the country estates.

During the last years of Charles II's reign, the Tories became the predominant party in Parliament. Rumors that the Whigs were plotting to overthrow the king hurt the Whig cause. In 1681, with Tory support, King Charles was able to dissolve Parliament and not recall it again during his reign.

## Charles II Converts and Dies

King Charles II was not the most honest of men—nor, as we have pointed out, did he always stand up for what he thought was right. Of course, he faced political enemies who were themselves not very **scrupulous**. Still, the king's court was notoriously immoral, and the king himself was unfaithful to his very faithful wife, Queen Catherine.

**scrupulous:** having moral integrity; high principled

Yet, if Charles did not live well, he died well. On the night of February 1, 1685, he apparently had some kind of convulsion. His problems continued for the next several days, and no remedy helped him. It appeared that the king would soon die, and the Anglican bishop and royal chaplain Thomas Ken offered communion to him. But the king refused it.

At that point Queen Catherine, Prince James, and Princess Mary Beatrice agreed to get a priest to Charles. On February 5, James whispered in Charles's ear the question, "Do you want a priest?" To which Charles said, "Yes, with all my heart."

The nearest priest, a member of Queen Catherine's household, was the same Father John Huddleston who had once saved Charles from being captured by Cromwell. When Huddleston came to him, Charles said, "You that saved my body are now come to save my soul." Charles answered Father Huddleston's questions clearly, made Confession, and received the Last Anointing. When it was time to receive the Holy Eucharist, Charles insisted on getting out of bed and kneeling. He held a crucifix while Father Huddleston said the prayers for the dying. King Charles II died at noon the next day.

# The "Glorious Revolution"

Many English Protestants were not happy when Charles II's Catholic brother, James II, became king in 1685. For several years, rumors of Catholic attempts to overthrow Protestantism in England had been common; in 1678, tales of a "popish plot" had led to persecution of Catholics and the murder of several prominent Catholics. Having a Catholic king only increased Protestant fears—and the fact that the Catholic king was also a believer in the divine right of kings only made matters worse.

King James II did little to **allay** such fears. Even the kings' allies, the Tories, were displeased by his decision to place Catholics as commanding officers in a standing army he was trying to create. And, of course, the Whigs were infuriated with the king. Then, in 1687, James issued the "Declaration of Indulgence," which guaranteed freedom of religion to all religious groups in England, Catholics and non-Anglican Protestants alike. In 1688, James reissued this declaration and ordered Anglican clergymen to read it to their congregations. Seven Anglican bishops refused, and James tried to have them convicted of sedition.

Still, England's Protestant leaders could console themselves with the thought that James, who was 55 in 1688, would not have a long reign. Better yet, he had no Catholic heir. James's Protestant daughter Mary, who was married to William, prince of Orange in the Netherlands, stood to inherit the throne. But then, in June 1688, Queen Mary Beatrice gave birth to a son, James Francis Edward Stuart. And, unlike her other children, this baby lived. He was now the heir to the throne—and he was baptized a Catholic.

Faced with the threat of another Catholic king, both Tories and Whigs in Parliament decided to take action. They were in contact with William of Orange. He was waiting only for

**allay:** to calm

**James II, king of England, Scotland, and Ireland**

**Parliament crowning William and Mary**

a "Protestant wind," as it was called, to set sail across the English Channel to England with his army.

The wind finally blew; Parliament invited William to take over the English throne, and he landed on the English coast on November 5, 1688. James's best general, John Churchill (soon to be made the duke of Marlborough), defected to William. With no one to fight for him, King James, with his wife and their baby son, fled London and found refuge in France. William of Orange marched triumphantly into the capital city.

Parliament offered the crown to William of Orange and King James II's daughter, Mary Stuart—thus making it clear that the new monarchs were receiving their authority from Parliament, not by inheritance or any right of their own. The Parliamentary monarchs were crowned as Queen Mary II and King William III in February 1689. This triumph of the power of Parliament over the king is called the "Glorious Revolution."

The same year that William and Mary came to power, Parliament passed the Declaration of Rights, also called the Bill of Rights. This law forbade the king from suspending laws passed by Parliament, to levy taxes, raise an army without Parliament's consent, or forbid the free speech of members of Parliament. Subjects, too, were given the right to petition the king. To make sure no Catholic Stuart would reign in England, the Bill of Rights said the king must belong to the Church of England. Parliament also passed the Toleration Act, which gave freedom of belief and public worship to English Protestant dissenters—but not to Catholics.

**Painting depicting the Battle of the Boyne, 1690**

The Glorious Revolution is considered a great landmark in English history. It set up once and for all England's constitutional monarchy, a system where the king is subject to the representatives of the English people and cannot rule absolutely. The fall of James II marked the end of the doctrine of the divine right of kings in England.

## The Death of Monarchs

William and Mary faced opposition in Ireland and Scotland from James II's supporters there, who called themselves Jacobites (from *Jacobus*, the Latin form of James). William defeated the Scottish Jacobites in 1689 at the Battle of Killiecrankie. With the aid of France, James II went to Ireland. At the Battle of the Boyne, however, the Irish Jacobites were soundly defeated, and James fled to France. There, he died in 1701.

Although the English people liked Queen Mary, they were not very fond of William. Queen Mary reigned until December 1694, when she died from smallpox. In 1702, King William died after a long illness. He was succeeded by James II's other daughter, Queen Anne. Like Mary, Anne was a Protestant.

# The United Kingdom of Great Britain

After Mary's death, King William had let Parliament rule England while he spent his time and energy fighting France on the continent of Europe. Queen Anne, however, was a more vigorous monarch. Though she did not seek to restore the doctrine of the divine right of kings, she vetoed acts of Parliament and chose Tories as her representatives (called the cabinet) in Parliament, even when the Whigs were in the majority. King William III had chosen his cabinet based on which party had the greatest number of members in Parliament. If the Whigs were in the majority, William's cabinet was made up of Whigs.

Perhaps the most important act of Queen Anne's reign was the uniting of the kingdoms of England and Scotland into one kingdom. Since James I, the kings of England had also been the kings of Scotland and Ireland. Scotland had its own parliament, separate from the English parliament, and was thus a separate kingdom. Fearing that the Scottish parliament would elect its own king after Anne's death, and so become completely independent, the English parliament forced it to accept the Act of Union in 1707. England and Scotland were thus united as one kingdom under the English parliament, which accepted Scottish members. This United Kingdom, henceforth, was called Great Britain.

## The Hanoverians

Queen Anne died, childless, in 1714. According to a law of Parliament, called the Act of Settlement, the next in line to the throne was Anne's cousin, Sophia, the wife of Ernest Augustus, the elector of the German state of Hanover. Sophia, however, had died shortly before Anne, and so the throne of Great Britain went to her son, George, the elector of Hanover. He became George I, king of Great Britain and Ireland, the same year Queen Anne died.

**Queen Anne**

Being German, King George I had little interest in British politics—he spoke no English—and allowed Parliament and the cabinet to govern Great Britain. His son, George II, who became king in 1727, spoke only broken English. Like his father had done, George II paid more attention to Hanover than England. Under the first two Hanoverian kings, Great Britain was indeed a monarchy, but Parliament was the real ruler.

Though Parliament was made up of two houses—the House of Lords and the House of Commons—its members were by and large aristocrats or controlled by aristocrats. Parliament was not a democratic body. Many places in England and Scotland were not represented at all; and most English, Scots, and Irish could not by law vote for members of Parliament. So it was that Parliament came to represent the interests of the wealthy classes in Great Britain and the Protestant landholders in Ireland.

Despite its aristocratic character, Parliament served as an example of representative government for Europeans of the 17th and 18th centuries. Representative government is government by lawmakers elected by the people of a region, class, or profession and serving as their voice in government.

King George II

Indeed, Englishmen were carrying the ideal of representative government outside the boundaries of Great Britain to the vast lands of the New World, called America.

Ever since the reign of Queen Elizabeth I, England had been establishing colonies in North America, chiefly along the Atlantic coastline. Jamestown (named after James I) was the first of these colonies, founded in 1607 in the area called Virginia. Then came the Puritan settlements of Plymouth and Massachusetts Bay. From these colonies, settlers moved into other parts of the region later known as New England. Under the subsequent monarchs of England and Great Britain, colonization of America continued. By 1750, Great Britain possessed 13 colonies stretching from Spanish Florida in the south to the St. Lawrence waterway in the north.

These British American colonies established their own little parliaments or assemblies, which had the task of making laws for each colony. Like the British parliament, these assemblies were not always democratic; but the colonists saw them as the way to maintain their rights and freedom as Englishmen. And for many decades, the English American colonies basically governed themselves, their assemblies making laws for them and voting taxes.

Great Britain's colonies in America—and its increasing power and wealth at home—brought it into frequent conflict, particularly with France. Beginning with George III, who became king of Great Britain in 1760, British power in the New World grew. Finally, the British held the entire North American continent—from the Mississippi River to the Atlantic Ocean and from Florida to the Hudson Bay. It would not be long, however, before Britain lost much of this vast territory in a struggle against its own colonies. These colonies would claim their right to the British ideal of representative government, which, they said, George III and Parliament were denying them. This struggle of the British colonies, first for their rights and then for independence, was the American Revolution—the war that gave birth to the United States of America.

The birth of the United States, however, would not come until Great Britain engaged in a struggle with the third great European power (besides

Chapter 19   Europe Before the Flood   **541**

**North America around 1750, showing British, French, and Spanish domains**

Jules Mazarin

itself and Spain) that held lands in the Americas. This power was France, which under its most powerful king (nicknamed the "Sun King") became not only the greatest nation in Europe but, in America, threatened to overwhelm Britain's colonies with destruction.

# The Age of the Sun King

The Thirty Years' War and the war with Spain that ended in 1659 made France the most powerful nation in Europe. Cardinal Richelieu's dream had been realized: the Habsburgs had been severely weakened, and the French king was supreme over all Christian monarchs. After Richelieu's time, France knew peace and plenty for half a century.

Yet, things might have gone differently for France. When King Louis XIII died in 1643, his throne passed to his four-and-a-half-year-old son, Louis XIV. Richelieu had made the king supreme in France, but there were still strong nobles who might take advantage of the fact that their new king was only a child. All of Richelieu's work might have come to nothing if not for Cardinal Jules Mazarin, who succeeded Richelieu as prime minister of France.

Though he was an Italian, and not at first a French citizen, Cardinal Mazarin had earned Richelieu's confidence. Like Richelieu would have done, Mazarin as prime minister worked to protect the young king in France and to promote the power of France in Europe. It was Mazarin who was able to crush a rebellion of the common people, who were trying to resist absolute monarchy, followed by a revolt of the French nobles. It was Mazarin who humbled Spain, making the Habsburg king promise to marry his daughter, Maria Theresa, to King Louis XIV. It was Mazarin who completed Richelieu's work, giving to Louis XIV a kingdom over which he could exercise absolute power.

### "I Am the State"

When Cardinal Mazarin died in 1661, the 22-year-old Louis XIV surprised his court by saying he would govern France himself, without a prime minister. In the following years, the king displayed great energy. He devoted at least eight hours a day to his kingly tasks, adding to those duties daily exercise and evening entertainments that often lasted well into the next morning. He took pride in exhausting his nobles and courtiers, who were expected to match his energy. But Louis's energy was not pointless or merely for show. He was determined to make himself and his France the wonder of the world.

Louis's motto was *L'état c'est moi*: "I am the state" (or "The State is me!") He was pleased when his flatterers called him *Le Roi Soleil*, which means "Sun King." He saw himself, like the sun, shining over France and the world.

Like the Stuarts, Louis XIV believed firmly in the divine right of kings. But, unlike the Stuart kings, he made this theory a reality. The French theory of the divine right of kings was developed by a brilliant theologian and bishop, named Jacques-Bénigne Bossuet. Bishop Bossuet said the king is sacred not only because he receives his right to rule from God, but because he has been consecrated by the Church. The king is like a father, said Bossuet, and his subjects owe him the obedience and respect children pay their fathers. It is thus a blasphemy to attack the king or resist him. Subjects may do nothing to oppose the king, even if he issues unjust commands or is a tyrant. They may only pray God to change the king's heart.

**Louis XIV**

Bossuet provided Louis XIV with a theory of the authority of the state over the Church. Both Bossuet and the king held that the king's temporal authority is completely independent of the pope and that the king also has power over the French or Gallican Church, whose bishops must for the most part act independently of Rome. Further, Bossuet and Louis held that a general council stands over a pope—a teaching condemned by the Council of Trent. These Gallican notions brought the king into conflict with Pope Innocent XI.

Louis XIV went further than Richelieu and Mazarin in bringing all power into the king's hands. He centralized the government by establishing a bureaucracy that oversaw all aspects of life in France. Under Louis, the French nobles lost their political power in their own domains. To keep a close eye on the nobles, Louis commanded them to live at his palace at Versailles for a part of every year. While at Versailles, they were obliged to attend theatrical events every evening from after dinner until the early morning hours. If a noble failed to remain at these entertainments for as long as the king did, he could earn the king's ill will. And the nobles did all they could to earn Louis's good will.

**French bishop and preacher, Jacques-Bénigne Bossuet**

### The Sun King's Show Palace

Louis XIV built several palaces and **châteaux** for himself, but the most extravagant was the hugely expensive Palace of Versailles outside Paris. Louis built this his pleasure palace in the village of Versailles, some 12 miles (a day's walk) from the outskirts of 17th-century Paris.

Among the extravagances of the palace were 1,000 orange trees; chimneys sheathed with copper; a zoo with leopards, lions, camels and elephants; enormous crystal chandeliers; 2,400 fountains; exotic birds; 2 million flowerpots (so that the flowers in the gardens could be changed every day, to suit Louis's moods); marble statues throughout the palace; and elaborate gardens where entertainments for the king's guests could be staged.

**château (plural, châteaux):** originally a feudal castle or fortress in France; later, a large country house or mansion

Entrance to the Palace of Versailles

Louis was called the "grand monarch" by the people of his time. The late 17th century has since his time been called the Age of Louis XIV. The fame and the glories of Louis's court were talked of in every European capital. To awe his people as well as his enemies, Louis lavishly displayed his wealth and power. Louis lived extravagantly and luxuriously. He surrounded himself with the leading men and women of his day. As Cardinal Mazarin had taught him, he encouraged dancing and theater as well as music and literature.

## Louis's Wars

Louis XIV wanted France to have every glory and power the other European nations had. This desire led him to work through his brilliant minister, Jean-Baptiste Colbert, to increase France's trade and make it a powerful mercantile nation. Louis also sought to increase the French presence in America. He did so by encouraging his subjects to people the settlements in Canada begun under his father, Louis XIII, and by claiming new lands.

It was during the reign of the Sun King that French explorers followed the Mississippi River from its source in what is now Minnesota to where it empties into the Gulf of Mexico. In 1682, René-Robert Cavelier, Lord of La Salle, claimed the entire Mississippi Valley and the lands lying along the banks of its **tributary** rivers for France and Louis XIV. In honor of the king, La Salle called these lands Louisiana.

**tributary:** a stream that feeds a larger stream, river, or lake

Louis XIV's interest in the New World was not entirely peaceful. He hoped that the wealth he gained from America (chiefly through fur trading) could pay for the wars he needed to fight in order to make France's borders secure and then to expand them by conquering new territory.

The Sun King increased the size of the French army and reorganized it into a complex military machine of more than 400,000 men. Louis never commanded troops in battle. Instead, he set up an efficient officer corps to command for him, much as his bureaucrats commanded other aspects of the French government. By obtaining modern weapons and using modern strategies, the French army became the best in Europe.

Louis used his army against Habsburg-controlled lands on France's eastern border. Since his wife was the Spanish king Philip IV's daughter, Louis decided he had a right to take the Spanish (or Belgian) Netherlands. And Louis might have done this had not Holland (the Protestant or independent Netherlands), England, and Sweden in 1668 threatened to enter the war on Spain's side. Faced with this threat, Louis ended the fighting.

Louis's next target was Holland—because it had stood in the way of his conquering the Spanish Netherlands and because it was a powerful trade rival. The war, which began in 1672, pitted France against Holland (under Prince William III of Orange) and its allies—the German emperor Leopold I, Spain, and several German states. By the end of the war, France gained from Spain the territory of Franche Comté, several strong fortresses in the Spanish Netherlands, and the duchy of Lorraine, which had been a German imperial territory.

The king of France, however, was not satisfied with these gains. He wanted to extend French territory all the way to the Rhine River—which he called one of France's "natural boundaries." Louis claimed he had the right to no fewer than 20 cities in the German empire. Based on this claim, the French army took the imperial city of Strasbourg, an important city on the Rhine.

Faced with France's push into his empire, Emperor Leopold formed a league with Spain, Sweden, and several German princes at Augsburg, Germany, in 1686. Despite this league, in 1688, Louis sent a French army into the Rhenish Palatinate, a state belonging to the empire. Thus began a new war, called the War of the League of Augsburg. As in his two previous wars, Louis thought he need not worry about England since its king was James II, who had received large sums of money from France. Louis, however, did not count on the Glorious Revolution, which drove James from the English throne. William III of Holland, who became the English king, was an old enemy of Louis, and he joined the allies against France.

During this war, which lasted 11 years, Louis and France alone fought the major powers of Europe—and Louis's army not only saved France from invasion but won several victories. In the Treaty of Ryswick, which ended the war in 1697, Louis lost no territory (though he had to give up his claim to Lorraine). He also was able to keep Franche Comté and Alsace, which France had gained in the Thirty Years' War. On the whole, the War of the League of Augsburg was a triumph for the Sun King.

## The War of the Spanish Succession

The Battle of Denain, in the War of the Spanish Succession

By 1700, the 62-year-old Louis XIV had achieved many of his longed-for goals. France was the greatest nation in Europe, feared and envied by the other European powers. In France itself, the king was the supreme, autocratic ruler; his once powerful nobles had become merely ornaments to adorn the royal palace at Versailles. Yet, all this had come at a cost. Louis's wars had increased the taxes his subjects had to pay; and, since the nobility did not pay taxes, the tax burden fell on the middle and lower classes. Colbert had tried to find ways to help these classes, but they were still discontent.

After signing the Treaty of Ryswick, Louis spent no time in enjoying his triumphs or seeking to solve the problems in his country. Instead, he turned his attention to making his family, the

Bourbons, the predominant ruling family in Europe. It was not enough that the Bourbons held France; Louis wanted the family to wear the crown of Spain as well. Louis thought he had a claim to the throne of Spain, since his wife was a Habsburg. When he had married Maria Theresa, Louis gave up any right his family might have to the throne of Spain in return for a very large dowry. But wars had made Spain poor, and the dowry was never paid. Louis used this debt as an excuse to claim Spain for himself.

Since 1665, Philip IV's son, Charles II, had been king of Spain. Charles was sickly and of weak mind; moreover, he was childless. The next in line to the Spanish throne was the Habsburg emperor Leopold I —a fact that did not please Louis XIV. The last thing he wanted was to see Spain and Austria united under a Habsburg king, as they had been under Charles V. By his charm and tact, Louis was able to convince the feeble-minded Charles II that it would be better if Spain were united to France rather than Austria. So it came about that, a month before he died in 1700, Charles II willed his kingdom to Philip of Anjou, Louis XIV's grandson.

The Austrian Habsburg Leopold, of course, opposed his cousin's decision, for it was a betrayal of the Habsburg family and its power. William III of England also was opposed, for he feared a union of France and Spain that would make Louis's Bourbon family far too powerful in Europe. To keep Philip of Anjou from becoming king of Spain, Leopold and William formed the Grand Alliance, which was joined by Holland, the duke of Savoy, and several German princes. The allies declared that not Philip but Archduke Charles von Habsburg, the son of Emperor Leopold, should become king of Spain.

The "War of the Spanish Succession" that followed in 1702 was fought in Germany, the Netherlands, Italy, and Spain—and even in North America, where it was called Queen Anne's War. In this war, fortune turned against Louis XIV, for the allies had England's greatest general—John Churchill, duke of Marlborough—as their commander. In 1704, at the Battle of Blenheim, Marlborough defeated the French army. With shocking French loss of life, the allies drove France's army from the German Empire. In 1706, Prince Eugene of Savoy drove the French from Italy; and by 1709, Marlborough had cleared them out of the Netherlands.

**Philip V of Spain**

**The Battle of Blenheim**

With these victories, it looked as if the allies would march on Paris itself. But Louis XIV refused to surrender. He appealed to the patriotism of the French people, who along with the Spanish rose up in defense of France and the Bourbon succession. By 1711, the allies were no closer to Paris than they had been two years before. Also in 1711, Archduke Charles von Habsburg became German emperor. Neither the English, the Dutch, nor the German princes wanted to see a Habsburg in control of both Spain and the empire, as would happen if Emperor Charles became king of Spain. So it was that both the allied and the French sides were willing to come to an agreement to end the war.

This agreement was the Peace of Utrecht. Signed in 1713, the Peace recognized Philip of Anjou as king of Spain, though it specified that France and Spain could never be united under one king. In return for giving up his claim to the Spanish throne, Emperor Charles VI received the Spanish Netherlands (which became known as the Austrian Netherlands) as well as Naples and Milan in Italy. France, on the other hand, lost some of its American possessions to Great Britain and gained nothing but the fact that a Bourbon, Philip V, was king of Spain. But this result alone spelled success for Louis XIV, for it increased the honor and glory of his family and of France itself.

## The Final Days of the Sun King

Though Louis XIV had done much to increase France's power and glory, his policies had dangerous consequences. Versailles, Louis's army and navy, and the four wars he fought in his reign had all been ruinously expensive. And, since he would not think of taxing the nobility or the wealthy churchmen of France, the French middle class—but still more, the French peasants—suffered under the ever-increasing tax burden laid on them.

Louis, however, cared little what his people thought—for, as the years passed, he had come to know less and less about them. Other French kings had traveled their kingdom, but Louis rarely left Versailles. The nobles, too, knew little of what was going on in their own parts of France, for they always had to be in attendance on the king. Among these nobles were France's great bishops and abbots—who, like the nobility, lived lives of luxury separate from the people and the hard-working priests they were called to shepherd.

So it was that when Louis XIV died on September 1, 1715, two years after signing the Peace of Utrecht, few of the common people mourned for him. As his dead body was carried from Versailles to the ancient burial place of the French kings at St. Denis in Paris, the common people only jeered and hooted at it.

# After Me, the Flood

After Louis XIV's death, his great-grandson, the five-year-old Louis XV, became king of France. Until he came of age to rule, the young Louis and France were at first under the direction of the king's cousin Philip, duke of Orléans, and then of Cardinal André-Hercule de Fleury. Philip of Orléans was more a lover of pleasure than a ruler, and he neglected the education and training of Louis XV. After Philip's death, Cardinal Fleury tried to repair the damage done to France by Philip and the Sun King before him. But Fleury was unsuccessful and even increased the peasants' discontent by forcing them to work on a series of roads spanning the kingdom.

Though Fleury sought peace with other nations, France became involved in a war in Poland in 1733. This war became mixed up with a

**The anointing of Louis XV as king of France**

struggle between the Bourbon king of Spain, Philip V, and Austria. It ended up being a fight between Russia and Austria on one side and France and Spain on the other. The war ended in 1738 as another victory for the Bourbons over the Habsburgs. Louis XV received the duchy of Lorraine from the German Empire, while Sicily and Naples passed from the Habsburgs to Philip V. The king of Spain made his son, Charles, king of Sicily and Naples. Now the Bourbons controlled three kingdoms—France, Spain (with its empire in the Americas and the Philippines), and southern Italy.

Despite the continuing glory of the Bourbon family, Louis XV was a weak and poor ruler. This became quite clear after Cardinal Fleury's death in 1743. Louis was uninterested in governing. Instead, he loved hunting, fine dinner parties, and beautiful women. He was unfaithful to his wife and had several mistresses—one of whom, Madame de Pompadour, was the power in the kingdom for 20 years.

All the evils that sprang up during the reign of the Sun King grew worse under Louis XV. The king knew nothing, and cared less, about the good of his people. His nobles lived a life of high culture and foolish pleasure, and all the while the common people suffered under heavy taxes and grinding poverty. Later in his reign, Louis was involved in long wars that made France bankrupt.

Still, on the surface, France appeared the wealthiest and most powerful nation in Europe. It had a large and well-trained army. Paris was the center of art and science, and the French nobility were considered the most elegant people in the world. Indeed, the French language had become the language of the upper classes and of diplomacy throughout Europe. The Bourbon family, too, ruled a good portion of Europe as well as most of North and South America.

Yet, the power of France and the Bourbons was hollow. Louis XV himself saw this. Looking at the France of his time, he knew all its glory could not last. It would all be destroyed, but after his time. *Après moi, le déluge*, he said—"After me, the flood." And, indeed, a great political, cultural, and religious flood was gathering. When it broke, it would sweep away not only the great kingdom founded by the Sun King but all that was left of Christendom. That flood was the terrible French Revolution that gave birth to modern Europe and to our present world.

# Chapter Review

## Summary
- King James I held to the doctrine of the divine right of kings, which said that kings are established on their thrones by God and so have absolute power in their kingdoms. James's attempts to achieve absolute power in England brought him into conflict with Parliament.
- King Charles I, like his father, James I, believed in the divine right of kings. In 1628, Parliament forced Charles to sign the Petition of Right, which said the king could not levy taxes without Parliament's consent. Because of its continued opposition to him, Charles dissolved Parliament in 1629.
- For 11 years Charles ruled without summoning Parliament. He raised the money he needed by collecting fines for the violation of old laws he revived and by collecting "ship money."
- Charles I's attempts to force bishops and the Anglican prayer book on the Presbyterian Church of Scotland led to a revolt of the Scottish Covenanters. In 1639, Charles was forced to sign the Peace of Berwick with the Covenanters.
- To subdue the Covenanters, Charles was forced to summon Parliament in 1639. He soon dissolved this Parliament (the Short Parliament); but when the Covenanters crossed into England in 1640, Charles summoned Parliament again (the Long Parliament). The Long Parliament forced the king to abandon several of his rights, including the power to dissolve Parliament itself. After Charles failed to arrest five of Parliament's leaders, the House of Commons rebelled against him. The king and his family fled London.
- From 1642 to 1649, the king's forces fought the forces of Parliament and the Covenanters in what is called the Great Rebellion. Under Oliver Cromwell, Parliament's army won the Battle of Naseby in 1645. Charles surrendered to Parliament, but in 1647 he escaped. At the Battle of Preston in 1649, Cromwell's army defeated the royalist forces, and Charles again surrendered to Parliament.

- Parliament set up a court to try King Charles. The court accused the king of being a tyrant, traitor, murderer, and public enemy and condemned him to death. Charles I was executed by beheading on January 30, 1649.
- After the death of Charles I, Cromwell and Parliament set up the Protectorate. But after twice dissolving Parliament, Cromwell ruled England, Scotland, and Ireland from 1655 to 1658 as dictator. When Cromwell died, the army forced the restoration of the Long Parliament.
- Charles II was restored to the English throne in 1661. In trying to keep his throne for himself and the Stuart family, King Charles II compromised with Parliament, giving in to its demands. He refused, however, to accept Parliament's demand that he divorce his Catholic wife and marry a Protestant; and he would not sign the Act of Exclusion that would have barred his brother James, who was Catholic, from the throne.
- English Protestants feared that King James II would overthrow the Protestant religion in England. Their fears increased when the king's second wife gave birth to a son, who was baptized Catholic. Parliament invited William of Orange and his wife, Mary Stuart, to England to take the throne. Abandoned by his own general, James II fled England in 1688. Parliament made William and Mary king and queen of England.
- Under King William and Queen Mary, then Queen Anne, and then the Hanoverian kings, Parliament increased its control of the English government. In 1707, Parliament forced the Scottish Parliament to accept the Act of Union, forming one kingdom of Great Britain.
- Louis XIV became king of France when he was only four-and-a half years old. During the first years of his reign, the young king was guided by Cardinal Jules Mazarin. When Mazarin died in 1661, Louis announced that he would rule France without a prime minister.
- King Louis XIV held to the doctrine of the divine right of kings. Louis centralized French government under his authority, using a bureaucracy that oversaw all aspects of life in France. The king lived lavishly and luxuriously, encouraging the arts of dancing, theater, music, and literature.
- King Louis XIV worked to make France a powerful mercantile nation. He encouraged the growth of France's American settlements and extended French territory down the Mississippi. The king built up the French army until it was 400,000 strong, and he armed its troops with the best and most modern weapons.

- Louis fought a series of wars to expand the borders of France and to weaken his neighbors. By 1700, he had achieved many of his goals and made France the most powerful nation in Europe. Louis's desire to extend the power of his family, the Bourbons, led to the War of the Spanish Succession. In the 1713 Peace of Utrecht, which concluded the war, Louis's grandson, Philip of Anjou, was recognized as king of Spain.

## Key Concepts

**divine right of kings:** the doctrine that kings receive absolute power over their kingdoms from God and are subject to no earthly authority; to resist the king is to disobey God, who gave him his authority

**High Church:** in Protestantism, favoring practices and ritual that are liturgical, traditional, and Catholic. Those favoring a simpler, less ritualistic worship are called *Low Church*.

**Puritans:** Calvinist reform party in England. They were called "Puritans" because they wanted to purify the Church of England of the traditional traces of Catholicism.

**Protectorate:** the name of the government of England, Scotland, and Ireland under Oliver Cromwell, who was called Lord Protector

**regicide:** killing a king, thought to be a great crime against God's ordinances and arrangement of political order

**Tory and Whig:** names for English political parties. The Tories were High Church and supporters of royal power; the Whigs, backed by Puritans and other dissenters, favored giving greater power to Parliament.

## Dates to Remember

**1625:** Charles I becomes king of England, Scotland, and Ireland
**1628:** Charles I signs the Petition of Right
**1638:** beginning of the Covenanters' rebellion
**1641:** beginning of the Great Rebellion in England and Scotland
**1643:** Louis XIV becomes king of France
**1649:** the execution of King Charles I
**1649–1658:** the Protectorate
**1661:** Restoration of Charles II
**1661:** Louis XIV comes of age
**1682:** founding of Louisiana
**1685:** James II becomes king of England, Scotland, and Ireland
**1688:** the Glorious Revolutions
**1707:** Act of Union forms the United Kingdom of Great Britain

**1701–1713:** the War of the Spanish Succession
**1715:** Death of Louis XIV; Louis XV becomes king of France

## Central Characters

**Charles I, Stuart (1600–1649):** king of England, Scotland, and Ireland; executed in the English revolution

**Oliver Cromwell (1599–1658):** leader of the Parliamentary army who became Lord Protector of England after the execution of Charles I

**Charles II, Stuart (1630–1685):** son of Charles I and king of England, Scotland, and Ireland during the Restoration period

**James II, Stuart (1630–1685):** Catholic king of England, Scotland, and Ireland; overthrown in the Glorious Revolution

**William III and Mary II, Stuart (reigned 1689–1702):** king and queen of England, Scotland, and Ireland; appointed by Parliament after the Glorious Revolution

**Anne Stuart (1665–1714):** English queen under whom Scotland and England were joined in the United Kingdom of Great Britain

**George I (1660–1727):** elector of Hanover who became king of Great Britain; founder of the Hanoverian line of British kings

**Cardinal Jules Mazarin (1602–1661):** Italian clergyman and statesman; Richelieu's successor as prime minister of France; served as regent for Louis XIV until he came of age

**Louis XIV (1638–1715):** the "Sun King" of France; he made France the most powerful state in Europe

**Bishop Jacques-Bénigne Bossuet (1627–1704):** French bishop who formulated a version of the divine right of kings; defender of Gallicanism

**Philip of Anjou (1683–1746):** grandson of Louis XIV who, as Philip V, became the first Bourbon king of Spain

## Questions for Review

1. What is the divine right of kings? Why was it not a successful doctrine in England? Where was it successful?
2. Why, unlike the Tudors, were the Stuart kings unable to control Parliament?
3. What events brought about open war between King Charles I and Parliament?
4. Why was the fact that Parliament invited William and Mary to take over the throne in England so significant to the long-standing rivalry between king and Parliament?
5. Why was Louis XIV called the Sun King?

6. What were the ways Louis XIV tried to make France the greatest nation in Europe?
7. What did Louis XIV mean by "*L'état c'est moi*" ("I am the State")?
8. What were Louis XIV and Bossuet's ideas about the relationship between the Church and the state in France?
9. What were the causes of the War of the Spanish Succession? How long did that war last, and who won? Who succeeded to the Spanish throne?
10. In what ways did Louis XIV leave France better than he found it? In what ways did he leave it worse than he found it?

## Ideas in Action

1. Find a photograph of the bust of Louis XIV by Bernini as well as later portraits of the king by other artists. What sort of character is captured in those features? Discuss the character of Louis and how the artists portrayed that character.
2. Discuss: Did Louis XIV fulfill Cardinal Richelieu's hopes for France? Why did French culture become the model for all other European nations of the 18th century?
3. Report on French gardens of the 17th and 18th centuries, particularly those of Versailles. How are they different from English gardens or American colonial gardens of the same period? Search for pictures and descriptions of both kinds of gardening. Report to class.
4. Draw a map of North and South America, using different colors to indicate what parts of those continents belonged to the Spanish, the English, the French, and the Portuguese.

# Highways and Byways

### Chamber Pots at Versailles

Louis XIV intended his palace at Versailles to be something like a huge luxury hotel. It had apartments for 1,000 nobles and 4,000 of their servants, as well as dining halls and dancing halls for the king's great feasts and fancy-dress balls. Versailles contained 1,252 chimneys and 67 staircases. The formal gardens designed by Le Nôtre stretched over many acres of flower beds and pruned hedges, with fountains and ponds and artificial hills and groves. Some 20,000 persons attached to the court were to be housed in the town, and 5,000 lived in the palace itself. Quarters for 14,000 soldiers and servants were built to house the royal guard and the palace staff. The result was a building several city blocks long and three blocks wide, containing over 2,000 rooms.

Among the rooms decorated in silk and gold leaf, there were, however, no facilities for the natural needs of the courtiers—no privy chambers (restrooms). This unfortunate lack was made up by hundreds of servants carrying and emptying a thousand chamber pots every two hours. The stairways and halls of the great hotel were said to smell as foul as the sewers of Paris in spring flood; and the nobles forced to reside at the palace carried perfumed oranges and other smelling salts with them at all times. Because of the overwhelming stench, both women and men fainted often in the halls and in the royal audience chambers. So a small mistake can make the greatest of human works comic. Power brought low by a chamber pot.

# LIGHT TO THE NATIONS

Part One

*The History of Christian Civilization*

## Supplemental Chapters

| | |
|---|---|
| China: The Middle Kingdom | 558 |
| Japan: The Land of the Rising Sun | 576 |
| Africa: The Enduring Continent | 588 |
| Latin America: Lands of Many Cultures | 604 |
| The Scientific Revolution | 624 |
| Two Revolutions: Industrial and Agricultural | 644 |
| The Age of Enlightenment | 653 |

# China: The Middle Kingdom

The ancient name for the land we call China is *Chung Kuo*—a name that means the "Middle Kingdom." The Chinese thought that their land was the center of the world. For thousands of years they met no civilized neighbors. Everything around ancient China was barbarian territory, at least as far as the Chinese were concerned.

Over the centuries, China expanded from a small kingdom along the Yellow River to cover much of southeastern and central Asia. China today stretches from the cold northern plains of Asia to the **tropical** jungles of Southeast Asia. China has some of the world's tallest mountains (the Himalayas), most **barren** deserts (the Gobi), and wildest rivers (the Yellow River and the Yangtze River). China has fertile lowlands and **arid** plateaus, snow-swept steppes and tropical jungles.

Two great rivers cross China from west to east—the Yellow River in the north and the Yangtze River in the south. Civilization in China grew up along these two rivers. The valley of the Yellow River, where Chinese civilization began, has rich farmland, with deep, but dry, **topsoil**. In the beginnings of China's history, grain crops such as millet and wheat grew abundantly in the Yellow River Valley. However, the Yellow River's annual floods have caused much hardship for the farmers and cities along the river. The valley of the Yangtze River, which is much farther south, is **semitropical** and surrounded by beautiful mountains. Rice growing made it a wealthy region. Farther south in China, tropical plants and flowers grow among the many farms and neatly ordered towns.

North of China lies Mongolia—a region of frozen plains and desert-like hills. Primitive tribes and nomads once lived in Mongolia, and the emperors of China built the marvelous "Great Wall" to keep them from invading China. In western China, the Gobi Desert and the Tibetan Mountains stretch for thousands of miles, from east to west. For centuries, these wild and desert lands made travel difficult between Europe and

**tropical:** a word referring to the area around the tropics
**barren:** not able to produce anything
**arid:** having very little rainfall; dry
**topsoil:** the upper part of the soil; the soil on the surface
**semitropical:** having hot summers and warm winters, with nearly no frost or snow

China and cut off almost all contact between them. The Silk Road, a great caravan route, stretched from China's capital, Changan, across the desert wastes. It ran from oasis to oasis all the way to Persia. Merchants traveling along this road brought treasured silk to the Mediterranean world in return for Western gold. Except for this trade, however, China had little contact with other civilizations. The Chinese mistrusted strangers so much that at times all foreigners were forbidden to set foot on Chinese soil.

# Early Chinese Dynasties

The Chinese divide their history into eras that are named for the principal royal families or dynasties that ruled them. Chinese history is said to have begun with mythical god-like rulers, called the *Three Rulers*. The Three Rulers are said to have invented civilization; and, if they existed at all, they lived sometime between 3000 and 2000 B.C. They were followed by human rulers, called the Five Emperors. The first dynasty for which we have certain historical evidence is the Shang Dynasty, which ruled northeastern China from about 1766 to 1022 B.C.

The dynasty that followed the Shang, the Zhou Dynasty, ruled China for an amazingly long time—900 years. Under the Zhou kings, who had their capital in north-central China, Chinese lords conquered lands to the south, west, and east. The Zhou Empire extended from the Pacific Ocean to the mountains of the west and included both the Yangtze and Yellow River Valleys. Farming practices improved during this period, and industry and commerce sprang up.

The culture of China under the Zhou Dynasty was rich. In religion, people worshiped, besides ancestors and spirits, a supreme God. This God, it was believed, loved good and just actions and hated evil deeds. The Zhou Chinese greatly honored the family, for they thought it the most important building block of society. China had schools, too, during this period, and artists who created works of literature, including poetry.

After a time, however, the Zhou kings grew weaker while the nobles grew stronger. The king could no longer rule the whole country and control the lords. Because a kind of feudal government developed during this period and different regions were constantly battling each other, this period of the Zhou Dynasty was called *Warring States*. Yet, it was during this period that the great thinkers of Chinese philosophy arose. The most important of these was a man called K'ung-tzu, whom we remember as Confucius.

## A Teacher of Tradition and Harmony

Confucius (551–479 B.C.) was an aristocrat from the small state of Lu in northeastern China. He wrote about morality, praising education and proper behavior toward one's parents, peers, superiors, and others. Confucius taught that one had to respect his elders and show obedience to his superiors. According to Confucius, a person became worthy of a great position, not because he had a noble parent, but by his own talents and moral character.

Confucius took on a small band of students, who followed him from Lu to other states and secured for him his first government post when he was old. He devoted his old age to collecting and writing down the great poetry and ideas of China under the Zhou Dynasty. Confucius is known for a compilation of poems called *The Book of Songs* and a history called the *Spring and Autumn Annals*. The work *Lunyu* (known in English as the *Analects*) contains sayings of Confucius that were probably brought together in a book by generations of his disciples.

Confucius gave China the social and moral ideas that have guided its civilization over the centuries since he lived. Confucius did not establish a religion, though he called on men to honor traditional religious rituals, especially reverence for ancestors. Rituals were important for Confucius, because he thought they joined people together in friendship and mutual respect.

Confucius did not come up with new ideas; rather, he saw himself as a preserver of the institutions and traditions of China. He rejected the idea that human beings are individuals that have no natural connection with one another. He wanted to give new life to the institutions that united people—the family especially, but also the local community, the school, and the kingdom. He opposed the kind of society where the rich and powerful for their own benefit rule and abuse the weak and poor.

Rulers, said Confucius, should seek first to become good men themselves and then govern more by their moral example than by force. Rulers are not to provide only for the physical needs of their people but to educate them as well. Formal education was very important to Confucius and his followers after him. Subjects, said Confucius, should show respect to their rulers, obey the laws, and participate in the rituals that tie society together. In turn, every person has the duty to show **piety** (or profound respect) to his parents, his superiors, and to the king.

**piety:** the showing of reverence to God and those in authority, especially parents

Every person must strive to discipline him or herself, said Confucius, and conform to the rituals of society. By striving to be virtuous, one was being true to himself. At the same time, a person had to be considerate of others, for only in this way could everyone in society be joined together in harmony. The maxim, "Do not do to others what you would not want others to do to you," was the golden rule of Confucius' thought.

# The Empire of the "Sons of Han"

In 249 B.C., the last Zhou king was removed from the throne. Three years later, a lord named Zheng made himself king of all China, calling himself the "First Emperor." He was the founder of the Qin Dynasty.

Zheng's reign began with terror. He killed local rulers to force the warring states to obey him alone. To keep his subjects from questioning him and his deeds, he forbade all his subjects to discuss philosophy. They were not to praise what had happened in the past or criticize what was happening in their own time. Zheng, in particular, did not like Confucianism, because it encouraged people to do good for its own sake. Zheng wanted his people simply to obey his laws and commands. He did not want them to think about whether doing so was right or wrong.

Zheng accomplished one of the wonders of the world: he built the first Great Wall to keep the fierce horsemen of Mongolia from invading China. The Great Wall today begins on the Pacific coast, at the Yalu River, and continues for 3,000 miles over the mountains and deserts to the sands of the western Gobi Desert. The first Great Wall was not so long, but it stretched for over 1,000 miles. Zheng forced thousands of peasants and political troublemakers to work on the wall. They had to ram dirt into frames to create bricks and haul great stones from quarries. Thousands died because of the extremely hard labor they were forced to do.

Zheng also forced peasants to dig a canal, linking rivers and lakes, so that shipping could move between the Yangtze and Yellow Rivers. The construction of the "Grand Canal," as it is called, took almost as many lives as the building of the Great Wall.

The Qin Dynasty did not last long after Zheng's death in 210 B.C. His reign had been too cruel and terrifying and so harmful to China that it brought about a rebirth of the Chinese love of tradition and sense of purpose. This led, finally, to one of the greatest periods of Chinese history—the empire of the Han Dynasty.

## The Han Dynasty (206 B.C.–A.D. 220)

Zheng's son tried to rule China after his father's death but was murdered in 207 B.C. Civil war then broke out until a peasant, called Liu Bang, won the command of the army and united central China. He proclaimed himself emperor of China (the first time a commoner had done so), and the Chinese people generally accepted him as their ruler. They had had enough of tyranny and civil war. Liu Bang was the founder of the Han Dynasty. So great was this dynasty that, not only did it rule China for 426 years, but it gave a name to the Chinese people. Ever since, the Chinese have called themselves the "Sons of Han."

The Han emperors did not try to control every aspect of life in China, like Zheng had done. For instance, the Han allowed some local aristocrats to go back to their lands and rule them in the name of the emperor. Han laws, too, followed the philosophy of Confucius. The Han emperors wanted people to obey the laws because it was the right thing to do, not just because they were afraid of punishment.

The Han dynasty united all of central China by learning rather than regulations. The Han emperors wanted the most capable men to serve as civil servants, and so the Han encouraged education. They were the first to use examinations to find the best minds in China for the civil service. Eventually, all of urban and rural China was included in this educational system. Though the civil service examination was open to all classes, it was expensive to prepare for it—which meant that few besides the wealthy could hope to take the test. Still, some poor men did pass the examination; in this way, even a poor peasant could become a leader in China. Also, over a period of several hundred years, the Chinese language spoken by the Han monarchs replaced local languages and customs.

The Han emperors carried on wars against the "barbarian" peoples in the lands northwest of central China and Central Asia. Under the Han, the Chinese conquered new lands in Central China and far into the south. They established trade routes that crossed thousands of miles of desert mountains and connected China with the countries of the Mediterranean. The Han Chinese traded with the Roman Empire, where Chinese porcelain and tea were greatly admired. The greatest Chinese trade item was silk, a fine cloth made from the cocoon web of a silkworm.

The Han Dynasty removed Zheng's ban on ancient books, and scholars began to copy them and write new works of their own. Poetry flourished under the Han Dynasty, as did the writing of history. Under the Han monarchs, the Chinese invented paper, water clocks, sundials, and instruments for use in studying the heavens. Painters, weavers, sculptors, and architects created beautiful works of art.

The Han Dynasty was one of the greatest periods in Chinese history. It created one of the most advanced civilizations the world has ever seen.

# A New Way for China

When the Han Dynasty came to an end around A.D. 220, it was followed by three-and-a-half centuries where China was divided into more than one kingdom. During this period, China suffered from civil wars and from invasions by Mongols, Turks, and people called the Hsiung Nu. China at last was reunited under the Sui Dynasty, which ruled from 589–618, and then the Tang Dynasty, which reigned from 618–907. The Tang united all the kingdoms of China and, under their rule, China became for a time the largest and strongest empire in the world. The Tang emperors conquered areas around China, including important trade routes that ran north of central China to Europe.

A new religion or philosophy came to China during the Han Dynasty and grew in popularity in the years China was divided. This religion was Buddhism.

Buddhism was not a native Chinese religion. It came originally from India and so its writings were originally written in Sanskrit, a language of India. The translation of the Sanskrit writings into Chinese was very difficult, and Buddhism at first grew slowly in China. It attained its greatest hold on China during the Tang dynasty and eventually became one of the most important religions of China.

## The Development of Buddhism

Buddhism has its roots in the religion of the Aryan people who invaded and settled India around 1500 B.C. Since the Aryans belonged to the larger family of Indo-European peoples (which include Europeans as well as Persians and other peoples), the heroic stories they told about their gods were similar to the stories the Greeks and Romans told about their gods and heroes. The chief Aryan gods were the three brothers, Brahman, Indra, and Varuna, who were similar in many ways to the Greek gods Hades, Poseidon, and Zeus.

Though the chief god of the Aryan people was Indra, the war god, the Aryan priests (called brahmins) worshiped Brahman, the god of enlightenment. The sacred books of the Aryans, called the *Vedas*, speak of some 33 gods, but the Aryans added the gods of conquered peoples to their **pantheon** until Indian civilization was worshiping hundreds of gods.

A major religious change occurred in Aryan society around the 600s B.C. While the Aryan lords called rajas and their warriors stole cattle and waged **petty** wars to strengthen their growing kingdoms, the brahmins became more influential among the people. The people honored the priests because they knew the complex rituals for controlling the gods. Kings had to listen to the brahmins' demands and buy their favor. In this way, the brahmins became the highest **caste** in Indian society. The religion of the brahmins is called Hinduism.

**pantheon:** a group of gods arranged in a family
**petty:** small and with little importance or value
**caste:** a social group that excludes everyone outside of itself; a distinct class

To escape the power of the brahmins, some men wandered off into the wilderness to live as hermits in search of spiritual knowledge. They undertook heroic fasts and acts of self-denial. They sang and performed sacred dances, unaware of anyone near them. They went into long trances. These hermits lived on what people gave them as they wandered from village to village, teaching their wisdom. Without using the ritual spells of the brahmins, the hermits blessed those who were kind to them.

The hermits' pursuit of religious wisdom transformed Indian life. Their teachings were set forth in a series of poems called the *Upanishads*, a word meaning the "meditations." The *Upanishads* say people should trust religious insight over what one can learn through study. They counsel people who want to escape from earthly desires and pains that they should practice self-denial instead of indulging in earthly pleasures.

According to the *Upanishads*, Brahman is the creator of the universe, and with him are two other gods—Shiva, the destroyer of creation, and Vishnu, who preserves the universe that Brahman creates. Shiva's wife (called Parvati, Kali, or Durga) was the most important god of the Hindu religion.

The *Upanishads* also speak of reincarnation. Reincarnation is the belief that after death the immortal soul does not go to live forever in a heaven or hell but is reborn in another creature. The Hindus believe the soul is "reincarnated" many times. How one will live in a future life depends on how well he or she lives in this life.

The *Upanishads* developed the idea of "the universal spirit." According to the *Upanishads*, the gods are just different "faces" of the universal spirit. Sometimes this universal spirit is called Brahman; sometimes it is presented as something greater even than Brahman.

## Siddhartha Gautama, the Buddha

In the 6th century B.C., an Indian prince named Siddhartha Gautama accomplished his own spiritual journey and taught a new way of spiritual enlightenment. This method of spiritual growth came to be called Buddhism from its founder, Siddhartha, who was later called Buddha, the "enlightened one."

**soothsayer:** one who foretells future events

According to Buddhist legend, at Siddhartha's birth, a **soothsayer** prophesied that the child would one day see signs that would convince him of the misery of the world. Seeing these signs, Siddhartha would choose to be either a teacher or a tyrant. To prevent this prophecy from coming true, Siddhartha's father tried to shelter him from all sickness and decay and surround him only with youth, beauty, and pleasure.

One day, however, Siddhartha was riding in his hunting preserve when he came upon a gnarled and feeble old man who had somehow wandered into the park. Having never seen an old person, Siddhartha asked his charioteer what this creature could be. It is "Old Age," the charioteer said. On the ride home, Siddhartha passed a beggar covered with sores and shivering with fever. "What is the matter with this man?" he asked. "Sickness," replied the charioteer. Just then a funeral procession rounded the corner, and seeing the corpse, Siddhartha asked, "What is this?" "Death," was the reply.

Troubled by these sights, Siddhartha left home at the age of 29 to learn the mystery of Old Age, Sickness, and Death. Finally, in his 36th year, he sat down under a great fig tree—which Buddhists call the *bodhi*, the tree of wisdom. He vowed to sit there until he had solved the three riddles of suffering. For seven weeks he sat, fasting and thinking. At last he entered a state of mind that seemed to be neither being or non-being. It was a timeless realm of meditation. Buddhism would later call that state of mind, *nirvana*—a word meaning "detachment." In that moment Siddhartha became *the Buddha*, the "Enlightened One."

Siddhartha wanted to know why there is sorrow and suffering in the world. His answer was that sorrow and suffering come from desire for pleasure and fear of pain. If people want to rid themselves of sorrow and suffering, said Siddhartha, they have to purify the spirit through right thinking and right conduct. Siddhartha did not abandon all the gods of Hinduism, but he taught that religious rituals are of no use. Men of all classes flocked to his message, and the new religion spread quickly throughout northern India.

People were attracted to the simple ideas of Buddhism and to the fact that, unlike Hinduism, it did not divide people into castes. Even though it did not entirely break off from Hinduism until later years, Buddhism was for several centuries the major rival to Hinduism in India.

## Buddhism in China

Missionaries carried Buddhism from its birthplace in India to Burma, Thailand, and Southeast Asia. They followed the trade routes from northwestern India into Central Asia, where Buddhism flourished for centuries until Islam replaced it there. Buddhism became the majority religion on the island of Sri Lanka, south of the Indian mainland. Today in Burma, Thailand, Cambodia, and Vietnam, most people are Buddhist.

Buddhism may have come to China as early as the third century B.C. Buddhist tradition, however, says that Mingdi, an emperor of the Han dynasty who reigned in the first century A.D., brought Buddhism to China after he dreamed of a flying god of gold that he thought was a vision of Buddha. Whether or not this story is true, Buddhism spread among many even of the common people of China, who added ideas from their own religion, Taoism, to it.

After the end of the Han Dynasty, when China was divided into more than one kingdom, non-Chinese rulers in northern China used Buddhist monks as counselors and magicians. Elsewhere in China, members of the upper classes and the learned studied and adopted Buddhist ideas and practices. In the fifth and sixth centuries, Buddhist schools and monasteries grew up in China, and even peasants adopted Buddhism. Under the Sui Dynasty (581–618), Buddhism became for the first time one of the official religions of the realm.

Chinese missionaries brought Buddhism into Korea in the late 4th century A.D. The people of Korea, who inhabit a peninsula that lies between the Yellow Sea and the Sea of Japan, had long been influenced by Chinese culture. This was especially true of northern Korea, which by the end of the first century B.C. was under direct Chinese rule. Though southern Korea remained outside of Chinese control, its culture was strongly influenced by Chinese culture.

By 300, Korea was divided into three independent kingdoms—Kogury (in northern Korea), Paekche (in southwest Korea), and Silla (in southeast Korea.) For about 700 years, these three kingdoms waged constant war on each other, while Silla itself suffered numerous attacks from Japan.

It was in this world of warring kingdoms that Buddhism made its first inroads into Korea. As was often the case in the ancient world, the new religion first found favor among the ruling classes. It was the aristocracy of the three kingdoms who first adopted Buddhist ideas and practices, which then gradually spread among the common people.

Korean Buddhism benefited from a number of remarkable teachers, among whom was Wonhy Daisa (617–686). Wonhy was a monk who studied not only Buddhism but the Chinese Taoist religion and Confucianism. In his earlier life he was a teacher for the royal family of Silla as well as the nobility; but later he abandoned his monk's robes, dressed as a common man, and lived the life of a wanderer. Using music, literature, and dance, he sought to spread Buddhist ideas among the common people. He tried as well to unite the various **sects** into which Buddhism had become divided.

**sect:** a group of people who have the same beliefs

It was during Wonhy's lifetime, in 660, that Silla united all the Korean kingdoms under its power. The unification of the peninsula helped Buddhism spread and flourish among the Korean people. Like Wonhy, the great thinkers of Korean Buddhism tended to seek for unity among the various schools of Buddhist thought and practice.

In the Middle Ages, however, Korean Buddhism fell away from its earlier, nobler ideals. The government, too, began to persecute Buddhists and remove privileges from the monks. Finally, by the 14th century, Confucianism replaced Buddhism as the official religious philosophy of Korea.

# The Golden Age of China

It was under the Tang Dynasty that China had its only official empress—Empress Wu Zhao, who took power in 690. With her beauty and wiles, Wu had married an emperor; then, after his death, she married his grown son from another marriage. She then poisoned her young husband and killed three of her own sons. After removing her fourth and last son from the throne, Wu declared herself a man and crowned herself emperor. She put to death anyone who opposed her.

Empress Wu ruled ably and extended the territory of her empire south and north. She made Buddhism the official religion of the realm and gave much wealth to Buddhist monasteries. In 705, however, she was overthrown, and her youngest son was made emperor in her place.

Seven years after Wu was overthrown, one of China's greatest emperors, Hsuan-Tsung, came to power. Emperor Hsuan-Tsung's capital city, Chang-an, in central China, became a brilliant center of culture and a fabulously rich city. The greatest Chinese poets and painters lived and worked in Chang-an—including the two poets Tu Fu and Li Po. Hsuan-Tsung supported thousands of musicians, dancers, and actors. He established China's first musical academy, called the "Pear Garden."

Trade between China and Central Asia, India, and Persia developed during the Tang Golden Age. The emperor's court sent ambassadors to the courts of Persia and, even, Constantinople. Because of this, many foreigners came to live in Chang-an—Syrians, Arabs, Japanese, Persians, Koreans, and Jews. These peoples enriched Chinese culture and practiced various religions, including Islam, Judaism, and the Christian faith. The first Christians had come to China in the 600s. These were heretical Christians, called Nestorians, who refused to call Mary the Mother of God. The Nestorians built the first Christian church in China in 636.

**sack:** to plunder (a captured town)

Hsuan-Tsung's reign, however, ended sadly. In 751, his armies were defeated by the Turks in western Asia, and in 755 a rebellion broke out against the emperor. The great capital, Chang-an, was **sacked**. After Hsuan-Tsung's death in 756, China suffered from invasions and civil wars. Millions of Chinese died. The empire lost a good amount of the territory it had gained under Empress Wu.

But even after 755, China under the Tang continued to experience growth and prosperity. People in the north of China entered the more fertile lands of the south where they grew, not only grain as they had in the north, but new crops such as tea and sugarcane. In the fertile Yangtze River Valley, farmers grew rice and cultivated new varieties of grain. Markets for both agricultural and other goods sprang up all over China, both in big cities and provincial towns. The growth of banking led to more widespread use of silver coins in place of silk, the traditional item used in payment for goods. Trade between foreign countries and China continued, though Arabs, Koreans, Persians, and others (not native Chinese) carried on such trade.

The Chinese civil service expanded greatly under Empress Wu and the Tang rulers that followed her. During this period, the civil service examinations became a way for younger sons in aristocratic families to enter the government. And, since students studied Confucian texts to prepare for the examinations, they became the means by which Confucianism came to dominate the government of China. When eventually candidates who passed the test began to be admitted to higher government offices, they began to take the place of aristocrats, who had been the chief hindrance to the emperor's power. Unlike the aristocrats, the new civil servants were faithful to the emperor. In this way, the power of the emperor increased, and government became more centralized.

# The Middle Kingdom in the Middle Ages

After the Tang Dynasty came to an end in 907, China was again divided between several governments. This lasted until 960, when the Song Dynasty reunited almost all of China. During the 300 or so years the Song emperors reigned, China fought continuous wars with a nomadic people called the Tatars and, later, the savage Mongols.

Yet, despite the wars, China under the Song Dynasty was prosperous and had the most advanced culture in the world. The wealthy lived lives of ease and beauty, and even poor farmers lived fairly well. But, under the Song emperors, only the wealthy were able to afford the training that was needed to take the civil service examinations. Thus, only the rich became civil servants. Yet, by the time the Song Dynasty came along, these civil servants had replaced the aristocracy in the government, thus bolstering the power of the emperor.

The growth of the Chinese population to over 100 million (the largest in the world) during the Song period meant more land had to be cultivated. Chinese farmers improved their tools and began planting crops that had much higher yields than anything the Chinese had previously known. Among these crops was an early ripening rice that had so short a growing period that farmers could harvest two and sometimes even three crops a year. Besides foodstuffs, Chinese farmers grew cotton, which provided clothing for rich and poor, and silk and hemp.

Mining of gold, silver, lead, and tin also increased during the Song Dynasty, as did manufacturing, especially, of porcelain. A network of state-maintained highways, as well as advances in bridge building, aided trade. Rivers continued to provide highways for merchants; large ships having multiple decks and propelled by paddles passed up and down China's interior waterways. Trade by sea was made easier and expanded because of the invention of accurate compasses and charts.

Another art that the Chinese brought to a high level of development during the Song Dynasty was printing. Since about the 2nd century A.D., the Chinese had been using paper; about 2,500 years before that, they had invented ink. Maybe sometime in the 6th century A.D., the Chinese were printing images to paper using a wood block. An artisan would carve a raised image of a text or picture into the wood, cover it with ink, and press the image onto the paper. It was not until around 1140, however, that the Chinese began to use movable type. Instead of using a single wood block, artisans would make individual characters or letters out of a mixture a clay and glue, hardened by baking. These figures would then be arranged on an iron plate to form texts. The figures then could be detached from the plate and rearranged to form a new text. Yet, though movable type printing was invented in China (some three hundred years before it was discovered in Europe), it did not become widely adopted there.

Besides such practical arts as shipbuilding and bridge construction, printing, medicine, and even gunpowder (for guns and fireworks), Song China produced fine poetry, beautiful paintings, and new ideas in philosophy. New discoveries were made as well in medicine, including acupuncture and treatments for diseases such as rheumatism and paralysis. Under the Song emperors, the teachings of Confucius became the chief philosophy of life, and so the Chinese valued scholarship and moral living.

## The Triumph of Neo-Confucianism

When he took power, the first emperor of the Song Dynasty, Taizu (960–976), tried to base his rule on the ideals of Confucius. He lived modestly in his personal life and, as emperor, he sought to learn from the wisdom of his counselors. Desiring to be a just and kindly ruler, he tried to ease the burden of the taxes the people had to pay. And even in war, Taizu sought justice and gentleness. He did not treat his defeated rivals with anything but kindness and generosity.

Confucian ideals underwent a revival in the years after the death of Emperor Taizu. Confucian scholars began to take on Buddhist ideas, as well as those of the native Chinese religion, Taoism. They began to dedicate themselves in a more intense way to philosophy, ethics, and politics, as well as individual self-discipline and refinement. The goals of these Confucians were to better the moral lives of the people and keep China a great and powerful land.

This movement has been called Neo-Confucianism. Its most important figure was a civil servant named Zhu Xi, who lived from 1130 to 1200. Zhu Xi thought the Chinese people needed to rediscover the true teachings of Confucius—and Zhu Xi believed his version of Confucianism embodied these teachings. His school of Confucian thought became known as the "School of the True Way" and, later, as the "School of Universal Principles."

Zhu Xi saw that the goal of education was to help people cultivate a sense of morality, teaching them to do what is right and avoid what is wrong. He was not content, however, with helping people be moral individuals; he sought to bring about a moral society which, he thought, would lead to good government. Zhu Xi believed followers of the True Way should reach out to the poor as well as the rich. The Neo-Confucians produced a kind of catechism as a means of teaching the way of virtue even to the simplest people. It was not long before storytellers and companies of actors and other performing artists were traveling about, spreading the teachings of the True Way.

But even though Zhu Xi and his followers did not seek political power for themselves, they earned the envy of powerful men in government, who thought the School of the True Way threatened the government. Because of this, Zhu Xi and many leaders of the True Way were banished to distant parts of the realm. Such treatment, however, made heroes of the Neo-Confucians, and after only a few years the government lifted the ban on the School of the True Way.

In the years following the lifting of the ban, Zhu Xi's teachings grew in importance and in the favor of the court. When, in the 1230s, the Mongols conquered parts of the northern China and established what they called a Confucian state, the Song government proclaimed Zu Xi's teachings the true, orthodox Confucianism. Thus, the True Way became the official philosophy of the schools, and from the schools spread to all of China.

## The Song is Sung

The need to protect China from foreign invaders was what finally ended the Song Dynasty. Needing protection against the Tatars and other enemies, the Song emperors became allies with the Mongols. The Mongols were masterful horsemen and the most skillful and brutal warriors of their time. A nomadic people, they traveled from place to place, killing or enslaving the peoples who lived on the lands they coveted.

The Mongol leaders, Genghis Khan and his son, Ogodei Khan, defeated China's enemies. But then, the Song emperors and the Mongols quarreled, and Ogodei invaded China. In 1260, Genghis Khan's grandson, Kublai Khan, set up his capital in Beijing, a city in northern China. Determined to become emperor, he invaded southern China and in a few short years conquered all of China. In 1279, the last Song emperor in despair flung himself into the sea, and Kublai Khan became emperor of China, establishing what he called the Yuan Dynasty.

# The Yuan Dynasty—Rule of the Mongols (1279–1368)

When he became emperor of China, Kublai Khan ruled a vast territory, stretching from Eastern Europe and Mesopotamia to the Pacific Ocean. As Chinese emperor, however, Kublai began adopting Chinese ways. His reign was thus brilliant and very prosperous. Under his rule, roads were built and farming flourished. Trade with Europe increased, though merchants had to cross long miles over land and sea to go to and from China. As a result of this trade, Chinese inventions in printing, gunpowder, and porcelain, as well as Chinese medical techniques, came into Europe. In Beijing, Kublai built for himself a magnificent palace called the Forbidden City.

During Kublai's reign, merchants from Europe traveled to China. The most famous of these merchants were Nicolo and Maffeo Polo of Venice and Nicolo's son, Marco Polo. Marco Polo remained in China for several years in the service of Kublai and later wrote a famous account of his travels throughout the Middle Kingdom. European Catholic missionaries also traveled to China during this period. The first of these missionaries was a Franciscan priest, John of Monte Corvino, who arrived in Beijing in 1294, where he set up China's first Catholic Church. John became archbishop of Beijing, and other missionaries came to China, including the pope's representative, John Marignolli.

## Kublai Khan and Marco Polo

In 1275, a young Italian merchant, Marco Polo, visited the court of Kublai Khan in China. He remained there for 16 years, serving as an official in Kublai's court and traveling widely throughout China. When Marco Polo eventually returned to Europe, he told stories of inventions and wealth no one would believe. He spoke of cities without crime or sewage in the streets. He said that the Chinese dug from their hills black rocks (coal) that burned with hot flame. The Chinese, he claimed, could print whole books using blocks that pressed images of letters on paper (a printing press). Chinese culture, too, said Marco Polo, was very refined. There were floating palaces and elegant dinners where the diners ate with long sticks of ivory and never touched the food with their fingers.

While they were ruling northern China and before they conquered the Song, the Mongols were not favorable to Confucianism, though they tolerated it as one of the religions of their realm. Kublai Khan, however, welcomed Confucian scholars into the imperial court, and Confucian teachings influenced his government and the empire's educational system. The Mongol court offered official state sacrifices to Confucius and encouraged the study of Confucian writings. Yet, the court also observed Buddhist rites as well as traditional Mongol religious ceremonies. Kublai Khan, however, dealt a serious blow to Confucian power by discontinuing the examinations for the civil service, with their study of Confucian texts.

The examinations were restored under the Mongol emperor Buyantu (r. 1311–1320); but the government discriminated against native Chinese in favor of Mongols and other foreigners, who came to hold the most important posts in the civil service. Buyantu ordered the study of Neo-Confucian writings in preparation for the examinations and thus made the True Way the primary school of thought. It would continue to be so for the next 500 years. Yet, Neo-Confucianism never achieved the same dynamism it had in the days of Zhu Xi. Neo-Confucian scholars did not explore new ideas but merely preserved the doctrines that had been handed down to them.

After Kublai's death in 1294, the Mongol empire began to disintegrate. The Mongols fought among themselves, and the Chinese rebelled against them. Finally, in 1368, a commoner named Hong Wu drove the Mongols out of China and made himself emperor. He set up a new, native Chinese dynasty, which he called Ming.

# The Ming Dynasty

Hong Wu's Ming Dynasty ruled China for 300 years. This was a period of peace for China. The Ming emperors encouraged agriculture and the development of new inventions. Architects built grand buildings, and artists created pottery of delicate beauty. Slavery was abolished and the lives of poor farmers improved because they did not have to pay high taxes; and when their time of serfdom ended, they were allowed to move to different regions of China and seek a better life. Future generations looked back on the Ming Dynasty as a golden age.

During the Ming Dynasty, China carried on trade with many foreign nations. From seaports of the Middle Kingdom, Chinese merchants sailed out to trade with Japan and southern Asia, as well as India, Persia, and Africa. Chinese legend says that, in the early 1400s, Admiral Zheng De sailed a fleet of giant ships, some 400 feet long with nine bamboo masts, to Sumatra and Borneo. From these lands, the fleet crossed the Pacific to the coasts of an uncharted land of "fiery mountains at the feet of the dawn." Will we one day discover that Chinese explorers reached the Pacific coast of America or at least the Hawaiian Islands several decades before Columbus landed in the New World?

At the same time, the countries of Europe were sailing eastward, and explorers from Portugal reached Asia, the Indies, and finally China. The Ming government tried to keep the Portuguese out of the Middle Kingdom, but they bribed their way in and eventually set up a profitable trade with China. The Spaniards and the Dutch soon followed and established their own trade with the Far East.

Catholic missionaries came to China with the Portuguese traders. The Catholic Church founded under the Mongols had disappeared from China, and the only Christians in China were a few Nestorian groups, who lived in the oldest Chinese cities. At first, however, no European was allowed to enter China; Portuguese traders had to stay in the port city of Macao in southwestern China. This changed in 1579, when the Chinese government allowed some Portuguese merchants to move further inland, to Canton. They were soon followed by Jesuit missionaries, one of whom was an Italian priest, Father Matteo Ricci.

## The Mission to China

Young Matteo Ricci was full of zeal for Christ and eager to bring the Catholic Faith to the rich and vast empire of China, so orderly and so respectful of learning and tradition. His own talents in science and mathematics won him the respect of powerful and learned men of China. Father Matteo had to learn to speak the elegant Chinese of the court and to adopt Chinese dress if he wished to be taken seriously. The Chinese knew only the roughest seamen and merchants from Europe; they thought of all Westerners as barbaric, unclean, and uneducated. Ricci and his fellow Jesuits showed the Chinese that Christian Europe, too, was a learned and civilized land. The work of the Jesuits was crowned with success when, in 1601, the emperor of China himself asked Ricci to come to Peking, the capital of Ming China.

Father Matteo was able to show the educated men of China that their ideas of right and wrong came from a Supreme Being, the Lord of Heaven. Ricci wrote a catechism, called *The True Doctrine of God,* in which he quoted Chinese writers, especially Confucius, to show that there is only one God, that the soul is immortal, and that other teachings of the Catholic Faith are true. Finally, he gained an audience with the emperor, after 16 years of trying, and only then because the clock he had brought from Italy caught the emperor's fancy.

Matteo Ricci died in 1610, but the work of the Jesuits continued. In 40 years time, they had assembled a Church of 150,000 people, made up both of the poor and the rich and learned Chinese. To aid their work, the Jesuits translated the liturgy and the Scriptures into Chinese so that the Chinese could read and pray in their own tongue. They allowed the new Chinese Christians, too, to continue to practice ancient ceremonies that honored their ancestors and Confucius, for the Chinese were very reluctant to abandon their ancient traditions. After much study, Ricci had decided that the Chinese were not practicing idol worship when they honored their ancestors and Confucius.

But some missionaries disagreed. They thought the Chinese practice of honoring ancestors and Confucius was idolatry or, at least, **superstitious**. They complained to the pope in Rome. Arguments went back and forth, some saying Ricci was right, others that he was wrong. In 1715, Pope Clement XI ordered the missionaries in China to stop allowing the practice of honoring ancestors, and they obeyed. The result was that educated Chinese from that time on rejected the Christian Faith. In 1724, the emperor began persecuting the Church and ordered all missionaries to leave China. The work of the Chinese missionaries, it seemed, was destroyed.

**superstitious:** having to do with superstition, an ignorant belief or trust in magic

Yet, the Chinese Catholic Church was not entirely destroyed. Jesuit missionaries for a while remained in the service of the emperor, who respected the priests' knowledge of mathematics and astronomy. Missionaries worked in secret among the Chinese, and native Chinese priests were ordained to minister to the people. Lay Chinese Catholics, too, catechized people in the Faith. The Church in China, however, did not grow again until the 1900s, when Christian missionaries were again allowed to work in the Middle Kingdom.

# The Last Dynasty of Old China

In the 1600s the Ming dynasty fought a long war with invaders from the north, the Manchus from Manchuria, and lost. By 1662, the Manchus had completely overcome the Ming. Taking over the empire, the Manchus called themselves the Ching Dynasty. The Ching Manchus made harsh laws to keep the native Han Chinese from rebelling against them.

The Ching emperors were able rulers for about 150 years. They not only ruled Manchuria and China but added new lands to the empire. They conquered Mongolia, Tibet, and Turkestan, and Korea was forced to pay tribute to the Manchu emperor. Beginning in the late 1700s, however, rebellions began breaking out throughout China. Though the Manchus had adopted Chinese culture, they never stopped treating the "Sons of Han" as a conquered people. The proud Han Chinese resented this and tried again and again to overthrow the Ching Dynasty.

Just like the Ming Dynasty, the Manchus had to deal with foreign merchants from Europe. First, it was the Portuguese and Spanish, and then the Russians. In the 1700s, Great Britain and France began trading with China. In 1784, the first ship from the United States entered a Chinese port. The Manchus feared these foreigners and would not allow them to travel from port cities into China itself. In the end, this only angered foreign countries. European countries and the United States were determined to enter China, whether the Manchu emperors liked it or not.

Throughout the 19th century and into the 20th century, European powers and the United States, as well as Japan, would continue to seek greater control of Chinese trade. What the Chinese learned from these powers, as well as their struggles against them, would lead ultimately to the overthrow of the imperial government that had ruled the Middle Kingdom for thousands of years.

# Chapter Review

### Summary
- The ancient name for China is the "Middle Kingdom," for the Chinese believed their land was the center of the universe.
- China's geographical features include extremes of climate, temperature, and terrain. Dangerous rivers, fertile farmlands, steppes, high mountains, cold northern plains, and southern jungles make up the diverse Chinese landscape.

- Chinese history is divided into eras named for the ruling families or dynasties. The first mythical dynasty was that of the Five Emperors, who were said to have invented civilization.
- The first historical Chinese dynasty was the Shang Dynasty (1766–1022 B.C.)
- The second dynasty was the Zhou Dynasty (1122 B.C.–A.D. 249) The Zhou dynasty saw the rise of Chinese philosophy and its most important thinker, Confucius.
- The Third Dynasty was the Qin Dynasty (A.D. 246–206), a brief period of terror and unification. The Emperor Zheng forced peasant armies to build the first Great Wall and the Grand Canal.
- The Fourth Dynasty, the Han Dynasty (206–220), supported Confucianism and spread literacy throughout the empire. A standard "Han culture" grew up in China. During this time, China established trade with the Mediterranean for the first time.
- The Fifth Dynasty, the Tang Dynasty (618–907), began with disunity; but the Tang united central China and added new lands. During the Tang, Buddhism became an important religion in China.
- The Sixth Dynasty, the Song Dynasty (960–1279), was an era of peace in China in which a luxurious civilization flowered. It was a time that saw developments in shipbuilding, poetry, medicine, science, and the arts.
- The Seventh Dynasty, the Yuan Dynasty (1279–1368), was the period during which the Mongols ruled China. The Mongols, led by Kublai Khan, overthrew the Song Dynasty in 1279.
- The Eighth Dynasty, the Ming Dynasty (1368–1662), arose after the Mongols were weakened by disease, Chinese opposition, and infighting. The Ming period is a high point of Chinese civilization, a golden age.
- Though China continued to trade with foreign countries, the Ming grew wary of foreigners in their port cities. The ports were closed to foreigners, except the Portuguese. The Jesuit priest, Father Matteo Ricci, entered China with Portuguese traders. Jesuit and other missionaries made much progress in converting the Chinese until controversy over the Jesuits' methods led the pope to condemn them.
- The last dynasty, the Ching dynasty (1644–1901), belonged to Manchus from northern China.

## Key Concepts

**Middle Kingdom:** the ancient name for China

**Confucianism:** a school of philosophy founded by the Chinese thinker, Confucius, that gave China the social and moral ideas that have guided Chinese civilization. Confucianism stresses that human beings are primarily members of communities—the family, especially, but also the local community, the school, and the kingdom. Confucianism teaches that rulers should govern more by moral example than by force. The people should honor ancestors, respect rulers, obey the laws, and participate in rituals that tie society together.

**Buddhism:** the religious philosophy ascribed to Siddhartha Gautama, the Buddha ("enlightened one"). Buddhism seeks to provide an answer to sorrow and suffering in the world, saying that they come from desire for pleasure and fear of pain. If people want to rid themselves of sorrow and suffering, they have to purify the spirit through right thinking and right conduct.

**Neo-Confucianism:** The name given to the revival of Confucianism during the Song Dynasty. Neo-Confucianism borrowed ideas from both Buddhism and the traditional Chinese religion, Taoism. One of the great Neo-Confucian teachers, Zhu Xi, taught that the goal of education is to help people cultivate a sense of morality. A moral society, he said, would lead to good government. Neo-Confucians sought to spread their ideas among the poor as well as the rich.

## Dates to Remember

**479 B.C.:** the death of Confucius
**A.D. 618:** the founding of the Tang Dynasty
**636:** the Nestorians build the first Christian church in China.
**960:** the Song Dynasty comes to power in China.
**1279:** Kublai Khan becomes emperor of China.
**1294:** John of Monte Corvina establishes the first Catholic Church in China.
**1610:** the death of Matteo Ricci
**1724:** the Chinese emperor orders the persecution of the Catholic Church in China.

## Central Characters

**Confucius (551–479 B.C.):** the founder of the religious philosophy that became the foundation of Chinese civilization
**Siddhartha Gautama, the Buddha (6th century B.C.):** the Indian religious thinker whose ideas became the basis of Buddhism, one of the most important religions of China and Korea
**Zheng (3rd century B.C.):** the first Qin emperor. Zheng united China and built the first Great Wall.
**Liu Bang (256–195 B.C.):** the first Han emperor. He made Confucianism the basis of law in China.
**Taizu (A.D. 927–976):** the first emperor of the Song Dynasty. He tried to base his government on Confucian ideals.
**Zhu Xi (1130–1200):** one of the founders of Neo-Confucianism
**Kublai Khan (1215–1294):** the Mongol conqueror of China who entertained Marco Polo
**Father Matteo Ricci (1552–1610):** a Jesuit priest who led a mission that converted 150,000 Chinese to the Catholic Faith during the Ming period

## Questions for Review

1. How did the Chinese emperors assure that their civil servants would be able men?
2. Who was Confucius? What was the golden rule of his thought?
3. Why was the Han Dynasty so important to Chinese history?
4. Where do sorrow and suffering come from, according to Siddhartha Gautama? How are people to rid themselves of sorrow and suffering?
5. Name three accomplishments of Tang China.
6. What were the goals of Neo-Confucianism?
7. Why is the Ming Dynasty remembered as China's golden age?

8. When did the first Christian missionaries come into China? Who were they?
9. Why were Matteo Ricci and the Jesuits so successful in converting the Chinese? Who disagreed with their methods and why?

### Ideas in Action
1. The Great Wall was built in phases over several dynasties. Look up the Great Wall on the Internet or in an encyclopedia and find out: how many building phases did it take to finish the Great Wall? When were the phases completed? When was the entire wall completed? How many miles long is it? How is the Great Wall used and preserved today? Make a map of the course of the Great Wall.
2. The Mongols once had the largest empire in the world. Use an encyclopedia or atlas to find the exact borders of the Mongol Empire at its height. Write a list of modern countries that were once under Mongol control. Did your ancestors in Europe, Asia, or the Middle East ever live under Mongol rule?
3. Ask students to find some of Confucius' sayings. Students should choose five Confucian sayings they like and explain whether they find his wisdom helpful in everyday life.
4. Chinese music is very strange to the Western ear. Listen to some Chinese music and compare its use of percussion, stringed instruments, and antique falsetto singing with Gregorian chant and Renaissance polyphony. Appropriate recordings can be found at the library, a music or book store, or the Internet.

# Highways and Byways

### The Chinese Language
The Chinese language is very different from the languages that have come from Europe. For instance, while English, French, and German words often have two or more syllables, Chinese words have only one syllable each. Chinese, too, has no plural nouns and no verb tenses. Chinese verbs are always in the present tense.

Chinese has several dialects, but the written Chinese language is the same everywhere. Chinese does not form words from an alphabet, like European languages do. Chinese is written in pictures, with each picture standing for an idea. Since each picture stands for an idea and not a sound (like our letters and words do), the same picture can be used for different words in the various Chinese dialects. An example of this is if we drew a picture of a fish to express the idea of a scaly water creature with fins. Such a picture could be understood by English speakers and Latin speakers, even though in English it would be called a "fish" and in Latin, *piscis*. In China, people could understand another person's writing, even if he could not understand his speech.

Chinese language drawings are called *ideograms*. People who read and write Chinese learn about 2,000 ideograms. Though each ideogram stands for a simple idea, it can be joined to other ideograms to express more complex ideas. The written languages of Japan, Korea, and Vietnam are based on Chinese characters. The characters are the same though the spoken languages sound completely different.

# Japan: Land of the Rising Sun

Japan is a necklace of islands that run from north to south and lie to the east of the coasts of Siberia, China, and Korea. West of Japan is the Sea of Japan, which separates the Japanese islands from the Asian mainland. East of Japan is the vast Pacific Ocean.

Our name, "Japan," comes from the Chinese name for the country. The people of Japan, however, call their country *Nippon,* a word that means "Land of the Rising Sun." When they spelled *Nippon,* the Japanese used the Chinese characters for "sun" and "source." In Chinese, those characters would be pronounced as JIH-PEN. Europeans, learning the name from Chinese speakers, called it Ja-pan.

**habitable:** fit to live in
**staple:** most important

Only a very small part of Japan is easily **habitable** by human beings. Today, Japan's over 100 million people inhabit the 15 percent of the country that is flat and fertile. The other 85 percent of Japan is mountainous, forested, and scenic. The mountains were formed from volcanoes, some of which are still active. The most famous is Mount Fuji, a beautiful, impressive volcanic mountain near Tokyo.

The soil from the volcanoes of Japan is rich, and the Japanese have learned how to get the most food they can from it. The largest crops are rice (a **staple** food of the Japanese diet), tea, soybeans, and fruit. The Japanese harvest fish from the abundant waters around the islands both for their own needs and to sell to other nations.

Japan is made up of four islands. The northernmost island is called Hokkaido. Sapporo is its capital. The island is known for its beauty. It has active volcanoes, hot mineral springs, and unspoiled lakes and forests. Its weather is cold and snowy in the winter and cool in the summer.

To the south of Hokkaido lies the Island of Honshu. Honshu is by far the largest of Japan's islands and is home to the nation's capital, Tokyo. Honshu is heavily populated and currently produces much of Japan's industrial goods (cars, boats, industrial machinery, etc.) and high-tech products (such as electronics).

The inhabitants of Honshu benefit from an unusual feature called the Inland Sea—a waterway between the southeastern part of Honshu and the northern part of Shikoku, the next island in the chain. The Inland Sea, with its numerous small coves, gives Japan a waterway that is screened from the Pacific Ocean.

Shikoku is the smallest of the four major islands. It is a beautiful land, covered with lush vegetation, though its mountains and valleys make farming very difficult. In summer, torrential rains and storms pound the Pacific side of the island. Snows cover the island during the winter, and rain falls often in torrents during the spring and especially the summer. These harsh rains sometimes grow into destructive **typhoons** in the Pacific Ocean.

The southernmost of the four main islands in the chain, Kyushu, is the third largest. It has a mountainous central region with coastal plains around it. Kyushu's climate is **subtropical**, with heavy rain. The northern part of the island houses industry, while the southern part produces abundant rice, potatoes, citrus, livestock, and fish.

Because its islands are volcanic, Japan experiences many earthquakes. Some release just a small amount of energy and cause inconvenience, while others are terribly destructive. Because their homes have been repeatedly destroyed by storms and earthquakes, the Japanese have learned to work together as an inventive and courageous team, ready to rebuild their homes as often as necessary.

> **typhoon:** a violent storm; hurricane
> **subtropical:** a region near the tropics, having hot summers and warm winters, with nearly no frost or snow; semitropical
> **Caucasian:** of or relating to the white race
> **mikado:** emperor of Japan

# Early History of Japan

The earliest inhabitants of Japan came to the islands in three waves of settlement. First came Stone Age **Caucasians** from Siberia; the next to arrive were Asian farmers. The third group of settlers was also Asian. They migrated into the south and began the process of nation building that produced Japan.

Around the 3rd century A.D., a tribe living in the Yamato Plain in central Honshu made itself the chief power over most of Japan. This tribe founded a dynasty of emperors that has continued without a break into our own time. This dynasty is called Sun, because the imperial Yamato family claimed that they were descended from the sun goddess, Amaterasu, who gave them three items that later became symbols of the emperor's power—a bronze mirror, a bronze sword, and a jeweled necklace.

The first emperor of the Sun Dynasty to rule Japan was Jimmu Tenno ("Divine Warrior"), who was called the **mikado** ("Honorable Gate") of Japan. Since Jimmu Tenno said he came from Amaterasu, all of the emperors of Japan have been considered descendants of the gods. The *mikado's* cousins became chieftains of the clans, which in Japan were groups of families. Later, Japanese clans formed industrial companies, such as Toyota, Mikasa, and Mitsubishi.

The oldest religion in Japan is Shinto, the worship of nature gods and ancestors. Shinto teaches that the gods founded Japan and will remain with the Japanese people as long as they are ruled by a *mikado* from the Sun Dynasty of Jimmu Tenno. Shinto continues the ancient practice of worshiping gods and spirits that are believed to inhabit such things as rivers and mountains. Shinto honors ancestors and encourages people to pray to them for aid. Even today, Shinto remains an important part of Japanese life in fostering **piety** and reverence for ancestors.

## China's Influence on Japanese Culture

Japan's nearest neighbors on the mainland of Asia were China and the little kingdoms of Korea. Korea had been civilized by the Chinese and was a very wealthy land in the eyes of the poor Japanese. Japanese clans began to raid Korea and try to conquer it. When they saw Chinese culture in Korea, the Japanese raiders thought it was superior to their own culture, and they began to imitate it. In that way, Chinese civilization first began to come into Japan.

One Korean king sent a number of gifts to the *mikado*. Among these gifts was an invaluable book, the *Thousand Character Classic*. Written in Chinese script, the book was a guide to learning and reading Chinese characters. Because only a few men in Japan were able to read, the *mikado* saw that the book would be very valuable to him. He sent to Korea for a scholar who might be able to teach the Japanese to read and write. The arrival of the Korean scribe Wa-ni in A.D. 405 was a new dawn for Japan. Chinese script became the first official written language of Japan.

Writing Japanese in Chinese characters (called ideograms) is very difficult. Unlike Chinese, Japanese is an inflected language; that is, it adds syllables to words to show they are plural or to indicate what tense they are. (For instance, in English, we add -s or -es to nouns to show they are plural and -ed to verbs to show past tense.) Chinese does not do this; its words do not change form at all, and so it is easy to use ideograms with it. Japanese words, on the other hand, change form, and so ideograms do not work as well with Japanese.

In the 9th century, a Japanese Buddhist monk named Kobo Daishi found a solution to how to use Chinese symbols for Japanese. Using the Indian language, Sanskrit, which has an alphabet, he came up with a **syllabary** for Japanese. Unlike a language, like our own English, which uses symbols (letters) for each sound, a syllabary uses symbols that represent syllables. English, for instance, uses *a* for the "aye" sound, *b* for the "bee" sound, *t* for the "tee" sound, etc. A language like Japanese uses one symbol for each syllable. A word such as *alphabet*, which has three syllables, would have three symbols, indicating each of the syllables *al*, *pha*, and *bet*.

Another import from Korea was Buddhism. Around 500, a Korean king sent an image of Buddha and sacred Buddhist books to the emperor of Japan. The emperor's family decided to adopt Buddhism, partly because it was considered to be the religion of the civilized world. The Japanese ruling clans, however, feared that Buddhism might offend their native gods, spirits, and divine ancestors. This conflict between Buddhism and Shinto was a violent one.

Buddhism was finally allowed into the country when the crown prince, Shotoku, decided to make China's great civilization the model for remaking Japanese society. His father, the *mikado*, had only a short a reign and

**piety:** being pious—that is, being reverent and respectful toward God, one's parents, other elders, and those in authority

**syllabary:** a set of written characters, each one representing a syllable

was succeeded by Shotoku's aunt, who in 593 allowed him to rule the kingdom as regent. To change his country, Shotoku insisted that his nobles learn and observe the moral laws of Confucianism. He wrote up laws for Japan, based on Confucius' teachings. He declared Buddhism to be the religion everyone should admire, thought he did not forbid people to practice Shintoism. Eventually, Buddhism became the chief religious philosophy of Japan, while Confucianism guided the laws, and Shinto directed the rituals of the court and was the religion of the people.

Under Shotoku's direction, Japanese who were skilled in the arts or Buddhist learning were sent to China to complete their studies. When they returned after 10 or 20 years of training at the Chinese court, they received important government posts in Japan. In this way, Shotoku introduced the Chinese civil service system into Japan. The crown prince also sponsored irrigation projects for farming and instituted government-supported measures to help the poor. Shotoku, who changed the life and culture of Japan and gave the imperial court its ceremony and philosophy, died at the age of 48. He had been the most powerful man in the realm, though he never himself became emperor. He was always just the crown prince.

# Japan in the Middle Ages

The full flowering of Chinese culture in Japan occurred during what is called the Heian period, which lasted from 794 to 1185. The *mikado's* court imitated the Chinese emperor's court and created poetry and music, artwork, and elegant calligraphy. In 793, a new capital city was built in the center of the Yamato plain. It was named Heian-kyo, or "Capital of Peace." Heian-kyo was the first true city in Japan. Its layout copied the Chinese capital city of Changan. It was rectangular, three miles long, and two and two-thirds miles wide. At the center of Heian-kyo sat the imperial palace. Parks and broad avenues, set at right angles, made it a lovely city. In time it came to be called simply, Kyoto, "the capital."

Though they imitated Chinese art styles, Japanese artists painted portraits that were more realistic and showed the individual character of people better than Chinese portraits did. Japan's oldest surviving portrait of an individual is the sculpture of the great Chinese Buddhist monk-missionary, Ganjin. It shows him as a **wizened** old man, wrinkled and worn, but meditating and tranquil of mind.

One of the great works of Japanese classical literature appeared only in 760, a short time before the Heian period. It was a collection of 4,500 poems called *Man'yoshu*, "Ten Thousand Leaves." Most of the poems in the collection are short, five-line poems called *waka*. A few are long poems, or *choka*—though long poems do not work well in the Japanese language and Japanese poets did not favor them. Poetry became very important during the Heian period. A **courtier**, for instance, was expected to be able to compose and recite a *waka* on command for any occasion, and to compose long poems for formal recitation when needed.

**wizened:** dry, shrunken, or wrinkled, usually on account of old age

**courtier:** a person present in the court of a king, emperor, etc.; a court attendant

> **prose:** writing in the ordinary form of speech; not poetry

In the 900s, **prose** romances became fashionable reading, and women writers made names for themselves by writing these works. Around 1002, one woman writer, Sei Shonagun, wrote the romance, *Pillow Book,* which is now recognized as a masterpiece. The greatest prose work of the period was by another court lady, Murasaki Shikibu. This work, called *The Tale of Genji* (written around 1015), is thought to be the world's first novel. Like many works written under the influence of Buddhism, *The Tale of Genji* gives one a sense of the impermanence of the world, though it contains skillful descriptions of human emotion and expresses the beauty of nature.

The Heian period enjoyed a kind of formal Buddhist dance that featured characters and told a story. It is said that a Korean named Mimashi had brought this dance, called *gigaku,* to the Japanese court in 612. *Gigaku* dancers wore masks to identify themselves as various characters. During 7th century, another dance, called *bugaku,* earned the favor of the court. *Bugaku* was and is a very formal dance performed by groups of four to eight male dancers to the accompaniment of bells, flute, lute, drums, and panpipe. During the Heian period, performers attached to temples and shrines began performing plays that included dancing, singing, and dialogue. Much later, in the 14th century, this joining together of dance, song, and drama became more highly developed in a form called *Noh.* Borrowing from the musical forms of both bugaku and *gigaku, Noh* also utilized Buddhist chanting. *Noh* plays have been continuously performed to our own time.

But while the arts at the court flourished, the imperial government was weakening. The imperial family came to rely on the Fujiwara family to help them govern, and the Fujiwara gradually replaced the emperors as the real rulers of Japan. They did not remove the emperors but forced them to stay in their palace in Kyoto while the Fujiwara took care of the government of Japan. But the Fujiwara could not stand up to the growing power of the warrior clans from the provinces, who gradually began to make themselves the masters of Japan.

Two warrior clans came to vie with each other for the control of the imperial family through marriages and military force. They were the Taira and Minamoto clans. The story of their long feud and struggle for control of the emperor is the subject a long story, called the *Heike Monogatori* (written about 1250). Stories from that conflict became subjects of Japanese drama.

# The Revenge of the First Shogun

The Minamoto family found favor at court and were given honors and wealth by the *mikado.* But, one night, their enemy, the Taira family, surprised them and slaughtered all the family except one small boy, Minamoto Yoritomo. He was the last of the Minamoto line, and when the guards were about to kill him, he spoke up and said, "My mother and father are dead, and who but I can pray for their happiness in the next world?" The young boy reminded the Taira grandmother of her own son who had died as a boy. Moved by the boy's **filial piety**, and

> **filial piety:** the piety shown by a son or daughter to his or her parents

remembering her own son who had died as a boy, the Taira grandmother begged for Yoritomo's life. The Taira spared him, but they banished him to an island in the faraway Izu province.

In his place of exile, Yoritomo was kept under close guard. Moreover, his guards had been given orders to kill him when he reached thirteen years. But a faithful servant raised Yoritomo and taught him **martial arts** in secret. When Yoritomo was thirteen, he was so **submissive** and seemingly helpless that the lord of the Taira allowed him to live. Yoritomo bided his time, waiting for the time he could take his revenge on his enemies, the Taira.

> **martial arts:** the art or skill of fighting; the arts suitable to a warrior
> **submissive:** obedient, humble

In order to get soldiers to help him carry out his revenge, Yoritomo decided to arrange a marriage with a powerful clan—which would make the clan his ally. There was one such clan, with two sisters, one ugly, the other, beautiful. To avoid notice and to gain the favor of the mother, Yoritomo decided he would ask to marry the ugly daughter. He thus wrote her a letter proposing marriage and sent it by his servant. But, as events turned out, the servant had other plans than his master.

One night, the ugly sister had a dream of a pigeon flying to her with a box of gold. When she awoke, she told her dream to the beautiful sister, Masago, who said, "Let me buy your dream, little sister, and I will give you my golden mirror in exchange." The homely sister agreed, but she had barely time to say "yes," before Yoritomo's servant appeared and handed his master's letter, not to the ugly sister, as he had been told to do, but to the beautiful one.

Masago eventually eloped with Yoritomo and began aiding him in his quest for revenge and the restoration of his house. The two of them set about collecting an army of followers and friendly lords, who were worried about the growing power of the Taira. The head of the Taira clan heard of Yoritomo's army and laughed. "For an exile to plot against the Taira is like a mouse going against a cat," he said.

But the laugh was soon Yoritomo's. Both sides gathered for battle on opposite sides of the Fuji River. On the night before the battle, two of the Taira warriors thought they would slip into Yoritomo's camp and assassinate him. They tried to cross the river through the wide shallows on their side, but their splashing stirred up the great flocks of ducks that were resting there. The sound of the birds flapping and quacking woke the Taira troops, who suspected a surprise attack by their enemy. In the confusion, many ran for safety and some fought their own men in the dark. In the morning, the Taira force was dead or fled from the field. Yoritomo had won a victory without striking a blow.

In time, Yoritomo and his beautiful wife Masago built a city for themselves and their followers at Kamakura, in a valley facing the open sea. There, Yoritomo and Masago made their own court more beautiful and attractive than the emperor's court in Kyoto. Indeed, Yoritomo became more powerful than the emperor. When Yoritomo died in his bed in 1199, his Minamoto family held control not only of the capital, Kyoto, but of the entire country.

## The Era of the Shoguns

Because Yoritomo had become the most powerful man in Japan, the emperor in Kyoto was forced to turn to him to subdue the other warrior-chiefs and bring peace to the country. In 1192, the emperor

> **shogun:** supreme general; a military ruler of Japan
> **samurai:** the art or skill of fighting; the arts suitable to a warrior
> **daimyo:** military lords of ancient Japan who controlled a number of private estates

gave Yoritomo a special title, **shogun**, or "supreme general," and with it the right to rule Japan for the emperor. The office of *shogun* became the chief power in the land. Under the *shogun*, warrior lords, called **daimyo**, came to control various private estates into which Japan had been divided. The emperors, though born of the ancient Sun Line, were mere figureheads without power or even enough wealth to keep up their palaces.

Yoritomo set up a system of government that was similar to feudalism in Europe. *Daimyo* and other nobles were to be loyal to their ruler, and the ruler to his nobles. Part of this system of loyalty was the warrior, called a **samurai**. The samurai followed the "code of the warrior," by which he was totally dutiful to his lord or master. A samurai's loyalty was absolute; he would unflinchingly die rather than face dishonor. The courage of the samurai may be compared to that of the Spartans. Yet, although the military skill of the samurai was legendary, they were much more than just warriors only. They were trained in writing and in politics as well.

The samurai were drawn to a sect of the Buddhist religion known as Zen. Zen Buddhism teaches that one can become enlightened through meditation and physical and mental discipline. Zen was blended with elements of the traditional Shinto religion to provide moral and artistic guidelines for the tough, yet loyal and artistic warriors—the samurai—of Japan. Other schools of Buddhism in Japan also flourished during the 12th and 13th centuries. With Zen they began to take on distinctively Japanese characteristics and traditions. Until the 12th century, Buddhism in Japan had been basically a Chinese religious philosophy transplanted in Japanese soil. After the 12th century, it took on the colors of Japanese culture.

The period of the *shoguns* brought some peace and prosperity to Japan. However, noble families constantly struggled for control of the country. Each powerful clan wanted to rule Japan in the name of the emperor. In the warfare, many lords died. Their orphaned samurai became *ronin*, or lordless samurai. They hired themselves out as warriors or wandered the country, taking whatever they needed by force.

# Traditional Japanese Arts

Influenced by the natural beauty of Japan, Shinto's appreciation of nature, and Buddhist contemplation, the Japanese developed very striking and unique arts: flower arranging (*ikebana*), the growing and pruning of miniature trees (*bonsai*), poetry, and the traditional tea ceremony.

Traditional Japanese flower arranging (*ikebana*) developed from the practice of offering flowers in Buddhist temples. These flower arrangements using natural flowers and other plant materials were afterward found in the homes of the upper classes and came to be recognized as an art form. The arrangements expressed the traditional Japanese idea of the balance of heaven and earth.

Traditional Japanese poetry expresses a strong, clear thought or emotion in verse that follows strict rules. Poetic ideas are inspired by natural objects, such as mountains, grass, or rain. The poet must express his thought in a very few words. The Japanese poetic form best known in the West today is *haiku*. A *haiku* poem has three unrhymed lines. The first line has five syllables; the second line, seven syllables; and the third line, five syllables again. In *haiku* the poet compares and contrasts what he sees here and now with the enduring patterns of nature. The reader is challenged to find the meaning of the poem by comparing permanent things with those that pass quickly away.

The Zen monk, Basho, wrote one famous example of *haiku*:

*This ancient pond here:*
*A frog suddenly plunges:*
*Plop of the water.*

To understand such a poem, you need to visualize the scene. Imagine yourself standing beside the oldest pond you can think of, seeing the lichen on the trees and rocks, and the color of the dark stones. Think of how long the pond has been there and of the men of prayer and thoughtfulness who have stood, like you, beside these waters. As you are drawn deeper and deeper into the contemplation of the deep water, a frog suddenly jumps in. You do not see him; he is too quick. But the sound of his hitting the water breaks your **reverie**, and in that moment the music of the rippling water reminds you that the ancient touches the now.

**reverie:** dreamy thoughts, dreamy thinking of pleasant things

Sometimes *haiku* can be used to express ideas of morality as well. Here is another poem by Basho:

*When a thing is said,*
*The lips become very cold*
*Like the autumn wind.*

"When a thing is said"—this is not just anything that is said, but a cold thing, cold enough to chill the lips that spoke it. How often do we regret having said an unkind word almost as soon as we have said it? Here, Basho thinks of that moment of regret as a cold autumn wind, turning the lips, and the heart, cold with sadness, and perhaps a little fear.

The Japanese tea ceremony or *chanoyu* takes place in a small, out-of-the-way room set aside for tea. Honored guests arrive to take part in what is more than simply a social gathering—it is a chance to purify the soul by appreciating nature. The ceremony is also an opportunity to appreciate the gardens surrounding the tearoom, the ceramic bowls used in the ceremony, and the decorative flowers. The tea ceremony, introduced from China, developed into its present form in the mid-1800s. It became an important form of social communication among the upper classes. The slow motions of the tea server, and the attention of the guests to every gesture, reflect the Japanese attitude to existence.

# Europe Comes to Japan

Around the year 1540, a Portuguese ship, driven by a storm, landed on an island lying south of Kyushu. This was the first contact Europeans had ever had with "The Land of the Rising Sun." Soon Portuguese merchants were trading with the Japanese.

In 1549, the Portuguese brought the Spanish Jesuit, St. Francis Xavier, to Japan. By his preaching and his holiness, as well as by many miracles, Francis Xavier won hundreds of Japanese to the Catholic Faith. He enthusiastically praised the spiritual understanding of the Japanese people and their openness to the Christian Faith. When Francis Xavier set out for China in 1551, other Jesuits came to Japan to carry on his missionary work. By 1587, there were about 200,000 Catholics in Japan.

By 1590, a Japanese feudal lord named Toyotomi Hideyoshi unified all of Japan under his power. Though at first Hideyoshi did not object to the Christians, he began to fear that Catholic priests were working to prepare Japan for conquest by Portugal or Spain. Hideyoshi feared, too, that his rivals, the samurai lords, would use the Christians against him. Hideyoshi thus began to persecute the Christians. He banished Christian missionaries from Japan and then made being a Christian a crime punishable by death.

Hideyoshi's wrath broke out against 20 Japanese Christians along with six Franciscan missionaries, whom he arrested. Among these were the Japanese Jesuits Paul Miki, James Kisai, and John de Goto. All 26 were crucified on a hill near Nagasaki on February 6, 1597. As he hung from the cross, Paul Miki preached to the crowds, inviting them to love Christ. All 26 men are today saints of the Catholic Church, known as the "Japanese Martyrs."

The desire of the Japanese government to keep Japan pure from outside influences led to further persecution of Christians from the 1600s until the middle of the 1800s. Thousands of Christians died rather than deny the Faith. Yet, despite all the persecution against Christians, the Church in Japan was not destroyed. When Catholic missionaries entered Japan in 1865, they found about 20,000 Japanese Christians who still practiced the Faith in secret.

## The Tokugawa Shogunate

Five years after Hideyoshi's death in 1598, Tokugawa Ieyasu (a descendant of Yoritomo) emerged as the *shogun* of all Japan. Ieyasu moved the capital to Edo, on the eastern shore of the island of Honshu—the place where Tokyo stands today. The emperor's court remained at Kyoto, but the *mikado* was totally powerless. Japan kept the emperor only because the Shinto religion taught that he was sacred.

The Tokugawa *shoguns* continued to try to keep Japan pure of all foreign influence. They persecuted Christians and forbade contact with all foreigners. The only nation they traded with was the Dutch. Ships from all other nations were forbidden to enter Japanese ports.

Under the Tokugawa *shoguns*, Japanese society was divided into three classes: the nobles of the court, the samurai, and the common people. The nobles with the *shogun* controlled the government, while the samurai served the nobles. The commoners were divided into farmers, artisans, and merchants, of whom farmers received the most respect and merchants the least. There was also a class of "outcasts," whom everyone despised and who did the worst jobs. It was practically impossible for anyone in Japan to move from the lower into the higher classes.

Because Japan was closed to the outside world, the changes that occurred in Europe, the Americas, and other parts of Asia in the 17th and 18th centuries did not affect it. By the mid-19th century,

Japan had none of the industry or technology that made the European countries world powers. Yet, by the end of the 19th century, Japan had adopted European-style industries and had built up a well-disciplined army and navy. Its samurai warrior tradition lived on into the 20th century and, armed with new weapons, challenged the great powers of the world.

# Chapter Review

## Summary
- The people of Japan call their country *Nippon*, meaning "Land of the Rising Sun." Our name Japan comes from the Chinese pronunciation of the written name, *Nippon*, pronounced in Chinese as JIH-PEN.
- Japan has four major islands: Hokkaido in the north, known for its cool climate, beauty, and hot mineral springs; next Honshu, the largest and most populated island, home to the capital city, Tokyo; next Shikoku, the smallest island, which has a harsh climate and is separated from Honshu by the Inland Sea; finally, in the south, Kyushu, where mountains rise in the center and separate an industrialized northern part from a southern agricultural plain.
- Japan was settled by Stone Age Caucasians from Siberia and two groups of Oriental farmers. The tribe living in central Honshu established itself as the dominant power of the island in the 3rd century B.C. This tribe established the Sun dynasty.
- The Japanese emperor is called the *mikado*, which means "honorable gate." He was thought to be a descendent of the sun goddess.
- The oldest religion in Japan is Shinto, the worship of nature gods and ancestors.
- Japanese learned Chinese civilization from Korea, which Japanese raiders invaded in A.D. 405.
- Japan developed its written language from Chinese script. A Buddhist monk, Kobo Daishi, invented a Japanese syllabary, or set of written characters each one representing a syllable.
- Buddhism was imported into Japan from Korea. After a violent conflict between Buddhism and Shinto, the crown prince Shotoku decided to remake Japanese society in the Chinese mode. Shotoku adopted Confucianism as the moral code, Buddhism as the philosophical or religious creed, and Shinto as the court and popular religion.
- During the Heian Period (A.D. 794–1185) Japanese culture experienced a golden age. It was a time of artistic development, poetry and literature.
- In 1192, Yoritomo became the first *shogun*, which means "supreme general." The *shogun* was the most powerful man in the land, and the emperor became a figurehead. There was some peace and prosperity during the period called the Shogunate, but noble families were constantly fighting each other. The fighting men of a lord's house were called samurai, and these warriors developed a strict code of loyalty, courage, and honor.
- In 1549, St. Francis Xavier brought the Christian faith to Japan when he arrived with Portuguese merchants. The Japanese people were very open to the Catholic Faith, and thousands converted.

- The *shogun* Hideyoshi opposed the foreign missionaries and regarded Christianity as a foreign threat and a power play by rival lords. Christians were banished, and persecutions began. St. Paul Miki and his companions were martyred near Nagasaki in 1597.
- Beginning in the 17th century, the Tokugawa shoguns isolated their country from foreigners, so modern developments in the rest of the world passed them by in the 17th and 18th centuries.
- Traditional Japanese arts include: flower arranging or ikebana, pruning miniature trees or *bonsai*, *haiku* poetry, and the Japanese tea ceremony. The ideas of Buddhism influence these arts, which emphasize meditation, bringing peace to the soul, and the difference between the transient and eternal things.

## Key Concepts

**mikado:** the name for the Japanese emperor, meaning "honorable gate"
**Shinto:** the oldest religion in Japan. Shinto worships nature spirits and ancestors and considers the *mikado* divine.
**shogun:** the supreme military ruler of Japan during the period called the Shogunate
**daimyo:** a warrior lord
**syllabary:** a set of written characters, each one representing a syllable
**Zen Buddhism:** a form of Buddhism that teaches that one can become enlightened through meditation and physical and mental discipline

## Dates to Remember

**250–350:** founding of the Sun dynasty as the dominant power of Japan
**593–604:** Prince Shotoku's reform of the imperial court and kingdom
**1192:** Minamoto Yoritomo establishes the Shogunate.
**1540:** The Portuguese arrive in Japan.
**1549:** St. Francis Xavier begins Jesuit missionary work in Japan.
**1597:** martyrdom of St. Paul Miki and companions
**1603:** Tokugawa Ieyasu seizes the Shogunate.

## Central Characters

**Jimmu Tenno (7th century B.C.):** the first *mikado*
**Shotoku (574–622):** the grand prince who remade Japanese society on the Chinese model
**Yoritomo (1147–1199):** last of the Minamoto clan; became the first *shogun*
**Basho (1644–1694):** major poet of Japan; a master of *haiku*
**St. Francis Xavier (1506–1552):** Catholic missionary to Japan
**Toyotomi Hideyoshi (1536–1598):** the *shogun* who opposed Christian missionaries
**St. Paul Miki:** a Japanese Jesuit, martyred during Hideyoshi's persecution
**Tokugawa Ieyasu (1543–1616):** the *shogun* who closed Japan to foreigners

## Questions for Review
1. List the names of the islands that make up Japan
2. Describe Shinto. What does Shinto teach about the *mikado*?
3. What did Shotoku do to make Japanese culture more like Chinese culture?
4. List and describe three arts of Japan.
5. What role did the *shogun* have in medieval Japan? What were the shogun's warriors called?
6. What might have happened in Japan if Hideyoshi had not suppressed the Catholic Faith in the 16th century?
7. Ponder the bravery of the Japanese Christians in keeping the Faith for 200 years. What does their endurance tell us about the character of the Japanese people?
8. Why do you think Japanese art is focused so much on the natural world?

## Ideas in Action
1. As a class, read and discuss the two *haiku* included in the text and read other examples of *haiku*. Two web pages that can be found on the internet and that may be helpful are: http://www.big.or.jp/~loupe/links/ehisto/ehisinx.shtml/*http://raysweb.net/haiku/pages/haikubythemasters.html.* Students should be encouraged to verbalize the links between the images in the *haiku* and then compose their own *haiku* from two juxtaposed images.
2. Teachers should find collections of Japanese painting and woodblock prints. Many collections can be found in libraries or bookstores. Students should be shown this artwork and instructed in the composition and color as representation of the Japanese spirit. Comparison should be made to Chinese painting and Byzantine icons and Western realistic and religious art.
3. View a film of performance of *bugaku* or *Noh* theatre. Discuss the differences between Japanese dramatic performances and those of our own culture.

# Highways and Byways

## Sesshu and the Mouse
Sesshu (1420–1506) was one of Japan's great artists. Originally, Sesshu studied to be a monk, but he was so busy drawing that he neglected his studies. As a punishment, his teacher tied him to a pillar at the temple. Sesshu's tears created a puddle at his own feet and, using only his toes, Sesshu drew a mouse in the mud. Legend has it that the mouse was so lifelike that his teacher, upon seeing it, gave Sesshu permission to study painting.

# Africa: The Enduring Continent

The continent of Africa provides many challenge to the people who live there. Africa's hot climate is one severe challenge. Most of the continent is open grassland, and the vast majority of Africa's soils are poor and not suitable for farming. Africa has many tropical diseases and voracious insects that torment the inhabitants of most areas of the continent. The Sahara, a huge desert, lies just south of the North African coast, making transportation by land from north to south extremely difficult. Also, since water is hard to obtain in many parts of Africa (not just the vast deserts), settled life is very difficult. With these challenges, the African peoples—both present and past—require fortitude, toughness, and teamwork just to survive.

## The Geography of Africa

Africa is the second largest continent in the world. It so huge that the United States, Europe, India, and Japan could easily fit into Africa with space left over. Oceans surround Africa on all sides, except for a small land bridge that connects it to Asia. The equator runs through the middle of the African continent, and all the areas of the continent are hot. In the center of the continent and along the western coast are the famous jungles of Africa.

Africa may be divided into six broad areas: North Africa, the Sahara Desert, West Africa, East Africa, Central Africa, and southern Africa.

**North Africa** is the part of Africa that touches the Mediterranean Sea. Its civilization has always been part of the greater Mediterranean world. The Nile Delta that was so important to ancient Egyptian civilization is part of the North African world. Along with Egypt, ancient Phoenicia, Greece, and Rome made North Africa part of the ancient civilized world. Later, in the 7th century, Muslim Arabs conquered the entire area. Because of its history, North Africa has developed differently from the rest of Africa. The modern-day countries that make up this area are Morocco, Algeria, Tunisia, Libya, and Egypt.

The Sahara lies below Africa's fertile and inhabited northern coast. The Sahara is by far the largest desert in the world and stretches from the Atlantic Ocean on the west to the Red Sea on the east. It covers three and one-half million square miles. The Sahara was once a grassland, or savannah, before the end of the last ice age. There is evidence that people in the Sahara once lived in tribes as nomadic herdsmen. As the ice age came to an end, the earth's climate changed, and hot, dry winds turned much of the Sahara into sand wastes. Today, the southern portions of Morocco, Algeria, Libya, and Egypt, the northern half of Sudan, as well as most of Mauritania, Mali, Niger, and Chad, lie within the Sahara Desert.

**savannah:** grassland containing scattered trees

**West Africa** is the region of the west coast of Africa, south of the Sahara, to just north of the equator, and eastward to Lake Chad. This fertile and rich area contains grasslands, rain forests, and farmlands. Many small states lie on the western coast of Africa: Senegal, Gambia, Guinea Bissau, Guinea, Sierra Leone, Liberia, Ghana, Burkina Faso, Togo, and Nigeria.

**East Africa** has high mountains that separate it from the Sahara to the north and west, and from the rainforests of western and Central Africa. The Great Rift valley, which runs down East Africa from north to south, is the meeting place of the African and Indian continental plates. Volcanoes are still active there. Mount Kilimanjaro is an active and growing volcano in Kenya as well as the highest mountain in Africa. The farmlands of this region are very fertile because of the rich volcanic soil of the mountains and the warm but wet climate. The countries of East Africa are Sudan, Ethiopia, Eritrea, Somalia, Kenya, Uganda, and Tanzania. East Africa is the home of two of the earliest African civilizations, Kush and Ethiopia.

**Central Africa** is the very large region drained by the Congo River, flowing west to the Atlantic, and the Zambezi River, flowing east to the Indian Ocean. The equator runs through Central Africa, and it contains thick forest jungles. Beyond the forested areas are bands of grassy savannahs.

**Southern Africa** is drier than Central Africa and less mountainous than East Africa. The Kalahari Desert divides it from its neighbors to the north. Southern Africa contains the nations of Namibia, the Republic of South Africa, Botswana, Zimbabwe, Lesotho, and Swaziland. Southern Africa is rich in minerals and developed farmland. The Republic of South Africa has industry like Europe and North America along with modern cities and transportation. Southern Africa is home to the Bushmen, a people that roamed the whole continent and parts of Europe in prehistoric times but now live only on the fringes of the Kalahari Desert.

## The Lakes and Major Rivers of Africa

In the deep chasms of the Great Rift valley in the eastern part of central Africa stand three large lakes: Lake Victoria, Lake Tanganyika, and Lake Malawi. The largest of the lakes is Lake Victoria, which is almost an inland sea, between Kenya and Uganda. Lake Victoria is only slightly smaller than Lake Superior in North America. The waters of Lake Victoria are the source of the southern branch of the Nile River. Lake Tanganyika drains west into tributaries of the Congo, and Lake Malawi drains

> **headwaters:** the sources or the upper parts of a river

south and east into the Zambezi River. These three lakes are high in the mountains and provide water for the lowlands below.

Four major rivers are an important part of the geography of Africa: the Nile, the Congo, the Niger, and the Zambezi. Although it is not a major river, the Okovango River in Botswana is very interesting, for it never reaches the sea. Instead, it ends in swamps in the Kalahari Desert in South Africa.

**The Nile** is the longest river in Africa, flowing approximately 4,160 miles from its farthest source until it reaches the Mediterranean Sea. The Nile starts in two places and for many miles has two branches: the western branch, called the White Nile, and the eastern branch, called the Blue Nile. The **headwaters** of the White Nile are at Lake Victoria in the mountains of Uganda. The Blue Nile begins at Lake Tana, in Ethiopia. The two branches flow northward until they meet at Khartoum, the capital of Sudan. From Khartoum, the Nile continues its long journey to the Mediterranean Sea.

The Nile provides water for living and farming for those on its banks. For centuries, it deposited the silt that made the Nile River Valley and the Nile Delta in Egypt some of the richest farmland in the world.

**The Congo** is the second longest river in Africa. It begins in the Katanga plateau in southern Africa and flows northward to the central part of the Democratic Republic of the Congo. The river then turns south and west and flows to the Atlantic Ocean. The Congo River does not form a delta like the Nile does but runs through a deep canyon to the ocean. The Congo River is the highway of the Democratic Republic of the Congo. From dugouts piloted by village people to modern riverboats and huge commercial transports, the Congo makes movement possible in the dense rain forests of Central Africa.

**The Niger** is Africa's third longest river. It begins in Guinea in West Africa and first flows northeast through Mali. It then turns south and flows through Benin and Nigeria, ending its journey to the sea at a large delta in Nigeria. This river is very important to the people of West Africa who live on its banks. Water from the river allows farming and commercial fishing.

**The Zambezi** is the fourth of the great rivers of Africa. It flows east from the same high country where the Nile and the Congo begin. It passes through thick forests in Zambia and Mozambique and at last empties into the Indian Ocean.

## African Resources and Food

Africa's most valuable resources are fossil fuels (such as oil and coal) and precious jewels, and metals, including abundant copper and gold.

Staple African foods—peanuts, sweet potatoes, okra—are so much a part of the cuisine of all lands today that their origin is unknown to most people. A world without the humble peanut and peanut butter is unthinkable. The sweet potato is used in many recipes. Okra and filé (a spice made from dried and ground sassafras leaves) are the essential ingredients in gumbo, and blackened meat and fish are now popular in all parts of North America.

# The African Peoples and their Cultures

Scientists say that Africa was the first home to all members of the human race, and from Africa our ancestors spread throughout the entire world. Roughly 30,000 years ago, human beings living in Africa were making sophisticated stone tools. These Africans were the Afro-Asians, Bantus, Pygmies, and Bushmen. They are ancestors of the peoples who are found on the continent today.

**The Afro-Asians** are ancestors of the people who live in northern Africa. They had light brown skin and were of medium height. Some older books refer to these people as "Caucasoid" or "Hamitic," but the term we use today is *Afro-Asian*.

**The Bantu** peoples have lived in the sub-Saharan plateau and along the fringe of the forest region. They are tall, large framed, dark ebony in skin color, and have wiry, tightly curled black hair. They are now called the blacks, or Bantu, and inhabit most of the continent today.

**The Pygmies** are similar to the Bantu except for their small stature—they are only about four and one-half feet tall. They have inhabited forest regions around the Congo basin and now are few in number. They have always lived by hunting and planting small plots of vegetables and maize.

**The Bushmen** have made their homes in Africa's eastern and southern savannahs. They are slight of build, of medium height, and have light, copper-colored skin. Their eyes are almond-shaped, like the eyes of East Asian peoples, and they have tightly curled dark hair. The Bushmen are a nomadic people, living by hunting and gathering only. Farming is still not their ordinary practice. Their paintings on the rock faces of cliffs and outcroppings of stone are very like the prehistoric paintings in the caves of Europe.

## A Religious Family Culture

Family and community are of the highest importance for all African societies. African peoples have believed it is one's duty to serve his group. Not only rich ancient cultures like Christian Ethiopia but less developed tribal societies have looked upon the good of the whole community as greater than what benefits individuals alone.

Working together has thus been an important part of African culture. A French traveler to Ethiopia in the 1830s noted that the Ethiopian Africans were proud of their spirit of cooperation: "A man with no fixed obligation to his society was, in their eyes, outside of society," he said.

Most black African peoples have always believed in a supreme being, a creator god who takes special care of human beings, who are his special creation. Because of this belief, it was not difficult for Africans to accept the monotheism of Islam and the Christian Faith. Africans, of course, worshiped other gods—spirits of nature and the elements. When Africans became Muslim or Christian, they often confused these gods with Christian saints or Islamic angels and prayed to them as if they were gods. African religions thus could be a mixture of paganism and Christian or Muslim beliefs.

African religion today still includes all the acts of daily life; every human action is thought to have a religious significance. Ceremony and ritual mark the great events of life: birth, marriage, successes and failures, and death. People offer things precious to the worshiper or sacred to a spirit to recognize the important event or the on-going life of the family. Special gifts are traditionally given to each god, including animal sacrifice and (at one time) human sacrifice. Whiskey and corn meal are the traditional gifts people offer to the ancestors of the family.

# Africa's Earliest Civilizations

Around 5500 B.C., the climate of the Sahara was wet and cool. Its grasslands were lush, and rivers ran across them southward into the Niger River and eastward toward the Nile River. (The dry riverbeds can still be seen in the desert.) Fish and game were plentiful, and generations of hunters and herdsmen lived comfortable lives. Then around 3000 to 2500 B.C. the climate changed. The rains stopped. The rivers dried up. The forests and grasses died.

The long disaster of the drying up of the Sahara helps explain the history of Africa after 2000 B.C. The peoples who lived in the once-bountiful Sahara migrated in three directions. Some went north to the coasts of the Mediterranean; some went east to the fertile valley of the Nile; and some went south into the heart of the continent.

In the Nile River Valley, the civilization of Egypt emerged. South of the Sahara Desert, people were cut off from the ideas of the peoples of the Mediterranean. They had to cope with heat, poor soil, dense jungles, and barren mountain slopes. The deep and broad rivers were full of predators and parasites. Everywhere, insects brought disease with their stings and bites.

## The Kingdoms of the Nile

Egypt was the first civilization in Africa, and it may have influenced two other kingdoms that grew up along the Nile River—the kingdoms of Kush and Axum. These kingdoms lay to the south of Egypt and included the lands of the modern states of Ethiopia, Sudan, and Eritrea.

Around 750 B.C., the princes of Kush made their capital at Napata, near the upper reaches of the Nile, and built a city influenced by Egyptian building styles. Greek writers referred to Kush as *Aethiopia* (Land of the Fire-Eyes) and called the Kushites, *Ethiopes*; but Kush lay to the north of what is today the nation of Ethiopia.

For a thousand years, the Kushites waged constant war with the Egyptians. Because of this contact with Egypt, the Kushites developed a civilization that looked Egyptian but had its own unique character. The Kushites, for instance, worshiped the Egyptian god Amun just as the pharaoh's court did; but the Kushites did not worship their king as a god as the Egyptians did the pharaoh.

Later, as the Sahara grew ever more dry and the pastures around Napata dried up, the Kushites shifted their capital farther south to Meroe and there built palaces and stone cities. In Meroe, the kings built pyramids that were not as grand as the pyramids of Egypt but nonetheless had a remarkable style and dignity. Iron was abundant around Meroe, and the kings of Kush made great use of the technology of iron working. The capital grew into a great metalworking center. Heaps of iron waste may still be seen in the ruins. The kings of Kush conquered their old foes, the pharaohs, in the 8th century B.C. and for a brief time ruled both Upper (southern) and Lower (northern) Egypt.

The Kushites managed to tame the African elephant, and they used elephants in war. In their art, they replaced pictures of Egyptian gods with those of lions and elephants. The kingdom of Kush loved new things and sent **emissaries** to all the lands of the Mediterranean. Kushite ships sailed from ports on the Red Sea as far as India. The Acts of the Apostles (Acts 8:26-40) in the Bible tells of how the deacon Philip met an official of the queen of Meroe on the road from Jerusalem and told him the Gospel of the Lord Jesus. The Bible calls the official an Ethiopian.

**emissary:** a person who is sent on an errand or mission

## The Kingdom of Nubia

Around A.D. 300, both the kingdom of Kush and the Kushite civilization seem to have faded after wild Nubian tribes and the kings of Axum, a realm in what is now called Ethiopia, invaded their lands. No one knows how Kush came to an end. The last king of the Kushites was buried in a tiny pyramid, a sad imitation of the tombs his ancestors had built. His name was Malequerabar. That is all that we known of him.

Two hundred years later, in the 500s A.D., the Nubian invaders in the Kushite towns produced their own culture, Christian Nubia. In the 300s or 400s, monks from a region of Egypt called the Thebaid had brought the Christian Faith to Nubia, and a Church was established there that had many of the same rituals as the Church in Egypt. In the 6th century, this Church adopted a heresy called *Monophysite*. The Monophysites taught that Christ is only truly God, not man. In Egypt, the Monophysite Church is called Coptic, after the ancient language used in its liturgy.

In the 7th century, the Church in Nubia was cut off from the rest of the Christian world by the Muslim conquest of Egypt. For centuries thereafter, Nubia's Christian kings and bishops knew nothing of the developments of the Christian world of Europe or Constantinople. Believing the rest of the world had fallen to the Muslims, they thought they alone were left to keep the Christian Faith alive. Nubian kings made constant war on the Muslim governors of Upper Egypt and declared themselves the protectors of Egypt's Coptic Christians.

Finally, the Muslims of Egypt under the sultan, Saladin, sent troops south to stamp out the Nubian nuisance. In 1276, the Muslims overcame the first of three Nubian kingdoms, and a second kingdom fell a century later. The last of the Nubian Christian kingdoms fell to the Muslims in the early 1400s. For nine hundred years, the Nubians of old Kush had held out against the Muslim armies.

## Axum

The kingdom of Axum arose to the south and east of Kush, in the mountains of Ethiopia. There is an Ethiopian legend that tells a strange legend about the people of Axum. The legend relates that the queen of Sheba, mentioned in the Bible, went up to Jerusalem to judge the reputation of Israel's King Solomon for wisdom. (1 Kings 10:1-13) There, Solomon fell in love with her, and she bore him a son whose name was Menelik.

The legend says that Menelik's relatives harassed him as he grew up, and he was forced to flee Sheba with the treasures that had belonged to his mother and father. He led his band of warriors into the mountains of Ethiopia, where he founded a kingdom and worshiped God like the Israelites did. Among the treasures Menelik took with him was Israel's sacred Ark of the Covenant. Solomon's Israelite son, says the legend, sent the ark to his half-brother, Menelik, to keep it safe. The legend says this Menelik became the founder of Ethiopia's line of kings. This royal line ruled Ethiopia into the 20th century. Its last emperor was Haile Selassie.

The legend of the queen of Sheba and her son, Menelik, is based on real history. "Sheba" is the land of the Sabaeans, a people who lived on the southern coast of Arabia. The Sabaeans set up trading posts on the African coast near their homeland. About 500 years before Christ, a number of Sabaean settlements on the African coast near the mouth of the Red Sea merged with the local peoples to develop a culture all their own. These peoples moved inland into the sparsely settled mountains of Ethiopia and built a city there safe from Red Sea pirates and wandering nomadic tribes. By A.D. 200, the city was called Axum, and the people of the mountains that it commanded were called Amharic.

The first Christian missionary to reach Axum was St. Frumentius—St. Athanasius of Alexandria, the great defender of the Trinity, had ordained Frumentius bishop of Axum around the year 330. In the 500s, a Monophysite priest, named Julian, was sent from Alexandria by the Byzantine empress Theodora (Emperor Justinian's wife) to Nubia and Axum to convert them to his heresy. Since then, the Church in Ethiopia has been Monophysite. In an extraordinary report to Constantinople, Julian said that the Christian king of Axum was dressed in white linen, adorned with gold and pearls and that his throne was a gilded chariot drawn by elephants. Julian claimed that Greek was the language of the Amharic court!

Whether the court spoke Greek or not, Ethiopia had its own literature written in Geez, a **literary language** spoken by the nobles and upper classes of Axum. Ethiopia even had its own translation of the Scriptures into Geez.

Axum also had unique architecture. In the 12th century, Axum's king, Lalibela, built some of the most unusual structures in the world. They were 10 churches chiseled out of the rock of the hills around his capital. Workers excavated down into the rock, hewing out a large, rectangular pit. In the center of this pit sits the church, sculpted out of a single rock. The roof of the church is level with the ground outside the pit. Within the churches, artisans carved out huge halls with pillars and arches, false windows and hidden rooms, just as if the churches had been erected above ground.

**literary language:** a form of a language that is more elegant than everyday speech

As with Nubia, the Muslim conquests cut Axum off from the rest of the Christian world. By the 1200s, Muslims and primitive pagan tribes surrounded the mountain kingdom, and Christian travelers from the mountains were forbidden to use ports on the Red Sea coast.

# The Sudanic Civilization

Fighting to survive in the hostile climates and terrain of the continent, African societies came up with different ways of staying alive and living joyfully. Like the Ethiopians, Africans south of the Sahara Desert (the area called Sudan by the Arabs) developed a unique culture we call the Sudanic civilization.

The Sudanic societies were tribes (which might be quite small or large), ruled by kings. Because the king was thought to be divine, he was kept from contact with the rest of the tribe. It was thought that the king needed to keep healthy to insure good weather and crops. The office of king was not passed down in families, from father to son. Instead, the king was the head priest, and the priestly class chose the king by election or **divination**.

> **divination:** the practice of trying to discover future events or hidden knowledge by means of magic

Because Sudanic societies thought their king was a divine being, he ruled his people with absolute power. His subjects provided him with wives, drink, food, crafts, and items for trade. He also controlled all trade.

This Sudanic order of society influenced all the peoples of West and Central Africa. It became the model for all the Bantu kingdoms of central and southern Africa.

The wealth and power of the kingdoms of the Sudan were built on gold, which can be found in great abundance in West Africa. In ancient times, the Africans had traded gold with the Phoenicians and the Carthaginians, and when the Arabs conquered North Africa in the 7th century, this trade continued. In particular, the Africans of Sudan traded gold for salt, which was priceless to the Africans. On trains of camels, the Arabs carried tons of salt to the south and brought home gold beyond their dreams. Salt was not only useful to make foods savory; it was essential for health among peoples who lost so much water through heavy perspiration in the intense heat.

Another Sudanic "product" that was not so savory was slaves. The great kingdoms of the Sudan conquered their neighbors to accumulate the gold and slaves that the traders demanded for their salt. Empires rose and fell as the price of salt and slaves went up or down.

Along with Arab merchants came Muslim teachers who converted the pagan tribes of the Sudan to Islam. The cities that grew up as trading centers and royal capitals in the Sudan became centers of Islamic learning. One such Islamic center, Timbuktu, grew world famous.

The empires of the Sudan also inspired the kingdoms on the forested western coasts of Africa to expand their borders and conquer their neighbors. The kings of Benin and Ashanti resisted Islam but waged wars to capture slaves to sell to the Muslim lands in North Africa. By the 1600s, the coastal kingdoms of West Africa were ready to trade with Europeans for gold and slaves, just as they long had done with their Muslim neighbors.

> **Burial of a Sudanic King**
>
> Kings in Sudanic cultures were not allowed to die a natural death, for the people thought that if a king died a natural death, the land would lose its fertility. Poisoning or ritual suffocation were used to hasten death when a king's time to die was near. The king would be buried with his favorite furniture, food, and the bodies of his servants and aides.

# The Empires of the Sudan

Much of what we know about the history of medieval West Africa we have learned through accounts written by Muslims from North Africa. West African "literature" was primarily oral—that is, it was unwritten but passed down through memory and recitation. This oral literature took the form of storytelling in tales, heroic poetry, epics, and histories. West African oral literature took the form of riddles, lyric poems, and proverbs. Through these—as well through the written literature in both the African languages and Arabic—the Sudanic peoples passed down their memories from generation to generation.

When Muslims first encountered the Sudanic peoples in the 9th and 10th centuries A.D., they found towns and cities surrounded by well-developed farmlands. The peoples of West Africa had a system of markets and carried on trade with one another. Though West Africa had tribal forms of government, it also had highly developed monarchies that grew up into empires. Four Sudanic kingdoms that grew into empires between A.D. 700 and 1800 were Ghana (not the modern country with that name), 700–1200; Mali (again, not the modern country), 1200–1500; Songhai, 1350–1600; and Kanem-Bornu, 800–1800.

The great Sudanic monarchies did not grow up in more fertile regions, such as the Niger River valley and around Lake Chad, but in the less fertile and drier lands that lie between these more fertile regions and the Sahara Desert. This indicates that these monarchies grew powerful through trade with the lands that lay along the Mediterranean coasts of North Africa. As the kingdoms grew wealthier, they extended their power over their neighbors from whom they obtained money (from taxes and tribute) as well as slaves for trade.

## Ghana

A kingdom called Ghana arose in the region along the border of what are now Mauritania and Mali. The lands of Ghana had a large population that supported itself by farming, irrigating crops by water obtained from wells. The king of Ghana lived in a walled palace and maintained a court that displayed his great power and wealth. The king's wealth came from a trade in gold (which came from further south) and slaves, as well as from taxes exacted from kings over whom his sway extended.

In the 10th century, Ghana's power began to extend over the nomadic tribes that lived to the north of the kingdom. These tribes, which lived by cattle raising, were disunited and so could not resist the power of the more powerful Ghana kingdom. Yet, these nomads had also been converted to Islam, a religion that allowed them to unite, in spite of their differences. It was under the zealous Muslim religious group called the Almoravids that these tribes united and began to expand their sway over the agricultural lands that lie on either side of the western Sahara and northward into Spain. Late in the 11th century it seems the Almoravids dominated Ghana itself. From that time onward the ruling and merchant classes of Ghana were Muslim, though paganism continued among the common people.

Throughout the 12th century, the Ghana empire grew ever weaker while the southern kingdoms that empire had dominated achieved their independence. One such kingdom was Mali, which lay in the well-watered and gold-rich lands of the upper Niger River valley. By around 1235, Mali had grown powerful enough to conquer what remained of Ghana.

## Mali and the Spread of Islam

The kingdom of Mali controlled not only the gold fields of the upper Niger River valley but the Niger River trade cities of Gao and Timbuktu. Controlling these cities allowed Mali to open up trade with other parts of West Africa. Up and down the river traveled merchants, who expanded their trade as

## The Slave Trade

In the 17th century, European colonists in the Americas demanded more and more slaves to work on their farms and plantations. To obtain slaves, European traders turned to West Africa. Many African chiefs collected slaves from their neighbors inland and traded them to slave traders on the coast in exchange for guns and other goods. Tribesmen convicted of a crime or who had debts (or whose family had debts) or whose chief did not like them, could be sold as slaves. When slaves became more valuable than gold, African kings on the coast made war on weaker neighbors to capture whole villages or peoples to sell to the slavers. The slaving wars disrupted Sudanic life and tribal allegiances for centuries.

The slave trade affected both eastern and western Africa. Arab slave traders on the east coasts set up slave-trading towns from Somalia to Mozambique. But the coming of the Europeans in the 1400s had the most destructive effect on African society, since the new plantations of Brazil and the Caribbean Islands seemed to have an endless appetite for new slave labor. The Portuguese, who had first explored the African coasts, stepped in to control the slave trade.

It is impossible to describe the horror of African slavery. Usually betrayed by a rival tribe, people were separated from their families and cultures, never to know them again. Then they were loaded aboard ships with too little air and space. If they survived the long trip across the ocean (and many did not), most slaves became agricultural workers with no rights, no pay, and no chance for improvement. Access to slaving areas was restricted, for it was feared that if Europeans not involved in the slave trade were to see it, it would be stopped.

The effects of the slave trade varied from place to place in Africa. Western Africa, with a large population, did not suffer terribly from the loss of people. But slaving harmed African morality, for it weakened family ties and damaged communities. In Central and East Africa, however, the loss of population was devastating. Slaving took its toll on those left behind. Villages starved because their young men and women were no longer there to work the fields.

far east as the lands of a Bantu people called the Hausa, who lived between Lake Chad and the Niger. The merchants soon were carrying their trade further south, along the Black Volta River and into what is now the modern African state of Ghana.

The Mali merchants, however, not only carried on trade but also took their Muslim religion with them. Because of their activities, Islam spread among the merchant classes of West Africa, and West African kings adopted the new religion. Though West African society remained basically pagan, it began to be highly influenced by the religion of the prophet Muhammad.

One effect of the expansion of Islam was the spread of the Arabic language in West Africa. Arabic was the language of Islam; Muslims of whatever race and language were expected to learn Arabic in order to read the Koran. In West Africa, Arabic became the language of trade and government, as well as of culture and learning. Arabic was for West Africa what Latin was for medieval Europe—the language of religion and scholarship and the means of uniting the disparate peoples of the region.

The use of Arabic spread literacy among the Sudanic peoples and brought them into contact with the riches of Muslim scholarship. Black Muslim scholars not only studied works of Muslim learning but produced learned works of their own. West Africa became rich not only with gold but numerous poets, historians, and scholars.

## Songhai

The Bantu people called the Songhai lived on the middle Niger River and had long made it difficult for Mali to control that region, which included the important trading city of Gao. In the 15th century, Mali lost control of Gao and, in the same century, a Songhai king arose who brought Mali's empire to an end. This king was Sonni Ali (r. 1464–1492), who rose up as a champion of his people's pagan religion against the Muslim faith of the Mali kings.

Fighting war after war against the Mali kingdom, Sonni Ali at last overthrew it and established his own empire, which he ruled from Gao. After Sonni Ali's death, however, the Songhai kingdom fell to one of his generals, Muhammad Askia (r. 1493–1528), who was not a Songhai pagan but a Muslim from the people of Mali. From this time forward, the Mali and Songhai continually struggled for control of the empire.

Yet, despite these struggles, the Songhai empire grew in power and influence. In the 16th century, it was strong enough to carry war and conquest into the Sahara to take control of the salt mines in the region. Such conquests, however, brought Songhai rule too close to the borders of the North African state of Morocco. In 1591, armed with firearms, a 4,000-strong Moroccan army invaded Songhai and conquered the cities of Jenne, Timbuktu, and Gao. This conquest brought an end to the Songhai kingdom.

# The Kingdom of Kongo

In 1482, the Portuguese adventurer Diego Cão, sailing down the west coast of Africa, became the first European to make contact with the kingdom of Kongo—the largest kingdom in Central Africa. Portuguese interest in Kongo grew rapidly. And the kings and nobles of Kongo found everything European fascinating. They entered into trade with the Portuguese for European cloth, tools, furniture, and wine. They offered high wages to Portuguese carpenters and masons to come and build new palaces and cities for the African kingdom. They also accepted the Catholic Faith. Nzinga a Nkuwu, the supreme king (or *manikongo*), became Catholic and was baptized as Hongo (João) II, in honor of the king of Portugal, King João I.

Kongo thus became a Christian kingdom, and in the early 16th century, Henrique, the grandson of the Manikongo Hongo II, became the first black African bishop in the Catholic Church. The nobles followed their king's lead and accepted the Faith. Many of the Bakongo people also were baptized, and a flourishing church seemed to be growing in the Congo River basin. Portuguese missionaries and Congolese converts set out into the interior of Kongo to preach the Gospel among the people there.

But Portuguese greed for gold and slaves worked steadily against the efforts of the Portuguese government and the Catholic bishops to make Kongo into a Christian kingdom. Throughout the 1500s, the slave trade grew, and local African warlords and magistrates sold their people as slaves or made war on their neighbors to collect enough slaves for sale.

Seeing the bad effects of slaving on his people, the *manikongo* tried to limit the effects of the slave trade on his subjects. But he lost control of his provinces and local governments, and slave traders were draining the Kongo of its manpower. In letters to the king of Portugal, the *manikongo* complained that the Portuguese had broken their word to his people. Committed as they were to the common good, Africans could not understand this disregard of honor.

After two centuries of Portuguese influence, Kongo was a Europeanized African kingdom; but the *manikongo* had little or no control over his provinces. Kongo's traditional morality was badly damaged, and its new Christian Faith had been distorted.

The desperate *manikongo* at last decided to drive the greedy and treacherous Portuguese slave traders and mercenary soldiers from his land. The king tried to gather the Kongo army from all the provinces, but fewer than half of the army answered the call. In 1665, in the Battle of Mbwila, the Portuguese defeated the Kongolese and the head of the *manikongo* was cut off. It was displayed in the chapel on the bay of Luanda, where the explorer Diego Cão had first landed in Kongo.

### A Warrior Queen

In the 1620s, Dona Anna de Souza Nzinga became a brilliant, warrior queen in the Kongo. She was the daughter of the king of Ndongo, a kingdom subject to Kongo. When Dona Anna's brother murdered her son, the heir to the throne, and made himself king, she fled to the bush and hid. When her brother found that he could not deal with the Portuguese, he called her back and made her his deputy to negotiate with the Europeans. Because of her efforts, the Portuguese made a peace treaty with Ndongo. At this time, Dona Anna accepted baptism.

Later, when the Portuguese betrayed their treaty with Ndongo, Dona Anna found allies among the Jaga, a fierce and less civilized people, and killed her brother to avenge her son. She raised a huge army of followers—her Jaga allies, her own countrymen, and hundreds of escaped slaves and displaced people.

Dona Anna kept a traditional-style royal court that moved with her and her army from camp to camp. Against African custom, she dressed like a man. Though through all these years she kept a priest at her side and heard Mass daily, her actions were in conflict with her faith. For nine years she fought the Portuguese until she was finally defeated in 1656. She remained queen of Ndongo until her death in 1663. Her sister, Dona Barbara, became queen after Dona Anna's death and made peace with the Europeans.

# The Age of Colonialism

As we have seen, the slave trade disrupted traditional African societies with their family-centered spirit of cooperation. This left the continent open to conquest by the European powers in the 19th century. European **colonialism** was the result.

**colonialism:** the control of a region by a more powerful foreign nation

By the end of the 19th century, almost all of the African continent was divided up into colonies controlled by one or other of the European powers. European governments and companies seized the wealth of African lands and often oppressed the people, but they brought stability, peace, and a degree of civilization to Africa as well. The many different nations of Africa did not become independent until after the Second World War. Traditional African social structures and royal lines, however, no longer exist.

# Africa and the World

**social mores:** the customs or practices of a society

The large numbers of slave workers who came from Africa to the Americas greatly affected life in the New World. Portuguese Brazil, along with islands in the Caribbean settled by the French, Spanish, and British, have large African populations and are extensions of African culture in the New World. African immigrants have influenced life in the United States more than the Native Americans have. Elements of African culture can be seen throughout Spanish America as well. African **social mores** and African religion have continued in Afro-American communities throughout the New World.

But African culture has not spread only in the Americas. European society both in the Americas and Europe has taken on characteristics of African musical forms and dance, as well African designs and images. For instance, early 20th century European artists imitated West African sculptures and paintings of the human form. Popular music in the United States, Europe, and in much of the world is now a blend of European melodies and African rhythms and harmonies. Bright colors in geometric patterns are so familiar in the decorative arts that it is almost forgotten that they came from Africa.

Africa's influence on art and music has been very important to the development of the culture of the world in which we live. African culture has truly become a world culture.

# Chapter Review

## Summary
- Africa is said to be the first home of the human race. It is the second largest continent. Africa can be divided into six regions: North Africa, the Sahara, West Africa, East Africa, Central Africa, and South Africa.
- The peoples who settled in Africa were the Afro-Asians, whose descendants live in North Africa; the Bantu, the tall, black people who inhabit the central plateau; the Pygmies of the Congo basin, who are short in stature; and the Bushmen, who live on the fringes of the Kalahari Desert.
- The early peoples of Africa lived in the Sahara region, before the lush grasslands dried up between 3000–2500 B.C. The Saharan people dispersed towards the Mediterranean, towards the Nile and towards the south, pushing the Bushmen farther and farther south.

- The high civilization of Egypt arose in the Nile River valley around 4000 B.C. Two other kingdoms existed on the Nile River: Kush (750 B.C.–A.D. 300), with its capital city in Meroe, and Axum or Nubia (A.D. 300–1400). Kush faded mysteriously and no one knows how the end came. Axum or Nubia arose in the mountains of Ethiopia. The kingdom of Nubia became Christian in the 500s but was cut off from the rest of the Christian world by the Muslim conquest of North Africa in the 600s.
- The Arabs established their empire in North Africa beginning with the conquest of Egypt in 639. All of North Africa became Muslim, and the Berbers there carried Islam to the Sudanic kingdoms.
- Arabs south of the Sahara developed the Sudanic civilization in the west of Africa. The four kingdoms of Sudan were Ghana (A.D. 700–1200), Mali (1200–1500), Songhai (1350–1600), and Kanem-Bornu (800–1800).
- The Sudanic kingdoms were ruled by tribal kings with absolute power. The wealth and power of these kingdoms came from the sale of slaves and gold. Along with Arab traders, who bartered salt for gold, came Muslim teachers who converted the Sudanic peoples to Islam. Sudanic capitals became centers of Islamic learning. By the 1600s, the kingdoms of West Africa traded with the Europeans and sent slaves to the Americas.
- Two regions were hit hard by the slave trade: West Africa, resulting in the weakening of communal ties; and Central and East Africa, where depopulation was so severe that villages starved from lack of labor. Those who became slaves were betrayed by rival tribes or sold by their chiefs.
- In 1482 Diego Cão made contact with the kingdom of Kongo. The king or *manikongo* converted, and Kongo became a Christian kingdom. The *manikongo's* grandson Henrique became the first black African bishop in the Catholic Church. The scandal of Portuguese greed and the slave trade weakened the Christian Church in the Kongo. Efforts to expel the Portuguese were defeated. During this period the Kongo had an unusual warrior queen, Donna Anna de Souza Nzinga, who was a baptized Christian but lived as a pagan king of the past.

## Key Concepts

**Afro-Asian:** the name for the ancestors of the people who live in northern Africa. They had light brown skin and were of medium height. Afro-Asians have been called "Caucasoid" or "Hamitic."

**Bantu:** the name for the peoples who have lived in the sub-Saharan plateau and along the fringe of the forest region. They are tall, large framed, dark ebony in skin color, and have wiry, tightly curled black hair.

**Bushmen:** the name for the peoples who have made their homes in Africa's eastern and southern savannahs. They are slight of build, of medium height, and have light, copper-colored skin. Their eyes are almond-shaped, like the eyes of East Asian peoples, and they have tightly curled dark hair. The Bushmen are a nomadic people, living by hunting and gathering only. Farming is still not their ordinary practice. Their paintings on the rock faces of cliffs and outcroppings of stone are very like the prehistoric paintings in the caves of Europe.

**savannah:** grassland containing scattered trees

**literary language:** a form of a language that is more elegant than everyday speech

**Sudanic civilization:** the civilization of the Bantu peoples who lived in the region south of the Sahara Desert
**colonialism:** the control of a region by a more powerful foreign nation

## Dates to Remember
**B.C. 3000–2500:** the Sahara grasslands dry up.
**ca. 750 A.D.:** the princes of Kush establish their capital at Napata.
**300s–400s:** Christian missionaries reach Axum.
**500s:** the Church in Nubia becomes Monophysite.
**900s:** Ghana begins to expand its power.
**1235:** Mali conquers what remained of Ghana.
**1276:** Muslims begin their conquests of the Nubian kingdoms.
**1482:** Diego Cão makes the first European contact with Kongo.
**1591:** Morocco brings an end to the Songhai kingdom.
**ca. 1600:** slave trade with the Europeans begins.

## Central Characters
**Menelik (ca. 950 B.C.):** the legendary son of King Solomon and the Queen of Sheba
**St. Frumentius (4th century):** the first Christian missionary to reach Axum
**Sonni Ali (r. 1464–1492):** pagan king of Songhai who championed his people's religion against the Muslim faith of the Mali kings
**Muhammad Askia (r. 1493–1528):** Muslim king of Songhai who seized power after the death of Sonni Ali
**Diego Cão (flourished 1480–1486):** a Portuguese explorer and the first European to make contact with the kingdom of Kongo
**Nzinga a Nkuwu, or Hongo (João) II (1470–1506):** the supreme king (or *manikongo*) of Kongo, who became Catholic
**Dona Anna de Souza Nzinga (1581–1663):** a queen of Ndongo (a kingdom subject to Kongo) who fought the Portuguese

## Questions for Review
1. Into what six regions can Africa be divided?
2. List the major rivers of Africa.
3. Name the four populations that make up Africa.
4. How does the drying up of the Sahara explain the history of Africa?
5. Who brought the Christian Faith to Axum? To what heresy did Axum convert? What did this heresy teach?
6. What role did the king play in Sudanic civilization?
7. When and through whom did Sudanic civilization adopt a written literature? In what language was this literature written?

8. How did the Sudanic peoples become Muslim?
9. How did the slave trade develop in West Africa?
10. Why was it difficult for the Catholic bishops of Kongo to make Kongo a Christian kingdom?

## Ideas in Action

1. Look up in the encyclopedia, or on the Internet, the kingdoms of the Sudan—Ghana, Mali, Songhai, and Kanem-Bornu. What were their cities? How did the people in these kingdoms live? Why did the kingdoms not continue into our times?
2. Look up Timbuktu. How old is that city? What is its importance? How was it looked upon by Europe?
3. Research the history of the Christian Faith in Africa in a good history of Africa or the encyclopedia. Which Christian groups sent missionaries to Africa? Who was David Livingstone (Protestant missionary)? Who were the first Catholic missionaries to evangelize Africa?
4. Make a list of African (as well as African-American) saints. Say a litany of the saints, naming the Africans. Find others besides St. Josephine Bakhita (February 8), St. Charles Lwanga and companions (June 3), Blessed Isidore Bakanja (August 8), Blessed Ghebere Mikha'el (September 2), St. Martin de Porres (November 3), Lalibela (Ghebere Misquel, Ethiopian emperor and saint of the Ethiopian Orthodox Church—October 27), Bl. Absalom Jones (an American, the first black American to receive ordination), and Pierre Toussaint (a 19th century American).
5. Writing Activity: Imagine you are a travel agent and you are creating an historic tour of Africa. Write a two-page "tour brochure" about historic places the tourists will visit.

# Highways and Byways

## The Legend of Prester John

During the late Middle Ages in Europe, a legend grew up of a great Christian kingdom in Africa on the other side of Muslim-controlled lands. A semi-magical king named Prester John, who, it seems, could live forever, ruled this mythical kingdom. Prester John, it was said, was waging war against the Muslims until the Christian crusaders of the West could join forces with him. Then, together, they could eliminate the Muslim threat.

In the 1400s, Portuguese explorers ventured into the mountains of East Africa in search of Prester John. They did not find the fabled king but discovered an Ethiopia that was in many ways like the kingdoms of medieval Europe. The Portuguese found proud and independent nobles, bound by oaths of loyalty to their king, along with lesser nobles and lords below them, and landless peasants laboring for all. Ethiopia had monks, abbots, and bishops with their parish clergy worshiping as Christians, but in strange and mysterious liturgies and in an ancient, sacred language.

# Latin America: Lands of Many Cultures

In Latin America, cultures mix like they do nowhere else in the world. Native Americans, Europeans, Africans, Japanese, Hindus and Muslims from India, all live and work together in the huge urban areas of the Latin American countries.

Latin American culture is found throughout Mexico, Central America, and South America, and in parts of the United States. In the 15th and 16th centuries, southern Europeans—especially Spaniards and Portuguese—began to settle in Latin America. These early settlers brought their Catholic religion and customs as well as their languages to their new homes. Since the languages of these settlers, Spanish and Portuguese, came from Latin, this cultural region of the world is called Latin America.

## The Geography of Latin America

Latin America has nearly every type of landscape: mountains, jungles, plains, deserts, and coast land. It also has abundant natural resources: vast **rainforests** and timber lands, rich grazing and farm lands, and large deposits of valuable minerals.

South America has a wide variety of landscapes, from tropical forests to dry desert, from temperate grasslands to icy cold mountaintops. The equator runs through northern Brazil, northern Ecuador, and southern Colombia; so, in general, the weather in these regions is warm throughout the year. Rainforests rise in the regions north and south of the equator. In contrast, the Atacama Desert in northern Chile is one of the driest places on earth. The weather is always cold in the high Andes Mountains, which are made up of incredibly high, snow-covered peaks and active volcanoes (many over 20,000 feet high). The Andes range stretches 4,500 miles along western South America from

**rainforest:** a tropical woodland that receives a very large amount of rain every year. Rainforests have very tall broad-leaved evergreen trees whose branches make an unbroken roof or canopy over the forest floor.

Venezuela in the north to Tierra del Fuego on the southern tip of the continent.

South America has two other major mountain regions. One of these, the Guiana highlands, runs from southeastern Venezuela, through Guyana, Suriname, and into French Guiana. The other range is about 1,500 miles to the south in Brazil, around the cities of São Paulo and Rio de Janeiro. Plateaus, plains, smaller mountain ranges and hills cover much of Brazil between the southern mountains and the great Amazon River Basin.

The largest tropical rain forest in the world is found in the Amazon River Basin. The Amazon River is the second longest river in the world. It flows 4,000 miles, eastward from the Peruvian Andes Mountains to the Atlantic. Only the Nile River in Africa is longer than the Amazon. The hot and moist Amazon Basin covers two-fifths of the South American continent and contains more kinds of plants than anywhere else in the world.

Extending eastward from the Andes, the Central Plains cover about three-fifths of South America. These plains are drained by the huge Amazon and Plate **river systems**, which empty into the Atlantic. Argentina and Venezuela, especially, have very fertile plains and grasslands, which support many prosperous ranches and extensive farms.

The boundary between South and North America is the narrow neck of land called the Isthmus of Panama. Between this isthmus and Mexico is the region called Central America, which includes the republics of Panama, Costa Rica, Nicaragua, Honduras, El Salvador, Guatemala, and Belize. Much of Central America is covered with high mountain ranges. Among the mountains are fertile valleys. Central America has a warm, tropical climate and tropical rainforests.

Mexico is geographically part of North America, but its history and traditions make it part of Latin America. Mexico's geography is rugged but hospitable to human life. The coastal plain along the Gulf of Mexico is semitropical forest. The central plateau rises rapidly to a mile above sea level. The eruption of volcanoes has left a layer of rich soil over the plateau.

Mexico has two major mountain ranges that run from north to south and are part of the Rocky Mountains of North America. One of these ranges, on the western side of the country, is called Sierra Madre Occidental; the other range, running on the eastern side of the country, is the Sierra Madre Oriental. The region of Mexico around the capital, Mexico City, is very mountainous, with peaks rising over 17,000 and 18,000 feet high. Northern Mexico is mountainous and arid, with two large deserts—the Chihuahuan and Sonoran deserts. A long peninsula on the west, Baja California, forms the western coastline of the Gulf of California, one of the richest marine-life regions of the world.

The islands of the Caribbean Sea also form a part of Latin America. These islands include Cuba (the largest of them all), Hispaniola (divided between the nations of the Dominican Republic and Haiti), Jamaica, Puerto Rico, and the Bahamas.

> **river system:** a term referring to a group of rivers that all flow into a common river. The Mississippi River system, for instance, is made up of the Mississippi River and all the rivers that flow into it. The Ohio, Red, and Missouri rivers are thus part of the Mississippi River system.

# Latin America Before Columbus

Sometimes we think of Native Americans as people living in tribes that travel from place to place and survive by hunting or gathering seed plants and nuts. Certainly, there were many Native American peoples who lived this way. Yet, North and South America also sheltered native peoples who farmed, lived in villages, and built permanent houses and villages. And in Central America and northwestern South America, native peoples built great civilizations that we can admire today.

Latin America's story includes the tale of these three great Native American civilizations: the *Maya* civilization of southern Mexico, the *Inca* civilization of Peru in South America, and the *Aztec* civilization in the highlands around what is now Mexico City. These civilizations are often called **Pre-Columbian**, because they existed before Christopher Columbus came to the Americas in 1492. Here, we shall discuss the Mayan and Inca civilizations. We shall address the Aztecs later in the chapter.

## The Maya

Of the three Pre-Columbian civilizations (Aztec, Maya, and Inca), the Mayan is the oldest. The Indian people called the Maya have lived on the Yucatan Peninsula for centuries, developing what became their great civilization. The Mayan civilization reached its full greatness between A.D. 300 and 900.

The Maya were a farming people, growing **maize** (their most important crop), cotton, and other crops. Farming was not easy where they lived, for the Yucatan is covered with tropical forests. In order to farm, the Maya had to clear away the forest—and then work constantly so that the dense jungle vegetation did not again overtake their fields. They terraced hillsides to provide more land for crops and developed rather advanced methods of irrigation.

It was in the cleared spaces of the jungle that the Maya raised their cities. At the peak of their civilization, the Maya had over 40 cities with populations of anywhere from 5,000 to 50,000 people. Mayan cities were more like groupings of religious temples than anything we think of as a city. These temples, made of stone, had a pyramid shape and could be lofty. One temple ruin discovered in the Yucatan is over 200 feet high. The Mayan temples are amazing not only because they were built so skillfully but because those who built them had only wood and stone tools to use in cutting the temple stones. The Maya too had no vehicles with wheels or large beasts (such as oxen) to drag the huge stones from the quarry to the building site. They possessed no machines to raise the stones one on top of another.

The Maya had other arts besides architecture. They carved beautiful figurines and ornaments out of **jade**. They developed painting, both for murals and pottery, as well as the arts of relief carving and sculpture. The Maya invented a written language that used hieroglyphics, which is a form of writing using pictures, or "glyphs." The pictures come to be associated with the sound of the name of a thing

**Pre-Columbian:** referring to the history of the Americas before Columbus and the Spaniards arrived in the New World

**maize:** a plant with grain growing on large ears; corn

**jade:** a hard stone used in jewelry and ornaments. Most jade is green.

the glyph represents. Along with the art of writing, the Maya developed the art of making paper, using the inner bark of the wild fig tree. They chiseled their hieroglyphs into stone, and it is from these inscriptions that we have come to know much of what we do know about Mayan civilization.

Like nearly all ancient peoples, the Maya worshiped many gods. Their gods were the gods of nature, and, along with the sun, moon, rain, and other natural things, the Maya honored maize as a god. A part of Mayan worship was human sacrifice—and it could be very brutal in the Mayan lands. Mayan warriors raided neighboring peoples, not only to get slaves but also to gather victims to sacrifice to their gods. These victims they tortured, mutilated, and then offered in sacrifice. Even Mayan rulers, as representatives of their people, had to offer themselves to the gods by drawing their own blood and torturing themselves. The Maya thought human sacrifice brought fertility to the soil. They also offered human beings to show their devotion to the gods. And the Maya thought that if they did not offer such sacrifices, disorder and chaos would strike not only their own land but all the world.

Priests had tremendous power in Mayan society, both because they represented the people before the gods and because they were believed to be able to tell fortunes and predict the future. To predict the future, the priests studied the stars and, especially, the movements of the sun, moon, and the planet Venus. In this way the Maya developed a knowledge of astronomy as well as mathematics. Among their great mathematical discoveries was the use of zero.

Their knowledge of astronomy and mathematics allowed the Maya to develop a complex and very precise calendar. The Maya's calendar was based on the **solar year**, which they divided into 18 months of 20 days each (360 days), with five days left over, which the Maya observed by fasting because they thought the days were unlucky. The Maya had another sacred calendar they used in conjunction with this calendar. The sacred calendar (of 260 days) was used to calculate when religious and ceremonial events would occur and as a means of **divination**. A third calendar was the Long Count, a cycle of time that began at a point in the distant past the Maya designated as zero. Most scholars name this zero point as 3113 B.C. If this is so, then the current cycle of the Long Count would have ended in A.D. 2011. The Long Count as well as precise observations helped Mayan astronomers predict solar eclipses.

> **solar year:** the period of time it takes for the earth to make one full revolution around the sun
>
> **divination:** the magical art or practice by which someone seeks to see into the future or discover hidden knowledge

After the year 900, the Maya abandoned many of their settlements—no one knows exactly why. Invaders from the north took control of Mayan settlements in north Yucatan and, it seems, changed Mayan society greatly. The older Mayan settlements had no walls to protect them from invasions, but later settlements did. Human sacrifice, too, seems to have increased in the new Mayan settlements. On the whole, it seems, because of the conquest, Mayan civilization became considerably more warlike than it had been before.

## The Realm of the Inca

The high mountain valleys of the Andes in Peru were the home of another great Pre-Columbian civilization. We call this civilization Inca after the title of its ruler, the Inca, who was believed to be a

> **thatch:** straw, rushes, or a similar material used as a covering or roof
>
> **aqueduct:** a man-made channel or pipe used to bring water from a distance

descendant of the sun god. Inca tradition says the first Inca, Manco Capac, was the son of the sun god and the moon goddess. It was Manco Capac who led his people to the Cuzco valley, where he established his capital city, named Cuzco, around the year A.D. 1200.

Like the Maya, the Incas built cities having great stone buildings. Unlike the early Mayan settlements, however, the Inca cities had walls made from uncut stones, very skillfully built without mortar. Unlike the Mayan pyramids and other buildings, the Incan structures had only one story; and, unlike Mayan buildings, which had stone roofs, Incan buildings had **thatch** roofs. Incan buildings are not as impressive as the Mayan structures, but the Incas showed their genius in building roads and canals to make travel over their wide realm easy and swift. Incan roads connected distant parts of the empire, though only government messengers and military could use them. The Incas, too, raised **aqueducts** to bring water to their settlements. They built all these structures without the aid of iron, machines, or beasts of burden.

The Incas were ingenious farmers, cutting terraces in the sides of hills and mountains in order to grow food. In growing crops, Incan farmers took advantage of the different climates of their realm. The low elevations along the Pacific coast were warm, while the weather grew colder as the Andes rose to their thousands of feet above the level of the sea. The Incas, thus, grew warm weather crops farther down the mountainsides and crops that did better in cooler climates, farther up.

The Incan government was very simple. The Inca was a complete despot, controlling the lives of all his subjects. Even the marriages of the humblest Peruvians were arranged by the Inca's government. Though, on the whole, the Inca was a rather gentle ruler, he took bitter revenge on anyone who dared to resist him. If he captured a city or region that had rebelled against him, he laid waste to it and slaughtered its inhabitants. No one was to rebel against the son of the sun.

Like the Maya, the Incas worshiped nature gods. Their chief god was the sun god, who had a magnificent temple in the city of Cuzco. The Inca was not only the king, but the highest priest, and he controlled religion just like he did everything else in his land. The Incas offered animals, grain, and flowers as sacrifices to their gods. On very solemn occasions they offered human sacrifices, generally a child or a beautiful maiden. Human sacrifice, however, was in no way as big a part of Incan religion as it was of the Mayan and Aztec religions.

Gold was very abundant in Peru and the Inca stored his houses with treasures of gold. It is said that no Inca passed his treasure down to his son. Each Inca thought he would need his treasures and even most of his houses in the next life. When the next Inca began his reign, he had to build new houses as well as gather his own treasury of gold. This gives one an idea of just how much gold was to be found in Peru.

Since the Incas passed on no written records, what we know of their history comes from the people's oral tradition that was committed to writing after the Spanish conquest. Before the conquest, officials called "memorizers" preserved Incan history from generation to generation.

The oral tradition says that it was the fourth Inca, Mayta Capac, who in the 14th century began to raid his neighbors for tribute and booty. The next Inca began expanding his sway outside the Cuzco valley; but it was the eighth Inca who instituted full-scale, permanent conquests, placing garrisons among the peoples he conquered. To prevent revolutions against his power, the Inca broke up tribes and dispersed their members throughout his realm. In the hundred years after 1438, the Inca empire entered its greatest period of expansion, reaching its greatest extent under the Inca Huayna Capac (1493–1525). But this empire was not destined to last long. Only ten years after Huayna's death, his empire fell under the conquering hand of the Spaniards.

# Europe Comes to Latin America

The modern history of Latin America began with Christopher Columbus' discovery of the American continents in 1492. In Chapter 16 of *Light to the Nations I*, we describe how, after much trying, Columbus was able to convince King Fernando and Queen Isabel of Spain to pay for an expedition to reach the Indies by sailing west over the Atlantic Ocean. Columbus' mission was to find gold and wealth for himself and Spain's "Catholic Monarchs" (as Fernando and Isabel were called). Yet he had a greater aim—to carry the Catholic Faith to the heathen overseas.

The land Columbus first discovered in October 1492 was only a small island, but it was just the beginning of his discoveries. In this, his first expedition and in others that he later made, Columbus discovered Hispaniola, Cuba, and the Virgin Islands. On his last expedition, he discovered the northern coast of South America. But to the day of his death, on May 10, 1506, Columbus thought he had reached the Indies instead of a "New World."

Not just Spain, but all of Europe took great interest in Columbus' discoveries. Portugal, which had been the first to reach the Indies by sea, was worried Spain would take some of its colonies in India and the Orient. To keep Spain and Portugal from quarreling over the new lands, Pope Alexander VI in 1493 set a dividing line in the Atlantic. The pope decreed that Spain could claim all lands in the Indies that fell west of this line, while Portugal could claim all the lands that fell east of the line. Because of the pope's decision, most of Latin America came under the power of Spain. Only Brazil, which jutted out east of the line, went to Portugal. This is why, even to this day, the people of Brazil speak Portuguese, while most of the rest of Latin America speaks Spanish.

Even during Columbus' lifetime, other adventurers set out to discover new lands in the "Indies." One of these was an Italian named Amerigo Vespucci, who explored the northern coast of South America. Because of a book that told of Vespucci's adventures, people in Europe began to call the newly discovered lands *America* after him. (*Americus* is the Latin form of the name Amerigo.)

In 1513, a Spanish captain, Vasco Nuñez de Balboa, plunged into the interior of Darien (Panama) with 170 men. On September 24, 1513, standing on a mountaintop, Balboa sighted a new ocean. He called it the South Sea; later, it would be called the Pacific. It was Balboa's discovery of the Pacific that showed that what Columbus had discovered and explored was not Asia or the Indies, but an entirely new world.

# The Conquest of Mexico

**conquistador:** Spanish word meaning "conqueror"

The Spanish explorers did not set out just to discover new lands, but to conquer them as well. Everywhere they went, these men, called **conquistadors**, claimed the lands for the crown of Spain. Like Columbus, they were eager to find riches; some, too, were interested in converting the Native Americans to the Gospel of Christ. Unfortunately, many of the explorers were cruel to the natives and forced them into slavery. They did so, even though Queen Isabel and, later, King Charles I, of Spain said the Indians should be treated with great gentleness.

One of the greatest of the Spanish conquistadors was a man named Hernán Cortés. In his youth, Cortés had been a bad student, wasting much of his time in foolish living. He dropped out of law school after only two years and then went to the Indies to seek his fortune. In 1518, Cortés became captain general of an expedition that was to seek for riches in what is now Mexico.

Cortés' fleet landed off the coast of Yucatán in February 1519. There, in what is now the state of Tabasco, Cortés' army of about 600 men fought and defeated a force of 40,000 Indians. Cortés made peace with these Indians and then sailed north along the coast of Mexico. In April 1519, he founded the first Spanish settlement on this coast, calling it Villa Rica de Vera Cruz.

At Vera Cruz, some of Cortés' men demanded that the expedition return to Cuba. They had learned that Cortés meant to march inland, to the realm of the mighty Aztecs. In response to these men, Cortés destroyed all but one of his 11 ships. Cortés' troops cried out that he had led them to Mexico to be butchered like cattle. But Cortés refused to listen to them. "I will remain here," he said, "while there is one to bear me company." If any of his men, he said, were cowards, they could take the one ship left and return to Cuba. There, said Cortés, they can remain and tell "how they deserted their commander and their comrades, and patiently wait until we return loaded with the spoils of the Aztecs."

These words filled his men with courage. Nearly all of them cried out: "To Mexico! To Mexico!" They were determined to match their force against the fearsome nation of the Aztecs.

## The Aztecs

The first Indians the Spaniards met when they came to the Americas were the gentle Taino people, who lived on many of the Caribbean islands. The Indians Cortés and his men had met in Tabasco were very different from the Taino. In this land the Native Americans called Anahuac, the native peoples raised buildings and temple pyramids of stone instead of the dwellings of stick and thatch the Taino built. The people of Anahuac were very numerous and lived in towns surrounded by well-cultivated fields of maize.

In the center of Anahuac, in a city built in the center of a lake, dwelt a powerful, warlike people—the Aztecs. By the time Cortés arrived, the Aztec king, Montezuma II, had conquered the tribes of Anahuac, making the Aztec empire greater than it had ever been before.

The Aztecs said that they had come to Anahuac from a land called Aztlán, far to the northwest, and had wandered into the south. In the 14th century, they came upon a lake in the high mountain valley of Mexico. There, on the shores of the lake, they beheld an eagle, perched on the stem of a prickly pear cactus, its wings spread to the rising sun and a serpent clutched in its **talons**. For the Aztecs, this was a sign that they should settle there. They called this place and the city they would build there, Tenochtitlán.

**talon:** the claw of a bird of prey, such as an eagle or hawk

The Aztecs were rather primitive when they arrived in Mexico. The neighboring city of Texcuco, however, had a high civilization, like that of the Maya, and it was from Texcuco that the Aztecs learned the arts of civilization. By the 16th century, the Aztecs had become skilled in agriculture (which allowed their population to become numerous and wealthy) and architecture. They planted beautiful gardens and built the glorious city of Tenochtilán in the center of the lake. They displayed their skill in making gold ornaments and developed hieroglyphic writing with which they wrote histories and beautiful poetry. Like the Maya and Inca, however, the Aztecs had not invented the wheel.

It was the Aztec ruler, Itzcóatl (r. 1428–1440), who initiated the period of his people's expansion. It was he who forged alliances with Tenochtitlán's neighboring cities, Texcuco and Tlacopan, and made the Aztecs the dominant power in central Mexico. By 1519, the Aztec empire had conquered over 400 small states and covered over 80,000 square miles. Tenochtitlán grew into a very large and populous city, with over 140,000 inhabitants. This great realm was ruled by the Aztec king and his military, who dominated the rest of society made up of various classes. Among the ruling classes of Aztec society were the priests and government officials. At the bottom were serfs, indentured servants, and slaves.

The Aztecs drew their religious beliefs from other peoples of central and southern Mexico, especially the Maya. (The Aztecs, for instance, developed their calendar from the Maya.) The Aztecs worshiped many nature gods, one of the most important of whom was Huitzilopochtli (witsy•lo•POCT•lee), the god of war and of the sun. It was to this god that the Aztecs offered human sacrifices, of which there were many. Indeed, one of the most important reasons the Aztecs went to war was to capture victims for sacrifice. The Aztecs had many religious festivals, and each one of them had to include sacrifices of human beings, whose bodies, afterward, were eaten by the worshipers. It is said that the Aztecs sacrificed about 20,000 victims each year.

Another important Aztec god was Quetzalcoatl (the "feathered serpent"), who was said to have white skin, dark hair, and a flowing beard. The legends say that Quetzalcoatl had taught people how to farm, use metals, and set up governments. The Aztecs said that under Quetzalcoatl Mexico had enjoyed a period of prosperity. But, at last, another god drove him out of Anahuac, and he went east across the sea. Quetzalcoatl promised his followers that, one day, he would return to Anahuac from the east, over the sea. It was said that when Quetzalcoatl returned, he would abolish human sacrifice.

## The Spaniards Arrive

The news of Cortés' landing at Vera Cruz filled Montezuma was fear—could the Spaniard be Quetzalcoatl returned from over the sea? The strangers were white-skinned and bearded, as Quetzalcoatl supposedly had been. What's more, whatever Native American cities the strangers entered, they freed the people who were to be sacrificed. Uncertain what to do, Montezuma invited Cortés to come to Tenochtitlán.

As the Spaniards approached the Aztec capital, they were joined by the Tlaxcalan Indians, who were enemies of the Aztecs. When Cortés and his men at last climbed the mountains surrounding Tenochtitlán, they saw below them the great Aztec city, with its towering temples. It was so beautiful that the Spaniards were in awe and fearful. Only a very powerful people, they thought, could build a city like that! It was Cortés' courageous spirit that encouraged his men to conquer their fear and move forward into the city.

Montezuma treated Cortés and his troops with hospitality. But though Montezuma was kind, Cortés did not trust him. Finally, fearing for his own safety, Cortés and his men seized Montezuma in his own palace. The Aztec king thus became Cortés' prisoner, though he continued to act as the king of Mexico.

The capture of their king was humiliating to the proud Aztecs. At last they rose up against the Spaniards. The streets and rooftops of Tenochtitlán were filled with armed Aztecs. Bloody fighting erupted, in the course of which Montezuma himself was killed by his own people. The Aztec king died on June 30, 1520.

Because of the uprising, the Spaniards faced certain death if they remained in the city. On the night of July 1, 1520, Cortés led his men and their Tlaxcalan allies in a retreat from Tenochtitlán. The Spaniards later named this night *La Noche Triste*—"the sorrowful night." The Aztecs in great numbers surrounded and attacked the fleeing Spaniards, taking some of them prisoner to sacrifice to the war god. Both the Spanish and the Tlaxcalans lost many men that night; all told, 450 Spaniards and 4,000 natives were killed. A few days later, a broken and discouraged army marched into Tlaxcala.

But though he had suffered defeat, Cortés was not discouraged. He immediately began making plans to return to Tenochtitlán. Though he at first did not know it, this time he had another ally to help him in his conquest—a disease called smallpox, which struck the Aztecs. Having no **immunity** against the disease, the Aztecs died in great numbers.

At Tlaxcala, Cortés ordered 15 small ships, called **brigantines**, to be constructed so that he could assault Tenochtitlán by the waters of the lake as well as by land. His total force consisted of 818 Spaniards, together with 87 cavalry and 25,000 Indian allies. The assault on the city began on April 28, 1521. It was very hard and bloody fighting. The desperate Aztecs withstood the Spaniards in every block and street of Tenochtitlán. Finally, to deprive the Aztecs of hiding places, Cortés ordered his men to destroy every house and building they came upon. When Cortés' army at last reached the center of Tenochtitlán, seven-eighths of the city had been laid waste. On August 13, 1521, the Spaniards overwhelmed what remained of the Aztec forces. Cortés had conquered Mexico.

**immunity:** the body's ability to resist catching a disease
**brigantine:** a ship with two masts

## The Beginnings of "New Spain"

In 1522, King Charles I of Spain made Cortés captain general and chief justice of "New Spain," as Mexico now was called. From 1522 to 1524, Cortés worked to rebuild Tenochtitlán, which became known as Mexico City. Using forced Indian labor, Cortés raised a city that was said to be more beautiful and rich than any city in Europe.

Encouraged by Cortés, many Spaniards came to settle in Mexico, where they mingled with the Native American population. Cortés zealously spread the Catholic Faith among the Native Americans. He requested the government to send over missionaries. Under Cortés, these missionaries established schools and colleges for the education of the Indians. The missionaries worked to destroy the native religion, but some of them translated Aztec hieroglyphics and so preserved the knowledge of Aztec institutions and history. On every site of human sacrifice, the Church performed **exorcisms** and erected churches to sanctify these terrible places.

In later years, Cortés fell out of favor with the court of Spain. In 1540, he returned to Spain to plead his case before the king. Frustrated with the **rebuffs** he received from Charles I, Cortés journeyed to Seville, planning to embark for Mexico. Instead, he fell sick in a town near Seville and there died on December 2, 1547.

**exorcism:** the act by which the Church drives demons from persons, places, or things

**rebuff:** resisting another person's attempts to help or seek help

# Spain and the Native Americans

In setting up governments in the lands they conquered in America, the Spanish monarchs faced a serious difficulty. Fernando and Isabel wanted the Native Americans to become Christians. They wanted to teach them European civilization so that they could fully participate in Spanish society. Only in this way, thought the monarchs, could Native Americans and Spaniards live peacefully side by side in America.

It was Columbus who came up with a way that was supposed to civilize the Native Americans and make them Christians. When Columbus was governor of the island of Hispaniola, he divided up the island's lands among his men and allowed them to use Native Americans to work the lands. Later, the Spanish crown took over what Columbus did and gave lands to Spanish settlers. These lands were called **encomiendas**—"complimentary land grants." Someone who received an *encomienda* was called an **encomendero**. According to Spanish law, an *encomendero* was not to treat the Native Americans on his encomienda as slaves, but he could make them work for him. In return, the encomendero had to take care of the Native Americans and educate them so that they could become Christians and learn the ways of European civilization. The idea behind this arrangement was that, in time, the Native Americans would take their place as full members of Spanish society.

Unfortunately, the *encomienda* plan did not better the lives of Indians. *Encomenderos* often treated their Indian workers like slaves and were cruel to them. On Hispaniola and other islands, the native peoples were not used to such heavy labor as farming and mining. Having no immunities against European sicknesses, thousands of Indians died.

As governor of New Spain, Cortés himself established *encomiendas*. Cortés was careful not to break up native tribes but allowed the Indians

**encomienda:** land that was given or granted by the Spanish king to some person

**encomendero:** a man who receives a land grant or *encomienda*

to live in their villages under their native chiefs. To insure that Indian workers were treated justly, Cortés passed laws setting the number of hours an Indian was allowed to work and how much he must be paid. Cortés also required *encomenderos* to provide suitable religious instruction to their Indian workers.

Nevertheless, just like in the Caribbean islands, Native Americans were often abused in Mexico. The system turned the natives of the continent into serfs, bound to their lands and enslaved to their landlords. Cortés was able to keep the abuses to a minimum, but they still occurred.

Some Spaniards defended the way the Spanish treated the natives in America. They claimed that Pope Alexander VI had divided the New World between Spain and Portugal, and so both nations had the right to conquer the Native Americans. But other Spaniards disagreed. They said the pope did not give either Spain or Portugal the right to conquer but only to convert the natives to the Catholic Faith. They condemned the way the way *encomenderos* were treating the Native Americans. Among the Spaniards who stood up for the Native Americans was a lawyer turned priest who would become known as the "Defender of the Indians." He was Bartolomé de Las Casas.

## Defender of the Indians

Bartolomé de Las Casas probably heard a sermon preached in a straw-thatched church on the island of Hispaniola in 1511. Commenting on the text, "I am a voice crying in the wilderness," the Dominican friar, Antonio de Montesinos, asked, "Are these Indians not men? Do they not have rational souls? Are you not obliged to love them as you love yourselves?"

Las Casas dedicated his life to the belief that the Native Americans should be treated with justice and Christian charity. For 40 years or so, he argued that, as human beings, Indians had equal rights with Spaniards. The Spanish crown, said Las Casas, had no right to conquer the Native Americans by force. He thought Spaniards could act as **overlords** to the Native Americans, but they could not abolish Native American governments or enslave natives. The *encomienda* system, he said, was little better than slavery and should be abolished. No one should use force in preaching the Gospel, Las Casas said.

In 1544, the Spanish king Charles I appointed Las Casas bishop of Chiapas in southern Mexico. There, Las Casas enraged colonists by setting rigid standards *encomenderos* must meet before he would **absolve** them from their sins. He basically forbade giving the Eucharist to anyone who exacted labor from Native Americans.

Las Casas was a stout defender of the Indians. Sometimes, though, in defending them, he exaggerated both Indian virtues and Spanish cruelty. His most famous work, *A Short Account of the Destruction of the Indies*, is filled with many exaggerations of Spanish cruelty. This work was translated into several languages, and from it came the "Black Legend" that has been used to this day to attack the reputation of colonial Spain.

In 1550, Las Casas was in Spain where he tried to convince the Spanish king to stop all conquests of America. King Charles I did stop conquests until theologians could decide whether they were just or not. The result

**overlord:** someone who is lord over someone else

**absolve:** to declare someone is free of sin or guilt

was that the king issued a new law for Spaniards in America. The law did not abolish conquests, but it tried to make life better for Indians in America and limit the cruelty of their Spanish rulers. It was a law inspired by the ideas of Bartolomé de Las Casas.

### Juan Diego and Our Lady of Guadalupe

Because he fought for justice for the Indians, Bishop Las Casas drew many native people to the Catholic Church. Unfortunately, this did not happen all over New Spain. Because of the bad treatment they had received, many Indians were not willing to accept the Catholic Faith. They thought it was a white man's religion, that it had nothing to offer the brown-skinned natives.

Then, on December 12, 1531, something miraculous occurred. The Virgin Mary appeared to the Indian Juan Diego on Tepeyac hill near Mexico City—the site where an Aztec temple to the goddess Tonantzin had once stood. Appearing, not as a white woman but as an Aztec princess, the Virgin told Juan Diego to ask the bishop of Mexico, Juan de Zumárraga, to build a church dedicated to her on Tepeyac hill. Bishop Zumárraga was, at first, unwilling to believe Juan Diego, but then a miracle changed his mind. On his third visit to the bishop, Juan Diego opened his **tilma**, or cloak, and a flood of roses poured forth from it. Not only was it wondrous that the Indian should find roses in December, but upon the *tilma* appeared the image of the lady. Bishop Zumárraga changed his mind and commanded that the church the Virgin ordered be built on Tepeyac hill.

Because of this **apparition** of the Virgin (whom we remember as Our Lady of Guadalupe), millions of Indians in Mexico were baptized into the Catholic Church. That Mary had appeared as an Aztec woman showed the Indians that the Faith was not just a white man's religion but was meant for them as well.

> **tilma:** a cloak made of cactus fibers
> **apparition:** the appearing of something that is unexpected, strange, or unusual

# The Conquest of Peru

Cortés' conquest of the mighty Aztec kingdom inspired another Spanish *conquistador* to find an empire of his own to conquer. His name was Francisco Pizarro; and, in 1532, he with his brothers set off on an expedition to Peru—an empire that rivaled the glory of the Aztecs.

Climbing high into the Andes, the Pizarro brothers and their men learned that the Inca, Atahualpa, was fighting a civil war against his brother. When the explorers arrived in the Peruvian city of Cajamarca, they beheld buildings that appeared to be roofed with gold. The walls and roof of the Temple of the Sun, the largest building in Cajamarca, and the walls of the Inca's palace were hung with plates of gold to reflect the life-giving rays of the sun god. Hungry for treasure, Francisco Pizarro planned to seize this gold for himself.

Pizarro and his men carried out their plan in the most treacherous way. They invited the Inca into their camp. When he entered with his bodyguard, the Spaniards slaughtered the Indians and took Atahualpa captive. Pizarro said he would release Atahualpa only if he agreed to fill a room with gold. The Inca and his nobles agreed and began bringing the shining metal into the throne room of the palace. But when, at last, the Inca fulfilled his promise and had filled the entire room with gold, the Spaniards killed him.

After the murder of Atahualpa, Pizarro had an Inca named Manco Capac crowned king of Peru. Manco Capac, however, wanted to drive the Spaniards from Peru. With his Indian armies, he laid siege to the Spaniards in the cities of Cuzco and Lima, a city Pizarro had founded in 1535. But in April 1537, the Spaniards defeated the Indians and put them to flight.

Francisco Pizarro, however, did not long enjoy his new riches and power. On June 26, 1541, he was assassinated in Lima by fellow conquistadors. The whole of rich Peru, however, remained part of the Spanish empire.

# Life in Spanish America

What was Spanish America? It was essentially a European society transplanted among the Native American people, who gradually transformed it, just as they were being transformed by it. It was an extension of Spain and Europe in the New World.

The kings of Spain saw their New World possessions not just as colonies to be exploited for the sake of the mother country, but as new kingdoms, equal to the old kingdoms of Spain—Castile, León, and Aragon. While the king did take a portion (the "royal fifth") of whatever gold, silver, or other wealth was found in America, he expended great sums of money in maintaining the colonies. The kings of Spain saw the free inhabitants of America, both natives and transplanted Spaniards, as equal subjects of the crown. The king believed it was his duty to Christianize and civilize the natives of America, and so he maintained any colony as long as there was progress in Christianizing and civilizing the Indians—even if the colony was a drain on the royal treasury.

The king of Spain tried to maintain a tight control over the government of his New World possessions, which he divided into "kingdoms." The highest authority in each kingdom (or **viceroyalty**) was a king's representative, or **viceroy**, who acted in the king's name. Along with the viceroy was the court called the *audiencia real*, or royal audience. While the viceroy took care of the administration of the viceroyalty, the *audiencia* took care of justice. Within the viceroyalty were provinces, each with its own governor and *audiencia*. Below the governor were a number of lesser officials. In the pueblos, or towns, some of these officials were elected, while others were appointed.

**viceroy:** an official who acts in the place of the king and in his name
**viceroyalty:** a region ruled by a viceroy
**mestizo:** a person of mixed Indian and Spanish heritage

## Spanish American Society

From the very beginning, the Spanish crown encouraged intermarriage between Spaniards and natives. From this intermingling of the races—what the Spanish called *mestizaje*—came a new racial type, the **mestizo**, or man of mixed European and Indian blood. After a time, the *mestizos* formed the largest single class in Spanish American society, outnumbering both Spaniards and Indians.

Spanish American society was clearly divided into classes based on race. The most influential and powerful were the European-born Spaniards, called **peninsulares**. These controlled all the higher offices of government in Spanish America. Below the *peninsulares* were the **creoles**, who were pure Spaniards, but born in America. The creoles could not hold the highest political offices, though they occupied the less influential and powerful ones. After a time the creoles, who were often rich, were able to buy their way into higher offices and some (though not many) even served as viceroys. As time passed, the creoles came to resent the power wielded by the *peninsulares*.

> **creoles:** American-born Spaniards
> **peninsulares:** Spanish-born people of New Spain
> **mulatto:** a person of mixed African and Caucasian heritage

As the *peninsulares* tended to look down on the creoles, so the creoles tended to look down on the *mestizos*. Even so, the *mestizo* population began to outnumber the ruling classes and even began to occupy many of the lowest offices, such as elective offices in the pueblos.

Next in order in Spanish-American society after the *mestizos* were the Indians. Though the Spanish crown considered them equal subjects to the Spaniards and tried to protect them, Indians were in practice often ill treated both by their *encomenderos* and by lower government officials. Spanish law, however, never called for transplanting Indians from their native lands or for placing them on reservations. The crown also opposed any attempts to exterminate the Native Americans. Though thousands of Indians did indeed die under Spanish rule, this was largely because they lacked immunities to European diseases. Smallpox, measles, whooping cough, scurvy, and influenza devastated Indian populations; in some cases, as on some Caribbean islands, disease wiped out the entire native population. In the 17th and 18th centuries, the crown tried again to change the *encomienda* system, to make it more just. King Philip V (r. 1700–1746) finally, in 1720, abolished the whole system in law, though it continued to exist in practice.

Spanish America had hundreds of thousands of black African slaves, imported from Africa every year from 1600 to 1750. These slaves suffered from cruel treatment in many parts of Spanish America, which led to a number of slave revolts. Though Spanish law had protections for slaves and said they could own property, a master held absolute power over his slave and could punish him with mutilation or even death. The law said the Church had to teach black slaves the Faith and give them the sacraments, including sacramental marriage. Spaniards intermarried with blacks, from which arose another social group, the **mulattos**. The zambos, or sambos, came from intermarriages between blacks and Indians.

Since slaves could buy their freedom, there were many free blacks in Spanish America. Communities of free blacks could be found in Cuba, Santo Domingo, Puerto Rico, and Colombia. Some black slaves from English territory escaped to the Spanish lands, fleeing their English masters.

## Life in New Spain

**reredos:** a stone or wood screen or wall of partition behind an altar. A reredos is often highly ornamented and adorned with pictures or statues of saints

By the 17th century, Central and South America had large, thriving cities with universities, theaters, mansions, and beautiful public buildings. These cities in some cases arose around ancient centers of Indian cultures. Spanish America had a rich culture. It was a Spanish, European civilization that was influenced by Indian cultures. Churches, cathedrals, monasteries, and palaces built in all the European styles rose throughout Mexico, Central America, and South America. The churches were dark but filled with colorful statuary and paintings. Ornately carved gilded **reredoses**, adorned with images of Our Lord, Our Lady, and the saints, filled church sanctuaries with brilliant color.

Much of the art of Spanish America was done in the service of the Church. A *mestizo* composer named Manuel de Zumaya composed beautiful music in the baroque style for church, as well as an opera called *Partenope* in 1711. Another great Mexican composer was Ignacio de Jerúsalem, who composed in the classical style popular in mid-eighteenth century Europe. A Mexican writer much admired today was the nun, Sor (sister) Juana Inés de la Cruz. Born in Mexico in 1648, Sor Juana wrote both secular and religious poetry, novels, and comedies, and engaged in scientific and classical literary studies.

The first colonists to come to Spanish America came to find gold. However, as time passed, agriculture became increasingly more important to the economy of the Spanish American realms. The Spanish introduced a number of crops to the New World—wheat, rye, barley, oats, sugarcane, coffee, peas, onions, melons, pears, plums, peaches, grapes, and many others. They also introduced plows and beasts of burden, such as oxen and horses. The Spanish introduced the wheel— an invention unknown to Native Americans.

The Spanish did not carry only gold and silver from America to Europe, but new foods cultivated by the Native Americans. Native American Indian farmers gave to the world their pink and lima beans, the potato, yellow squash and acorn squash, chili pepper, maize corn of many types, chocolate, and the tomato.

The Catholic Church was central to the life and culture of Spanish America. One of the main goals of Spanish exploration and settlement in the New World was the conversion of the natives to the Catholic Faith. Missionaries from religious orders, such as the Domincans, Franciscans, and Jesuits, traveled into the mountains, deserts, and jungles of the New World to spread the Gospel of Christ. Everywhere they established missions under the patronage of the Spanish king.

The Church influenced the whole way of life in Spanish American society. Pueblos were built around the parish church. The Church worked to civilize the Indians, teaching them how to engage in civic life and how to farm. The Church fought those who tried exploit the Indians or even exterminate them. Though there were clergymen who mistreated the Indians, the Church from the beginning upheld the dignity and rights of the American natives.

As in Europe, the Church in America dispensed charity to the poor and the sick. Bishops, priests, and religious orders founded and staffed schools and hospitals, as well as the missions. The Spanish crown gave the Church wealth to carry out its task—which made the colonial Church one of the largest landholders in America. This was not always good for the Church, for some bishops and priests grew too comfortable and even corrupt. Yet, many were the clergy and religious who took their vows seriously and worked for the good of their people. Many even suffered martyrdom for the sake of the Gospel.

Formed as it was by European and Native American cultures, as well as the Catholic Church, Spanish America became a rich, beautiful, and diverse civilization. Its legacy lives on today in the various nations and peoples that live in the lands that stretch from Tierra del Fuego (the southern tip of South America) to the northern borders of Mexico.

# Chapter Review

## Summary

- Latin America has vast natural resources and a growing population. The languages of these regions—Mexico and Central America, and South America—are Spanish and Portuguese.
- Latin America has diverse climates and landscapes, with deserts, high mountain ranges, tropical rain forests, and plains. Latin America extends from Mexico to Tierra del Fuego.
- Latin America's story includes the tale of three great Native American civilizations: the *Maya* civilization of southern Mexico, the *Inca* civilization of Peru in South America, and the *Aztec* civilization in the highlands of what is now Mexico City. These civilizations are often called Pre-Columbian.
- The Maya, who lived on the Yucatan Peninsula, were a farming people. They raised cities, which were more like groupings of religious temples than anything we think of as a city. The Mayan arts included architecture, the making of beautiful figurines and ornaments, painting, as well as relief carving and sculpture. The Maya invented a written language that used hieroglyphics. They developed the art of making paper. Their knowledge of astronomy and mathematics allowed the Maya to develop a complex and very precise calendar. The Maya worshiped many gods and practiced human sacrifice.
- Like the Maya, the Incas built cities having great stone buildings, built from uncut stones very skillfully joined without mortar. The Incas built roads, canals, and aqueducts. They were ingenious farmers. Their ruler, the Inca, was a complete despot, controlling the lives of all his subjects. The Inca was not only the king but the highest priest of his people, who worshiped many gods. Though the Incas practiced human sacrifice, it was not as big a part of Incan religion as it was of the Mayan and Aztec religions.
- The modern story of Latin America begins with Christopher Columbus' discovery of America in 1492. One of Columbus' motives was to convert pagans to the Christian Faith.
- Pope Alexander VI set up a demarcation line that split territories in the New World between Portugal and Spain for purposes of evangelization as well as empire.
- In 1518, Hernán Cortés captained an expedition to the mainland of North America. He intended to bring the Aztec kingdom of Mexico under the authority of the kings of Spain.

- The dominant native people in Mexico were the Aztecs. According to legend, they came from a land in the northwest called Aztlán to the high mountain valley of Mexico. By the sixteenth century, the Aztecs had become an advanced civilization.
- The most important Aztec god was Huitzilopochtli, the god of war. But another important deity was Quetzalcoatl, the god of the air, who, legends said, had white skin, dark hair, and a flowing beard. Quetzalcoatl, it was said, would return from the east and abolish human sacrifice, commonly practiced by the Aztecs.
- Reports of Cortés' landing filled the Aztecs and Montezuma with fear, because they thought he was Quetzalcoatl. Montezuma received Cortés and his troops at Tenochtitlán, but Cortés placed Montezuma under house arrest. The Aztecs rose up against the Spanish and Montezuma was killed by his own people. In their retreat from the city, the Spaniards lost 450 men.
- In August 1521, Cortés captured Tenochtitlán. In 1522, he became captain general of Mexico, called New Spain. He brought in missionaries and built churches.
- Columbus began the Spanish land grant system in America by rewarding his men with land. The Spanish crown continued this practice with *encomiendas*, which in practice included control over the Indians on the lands the government gave into the charge of a Spanish landowner. The system was abused, and a priest named Bartolomé de las Casas fought to protect the Indians abused by landowners.
- On December 12, 1531, the Virgin Mary appeared to St. Juan Diego, an Indian, at Tepeyac hill, near Mexico City. This apparition of the Virgin led to an increase of native baptisms.
- Francisco Pizarro and his brothers conquered Peru in 1532. Pizarro had the Inca treacherously killed. Pizarro then proceeded to conquer the Inca's realm.
- Spanish America was essentially a European society transplanted among an alien people and was being transformed by those people. The kings of Spain saw their New World possessions, not just as colonies to be exploited for the sake of the mother country, but as new kingdoms, equal to the old kingdoms of Spain. The king of Spain tried to maintain a tight control over the government of his New World possessions, which he divided into "kingdoms."
- In Spanish American society, slaves were the lowest class. Then came the Indians. *Mestizos*, those of mixed Indian and Spanish blood, had the largest population. The creoles, or American-born Spaniards, held a higher position in society than the *mestizos*. Highest of all were the *peninsulares*, those born in Spain, who controlled the political offices.
- By the 17th century, Central, and South America had large, thriving cities with universities, theaters, mansions, and beautiful public buildings. The first colonists to come to Spanish America came to find gold. However, as time passed, agriculture became increasingly more important to the economy of the Americas. The Spanish introduced new crops, tools, and the wheel to America. But Native Americans contributed new crops to Europe, such as the potato, chocolate, and the tomato.
- The Catholic Church was central to the life and culture of Spanish America. One of the main goals of Spanish exploration and settlement in the New World was the conversion of the natives to the Catholic Faith. Formed as it was by European and Native American cultures, as well as the Catholic Church, Spanish America became a rich, beautiful, and diverse civilization.

## Key Concepts
**river system:** a term referring to a group of rivers that all flow into a common river
**Pre-Columbian:** referring to the history of the Americas before Columbus and the Spaniards arrived in the New World
**solar year:** the period of time it takes for the earth to make one full revolution around the sun
**conquistador:** Spanish word meaning "conqueror"
**encomienda:** a land grant system established by Spain in America by which landholders, called *encomenderos*, were given land along with control over the Indians in that territory
**mestizos:** those of mixed Indian and European blood in Spanish America
**creoles:** American-born Spaniards in Spanish America
**peninsulares:** Spanish-born inhabitants of Spanish America, who controlled the political offices

## Dates to Remember
**300–900:** the period in which Mayan civilization reached its full greatness
**ca. 1200:** the Inca, Manco Capac, establishes his capital at Cuzco
**1300s:** the Aztecs arrive in Mexico
**1438–ca. 1537:** the period of the Incan empire's greatest expansion
**1492:** Columbus lands on an island in the Americas.
**1513:** Vasco Nuñez de Balboa sights the Pacific Ocean from Panama.
**1521:** Hernán Cortés conquers Tenochtitlán.
**1531:** The Virgin Mary appears to St. Juan Diego at Tepeyac.
**1537:** Francisco Pizarro conquers Peru.

## Central Characters
**Manco Capac (flourished ca. 1200):** the first Inca, who established his capital at Cuzco
**Huayna Capac (1493–1525):** the Inca under whom the Incan empire reached its greatest extent
**Itzcóatl (r. 1428–1440):** the Aztec ruler who began his people's period of expansion
**Huitzilopochtli:** the Aztec god of war and of the sun to whom the Aztecs offered human sacrifices
**Quetzalcoatl:** (the "feathered serpent"), an Aztec god who was said to have white skin, dark hair, and a flowing beard. The legends say that Quetzalcoatl had taught people how to farm, use metals, and set up governments.
**Montezuma II (1466–1520):** the Aztec ruler of Mexico who welcomed Cortés to Tenochtitlán
**Hernán Cortés (1485–1547):** Spanish conqueror of Mexico
**Francisco Pizarro (ca. 1475–1541):** Spanish conqueror of Peru
**Atahualpa (ca. 1502–1533):** the Inca who was killed by Pizarro and his brothers
**Bartolomé de Las Casas (1474–1566):** Spanish bishop of Chiapas and defender of the Indians, who fought the *encomienda* system

## Questions for Review
1. What three major Indian civilizations were in America when the Europeans arrived?
2. How were the Pre-Columbian empires of Latin America alike? How did they differ?

3. What Native American empire did Cortés overcome? What American Indian empire did Pizarro conquer?
4. How were the Spanish conquistadors, Cortés and Pizarro, alike? How did they differ?
5. Why did the Spanish set up the *encomienda* system? Was it successful? Why or why not?
6. What did the appearance of the Virgin Mary at Tepeyac tell Native American peoples about the Catholic Faith?
7. Give three examples of how the Catholic Church influenced life in Spanish America.
8. List and describe the four social classes of Spanish America.
9. What are the two major languages spoken in Latin America today?

## Ideas in Action
1. Watch a documentary on Our Lady of Guadalupe and learn about the actual *tilma* hanging in Mexico City today. How did the apparition at Guadalupe change Mexico? What does this documentary teach us about God's action in history? About miracles? How does the miracle of Tepeyac, which we can see with our own eyes, change our thinking about the miracle of the Incarnation? Are there ways that we can experience the Incarnation in our own lives? Does Our Lady of Guadalupe still change history? How?
2. Ask students to list foods, fashions, music, words, and customs imported from Latin America to the United States and other non-Hispanic regions. Have students write a paragraph or two summarizing the impact of Hispanic culture on American culture.
3. Teach students some basic Spanish vocabulary words and phrases. (Use a Berlitz guide to Spanish to find common phrases, such as "what is your name?") Make flash cards of the words, ask students to speak/repeat the words and phrases, and ask them to illustrate the meanings of certain Spanish words and phrases with pictures.
4. Look up the ancient city of Cuzco in an encyclopedia or on the Internet. Assign class reports, including: some of the advances of Inca civilization; some facts about the way the Inca people lived, what they ate, what they wore, and so on. Does this civilization have any counterparts anywhere in the world, i.e. has there ever been such an advanced mountain-dwelling people anywhere else, in Europe, Asia, Australia, or Africa?
5. Look up the history of the civilizations that came before the Aztecs in Mexico and Yucatan. Assign reports on the Olmecs, the Toltecs, the pyramids at Teotihuacan, and the cities of Yucatan.

# Highways and Byways

## Saints of South America

Following the conquest of the Inca, the conquistadors set up *encomiendas* in Peru. The native Indians were treated as serfs, bound to the land of their villages, and forced to work in mines and building projects. Thousands died in the first ten years of the colony. A feudal kingdom was created, rich, cruel, and far from the control of Spanish law and Spanish justice. The Church alone tried to help the Indians and improve their lot.

But despite all the evils of the time, Peru produced many holy men and women in colonial days. St. Rose of Lima (1586–1617) and St. Martin de Porres (1579–1639) are the best known.

A healer and wonder-worker, St. Martin was the son of an African slave-woman and a Spanish owner. He brought comfort to the poor of Lima and inspired the rulers of the city to help their Indian serfs.

St. Rose, the patroness of South America and the Philippines, is remembered for the love of Christ that led her to a life of prayer and hard penance. Though she lived as a recluse, St. Rose knew of the sufferings of the Indian poor of Peru and spoke out against the cruelty of those who showed so little respect for their brothers and sisters.

St. Toribio de Mongrovejo (1538–1606), the bishop of Lima, risked his life fighting for Native American rights and justice. His efforts were finally rewarded when the king of Spain, Philip III, outlawed Native American servitude in 1601.

St. Francis Solano (1549–1610) carried the Gospel deep into the Chaco jungle, over the mountains, to the hostile and primitive people who lived there. In old age he returned to Lima to preach to the wealthy of the city. His message brought about a revival of Christian faith and morality among the ruling classes of Peru.

# The Scientific Revolution

By the beginning of the 16th century, a new Europe was rising from the ashes of the Middle Ages.

For all its problems and sins, the old medieval society had been centered on the Christian Faith as revealed through the teachings of the Catholic Church. All of life found its meaning and purpose in attaining the life that is to come—union with God, through Jesus Christ. Medieval men, of course, did not neglect the good things of this life. They sought to create societies based on law and justice; they developed the practical arts of agriculture and manufacturing; they cultivated the fine arts of architecture, painting, sculpture, poetry and music; and they sought to understand the world around them through the study of philosophy. But for the people of the Middle Ages, all these earthly goods were seen to have one great purpose; they were to help lead men and women to God. For medieval man, the Church and the Faith were at the center of human life.

The Renaissance changed all this. Beginning in Italy in the mid-14th century, scholars, poets, and artists discovered a new interest in the classical civilizations of ancient Greece and Rome. The ancient world became for them the model of a perfect society; classical art, they thought, was the model of true beauty. This new fascination with classical civilization caused people to despise the Middle Ages as barbaric; they thought of it as just a "middle period" between the glories of the ancient world and the rebirth (which "renaissance" means) of classical culture in the 14th century. First the Italian city of Florence, and then Rome herself became the center of the Renaissance and of humanism—the belief that mankind's goal in life is to attain the good things of this earth.

Renaissance humanism was not necessarily contrary to Christian culture, any more than reason is contrary to faith. Many of the original humanists had been devout Catholics who saw humanism as a way of enriching their religion, not replacing it. Yet, humanism became increasingly more atheistic—not because humanists did not believe in God, but because they more and more began to ignore him.

Interest in religion, however, did not die out in the Renaissance. Humanists were among the chief critics of the corruption in the Church; they hoped for a renewal of the true Christian faith in all its purity. It is not surprising, then, that many humanists joined Martin Luther in his revolt against the Church, which began in 1517. Soon large sections of Germany, England and Scotland, Scandinavia, and even many areas of France became Protestant. This Protestant Reformation or Revolution destroyed the unity of Christendom and led to bitter wars of religion that shook France and destroyed large sections of Germany. The Protestant Reformation, too, ended the Renaissance.

The end of the Renaissance, however, was the beginning of another kind of "renaissance"—the renaissance of what today we call "science." This scientific renaissance was not, like the earlier renaissance, centered on literature, art, and culture. Though it was inspired by the ideas of certain ancient Greek thinkers, it did not seek to return to an earlier, more perfect age. It was, indeed, more of a revolution than a rebirth, for it wanted to cast away the philosophy and science of the Middle Ages and to create new ways of thinking about the world. The "scientific revolution" was to change the world even more than the Renaissance did. It was the first of many revolutions that ultimately gave birth to our modern world and changed the face, not only of Christendom, but of every culture and civilization on earth.

# Philosophy and Science

Though today we think of *science* and *philosophy* as very different studies, people in the 16th and 17th centuries did not. Then, the terms "science" and "philosophy" were used interchangeably. Philosophers saw themselves as seekers after *scientia* (the Latin word for *knowledge*), and the men we would today call scientists said their interest was in "natural philosophy." Furthermore, in the 16th and 17th centuries, the men we would today call scientists also busied themselves in what we today would call philosophy, and many a philosopher carried on studies in what we call science.

Yet though they saw little or no difference between science and philosophy, the people of the 16th and 17th centuries had begun to distinguish between different ways or methods of coming to know the world around them. As they saw it, there were two basic paths of knowledge one could follow. One was the old path, blazed by the Greek philosophers Plato and Aristotle and continued by the Scholastics of the Middle Ages. The other path was also, in a sense, old—it came from the ancient Greek world, from philosophers who had lived before Plato and Aristotle. But, as the 16th and 17th century thinkers saw it, the path from that ancient Greek world to their own had become overgrown and nearly lost over the centuries. These 16th and 17th century thinkers saw it as their task to clear a new path through the "weeds" and "confusion" of the Middle Ages, a path that would lead them more certainly to true knowledge about the world.

## The "Old Way"

One of the hallmarks of the Middle Ages had been Western Europe's rediscovery of the works of the Greek philosopher, Aristotle. Many greeted the rediscovery of Aristotle as a kind of renaissance in learning. Indeed, in the 13th century, Aristotle was seen as a radical philosopher, so radical that some devout Catholics rejected his works outright, for they saw his teachings as dangerous to the Catholic Faith.

> **ossified:** opposed to change, as if turned to bone (from the Latin word, *os*, meaning bone)
>
> **inanimate:** without a soul or life (from the Latin word *anima*, meaning "soul" or "life.")

It was the two great medieval thinkers, St. Albert the Great and St. Thomas Aquinas, who demonstrated that, though some of Aristotle's conclusions are contrary to the Catholic Faith, his way of doing philosophy is not. In fact, Aristotle's philosophy was seen to be the best way to understand the world around us. Many thinkers thought Aristotle gave theologians the best intellectual tools possible to explain the mysteries of religion. Both Albert and Aquinas turned Aristotle's philosophy from being an enemy of the Faith to become the handmaiden of theology.

But, over the centuries after the days of Albert and Thomas, Aristotelian philosophy had become **ossified**. Scholars did not question Aristotle—nor, for that matter, did they question other ancient thinkers, such as the Roman physician Galen and the Alexandrian astronomer, Ptolemy. By the 16th century, many scholars thought that, to know truth, all one had to do was read the works of these thinkers—that what, for instance, Aristotle said was true because Aristotle said it. One did not need to find out for himself whether or not what Aristotle and other ancient thinkers said was true or not. One only had to accept it.

Such an attitude was contrary to what Aristotle himself had said was the true way to come to knowledge. For Aristotle (as well as for Albert and Thomas Aquinas), all knowledge begins with what we experience. The mind of every person begins as a "clean slate"—we are not born with knowledge but come to knowledge as we grow older by understanding the things we experience in the world. Through our senses of sight, hearing, and touch, we come into contact with the world around us; and by thinking about the things we sense, we are able to understand them, to have knowledge about them. We do not learn primarily from books but by coming into contact with all the wonders that surround us.

An example of how the "old way" of knowledge worked is the way people come to know about who and what we are. Human beings only know themselves by what they experience about themselves and about other things. As a person grows, he experiences other beings besides himself—not only his mother and father, family members, and other human beings, but beasts, plants, and such **inanimate** objects as rocks, water, and soil. Perhaps he first understands that the non-human creatures he sees, hears, tastes, and touches are in some ways very much like himself; but soon he begins to perceive that he is very different from them, as well. He sees, for instance, that he is made of "stuff," like they are, though often of a very different kind of stuff. Then, he notices that he is more like plants and animals than rocks and water, because, like plants and animals, he grows and develops. He then sees that he is more like beasts than plants, because, like the beasts, he can move about from place to place and has senses like they do. After a time, however, he learns that he is quite unique from anything else in the world; for, unlike all other creatures, he can form ideas and think about those ideas.

All these experiences are the beginnings or "principles" of understanding and knowledge. They are the beginnings of science. And these experiences encourage the philosopher to give answers to the question, "what am I?" Understanding that he has a body, five senses, and even emotions and passions, just like the beasts have, the philosopher realizes that he is an *animal*. Then, seeing that, unlike the beasts, he can think and reason, and even use his reason to make tools by which he can cultivate the soil or build the most marvelous machines, he understands that he is more than just an animal. He comes to understand that he is a *rational animal*, a being with a body, senses, and a mind that understands and makes connections between things.

After answering the question, "what am I?" the philosopher makes other **queries**. His next question, perhaps, is "why do I exist? What is the purpose for which I exist?" Because he is different from other creatures, he comes to understand that his purpose for existing must be different from that of all other creatures. He comes to understand that, because he can reason and know, and use his reason and knowledge to make new things, his purpose in life is to understand the world around him and be a maker and creator.

"Why do I exist," however, is not the final question the philosopher asks. He does not simply want to know *what* he is, or *why* he exists, but he seeks to discover *where* he comes from. In asking the question, "Where do I come from? Who made me?" the medieval philosophers after much thought, gave the answer, *God*. It is God, they said, who is the source from which they and all things come to be.

This method of reasoning is called **deduction**. It begins with **principles** that one discovers by thinking about his experience (and what others have said about their own experiences); one then draws conclusions from those principles by asking questions.

To understand deduction, we have used the example of a philosopher coming to know what a human being is. But medieval philosophers used deduction to understand many other things as well, including mathematics, morality, politics, and who God is. By using deduction, of course, different philosophers came to different conclusions on any number of questions; but, for centuries, nearly all philosophers thought deduction was the chief and best way to understand the world, themselves, and God.

> **query:** a question or inquiry
> **deduction:** a method of reasoning where one begins with principles and, by asking questions, draws conclusions from those principles
> **principle:** the first ideas in thinking, from which one draws conclusions

## The "New Way"

Though the best of medieval philosophers valued deduction as the means of coming to the truth about the world, they insisted that all reasoning had to start with experience. St. Thomas Aquinas, for instance, said that an argument based on authority (for instance, "this is true because Aristotle says it's true") is the weakest kind of argument in philosophy. Thomas, like other medieval thinkers —like his teacher St. Albertus Magnus—insisted that all proofs in philosophy had to be rooted in *experimentum*—the Latin word for "experience."

It was Albertus Magnus, however, who suggested another kind of *experimentum*—the kind indicated by our English word, "experiment." What is an experiment? Firstly, it is a kind of experience, but a carefully controlled experience. It is a testing of a thing to see what it does or how it behaves under very controlled circumstances. Experiment can take the form of careful observation; for instance, a philosopher or scientist may watch spiders to understand how they kill their prey. He might choose several species of spiders to watch, and in observing them, note down every detail of their movements he can discern. He will then compare his observations, carried out over a period of time, and come to some conclusions—for instance, that spiders inject a poison into their prey to paralyze them before eating them.

A scientist may do more than merely observe natural things. While observing them, he may actively test them. For example, in watching ants move in single file along a path leading to and from their anthill, the scientist wonders what makes them infallibly follow this path? Is it their sense of sight or smell, or something else? To discover this, he may brush away the soil over which the ant path crosses. He notices that the ants suddenly appear confused and wander about as if they had lost their direction. From this trial, the scientist may conclude that it is the ants' sense of smell, rather than their sight, which keeps them on their path.

The scientist or philosopher, however, does not simply accept his conclusion as true. He continues to test his idea by more and more experiments. Other scientists, too, may carry out similar experiments to test one scientist's conclusions. If future experiments do not give the same results, then scientists come up with new ideas to describe what they have experienced. Only after many experiments give the same results do scientists decide that their conclusions are really true.

Experiment is merely another kind of experience that we can use to understand the world. But though it gives us much useful information, experiment alone cannot tell us everything we need or want to know. Though experiment can show us, for instance, how the human body is constructed or how it works, it cannot by itself tell us about the human soul or the purpose for which human beings exist; for these realities cannot be perceived by the senses or measured with instruments. To understand these realities, we need the "old way" of traditional philosophy.

Because philosophers had for so long neglected experiment as a means of understanding the world around them, the thinkers who rediscovered experiment in the 16th century thought they had happened upon something new. For these philosopher-scientists, the way of experiment became the new way of "natural philosophy." And because what they came to discover through experiments were so astounding and, sometimes, contrary to what everyone had thought before, 16th century thinkers began to reject the "old way" of philosophy in favor of the "new way" of experimental science. They began to think that experimental science was the only way to come to a certain knowledge about the world.

# The Copernican Revolution

Amid all the turmoil of religious revolt and war of 16th century Europe, one man lit a flame that would ignite all of Europe. This man was a native of Poland, Nicolaus (Nicholas) Copernicus. Born in 1473, Copernicus later studied at the University of Krakow in Poland and the University of Bologna in Italy. At Bologna he became a member of the clergy, though not a priest, and studied canon law and Greek. Though he would later add medicine and law to his areas of study, Copernicus' chief interest was astronomy. In 1500, he gave lectures on astronomy in Rome, and wherever he lived he pursued careful observations of the stars and the planets.

Copernicus was the father of the **heliocentric** theory of the universe. For centuries, all learned men had accepted the theory of the Alexandrian astronomer Ptolemy that the earth sits at the center of the universe and is the unmoving point around which the sun, the planets, and the starts revolve in perfect circles. Ptolemy's great work of astronomy, the *Almagest*, explains the motions of the heavenly bodies using complicated mathematics and giving ingenious explanations for why some heavenly bodies appear to move more slowly during some parts of the year and more quickly during others.

**heliocentric:** sun-centered (From the Greek word, *helios*, meaning "sun.")
**geocentric:** earth centered (From the Greek word, *Ge* or *Gaia*, signifying the earth

Ptolemy's **geocentric** theory, however, had problems. For one thing, his explanations for certain motions of the heavenly bodies were very complex. Following the lead of Aristarchus, an ancient Greek philosopher who held to the heliocentric theory, Copernicus discovered that if one assumed that the sun, not the earth, is the center of the universe, one could come up with simpler explanations for why the heavenly bodies move as they do. For 25 years, Copernicus worked on his theory; but when he had finally finished his great work, *On the Revolution of the Heavenly Spheres*, he refused to have it published. His friends urged him to publish the work, but Copernicus would not. He feared that those who did not understand it would treat it with contempt.

Why was Copernicus so hesitant to publish his discoveries? It is perhaps hard for us to understand—we, who think we know that the earth moves around the sun. But in the 16th century and, indeed, for many centuries before, the idea that the sun, planets, and stars move around the earth seemed obvious. After all, does it not *appear* to us that the sun moves around us, not we around the sun? To people of the 16th century, moreover, the theory that the earth is the center of the universe seemed to agree with Sacred Scripture, which in places speaks of the earth as stationary and the sun as moving around it. Also, many 16th century people thought that, if man is God's chief and greatest creature, is it not most fitting that man's home, the earth, be the physical center of all creation?

For many people, Copernicus' heliocentric theory was revolutionary. Ironically it was the religious revolutionaries (men like Martin Luther and his associate, Philip Melancthon) who were Copernicus' biggest opponents. The Protestant reformers thought the heliocentric theory clearly contradicted Scripture. Copernicus, however, received encouragement from bishops and learned Catholics to publish his work on the heliocentric theory.

Though Copernicus understood the controversy his heliocentric theory would lead to in his own day, he could not foresee the revolution it would help create in the years to come. Many would come to see Copernicus' ideas as a challenge to religion and would use it as an example of how science contradicts religion, and religion, science. So, though Copernicus himself was a faithful Catholic, other, less faithful thinkers would use his heliocentric theory to justify rebellion against the Catholic Church and all of Europe's past. It is for this reason that Copernicus' discovery of the heliocentric theory has been called a revolution—the "Copernican Revolution."

# The Renaissance of Science

Despite the interest shown in Copernicus' heliocentric theory, astronomy and natural science were not the major focuses of interest in the second half of the 16th century. Religious controversies between Protestants and Catholics, reform of the Church, how to protect Europe from Turkish invasion—these questions were of greater importance to Europeans than whether the earth moves around the sun, or the sun around the earth.

Interest in astronomy or in experimental science, however, did not die out in the 50 or so years after Copernicus' death. Astronomy helped bring about an important development—the reform of the calendar. Improved observations of the stars and better knowledge of astronomy made it possible to draw up a new calendar that better followed the course of the year. In 1582, a new calendar, called the "Gregorian Calendar," replaced the Julian Calendar that had been in use since the days of Julius Caesar.

The astronomy that brought about the Gregorian Calendar, however, was not based on Copernicus' heliocentric theory. Most astronomers continued to explain the universe using Ptolemy's astronomy, and for one simple reason—Copernicus' theory had not been proven to be true. It was an *hypothesis*, just like Ptolemy's theory. A hypothesis is something like an educated guess, an idea presented as a way of explaining what one experiences. A hypothesis only becomes more certain the more it is tested. Copernicus offered the heliocentric hypothesis as a way of explaining the motions of stars and planets as one sees them from the earth. He thought his hypothesis was better than Ptolemy's in explaining these motions, but not every one agreed with him. One of those who did not agree was a Jesuit, Christoph Clavius (1538–1612), highly esteemed as both a mathematician and astronomer by the greatest scholars of his time.

## The Wonder of Florence

The city of Florence in Italy had long been an important center of European culture. The home of Dante Alighieri (who wrote the *Divine Comedy*) and of Leonardo Da Vinci, Florence had become famous for art and poetry. But another of Florence's sons, Galileo Galilei (1564–1642), would make it renowned for its contributions to natural science.

Even as a young boy, Galileo had shown a remarkable aptitude for mathematics and even **mechanics**—traits he may have learned from his father, Vincenzo Galilei, who had gained some fame as a musician and mathematician. Yet, though a nobleman, Vincenzo was not wealthy, and he wanted his son to learn a profession that would bring him some wealth. But Galileo resisted his father's pressure to study medicine. Galileo's interests were mathematics, mechanics, and astronomy—and these interests he was determined to pursue.

In 1589, at the age of 25, Galileo became professor of mathematics at the University of Pisa. It was there that he challenged Aristotle himself and proved that, in one area, at least, the great philosopher was wrong. In his treatise, *De Coelo* ("On Heaven") Aristotle seemed to say that the larger

**mechanics:** a branch of physical science that deals with physical forces and their effect on bodies

## A Tale of Two Astronomers

Another of the "greatest scholars" who disagreed with Copernicus was Tycho Brahe of Denmark. Tycho, who was born three years after Copernicus died, came from an aristocratic family. While studying at the university in Copenhagen, Denmark, he discovered Ptolemy's *Almagest.* Forever after, astronomy became the chief interest of Tycho's life.

Having inherited a fortune from his uncle, Tycho was able to transfer to the University of Wittenberg in Germany to study mathematics and astronomy. To escape a plague, he left Wittenberg for Rostock, and there lost part of his nose in a duel. (No matter, Tycho had a silver and gold nose made for him, and he wore it for the rest of his life.) After traveling in Germany, Tycho returned to Denmark where, in 1572, he discovered a *nova stella* (a blast of light from the destruction of a star) in the constellation Cassiopeia—a discovery that made him famous throughout Europe.

Tycho's fame helped him convince King Frederik II of Denmark and Norway to build him an observatory. The king gave him the island of Hveen (meaning "Venus"), off the coast of Denmark, and a good deal of money. Tycho used the money to build a castle and gardens, complete with a library, observatories, and a workshop. There—and later in Prague, where he was employed by Emperor Rudolf II—Tycho carefully observed the stars, cataloging them and marking them on a great globe of the heavens.

Tycho's observations proved of great use to astronomers throughout Europe, but especially to the laboratory assistant who joined him in Prague in 1600. Johannes Kepler was born near Stuttgart, Germany, the son of an army officer who became a tavern keeper. Sent by the duke of Württemberg to study for the Lutheran ministry at the University of Tübingen in Germany, Kepler there learned of Copernicus' theory and became so enamored of astronomy that he decided to abandon the ministry in order to spend his time studying the stars.

When Kepler arrived in Prague, Tycho had not long to live. After the old astronomer died of a burst bladder in 1601, Kepler inherited his instruments and the books in which Tycho had recorded his observations of the heavens. But Kepler did not agree with Tycho's rejection of Copernicus. Using Copernicus' heliocentric theory, Kepler studied the movement of Mars and came to the conclusion that the planet did not move around the sun in a perfect circle as Copernicus said it did, but in an oval called an ellipse. But if this were true of Mars, why would it not be true of other planets? Kepler eventually concluded that all the planets move in elliptical paths around the sun.

Unlike a planet following a circular path (where it will always be equally distant from the sun), a planet following an elliptical path will sometimes be closer to the sun than at other times. In 1609, Kepler published a work showing that a planet will move more quickly along its elliptical path when it approaches nearer the sun. Kepler said this was because the sun acted like a giant magnet, attracting the planet. By 1621, Kepler had compiled his findings in a work he called the *Epitome of the Copernican Astronomy*.

Kepler's observations of the heavens led him to think that the heavenly bodies always move according to certain patterns. These patterns, called "laws," he said, are what govern the universe. Unlike later thinkers, however, Kepler did not think these laws replaced the providence of God. Kepler thought the order of the universe shows the power and wisdom of God. A pious Protestant, Kepler wrote, "My wish is that I may perceive the God whom I find everywhere in the external world in like manner within me."

> **parabolic:** Having the shape or form of a curve called a parabola
>
> **physics:** the experimental science that studies and measures the motion of bodies
>
> **optician:** a grinder of lenses for spectacles or glasses

a body of gold, lead, or any other material is, the faster it will fall to the ground. Galileo proved this idea wrong by various experiments. Several times, says one account, he dropped similar bodies of unequal size from the top of the leaning tower of Pisa, demonstrating that the larger body did not fall more quickly than the smaller one, but both fell at the same rate.

Both at Pisa and at the University of Padua, where he went to teach in 1592, Galileo made important discoveries in mechanics and **physics**—the science that studies and measures the motion of bodies. Among other important discoveries, Galileo demonstrated that a body thrown or shot through the air always travels in a **parabolic** curve.

Yet, despite the fact that Galileo's most important discoveries were in physics, he is more famous for his contributions to astronomy. In 1609, Galileo learned that an **optician** in the Netherlands had invented an instrument that allowed one to see distant objects more closely. After a single night of thinking how this could be done, Galileo designed an instrument that could make distant objects appear three times larger than they appeared to the naked eye. This power was soon increased to 32-times, and Galileo began using this invention, called the *telescope*, to look at the heavens.

Looking through his telescope, Galileo saw what no human being had ever seen before. He discovered that the Pleiades constellation, which appears to the naked eye as seven stars (the "Seven Sisters"), contains, instead, 36 stars. The Milky Way, he found, is not just a swath of light across the night sky but is made up of innumerable stars. Turning his telescope on the moon, Galileo noticed that it was covered with what appeared to be seas and mountains and valleys. But perhaps more significant were his discoveries that the planet Jupiter had moons revolving around it and that Venus and Mercury have phases like the moon does. These last discoveries provided more evidence that Copernicus' heliocentric theory of the universe was true.

In defending and promoting Copernicus' ideas, Galileo won undying popular fame; for his zeal for the heliocentric theory brought him into conflict with the Catholic Church. This conflict gave Galileo the reputation as a "martyr for science" and has made the Church appear to be an enemy of scientific research, learning, and all progress. It is to this conflict we now turn our story.

## "But It Does Move!"

At times Galileo seemed quite a humble man. For instance, he wrote, "I have never met a man so ignorant that I could not learn something from him." Yet, despite such statements, Galileo was proud and could be quite harsh with those who disagreed with him. Firmly convinced that his discoveries had proven that the Copernican heliocentric hypothesis was true, Galileo showed little patience with those who thought otherwise. For instance, writing in the margin of a book written to defend the Ptolemaic system, Galileo called the book's author (the Jesuit Antonio Rocco) an "ignoramus, elephant, fool, dunce…"

But though he had little respect for Rocco, Galileo was on good terms with other Jesuits—at least for a time. Jesuits had been among the foremost scientists of Galileo's day. The Jesuits in Rome were quite interested in Galileo's discoveries. In 1611, they welcomed him to Rome and allowed him to stay in their house in the city. What's more, Church prelates and Pope Paul V himself showed the astronomer every sign of favor.

What then happened to sour Galileo's friendship with the Church? As we have seen, it had been churchmen who had urged Copernicus to publish his work, and churchmen (particularly the Jesuits) had been eager students of natural science and had made important discoveries themselves. (For instance, the Jesuit Christoph Scheiner of Ingolstadt, had discovered sunspots in 1610—even before Galileo himself did.) Why, then, did churchmen, and the Jesuits in particular, become Galileo's opponents?

The reason is that Galileo and the churchmen differed in how they understood the importance of Copernicus' ideas. For even the most scientific Jesuits thought Copernicus' heliocentric idea was an hypothesis, and only an hypothesis. That is, they thought the heliocentric idea might be a useful instrument to help astronomers describe the universe and make predictions about when solar eclipses and other phenomena would occur. The Copernican hypothesis was a good tool, they thought, but it did not necessarily describe the universe as it truly is.

Churchmen and, indeed, many of the most learned men of Europe, continued to hold to the notion that the earth does not move and is the center of the universe. They thought the idea that the earth moves and the sun is stationary contradicted common sense. More importantly, they thought it contradicted Sacred Scripture, which in some places seems to teach very clearly that the earth does not move. Finally, in Galileo's day, Copernicus' hypothesis had not been thoroughly proven—there were still good reasons to think it might be a false way of describing the universe.

Galileo thought differently. He was so convinced that his discoveries proved that Copernicus' hypothesis was true that he would not rest until he convinced everyone else of it as well. He even began to suggest ways to interpret the Bible to take care of the troublesome passages that seemed to say the earth is stationary. Some churchmen thought Galileo was going too far in insisting on the truth of the Copernican hypothesis (and interpreting Scripture), and an intemperate Dominican named Tommaso Caccini began calling the Copernican system a heresy. Caccini tried to get the **Holy Office of the Inquisition** in Rome to try Galileo as a heretic but was unsuccessful. Galileo was merely told to insert some lines into his works saying that the Copernican theory was an hypothesis. And when Galileo refused to do this, the Holy Office seemed not to care.

For his part, however, Galileo would not let the matter drop. Fearing further investigations by the Holy Office, he went to Rome in late December 1615. In Rome, Galileo approached various Church authorities, trying to convince them about the truth of his and Copernicus' ideas.

Finally, in late February 1616, after Galileo and his ideas had become the talk of Rome, the Holy Office took action. On March 5, it issued a decree

**Holy Office of the Inquisition:** an office of the curia (the pope's officials in Rome) that issued doctrinal decrees and condemned heretical teachings. Its purpose as to protect the purity of the Catholic Faith.

calling the Copernican view "foolish, philosophically false, and utterly heretical, because contrary to Holy Scripture" and commanded Galileo to reject the heliocentric theory and teach it no longer. Another decree forbade anyone to read Copernicus' work until it was corrected. The Holy Office called for the removal of nine sentences from Copernicus' book, *On the Revolution of the Heavenly Spheres,* that referred to the heliocentric view as a fact and not merely as an hypothesis. The Holy Office approved the publication of the corrected text of Copernicus' work in 1620.

Galileo agreed to obey the Holy Office and returned to Florence. For seven years, he carried on his researches and studies. Then, in 1623, Galileo learned that Cardinal Barberini had been elected pope as Urban VIII—news that filled the astronomer with hope, for Barberini had been one of three cardinals in the Holy Office who had opposed silencing Galileo in 1616. Galileo was able to meet with the new pope, hoping he would remove the Holy Office's decree. Urban did not do this, but three years later the pope permitted Galileo to publish a work comparing the Ptolemaic and Copernican systems. Galileo had only to present the Copernican system as an hypothesis, not as fact, said the pope. To this, Galileo agreed.

This work, published in 1632, was written in the form of a dialogue (conversation) between three men. Two of the men, who defended the Copernican ideas, were presented as clever, insightful, and intelligent; the one who defended the Ptolemaic theory was presented as a fool, and was even called Simplicio—"simpleton." Worse yet, Simplicio gave arguments that were very similar to the ones Pope Urban VIII had used in defending the Ptolemaic system to Galileo. Learning of all this, Pope Urban ordered the Holy Office to examine the dialogue. In August 1632, the Holy Office forbade any further sales of the dialogue and in September ordered Galileo to present himself for trial

The now aged Galileo appeared before the Holy Office in February 1633 and was charged with having broken his word by publishing a work presenting the Copernican system as true. Galileo said he was innocent, but he had to remain in the palace of the Holy Office, where he was well treated and lived in comfort, for the next several months. Finally, after several hearings, the Holy Office declared on June 22 that Galileo was guilty of heresy and disobedience. Kneeling, he had to declare that Copernicus was wrong, that the sun is *not* the center of the universe, and the earth does not move. He was then sentenced to be imprisoned and ordered to pray the seven penitential psalms once a week for the next three years. According to a later legend, as Galileo left the tribunal of the Holy Office, he muttered to himself, *Eppur si muove!*—"But it [the earth] does move!" Despite his **recantation**, Galileo still held to the Copernican view that the sun, not the earth, is the center of the universe.

Galileo's "imprisonment" in the palace of the Holy Office lasted three days more. By order of Pope Urban, he was then moved to a rich villa and from there to comfortable quarters belonging to a friend in Siena. Finally, in December 1633, he was allowed to return to his own villa near Florence. There he spent the remaining years of his life, receiving visitors, studying, teaching, and writing books. Galileo died at the age of 78, in 1642.

Since the 17th century, many have used the trial of Galileo to attack the Catholic Church. Protestants, for instance, have said the Holy Office's condemnation of the Copernican theory disproves the Church's teaching

**recantation:** a formal rejection of a statement or idea

that the pope is infallible. Yet, what these critics miss is the fact that, neither in 1616 nor in 1633, did the pope sign the decrees condemning the Copernican viewpoint. And even if the popes had signed the decrees, such decrees do not qualify as infallible teaching, as defined by the Church.

More serious, however, has been the charge that the Church persecuted Galileo because she is opposed to science and progress. Such a charge is unhistorical. As we have seen, far from opposing natural science, the Church in the 16th and 17th centuries actively supported it. In condemning Galileo, the Holy Office was not condemning science but what its members thought was a viewpoint that contradicted Sacred Scripture. And it is important to recall that Galileo was wrong to think that he had proven the Copernican view of the universe to be true.

Still, the trial of Galileo continues to this day to be used as an example of how the Catholic Church opposes science and human freedom. Beginning in the 17th century, many scientists and thinkers would adopt this false notion about the Church and come to think that all religion stood in the way of human progress. The story of Galileo's trial thus came to symbolize for many the rebellion of the "modern," scientific mind against what they saw as the ignorance and superstition of the Catholic Church and all traditional religion.

# The Philosopher of Science

Copernicus, Tycho Brahe, Kepler, and Galileo were not the only ones in the late 16th and early 17th centuries to seek out the mysteries of nature through experiment and observation. All over Western Europe, men were studying the natural world and prodding it to reveal its wonders—and not only in astronomy, mechanics, and physics. Some investigators were turning their thoughts, not to the outside world, but to the inner world of the human body.

One of these thinkers was Sir William Harvey, who discovered how blood circulates in the human body. Harvey had developed a theory in 1615 and, in 1628, published it in the work *Anatomical Investigation Concerning the Motion of the Heart and Blood in Animals*. Harvey's theory, however, was not generally accepted, in part, because it contradicted the theory of the second century Greek physician, Galen. For centuries, Europeans and Arabs alike had treated Galen as an authority in medicine and **physiology**. That he might be wrong was for many a shocking idea.

Galileo's demonstration that Aristotle had been wrong about falling bodies, along with Harvey's discovery about the motion of blood in the human body, led many to reject the authority of these ancient thinkers. More and more, men began to think that the old way of philosophy had to give way to the new way of experimental science. One of the greatest champions of the "new way" was Sir Francis Bacon, a lawyer who, in 1618, had been appointed chancellor of England by King James I.

Despite his friendship with King James, Bacon did not long survive as chancellor. Both as chancellor and as a judge he had accepted bribes—not an uncommon thing in 17th century England. Still, Bacon had served his king well, even if dishonestly, and this angered Parliament, which was opposed to King James' claims to absolute authority. In 1621, Parliament impeached and

**physiology:** the study of the structure and functions of the body

convicted Bacon on 23 charges of corruption. He had to resign as chancellor, was forbidden to hold public office ever again, was fined, and was imprisoned in the Tower of London. His good service to King James, however, paid off, for the king soon released Bacon from prison and from paying the fine as well.

Bacon's impeachment turned him away from politics and allowed him to devote himself to "philosophy," which had been his interest for many years. By philosophy, however, Bacon did not mean the study of Aristotle or Plato or any of the medieval thinkers. Bacon thought all this kind of philosophy had to be swept away and an entirely new system of philosophy put in its place. He wanted to bring about what he called an *Instauratio Magna*, or "Great Restoration," of philosophy. This *Instauratio*, he wrote in 1620, was to be the beginning of "a total reconstruction of sciences, [practical] arts, and all human knowledge, raised upon the proper foundation..."

The "proper foundation" of science had to begin with "a more perfect use of reason," as Bacon wrote in 1620 in his work, *Novum Organum*. This work was so named because Bacon wanted it to replace Aristotle's work on logic, called the *Organon*. Bacon rejected deduction as utterly useless. Instead, said Sir Francis, all true knowledge comes through experiment alone. In the *Novum Organum*, Bacon gave a description of the form of experiment called *induction*, which has become the basis of modern scientific research.

But Bacon did not simply call for new ways of doing science; he proposed a different purpose for pursuing knowledge.

For Plato, Aristotle, and the great medievals, the purpose of learning is simply to know, for knowledge was seen as good in itself. Human beings desire to know, said these ancient and medieval thinkers, simply because they are rational creatures. We do not study geometry primarily to use it in building or constructing roads but because the truths of geometry are good to know in themselves. And, finally, for the Christian mind, the joy of heaven is found in seeing God—that is, knowing him as he is.

Bacon, however, did not think one should seek knowledge because knowing is good in itself; rather, he thought man should seek knowledge in order to use it to subjugate and control the world. "Knowledge and human power are synonymous," he wrote in the *Novum Organum*. Elsewhere, he said, *ipsa scientia potestas est*—"knowledge itself is power." As far as Sir Francis was concerned, men are to discover the mysteries of nature in order to control nature. And men control nature, he thought, in order to make human life on earth longer, more productive, and more comfortable.

But if the purpose of knowing is purely practical, what about the knowledge of God? Do we seek to know God only to have a better and happier life in this world? As a member of the Church of England, Bacon did not deny the existence of God or reject the Christian Faith. But he did revive the old notion of the "two truths"—that truths discovered by reason and science might contradict the truths revealed by God, but both remain equally true. The Bible, for instance, might teach that the world was created from nothing—and this may contradict a finding of science that the universe is eternal. For Bacon, this posed no problem. As a scientist, he would say that the universe is eternal while, as a Christian, he would claim that he believed it was created.

## What is Induction?

In induction, the scientist begins with a hypothesis and does experiments to test whether the hypothesis makes sense. For instance, a scientist, like Galileo, may start with the hypothesis that two bodies made of similar material but differing in size fall to the ground at the same rate. To test this, he drops two such bodies from a tower, and if they hit the ground at the same time, the scientist has grounds for thinking his hypothesis is true. But while such an experiment gives support to a hypothesis, it does not prove it, because there might be other circumstances where the same experiment would not produce the same result. The more the hypothesis is tested and is found to fit the facts, the more certain it becomes.

Sometimes some facts will support a hypothesis while others do not. Copernicus' heliocentric hypothesis provided a simpler explanation for the motions of the heavenly bodies and was useful to predict certain facts that were able to be verified by observing the heavens through telescopes. But other observations seemed to contradict the hypothesis. For instance, in the 17th century, some argued that if Copernicus was right, and the earth revolved around the sun, the distant stars should appear to us to alter their positions slightly. Such a movement, called a parallax, could not be seen until long after the 17th century. As long as no one could see a parallax, scientists had a reason to doubt that the Copernican hypothesis was true.

Such ideas (that true knowledge comes only through experiment and that the purpose of science is to make life on earth easier and better) have dominated the minds of European philosophers and scientists from Bacon's time to our own. Though Bacon himself only dabbled in experiments, his philosophy of science was to influence many experimental scientists. It became the basis of **rationalism** and **empiricism**, twin ideas that hold that truth can be found only by human reason through experimental science, and that whatever cannot be known by reason and experiment is unimportant. After Bacon, many came to see experimental science as the only sure foundation on which to erect the temple of human thought.

# The Recluse of Cambridge

In 1642, the year Galileo died, a small, sickly boy child was born on a little farm in Lincoln County, England. So sickly and small was this child that no one thought he would live beyond a few days. Yet, he survived, and from such a humble and precarious beginning, went to become one of the most influential men of thought Europe and the world have ever known.

As a boy, Isaac Newton was not a dependable worker on his mother's farm, nor, when he went to school at age 12, was he a very diligent student. Instead of working or attending to his studies, he read books that caught his interest, did math, or spent time working on mechanical

> **rationalism:** the theory that truth can be known and problems solved only by the use of human reason and by experience. Rationalism denies that inspiration or faith is a path to truth.
> **empricisim:** the theory that truth can only come through experience and experiment

> **recluse:** one who avoids contact with others; a hermit; one who lives like a *recluse* is said to be reclusive
> **alchemy:** a supposed science that sought to change base metals into gold
> **refract:** to turn from the path of a straight line, to "bend"

contrivances, such as water wheels and clocks. Though he must have been frustrating to his mother and his teachers, one of his uncles saw his potential and made sure he finished school. In 1661, this uncle was able to send the 19-year old Isaac to Trinity College, Cambridge University. Newton took his degree there four years later, and in 1669 (at the age of 27) was appointed a Cambridge teacher in mathematics. Newton would remain at Cambridge for the next 35 years, living the life of a **recluse**, dedicated to study and research.

Newton was not a popular teacher. Few students attended his lectures, and sometimes he faced an empty lecture hall. He was something of an oddity, so absent-minded that he walked about in disheveled clothes and skipped meals because he was struck by an idea that drove all thought of food from his mind. Indeed, Newton's mind was full of ideas and questions. He thought about mathematical problems, came up with numerous hypotheses about such matters as the nature of light and how the earth and other planets move around the sun. He spent most of his time in his room or in the laboratory he built at Cambridge, where he carried on experiments, often in **alchemy**—the supposed science that sought to change base metals into gold.

Newton's absent mind came to a number of important discoveries. One was the mathematical discipline called the differential calculus, used in the science of physics. (The German Gottfried Leibnitz also came up with differential calculus at the same time and apart from Newton.) Experimenting with a prism he bought at a fair in 1666, Newton discovered that when sunlight passes through the crystal, it appears as a row of colored bands—red, orange, yellow, green, blue, indigo, and violet. He also noted that each of the colors is **refracted** by the prism at a different angle. These discoveries led him to a theory of the nature of light and how we see color. Published in 1704, in a work called Opticks, these theories later helped astronomers come up with methods by which they could determine a star's chemical composition and its distance from the earth.

## Theory of Gravitation

In 1666, the year he was experimenting with his new prism, Newton fled Cambridge to escape the plague. He retired to his family's farm in Lincoln where, according to some old stories, he discovered his theory of gravitation when he was struck on the head by a falling apple.

Whatever the truth of such stories, by 1666 Newton had probably come a long way in working out what is called his theory of gravitation. From other mathematicians, he had learned the mathematical formula for the gravitational pull of the sun on a planet—that the force of gravitation varies inversely with the square of a planet's distance from the sun. (That is, very roughly, the farther a planet is from the sun, the less pull the sun has on a planet, and the closer it is to the sun, the more pull it has on it.) Newton did not come up with the idea of gravity or gravitational force; astronomers as early as the 15th century were saying the heavens pull on the earth in the way a magnet pulls on a piece of metal. Such ideas were not original with Newton.

What was original with Newton was how he worked out mathematical demonstrations to account for the motion of all bodies in the universe based on three "laws" of motion. Newton set out his gravitational theory in the first book of what became his greatest work, *Philosophiae Naturalis Principia Mathematica* (the Mathematical Principles of Natural Philosophy), presented to a group of scientists, called the Royal Society of London, in 1686.

**mass:** expanse or bulk of a body

In the *Principia*, Newton set out the "laws of motion," which served as the bases of his mathematical descriptions of the paths planets take. For instance, Newton's first "law" of motion states that "every body continues in its state of rest or of moving uniformly in a straight line, unless it is forced to change that state by forces impressed on it." From this law, we understand that a planet moves continuously in a straight line until it encounters the downward, or gravitational force, of the sun. The planet does not fall into the sun, because the planet's motion is strong enough to withstand such a force. But the planet may not continue moving in a straight line, because the sun is pulling the planet towards itself. The result is that the planet takes a curved path around the sun. Newton was able to describe this path mathematically from the two forces—the "gravitational" pull of the sun and "inertia"—the planet's tendency to keep to the state it is in. In this case, the state of motion.

In the *Principia*, Newton showed how all heavenly bodies exert a gravitational influence on each other. Thus, the sun not only pulls on the earth, but the earth pulls on the sun, and all the heavenly bodies pull on each other. Newton was able to demonstrate how his calculations agreed with the discoveries made by astronomers—particularly Kepler. Newton also was able to calculate the **mass** of each planet and he explained the ocean tides by the gravitational pull of the moon and the sun. The *Principia* is an amazing work, accounting for motion with mathematical demonstrations based on three principles or "laws of nature."

## The Search for Laws, and More Laws

Newton's *Principia* did not escape criticism. Some said he had made gravitation such an important force in the universe but had failed to say what exactly gravitation is. As far as it went, this criticism was certainly true—and Newton himself admitted it. *Gravitas*, the Latin word Newton used and which we translate as "gravity," means simply "heaviness." What makes a body move toward another body? Do the bodies pull each other toward each other? Is something or someone pushing them toward each other? And if so, how? Newton did not know. He later wrote that the point of the *Principia* was to describe *how* bodies move, not *why* they move.

Others criticized Newton's work because it seemed to describe the universe as a great machine that operated by fixed and unchangeable laws. It seemed to say that the heavenly bodies moved by themselves and did not need God to keep them in motion as the Christian Faith had always said they did. A machine that moves automatically has no need for an operator. And if the universe always existed (as many in Newton's time were beginning to think) the bodies in it have always been moving and so have no need for a being to start them in motion. They certainly do not need a creator.

Newton denied that his ideas removed the need for God. "This most beautiful system of the sun, planets, and comets," he wrote, "could only proceed from the counsel and dominion of an intelligent and powerful Being." Newton argued that the universe not only needed God to set it in motion and to correct irregularities in the motions of bodies, but to keep the energy in the universe from running down.

Despite Newton's defense of the need for God, many who read his *Principia* both in his lifetime and afterward saw it as presenting a purely mechanical universe that did not need God, at least, to keep it in operation. The idea of God, they thought, was not necessary to explain the workings of the world. The key to understanding the world lay, they thought, in discovering the unchanging and eternal laws by which everything worked.

And, many wondered, if the motions of bodies in the universe ran according to fixed laws, like the parts of an immense machine, might not everything else operate in the same manner? Might it not be that everything—absolutely *everything*, even man—works like a machine, according to fixed laws? Newton's *Principia* inspired philosophers in every discipline to search for laws to explain everything, from the growth of plants to chemical reactions to human morality and religion. In the 18th century, Newton's *Principia*, for countless thinkers, became the model for all sciences.

# Among the Most Honored

Sir Isaac Newton (he was knighted in 1705 by Queen Anne) was a great natural scientist but also a complex and troubled man. He was timid and reclusive. He was also moody, suspicious, and proud. Throughout his life he engaged in bitter controversies with fellow scientists who said that he had taken some of their ideas and claimed them as his own. Though Newton would at times admit he had learned from others, he could also defend himself with bitterness and **invective**.

Newton's interests extended beyond natural science and mathematics. Until at least 1692, he continued his experiments in alchemy, writing a great deal on the subject. At the same time, he was a zealous student of the Bible and by the end of his life had written more on theological topics than on natural science and mathematics together. Though he did not seem to think that the Son of God is equal to the Father, Newton believed that every word of the Bible is literally true. Like most Englishmen of his day, he was quite anti-Catholic, and in a commentary he wrote on the Apocalypse, he identified the antichrist with the pope.

In 1692, Newton suffered a mental breakdown that lasted two years and spelled the end of his days of solitude at Cambridge. In 1695, at the urging of his friends, who thought Newton needed to spend time away from his laboratory, King William III made him warden of the royal mint and, four years later, master of the mint. As master of the mint, Newton undertook a campaign against forgers and counterfeiters, personally attending their trials, torture, and hangings.

Newton's new position gave him an annual salary on which, along with his savings, he ultimately was able to enter and enjoy London society. When he died at the ripe old age of 85, he was perhaps one of the most honored men, not only in Great Britain, but all of Europe. He was buried in London's Westminster Abbey, the burial place

**invective:** insult or abuse

of England's royalty, and his funeral was attended by philosophers, statesmen, and nobles. As if for a king, dukes and earls bore Newton's funeral pall.

# Chapter Review

## Summary
- The period called the Renaissance began in the 14th century and brought with it a new interest in classical culture.
- The Protestant Reformation ended the Renaissance. The end of the Renaissance marked the beginning of the "scientific revolution."
- The scientific method differs from the older method of philosophy. The scientific method is based on *induction*, while the older way of philosophy is based on *deduction*.
- Copernicus' heliocentric theory was the beginning of the scientific revolution. Because many Christians of the time thought the theory contradicted Sacred Scripture, they either rejected the theory or thought it could be used as an hypothesis, not a true account of reality.
- Galileo Galilei is remembered for his contributions to the sciences of physics and astronomy. A promoter of Copernicus' theory, he was tried and found guilty by the Holy Office for writing about the theory as fact.
- Francis Bacon rejected deduction as a way to knowledge. Induction, he said, is the only true foundation of knowledge. Bacon held the purpose of science is to subjugate and control the world.
- Newton's *Principia Mathematica* inspired philosophers in every discipline to search for laws to explain everything, from the growth of plants to chemical reactions to human morality and religion.

## Key Concepts
**Renaissance:** the rebirth of classical culture in the 14th century
**humanism:** the belief that mankind's goal is to attain the good things of this earth
**scientific revolution:** a movement that was concerned exclusively with the natural world as it can be measured and observed by experiment
**Ptolemy's geocentric theory:** the idea that the earth is the center of the universe around which the planets, stars, and sun revolve
**Copernican Revolution:** a rebellion against religion centered on Copernicus' discovery of the heliocentric theory
**deduction:** a method of reasoning where one begins with principles drawn from experience and, by asking questions, draws conclusions from those principles
**induction:** a form of experience in which a scientist begins with a hypothesis and then performs experiments to prove it. This form is the basis of modern scientific research.

## Dates to Remember
**1517:** Martin Luther's revolt against the Church
**1543:** death of Copernicus
**1582:** A new calendar, called the Gregorian calendar, replaces the Julian calendar that had been in use since the days of Julius Caesar.
**1616:** The Holy Office says Copernicus' heliocentric theory is heretical.
**1620:** Francis Bacon writes his *Instauratio Magna* ("Great Restoration") and *Novum Organum*.
**1633:** The Holy Office finds Galileo guilty for publishing a work depicting the Copernican theory as a fact.
**1686:** Newton presents his *Principia Mathematica* to the Royal Society of London.

## Central Characters
**Aristotle:** an ancient Greek philosopher whose philosophy was considered the best way to understand the world in the high Middle Ages
**Nicolaus (Nicholas) Copernicus (1473–1543):** a Polish clergyman who theorized about a heliocentric universe—a universe centered on the sun
**Tycho Brahe (1546–1601):** a Danish nobleman and astronomer whose observations of the stars were of great use to astronomers across Europe. He disagreed with Copernicus' theory.
**Johannes Kepler (1571–1630):** a German astronomer who accepted Copernicus' theory and discovered that the planets moved in elliptical paths around the sun. He believed that the order of the universe reflects the wisdom of God.
**Galileo Galilei (1564–1642):** Born in Florence, Galileo studied mathematics, astronomy, and physics. He is known for inventing the telescope. Galileo promoted Copernicus' Theory; he was tried and found guilty by the Holy Office for presenting the theory as fact.
**Francis Bacon (1561–1626):** statesman, nobleman, and chancellor of England who tried to bring about a "great restoration" of philosophy. He believed that all knowledge comes from experience alone and should be used to subjugate and control the world. His method of scientific inquiry is now known as the scientific method.
**Sir Isaac Newton (1642–1727):** English scientist and author of the *Principia Mathematica*, a work that gives mathematical descriptions of the motion of bodies, based on natural laws

## Questions for Review
1. Did people in the 16th and 17th centuries see any difference between science and philosophy? Why or why not?
2. What is meant by scientific method?
3. What led to the split between science and faith? How could this have been prevented?
4. What was the Gregorian calendar? Is it still being used today?
5. If Isaac Newton believed in God, why did his *Principia Mathematica* lead others to reject the idea of God?

## Ideas in Action

1. Using the *Catechism of the Catholic Church*, research what the Catholic Church teaches about human nature. Does the idea that human beings are rational animals contradict the Church's teaching that they are made in the "image and likeness of God"? Why or why not?
2. Discuss the difference between a hypothesis and a theory. Find examples of each.

# Highways and Byways

## Robert Hooke and England's Royal Society

The oldest scientific organization still in existence may be the Royal Society of London for the Improvement of Natural Knowledge. The society is called "royal" because in 1662, King Charles II granted it a charter. The Royal Society, however, originated some 17 years earlier when a group of students at Oxford University met clandestinely to talk about "natural philosophy" and the ideas of Francis Bacon. These meetings were hidden, for at the time the Puritan Oliver Cromwell ruled England. His Protectorate government forbade the study of natural philosophy. When Charles II became king in 1661, scholars could again discuss scientific subjects freely and in the open.

The Royal Society was a gathering of gentlemen scholars to talk about natural science, show experiments, and share discoveries. One member was not, however, a wealthy gentleman. This was Robert Hooke, who had been a "poor scholar" (that is, a servant) for one of the original members of the Oxford group, Robert Boyle. Hooker had supplied the inspiration for Boyle's scientific research and contributions. The gentlemen of the Royal Society recognized Hooke's brilliance and created a paid position, "curator of experiments," so that he could be a member of the society.

Hooke was extraordinarily creative and a very talented artist. In addition to his remarkable skill in drawing, Hooke knew several languages and was an accomplished mathematician; he also knew music and could sing beautifully. In natural philosophy, Hooke was unsurpassed in inventiveness and brilliance. In his earlier years, he did not hesitate to share his ideas with others, and it may have been Hooke who suggested the formula for gravity to Isaac Newton. At least Hooke claimed this was the case, and his statement led to a bitter controversy with the more powerful and wealthy Newton.

Hooke became melancholy and isolated after his bitter fight with Newton, but he continued his work as if it was a religious discipline. In many ways, it was faith in science that sustained him. A devout Christian and son of a Protestant pastor, Hooke saw no contradiction between faith and science. He did not think that God could be absent from His "Grand Design" of the created world. Since man was created in God's image, said Hooke, man's intelligence should be able to grasp the "Grand Unifying Principle" of the universe. Hooke pursued this worthy goal all of his life.

Although scant recognition and credit has been given to Robert Hooke, he was one of the most outstanding scientists of all time. He was the very "soul" of the Royal Society, where he was too poor to be a regular gentleman member.

# Two Revolutions: Industrial and Agricultural

It was not just ideas that were bringing change to Europe in the 17th and 18th centuries. Other forces were at work. In particular, European exploration and colonization of the New World and Asia brought new sources of wealth to some in Europe and changed relationships of power between the wealthy and those with fewer resources. Those who possessed wealth could use it to take advantage of new scientific discoveries and inventions that led to what history calls the Industrial Revolution. This revolution, centered at first in Great Britain, was destined to have far reaching effects, not only in Europe, but eventually over the entire world.

## The Rise of Capitalism

Following the end of what is called the Seven Years War in 1763, Great Britain became the most powerful nation in Europe. In this war, it had won from France all of Canada and France's possessions in India. The war, too, had left Great Britain the mistress of the seas. No European power could vie with the British navy. Great Britain had colonies in the Americas and in Asia, from which ever greater amounts of wealth flowed into the island kingdom.

Trade with these colonies, along with the involvement of British seamen in the African slave trade, the plunder of British privateers (pirates), and the mining and importing of gold and silver, enriched Great Britain (especially England) in the 18th century. Men of modest means won so much wealth in the colonies that they were very wealthy when they returned to Britain. Some were even made peers, as members of the aristocracy were called. Money lending increased, as did the number of banks. London, Bristol, and Liverpool in England as well as Glasgow in Scotland grew into important ports for the Atlantic trade.

All this new wealth was not spent on the building of palatial mansions or in increasing the luxuries of the rich. Unlike the aristocracy in other lands, who had lived solely off the wealth of their country estates, the British nobility invested their wealth in commerce and trade, by which they increased their already great fortunes. Members of the middle class did the same; and, having become wealthy, they began marrying into aristocratic families. The merchant aristocracy and middle class came to wield great power in Parliament—a power they used to further their own interests.

All this commercial activity represented an economic system called **capitalism**. What is capitalism? It is the large-scale organization of business, where those who possess a store of wealth or capital (which includes money, raw materials, tools, land, factories, etc.) hire laborers to engage in activities that increase wealth. In mining, for instance, the capitalist is the man who has the money to buy the mine, purchase tools, and hire workers. In capitalism, a few own and control wealth-producing enterprises, while the vast majority of the people engaged in those enterprises (the workingmen) control only their labor, which they sell to the capitalists for a wage.

> **capitalism**: the large-scale organization of business, where those who possess a store of wealth or *capital* (which includes money, raw materials, tools, land, factories, etc.) hire laborers to engage in activities that increase wealth.

Capitalism had not been the chief economic system of Europe, at least until the 17th century. More typical were the medieval guilds, which organized workers in a single trade (stonemasons, cobblers, weavers, musicians, etc.) and allowed more than just a very few men to own wealth-producing enterprises (businesses). Guilds provided for the spiritual and material needs of members as well. Guilds still existed in the 18th century, but in many cases had themselves become capitalistic by restricting the number of those (called masters) who could actually attain ownership of wealth-producing enterprises.

Revolutionary France abolished guilds. In Great Britain, the guilds were dying out. Without enough capital to obtain raw materials from the colonies, guild masters could not compete with "projectors"—men possessing the capital not only to purchase raw materials but to fund business enterprises. Projectors, too, had this advantage over guild masters—they were not controlled by guild regulations that discouraged competition between guild members. Nor did projectors have to share new inventions with others, as did individual guild members, who were supposed to offer their inventions for the common use of the guild. Such regulations had originally existed to prohibit one guild member from driving other guild members out of business as well as to make sure that high-quality goods were being produced; but because projectors were not bound by such regulations, it was harder for guild masters to compete with them.

## The Industrial Revolution

Among the advantages projectors and capitalists had was their ability to invest in the new inventions that were transforming manufacturing in England and Scotland in the 18th century. More than any other European nation, England excelled in the invention of machinery that could save labor and greatly increase industrial production. Scientists of London's Royal Society, who had always had a more practical bent than scientists on the European continent, had made discoveries about the uses

> **textile:** cloth; especially, a woven or knit cloth

of steam and the properties of gases that would prove to have very practical uses. This, and the discovery in the mid 18th century of less expensive ways of smelting iron, set the stage for what has been called the Industrial Revolution.

An important impetus for the development of new machinery was the great demand for **textiles** in mid-18th-century Europe. The traditional ways of manufacturing cotton and wool cloth on looms, in small, often family-owned shops with a few employees, were not meeting the demand for cotton fabric. To meet this demand, inventors looked for ways to increase production of cloth while reducing the number of weavers employed in its production.

As early as 1733, mechanical weaving devices began to be invented in England. In 1765, James Hargreaves of Blackburn, in Lancashire, had found a way to spin eight threads at one time. Hargreaves continued to develop this Spinning Jenny (as it was called) by adding more power and spindles until he was able to spin 80 threads at once. In 1769, Richard Arkwright developed a machine using rollers for producing yarn from cotton fibers. In 1774, by combining the Spinning Jenny and Arkwright's water frame, Samuel Crompton greatly increased textile production.

Production of textiles took another giant leap forward in 1765 with James Watt's development of the first true steam engine. Before this invention, looms were powered by water and so were placed by streams. Textile factories thus spread over the English countryside. With the invention of the steam engine, however, factories were freed from waterpower and could be placed in more centralized locations. Cities such as Birmingham, Manchester, and Leeds became centers for manufacturing, filled with factories belching smoke from the coal burned to supply power for the steam engines.

Because of the revolution in industry, large factories came to replace traditional, small manufacturing shops throughout England, Scotland, and Wales. Unlike small shops, factories required a great deal of capital to build; and to obtain this capital, industrialists looked to men of means—the capitalists. As the costs of production increased, factory owners had to rely on loans from banks, which thus grew in importance and influence in British society.

## The Industrial Workers

The huge factories, of course, required a large number of workers to man the machines. These workers were drawn from the older industries put out of business by the new machinery or from the rural districts.

The new factories were very different from the older, smaller shops. The old shops were intimate and allowed the owner and his employees to be friends. Hard masters there were, but many others treated their workers with kindness, as if they were members of the family. The new factories, however, were very impersonal. Workers labored typically 14 hours a day, 6 days a week—for very low wages. Packed into poorly built factory buildings, workers succumbed to disease or were injured in accidents with the machines. A laborer who was no longer able to work was fired; his employer did not need to keep him on, for many unemployed men could take his place. Women and children, too, worked in the factories and received even lower wages than the men. Many of the children were orphans or from poor families farmed out to the factories by parish organizations that had, by law, to care for the unfortunate. In 1788, England's textile mills employed 59,000 women and 48,000 children.

The capitalist class found justifications for their treatment of the workers. "Everyone but an idiot," said an English aristocrat, Arthur Young, "knows that the lower classes must be kept poor, or they will never be industrious." Enlightenment thinkers, however, had provided another justification. *Laissez-faire!* ("Let them do as they will!") was the motto of the French economist François Quesnay (1694–1774), who thought that economic activity should be allowed to follow the natural laws that govern it. Nothing, neither government nor guilds, should dare to restrict wealth making, according to Quesnay. His ideas were further developed by the Scotsman Adam Smith in his 1776 work, *Wealth of Nations*. In that work, Smith said that governments should not try to control economic activity by regulating wages or prices or by any restriction whatsoever. Each person should be allowed to follow his own personal interest in the creation of wealth for himself. Indeed, said Smith, each person *should* consider only his personal interest, for only in that way will the economic life of society be "led by an invisible hand" to wealth and prosperity.

> **tenement:** a house used as a dwelling; an apartment or flat
>
> **pauperism:** the state of being a pauper, or poor
>
> **strike:** a refusal by workers to work, in an effort to bring employers around to give into their demands

The invisible hand, however, did not hold out prosperity for the new class of industrial workers. Housed in dismal **tenements** in slums that began spreading out from the factory towns of England, Scotland, and Wales, the workers and their families suffered from hunger, cold, and disease. The threat of losing their jobs was always present, for an employer could fire his workers at will. Or, if the factory produced more goods than there were buyers for the goods, the employer would lay off his workers. Throughout England, **pauperism** spread. In 1742, the amount of money spent on relief for the poor was 600,000 pounds; in 1784, it had risen to 2 million pounds.

The poor in England, however, did not submit to the new state of things without some resistance. The older craftsmen, seeing the threat the factories posed to their jobs, took out their anger on the new machines. In 1779, factory workers in Lancashire County formed a mob that as it went swelled from 500 to 8,000 members. These workers wrecked one factory and smashed the equipment at another until troops from Liverpool put them to flight. Those who were caught were hanged. Other workers began organizing themselves to fight for better wages. The groups they formed staged **strikes** that involved violence from both the employers and the workers. In these struggles, Parliament in the end came down on the side of the employers. In 1799, the House of Commons passed a law making it illegal for any association of workers to push for higher wages or change the quality of work. Those who formed such associations would be imprisoned.

# Revolution in Agriculture

It is, of course, not surprising that Parliament came down on the side of employers in the matter of workers' organizations: Parliament was controlled by those who benefited from paying

> **arable:** able to be plowed and planted with crops
>
> **yeoman:** a small farmer who cultivates his own land; a freeholder
>
> **cereal crops:** crops such as wheat, rye, barley, and corn
>
> **crop rotation:** the practice of growing different crops in succession on the same piece of land in order to preserve and enhance soil fertility
>
> **subsistence farming:** a kind of farming that provides all or most of what is needed by a farm family, and where much of the crop is not put up for sale on the market

workers low wages. Another area where parliamentary laws benefited the rich at the expense of the poor was in the matter of the rural commons and open fields.

The commons was wasteland or pasture adjoining farmland. It was called commons because, since the Middle Ages, peasant farmers had a common right to use such land as pasture for their cattle, pigs, geese, and beasts of burden. The open field was **arable** land held in common by a farming village. Each farmer received strips of the common land for cultivation. The strips belonging to any one farmer were as a rule scattered and separated from each other by the strips belonging to other farmers. Some farmers held more of these strips than others. Farmers called yeomen had actual ownership of the strips, while others paid rent for cottages and the right to use arable land. Such land divisions had for centuries characterized all of European farming, but two developments in the 18th century seemed to demand an end to this method of dividing property and rights.

The first of these developments was what has been called the agricultural revolution. In England, aristocratic gentleman farmers had developed methods of farming that were more "scientific" than those practiced by the peasant or **yeoman** farmers. These methods included a wider and better use of fertilizers, the planting of crops (such as grasses, clover, or turnips) that helped replenish nutrients in the soil, methods of planting **cereal crops** in rows to make weeding easier, the development of **crop rotation** techniques, better methods of breeding cattle, and the invention of new machines that made farm labor more efficient. Such methods dramatically increased crop yields which, at the time, added to profits made from farming.

And profits there were to be made. The population of the British Isles had doubled in the 18th century, and all these people (especially the growing number of workmen in the cities) needed food. Wars in Europe had cut off shipments of agricultural produce to England from France, increasing the need for English farms to produce food for the market. The open-field method of farming, it seemed, could not produce the food needed to feed both the growing population and the armies Great Britain was outfitting for war on the continent.

Traditional agriculture had been for **subsistence**; that is, farmers worked to feed their families first and sold only what they did not need. But now the desire was for farms that produced primarily for distant markets. Besides, it was harder—seemingly impossible—to use the new farming techniques and farm machinery on the traditional strip divisions. The gentleman farmers thought commons and wasteland could be converted into cropland; and, instead of being divided into strips, farmland could be sectioned into fenced-off, compact holdings. Such holdings could be used for growing crops or as grassland to pasture cattle.

## The Enclosures

To convert strip fields into compact holdings, landholders resorted to the practice of enclosure. Enclosure had two parts. The first was abolishing the village's common. The second was redividing the common and the village's arable fields into compact farmsteads. Those who had a claim to strips in the common field would now receive an equivalent amount of land as a compact farm, which they would then be required to fence off, or *enclose*.

Enclosures were not new in English history; they had occurred in the 16th and 17th centuries. The new thing about enclosures in the 18th century, however, was that they were being ordered by Parliament. In the course of the 18th century, Parliament ordered thousands of enclosures that affected over 5 million acres of land.

Lands were enclosed in this way. After at least three-fourths of village landowners agreed to an enclosure of their lands, they filed a petition with Parliament and then posted a notice announcing the enclosure on the door of the village church. Parliament then considered the petition and, if it was accepted, appointed commissioners to supervise the enclosure. The commissioners considered the legal claims of individual landowners and then divided the land based on those claims.

This process seemed fair and just; it was, however, subject to abuses. The larger and richest landowners could use the process to their own advantage. They worked up the petition and the plan for enclosure and obtained signatures in secret. Since the costs of the whole process were very high, those who opposed the enclosure plan were unable to put forward a plan of their own. They could not afford to hire lawyers to oppose the plan in Parliament; further, the parliamentary committee considering enclosures was made up of large landowners who rarely considered petitions filed against a plan drawn up by other large landowners.

The actual enclosure of the land benefited only those who could prove they had owned legal village farmlands. Those who had been non-owning tenants of farmland, but who had customary rights to the use of land, did not receive farmsteads. And with the abolishing of the commons, they had no place to graze whatever pigs, cows, geese, or poultry they owned. Such tenants were forced henceforth to work for wages, which were often too low to keep them sufficiently fed or clothed. If the newly divided farmland was used for cattle (which required less labor), these former farmers were forced to leave their native districts for other areas or go to the cities, where they were reduced to an even crueler poverty.

Of those farmers who received farmsteads, many now ended up with holdings so small that they could not produce enough wealth to pay the costs of fencing in their lands. Without the common on which to graze their livestock or gather fuel, they relied more and more on purchasing their food and cooking it—not in their own homes, but at the baker's shop. Such farmers too were in the end forced to sell their lands and either labor for other men or go to the cities.

Though it did not happen immediately, the enclosure movement ended in drastically reducing the number of people who lived in the countryside of England and Wales. In many places, whole villages were abandoned and long-standing communities were destroyed. The class of stout, freedom-loving yeomen who had for centuries been the backbone of English culture began to disappear.

> **poor rates:** taxes raised to support the poor
> **workhouse:** a house set up to care for the poor at public expense

The enclosure movement, too, had sad effects on public morality. Village commons had given poorer tenant farmers an opportunity to better their condition. By raising geese or poultry on the common, they could feed themselves as well as earn money to buy a cow and, eventually, even a small plot of land. After enclosure, this was impossible. Even if they could save money from their paltry wages, they could not hope to buy land, for the farm holdings were too large and thus too expensive for them to buy. They could not make money by handicrafts, for the factories in the cities now produced what formerly rural craftsmen had made. The incentives for saving were gone; instead of working for extra pay, or tending his flock of poultry, or gathering fuel for his family's hearth, the common laborer often grew slothful and took to drink.

Even such a defender of agricultural improvements and enclosures as the writer Arthur Young could see the sad effects enclosures had on the morality of the rural poor. He wrote:

> Go to an ale-house kitchen of an old enclosed country, and there you will see the origin of poverty and the **poor rates**. For whom are they to be sober? For whom are they to save? (such are their questions.) For the parish? If I am diligent, shall I have to build a cottage? If I am sober, shall I have land for a cow? If I am frugal, shall I have half an acre of potatoes? You offer no motives; you have nothing but a parish officer and a **workhouse**. Bring me another pot [of ale].

# Chapter Review

## Summary

- Trade with the Great Britain's overseas colonies allowed middle-class people in Great Britain to become very rich. The aristocracy invested their wealth and became even wealthier. The merchant aristocracy and middle class came to wield great power in Parliament—a power they used to further their own interests.
- The increased commercial activity in Great Britain developed into capitalism, the large-scale organization of business, where those who possess a store of wealth or capital hire laborers to engage in activities that increase wealth. In capitalism, a few own and control wealth-producing enterprises, while the vast majority of the people engaged in those enterprises (the workingmen) control only their labor, which they sell to the capitalists for a wage.
- Capitalists invested in new machinery and developed large industries, against which smaller manufacturers and the manufacturing guilds could not compete. The development of capitalism thus led to the destruction of the guild system in Great Britain.
- Capitalism led to what is called the Industrial Revolution. Though this revolution brought about an amazing growth in the manufacture of goods, it brought misery and poverty to many laborers. Capitalists justified their treatment of workers by the Liberal economic doctrine called *laissez-faire*. Workers reacted with strikes and violence. Parliament sided with employers against the workers.

- Large landowners in Great Britain, wanting to consolidate lands to make it easier to practice "scientific" agriculture, pushed for the enclosure of agricultural lands. Parliament mandated enclosures, which led to a drastic reduction in the rural population of England and Wales and devastated rural communities.

## Key Concepts
**Industrial Revolution:** a rapid change in 18th-century England that arose because of the introduction of steam-driven machinery and greater efficiency in the textile industry. It is called a "revolution" because the economy of British society and its social structure were changed radically by the introduction of power-driven machinery.
**crop rotation:** the practice of growing different crops in succession on the same piece of land in order to preserve and enhance soil fertility
**enclosure:** division of common grazing land or wasteland into small farms, which then had to be enclosed or fenced. In the 18th century, Great Britain's Parliament ordered over 5 million acres enclosed. Enclosure was subject to much abuse by those who were wealthiest, and it drove many poor tenant farmers into deeper poverty.
**workhouse:** a house set up to care for the poor at public expense

## Dates to Remember
**1765**: James Hargreaves invents the Spinning Jenny.
James Watts develops the first true steam engine.
**1776**: Adam Smith publishes the *Wealth of Nations*.
**1779**: Workers rise in Lancashire County, England.
**1799**: The British parliament declares workers' associations illegal.

## Central Characters
**James Hargreaves (d. 1778):** inventor of the Spinning Jenny
**Richard Arkwright (1732–1792):** inventor of the water frame
**Samuel Crompton (1753–1827):** an inventor whose combination of the Spinning Jenny and Arkwright's water frame led to a increase in textile production
**François Quesnay (1694–1774):** a French economist who promoted the economic principle of *laissez-faire*—"Let them do as they will." Quesnay believed that economic activity should be allowed to follow the natural laws that govern it and that neither government nor guilds should dare to restrict wealth making. Quesnay influenced Adam Smith.
**Adam Smith (1723–1790):** author of the *Wealth of Nations*, in which he argued that governments should not try to control economic activity by regulating wages or prices or by any restriction whatever

## Questions for Review
1. Why did the Industrial Revolution cause such social upheaval in England?
2. What is capitalism? How does capitalism differ from the guild system?

3. How did the increase of aristocratic and middle class wealth in England bring about the rise of capitalism?
4. What does *laissez-faire* refer to?
5. What are strikes? Why did workers in Great Britain strike? Were their strikes successful?
6. What is meant by the agricultural revolution?
7. What were enclosures? What were the effects of the enclosures on farmers in Great Britain?

## Ideas in Action
1. Research the workhouses of England and discuss the pros and cons of such public housing for the poor.
2. List the good effects of work. Explain what keeps people from getting work.
3. Have students bring in poems or songs written in the 18th century about the conditions of the Industrial Revolution and the desire for a pristine natural world. Read the poems aloud and discuss them.

# Highways and Byways

## The Deserted Village
In 1770, in his long poem, "The Deserted Village," the poet Oliver Goldsmith described the effects of the enclosures on rural villages. The village he describes, Auburn, is imaginary; but as Goldsmith said in a letter of dedication, all that he wrote about Auburn was based on villages he had seen "in my country excursions, for these four or five years past." In his poem, Goldsmith attacks the greed for land, the love of wealth and luxury that he says impelled the rich and powerful to seek and seize the lands of the poor. He praises the life of the rural peasant, his innocence and simple joys. The following lines from the poem are among the most famous.

*Ill fares the land, to hastening ills a prey,*
*Where wealth accumulates and men decay;*
*Princes and lords may flourish or may fade;*
*A breath can make them as a breath has made;*
*But a bold peasantry, their country's pride,*
*When once destroyed, can never be supplied*

*A time there was, ere England's griefs began,*
*When every rood of ground maintained its man;*
*For him light labor spread her wholesome store,*
*Just gave what life required, but gave no more;*
*His best companions, innocence and health;*
*And his best riches, ignorance of wealth.*

*But times are altered; trade's unfeeling train*
*Usurp the land, and dispossess the swain;*
*Along the lawn, where scattered hamlets rose,*
*Unwieldy wealth and cumbrous pomp repose;*
*And every want to opulence allied,*
*And every pang that folly pays to pride.*

# The Age of Enlightenment

When the terrible Thirty Years War had only just begun, a young man took up a private struggle, a fearful struggle, of his own. This young man, named René Descartes, had joined the army of Duke Maximilian of Bavaria. The duke was fighting on the side of the German emperor, Ferdinand I, against Protestant forces in Bohemia. A devout Catholic, Descartes was filled with doubt, but not about his faith. Instead, he wondered how he could know the truth about the world, whether what he sensed and experienced was really true or not. He even wondered how, apart from faith, anyone could know if God exists.

## The Troubled Philosopher

Descartes was born in 1596 at La Haye, in the region of Touraine in southern France. As a boy, he studied at the Jesuit school of Henri-Le-Grand at La Flèche. During his eight years at the school, Descartes studied Latin and Greek, mathematics, and other classical studies. But the subject he loved most was mathematics.

Though he was a sickly youth, Descartes's physical weakness did not hinder him from continuing his studies. In 1613, at the age of 17, Descartes entered the University of Poitiers, where he earned his law degree three years later. But Descartes did not want to be a lawyer; instead, he longed for military glory and so became a soldier.

While serving as a soldier in Bavaria, Descartes continued to study mathematics and another subject he deeply loved, philosophy. But philosophy introduced him to some troubling questions. How can man come to the truth, he asked himself? How can man know he has come to the truth? These questions deeply troubled Descartes. Only by answering them could he hope to find peace.

Burning for answers to his questions, Descartes shut himself up in what he called a "stove" (probably a small, well-heated room) and prayed for "light." Throughout his life, he had found joy in the study of mathematics, for mathematics offered certain truth. And it was in contemplating how mathematicians

> **Jubilee:** a holy year proclaimed by the pope, usually every 25 years, in which pilgrims to Rome receive special graces

come to their conclusions that, on November 10, 1619, Descartes said he found "light." Mathematicians, he knew, begin with very simple, clearly understood concepts and, by deduction, arrive at certain conclusions. In a flash of inspiration, Descartes thought he discovered that if a philosopher followed the mathematical method in any subject, he could find certain truth. In thanksgiving for this discovery, Descartes vowed to make a pilgrimage to the Holy House shrine of Our Lady at Loreto in Italy—a vow he fulfilled in 1624.

## Descartes's Method

After visiting Loreto, Descartes remained in Italy for the **Jubilee** of 1625 and then returned to France. Upon settling in Paris, he found that city life distracted him from thinking; and so, in 1628, he moved to Holland. There, in solitude, he hoped he could continue to develop his philosophical ideas and pursue studies in mathematics and natural science. While in Holland, Descartes wrote his *Discourse on Method*—a book he finished in 1629 but did not publish for another eight years.

In the *Discourse*, Descartes described how, beginning in the darkness of doubt, he had come to the light of truth. The truths we think we know, he wrote, are nothing but "prejudices" we learn as children. Only when we realize this, he said, can we understand that we must doubt anything and everything we think we know. "All things must be doubted," declared Descartes.

But how do we finally escape doubt? We escape doubt, said Descartes, by realizing that only a thinking being can have doubt, for doubt is a thought. Moreover, if I am a thinking being, Descartes continued, I must also exist; for, how could I think if I did not exist? This was the "light" Descartes was seeking—*cogito ergo sum*—"I think, therefore I am." He had proven his own existence. Everything was not an illusion!

Once he discovered that he existed, Descartes came to other conclusions. One of his thoughts, he noted, was of a perfectly good being, of God—and where does such an idea come from? Descartes knew that such a thought could not come from himself, for he was not perfectly good. But from what, then? Descartes concluded that the idea of God could come only from God himself and, therefore, God must exist. And if God exists and is perfectly good, he cannot lie. Therefore, said Descartes, everything I feel, hear, taste, and see must also exist. From understanding that he himself existed, and that God exists, Descartes concluded that the world outside himself also exists.

Using his method, Descartes decided that the human soul is very different from the rest of the world. Only the human soul is free, said Descartes; only human beings have free will, because the human mind and will are not material. The material world, however, and the human body itself, are not free but operate according to fixed and eternal laws that cannot be broken or changed. The material world, said Descartes, is like a vast machine, set in motion by God. But once God set the world in motion, it continued like a machine without any help from God. Descartes said that God gave the universe its first push, but then left it to run on its own and all by itself.

Descartes thought his method would be helpful to the Catholic Faith by proving the existence of God. But his philosophy actually helped bring about a revolution in European thought. By describing the universe as a machine that operated without God's help, Descartes undermined the Catholic belief in Divine Providence—that God not only created the world but continually keeps it in existence and cares for human beings and all creation. Descartes's **mechanistic** view of the universe, too, did not offer any place for miracles. So it was that most Catholics came to reject Descartes's philosophy. In 1663 (13 years after Descartes's death), the Holy Office placed his works on the **Index of Forbidden Books**.

But the Church's condemnation of Descartes's works did not stop the spread of his ideas. They would continue to influence many in France and all Europe. Though Descartes did not wish it, his philosophy opened the way for *rationalism* and *skepticism*, two doctrines that would undermine the influence of the Catholic Faith and give rise to our modern world.

> **mechanistic:** working like a machine
>
> **Index of Forbidden Books:** the list of those books the Church considered dangerous to the Catholic Faith and forbade Catholics to read
>
> **skeptic:** one who advocates *skepticism*, the doubt that anything can be known for certain to be true
>
> **libertine:** a freethinker, or one who acts without regard to a moral law

## Skeptics and Libertines

Descartes had not been the first one in his time to doubt if he knew anything—though, maybe, he was the only one who went so far as to doubt even his own existence. Indeed, Descartes expressed what other philosophers of his age were thinking. These philosophers, called **skeptics**, thought no one, no matter how hard he tried, could come to a certain knowledge of truth. One must doubt everything that people think to be true, said the skeptics, because no one can be certain that what he thinks is true.

Before coming up with his method, Descartes had been a skeptic; he thought his method had saved him from remaining a skeptic. Descartes's method, however, could not overcome skepticism, for not everyone found the method convincing. In fact, by encouraging people to begin their thinking by doubting everything, Descartes was encouraging skepticism.

It would be wrong, however, to blame skepticism on Descartes alone. Europe had long been prepared for it. Indeed, the roots of skepticism go far back into the 14th century, when the Church began to lose the respect of the peoples of Christendom. The Renaissance further weakened devotion to the Church, and then came the Reformation. The Protestant doctrine of private interpretation of Sacred Scripture produced several different versions of the "true religion." All Europeans no longer acknowledged one church as the source of the truths of the Faith, and this led some to wonder if anyone could come to certain knowledge of religious truth. It was not long before people began to think there was no religious truth at all.

The new interest in experimental science in the 17th century also encouraged a skeptical spirit. It was not that experimental science itself made men skeptics—not at all. Rather, it was because the new scientists began their studies by doubting anything that had not been proven by experiment. Other men besides natural scientists themselves not only began doubting, but never stopped doubting. Nothing can be known for certain, said these thinkers; and because nothing can be known for certain, everyone should be allowed to think or even say openly what he thinks without fear of being silenced or punished by church or state. Because these skeptical thinkers thus called for freedom of thought and expression, they became known as **libertines** and, later, "freethinkers." Some libertines called for freedom of thought as well as freedom from the moral law. Thus, the 17th century saw the rise not only of intellectual, but moral libertines—people who thought they could ignore what the churches and social custom said was the proper way to behave.

In the 16th century, libertines and skeptics made up only a very small part of the population of Europe. They were found only in the upper classes and among intellectuals and writers. The vast majority of Europe's population continued to follow the teachings of their religion and to acknowledge the moral law, even if they did not always obey it. But though this would remain the case throughout the 17th century and into the 18th century, the number of skeptics and libertines continued to grow and threaten the civilization of Christendom.

# A New "Religion"

As we have said already, Descartes himself saw his method of philosophy as a help to the Christian faith. Others agreed with him, and even faithful Catholics began to adopt Descartes's method. Others thinkers, however, thought Descartes's philosophy made it easy to reject the Christian God. Since Descartes's ideas had made God unnecessary for the day-to-day running of the universe, some people thought they did not have to pay attention to God. If God did not change things in the universe, praying to him is useless, they said. So it was that many followers of Descartes just ignored God, or they came up with ideas of God that differed radically from the Christian teaching about God.

It was in England that a new idea of God took strong hold. Tired of the doctrinal fights between Protestants and Catholics, and between the different Protestant sects, some English intellectuals began to look for a new religion to replace the Christian Faith. The new religion would admit only the existence of God, but not of a God who intervened by his providence in the affairs of the world. The God of the new religion would be the God of Newton's science and Descartes's philosophy—the God who set the machine of the universe in motion and left it alone to continue moving by the laws of nature.

This religion, known as *Deism*, was the religious side of rationalism. Because rationalists thought reason is the only judge of what is true, they said reason must judge religion as well as science. So it was that Deists, while accepting Jesus Christ as a great ethical teacher, did not acknowledge him to be God. Deists thought beliefs such as the Incarnation or the Trinity were irrational. Nor did they accept the resurrection and virgin birth of Jesus, or the possibility of miracles. Such things could never occur, said the Deists, in a world that operates according to unchanging laws.

Those who accepted Deism were not necessarily moral libertines. They did not reject the moral law but held that it had to be rational. Human beings, said the Deists, do not learn how they ought to behave by receiving any divine revelation, but by using their reason to come to a better understanding of the laws of nature. For Deists, in fact, the moral law was the only truly important aspect of religion. Deists did not want formal worship services or a church structure, for they thought such things were irrational. True religion, said the Deists, required men to worship God by living a moral life.

Some Deistic thinkers did not reject the Christian Faith outright; they thought it was a useful tool for controlling the common people. Only educated freethinkers should be allowed to be Deists, they said; everyone else needs to be controlled by means of established churches.

The God most Deists accepted was a spiritual being utterly separate from the universe he created—and that, after its creation, he abandoned. This God was like a watchmaker who, having made a watch and wound it, left it alone to operate by itself. Other rationalist thinkers, however, came to different conclusions about God. One of these thinkers was Baruch (Benedict) Spinoza, who was born in 1632 to a Jewish family in Amsterdam, Holland. As a youth he discovered the new rationalist and scientific philosophy, which led him to reject many of the teachings of Judaism. In 1656, the leaders of his synagogue in Amsterdam excommunicated Spinoza for "abominable heresies that he practices and teaches."

**Huguenot:** a French Protestant who accepted Calvinist beliefs

Cut off from his people and his past, Spinoza made his living from grinding and polishing lenses. His main occupation, however, was philosophy. In 1670, he began to publish his "abominable heresies" in a work called the *Theological-Political Treatise*. In this work he argued that, because religion is a purely private affair, the state should tolerate the beliefs and practices of all religions. This was a radical idea in a time when governments protected religion and punished heresy. Even the Dutch, though they offered freedom of religion, were still deeply Calvinist and so were shocked by Spinoza's claim. More shocking still, though, was Spinoza's claim that one had to accept only the Bible's moral teachings; everything else in the Bible could be rejected as false. Even worse was Spinoza's opinion that religion had nothing to do with truth, and anyone looking for truth should turn instead to philosophy.

But Spinoza's most radical ideas were to be found in his *Ethics Demonstrated In The Manner of Geometry*, which was published after his death in 1677. In this work, Spinoza, like Descartes, said the material universe works like a machine, according to unalterable laws. Unlike Descartes, however, Spinoza said the mind is material and so is not free. Mind and matter in the universe, said Spinoza, are really one thing, and that is God. The universe is God, and the natural laws by which the universe runs are the will of God.

Such rationalist and Deistic ideas could powerfully shake and finally destroy the faith of religious souls. An example of this is Pierre Bayle, who was born in 1647 at the foot of the Pyrenees Mountains in southern France. Though a **Huguenot** minister, Pierre's father sent him to a Jesuit college at Toulouse. Pierre's father probably regretted this, for, impressed by his teachers, Pierre decided to enter the Catholic Church. He even tried to convert his father and brothers to the Catholic Faith; but Pierre was so unsuccessful in converting his family that he himself converted back to Huguenotism. Fearing that the French government would punish Pierre for abandoning the Catholic Faith, his father sent him to Calvinist Geneva (in western Switzerland), where he was certain Pierre's faith could not again be shaken.

If the Geneva Calvinists kept Pierre Bayle safe from Catholicism, they could not shield him from doubts about religion. For, at Geneva, Bayle discovered the works of Descartes and began to doubt not only Calvinism, but the Christian Faith itself.

Having completed his studies, Bayle served as a tutor and then as a professor at a Calvinist seminary in France. When France's king, Louis XIV, closed the seminary in 1681, Bayle sought refuge at Rotterdam in Holland. There he became a professor of history and philosophy.

The years 1661 to 1665 were a particularly bitter time for the French Huguenots. Since 1598, when France's King Henri IV issued the Edict of Nantes guaranteeing them religious liberty, the Huguenots

**revoke:** to annul, to take back, to rescind

had prospered in France. But France, united under one king and one law, needed also to be united under one religion—or so thought King Louis XIV. To bring about religious unity in his kingdom, Louis in 1661 began repressing Protestantism there. Over the next four years, Huguenots suffered bitterly, and thousands fled France to other lands, especially England and Holland. Finally, on October 17, 1685, King Louis XIV **revoked** the Edict of Nantes. From then on, any Huguenot who refused to stop practicing his faith in public could be imprisoned. Huguenots who became Catholic but then returned to Calvinism could be put to death. Bayle's family underwent harsh sufferings during this period. On account of the persecutions, Bayle lost his mother and father, and his brother died in 1685 from the cruel treatments inflicted on him in a French prison.

In response to the persecution of the Huguenots, Bayle in 1686 published a work in which he called for religious tolerance, even for Jews, Muslims, and Catholics, and condemned all religious persecution. Because Bayle argued that no religion really expresses any truth, some accused him of being an atheist.

Whether he was an atheist or not, Bayle was certainly a religious skeptic. This skepticism inspired him to write his most important work, *The Historical and Critical Dictionary*, which he began publishing in Rotterdam in 1696. The *Dictionary* was not a dictionary as we understand it—a catalogue of words and their meanings. It was more like an encyclopedia, offering a collection of articles on history and historical and biblical figures, theology, ethics, geography, mythology, literature, and philosophy. In this work, Bayle did not directly attack religion, yet he gave arguments that could move readers to doubt the truth of Scripture or question religious authorities.

Bayle's *Dictionary* was a powerful tool in spreading skeptical doubt. In Holland, France, Germany, and England, intellectuals as well as refined gentlemen and ladies eagerly read it. Bayle's chief importance, however, lies in the influence he had on the next generation of philosophers, the major figures of what has become known as the "Enlightenment." Men like the French thinkers Diderot, Montesquieu, and Voltaire read the *Dictionary* and took inspiration from it. For this reason, Pierre Bayle has become known as the "Father of the Enlightenment."

# The Rise of Liberalism

It is probably not surprising that the Englishman Thomas Hobbes was timid and fearful all his life. He was born prematurely on April 5, 1588, after his mother became frightened by news of the Spanish Armada. His father, an Anglican minister, abandoned Thomas, his mother, and two siblings when Thomas was still a child. Such experiences could well make one timorous and pessimistic in later life.

Following his father's flight, young Hobbes and his siblings were raised by a well-off uncle. At age 4, Hobbes himself was sent to a church school and then attended a private school. At the age of 15, he entered Magdalen College, at Oxford University, where he studied the Greek and Latin classics and ignored philosophy. After graduating at age 20, Hobbes served as a tutor to William Cavendish, the second Earl of Devonshire, and then for a time as secretary to Francis Bacon.

Was it his timidity that moved Hobbes, at the age of 52, to flee England for France? Hobbes was a staunch supporter of King Charles I of England against the king's Puritan enemies in Parliament. In 1640 (even before the Great Rebellion against the king broke out), Hobbes decided France was a safer place for royalists than England. In France he met French thinkers and read Descartes. For two years he served as tutor to the Prince of Wales, Charles II—who, with other English royalists, was in exile in France after the Great Rebellion.

Hobbes's timid disposition, however, did not stop him from writing a work that could have gotten him into a good deal of trouble—and almost did. This work, published in 1651, was called *The Leviathan, or the Matter, Form, and Power of a Commonwealth, Ecclesiastical and Civil*. The word *Leviathan* in the title refers to the leviathan of Scripture—a fearsome serpent that lives in the depths of the sea. *Leviathan* is a fitting name for this work, for it comes to conclusions that most readers would find very terrible. After the publication of this book, though Hobbes became a celebrity in England and Europe, he was widely criticized. At one point, Anglican bishops in England's Parliament wanted to burn him as a heretic. That might have been Hobbes's fate; but his former pupil, Charles II, then reigning as king, decided to protect him.

Despite, or because of, the attacks against it, Hobbes's *Leviathan* was an influential work. In both England and the European continent, it influenced some of the leading intellectuals of the late 17th century, including Pierre Bayle—the Father of the Enlightenment—himself. It was Bayle who called Thomas Hobbes "one the greatest geniuses" of his time.

## Leviathan

Thomas Hobbes's *Leviathan* is a dark work that presents a very pessimistic view of human nature. According to Hobbes, a human being is merely a kind of machine, lacking both an immaterial soul and a free will. Left to themselves, people will do only what pleases them without thinking about morality. According to *Leviathan*, at one time people were left entirely to themselves—a time Hobbes called the "state of nature." In the state of nature, people had no "notions of right or wrong, justice or injustice," said Hobbes, and life was "a war of every man against every man."

So terrible was the state of nature, said Hobbes, that people decided to escape it by banding together under a common government. To defend themselves against strong and cruel men, they made a "social contract" with a sovereign ruler. They gave up to this ruler all the freedoms they enjoyed in the state of nature in return for peace and security. The social contract gave this ruler absolute power over his subjects and allowed him to do whatever he needed to do to keep order. His subjects were never allowed to disobey or resist him, but must obey him in every particular.

In *Leviathan*, Hobbes said the purpose of religion is to help the sovereign ruler keep order. Religion is the servant of the government, according to Hobbes, and must remain under the absolute control of the sovereign, who even can tell people how to worship and what to believe. For Hobbes, the state, or as he called it, "that great LEVIATHAN," holds unlimited sway both over what belongs to man and what belongs to God.

**divine right of kings:** the doctrine held by some Christians that God places kings on their thrones and gives them absolute power in their kingdoms

**meteorology:** the science that deals with the atmosphere, with weather and predicting weather

## The Social Contract and Freedom

Thomas Hobbes was not the last philosopher to talk about a state of nature. Many other political philosophers were saying there was a time when individuals lived completely free, without law and without any connections to one another. But while some political philosophers agreed with Hobbes that a social contract can give governments unlimited power and control over individuals, other thinkers thought a social contract actually protects the freedoms citizens enjoy.

The foremost defender of the idea of freedom in the late 17th century was an Englishman named John Locke. Locke was 16 years old when Parliament executed King Charles I, who believed in the **divine right of kings** to hold absolute power in government. Locke's father was a small landowner and attorney, as well as a strict Puritan, who had fought with the "Roundhead" forces of Parliament against Charles I. Following in his father's footsteps, Locke was himself a convinced Puritan and Roundhead.

Having entered Christ College, Oxford, in 1652, Locke was a student during Oliver Cromwell's rule of England. Before long, however, Locke found himself at odds with the radical Puritans at Oxford, who did not tolerate people of any other religion. Because of this experience, Locke became a champion of religious liberty and tolerance. Locke continued at Oxford after earning his Masters degree in 1658, and he became a lecturer there.

At Oxford, Locke studied chemistry and **meteorology** and decided on medicine as a profession. During this period, he read Descartes and discovered a new interest—philosophy. After leaving Oxford, Locke got involved with people the government thought were dangerous. In 1683, to escape arrest for treason, Locke fled to Holland, where he joined other English political exiles. Holland at the time was the refuge for all sorts of freethinkers and literary men (including Pierre Bayle). In Holland, Locke's writings first appeared in print in a journal dedicated to radical ideas.

While in Holland, Locke joined other English exiles in support of William, the prince of Orange, and his invasion of England in November 1688. More than a year after William's "Glorious Revolution" drove King James II from the English throne, Locke returned to England—on the very ship that carried William's wife, Princess Mary, who was to share the rule of England, Scotland, and Ireland with her husband.

One of John Locke's most important works, the *Two Treatises on Government*, was published in London in 1690. He had written the work, he said, to "establish the throne of our great restorer, the present King William, to make good his title in the consent of the people."

In his *Two Treatises*, Locke—like Hobbes—said that mankind originally lived in a state of nature in which individuals were completely free to do as they saw fit. Each person in the state of nature possessed three natural rights, according to Locke—goods that no one could justly take from him. These were life, liberty (one's ability to do what seems good to him), and property (land or other material goods needed for maintaining life and exercising one's liberty.) Unlike Hobbes, however, Locke said that in the state of nature human beings followed a moral law, a "natural law," that required them to respect the rights of others. Locke did not think that people in the state of nature were always cruel, selfish creatures, but he did think that their rights were not entirely secure. They always faced the threat of losing their life, liberty, or property to the more powerful and unscrupulous among them.

**monarchy:** government by a monarch or ruler—a king, queen, or emperor

To secure their rights, said Locke, individuals made a social contract with each other and formed the state or "commonwealth." In doing so, individuals agreed to give up only some of their liberties (but not liberty itself) in order to preserve their life and property. The commonwealth, in turn, said Locke, is bound by natural law to respect life, liberty, and property—but, especially, property. "The great and chief end . . . of men uniting into commonwealths and putting themselves under government," wrote Locke, "is the preservation of property."

In emphasizing the right to property, Locke was speaking for his social class—the English merchants and businessmen who formed the Whig party in English politics. The Whigs had led the "Glorious Revolution," placing William of Orange on the throne of England and establishing Parliament as the supreme power in England. For Locke, this situation was perfectly right and proper. Though he did not reject **monarchy** as a form of government, Locke said that the government most likely to protect property is a government controlled by the majority of the free citizens, who rule through a representative assembly, such as Parliament. Further, said Locke, whenever a government violates the rights of individuals, the citizens have the right to overthrow that government and establish a new one in its place.

Just as Isaac Newton had convinced the scientific world that the universe is a material machine, operating according to fixed laws of motion, so Locke provided a theory of government that has become the basis of most political thinking from his time to our own. In doing so, Locke laid the foundations of the system of political thought called Liberalism.

## What Is Liberalism?

Before we say what Liberalism is, we must say what it is not. Liberalism is not simply those political ideas held by the people and political parties we today call "liberal." In the 17th, 18th, and 19th centuries, Liberalism had a much broader meaning. Indeed, many of those we call "conservative" in our time would have been called "Liberals" in those earlier centuries.

Liberalism, as it developed in the 17th and 18th centuries, was a political and social philosophy that emphasized the freedom of individuals to follow their own desires in their social, religious, and economic life. To the Liberal way of thinking, human beings by nature are individuals who live unconnected to anyone and have no obligation to obey anyone. Since by nature, every person is born completely free, every person is equal to every other person. In the state of nature, no one has a superior who may tell him what to do.

To the Liberal thinker, government exists to make sure that every person may exercise his rights with as much freedom as possible. Indeed, this was why people left the state of nature—because in the state of nature, they could not exercise their rights securely. But, according to Liberalism, no one enters society to become unfree. They certainly give up some of their freedoms when they enter society, but they still want to achieve their own personal goals. So, according to the Liberal way of thinking, society and government exist so that each person can attain the goals he sets for himself without, however, harming the rights of other individuals. As in the state of nature, so in society: individuals first and foremost work for themselves, for their own private benefit. The function of government is to make sure everyone may work for himself and his interests without hindering other individuals from working for themselves and their interests.

Catholic thinkers in the Middle Ages had arrived at very different conclusions about the individual and the society he lives in. To the medieval mind, human beings are persons who are made by God to live in society with others. Only in society, in fact, can people achieve the "common good," which is the best good for man. The common good includes the ability to obtain the things that sustain life, such as food and shelter, but it is much more than that. Finally, the common good includes peace, wisdom, virtue, and, ultimately, the greatest common good of all: everlasting union with God in heaven. The common good includes those good things everyone needs to live a fully human life. It is *common* because all share the common good together.

Liberals tended to think of government as a necessary evil—if we could live without it, we would. But the medieval ideal said that government is a positive good. It does not exist just to keep individuals from hurting one another but to help form the type of society where everyone can together achieve what is necessary to make him fully human.

Medieval thinkers thought governments were supposed to help people achieve the greatest of all goods—eternal life. Because of this, medieval thinkers held that rulers had to protect and foster the one true religion by actively supporting the mission of the Church, on the one hand, and fighting immorality and heresy, on the other. Medieval rulers did not think false religions should have full public freedom; to the medieval mind, false religions threatened the common good of society by spreading error. Religious error, it was believed, kept men from achieving the common goods of truth and virtue. It ultimately destroyed the very purpose of human society.

Because Liberals tended to deny that religions teach truth, they treated religion as if it were just a matter of private opinion. Governments, said the Liberals, should not be in the business of forcing one group's private opinions on other people. Liberals, therefore, insisted that governments should permit freedom of thought and expression. Individuals should be permitted to speak and to publish their opinions, no matter what they were.

Believing as they did in freedom of thought, not all Liberals held the same set of ideas. Some thought that individuals gave up their liberty entirely when they formed a social contract; others, like Locke, insisted that people gave up only some of their liberties but not others. Some Liberals spoke of a right to revolution, while others said that no one had the right to resist the power of government.

Liberalism was in some ways a very mixed bag of ideas, and Liberal freedoms often were applied quite selectively. But a common thread of all Liberal thought was to replace the idea of the common good with the ideal of individual liberty. The only just society, according to Liberals, is one that allows the individual the greatest scope to achieve his personal goals and desires.

# The "Enlightenment"

On September 1, 1715, King Louis XIV of France died. With his passing, the "Great Century" (the age of Louis XIV) came to an end. During that monarch's reign, France became not only the most powerful nation in Europe but the undisputed leader of European culture. Throughout Europe, aristocrats took on French ways and spoke the French language. They built houses and public buildings in the French style, and the artists and writers they patronized imitated the patterns of French art and literature. Louis XIV may have been the most feared ruler in Europe, but he was also the most envied and imitated.

Louis XIV gave Europe the example of a successful absolute monarch. Believing as he did in the divine right of kings, he tried to bring every French institution under the control of the crown—including the Catholic Church in France. In Louis's mind, the Church had to do the king's bidding. Yet, even though Louis used the Church in France to advance his political goals, he was a true believer in the truths of the Catholic Faith. He fought against heresy in his dominions, using a police force and the courts to crush opposition to the Church. Authors of heretical books, and even the readers of these books, could be imprisoned or condemned to serve in the galleys. In his personal life, Louis XIV attended to his devotions and even heard daily Mass as often as he could.

But Louis XIV was a contradictory character. Though devout, he appointed unfit men to serve as bishops in the French Church, and he himself lived an immoral life. And while he actively suppressed heresy and the spreading of anti-Catholic ideas in his kingdom, many of the nobles of his court were skeptics and moral libertines.

**dissenter:** one who dissents or disagrees with the ideas of another
**salon:** a gathering of fashionable notables (such as artists, writers, thinkers, government leaders, and others) in the home of an important person
**provincial:** belonging to a province
**irreligion:** the state of being without religion
**The Hague:** a city in the Netherlands (in Dutch, *Den Haag*)

Not much changed under Louis XIV's successor, King Louis XV. Like his grandfather, the new king suppressed bad books and punished **dissenters** against the Church. Yet, despite these measures, anti-Catholic books continued to be published in France and were even promoted by government officials. Members of the nobility avidly read these books, while elegant ladies formed **salons** where Liberal and irreligious ideas were openly and enthusiastically discussed. Paris itself had Liberal discussion clubs, and societies in the **provincial** French towns offered lectures on the new ideas.

The Paris salons drew more than just aristocrats. Middle-class intellectuals who promoted Liberalism found their way into these gatherings, where they earned the friendship and support of the aristocracy. With the support of the ruling classes, these thinkers, called *philosophes* (or philosophers), spread **irreligion** and Liberalism into the middle class.

Among the Parisian *philosophes* was a notary's son who, by wit and cunning, became the age's greatest popularizer of Liberal thought, not only in France, but across Europe and even into Europe's American colonies. His name was François Marie Arouet, but he came to be known more commonly by his pen name—Voltaire.

## "Crush the Infamous One!"

In the Paris salon of the Duchess of Maine, François-Marie Arouet began the literary career that would make him the most famous *philosophe* in Europe. The year was 1715, and Arouet had just returned to Paris from **The Hague** in the Netherlands. Arouet had mixed with aristocratic

> **lampoon:** a harsh, bitter literary piece that uses ridicule
> **Bastille:** a fortress tower in Paris; used as a jail
> **speculation:** the buying of property or goods in the hope of selling them at a higher price than when they were bought
> **creditor:** someone to whom one owes money; someone who makes a loan to another person
> **chevalier:** a title for a French nobleman. It means "knight."

freethinkers before going to The Hague; for though he belonged to the middle class, his mother had friends among the nobility.

The duchess of Maine's salon was a distinguished one, but also quite dangerous for a young man like Arouet. The Duchess was a bitter enemy of the Duke of Orléans (the regent of King Louis XV, who in 1715 was still only a boy). Under the duchess's influence, Arouet wrote poems mocking the regent—a dangerous thing to do, as Arouet soon learned. Because of his **lampoons**, Arouet was forced to leave Paris in May 1716. Shortly afterward, he was allowed to return; but in 1717 he was arrested and sent to the **Bastille**. Some anonymous lampoons had surfaced, and the government thought Arouet had written them.

Arouet might have gotten on better if he had followed his father's advice and become a lawyer. But the young man loved literature, especially stage plays, and he was eager to earn fame as a writer. While in the Bastille, he spent his time working on two plays that he hoped to publish under a pen name he had chosen for himself—Arouet de Voltaire.

Voltaire saw the first of his plays performed at the Théatre Français after his release from the Bastille in April 1718. The play was a great success. Other plays followed; some successful, others not. But Voltaire did not just rely on his plays and other literary works to make a living. Throughout his life, he engaged in financial **speculation** and investments. He courted aristocrats and used flattery to gain their favor. Voltaire eventually became a wealthy man—wealthier than many a nobleman whose favor he had sought in his younger days. Indeed, many of these noblemen, under heavy debt, would take loans from Voltaire to pay off their **creditors**.

Yet Voltaire, it seems, could not control his often bitter, sarcastic tongue. In 1725, he insulted an important noble, the **Chevalier** de Rohan, who had insulted *him*. Shortly afterward, several men attacked Voltaire and beat him with sticks while Rohan stood by, watching. This was an affront Voltaire could not ignore. He challenged Rohan to a duel, and the chevalier accepted. But on the morning of the duel, police arrested Voltaire and placed him in the Bastille. He remained there two weeks until, at his own request, he was sent from France to England.

## The Playwright Becomes a Philosopher

During his stay in England (1726–1729), Voltaire discovered that English society differed in many ways from that of his native France. Unlike France, England offered freedom of religion, at least to Protestants, and the English government was far more tolerant of freethinking than was the government of Louis XV. And the government of England itself, in Voltaire's mind, offered a superb model of how to keep order and preserve freedom at the same time. England's king was not all-powerful, as was the French king; Parliament, a government by representatives of at least *some* of the people, severely limited the power of the then reigning King George II. In England, Voltaire discovered the work of the English scientist Isaac Newton and the English philosopher John Locke. Voltaire came to think that Locke showed the way to remedy France's political and religious "tyranny."

Though Voltaire left France as a playwright, he returned as a philosopher. He continued to write poems and plays, but along with these he wrote commentaries on politics and, especially, works against religion. The first of these was *Philosophical Letters on the English*, published in 1732. In this work, Voltaire used his sharp wit to praise England's government and toleration of religion while he attacked the French Church and state. When on June 10, 1734, the government of Louis XV condemned the *Philosophical Letters* and ordered its author arrested, Voltaire fled Paris to the independent duchy of Lorraine, where he would be safe from French authorities.

Inspired by Newton's example, Voltaire set up a laboratory at Cirey, his estate in Lorraine, and performed experiments. He continued to write dramas and poetry, but turned more and more to works on science, philosophy, and politics. None of these works offered any original ideas, but they made Liberal ideas more popular and spread Locke's political ideas among the *philosophes* in France. Voltaire's clear, witty, and refined style could capture a reader's attention, and his cruel satire could make the ideas of his opponents appear ridiculous. Voltaire would stop at almost nothing—even outright lies (and he told many of them)—to promote his ideas and destroy those of others. He stopped at nothing to destroy what he called *l'infame*—"the infamous one."

What was the so-called infamous one? It was what we call religion; Voltaire called it superstition. Voltaire rejected all traditional religion as foolish. Himself a Deist, Voltaire thought everything, including the human soul, was composed of matter; and so he denied the immortality of the soul. Moreover, Voltaire was a rationalist and a proponent of free thought and moral libertinism. Voltaire's chief enemy, however (the most infamous of all the infamous ones in his mind) was the Catholic Church. The Church, he said, pretended it was the one, true religion just to fool the masses and keep them under the clergy's control.

Voltaire thought religion might be fine for ignorant, common people. But, he said, educated men—and especially rulers—should look to science and reason, not "superstition," for guidance on how to live in and govern society. A rational and scientific society, according to Voltaire, would not try to crush religion, but it would not promote one religion over another.

So it was that Voltaire became perhaps the greatest advocate of religious tolerance in the 18th century. And he proposed other "rational" reforms—abolishing torture, for instance, and ending the death penalty, at least for offenses such as forgery, theft, and smuggling. Yet Voltaire was not a revolutionary. He opposed democracy, for, he thought, the common man (whom he called *canaille*—"the rabble, riffraff") could never be enlightened. His ideal government was an absolute monarch, rather like Louis XIV, but without that king's attachment to "superstition" and persecution of those who did not agree with him.

## "Enlightenment" in France and Abroad

Voltaire called for "enlightenment." He thought reason and science should reform all of life, and religion should be allowed to wither and die. Voltaire's ideas inspired younger writers and thinkers who became famous during the reign of Louis XV. Like Voltaire, these *philosophes* were rationalists and materialists. But unlike Voltaire, they rejected Deism and embraced full-blown atheism.

The leader of these younger *philosophes* was Denis Diderot, a traveling book salesman and translator. Inspired by Bayle's *Dictionary*, Diderot came up with an idea for a similar work that would give a

> **collaborator:** a person who works together with others
>
> **hospice:** a lodging for travelers, youth, or the poor, often kept by a religious order

"general picture" of all the human mind had discovered, created, or conceived in the arts, science, religion, and politics. He called the work the *Encyclopedia*. Like all encyclopedias since its time, Diderot's *Encyclopedia* was divided into separate articles, written on a variety of subjects. Diderot himself wrote many of these articles, but he also received contributions from the leading *philosophes* of his day, including Voltaire. The first volume of the *Encyclopedia* came out in 1751. When it was finished in 1772, the *Encyclopedia* consisted of 12 full volumes, along with four supplemental volumes, and 11 volumes of illustrations.

Though written by Deists and atheists, the *Encyclopedia* was not obviously anti-Christian. Yet, Diderot was sly; many of the articles in the *Encyclopedia* hinted that religious ideas were foolish or irrational and directed readers to read works by atheistic or Deistic authors. The *Encyclopedia's* anti-Christian character did not escape the notice of the French authorities both in the Church and state, and in 1757 they forbade the publication of the remaining volumes. But Diderot had friends in high places and so was able to complete the work.

The *Encyclopedia* spread the antireligious ideas of the Enlightenment more widely among the upper and middle classes. Editions of the *Encyclopedia* appeared in Geneva and Italy, and the work was even smuggled into Spain. Diderot's work was instrumental in undermining the influence of religion and tradition among an ever-increasing number of people in Europe.

# The Prophet of Democracy

In August 1742, a 30-year-old musician from a French provincial town made his first visit to Paris. He had come to the capital to present to the Academy of Sciences a new system of musical notation he had devised. Though the academy rejected his system, which they said was ingenious but impractical, our musician decided to remain in the city. There he met Diderot and other prominent *philosophes* and was accepted as one of their colleagues and **collaborators**. He was to become one of the most prominent and influential thinkers of the 18th century.

Our musician, Jean-Jacques Rousseau, was born in 1712 in Calvinist Geneva, an independent, French-speaking city in Switzerland, on the border with France. Rousseau started life unhappily—he lost his mother when he was only a week old and was abandoned as a boy by his father. When he was 16 years old, he fled Geneva after being beaten by an engraver to whom he was apprenticed. He eventually found refuge with Madame de Warens, a noblewoman in Savoy. Herself a convert to the Catholic Faith, Madame de Warens sent Rousseau to a **hospice** in Turin. There, in 1728, he abandoned Calvinism and became a Catholic.

For the next several years, Rousseau was a wanderer. In 1729, Madame de Warens sent him to a seminary to study for the priesthood. But he could not tolerate his Latin lessons, so he was dismissed. Rousseau then went to work for the organist at the cathedral in Annecy, a town in Savoy. When the organist died, Rousseau no longer had any employment. He began a series of wanderings through the beautiful countryside of northern Savoy, Burgundy, western Switzerland, and Lyonnais. In the city of Lyons, he settled for a time and earned his living by copying music.

In 1732, Rousseau returned to Madame de Warens and was received into her household. Like many noblewomen of her time, Madame de Warens was not a very strict Catholic. She read the works of Deist authors, particularly Voltaire, and was something of a moral libertine. While living in her household, Rousseau not only began to study Latin, but delved into the works of Newton, Bayle, and Voltaire. Voltaire's works, in particular, he said, "Inspired me with a desire to write elegantly, and caused me to endeavor to imitate the colorings of that author, with whom I was so enchanted." It is not surprising, that by 1738, Rousseau's faith began to falter. Since his youth he had conceived a deep love for the beauty of nature, and now he began to think nature was God.

> **foundling:** an infant abandoned by its parents and found by others. A *foundling hospital* is a place where foundlings are sheltered and cared for.

For the first few years after arriving in Paris in 1742, Rousseau lived in poverty. There he formed a relationship with a poor, simple, hotel laundress named Thérèse Levasseur and spent the rest of his life with her. The two had five children together. At each child's birth, Rousseau abandoned the infant to a **foundling** hospital.

Yet, despite his own moral failures—as well as the immorality of others he had known in his life—in Paris Rousseau began to think that human beings are basically good. What, then, makes them bad? Rousseau's answer was that Society makes people bad. Government, laws, religious institutions, even the arts and sciences corrupt men and make them immoral, he said. The savage, who lives closest to nature, is far superior to the civilized man, he thought. In 1750, Rousseau published these ideas in his first published work, called *The Discourse on Arts and Sciences*.

Inspired by his own ideas, Rousseau abandoned the dress of the upper class, which he had adopted, and donned the clothing and wig of the middle class. In 1754, he even returned to his native Geneva, which he admired for its republican form of government. (In Geneva, 1,600 out of the city's 20,000 inhabitants voted for the members of the "Council of 25," who made the laws and governed the city and its surroundings.) In Geneva, Rousseau abandoned the Catholic Faith and reaffirmed his belief in Calvinism (though, privately, he did not accept the divinity of Christ and other Christian doctrines). Yet, despite his pride in being a Geneva citizen, Rousseau spent only a few months there. In October 1754, he was again in Paris.

## Rousseau the Philosopher

In his first published work, Rousseau had held up the savage life as the ideal life for man. He abandoned this idea in his second work, the *Discourse on the Origins and Foundations of Human Inequality*, published in June 1755. In this work, instead of the savage, Rousseau praised societies based on the family, which he called the only "natural" society. According to the second *Discourse*, mankind was at its best, and happiest, when people lived in small, family-centered, tribal groups and shared the goods of the earth in common. This was how men had lived in the "state of nature," he said. It was private property, Rousseau said, that made society corrupt and made people unequal and led to the oppression of the poor by the rich. To protect their property, Rousseau said, people began to rely on the use of force. The next step was setting up the rule of law, which the strong in society used to oppress the weak.

> **satire:** a literary work that uses ridicule and scorn to attack human vices

In this second *Discourse*, Rousseau said that he opposed revolution because it did nothing to fight evil in the world. Instead of revolting against the government, families, he said, must return to the land and take up farming. Private property must be maintained, but it should be controlled by what he called the "general will" of the families who make up the state. In this way, everyone can obtain an equal share of property.

Rousseau thought religion is important to the state, but he did not espouse any traditional Christian religion. The state's religion (which, Rousseau said, had to remain under the control of the "general will") should insist only that people hold a few doctrines. These doctrines are that God exists, that by his providence he cares for the world, and that those who act well will receive rewards in an afterlife (and punishments if they do ill.) Rousseau rejected the Catholic Faith because it placed the state under the Church.

The ideas of his second *Discourse* moved Rousseau farther from his friends, the *philosophes*. Voltaire thought Rousseau's two discourses were raving nonsense. Still, for a time, Rousseau remained friends with Diderot and other *philosophes*; he even contributed articles to the *Encyclopedia*. But in the end, his difficult temperament undermined these friendships. Rousseau eventually made Voltaire his bitter enemy. After 1757, Rousseau became more and more isolated from all those who had ever shown him friendship and support.

## Two Philosophers

Voltaire also had something of a difficult temper. For a time, he lived at the court of King Friedrich the Great of Prussia, but the philosopher's bitter tongue and dishonesty earned him the king's displeasure. In the end, Voltaire had to leave the Prussian court.

Voltaire eventually found a home in Geneva, where he bought a house close to the French border. There he built a theater where he staged productions of his plays. In 1755, Voltaire published *Pucelle*, a rather nasty poem on the life of St. Joan of Arc. In Geneva, he wrote his most famous tale, *Candide*, a **satire** that bitterly attacked *l'infame*—the Catholic Church. But even in Geneva Voltaire could not live in peace, for the republic had laws against the staging of plays. So in 1758, he bought two estates, four miles from the Geneva border, in France. As part of the purchase price, he became a nobleman, the "Count of Tourney." He settled at one of the estates, named Ferney. From there, he thought, he could escape into Geneva if the French authorities sought to arrest him.

But no one tried to arrest Voltaire. Instead, his home at Ferney became a center of pilgrimage for nobility and philosophers—all those who honored the old man, who was now in his sixties. He continued to write volumes of letters, plays, poems, histories, stories, and works of social criticism.

During his stay at Ferney, Voltaire became famous for championing the cause of individuals who suffered persecution from Church and state in France. So, more than ever, Voltaire became the toast of Europe. Nor did he neglect his estates. He planted thousands of trees and cultivated the land. He built houses for his peasant workers, loaned them money at low interest rates, fed them in a time of famine at his own expense, and worked to free the serfs in the neighboring province of Gex. He even built a church for his peasants and, at times, attended Mass there. "I am becoming a patriarch," he boasted. Indeed, he became known as the "Patriarch of Ferney" and was well beloved by his peasants and servants as well as by others who benefited from his generosity.

At one point, Voltaire, hearing of Rousseau's poverty, offered him a home at Ferney. But Rousseau was becoming mentally unstable. In a piece of writing, he revealed that Voltaire had written a tract that could land him in prison if he was identified as the author. This was too much! The Patriarch finally turned on Rousseau. Voltaire could no longer tolerate Rousseau, and he never could tolerate Rousseau's ideas. He called him "a mad dog who bites everybody" and "a Judas who betrayed philosophy."

By 1757, Rousseau had lost all his friends, except some members of the nobility who respected him as a philosopher. He achieved more fame in 1761 by publishing a sentimental novel—called *Julie, or the Novel of Héloïse*—that glorified faithful, marital love. But Rousseau was not finished with philosophy, and in 1762 he published his most important and influential work, *The Social Contract*.

"Man is born free, and he is everywhere in chains"—so Rousseau opened this eloquent and stirring work on the foundations of the social order. In *The Social Contract*, Rousseau developed his idea that the authority of the state comes from the combined will of the citizens. The sovereign power, he said, does not belong to rulers—whether they be kings or parliaments—but to the people. Rousseau said that, to preserve their lives and goods, individuals join together and make a social contract with each other. In doing so, they lose all their liberties and agree to be ruled by the "general will" of all.

Rousseau's ideal form of government is a republic, but a very small republic, where citizens gather in an assembly to make the laws. Such a republic would have to be very small, indeed; for who could imagine the millions who lived in France gathering in one place to make laws? Rousseau, however, did not want large nations like France, but a republic more like Geneva. "The larger the state," he said, "the less the liberty."

The ideas expressed in *The Social Contract* were not very realistic, given Europe as it was at the time. Even so, *The Social Contract* was destined to become a highly influential book in the years to come. It would make Rousseau a champion not of Enlightened reform, like Voltaire, but of a movement that would shake the monarchies of Europe and change Christendom forever. Although Rousseau did not call for revolution, his championship of the small farmer and craftsman inspired a movement from which Voltaire and all the *philosophes* would have shrunk with horror. That movement is *democracy*.

# The Death of Philosophers

In the years following the publication of *The Social Contract*, Rousseau again became a wanderer. In 1762, to escape imprisonment in France, he fled first to Switzerland and then to England. But even in Voltaire's land of freedom, Rousseau found no peace. He suffered a mental breakdown, which became worse when his old friends, including Diderot and Voltaire, attacked him in print. Rousseau eventually returned to France, and with Thérèse (whom he finally married) continued his wandering life, which ended in Paris in June 1770.

In Paris, Rousseau and Thérèse lived in poverty. But dwelling among the poor and suffering bitterly from the guilt of having, years earlier, abandoned his children, Rousseau turned once again to religion. He began attending Catholic services and took to visiting the sick and giving alms. Still, he complained, he could not believe. "Ah, how happy the man who can believe!" he cried.

He felt no envy when, in February 1778, the 86-year-old Voltaire made his triumphant entry into Paris. It had been 28 years since Voltaire set foot in the city. He came to see the premiere of his latest play, a tragedy called *Irène*. King Louis XV had died in 1777, and King Louis XVI's wife, Queen Marie Antoinette, was a fan of Voltaire's plays and had become his protector. The literary academy of Paris, the nobility, foreign dignitaries, even the common people enthusiastically greeted the Patriarch of Ferney's arrival in the capital.

But all this glory was too much for Voltaire. He suffered a hemorrhage two weeks after entering Paris. Following this bout of sickness, however, Voltaire recovered and was strong enough to attend a performance of *Irène*, where the crowd hailed him enthusiastically and crowned him with laurels—the way people acclaim a great poet.

In the middle of May, Voltaire again fell sick. This time it seemed he would not recover. Priests were called, and three of them visited the old man's sick room. What happened is unclear. One account relates that when Voltaire saw the priests, he complained, "Let me die in peace!" Another account says he waved them away. The most commonly accepted account, however, says the priests found him delirious and left before giving him last rites. That same night, Voltaire died.

Hearing of Voltaire's death, Rousseau said, "our lives were linked to each other; I shall not survive him long." In this he was prophetic. On July 2, 1778, a little over a month after the death of his former enemy, Rousseau suffered a stroke and fell to the ground, gashing his head open on the tile floor. Shortly after this accident, Rousseau died.

Sixteen years after the deaths of these two philosophers, after a fierce revolution had shaken France's Church and state to its foundations, the remains of Rousseau and Voltaire were buried, side by side, in a former Parisian church renamed the Panthéon. Side by side lay the two men—former enemies, but joined in a common cause. Both had fought a common enemy—Christendom—and inspired a revolution, one that would end, it seemed, in the utter destruction of the Christian order of Europe.

# Chapter Review

## Summary

- In his *Discourse on Method*, Descartes claimed he had discovered a new basis for philosophy. Man could be certain of the existence of God and of the universe, he said, because he is first certain of his own existence. Though he thought he was defending the Catholic Faith, Descartes's work helped pave the way for rationalism and skepticism.
- Descartes's idea that the universe operates like a machine gave support to Deism, the belief that God set the machine of the universe in motion and left it alone to operate by the laws of nature.
- Baruch Spinoza was influenced by Descartes and Deist ideas. Spinoza taught that the universe is God, and the laws by which the universe runs are the will of God.
- The Frenchman Pierre Bayle promoted religious skepticism though his work, *The Historical and Critical Dictionary*.

- In his famous work, *Leviathian*, Thomas Hobbes said that mankind once lived in a "state of nature" in which people had no "notions of right or wrong, justice or injustice" and life was "a war of every man against every man." To escape this state of nature, people made a "social contract" with a sovereign, to whom they gave up their liberties.
- In his "Two Treatises on Government," John Locke laid the foundation for Liberalism: the social philosophy that emphasizes the freedom of the individual. Locke accepted the idea of a state of nature but thought the social contract did not remove all freedoms from people.
- Irreligion and Liberalism spread throughout the French middle class. One of the most influential popularizers of skepticism, irreligion, and Liberalism was the French playwright, Voltaire.
- Denis Diderot's *Encyclopedia* attacked the Christian Faith and helped spread Liberal ideas throughout Europe.
- In his various works, Jean-Jacques Rousseau argued that the authority of the state comes from the combined will of the citizens. Rousseau thus inspired the movement toward democracy.

## Key Concepts

**Descartes's mechanistic view of the universe:** the belief that God created the world like a machine, to run without divine help. This idea undermined the Catholic belief in Divine Providence.

**Divine Providence:** Catholic belief that God created the world and continually cares for it.

**skeptic:** one who doubts that anything can be known for certain to be true. Skeptics who wanted freedom of thought and expression became known as *libertines*.

**Deism:** the religious idea that God set the machine of the universe in motion and left it alone to continue moving by the laws of nature. Deists did not acknowledge the teaching that Jesus is God, because they believed it to be irrational.

**Liberalism:** the political idea that individuals should have the freedom to work for their own benefit in any way they see fit as long as they do not harm the rights of others

**state of nature:** a theoretical time of human history in which people lived without government and each person possessed all rights and complete liberty

**social contract:** an agreement by which people give up some or all of their liberty and rights to a government in return for peace and security

## Dates to Remember

**1598:** Edict of Nantes issued, guaranteeing French Huguenots religious freedom in France

**1629:** Descartes completes his *Discourse on Method*.

**1651:** Hobbes publishes *The Leviathan*.

**1685:** The Edict of Nantes is revoked in an effort to unite France under one religion.

**1690:** Publication of Locke's *Two Treatises on Government*

**1696:** Bayle began publishing *The Historical and Critical Dictionary*.

**1751:** Publication of the first volume of the *Encyclopedia*
**1762:** Publication of Rousseau's *The Social Contract*

## Central Characters

**René Descartes (1596–1650):** a Frenchman whose passion for philosophy and mathematics inspired him to look at philosophy in a mathematical way. He wrote *Discourse on Method*.

**Pierre Bayle (1647–1706):** a French philosopher who wrote the *Historical and Critical Dictionary*, an encyclopedia of historical, biblical, and mythical events that spread antireligious ideas. He became known as the "Father of the Enlightenment."

**Thomas Hobbes (1588–1679):** an Englishman and author of *The Leviathan*. In this work, Hobbes claims that humans operate like a machine, without a soul or free will. Left to themselves, people have no morality. To escape the state of nature, said *The Leviathan*, people form a social contract with a sovereign ruler.

**John Locke (1632–1704):** an Englishman and author of *Two Treatises on Government*. In this work, Locke argues that man has three natural rights: life, liberty, and property. When they enter into a social contract, persons do not lose these rights. Unlike Hobbes, Locke said humans have a moral law that requires them to respect the rights of others.

**Voltaire (1694–1778):** the penname of Francois-Marie Arouet, perhaps the greatest popularizer of Liberal ideas in the 18th century. Voltaire wrote revolutionary satire, plays, and poems mocking the traditional society of his time and religion, especially the Catholic Church. Voltaire wanted greater freedom and tolerance of different religions in society and favored the English government over the French system.

**Denis Diderot (1713–1784):** the leader of a group of atheist philosophers. He published the *Encyclopedia*, which spread antireligious views across Europe.

**Jean-Jacques Rousseau (1712–1778):** a musician accepted into Diderot's atheist group. He wrote *Discourse on the Origins and Foundations of Human Inequality*, where he praised small, family-based societies. He later wrote *The Social Contract*, which inspired the movement toward democracy.

## Questions for Review

1. Why did Descartes's view of the mechanical universe undermine the Catholic Faith?
2. How did Hobbes's and Locke's philosophies of government differ?
3. What is the function of government, according to Liberalism? Whose theory of government inspired Liberalism?
4. In what ways does Rousseau's "natural society" differ from modern American society?
5. Why were people in France so divided in their worldview and politics?

## Ideas in Action

1. Look at the portraits of the people who lived at the time of the Enlightenment. Discuss what work would have been required to wear a wig, heavy makeup, dresses for women and costumes for men, shoes, hat, and accessories.
2. Research and discuss what a school of the Enlightenment period would have looked like in structure, size of classroom, and subjects studied.
3. Listen to 18th-century music from Europe and England. Does any of it have the "Enlightenment spirit"?
4. Research and deliver short presentations on European architecture, painting, drama, and poetry of the Enlightenment period.
5. Discuss the differences between the Enlightenment in England and the Enlightenment in France and the rest of Europe.
6. Imagine that you were a physician to one of the Enlightenment thinkers who had fallen ill. Write a diary of your patient's illness, progress, and frame of mind as regards medical treatment and the possibility of death. (Comment on the medicine available and the sort of medicine or treatment you would administer to your patient.)

# Highways and Byways

## Good Eats in the 17th Century

Beginning in the 17th century, the people of Europe, from royalty to peasant, saw an amazing increase in the amount and variety of food they could enjoy. Spices, tea, and coffee began to be available. General prosperity through worldwide trade created general affluence and demand for luxury goods and foods. Fine wines from France, Spain, and Italy made their way to celebrations everywhere.

Europeans of the time were amazed at the amount, variety, and novelty of foods the trading empires of England, the Netherlands, Spain, Portugal, and France brought them. Local farming and fishing were a part of every culture, but exotic fruits and vegetables, along with meats of every sort, inspired a fever to cook the most delicious and unusual dishes. In Protestant England and Northern Europe, the lost Catholic religious feast days were soon replaced by secular celebrations of human life—weddings, births, funerals—as well as more materialistic celebrations—a successful business venture, the purchase of property, the arrival of a merchant ship. Painters began to immortalize the banquets of the time, giving rise to a new subject for art. Still life paintings, portraits, and genre scenes became the order of the day, as in this painting titled *Banquet Piece*, by the 17th-century Dutch artist Abraham van Beyeren.

# 674 Credits

*Credits continued from page iv*

p. 119 © Anna Stasevska/Shutterstock; p. 119 © Anna Stasevska/Shutterstock; p. 120 © Wikipedia; p. 121 © KarSol/Shutterstock; p. 122 © Renata Sedmakova/Shutterstock; p. 124 © Wikipedia; p. 125 © Vladislav Gurfinkel/Shutterstock; p. 126 © Wikipedia; p. 127 © khd/Shutterstock; p. 128 © Renata Sedmakova/Shutterstock; p. 129 © Everett Historical/Shutterstock; p. 130 © Wikipedia; p. 133 © vvoe/Shutterstock; p. 140 © Shutterstock; p. 141 © Ozgur Guvenc/Shutterstock; p. 142 © Shutterstock (tl); p. 142 © Filip Fuxa/Shutterstock (br); p. 144 © nito/Shutterstock; p. 146 © Artur Bogacki/Shutterstock; p. 147 © SmarterMedium/Shutterstock; p. 148 © Wikipedia; p. 149 © M Reel/Shutterstock; p. 150 © Wikipedia; p. 151 © Wikipedia (t); p. 151 © Wikipedia (b); p. 153 © Wikipedia; p. 154 © m.bonotto/Shutterstock; p. 155 © Cliff Lloyd/Shutterstock; p. 156 © Tupungato/Shutterstock; p. 157 © Wikipedia; p. 158 © Wikipedia; p. 159 © Wikipedia; p. 160 © Wikipedia; p. 167 © Chubykin Arkady/Shutterstock; p. 168 © Mi.Ti./Shutterstock; p. 169 © mikhail/Shutterstock; p. 171 © Marzolino/Shutterstock; p. 173 © Morphart Creation/Shutterstock; p. 174 © Shutterstock; p. 175 © Shutterstock; p. 176 © Zurijeta/Shutterstock; p. 177 © Wikipedia; p. 179 © Waj/Shutterstock; p. 182 © Wikipedia; p. 185 © Shutterstock; p. 186 © Wikipedia (t); p. 186 © Wikipedia (b); p. 187 © Wikipedia; p. 188 © Wikipedia; p. 193 © PavleMarjanovic/Shutterstock; p. 195 © Mikhail Markovskiy/Shutterstock; p. 196 © Artur Bogacki/Shutterstock; p. 198 © Rodrigo Garrido/Shutterstock; p. 199 © Wikipedia; p. 202 © Wikipedia; p. 203 © ronnybas/Shutterstock; p. 205 © Granger; p. 206 © Wikipedia; p. 207 © Wikipedia; p. 211 © Wikipedia; p. 213 © Wikipedia; p. 219 © Wikipedia; p. 220 © Wikipedia; p. 234 © daulon/Shutterstock; p. 225 © Fernando Cortes/Shutterstock; p. 226 © Marzolino/Shutterstock; p. 228 © Wikipedia; p. 229 © Wikipedia; p. 232 © Alan Egginton/Shutterstock (tl); p. 232 © Nikonaft/Shutterstock (tr); p. 233 © Nikonaft/Shutterstock; p. 234 © pedrosala/Shutterstock; p. 235 © Marzolino/Shutterstock; p. 236 © Max Topchii/Shutterstock; p. 237 © Corbis; p. 238 © Wikipedia; p. 243 © Claudio Giovanni Colombo/Shutterstock; p. 245 © ventdusud/Shutterstock; p. 246 © Wikipedia; p. 247 © Wikipedia; p. 248 © Wikipedia; p. 252 © Granger (t); p. 252 © Wikipedia; p. 253 © Renata Sedmakova/Shutterstock; p. 254 © Wikipedia; p. 255 © Wikipedia; p. 256 © Wikipedia; p. 257 © Bettmann/Getty Images; p. 258 © Granger; p. 259 © Public Domain; p. 261 Nicku/Shutterstock; p. 267 © A.S.Floro/Shutterstock; p. 268 © Anibal Trejo/Shutterstock; p. 269 © foto-sub/Shutterstock; p. 270 © Kutlayev Dmitry/Shutterstock; p. 272 © MG photos/Shutterstock; p. 273 © Wikipedia; p. 274 © David Fowler/Shutterstock; p. 275 © Wikipedia; p. 276 © Wikipedia; p. 277 © Wikipedia; p. 279 © Wikipedia; p. 280 © Bettmann/Getty Images; p. 281 © Georgios Kollidas/Shutterstock; p. 282 © Wikipedia; p. 283 Georgios Kollidas/Shutterstock; p. 284 © Bettmann/Getty Images; p. 286 © Wikipedia; p. 287 © PHB.cz (Richard Semik)/Shutterstock; p. 288 © Wikipedia (tl); p. 288 © Wikipedia (br); p. 295 © Wikipedia; p. 296 © Wikipedia; p. 297 © Leonard de Selva; Corbis; p. 298 ©Wikipedia; p. 300 © Vladimir Korostyshevskiy/Shutterstock (t); p. 300 © Pavlov Valeriy/Shutterstock (b); p. 301 © Wikipedia; p. 303 © Wikipedia; p. 304 © Bettmann/Getty Images; p. 307 © Jarno Gonzalez Zarraonandia/Shutterstock; p. 308 © Artur Bogacki/Shutterstock; p. 311 © Wikipedia; p. 312 © nito/Shutterstock; p. 313 © Wikipedia; p. 316 © Lenar Musin/Shutterstock; p. 318 © vvoe/Shutterstock; p. 320 © Luca Grandinetti/Shutterstock; p. 321 © Wikipedia; p. 327 © jorisvo/Shutterstock; p. 328 © Slimewoo/Shutterstock; p. 329 © Steve Estvanik/Shutterstock; p. 330 © Peter Zurek/Shutterstock (t); p. 330 © Kathie Walters/Shutterstock (b); p. 331 © Claudio Giovanni Colombo/Shutterstock; p. 332 © Wikipedia; p. 334 © Wikipedia; p. 335 © Mirek Hejnicki/Shutterstock; p. 336 © Wikipedia; p. 338 © Wikipedia; p. 339 © Zvonimir Atletic/Shutterstock; p. 340 © Wikipedia; p. 341 © Corbis; p. 343 © Michel Setboun/Corbis; p. 344 © Wikipedia; p. 345 © Wikipedia; p. 347 © roberaten/Shutterstock; p. 348 © Wikipedia; p. 349 © Corbis; p. 350 © Wikipedia; p. 352 © Wikipedia; p. 353 © Wikipedia; p. 359 © Wikipedia; p. 362 © Georgios Kollidas/Shutterstock; p. 364 © Granger; p. 365 © Boris Stroujko/Shutterstock; p. 367 © Shutterstock; p. 368 © Renata Sedmakova/Shutterstock; p. 369 © Wikipedia; p. 370 Fabio Bernardi/Shutterstock; p. 372 © ullstein bild/Granger; p. 373 Jeff Whyte/Shutterstock; p. 374 © fstockfoto/Shutterstock; p. 376 © Wikipedia; p. 381 © Leonid Andronov/Shutterstock; p. 382 © Serge Vero/Shutterstock; p. 383 © alexsol/Shutterstock; p. 384 © Wikipedia; p. 386 © Marco Saracco/Shutterstock; p. 388 © Wikipedia; p. 391 © Corbis; p. 393 © Wikipedia; p. 394 © Georgios Kollidas/Shutterstock; p. 395 © Georgios Kollidas/Shutterstock; p. 396 © Wikipedia; p. 397 © Wikipedia; p. 399 ©Wikipedia; p. 400 © Granger; p. 401 © Granger; p. 404 © fpolat69/Shutterstock; p. 413 © Pecold/Shutterstock; p. 414 © Wikipedia; p. 416 © Wikipedia; p. 417 © Wikipedia; p. 418 © Wikipedia; p. 419 © Wikipedia; p. 420 © Wikipedia; p. 421 © Janaka Dharmasena/Shutterstock; p. 422 © javi_indy/Shutterstock; p. 422 © jorisvo/Shutterstock; p. 423 © Wikipedia; p. 424 © airphoto.gr/Shutterstock; p. 425 © Wikipedia; p. 428 © Granger; p. 430 ©

# Credits

Vadim Petrakov/Shutterstock; **p. 431** © Shutterstock; **p. 432** © Marzolino/Shutterstock; **p. 434** © Wikipedia; **p. 436** © Philip Lange/Shutterstock; **p. 443** © Wikipedia; **p. 444** © Wikipedia; **p. 445** © Wikipedia; **p. 446** © Wikipedia; **p. 448** © ArTono/Shutterstock; **p. 450** © Wikipedia; **p. 451** © Wikipedia; **p. 452** © m.wolf/Shutterstock; **p. 453** © Christian Draghici/Shutterstock; **p. 455** © Wikipedia; **p. 456** © Shutterstock; **p. 457** © Georgios Kollidas/Shutterstock; **p. 458** © Wikipedia; **p. 461** © Wikipedia (tl); **p. 461** © Wikipedia (tr); **p. 462** © Wikipedia; **p. 464** © Everett Historical/Shutterstock; **p. 465** © Everett Historical/Shutterstock; **p. 466** © Everett Historical/Shutterstock; **p. 467** © Georgios Kollidas/Shutterstock; **p. 468** © Wikipedia; **p. 469** © Wikipedia; **p. 470** © Wikipedia; **p. 472** © Wikipedia; **p. 473** © Wikipedia; **p. 474** © Wikipedia; **p. 476** © Wikipedia; **p. 483** © Marzolino/Shutterstock; **p. 486** © Wikipedia; **p. 487** © Wikipedia; **p. 489** © Wikipedia; **p. 490** © Wikipedia (t); **p. 490** © Wikipedia (b); **p. 491** © Georgios Kollidas/Shutterstock (t); **p. 491** © BorisVetshev/Shutterstock (b); **p. 493** © Wikipedia; **p. 494** © Sergey Kohl/Shutterstock; **p. 495** © Wikipedia; **p. 496** © Wikipedia; **p. 498** © Wikipedia; **p. 500** © Wikipedia; **p. 501** © Wikipedia; **p. 502** © Wikipedia; **p. 505** © Wikipedia; **p. 506** © IgorGolovniov/Shutterstock (t); **p. 506** © IgorGolovniov/Shutterstock (b); **p. 508** © Granger; **p. 510** © Wikipedia; **p. 512** © Wikipedia; **p. 513** © Wikipedia; **p. 522** © Wikipedia; **p. 524** © Wikipedia; **p. 525** © Wikipedia; **p. 526** © Wikipedia; **p. 529** © Georgios Kollidas/Shutterstock; **p. 530** © Granger; **p. 532** © KevinTate/Shutterstock; **p. 532** © Georgios Kollidas/Shutterstock; **p. 533** © Granger; **p. 534** © Wikipedia; **p. 536** © Wikipedia; **p. 537** © Corbis; **p. 538** © Wikipedia; **p. 539** © Wikipedia; **p. 540** © Wikipedia; **p. 542** © Wikipedia; **p. 543** © Wikipedia (t); **p. 543** © Georgios Kollidas/Shutterstock (b); **p. 544** © Phillip Minnis/Shutterstock; **p. 546** © Wikipedia; **p. 547** © Wikipedia; **p. 548** © Wikipedia; **p. 550** © Wikipedia.

# Index

## A

Abbasids, 187–189
Abbey of Cîteaux, 246–247
Abbey of Cluny, 245–246
Abbey of Monte Cassino, 155, 157, 164, 350
Abbey of Montserrat, 491
Abbey of St. Denis, 285–286
Abd-ar-Rahman (Caliph), 201, 210
Abd-ar-Rahman (Emir), 201, 202
abdicate, 371
absolve, 364
Abu Abd Allah Muhammad Al-Nasir, 310–312
Abu Bakr, 177–178, 191
abuses, 488
academia. *See* liberal arts; schools
Acre, 303
Act of Settlement, 539
Act of Supremacy, 480
Act of Uniformity, 473
Acts, 32, 33, 37, 46, 244
A.D. *See Anno Domini*
Adalbert of Prague, 255
Adam, 1, 12, 102, 417, 424
Adeodatus, 101
adjourn, 486
Adolphus, Gustavus, 517
Adrian I, 209
Adriatic Sea, 103, 306
*Advantage of Death*, 200
Aegean Sea, 404
*Aeneid, The*, 49, 50
Africa, 57, 63, 90, 98, 100, 108–109, 115, 124–126, 126, 143, 181, 204, 222, 235, 271, 320
Africanus, Apuleius, 348
Agincourt, 393–395

Agricultural Revolutions, 231
agriculture, 2, 7, 15, 230–231. *See also* feudalism
Agrippina, 54
Al-Andalus, 203–204, 215, 309–312
Alaric, 104, 105, 111, 121, 135
Albert of Brandenberg, 445–446
Albert the Great, 351, 352
Albertus Magnus. *See* Albert the Great
Albigensians, 289, 313, 314, 317, 324, 340, 417
Albinus, 151
Alcuin, 216
Alexander, 90
Alexander III, 262
Alexander the Great, 3
Alexander V, 370
Alexandria, 77, 90, 94, 181
Alfonso II, 267
Alfonso III, 292
Alfonso IX, 334–335, 340
Alfonso VI, 269–271, 292
Alfonso VIII, 310, 325–326
Ali, 183–184, 191
Alighieri, Dante, 361–362, 378
"All Creatures of Our God and King", 358
Allah, 172, 190
allay, 536
*Almagest*, 60
Al-Mansour, 325–326
Almohads, 317
Almoravids, 271
Al-Qadir, 269–271
Al-Saffah, 187–188
Amalasuntha, 133, 143–144
Amalings, 131–133

Amalric, 133
Ambrose, 98–99, 111
Ambrose of Milan, 200
America, 438, 540–542
Amorium, 193
Amr, 181
Anabaptists, 455, 488
Anatolia, 193
Andrew, 35
Andrew II, 318
Angel of the Annunciation, 1
Angles, 131, 160
Anglican, 488
Anglican church, 524–525. *See also* Protestant Reformation
Anne Boleyn, 467–469, 477, 480
Anne Stuart, 538–539, 554
*Anno Domini*, 2
annulment, 467, 479
Anselm, 275–276
Antioch, 88, 96, 181, 299, 301
antipope, 260, 264, 369
Antoninus, 59, 66
Antwerp, 513
Apocalypse, 72
Apostle of Germany, 200
*Apostle Saint Paul, The*, 37
apostles, 13, 25–26, 28, 34–35, 43, 44
*Appeal to the German Nobility, An*, 450
apprenticeships, 237
aqueduct, 144, 186
Aquinas, Thomas. *See* Thomas Aquinas
Aquino, 350
Aquitania, 105, 222, 393
Arabia, 170–172, 204
Aragon, 309–312, 432

677

*Arbiter Elegantiae*, 54
Arcadius, 96, 103–104, 104
Arch of Titus, 56
archaeology, 3
architecture, 7, 328–330
Arians, 90–92, 94, 99, 103–104, 106, 108–109, 111, 112, 121, 132, 199, 200
aristocracy, 55
Aristotelianism, 348, 356
arithmetic, 150, 332
Arius. *See* Arians
armada, 477
Armenia, 10, 11, 58
armistice, 526
Arsuf, 304
art, 7, 327–330, 421–422
Arthur (King), 279, 411–412
Arthur Tudor, 466
Articles of Union, 553
ascension, 30–32, 35
*Ascension of Christ*, 32
ascetic, 75
Asia Minor, 10, 11, 36, 38, 41, 52, 62, 69, 90, 97, 139, 141, 146, 169, 193, 295, 296, 301
Assumption of the Blessed Virgin, 194
Assyria, 58
astronomy, 150, 332, 519–520
Asturias, 216, 267
Athalaric, 143–144
Athanagild, 121
Athanasius, 94–95, 111
Athaulf, 121
atheist, 71
Athenagoras, 76
Athens, 76
Attila the Hun, 107–108, 111, 130
Augsburg, 248
Augustine of Canterbury, 158–159, 161, 165
Augustine of Hippo, 98, 100–103, 106, 111, 208, 247, 349
Augustus, 3, 47–51, 65, 83
Aurillac, 254–255, 265–266

austerity, 299
Austrasia, 199, 201, 206, 222
*Authorized Version*, 440
autocracy, 418, 440
Avars, 132
*Ave Maria*, 331
Avignon, 364, 368
Avitus, 128

# B

Babylon, 57
Babylonia, 10
Bactria, 10
Baghdad, 188–189
Balkan Peninsula, 62, 96, 103–104, 296
Baltic Sea, 59, 116, 429
Baptism, 23, 92, 487
*Baptism of Christ, The*, 23
*Baptism of Saint Prince Vladimir, The*, 383, 384
Barabbas, 29
Barbarossa. *See* Frederick I
Barcelona, 491
Barebone, Praisegod, 531
"Barebone's Parliament", 531
Barocci, Federigo, 339
Barrada River, 179
Bartholemew, 35
Basil, 97
basilicas, 89
Basques, 210
Bassano, Leandro, 33
bastion, 404
Battle of Blenheim, 547–548
Battle of Bosworth Field, 403
Battle of Breitenfeld, 508–511
Battle of Crécy, 393, 409
Battle of Denain, 546–549
*Battle of Las Navas de Tolosa*, 311
*Battle of Lepanto*, 496
Battle of Lepanto, 496–498, 517
Battle of Lützen, 517
Battle of the Boyne, 538
Battle of Tours, 201–202
Battle of Worcester, 528–529

Battle of Yarmouk, 179, 191
Batu, 343–344, 388
Bavaria, 212, 248–249, 506
B.C. *See* Before Christ
Bec, 274
Becket, Thomas, 277–281, 292
Bede the Venerable, 205–206, 216
Bedouin, 171, 204
*Before Christ*, 2
Begarelli, Antonio, 349
Belgium, 513, 545
Belisarius, 143–146, 164
Bellini, Giovanni, 31, 340
Benavente, 345
Benedict of Nursia, 152–155, 164, 165, 334
Benedict VII, 253
Benedict XI, 364
Benedict XIII, 371
Benedict XV, 398
benefice, 244, 264
Berbers, 204
Berengaria, 334–335
Bernard of Clairvaux, 252, 286, 287–288, 293, 301, 313
Bethlehem, 20, 100
Bible. *See* Holy Bible
Bingen, 252
bishops, 243–244, 487
*Bishops' Bible*, 440
Bithynia, 38
Black Death, 377
Black Sea, 59, 63, 103, 139, 383
Blessed Virgin. *See* Mary
Blood of Christ, 28, 335, 449, 457, 487
"Bloody Mary", 471–472
Boadicea (Queen), 54
bodies, 73
Body of Christ, 28, 335, 449, 457, 487
Boethius, 150–151, 164
Bohemia, 249, 370, 373, 504, 505–506
Boleyn, Anne, 467–469, 477, 480
Bologna, 342
Bonaventure, 349–350, 356

## Index

Boniface, 200, 216, 217–218
Boniface VIII, 359–363, 375, 377, 378
*Book of Common Prayer*, 471, 473, 525–526
Book of Kells, 150
books, 333
Borromeo, Charles, 490
Bosporus straits, 63
Bossuet, Jacques-Bénigne, 542–549, 554
Botticelli, Sandro, 13, 20
Bourbons, 499, 500–501
Britain, 11, 54, 58, 63, 97, 147–150, 204–206, 219, 273–284, 402, 538–542. *See also* England; Ireland; Scotland; Wales
"the Bruce", 283
Brunelleschi, Filippo, 421–422
Bruno, 247
bubonic plague, 377
Bucer, Martin, 456
Buda, 460
bull, 360, 377
"Bull Against Martin Luther and Followers," 450
bureaucrat, 49
Burgundians, 131, 132
Byzantine, 145
Byzantine Empire, 140–142, 145, 164, 168–170, 193, 253, 254, 295, 381, 405–406, 428. *See also* Russia

### C

Cádiz, 347
Caesar. *See* Julius Caesar
Caesarea, 97
Cairo, 171, 182
Calais, 393
Calatrava Castle, 310
Caligula, 51, 52–53
caliph, 191. *See also specific caliphs*
Caliph Ali. *See* Ali
Caliph Omar. *See* Omar ibn al-Khattab
Caliph Othman. *See* Othman

calligraphy, 174
Callistus III, 398
Calvin, John, 456–457, 471, 475, 480, 498, 523, 525
Calvinism. *See* Calvin, John
Cana, 23
Canisius, Peter, 495, 518
cannons, 392
canon, 99, 247
canon lawyer, 260
Canterbury, 276, 280
*Canterbury Tales, The,* 369
"Canticle of the Sun," 357
Capets, 284
Capistrano, John, 426, 441
Cappadocia, 38
Carcassonne, 316
Carloman, 206
carnal, 523
Carolingian, 129, 135, 207
*Carolus Magnus. See* Charlemagne
Carthage, 101, 108–109, 111, 143, 185, 186
Carthusian Order, 247
Casimir, 318
Castagno, Andrea del, 416
Castel Sant' Angelo, 58, 59, 260
Castile, 309–312, 344, 432
Castle Church, 452
castle design, 225
catechism, 495, 516
catechumen, 89
Cathar, 324. *See also* Albigensians
*Cathari,* 312
Cathedral of Hagia Sophia, 140–141, 146, 308, 424–425
Cathedral of Santiago de Compostela, 325–326
Cathedral of Seville, 347
Cathedral of St. Basil the Blessed, 386
Cathedral of St. Denis, 285–286
Cathedral of St. Peter, 330
Cathedral School of Reims, 247
*Catherine de Medici,* 498
Catherine de Medici, 498–499

Catherine of Aragon, 466, 468, 472, 479, 480
Catherine of Braganza, 534–535
Catherine of Siena, 368, 370
Catholic epistles, 38
Catholic League, 499–500, 505–506, 509
Catholicism
  Arians and, 122–124
  Germany and, 126–129
  reform of, 463–465
  renewal of, 483–514
Caucasus Mountains, 47
cavalier, 528
Cavaliers, 528
Cavelier, René-Robert, 545
celibate, 97
Celtic tribes, 54. *See also* Gaelic Christians
cenobites, 97
census, 19
Ceolfrith, 205
Cephas. *See* Simon Peter
Chalcedon, 169
chamber pots, 556
chancellor, 128
Charlemagne, 207–214, 216, 222–223, 248, 318
Charles (son of Charlemagne), 214
Charles I, 457, 523–531, 553, 554
Charles II, 532–536, 553, 554
Charles IV, 376
Charles IX, 499
Charles Martel, 129, 199–202, 216
Charles the Fat, 223
Charles the Great. *See* Charlemagne
Charles the Hammer. *See* Charles Martel
Charles V, 393, 457–465, 463, 464–465, 468, 472, 480, 484–485, 498
Charles VI, 395
Charles VII, 395, 397, 398–399
Charles von Hapsburg, 547
Chartres, 500
Chartres Cathedral, 161

Chartreuse, 247
château, 544
Chaucer, Geoffrey, 369, 378
Chi Rho, 82, 83
Chiari, Bartolomeo, 25
Childeric III, 206
chimneys, 233
China, 9
chivalry, 227, 277–284
*Christ Preaching*, 25
Christendom
    defense and building of, 193–214
    defined, 115
    founders of, 139–162
    rebirth of, 248–255
Christian Church, 13
Christian Empire, 85, 89–109
Christian martyrs. *See* martyrs
Christmas, 339
Church of S. Savior, 424
Church of the Holy Sepulcher, 89, 169
Church of the Holy Sepulchre, 295, 298
Church of the Holy Wisdom, 140–141, 146
Churchill, John, 547
Cistercian monastery, 353
Cîteaux, 246–247, 287–288, 340
cities, 2, 234–236. *See also specific cities*
civilization, 4–8, 15
    defined, 8
    early, 8–13
    Jesus' gifts to, 42
Clairvaux, 252, 287–288
clan, 148, 164
Claudius, 51, 53
Claudius Ptolemy, 60
Clement, 77
Clement V, 364–365, 378
Clement VII, 370, 461, 468–469, 484
*Clement VII & Francis I*, 461
cloistered, 154
Clovis, 126, 127–128, 136
Cluniac reform, 254, 257, 264

Cluny, 245–246
code, 142
codex, 142
Codex Calixtinus, 267
Codex Justinianus, 143, 164
*Coeur de Lion*. *See* Richard I ("Lion-Heart")
College of Cardinals, 256–257
Cologne, 247, 351
Colossians, 38
Columbus, Christopher, 326, 433, 436–438, 441
*comes*. *See* count
Commandments, 12
Commodus, 60
common lands, 230
communion. *See* Eucharist
Company of Jesus, 492–494, 517
Compiègne, 397
conciliar theory, 371, 377
Concordat of Worms, 260–261
concubine, 175
Confirmation, 487
Conrad III, 301
*Consolation of Philosophy*, 151
Constance, 262
Constans, 93, 94
Constantine, 81–85, 85, 87, 89, 90, 92–93, 113–114, 169
Constantine II, 93, 94
Constantine V, 197
Constantine VI, 197
Constantine XI Palaiologos, 424, 430
Constantinople, 85, 90, 95, 104, 131, 142, 145, 146, 156, 168, 179, 181, 188, 194–195, 221, 295, 306–307, 308, 381, 422–428, 440
Constantius, 63, 81
Constantius II, 93, 94
consubstantial, 92, 112
Controversy over the Exclusion Act, 535
convent, 338
convoke, 483
Copernicus, Nicholas, 519–520

Corbis, 243, 544
Cordoba, 203–204, 325–326, 345–346
Corinthians, 12, 33, 38, 39
corrosive, 417
Corsica, 125
Cossacks, 387
Council of Constance, 370–372, 372, 373, 377, 378
Council of Constantinople, 95
Council of Florence, 440
Council of Nicaea, 93, 111
Council of Toledo, 123–124, 135
Council of Trent, 480, 483–488, 490, 517
count, 212, 216
Counter-Reformation, 488–490, 516
courage, 137
Cova Dominica, 198
Covadonga, 198
covenant, 10
Covenanter flag, 526
Covenanters, 525–531, 553
craftsmanship, 237–238
Cranmer, Thomas, 468, 469, 470, 472, 480
crèche, 339
Crécy, 393
creed, 92
Crete, 38
Cromwell, Oliver, 529, 531–533, 554
Cromwell, Thomas, 469
crosiers, 243
Cross, 89. *See also* crucifixion
Crotona, 253
Crown of Recceswinth, 122
crucifixion, 29–30
crusade, 323
Crusades, 286, 289, 295–322. *See also* Islam
*crux*, 297
Ctesiphon, 60
cuirass, 226
*Cur Deus Homo*, 276
curia, 444

# Index

currency, 79
Cypress, 38
Cyprus, 10, 57, 320, 496

## D

da Gama, Vasco, 435–436
da Modena, Tommaso, 352
Da Vinci, Leonardo, 421–422
Dacia, 11, 57, 95
Dalmatia, 143, 306
Damascus, 100, 170–172, 179, 184, 185, 302
Danes, 220. *See also* Vikings
Dante Alighieri, 361–362, 378
Danube River, 57, 58, 59, 78, 84, 95, 104, 107, 248, 460
Dark Ages, 115, 329
Dauphin, 393
David, 2
*David*, 422
d'Azevado, Diego, 340
*De Civitate Dei*, 106
de Coligny (Admiral), 499
de Guzman, Dominic, 313, 340–342, 356
de Lusignan, Guy, 320
de Montfort, Simon, 282
de Nogaret, Guillaume, 361
de Troyes, Chrétien, 279, 284
de Zurbaran, Francisco, 336
deacons, 36
"Death of Arthur, The," 411–412
Decius, 78
*Deeds of Otto*, 252
"Defender of the Faith," 466
defenestration, 505
demigod, 118
Denmark, 210
depose, 94
Despenaperros, 312
Deuteronomy, 26
di Bondone, Giotto, 413
di Tito, Santi, 498
*Dialogues, The*, 162
Diaz, Rodrigo, 272

diet, 253
Diet of Augsburg, 462
Diet of Tribur, 258
Diet of Worms, 450–452, 479
Diocletian, 62–64, 65, 66, 80, 87, 90, 113
disciples. *See* apostles
disputations, 333
dissolution, 469
*Divine Comedy*, 361–362, 379
Divine right of kings, 521–523, 553
*djinns*, 171
*Domini canes*, 340–342
Dominic, 313, 340–342, 356
Dominicans, 340–342, 356
Dominic's Order of Preachers, 340–342
Domitian, 56, 71
Don Juan, 496–497, 518
Don Pelayo, 216, 267
Donatists, 90, 102, 112
Donskoi, Dmitri, 389, 410
Doré, Gustave, 297, 298
*Douai-Reims* Bible, 440
dour, 523
dowry, 466
Drogheda, 533
Druids, 148
du Guesclin, Bertrand, 393
duchy, 209
Dürer, Albrecht, 70
Durham Cathedral, 531

## E

Easter, 30
Eastern Europe, 141
Eastern Orthodox Church, 350, 423. *See also* Byzantine Empire; Russian Orthodox Church
East-Goths, 95
*Ecclesiastical History of the English People*, 205
ecumenical, 90
ecumenical councils, 90, 112
Edessa, 61, 299, 301

Edgehill, 528
edict, 79
Edict of Milan, 83–84, 86
Edict of Nantes, 500–501, 517
Edict of Restitution, 507–508
Edict of Toleration, 79–80, 82
Edict of Worms, 451–452, 462
Edward I, 282–284, 293, 360
Edward II, 283–284
Edward III, 366–367, 390–391, 400, 410
Edward IV, 403, 481
Edward V, 403
Edward VI, 471
Egypt, 9, 10, 11, 56, 57, 62, 139, 146, 181, 182, 305, 319
Egyptian civilization, 2
El Cid Campeador, 272, 292
Eleanor of Aquitaine, 277–278, 279, 281, 292
Elizabeth I, 403, 473–477, 480, 521
*emirs*, 178, 191
emperor, 48, 65
Emperor of the Romans, 216. *See also* Charlemagne
*Emperor Theodosius and Saint Ambrose, The*, 98
England, 8, 148, 219, 236, 273–284, 366–367, 389–399, 399–403, 465–477, 545. *See also* Britain
*Entry of Joan of Arc into Orleans*, 395
Ephesians, 38
episcopal, 523
epistles, 38, 39
Erasmus, Desiderius, 448
*Erec and Enide*, 279
Erpingham, Thomas, 395
established church, 474–475
eternal life, 13
Ethelbert of Kent, 159
*Etymologies*, 124
Eucharist, 28, 33, 43, 335–336, 356, 449, 457, 487
Eugenius IV, 423–424
Euphrates River, 8, 9, 58

Eusebius, 94
Eustochium, 100
Eve, 1, 424
evil, 103
excommunication, 450
Exodus of Israel, 2
Extreme Unction, 487

**F**

fairs, 238
Faith, 103, 487
farming. *See* agriculture
fasting, 176
Father. *See* God the Father
Feast of the Dormition of the Virgin, 194
Felicity, 72
feod, 223–224
Ferdinand II, 504–505, 511, 518
Ferdinand III, 345–347, 356, 512–514
Ferdinand of Aragon, 432, 440, 441
*Fernando and Isabella*, 432
Ferris, Jean Leon Gerome, 431
feudalism, 219–238, 240, 289–290, 321, 387–388
fiat, 1
fief, 223–224, 240
Fifth Lateran Council, 443–445
First Agricultural Revolution, 231
First Jewish War, 55
Fisher, John, 469
Five Pillars of Islam, 176, 191
flagship, 436
Flanders, 236
Flatters, 102
Flavius Vespasian, 55, 55–56
Fleury, André-Hercule de, 549–550
Flicke, Gerlach, 470
Florence, 235, 419
Florentina, 122
forfeiture, 391
forgery, 360
forgiveness of sins, 35
Fossanova, 353
*Four Leaders of the First Crusade*, 297

Fourth Lateran Council, 335–336
France, 220, 222, 223, 236, 246–247, 279, 284–290, 364, 370, 375–376, 389–399, 390, 483–488, 498–502, 542–551. *See also* Gaul
Franche Comté, 545
Francis I, 461, 463, 484, 498
Francis of Assisi, 336, 337–340, 349, 356, 357–358
*francisca*, 126
Franciscans, 337–340, 349, 356
Franconia, 249
Franks, 95, 124, 126–127, 131, 199, 201, 206, 210–211
fratricidal, 403
*Fratres Minores*, 337–340
Frederick I, 261–262, 375
Frederick II, 319, 334–335, 351, 375
Frederick III, 448, 452
French Revolution, 536–551, 553
fresco, 420
friar, 356
Friars Minor, 337–340
Fribourg, 455
Frisians, 199, 200, 220
Fulgentius, 122

**G**

Gaelic Christians, 147–150, 159–161
Gaius. *See* Caligula
Gaius Julius Caesar. *See* Julius Caesar
Gaius Julius Caesar Octavianus. *See* Augustus
Galata Bridge, 193
Galatians, 38
Galba, 55
Galerius, 80, 81, 82, 87, 113
Galicia, 267
Galilee, 22, 23
galley, 497
Gallican, 486
Gallienus, 61–62
Gamaliel, 36
Gandersheim, 252
Garonne River, 220

garrison, 125
Gaul, 11, 52, 63, 72, 82, 96, 108, 120–121, 124. *See also* France
Geffels, Frans, 462
Genesis, 4
*Geneva Bible*, 440
Genghis Khan, 342–344, 343, 381, 386
Genoa, 235
Genseric, 108–109, 111, 125, 125–126
geocentric theory, 519
Geoffrey (son of Henry II), 278
Geoffrey Plantagenet, 277
*Geographical Outline*, 60
geometry, 150, 332
George I, 539, 554
George II, 540–542
Gerbert of Aurillac, 254–255, 265–266
Germany, 95, 103–106, 108, 115–133, 168, 200, 248–262, 263, 301, 334–335, 351, 545. *See also* Luther, Martin
Gibraltar, 186
gilded, 384
Giovanni, 349
"Glorious Revolution," 536–551, 553
Gnosticism, 73, 76, 86
God the Father, 12–13, 90, 91–93, 103
Godfrey of Bouillon, 324
gods, 12, 56, 71, 78, 119–120
"Golden Age", 85
"Golden Horde," 386–389
Golden Horn, 195, 215
Golden Legend, 491
"Good Queen Bess," 473–477
Gospels, 17, 157
Gothic architecture, 329, 355, 415
Goths, 59, 62, 95–96, 103, 107
Gozzoli, Benozzo, 21
grace, 1
Grace, 449, 487
Grail. *See* Holy Grail
grammar, 150, 332
Granada, 326, 433–438, 440

# Index

"Grand Delinquent," 530
Gratian, 95, 96, 124
Great Britain. *See* Britain
Great Century, 327–354
Great Mosque at Cordoba, 203–204
Great Mosque of Damascus, 185
Great Schism, 368–375, 377
Greece, 10, 11, 115, 139, 141, 146, 307
Greek Empire, 10
Greek fire, 195
Gregory II, 200
Gregory IX, 319
Gregory the Great, 155–162, 164, 165, 167
Gregory VII, 257–259, 264
Gregory XII, 371
Gregory XIII, 490
Guadalquivir River, 347
Guadiana River, 312
*Guanahani*, 438
guilds, 237–238, 240
Gustavus II Adolphus, 508–510, 518, 529
Gutenberg, Johannes, 431, 440

## H

Hadrian, 58–59, 66
hair shirt, 359
*hajj*, 176
Hanovers, 539, 554
Habsburg Empire, 459, 503, 547
Harold, 273
Hasan, 184
hauberk, 226
Hebrews, 38
*Hegira*, 173, 191
*Hejra*, 173
Helena, 90, 169
heliocentric theory, 519–520
Helios, 56
helmet, 226
Henrietta Marie, 523–524
Henry de Bourbon. *See* Henry IV (France)
Henry de Guise, 499

Henry I (England), 276
Henry II (England), 276–278, 292
Henry II (France), 485
Henry II (Germany), 255
Henry III (England), 282, 288–289
Henry III (France), 499
Henry III (Germany), 257
Henry IV (England), 367, 394, 400
Henry IV (France), 499, 500–501, 517, 518
Henry IV (Germany), 257–260, 264
Henry V (England), 367, 394–395
Henry V (Germany), 261
Henry VI (England), 400–403, 410
Henry VI (Germany), 262, 351
Henry VII (England), 403, 466
Henry VIII (England), 467–471, 479, 480, 481, 488
Heraclius, 170, 191
Hereford, Henry, 394
heresiarch, 94
heresy, 73–76, 86, 324, 366–367, 470–471
Hermenegild, 122
Hermes, 12
hermitage, 96, 97
hermits, 96, 97
Herod Antipas, 22, 24, 29
Herod Archelaus, 22
Herod the Great, 18–19, 21, 24, 44
Herodias, 24
Hieromax River, 179
High Church, 524–525, 553
Hildebrand. *See* Gregory VII
Hildegard of Bingen, 252
Hildesheim, 254
Hillel, 36
Hippo, 98, 100–101, 208, 247
Hispania, 63, 96, 105, 106, 120, 132
history, 3, 15
Hohenstaufen line, 375
Holland, 545
Holy Bible, 431, 440, 474
Holy Grail, 279
Holy Isle of Lindisfarne, 205, 219

Holy Land, 323. *See also* Crusades; specific cities and countries
Holy Office, 489, 516
Holy Orders, 487
Holy Roman Empire. *See* Roman Empire
Holy Spirit, 75, 103. *See also* Trinity
Holy Trinity-St. Sergius monastery, 429
*homoousios*, 92
Honorius, 96, 103, 104, 105
Honorius III, 318–319, 341
Horace, 50
horse collars, 232–233
Hospitallers, 299–301, 324, 458
Hounds of the Lord, 340–342
House of Commons, 399, 409, 539
House of Lords, 399, 409, 539
Hrolf, 241
Hroswitha of Gandersheim, 252
Huddleston, John, 531–533, 536
Hugh, 517
Hugh (Capet), 247, 284
Huguenots, 498–502, 517
Humanism, 414–418, 440
Hundred Years' War, 389–399, 409
Hungary, 251, 370
Huns, 106–108, 111, 112, 132, 145–146
Hunyadi, John, 424
Hus, John, 373, 378

## I

Iberian Peninsula, 120–124, 210, 309. *See also* Spain
iconic painting, 141
iconoclasm, 196, 215
Ignatius, 88
Ignatius of Loyola, 491–494, 517
*imam*, 178
impeach, 400
Imperial Diet of Augsburg, 462
impregnable, 423
*in carne*, 15
*In Defense of the Seven Sacraments*, 466

incarnation, 1, 15, 35
Index of Forbidden Books, 489, 516
*Index of the Royal Privileges*, 345
India, 8, 9, 434–436
indict, 400
Indies, 436–438
indulgence, 443, 445, 479
Indus River, 9
Ingeborg, 334–335
Innocent III, 305–307, 310, 313, 314–315, 317–318, 324, 333–336, 338, 356, 366
Inquisition, 324
*Institutes of the Christian Religion*, 456, 480
interdict, 334
inventions, 231–232
investiture, 244, 256–260, 264
investment, 227
Iran. *See* Persia
Ireland, 147–150, 533. *See also* Britain
Irenaeus, 86
Irene, 197
"Ironsides," 529
Isabel of Castile, 432, 440, 441
Isauria, 194
Isidore, 135
Isis, 56
Islam, 167–189, 191, 197–199, 222, 268–272, 286, 333, 345–347, 381, 403–407, 433–438, 461–462. *See also* Crusades
Israel, 2, 3
Istanbul. *See* Constantinople
Italy, 11, 40, 132, 142, 143, 144–145, 152, 220, 222, 236, 253, 262, 274, 485
Ivan III, 428, 430–432, 440, 441

# J

Jacobites, 538
James, 35, 38, 267, 292
James I, 521–523
James II, 536–538, 554
James the Less, 35
James V, 475
James VI, 521–523
Jamestown, 540
Jane Seymour, 471
Janissaries, 406
Jarrow, 205
Jerome, 98, 111, 157, 161
Jerusalem, 19, 27, 32–36, 39, 56, 76, 181, 295, 298, 299, 301, 317–318. *See also* Crusades
*Jerusalem Bible*, 46
Jesuits, 492–494, 517
Jesus Christ
 birth of, 17, 19–20, 44
 civilization and, 42
 crucifixion of, 29–30
 death of, 3
 hidden life of, 21–22
 Incarnation of, 1
 infancy of, 21–22
 ministry of, 22–32
 passion of, 27–30
 public life of, 22–32
 relation to God and, 90, 91–93
 renewal through, 12
 resurrection and ascension of, 30–32, 35, 44
 resurrection of, 3
 sacrifice of self, 13
 Trinity and, 103. *See also* Trinity
*Jihad*, 173–174, 191
Jiménez, Francisco, 448
Joan of Arc, 395–398, 410
*Johannes Gutenberg*, 431
John, 17, 29, 30, 35, 38, 42, 71–72
John (King), 244, 267, 335, 522
John (Lackland), 281–282, 289, 292
John Capistrano, 426
John II, 391–393
John of Brienne, 319
John of Gaunt, 366–367
John the Baptist, 23, 24, 44
*John the Baptist Rebukes Herod*, 24
John VIII Palaiologos, 423
John XI, 251
John XII, 251
John XIII, 251, 255
John XXIII, 370–371
Jordan, 179
Joseph, 20, 22, 44
Joseph of Arimathea, 30
journeymen, 237
Judaism, 204
Judas Iscariot, 34, 35
Jude, 35, 38
Judea, 18–19, 22, 52
Judgment. *See* Last Judgment
Judith, 223
Julian family, 47
Julian the Apostate, 94
Julius Caesar, 3, 47, 49, 65, 205
Julius II, 443–444
Julius III, 485–486
Justin Martyr, 75, 76, 87
Justinian, 139–146, 164
Justinian Code, 143, 164

# K

Kaaba, 171, 175, 190
Kalikovo Pole, 389, 410
Karlstadt, 455
Katherine, 97
Kekova Island, 404
Ken, Thomas, 534–535
Kent, 204
Khalid, 179
khanate, 428
Khara Khorum, 343–344
Kharijites, 184
Khazars, 185
Kherson, 383
Khwarazmians, 319
Kiev, 221, 383–384
king, 135, 291
*King James Bible*, 440
"Knight of the Cart," 279
"Knight of the Lion," 279
knighthood, 226–227, 240, 299–301
Knights of St. John, 300–301, 324
Kniva, 59

Koran, 173, 174, 191
Kosovo, 407, 410, 424
Krak des Chevaliers, 300
Krakow Cathedral, 519–520
Kremlin, 430
Kublai Khan, 344
Kunigunde, 255

# L

La Mancha, 268, 310
*La Pucelle*, 395–398
Lactantius, 80
Lake Galilee, 34
Lake Priapus, 388
*Lamentation, The*, 413
Lancasters, 394, 400–403, 522
*Lancelot*, 279
Lanfranc, 274
Langton, Stephen, 335
Languedoc, 314, 315–316, 340–341
Las Navas de Tolosa, 310–312
Last Judgment, 102
Last Supper, 28, 33, 279
*Last Supper* fresco, 421–422
*Last Supper, The*, 33
Lateran Councils, 335–336, 443–445
Latin Vulgate, 487
Laud, William, 525–526, 527–528
lay, 146
lay investiture, 244, 264
Lazar, 406–407
*Le Morte D'Arthur*, 411–412
Lech River, 248, 510
lectures, 333
legate, 257
legion, 49, 65
Lent, 197
Leo I, 106–108, 111, 125
Leo III, 212
Leo III the Isaurian, 193–197, 216
Leo IV, 197
Leo V, 197
Leo VIII, 251
Leo X, 444–445, 448, 467, 480
León, 309–312, 340, 345
Leopold, 547

Leovigild, 122, 135
Letts, 234
Leviticus, 26
levy, 524
liberal arts, 150, 332
Licinius, 84
liege, 224–225, 240
light, Jesus Christ as, 1
Lindisfarne. *See* Holy Isle of Lindisfarne
"Lion-Heart". *See* Richard I ("Lion-Heart")
liturgy of the Mass, 157, 161, 487–488
logic, 150
*Logos*, 75
Loire River, 121, 127, 132
Lollards, 367, 377
Lombard warrior, 157
Lombardy, 222
"Long Peace", 79
longbows, 392–393
Longfellow, William Wadsworth, 379
"Longshanks," 282–284
Lothair, 222, 223
Lotharingia, 249
Louis (son of Louis the Pious), 223
Louis IX, 289–290, 293, 319–321, 375
Louis the Pious, 212, 214, 222–223, 241
Louis VI, 285
Louis VII, 285–286, 301
Louis X, 376
Louis XI, 399, 410
Louis XIII, 500–501, 512, 524
Louis XIV, 542–549, 553, 554, 555–556
*Louis XIV on Horseback*, 542–549
Louis XV, 549–551, 554
Louisiana Territory, 545, 553
love, 26
Low Church, 525, 553
Lucca, 235
Lucerne, 455
lucrative, 523
Luke, 17, 26, 29, 34

Luther, Martin, 447–454, 464, 480. *See also* Protestant Reformation
Lyons, 72

# M

Macedonia, 10, 11, 38, 63
Machiavelli, Niccolò, 417, 418
*Madonna*, 422
Magna Carta, 282, 292, 315, 335, 522, 533
magnate, 253
"Magnificat," 34
Magyars, 222, 248, 251
Mahomet II, 425–428, 440
Main River, 126
Mainz, 254
Malory, Thomas, 411–412
Malta, 39
"Man of Blood", 530
Manicheanism, 101, 112
manors, 228–230, 240
maps
    13th-Century Europe, 361
    16th Century England, 447
    Anglo-Saxon kingdoms, 160
    Arabia, 171
    Battle of Tours, 201
    Bohemia, 507
    Britain, 402
    Charlemagne's empire, 208
    China, 9
    Christopher Columbus's route, 437
    Crusades, 299, 305
    Eastern Roman Empire, 139
    Egypt, 9, 319
    England, 527
    France, 285, 390, 499
    Germanic kingdom, 131
    Germanic movements, 117
    Hapsburg Empire, 459, 503
    human migration patterns, 6
    India, 9
    Islam, 180
    Italy, 152, 485

journey of St. Paul, 38
Languedoc, 314
medieval Spain, 269
Mediterranean Sea, 194, 316
Mesopotamia, 9
Mongol Empire, 343
North America, 541
Ostrogoth Italy, 143
Ottoman Empire, 405, 427, 497
Palestine, 18, 319
Roman Empire, 11, 48, 84
Russia, 385
Scotland, 527
Spain, 346, 433
Switzerland, 454
Vasco da Gama's route to India, 435
Viking routes, 221
Marc Antony, 47
Marcellus II, 485–486
march, 222
Marcionism, 73, 75, 86
Marco Polo, 344
Marcus Aurelius, 59–60, 66, 72
Marcus Lepidus, 47
*Mare Nostrum*, 11
Margaret of Anjou, 401
Maria Theresa, 546–549
Marie de Champagne, 279
maritime, 235
Mark, 17, 26–27
markets, 238
Marriage, 487
Marston Moor, 529
*Martellus. See* Charles Martel
Martha, 35
Martin Luther. *See* Luther, Martin
Martin of Tours, 161
Martin V, 372–373
*Martyrdom of the Ten Thousand*, 70
martyrs, 43, 69–85, 86
  Saint Ignatius, 88
  Saint Paul, 3, 40–41
  Saint Peter, 3, 40–41
  Saint Stephen, 36
  St. Justin Martyr, 75

Marus, 154
Mary, 1, 20, 22, 29, 34, 44, 228, 331
Mary (mother of James), 30, 34
Mary, Queen of Scots, 474–475, 523
Mary Beatrice d'Este, 534–535
Mary II, 536–538, 554
Mary Magdalene, 29, 30, 35
Mary of Bethany, 34–35
Mary Tudor, 471–472, 480
Masaccio, 35
Masalama, 193–196
*Mass of Saint Gregory, The*, 158
Massachusetts, 540
Massacre at Drogheda, 533
Massacre of Verden, 211
Matilda, 277
Matthew, 17, 21, 26, 26–27, 30, 32, 34, 35
Matthias von Hapsburg, 504
Mauretania, 11
maxim, 416
Maximian, 62, 81
Maximilian, 506
Maximinus Daia, 81, 82, 83
Mazarin, Jules, 542, 554
Mecca, 170–172, 173, 188
Media, 10
Medici, Giovanni de. *See* Leo X
Medici, Lorenzo di, 419, 440
Medicis, 419, 440, 444
Medieval Reformation, 243–262
Medieval times. *See* Middle Ages
Medina, 172–173, 188
Mediterranean, 11, 52, 57, 121, 194, 316
*Meeting of Attila the Hun and Pope Leo I, The*, 107
megaliths, 8
mendicant, 338
Menno, Simons, 455–456
Mennonites, 455–456
menorah, 125
mercenary, 92
Merica, 204
Merovech, 127, 135

Merovings, 127–129, 135, 206, 384
Mesopotamia, 2, 3, 8, 9, 10, 11, 58, 60, 61, 62, 84, 139, 168, 181, 188
Messiah, 26, 27, 43
*Metamorphoses, The*, 50
metropolitan, 389
Michaelangelo di Buonarroti, 417, 422, 440
Middle Ages, 228–230, 230–238, 327–354, 359–376, 413–414. *See also* feudalism
Mignard, Pierre, 542–549
migration patterns, 6
Milan, 85, 99, 104, 235, 262
militia, 526
Milton, John, 102
minnesingers, 279
Miramamolin, 310–312
Mirandola, Gianfrancesco Pico della, 445
*Missale Romanium*, 157
*missi dominici*, 212
Mississippi River, 545
Missorium of Theodosius, 96
Mithras, 56
Mohács, 460
*Mona Lisa*, 421–422
monarch, 291
monasteries, 97, 121–122, 153–155, 205–206, 244–247, 469–470
Monasticism, 97
Mongolia, 106–108, 342–344, 381, 386–387, 409. *See also* Russia
Monica, 101
monk, 97
"Monomakh", 385
monotheist, 172
Montanists, 75, 86
Monte Cassino, 155, 157, 164, 350
Moors, 197, 433. *See also* Crusades; Islam
More, Thomas, 448, 469
Moro, Antonio, 471–472
*Moros*, 197

mosaic, 164
Moscow, 388–389, 428–432, 440
Moses, 12
Mount of Olives, 32
Mount Sinai, 97
Mount Vesuvius, 56
*Mozarabes*, 204
Mu'awaiya, 184
Muhammad, 172–177, 191
*mullahs*, 178
Murad I, 407, 423
Muscovite, 428. *See also* Moscow
Muscovy. *See* Moscow
music, 150, 328, 332
Muslims. *See* Islam
*Mystic Nativity*, 13, 20
Mytens, Daniel, 522

# N

Nain, 25
Nantes, 220
Naples, 105
nationalism, 409
nation-state, 283, 292
Nativity, 339
Navarre, 210, 309–312, 370
Nazareth, 22
Neolithic, 4, 5
nepotism, 364
Nero, 41, 51–52, 53–54, 65
Netherlands, 511–513, 545.
    *See* Frisians
Neustria, 199, 222
Nevski, Alexander, 388, 410
New Scipio, 170
New Stone Age, 2, 4, 5, 231
New Testament, 18, 73, 99
New World. *See* America
Nicaea, 90, 93, 197, 301
Nicene Creed, 93, 111, 112
Nicholas, 257, 259
Nicholas V, 420, 424, 440
Nicomedia, 63, 94
Nika Revolt, 140
Nile River, 8, 9, 319, 320
*Niña*, 436

Ninety-five Theses, 446, 479
Nis, 62
Norbertines, 247
Normandy, 274–275, 284, 394
Norse gods, 119–120
North Africa, 57, 63, 90, 98, 100,
    108–109, 115, 124–126, 126,
    143, 181, 222, 235, 271, 320
North America, 541
Northmen. *See* Vikings
Northumbria, 204–205
Notre Dame Cathedral, 330
*Nova Roma*, 85, 145
Novgorod, 383, 387–388, 429–430
Numidia, 11
Nuremberg, 460–462

# O

Oath of Supremacy, 473
Obeida, 179
Octavia, 54
Octavian. *See* Augustus
Odilo of Cluny, 245
Odin, 119
Odoacer, 130, 131–132
Ogodei Khan, 343–344
Old Stone Age, 5–6, 7
Old Testament, 12, 18, 73, 75
Olga, 383
Omar ibn al-Khattab, 178, 180,
    181–182, 191
*On the Revolution of the Heavenly
    Spheres*, 520
open-field system, 230–231
*Optimus*, 57
orders
    Holy, 487
    monastic, 246–247
Orestes, 130
Origen, 41, 77, 87
*Origin of the Abbey of Gandersheim*,
    252
Original Sin, 102, 449, 487
Orkhan, 405–406, 409, 410
Orleans, 395
orthodox, 92, 112

Orthodox, 194, 215
Osma, 340
Osman, 405
Ostrogoths, 95, 129–133, 131, 143
Oswy, 161
Othman, 182–183, 191, 425
Otho, 55
Otto I, 248–253, 258, 264
Otto II, 253, 264
Otto III, 254, 255, 264, 334–335
Ottoman Empire, 404–407, 409, 427,
    459, 494–498
Our Lady. *See* Mary
Outremer, 299, 317–321
Ovid, 50
Oxford University, 366–367

# P

pacific, 213
padded horse collars, 232–233
paganism, 12, 56, 71, 75, 77, 78, 79,
    94, 106, 119–120, 148, 171,
    199, 200, 218, 234
Palatine hill, 54
Palazzo Farnese, 423
Paleolithic, 5–6, 7
paleontology, 3
Palestine, 18, 146, 179, 181, 319, 320
*Pange Lingua*, 354
pantheon, 119
papistical, 454
Paraclete, 75
*Paradise Lost*, 102
paragon, 305
parchment, 340
Parentucceli, Tommaso. *See*
    Nicholas V
Paris, 127, 223
*Parlement de Paris*, 292
Parliament, 292, 399, 409, 539
Parthia, 10, 60, 220
*Parzifal*, 279
Paschal II, 260
passion, 27–30
Passover, 27, 43
*Pastoral Rule*, 162

Patrick, 147–150, 164
patronize, 189
Paul, 3, 33, 36–41, 42, 44, 52, 89
Paul III, 483, 493, 517
Paula, 100
Pavia, 274
*Pax Romana*, 49
Peace of Alais, 502, 517
Peace of Augsburg, 464–465
Peace of Madrid, 460
Peace of Utrecht, 548
Peace of Westphalia, 513–514, 517
Peasants' Crusade, 296
Pelagianism, 112
Pelagius, 102, 198–199
Penance, 487
Pentecost, 32–36, 45
Pepin, 129
Pepin (son of Charlemagne), 214
Pepin (son of Louis the Pious), 222–223, 223
Pepin the Short, 129, 136, 206–207, 216
*Perceval*, 279
perjury, 317
Perpetua, 72
Persia, 56, 61–62, 101, 168–170, 181
Persis, 10
Perugino, Pietro Vannucci, 23
Peter, 3, 26–27, 30, 34, 35, 38, 40–41, 44, 45, 71, 76, 89, 244
Peter Canisius, 495
Peter II of Aragon, 310
Peter of Aragon, 315
Peter of Castelnau, 314–315
Peter the Hermit, 296
Petrarch, Francesco, 416, 440
Petronius, 54
Pharisees, 19, 30, 36
Philemon, 38
Philip, 24, 35
Philip II, 472, 477, 488, 496, 512
Philip II "Augustus," 288–289, 293, 302, 334–335
Philip IV, 505–506, 512–513

Philip IV "the Fair," 283, 359–366, 375, 376
Philip of Anjou, 547–549, 554
Philip V, 376
Philip VI, 389–390
Philippians, 38
philosophy, 12
Phoenicia, 38
Piacenza, 235
*Pietà*, 331
Pilgrimage of Grace, 470
pillage, 507
Pino, Marco, 37
*Pinta*, 436
Pisa, 235, 371
*Pius*, 59
Pius IV, 486, 517
Pius V, 473, 480, 517
Plantagenets, 277–284, 522
Platonism, 77
Plessis, Armand-Jean du. *See* Richelieu
Pliny the Elder, 56
plows, 232
plunder, 507
Plymouth, 540
Poland, 251, 549
Pole, Margaret, 481
Pole, Reginald, 481–482
Polycarp, 69, 70, 76, 86
polygamy, 175
polyphony, 328
Pomerania, 318
Pompeii, 56
Ponthieu, 393
Pontius Pilate, 29–30, 44, 52
Popes
    Adrian I, 209
    Alexander III, 262
    Alexander V, 370
    Benedict VII, 253
    Benedict XI, 364
    Benedict XIII, 371
    Benedict XV, 398
    Boniface VIII, 359–363, 375, 377, 378

    Callistus III, 398
    Clement V, 364–365, 378
    Clement VII, 370, 461, 468–469, 484
    Damasus, 100
    defense of the West and, 106–109
    Eugenius IV, 423–424
    Gregory II, 200
    Gregory IX, 319
    Gregory the Great, 155–162, 164, 165, 167
    Gregory VII, 257–259
    Gregory XII, 371
    Gregory XIII, 490
    Honorius III, 318–319, 341
    Innocent III, 305–307, 310, 313, 314–315, 317–318, 324, 333–336, 338, 356, 366
    John XI, 251
    John XII, 251
    John XIII, 251, 255
    John XXIII, 370–371
    Julius II, 443–444
    Julius III, 485–486
    Leo I, 106–108, 111, 125
    Leo III, 212
    Leo VIII, 251
    Leo X, 444–445, 448, 467, 480
    Marcellus II, 485–486
    Martin V, 372–373
    Nicholas, 257, 259
    Nicholas V, 420, 424, 440
    Paschal II, 260
    Paul III, 483, 493, 517
    Pius IV, 486, 517
    Pius V, 473, 480, 517
    Sixtus IV, 350
    Sylvester, 90
    Sylvester II, 254–255
    Urban II, 247, 256, 295–296, 324
    Urban VI, 368–370
Poppaea Sabina, 54
Porritani, Gilberti, 348
Portugal, 309–312, 434–436
power, 162, 164
Praemonstratensians, 247

Praetorians, 55
Prague, 255, 504–505
prayer, 176
predestination, 457
prehistory, 4
prelate, 282
Presbyterianism, 475. *See also* Calvin, John
priests, 487
Prignano, Bartholomew, 368–369
primatial, 149
*Prince, The*, 417
prince elector, 448
Prince of Wales, 283
principate, 47–51, 65
printing press, 431
prior, 245
*Procession of the Magi, The*, 21
promontory, 225
promulgate, Italy, 485
prophets, 12
Protectorate, 531–533, 553
Protestant, 479
Protestant Reformation, 443–477
Provençal, 279
Providence, 151
Provincia, 105
Prussians, 234
Ptolemy, 519
Publius Aelius Hadrianus. *See* Hadrian
Puritans, 523, 553
Pym, John, 526
Pyrenees mountains, 105, 199, 203, 210

# Q

*quadrivium*, 332
Quran, 173, 174, 191

# R

Radonezh, 429
Raphael di Santi, 107, 415, 422, 440, 443, 444
Ravenna, 104, 129, 130, 142
*Ravnoapostol*, 383

Raymond of Toulouse, 314–315
recant, 373
Reccared, 123, 135
*Reconquista*, 198–199
Reformation
  Medieval, 243–262
  Protestant, 443–477
regalia, 131
regent, 133
regicide, 521, 532–538, 553
Reims, 127, 247, 255, 287
Reims Cathedral, 328
*Religion Crushing Heresy*, 74
Remi, 128
Remigius, 128
Renaissance, 415–438, 440
responsum, 348–349
Restoration, 533–536
resurrection, 3, 30–32, 35
*Resurrection of Christ*, 31
Revelation, 72
rhetoric, 76, 150, 332
Rhine River, 52, 62, 63, 108, 124, 126, 127, 199, 201, 545
Rhodes, 38, 57, 320
Rhône River, 72
Ricci, Sebastiano, 32
Richard (Plantagenet), 278
Richard I ("Lion-Heart"), 281–282, 289, 302–304, 305, 324
Richard II, 393–394, 400
Richard III, 402–403
Richard IV, 402
Richard of York, 401–403
Richelieu, Armand-Jean de, 501–504, 509–512, 518. *See* Plessis
rings, 243
Rio Duero Castillo, 269
River Elbe, 234
Robert, 276
Robert I, 283
Robert of Locksley, 294
Robin Hood, 294
Rock of Gibraltar, 186

Roman Empire, 11, 13, 47, 72, 84, 115–116, 139, 263, 364, 375–376, 457–465
  Antonines and, 57–60
  Augustus and, 47–51
  Diocletian and, 62–64
  fifty years of fifty emperors and, 61–62
  Flavians and, 55–56
  Julians and, 51–55
Roman gods, 119
Roman Republic, 3. *See also* Julius Caesar
Roman Rite, 157
romance, 277–284, 279
Romanesque architecture, 329, 355
Romans, 38
Rome, 12, 22, 29, 35, 39, 41, 63–64, 78, 85, 88, 105–106, 111, 152, 181, 212, 222, 307, 308, 420, 460–462, 479. *See also* Roman Empire; Roman Republic
Romulus Augustulus, 130, 136
Roncesvalles, 210
Rouen, 127
Rubens, Peter Paul, 98
rue, 527
Ruhr River, 200
*Rule of St. Augustine*, 247
*Rule of St. Benedict*, 153–155, 157, 161, 164, 205
"Rump, The," 530
Rump Parliament, 530, 531
Rurik, 221, 241, 382
Rus. *See* Russia
Russia, 141, 221, 307, 381–389, 409, 440
Russian Orthodox Church, 388, 428–432. *See also* Byzantine Empire; Eastern Orthodox Church

# S

Sacchi, Andrea, 156
sacramental, 449

Sacraments, 336, 487. *See also* Eucharist
Sacred Tradition, 449, 486
*Sadducees*, 19
*Saint Augustine and the Child*, 101
*Saint Dominic*, 340
*Saint Francis of Assisi*, 336
*Saint Francis Receiving the Stigmata*, 339
Saint Patrick's Cathedral, 149
Saint Petersburg, 388
Saints. *See specific names*
Saladin, 302–304, 305, 324
*salat*, 176
Salome, 30
salvation, 73
Salviati, Francesco, 423
San Damiano, 337
Sancho VII, 310
Sanhedrin, 30
*Santa Maria*, 436
Santiago, 292, 325–326. *See also* James
Saracens, 222
Saragossa, 210
Sardinia, 125
Sassanids, 61–62
satirist, 54
Saul. *See* Paul
*sawn*, 176
Saxons, 131, 159, 160, 199, 208–211, 248
Scherrer, J.J., 395
Schism of 1054, 308
schismatic, 90, 112, 470–471
Schlosskirche, 452
Schmalkaldic League, 462
Scholastica, 153
*School of Athens, The*, 415
schools, 76–77, 348–354, 355
Schwyz, 455
scion, 403
Scotland, 148, 219, 284, 525–531. *See also* Britain
scourging, 29

Scriptures, 19, 43, 75, 80, 99, 100, 111, 449, 486. *See also specific books*
scrupulous, 535
Sea of Galilee, 25, 302
Sea of Tiberias. *See* Sea of Galilee
Second Agricultural Revolution, 231
*Second Assault of Jerusalem: The Crusaders Repulsed*, 298
sect, 51
secular, 243, 264, 414. *See also* Humanism
sedition, 196
see, 149
self-denial, 75, 101, 102, 112
Selim II, 496
Seljuks, 295
Senate, 65
Sens, 223
sensualism, 416
Sephardic Jews, 204, 268
Sephardim, 268
Septimius Severus, 61, 72, 77
Serbia, 407, 410
serfdom, 234, 240. *See also* feudalism
Sergius of Radonezh, 429
*Servus Servorum Dei*, 164
seven liberal arts, 150, 332
Seventh Ecumenical Council, 197
Severianus, 122–123
Seville, 347
Seymour, Jane, 471
*shehada*, 176
Shiites, 184, 187–189, 191
Sicily, 11, 40, 125, 262, 334–335
*Siege of Vienna*, 462
Sigismund, 373
Simon IV de Montfort, 315
Simon Magus, 244
Simon Peter. *See* Peter
Simon the Zealot, 34, 35
Simon V de Montfort, 315
simony, 244
Simony, 257
simony, 264
Sistine Chapel, 417

Sixtus IV, 350
Slav, 234
Slavata, Wilhelm, 504–505
Sleipnir, 119
Slovakia, 224
Society of Jesus, 492–494, 517
Soissons, 127
*sola fide*, 449, 479
*sola gratia*, 449
*sola scriptura*, 449
Solomon, 3
Son. *See* Jesus Christ
*Song of Roland*, 210
Sophia Palaiologos, 430
sortie, 397
South America, 115
Spain, 11, 55, 90, 95, 96, 197–199, 203–204, 210, 215, 220, 268–272, 309–312, 345–347, 433, 457, 491, 546–549
Spanish Armada, 477, 480
"Spider King," 399
spiritual power, 162, 164
St. Bartholomew's Day Massacre, 499–500
St. Bernard's Abbey of Cîteaux, 340
*St. Bonaventure*, 349
St. Denis monastery, 549
*St. Jerome in His Study*, 100
St. Mark's Cathedral, 262, 307
St. Peter's Basilica, 41, 213
St. Stephen's Crown, 255
stained glass, 327
standing army, 536
Stephen, 36, 37, 255
steppe, 381
Stilicho, 103–104, 111
Stoic philosophy, 60
Stone Age, 2, 5–6
Stonehenge, 8
"Story of the Holy Grail," 279
Stuarts, 523–539, 554
Subedei, 343–344
Suger, 285–287, 293
Suleiman, 193, 458–459
Suleiman's Mosque, 195

sultan, 295, 324
*Summa Theologica*, 352
Sun King, 542–549
Sunnis, 184, 191
*sura*, 173
Swabia, 249
Sweden, 221, 508–511, 545. *See also* Vikings
Switzerland, 454
Sybil of the Rhine, 252
Sylvester, 90
Sylvester II, 254–255, 264
Symmachus, 150–151
synod, 161
Synod of Whitby, 161, 164
Syria, 10, 11, 56, 62, 139, 168, 179, 181, 185, 204, 300

# T

table-monks, 97
tactician, 303
Tagaste, 101
Tagus River, 269–271, 271
Tarik, 197, 216
Tarsus, 36
Teano, 350
Templars, 299–301, 323
temporal power, 162, 164
Tertullian, 87. *See* Perpetua
Test Act, 534
testament, 18, 43
Tetzel, 445
Teutonic Knights, 388
textiles, 235–236
theocracy, 177
Theodora, 140, 145, 164, 197, 350
Theodoric, 131–133, 136, 151
Theodorus, 179
Theodosia, 122
Theodosius, 96, 98, 103, 111
Theophano, 253, 254
Theory of Courage, 137
Theotokos, 196
thesis, 351
Thessalonians, 38
Thessalonica, 63

Thessaly, 38
Third Council of Toledo, 123–124
Third Rome, 440. *See also* Russian Orthodox Church
Thirty Years' War, 503, 517
Thomas, 32, 35
Thomas Aquinas, 349–350, 350–354, 356, 415
Thor, 120
Thrace, 38, 139
Tiberius, 51, 52–53, 65
Tiepolo, Giovanni Battista, 74
Tigris River, 8, 9
Tilly (Count). *See* Tserclaes, Johann
time, 2–3
Timothy, 38
Titian, 483
Titus, 38, 55–56
Titus Aurelius Antonius. *See* Antonius
Toledo, 96, 123–124, 135, 197, 269–271, 271, 310
toleration, 79
Toleration Act, 538
Tolkein, J.R.R., 137
Tolosa, 105
Tomb of Charlemagne, 318
Torah, 19
Tory, 538, 553
Tours, 201–202
towns, 234–236
trade, 235–236
Tradition, 449, 486
*traditores*, 90
Trajan, 57, 66, 88
transubstantiation, 28, 335–336, 356, 449
Treaty of Ryswick, 547
Treaty of Troyes, 394–395
tributary, 271, 545
*Tribute Money, The*, 35
Tridentine, 489
Tridentine Rite, 489, 517
Trier, 63
Trinity, 76, 94, 103
Tripoli, 299

Triumph of Orthodoxy, 197
*trivium*, 332
troubadours, 279, 413
Tserclaes, Johann, 506–507, 509, 518
Tudor, Arthur, 466
Tudors, 403, 465–477, 521–522
Tunis, 320
Turkey, 296, 404, 494–498. *See also* Ottoman Empire
Turks, 185
Twelve Apostles. *See* apostles

# U

Uberti, Lucantonio degli, 419
Ultramontane, 486, 516
Umayyad Mosque, 185
Umayyads, 184–187, 201, 203
uniformity, 473, 479
Universal epistles, 38
universities, 331–333, 356
University of Naples, 351
University of Paris, 349, 456
University of Wittenberg, 443–477
unscrupulous, 417
Unterwalden, 455
Ural River, 381
Urban II, 247, 256, 295–296, 324
Urban VI, 368–370
Uri, 455
usurper, 306

# V

Valencia, 123, 272
Valens, 95
Valentinian I, 95, 96, 99
Valentinian III, 129
Valerian, 61–62
Valhalla, 119
van Cleve, Joos, 100
Van Halen, Francisco, 311
Vandals, 95, 103–104, 108–109, 111, 112, 124–126, 131, 143
vanguard, 193
Varangian Guard, 221
Vasari, Giorgio, 461
Vasili III, 431–432

Vasnetsov, Viktor, 383, 384
vassal, 224–225, 240, 243
Venice, 235, 262, 305
venue, 484
Veronese, Paolo, 496
Versailles, 544, 555–556
Verus, 60
Vespasian. *See* Flavius Vespasian
Vespers, 280
viaticum, 353
Vibia Perpetua. *See* Perpetua
viceroy, 201
Vienne, 128
Vikings, 219–222, 240, 248, 382
Vincennes, 289
Vindabona, 60
Virgil, 50
Virgin Mary. *See* Mary
Virginia, 540
Visigoths, 95, 103–104, 105, 111, 120–124, 131, 197, 198–199
Vitellius, 55
Vladimir, 383, 409, 410
Vladimir II, 385–386
von Eschenbach, Wolfram, 279

# W

Wales, 148, 283. *See also* Britain
Wallenstein, Albrect von, 506, 518
War of the Spanish Succession, 546–549, 554
Wars of Religion, 498–502
Wars of the Roses, 400–403, 409, 410
Weesop, 530
Wends, 234
Weser River, 200, 210
Western Orthodox Church, 350
West-Goths, 95
Westphalia, 513–514, 517
Whigs, 538, 553
"White Knight of Wallachia," 424
"Why did God become Man?," 276
William (Plantagenet), 278
William, Prince of Orange. *See* William III
William II "Rufus", 275–276
William III, 536–538, 554
William of Holland, 375
William of Normandy, 284
William the Conqueror, 273–275, 292
William X of Aquitaine, 277–284, 279
windmills, 234
Wittekind, 210, 211
Wittenberg, 452
Wodin, 119
Wolsey (Cardinal), 467–468
women, 175, 228, 252
Wooton, John, 548
Worms, 260–261, 450–452
Wormwood. *See* Clairvaux
writing, 2, 3
Wulfilas, 95

Wycliffe, John, 366–367, 373, 377, 378

# Y

Yarmouk River, 179, 191
Yaroslav, 384–385
Year of the Four Emperors, 55
*Yehoshua*, 21
Yellow River, 9
*Yeshua*, 21
York Minster, 330
Yorks, 400–403
Ysenbrandt, Adrien, 158
*Yvain*, 279

# Z

Zacharias, 169
Zahara, 433
*zakal*, 176
Zamora, 269
Zara, 306
Zeno, 131–132
Zug, 455
Zwingli, Ulrich, 454–455, 480
Zwinglians, 455